WOMEN OF COLOR

GARLAND REFERENCE LIBRARY
OF SOCIAL SCIENCE
(VOL. 173)

Lupe Velez

WOMEN OF COLOR
*A Filmography of Minority
and Third World Women*

Maryann Oshana

GARLAND PUBLISHING, INC. · NEW YORK & LONDON
1985

Library of Congress Cataloging in Publication Data

Oshana, Maryann.
Women of color.

(Garland reference library of social science ; vol. 173)
Bibliography: p.
Includes indexes.
1. Women in moving-pictures—Catalogs.   2. Minority women in motion pictures—Catalogs.   3. Developing countries in motion pictures—Catalogs.   I. Title.
II. Series: Garland reference library of social science ; v. 173.
Z5784.M9084   1985   791.43′09′09352042   82-49143
[PN1995.9.W6]
ISBN 0-8240-9140-X (alk. paper)

Cover design by Donna Montalbano

Printed on acid-free, 250-year-life paper
Manufactured in the United States of America

To my parents
Sam and Rita Nova

CONTENTS

INTRODUCTION

This book aims to acquaint the reader with English-language films whose characters include a woman of color, specifically an American woman character who belongs to a minority group or a woman of the Third World. However, this filmography is not limited to films in which minority and Third World women play these characters. In fact, the minorities in question have usually been played by white women. Coverage includes films released from 1930 through 1983; most were produced in the United States, but a few from Great Britain are included. Silent films were not included because they are so numerous, and the time and space necessary for thorough research and coverage were not available.

The study does not attempt to be comprehensive, an almost impossible aim given the great number of films in which Black and Hispanic women were depicted as maids and servants. Nevertheless, many of the maid roles are included to give the reader an idea of the limited roles available to minority women throughout film history. Films were selected for inclusion to suggest the variety and types of characters to which women of color have been relegated.

In selecting films for inclusion I have identified three role/character types:

1. The leading character: the film focuses on this woman, often with another major plot development.
2. Supporting character: this woman is usually a significant character but the focus is not on her; or because of the nature of the role, even if rather minor, she stands out in the film.
3. Stereotypical character: this is a much broader category which can be divided into three subdivisions—(a) A "token" minority type: for example, Hattie McDaniel and Louise Beavers played maids throughout their film careers. Not all of these films can be listed here; a random sample is provided to indi-

cate this fact. (b) Specialty roles: these occur in films set in a specific time or place where a token native is needed to add local color. (c) Specialty numbers: this refers to films in which the woman is used specifically for a song or dance. Any other character development is incidental. Carmen Miranda is probably best known for such roles.

How to Use This Filmography

Films are listed alphabetically by title. Each entry contains, whenever possible, the following information: production company, running time, year of release, producer, director, screenwriter, cameraperson, editor, music director, principal cast members, and the minority/Third World classification. In each entry the principal woman of color in the film is designated by italic capital letters; where there is only one woman of color in a given film, capital letters are not intended necessarily to suggest that the character is prominent. If more than one woman is a major character, both names are capitalized and italicized. Also italicized but not capitalized are additional minority/Third World women characters; in most cases the parts such women played are not described. Plot summaries have been provided for almost all films listed. However, some films were unavailable for viewing and information was not available from other sources; such cases are so identified in the filmography. At the end of the filmography are indexes according to actress (in a minority role), director, and minority/Third World classification.

Whenever possible the character's country of origin is listed. For the most part it was necessary to be rather general and list only the broad geographic area, for example, Asia, Latin America. A difficulty arose with Native Americans or American Indians and the Indians of Canada and Mexico. For the United States I designated them as Native Americans while also referring to American Indians in film descriptions. When necessary I also listed these groups as Mexican Indians and Canadian Indians to designate the differences between these groups and to designate the differences in Mexico between Mexican and Indian populations, and in Canada the difference between the Indian population and the Metis.

Another classification which may be confusing is Arabian Nights. This was used to distinguish between films with Arab women and the fantasy world of the Arabian Nights—the latter far outnumbers the Arab women classification and indicates the types of characterizations to which Arab women have been relegated.

The following classifications are used in this filmography:

Asian—This includes all women who are of Asian descent, without reference to a specific country of origin. This category includes; *Chinese, Eurasian, Filipino, Japanese,* and other specific southeast Asian countries.

Arabian Nights—This includes films set in the Middle East but specifically in the fantasy world of the Arabian Nights. These women are Arabic in character but within the fantasy world of the Arabian Nights.

Blacks—This category is subdivided into *American Black, African Black, West Indian,* and *Jamaican.*

Latin American—This includes all women of Hispanic origin who are not referred to a specific country. This category also includes specific South and Central American countries and Mexico.

Middle Eastern—This includes Arab women with no specific country of origin as well as those with specific countries. It also includes *Afghan, Persian,* and *Turkish* women.

Native American—This includes all Indians in the United States proper, with tribal affiliation given whenever possible. Also included in this category are Mexican and Canadian Indians.

South Sea Island—This includes the islands of the South Pacific.

Miscellaneous Groups—Included here are *Cajun, Creole, Gypsy, Indian, Jungle Exotic* (a woman who lives in a jungle or comes from a jungle environment with no other specific background) *Island Exotic* (as with *Jungle Exotic*).

My primary reference sources were *Variety, The New York Times, BFI Monthly Film Bulletin, Film Daily, Screen World,* and *Film Facts.* I wish to thank the Northwestern University Library for allowing me access to their resources. I would like to thank the following friends and associates for their help and assistance: Thomas Erffmeyer for his support in the early stages of this project and his assistance in the classification of types; Stuart Kaminsky, Jack Ellis,

Chuck Kleinhans, and Michelle Citron, film faculty in the Department of Radio/TV/Film at Northwestern University; Suzi Doll and David Oshana for helping me in ways they will never know. My special thanks go to Carol Slingo, one of the most knowledgeable women I know, for providing me with countless film titles and sources which I would never have found on my own. Without the help of these people this work could not have been accomplished.

AARON LOVES ANGELA   Puerto Rican   1975/Drama

Columbia; 98 min.; *Producer*: Robert J. Anderson; *Director*: Gordon
Parks, Jr.; *Screenplay*: Gerald Sanford; *Music*: Jose Feliciano;
Camera: Richard Kratina; *Editor*: William E. Anderson; *Cast*: Kevin
Hooks (Aaron); *IRENE CARA (ANGELA)*; Moses Gunn (Ike); Robert Hooks
(Beau); *Ernestine Jackson (Cleo)*; Leon Pinkney (Willie).

    Aaron, a black Harlem youth, is in love with Angela. Their
meeting place is a deserted tenement, also used by drug dealers, who
kill each other there. Before he dies, one of the pushers gives
Aaron a quarter of a million dollars. Aaron wants to keep the money
but Angela wants to turn it over to the police. Aaron's solution is
to dump the money from an el platform into the streets of Harlem.

ABBY   Black   1974/Thriller

American International; 91 min.; *Producers*: Mike Henry/G. Cornell
Layne; *Director*: William Girdier; *Screenplay*: G. Cornell Layne; *Music*:
Robert O. Ragland; *Camera*: William Asman; *Editors*: Corky Ehlers/Henry
Asman; *Cast*: William Marshall (Rev. Dr. Garnet Williams); *CAROL SPEED
(ABBY)*; Terry Carter (Rev. Emmett Williams); Austin Stoker (Cass
Potter); *Juanita Moore (Mamma Potter)*; Charles Kissinger (Dr. Henn-
ings); Elliott Moffitt (Russell).

    Abby is possessed by demons after her father-in-law uncovers
some artifacts in Nigeria. She is saved by exorcist Rev. Dr. Garnet
Williams.

ACROSS THE WIDE MISSOURI   Native American   1951/Western

MGM; 78 min.; *Producer*: Robert Sisk; *Director*: William A. Wellman;
Screenplay: Talbot Jennings; *Music*: David Eskain; *Camera*: William
Mallor; *Editor*: John Dunning; *Cast*: Clark Gable (Flint Mitchell);
Ricardo Montalban (Ironshirt); John Hodiak (Brecan); Adolph Menjou
(Pierre); *MARIA ELENA MARQUES (KAMISH)*; J. Carrol Naish (Looking
Glass); Jack Holt (Bear Ghost); Alan Napier (Capt. Humberstone Lyon);
George Chandler (Gowie); Richard Anderson (Dick).

    Kamish is purchased by Flint Mitchell, much to his dismay, to
protect his trading alliance with her tribe. Kamish speaks no English
but learns to play Flint's favorite song, "Skip to My Lou," on his
mouth harp. Eventually he falls in love with her and they have a son.
Then Kamish is killed by a rival Indian tribe and Flint is left to

bring up his son alone in the wilderness.

ACTION IN ARABIA   Arab--Syrian   1944/Spy Drama

RKO; 90 min.; *Producer*: Maurice Geraghty; *Director*: Leonide Moguy;
Screenplay: Philip MacDonald/Herbert Biberman; *Music*: Roy Webb;
Camera: Roy Hunt; *Editor*: Robert Swink; *Cast*: George Sanders (Gordon);
Virginia Bruce (Yvonne); *LENORE AUBERT (MOUNIRAH)*; Gene Lockhart
(Danesco); Robert Armstrong (Reed); Alan Napier (Latimer); H.B. War-
ner (Rashid); Rafael Storm (Hotel Clerk).

   The setting is 1941 Damascus. Syria is a hotbed of political
intrigue as a power struggle develops between the allies and the axis
powers. Mounirah is involved with the volatile politics of the day
as well as with American reporter Gordon.

THE ADVENTURERS   South American   1970/Adventure

Avco Embassy/Paramount; 171 min.; *Producer/Director*: Lewis Gilbert;
Screenplay: Michael Hastings/Lewis Gilbert; *Music*: Antonio Carlos
Jobim; *Camera*: Claude Renoir; *Editor*: Anne V. Coates; *Cast*: Bekim
Fehmiu (Dax Xenos); Charles Aznavour (Marcel Campion); Alan Badel
(Rojo); Candice Bergen (Sue Ann Daley); Thommy Berggren (Sergei
Nikovitch); Delia Boccardo (Caroline de Coyne); *LEIGH TAYLOR-YOUNG
(AMPARO)*; Olivia De Havilland (Deborah Hadley); Anna Moffo (Dania
Leonardi); Ernest Borgnine (Fat Cat); Rossano Brazzi (Baron de Coyne);
Fernando Rey (Jaime Xenos); John Ireland (Mr. Hadley).

   Amparo, the daughter of revolutionary leader Rojo, bears Dax a
son. Soon after Dax attempts to set up a democratic government, he
is assassinated by a rival revolutionary group.

THE ADVENTURES OF FRONTIER FREMONT   Native American   1976/Western

Sunn Classic; 96 min.; *Producer*: Charles E. Sellier; *Director*: Richard
Friedenberg; *Screenplay*: David O'Malley; *Camera*: George A. Stapleford;
Music: Bob Summers; *Editors*: Sharron Miller/Steve Siegel/Stephen W.
Gray; *Cast*: Dan Haggerty (Jacob Fremont); Denver Pyle ("Big Bill"
Diggers); Tony Miratti (Kemp); Norman Goodman (Williams); *TERI
HERNANDEZ (INDIAN MAIDEN)*; Bryan Frasier (Indian Boy); Don Shanks
(Young Warrior); Henry Tyler (Medicine Man); Douglas Carson (Chief).

   Not enough information was available to describe this role
accurately.

THE ADVENTURES OF HAJJI BABA   Arabian Nights   1954/Fantasy

20th Century-Fox; 92 min.; *Producer*: Walter Wanger; *Director*: Don
Weis; *Screenplay*: Richard Colling; *Music*: Dimitri Tiomkin; *Camera*:
Herald Lipstein; *Editor*: William Austin; *Cast*: John Derek (Hajji
Baba); *ELAINE STEWART (FAWZIA)*; *Rosemarie Bowe (Ayesha)*; Thomas Gomez

(Osman-Aga); Paul Picerni (Nur-el-Din); Donald Randolph (Caliph); *Amanda Blake (Banah); Linda Danson (Fabria).*

Princess Fawzia is on her way to marry Prince Nur-el-Din when she meets barber Hajji Baba, who joins her on her journey to meet the Prince. When they meet him, they realize that he is interested in Fawzia only so that he may advance himself politically. Hajji Baba fights the Prince and wins Fawzia for himself.

ADVENTURES OF MARCO POLO   Chinese   1938/Adventure

United Artists; 100 min.; *Producer*: Samuel Goldwyn; *Director*: Archie Mayo; *Screenplay*: Robert E. Sherwood; *Music*: Alfred Newman; *Camera*: Rudolph Mate; *Editor*: Fred Allen; *Cast*: Gary Cooper (Marco Polo); *SIGRID GURIE (PRINCESS KUKUCHIN)*; Basil Rathbone (Ahmed); George Habier (Kublai Khan); Binnie Barnes (Nazama); Ernest Truex (Binguccio); Alan Hale (Kaidu); H.B. Warner (Chen Tsu).

The story of explorer Marco Polo and his love for Princess Kukuchin. She is betrothed to a Persian prince and is desired by the evil Ahmed as a step toward the throne, but she has eyes only for Marco Polo. Ahmed's plot to get rid of Polo and seize the Princess and the throne brings about his destruction, and Polo claims the Princess for himself.

AFFAIR IN HAVANA   Cuban   1957/Drama

Allied Artists; 71 min.; *Producer*: Richard Goldstone; *Director*: Laslo Benedek; *Screenplay*: Burton Lane/Maurice Zimm; *Music*: Ernest Gold; *Camera*: Alan Stenvold; *Editor*: Stefan Arnsten; *Cast*: John Cassavetes (Nick); Raymond Burr (Mallabee); Sara Shane (Lorna); *LILLA LAZO (FINA); Celia Cruz (Fiesta Singer)*; Jose Antonio Rivero (Rivero); Sergio Pena (Valdez); Miguel Angel Blanco (Police Captain).

Fina is a servant's wife.

AN AFFAIR OF THE SKIN   Black   1963/Drama

Zenith International; 102 min.; *Producers*: Helen Levitt/Ben Maddow; *Director/Screenplay*: Ben Maddow; *Music*: Shiko Ozaki/Leroy Vinnegar; *Camera*: Roger Barlow/David Shore; *Cast*: Viveca Lindfors (Victoria); Kevin McCarthy (Allen McCleod); Lee Grant (Katherine McCleod); *DIANA SANDS (JANICE)*; Herbert Berghof (May); Nancy Malone (Claire); Osceola Archer (Mrs. Cluny).

Janice is a photographer interested only in her work. Max tries to fix her up with Allen who is married. When Allen, in a drunken stupor, brings a prostitute to her studio she makes him confess his philandering in letters of atonement to his wife and mistress.

AGAINST A CROOKED SKY   Native American   1976/Western

Doty-Daton; 88 min.; *Producer*: Lyman D. Dayton; *Director*: Earl
Bellamy; *Screenplay*: Douglas C. Stewart/Eleanor Lamb; *Music*: Lex de
Azevedo; *Camera*: Joe Jackman; *Editor*: Marsh Hendry; *Cast*: Richard
Boone (Russian Habbakuk); Stewart Petersen (Sam Sutter); Jewel Blanch
(Charlotte Sutter); Gordon Hanson (Shumeki); Clint Ritchie (John
Sutter); Shannon Farnon (Molly Sutter); *BRENDA VENUS (ASHKEA)*; Henry
Wilcoxon (Cut Tongue); Geoffrey Land (Temkai); Vincent St. Cyr
(Shokobob); Margaret Willey (Old Hag); Norman Walke (Milt Adams).

Ashkea befriends white captive Charlotte Sutter. Charlotte is
pregnant by her Indian husband, but when it is thought that she has
betrayed the tribe, she is sentenced to be executed. Ashkea takes
Charlotte's place at the execution, and Charlotte returns home with
her newborn baby.

ALADDIN AND HIS LAMP   Arabian Nights   1952/Fantasy

Monogram; 67 min.; *Producer*: Walter Wagner; *Director*: Lew Landers;
Screenplay: Howard Dimsdale/Millard Kaufman; *Music*: Marlin Skiles;
Camera: Gilbert Warrenton; *Editor*: Jack Ogilvie; *Cast*: *PATRICIA MEDINA
(JASMINE)*; John Sands (Aladdin); Richard Erdman (Mirza); John Dehner
(Bokra); Billy House (Kafan); Ned Young (Hassan); *Noreen Nash
(Passion Flower)*; Rick Vallin (Capt. of the Guard); Charles Horvath
(Genie); *Sujata (Dancing Slave Girl)*; *Arabella (Maid-in-waiting)*.

Pickpocket Aladdin falls in love with Jasmine, the Caliph's daughter.
Bokra is also interested in Jasmine, but only because he wants to
become Caliph. With the help of his magic lamp and the genie, Aladdin
wins the Princess.

ALEX AND THE GYPSY   Gypsy   1976/Drama

20th Century-Fox; 98 min.; *Producer*: Richard Sheperd; *Director*: John
Korty; *Screenplay*: Lawrence B. Marcus; *Music*: Henry Mancini; *Camera*:
Bill Butler; *Editor*: Donn Cambern; *Cast*: Jack Lemmon (Alexander Main);
GENEVIEVE BUJOLD (MARITZA); James Woods (Crainpool); Gino Ardito (The
Golfer); Robert Emhardt (Judge Ehrlinger); Tito Vandis (Treska); Bill
Cort (Public Defender); Todd Martin (Roy Blake).

Maritza is sent to jail for assaulting her lover. Alex is the bail
bondsman who posts her bond. She goes home with him and they become
lovers. Alex, realizing that her going to jail will cause her great
psychological damage, allows her to jumb bail, although he will thereby lose his job.

ALI BABA AND THE FORTY THEIVES   Arabian Nights   1944/Fantasy

Universal; 87 min.; *Producer*: Paul Malvern; *Director*: Arthur Lubin;
Screenplay: Edmund L. Haktmann; *Music*: Edward Ward; *Camera*: George
Robinson; *Cast*: *MARIA MONTEZ (AMARA)*; *Yvette Dugay (Amara at 10)*;

Jon Hall (Ali); Scotty Beckett (Ali at 12); Turhan Bey (Jamiel); Kurt
Katch (Hulagu Khan); Andy Devine (Abdullah); Frank Publia (Cassim);
Moroni Olsen (Hassan); Fortunio Bonanova (Old Baba); Harry Cording
(Mahmoud); *Ramsay Ames (Nalu)*.

A typical juvenile version of the Arabian Nights. Amara agrees
to marry the evil Mongol lord Hulagu Khan to save her father's life.
However, her father is actually involved in a plot with the Khan, and
is responsible for the overthrow of Ali Baba's father as caliph of
Bagdad. Ali Baba and his thieves enter Bagdad at the time of the
wedding and overcome the Mongols.

ALI BABA GOES TO TOWN   Arabian Nights   1937/Fantasy

20th Century-Fox; 81 min.; *Producer*: Darryl F. Zanuck; *Director*:
David Butler; *Screenplay*: Harry Tugent/Jack Yellen; *Music*: Louis
Silver; *Camera*: Ernest Palmer; *Editor*: Irene Butler; *Cast*: Eddie
Cantor (Ali Baba); Tony Martin (Yusuf); Roland Young (Sultan); *JUNE
LANG (PRINCESS MIRIAM)*; *Louise Hovic (Sultana)*; John Carradine
(Ishak); Virginia Field (Diana); Alan Dinehart (Boland); Douglas
Dumbrille (Prince Musah); Maurice Cass (Omar, the rug maker).

Ali Baba (who is actually a 20th-century American transported
back to ancient Bagdad after taking too many pain killers) introduces
modern ideas into Bagdad and becomes involved with the sultan, Princess Miriam, and Sultana—one of the sultan's hundred wives.

ALICE'S RESTAURANT   Asian   1969/Comedy

United Artists; 110 min.; *Producers*: Hillard Elkins/Joe Manduke;
Director: Arthur Penn; *Screenplay*: Venable Herndon/Arthur Penn;
Music: Arlo Guthrie; *Camera*: Michael Nebbia; *Editor*: Dede Allen;
Cast: Arlo Guthrie (Arlo); Pat Quinn (Alice); James Broderick (Ray);
Michael McClanathan (Shelly); Geoff Outlaw (Rogers); *TINA CHEN (MARI-
CHAN)*; Kathleen Dabney (Karin); William Obanhein (Officer Obie); Seth
Allen (Evangelist).

In this film based on Arlo Guthrie's song "Alice's Restaurant,"
Mari-Chan is Arlo's girlfriend.

ALL THE BROTHERS WERE VALIANT   Island Exotic   1953/Adventure

MGM; 94 min.; *Producer*: Pandro S. Berman; *Director*: Richard Thorpe;
Screenplay: Harry Brown; *Music*: Miklos Rozsa; *Camera*: George Folsey;
Editor: Ferris Webster; *Cast*: Robert Taylor (Joel Shore); Stewart
Granger (Mark Shore); Anny Blyth (Priscilla Holt); *BETTA ST. JOHN
(NATIVE GIRL)*; Keenan Wynn (Silva); James Whitmore (Fetcher); Kurt
Kasznar (Quint); Lewis Stone (Capt. Holt); Robert Burton (Asa
Worthen); Peter Whitney (James Finch).

Shipwrecked Mark Shore has a romance with Native Girl.

ALL THE FINE YOUNG CANNIBALS   Black   1960/Drama

MGM; 122 min.; *Producer*: Pandro S. Berman; *Director*: Michael Ander; *Screenplay*: Robert Thom; *Camera*: William H. Daniels; *Editor*: John McSweeney, Jr.; *Cast*: Robert Wagner (Chad Bixby); Natalie Wood (Salome/Sara Davis); Susan Kohner (Catherine McDowall); George Hamilton (Tony McDowall); *PEARL BAILEY (RUBY JONES)*; Jack Mullaney (Putney Tiner); Onslow Stevens (Joshua Davis); Anne Seymour (Mrs. Bixby); Virginia Gregg (Ada Davis); Mabel Albertson (Mrs. McDowall); *Louise Beavers (Rose)*; Addison Richards (Mr. McDowall).

Trumpet player Chad Bixby is the protege of blues singer Ruby Jones. Ruby and Chad go to New York where she helps him to become successful. Ruby dies of alcoholism.

ALOMA OF THE SOUTH SEAS   Island Exotic   1941/Adventure

Paramount; 77 min.; *Producer*: B.G. DeSylva; *Director*: Alfred Santell; *Screenplay*: Frank Butler/Lillian Hayward/Seena Owen; *Music*: Andrea Setaro; *Camera*: Karl Strauss; *Editor*: Arthur Schmidt; *Cast: DOROTHY LAMOUR (ALOMA)*; Jon Hall (Tanoa); Lynne Overman (Corky); Philip Reed (Bevo); *Katherine de Mille (Kari)*; Fritz Leiber (High Priest); *Dona Drake (Nea)*; *Esther Dale (Taruga)*; Pedro de Cordova (Raulti); John Barclay (Ikall).

As children Aloma and the chief's son, Tanoa, were betrothed. Tanoa left the island to receive an education in white society. On his return 15 years later he is unwilling to agree to the marriage. However, he and Aloma meet accidentally and fall in love. During the marriage ceremony trouble is caused by Bevo, Tanoa's jealous cousin, and by a volcanic eruption. When the fireworks are over, Tanoa and Aloma live happily ever after.

ALONG THE NAVAJO TRAIL   Gypsy   1945/Western

Republic; 66 min.; *Producer*: Edward J. White; *Director*: Frank Mac Donald; *Screenplay*: Gerald Geraghty; *Camera*: William Bradford; *Editor*: Tony Martinelli; *Cast*: Roy Rogers; Dale Evans (Lorry Alastair); George "Gabby" Hayes (Gabby Whittaker); *ESTELITA RODRIGUEZ (NARITA)*; Douglas Fowley (J. Richard Bentley); Nester Paiva (Janza); Sam Flint (Breck Alastair).

Deputy marshall Roy Rogers is assigned to investigate crimes against Breck Alastair's ranch. Narita is a member of a gypsy caravan who is competing with Lorry Alastair for Roy's attentions. Roy sets everything right and wins Lorry in the end.

AMAZING GRACE   Black   1974/Comedy-drama

United Artists; 99 min.; *Producer*: Matt Robinson; *Director*: Stan Lathan; *Screenplay*: Matt Robinson; *Camera*: Sol Negrin; *Cast: Moms MABLEY (GRACE)*; Slappy White (Forthwith Wilson); Moses Gunn (Welton J.

Waters); *Rosalind Cash (Creola Waters)*; Jim Karen (Jim Annenberg); Stepin Fetchit (Cousin Lincoln; *Butterfly McQueen (Clarine)*.

Grace decides to campaign vigorously for the Black candidate for mayor of Baltimore.

AMBUSH AT CIMARRON PASS   Mexican   1958/Western

20th Century-Fox; 73 min.; *Producer*: Herbert E. Mendelson; *Director*: Jodie Copelan; *Screenplay*: Richard G. Taylor/John Butler; *Music*: Paul Sawtell/Bert Shefter; *Camera*: John M. Nickolaus, Jr.; *Editor*: Carl L. Pierson; *Cast*: Scott Brady (Sgt. Matt Blake); *MARGIA DEAN (TERESA)*; Clint Eastwood (Keith Williams); Irving Bacon (Stan Field); Frank Gerstle (Sam Prescott); Dirk London (Johnny Willows); Baynes Barron (Corbin); Ken Mayer (Corp. schwitzer).

Teresa is a captive of the Apaches whom is left behind when they steal a herd of horses belonging to a group of ranchers and cavalry soldiers. Teresa and the men are forced to travel by foot to the safety of the army fort.

AMBUSH AT TOMAHAWK GAP   Native American-Apache   1953/Western

Columbia; 73 min.; *Producer*: Wallace MacDonald; *Director*: Fred F. Sears; *Screenplay*: David Lang; *Music*: Ross Dimaggio; *Camera*: Henry Freulich; *Editor*: Aaron Stell; *Cast*: John Hodiak (McCord); John Derek (Kid); David Brian (Egan); *MARIA ELENA MARQUEZ (INDIAN GIRL)*; Ray Teal (Doc); John Qualen (Jonas P. Travis); Otto Hulett (Stranton); Percy Helton (Marlowe); Trevor Bardette (Sheriff).

After serving five years in prison for robbery, four men return to the ghost town of Tomahawk Gap to recover the stolen money. Indian Girl is a resident there.

THE AMERICANO   Brazilian   1954/Adventure

RKO; 85 min.; *Producer*: Robert Stillman; *Director*: William Castle; *Screenplay*: Guy Trosper; *Music*: Roy Webb; *Camera*: Harry Marker; *Editor*: Harry Marker; *Cast*: Glenn Ford (Sam Dent); Frank Lovejoy (Bento Hermanny); Cesar Romero (Manoel); *URSULA THIESS (MARIANNA FIGUERIDO)*; *Abbe Lane (Teresa)*; Rodolfo Hoyos, Jr. (Cristino); Salvador Baguez (Capt. Gonzales); Tom Powers (Jim Rogers); Dan White (Barney Dent); Frank Marlowe (captain of ship).

Marianna Figuerido is slowly being driven off her ranch by Bento Hermanny. Help comes from Texan Sam Dent.

ANNA AND THE KING OF SIAM   Asian   1946/Biography

20th Century-Fox; 128 min.; *Producer*: Louis D. Lighton; *Director*:
John Cromwell; *Screenplay*: Talbot Jennings/Sally Benson; *Music*:
Bernard Herrmann; *Camera*: Arthur Miller; *Editor*: Harmon Jones; *Cast*:
Irene Dunne (Anna Owens); Rex Harrison (King Mongkut of Siam); *LINDA
DARNELL (TUPTIM); Gale Sondergaard (Lady Thiang)*; Lee J. Cobb
(Kralahome); Mikhan Rasumny (Alak); Dennis Hoey (Sir Edward); Tito
Renaldo (Prince); Richard Lyon (Louis Owens); William Edmunds
(Moonshee); John Abbott (Phya Rhrom); Mickey Roth (younger prince).

Tuptim is given to the King of Siam as a gift and she becomes
his favorite wife. She falls in love with one of the King's couriers
who brought her to Siam. Their meet secretly and plot to run away
together. Their plot is uncovered and he is killed and because of
her infidelity she is burned at the stake.

ANNA LUCASTA   Black   1959/Drama

United Artists; 97 min.; *Producer*: Sidney Harmon; *Director*: Arnold
Laven; *Screenplay*: Philip Yordan; *Music*: Elmer Bernstein; *Camera*:
Lucien Ballard; *Editor*: Richard C. Meyer; *Cast*: *EARTHA KITT (ANNA
LUCASTA)*; Frederic O'Neal (Frank); Sammy Davis, Jr. (Danny Johnson);
Henry Scott (Rudolph Slocum); Rex Ingram (Joe Lucasta); *Georgia
Burke (Theresa Lucasta)*; James Edwards (Eddie); *Rosetta Lenoire
(Stella)*; *Isabelle Cooley (Katie)*; Alvin Childress (Noah).

After throwing Anna out of the house because of her promiscuity,
Joe Lucasta brings her home so she can marry Rudolph, an old friend
of the family, who has money and is looking for a wife. Rudolph, is
a well-educated man, falls in love with Anna. She tells him about
her past, but he still wants to marry her. They marry but Joe,
determined to ruin Anna, tells Rudolph's future employer about Anna's
past. Anna then runs away with her ex-lover, Danny. When they
return to get money, they find Joe dying. Joe makes peace with Anna,
and Danny leaves, knowing Rudolph and Anna will now find happiness.

APACHE   Native American--Apache   1954/Western

United Artists; 91 min.; *Producer*: Harold Hecht; *Director*: Robert
Aldrich; *Screenplay*: James R. Webb; *Music*: David Raksin; *Camera*:
Ernest Laslo; *Editor*: Alan Crosland, Jr.; *Cast*: Burt Lancaster
(Massai); *JEAN PETERS (NALINLE)*; John McIntire (Al Sieber); Charles
Bronson (Hondo); John Dehner (Weddle); Paul Guilfoyle (Santos); Ian
MacDonald (Glagg); Walter Sande (Lt. Col. Beck); Morris Ankrum
(Dawson); Monte Blue (Geronimo).

Nalinle is the wife of Massai, who is waging a one-man war
·against the United States Cavalry. Although Massai does not want her,
Nalinle insists on being with him while the army is tracking him down.
When Nalinle gives birth to his child, he realizes the futility of his
fight and agress to end his vendetta.

APACHE AMBUSH   Mexican   1955/Western

Columbia; 68 min.; *Producer*: Wallace MacDonald; *Director*: Fred F.
Sears; *Screenplay*: David Lang; *Music*: Mischa Bakaleinikoff; *Camera*:
Fred Jackman, Jr.; *Editor*: Jerome Thoms; *Cast*: Bill Williams (James
Kingston); Richard Jaeckel (Lee Parker); Alex Montoya (Joaquin
Jironza); *MOVITA (ROSITA)*; Adelle August (Ann); Tex Ritter (Trager);
Ray "Crash" Corrigan (Mark Calvin); Ray Teal (Sgt. O'Roarke); Don C.
Harvey (Major McGuire); James Griffith (Mr. Lincoln).

     Rosita is the girlfriend of Mexican outlaw Joaquin Jironza.

APACHE CHIEF   Native American   1949/Western

Lippert; 59 min.; *Producer*: Leonard S. Picker; *Director*: Frank Mac
Donald; *Screenplay*: George D. Green; *Camera*: Benjamin Kline; *Editor*:
Stanley Frazon; *Cast*: Alan Curtis (Young Eagle); Tom Neal (Lt. Brown);
CAROL THURSTON (WATONA): Russell Hayden (Black Wolf); Fuzzy Knight
(Nevada Smith); Trevor Bardette (Big Crow).

     Young Eagle believes that whites and Indians can live in peace,
but he is opposed by Black Wolf, who wants to go to war. Watona is
romantically undecided between them until Young Eagle defeats Black
Wolf and proves peace is better than war.

APACHE RIFLES   Native American--Kiowa   1964/Western

20th Century-Fox; 92 min.; *Producer*: Grant Whytock; *Director*: William
H. Witney; *Screenplay*: Charles B. Smith; *Music*: Richard La Salle;
Camera: Arch R. Dalzell; *Editor*: Grant Whytock; *Cast*: Audie Murphy
(Jeff Stanton); Michael Dante (Red Hawk); *LINDA LAWSON (DAWN GILLIS)*;
L.Q. Jones (Mike Greer); Ken Lynch (Hodges); Joseph A. Vitale
(Victorio); Robert Brubaker (Sgt. Cobb); Eugene Iglesias (Cpl.
Ramirez); J. Pat O'Malley (Capt. Thatcher).

     Having mistaken her for a captive of the Apaches, Jeff Stanton
is shocked to learn that Dawn Gillis is a missionary living willingly
among them. His attitude prevents her from telling him of her Kiowa
background as they begin to fall in love. When he learns the truth he
is at first repelled but soon confronts his bigotry and accepts his
love for Dawn.

APACHE WARRIOR   Native American--Apache   1957/Western

20th Century-Fox; 73 min.; *Producer*: Regal Film Production; *Director*:
Elmo Williams; *Screenplay*: Carroll Young/Kurt Neumann/Eric Norden;
Music: Paul Dunlap; *Camera*: John M. Nickolaus; *Editor*: Jodie Copelan;
Cast: Keith Larsen (Apache Kid); Jim Davis (Ben); Rodolfo Acosta
(Marteen); John Miljan (Nantan); Eddie Little (Apache 1); Michael
Carr (Apache 2); *EUGENIA PAUL (LIWANA)*; George Keymas (Chato); Lane
Bradford (Sgt. Gaunt); Damian O'Flynn (Major);

The Apache Kid is an Indian scout for the United States cavalry. When he kills the Indian who murdered his brother, he is hunted by Ben. Liwana is the Apache Kid's wife who helps the Kid clear his name. Ben soon realizes that the Kid was justified (according to Indian custom) and abandons his search for the Apache Kid and his wife. They then escape into Mexico.

APACHE WOMAN   Native American--Apache   1955/Western

American Releasing Corp.; 82 min.; *Producer/Director*: Roger Corman; *Screenplay*: Lou Rasoff; *Music*: Ronald Stein; *Camera*: Floyd Crosby; *Editor*: Ronald Sinclair; *Cast*: Lloyd Bridges (Rex Moffet); *JOAN TAYLOR (ANNE LIBEAU)*; Lance Fuller (Armand); Morgan Jones (Macey); Paul Birch (Sheriff); Jonathan Haze (Tom Chandler); Paul Duboy (Ben); Lou Place (Carrom).

Anne Libeau is the sister of the crazed, college-educated Armand who is leading a small band of renegades against the local settlers. She is attracted to Rex Moffet, who is trying to track down her brother.

THE APPALOOSA   Mexican   1966/Western

Universal; 99 min.; *Producer*: Alan Miller; *Director*: Sidney J. Furie; *Screenplay*: James Bridges/Roland Kibbee; *Music*: Frank Skinner; *Camera*: Russell Metty; *Editor*: Ted Kent; *Cast*: Marlon Brando (Matt Fletcher); *ANJANETTE COMER (TRINI)*; John Saxon (Chuy Medina); Emilio Fernandez (Lasaro); Alex Montoya (Squint Eye); *Miriam Colon (Ana)*; Rafael Campos (Paco); Frank Silvera (Ramos); Larry D. Mann (Priest); *Argentina Brunetti (Yaqui Woman)*.

Trini, sold by her parents to bandit Chuy Medina, continually tries to run away from him. During one of her escape attempts she steals Matt Fletcher's horse--a prized appaloosa. She is caught and Chuy tries to buy the horse from Matt to save face. Matt refuses. Soon Trini becomes the prize in the conflict between the two men. Matt sacrifices the appaloosa and kills Chuy, thereby winning Trini for himself.

ARABESQUE   Arab   1966/Thriller

Universal; 105 min.; *Producer/Director*: Stanley Donen; *Screenplay*: Julian Mitchell/Stanley Price/Pierre Martin; *Music*: Henry Mancini; *Camera*: Christopher Challis; *Editor*: Frederick Wilson; *Cast*: Gregory Peck (David Pollock); *SOPHIA LOREN (YASMIN AZIR)*; Alan Badel (Beshraavi); Kieron Moore (Yussef); Carl Duering (Hassan Jena); John Merrivale (Sloane); Duncan Lamont (Webster); George Coulouris (Ragheeb); Ernest Clark (Beauchamp); Harold Kasket (Mohammed Lufti); Gordon Griffith (Fanshaw).

David Pollock becomes involved with spies and Yasmin Azir, who is mistress to oil magnate Beshraavi, because Pollock is able to decipher a hieroglyphic message which tells of the assassination of the

prime minister of a Middle Eastern country. Pollock is never sure of
Yasmin's loyalties because of the lies she tells. She finally admits
that she is a spy for the prime minister of her country. She and
Pollock expose Beshraavi, the real spy, and return to David's home in
England.

ARABIAN ADVENTURE   Arabian Nights   1979/Fantasy

Warner Brothers/Orion; 98 min.; *Producer*: John Dark; *Director*: Kevin
Connor; *Screenplay*: Brian Hayles; *Music*: Ken Thorne; *Camera*: Alan
Hume; *Editor*: Barry Peters; *Cast*: Christopher Lee (Alquazar); Milo
O'Shea (Khasim); Oliver Tobias (Prince Hasan); *EMMA SANDS (PRINCESS
ZULEIRA)*; Puneet Sira (Majeed); Peter Cushing (Wazar Al Wuzara);
Capucine (Vahista); John Wyman (Bahloul); John Ratzenberger (Achmed);
Shane Rimmer (Abu); hal Galili (Asaf); Mickey Rooney (Daad El Shur).

    The evil magician Alquazar, ruler of Jadur, promises Princess
Zuleira's hand in marriage to Prince Hasan if he performs a certain
task that will insure Alquazar unlimited power. After several magical trials and tribulations Hasan manages to overthrow Alquazar and
marry Princess Zuleira.

ARABIAN NIGHTS   Arabian Nights   1942/Fantasy

Universal; 86 min.; *Producer*: Walter Wanger; *Director*: John Rawlins;
Screenplay: Michael Hogan; *Camera*: Milton Krasner; *Editor*: Philip
Cahn; *Cast*: Jon Hall (Haroun-Al-Raschid); *MARIA MONTEZ (SCHEHERAZADE):*
Sabu (Ali Ben Ali); Leif Erikson (Kamar); Bill Gilbert (Ahmad); Edgar
Barrier (Nadan); Richard Lane (Corporal); Turhan Bey (Captain); John
Qualen (Aladdin); Shemp Howard (Sinbad); Wm "Wee Willie" Davis
(Valda); Thomas Gomez (Hakim); *Acquanetta (Ishya)*.

    Scheherazade is a dancing girl who wants to marry a caliph.
Haroun-Al-Raschid and his brother Kamar are fighting over the caliph-
ate. Kamar plots to get rid of Haroun. Haroun, fleeing for his life
and presumed dead, meets Scheherazade and her carnival. They fall in
love, and Haroun confronts his brother and becomes caliph.

ARCTIC MANHUNT   Eskimo   1949/Western

Universal-International; 69 min.; *Producer*: Leonard Goldstein;
Director: Ewing Scott; *Screenplay*: Oscar Brodney/Joel Malone; *Music*:
Milton Schwarzwald; *Camera*: Irving Glassberg; *Editor*: Otto Ludwing;
Cast: Mikel Conrad (Mike Jarvis); *CAROL THURSTON (NARANA)*; Wally
Cassell (Tooyuk); Helen Brown (Lois Jarvis); Harry Harvey (Carter);
Chet Huntley (Landers); Paul E. Burns (Hotel Clerk); *Quianna (Eskimo
Girl)*.

    Convict Mike Jarvis is paroled from prison and retrieves the
money he stole. He then flees to Alaska. He loses the money along
the way and poses as a dead minister. He stops at an Eskimo village
where he falls in love with Narana, who assists him as a nurse and

helps with his ministry. The stolen money turns up, as does an in-
surance agent who has been tracking Mike. Mike takes off over the
frozen tundra and loses his life when the ice breaks.

THE ARIZONA KID   Mexican   1930/Western

Fox Film Corp.; 84 min.; *Producer*: William Fox; *Director*: Alfred
Santell; *Screenplay*: Ralph Block; *Camera*: Glen MacWilliams; *Editor*:
Paul Weatherwax; *Cast*: Warner Baxter (The Arizona Kid); *MONA MARIS
(LORITA)*; Carole Lombard (Virginia Hoyt); Theodore Von Eltz (Nick
Hoyt); Arthur Stone (Snakebite Pete).

The Arizona Kid is a bandit-hero who loves Lorita until blonde
Virginia Hoyt arrives on the scene. Virginia and her brother (who is
really her husband are using the Kid for their own profit. When the
Kid realizes he is being used, he and Lorita ride off together.

ARIZONA RAIDERS   Native American--Yaqui   1965/Western

Columbia; 88 min.; *Producer*: Grant Whytock; *Director*: William Witney;
Screenplay: Alex Gottlieb/Mary Willingham/Willard Willingham; *Camera*:
Jacques Marquette; *Editor*: Grant Whytock; *Cast*: Audie Murphy (Clint);
Michael Dante (Brady); Ben Cooper (Willie Martin); Buster Crabbe
(Capt. Andrews); *GLORIA TALBOTT (MARTINA)*; Ray Stricklyn (Danny
Bonner); George Keymas (Montana); Fred Krone (Matt Edwards); Willard
Willingham (Eddie); Red Morgan (Tex); Fred Graham (Quantrell).

Members of Quantrell's Raiders Kidnap Martin, daughter of the
chief of a band of peaceful Yaqui Indians. Clint and Willie, former
members of Quantrell's Raiders, help rescue Martina.

ARRIVEDERCI, BABY! [See DROP DEAD, DARLING]

ARROWHEAD   Mexican/Apache   1953/Western

Paramount; 105 min.; *Producer*: Nat Holt; *Director*: Charles Marquis
Warren; *Screenplay*: Frank Bracht; *Music*: Paul Sawtell; *Camera*: Ray
Rennahan; *Cast*: Charlton Heston (Ed Bannon); Jack Palance (Toriano);
KATY JURADO (NITA); Brian Keith (Capt. North); Mary Sinclair (Lela
Wilson); Milburn Stone (Sandy Mackinnon); Richard Shannon (Lt. Kirk);
Lewis Martin (Col. Weybright); Frank de Kova (Chief Chattez); Robert
Wilke (Sgt. Stone); Peter Coe (Spanish); Kyle James (Jerry August);
John M. Packard (John Gunther); Pat Hogan (Jim Eagle).

Nita is attracted to Ed Bannon, army scout. She is spying on
him for the Apaches.

ASHANTI   Black   1979/Drama

Columbia; 117 min.; *Producer*: Georges-Alain Vuille; *Director*: Richard

Fleischer; *Screenplay*: Stephen Geller; *Camera*: Aldo Tonti; *Cast*:
Michael Caine (Dr. David Linderby); Peter Ustinov (Suleiman); *BEVERLY*
JOHNSON (ANANSA LINDERBY); Kabir Bedi (Malik); Omar Sharif (The
Prince); Rex Harrison (Brian Walker); William Holden (Jim Sandell);
Zia Moyheddin (Djamel); Winston Ntshona (Ansok); Tariq Yunus (Faid);
Tyrone Jackson (Dongaro); Jean-Luc Bideau (Marcel).

Anansa is kidnapped by slave trader Suleiman while in Arica.
Her husband, Dr. David Linderby, sets out to retrieve her.

BABES IN BAGDAD   Arabian Nights   1952/Fantasy

United Artists; 79 min.; *Producer*: Danziger Brothers; *Director*: Edgar
G. Ulmer; *Screenplay*: Felix Feist/Joe Anson/Edith Lenny; *Music*: J.
Leoz; *Camera*: Joe Cox; *Editor*: Edith Lenny; *Cast*: *PAULETTE GODDARD*
(KYRA); *Gypsy Rose Lee (Zohara)*; Richard Ney (Ezar); John Bales
(Hassan); Thomas Gallagher (Sharkhan); Sebastian Cabot (Sinbad);
Macdonald Parke (Caliph); *Natalie Benesh (Zelika)*; Hugh Dempster
(Omar); Peter Bathurst (Officer).

Unusual Arabian Nights fare. Kyra and Zohara, members of a
harem, start a rebellion after deciding that they want some independence.

BACKTRACK   Mexican   1969/Western

Universal; 95 min.; *Producer*: David J. O'Connell; *Director*: Earl
Bellamy; *Screenplay*: Borden Chase; *Camera*: Benjamin H. Kline/John L.
Russell/Andrew Jackson; *Editor*: Michael R. McAdam; *Cast*: Neville Brand
(Reese); James Drury (Ramrod); Doug McClure (Trampas); Peter Brown
(Chad); William Smith (Riley); Philip Carey (Capt. Parmaler); *IDA*
LUPINO (MAMA DELORES); *·RHONDA FLEMING (CARMELITA)*; Fernando Lamas
(Capt. Estrada).

Carmelita is a saloon singer being fought over by Trampas and
Chad, Reese and Riley--Texas Rangers. Mama Delores is a cantina owner
who wants to marry Reese. In the end both women are abandoned by the
adventurous men.

THE BADLANDERS   Mexican   1959/Western

MGM; 85 min.; *Producer*: Aaron Rosenberg; *Director*: Delmer Daves;
Screenplay: Richard Collins; *Camera*: John Seitz; *Editor*: William H.
Webb/James Baiotto; *Cast*: Alan Ladd (Peter Van Hoek); Ernest Borgnine
(John McBain); *KATY JURADO (ANITA)*; Claire Kelly (Ada Winton); Kent
Smith (Cyril Lounsberry); Nehemiah Persoff (Vincente); Robert Emhardt
(Sample); Anthony Caruso (Comanche); Adam Williams (Leslie); Ford
Rainey (Warden); John Day (Lee).

Anita becomes involved with Peter and John in a plan to rob a
gold mine.

BAGDAD   Arab   1949/Adventure

Universal-International; 82 min.; *Producer*: Robert Arthur; *Director*:
Charles Lamont; *Screenplay*: Robert Hardy Andrews; *Music*: Milton
Schwarzwald; *Camera*: Russell Metty; *Editor*: Russell Schoengarth;
Cast: MAUREEN O'HARA (PRINCESS MARJAN): Paul Christian (Hassan);
Vincent Price (Pasha Ali Nadim); John Sutton (Raizal); Jeff Corey
(Mohammed Jad); Frank Puglia (Saleel); David Wolfe (Mahmud); Fritz
Leiber (Emir); Otto Waldis (Marengo); Leon Belasco (Beggar).

Princess Marjan, educated in England, discovers on her return
home that her father, a tribal leader, has been murdered. Marjan tries
to find the murderer so she can have revenge.

BAHAMA PASSAGE   West Indian   1942/Adventure

Paramount; 83 min.; *Producer/Director*: Edward H. Griffith; *Screenplay*:
Virginia Van Upp; *Camera*: Leo Tover; *Editor*: Eda Warren; *Cast*:
Madeleine Carroll (Carol Delbridge); Sterling Hayden (Adrian Ains-
worth); Flora Robson (Mrs. Ainsworth); Leo G. Carroll (Delbridge);
Mary Anderson (Mary); Cecil Kellaway (Capt. Jack Risingwell); Leigh
Whipper (Morales); DOROTHY DANDRIDGE (THALIA).

Not enough information was available to accurately describe this
role.

THE BALCONY   Black   1963/Drama

Continental Distributing; 84 min.; *Producers*: Joseph Strick/Ben
Maddow; *Director*: Joseph Strick; *Screenplay*: Ben Maddow; *Music*: Igor
Stravinsky; *Camera*: George Folsey; *Editor*: Chester W. Schaeffer;
Cast: Shelley Winters (Madam Irma); Peter Falk (Police Chief); Lee
Grant (Carmen); RUBY DEE (THIEF); Peter Brocco (Judge); Kent Smith
(General); Jeff Corey (Bishop); Joyce Jameson (Penitent); Arnette
Jens (Horse); Leonard Nimoy (Rebel Leader).

Thief is a prostitute in a bordello called "The Balcony," which
caters to various fantasies of its male customers.

BAND OF ANGELS   Black   1957/Drama

Warner Brothers; 125 min.; *Director*: Raoul Walsh; *Screenplay*: John
Twist/Ivan Goff/Ben Roberts; *Music*: Max Steiner; *Camera*: Lucien
Ballard; *Editor*: Folmar Blangsted; *Cast*: Clark Gable (Hamish Bond);
YVONNE DE CARLO (AMANTHA STARR); Sidney Poitier (Rau-Ru); Efrem
Zimbalist, Jr. (Ethan Sears); Patrick Knowles (Charles de Marigny);
Rex Reason (Seth Parton); Torin Thatcher (Capt. Canavan); Andrea King
(Miss Idell); Ray Teal (Mr. Calloway); Russ Evans (Jimmee); *Carolle
Drake (Michele)*; Raymond Bailey (Stuart); Tommie Moore (Dollie);
William Forrest (Aaron Starr); Noreen Corcoran (Young Manty).

After Amantha Starr's rich father dies, a jealous neighbor re-

veals that her mother was a Black slave. Amantha is then sold at
auction to Hamish Bond. Bond allows her to live as a lady,
replacing his previous Black mistress, Michele. He falls in love
with Amantha but refuses to marry her. With the advent of the Civil
War and the fall of the South, Amantha gains her freedom and moves to
New Orleans where Ethan Sears, thinking she is white, falls in love
with her. Amantha, however, loves Bond and leaves New Orleans to
search for him. She finds him and they set sail, managing to escape
the encroaching Union Army.

BANDOLERO!   Mexican   1968/Western

20th Century-Fox; 106 min.; *Producer*: Robert L. Jacks; *Director*:
Andrew V. McLaglen; *Screenplay*: James Lee Barrett; *Music*: Jerry
Goldsmith; *Camera*: William H. Clothier; *Editor*: Folmar Blangsted;
Cast: James Stewart (Mace Bishop); Dean Martin (Dee Bishop); *RAQUEL
WELCH (MARIA STONER)*; George Kennedy (Sheriff Johnson); Andrew Prine
(Roscoe Bookbinder); Will Geer (Pop Chaney); Clint Ritchie (Babe);
Denver Pyle (Muncie Carter); Tom Heaten (Joe Chaney); Rudy Diaz
(Angel Munoz).

Maria Stoner is taken captive by the outlaw, Dee Bishop, who
murdered her husband. She eventually falls in love with him. They
plan to settle down, with Bishop giving up his life of crime. However, he is pursued by Sheriff Johnson who also loves Maria. Bishop
is eventually killed by Johnson, who takes Maria back with him to
town.

THE BARBARIAN   Arab--Egyptian   1933/Drama

MGM; 67 min.; *Director*: Sam Wood; *Screenplay*: Anita Loos/Elmer Harris;
Music: Herbert Stothart; *Camera*: Harold Rosson; *Editor*: Tom Held;
Cast: Ramon Novarro (Jamil); *MYRNA LOY (DIANA)*; Reginald Denny
(Gerald); Louis Closser Hale (Powers); C. Aubrey Smith (Cecil);
Edward Arnold (Achmed); Blanche Frederici (Mrs. Hume).

Diana is the daughter of an Egyptian woman and an American man,
who is torn between these two different worlds. When she returns to
Egypt with her white fiance she looks and acts American. When she
meets Jamil, an Egyptian guide, she is drawn to her Arab heritage.
She begins to wear the traditional dress of Egyptian women, falls in
love with Jamil, and leaves her white fiance. In the end it is revealed that Jamil is really a prince in disguise.

THE BARBARIAN AND THE GEISHA   Japanese   1958/Drama

20th Century-Fox; 195 min.; *Producer*: Eugene Frenke; *Director*: John
Huston; *Screenplay*: Charles Grayson; *Camera*: Charles G. Clarke;
Editor: Stuart Gilmore; *Cast*: John Wayne (Townsend Harris); *EIKO ANDO
(OKICHI)*; Sam Jaffe (Henry Heusken); So Yamamura (Tamura); Norman
Thomson (Ship Captain); James Robbins (Lt. Fisher); Morita (Prime
Minister); Kodaya Ichikawa (Daimyo); Hiroshi Yamato (Shogun).

   Okichi is sent to spy on Townsend Harris, the first American
Consul to Japan. Okichi falls in love with him and cannot betray him.
She also prevents an attempt on his life. Realizing that she is a
deterrent to his accomplishing his mission, she leaves him.

THE BARRIER   Native American   1937/Western

Paramount; 90 min.; *Producer*: Harry Sherman; *Director*: Leslie Selan-
der; *Screenplay*: Bernard Schubert/Harrison Jacobs/Mordaunt Shairp;
Music: Boris Morros; *Camera*: George Barnes; *Editors*: Thomas Neff/
Robert Warwick; *Cast*: Leo Carillo (Pollon Doret); *JEAN PARKER (NECIA)*;
James Ellison (Lt. Burrell); Robert Barrat (John Gale); Otto Kruger
(Stark); Andy Clyde (No Creek Lee); Addison Richards (Runnion); Sara
Haden (Alluna); J.M. Kerrigan (Sgt. Thomas); Sally Martin (Molly);
Fernando Alvarado (Johnny).

   Jilted by his Indian mistress, John Gale kidnaps her daughter,
Necia, and brings her up as his own. When she wishes to marry Lt.
Burrell, Gale tells her of her Indian heritage and she is prevented
from becoming Burrell's wife.

BATTLE AT APACHE PASS   Native American--Apache   1952/Western

Universal-International; 85 min.; *Producer*: Leonard Goldstein;
Director: George Sherman; *Screenplay*: Gerald Drayson Adams; *Music*:
Hans J. Salter; *Camera*: Charles Boyle; *Editor*: Ted J. Kent; *Cast*:
John Lund (Major Jim Colton); Jeff Chandler (Cochise); Beverly Tyler
(Mary Kearny); Bruce Cowling (Neil Baylor); *SUSAN CABOT (NONA)*; John
Hudson (Lt. George Bascom); Jimmy Best (Corp. Hassett); Regis Toomey
(Dr. Carter); Richard Egan (Sgt. Bernard); Hugh O'Brian (Lt. Harley);
Palmer Lee (Joe Bent); William Reynolds (Lem Bent); Jay Silverheels
(Geronimo); Tommy Cook (Little Elk); Jack Elam (Mescal Jack); Richard
Garland (Culver); Jack Ingraham (Johnny Ward); John Baer (Pvt. Bolin);
Paul Smith (Ross).

   Nona is the pregnant wife of Cochise.

BATTLE FOR THE PLANET OF THE APES   Asian   1973/Science Fiction

20th Century-Fox; 86 min.; *Producer*: Arthur P. Jacobs; *Director*: J.
Lee Thompson; *Screenplay*: John William Corrington/Joyce Hooper
Corrington; *Music*: Leonard Rosenman; *Camera*: Richard H. Kline;
Editors: Alan L. Jaggs/John C. Horger; *Cast*: Roddy McDowall (Caesar);
Claude Akins (Aldo); Natalie Trundy (Lisa); Severn Darden (Kulp); Lew
Ayres (Mandemus); Paul Williams (Virgil); *FRANCE NUYEN (ALMA)*; Austin
Stoker (McDonald); Noah Keen (Teacher); Richard Eastham (Mutant Cap-
tain); Bobby Porter (Cornelius).

   Not enough information was available to describe this role
accurately.

BAYOU   Cajun   1957/Drama

United Artists; 85 min.; *Producer*: M.A. Bates; *Director*: Harold
Daniels; *Screenplay*: Edward L. Fessler; *Camera*: Ted & Vincent Sairis;
Editor: Maury Wright; *Cast*: Peter Graves (Martin); *LITA MILAN (MARIE)*;
Douglas Fowley (Herbert); Tim Carey (Ulysses); Jonathan Haze (Bos);
Edwin Nelson (Edenne); Eugene Sondfield (Jean Tithe); Evelyn Hendrick-
son (Doucelle); Milton Schneider (Cousine); Michael R. Romano
(Felician).

Marie falls in love with architect Martin who becomes involved
with the Cajun community.

THE BEAST OF HOLLOW MOUNTAIN   Mexican   1956/Science Fiction

United Artists; 81 min.; *Producers*: William & Edward Nassour;
Director: Edward Nassour; *Screenplay*: Robert Hill; *Music*: Raul La
Vista; *Camera*: Jorge Stahl, Jr.; *Editors*: Holbrook Todd/Maury Wright;
Cast: Guy Madison (Jimmy Ryan); *PATRICIA MEDINA (SARITA)*; Eduardo
Noriega (Enrique Rios); Carlos Rivas (Felipe Sanchez); Mario Navarro
(Panchito); Pascual Garcia (Pena Pancho); Julio Villareal (Don Pedro);
Lupe Carriles (Margarita); Manuel Arvide (Martinez); Jose Chavez
(Manuel); Margarito Luna (Jose); Roberto Contreras (Carlos); Lobo
Negro (Jorge).

Sarita is the daughter of a mayor whose town is being terrorized
by a prehistoric dinosaur. Sarita is being romanced by American
Jimmy Ryan, much to the distress of her jealous boyfriend, Enrique
Rios.

BEAUTY AND THE BANDIT   Mexican   1946/Western

Monogram; 77 min.; *Producer*: Scoot R. Dunlap; *Director*: William Nigh;
Screenplay: Charles Belden; *Music*: Edward J. Kay; *Camera*: Harry
Neumann; *Editor*: Fred Maguire; *Cast*: Gilbert Roland (Chico Via);
Martin Garralaga (Valegra); Frank Yaconelli (Baby); Ramsay Ames (John
DuBois); *VIDA ALDANA (LOLITA)*; George J. Lewis; William Gould; Dimas
Sontello; Felipe Turich; Glen Strange; Alex Montoya; Artie Ortego.

Lolita is a waitress who lusts after Chico Via, who is more
interested in John DuBois, a woman disguised as a man.

BEHIND THE RISING SUN   Japanese   1943/War Drama

RKO; 89 min.; *Director*: Edward Dmytryk; *Screenplay*: Emmet Lavery;
Music: Lennie Hayton; *Camera*: Russell Metty; *Editor*: Blanche Sewell;
Cast: *MARGO (TAMA)*; Tom Neal (Taro); J. Carrol Naish (Publisher);
Robert Ryan (Lefty); Gloria Holden (Sara); Don Douglas (O'Hara);
George Givot (Boris); Adeline DeWolf Reynolds (Grandmother); Leonard
Strong (Tama's father); *Iris Wong (Secretary)*; Wolfgang Zilzer (Max).

Tama is a half-caste in love with Taro, the American-educated son of a respected Japanese publisher. At his father's urging Taro reluctantly joins the Japanese army, on the brink of World War II. Taro takes the war very seriously and much to his father's and Tama's dismay he becomes a merciless killer.

BEHOLD MY WIFE   Native American   1935/Melodrama

Paramount; 79 min.; *Producer*: H.P. Schulberg; *Director*: Mitchell Leisen; *Screenplay*: Grover Jones/Vincent Lawrence; *Camera*: Leon Shamroy; *Cast*: *SYLVIA SIDNEY (TONITA STORMCLOUD)*; Gene Raymond (Michael Carter); Julietta Compton (Diana Carter-Carson); Laura Hope Crews (Mrs. Carter); H.B. Warner (Mr. Carter); Monroe Owsley (Rob Prentice); Kenneth Thomson (Jim Carson); Ann Sheridan (Mary White); Dean Jagger (Pete); Charlotte Granville (Mrs. Sykes); Eric Blore (Benson); Charles B. Middleton (Juan Stormcloud); Ralph Remley (Jenkins); Cecil Weaton (Gibson).

Michael Carter marries Tonita Stormcloud, daughter of a chief, to get even with his parents for not letting him marry his true love, Mary White. Soon Tonita realizes that Michael doesn't love her. She leaves his house so that she can avenge herself but she is unsuccessful and dies.

BELA LUGOSI MEETS A BROOKLYN GORILLA   Jungle Exotic   1953/Comedy

Realart; 74 min.; *Producer*: Jack Broder (Maurice Duke); *Director*: William Beaudine; *Screenplay*: Tim Ryan; *Camera*: Charles Van Enger; *Editor*: Phil Cahn; *Cast*: Bela Lugosi (Dr. Zabor); Duke Mitchell (Duke); Sammy Petrillo (Sammy); *CHARLITA (NONA)*; Muriel Landers (Salome); Al Kilume (Chief Rakon); Mickey Simpson (Chula); Milten Newberger (Bongo); Martin Garralaga (Pepe Bordo); Ramona, the chimp.

This film provides the audience with Dean Martin and Jerry Lewis look-alikes. The comedy is set in a tropical jungle where Duke and native girl Nona become romantically involved, much to the distress of Dr. Zabor, who lusts after Nona. Dr. Zabor injects Duke with a serum, turning him into a gorilla. All is well when Sammy awakes from his jungle nightmare.

BELLE OF OLD MEXICO   Mexican   1950/Western

Republic; 70 min.; *Producer*: Edward J. White; *Director*: R.G. Spring- steen; *Screenplay*: Bradford Ropes/Francis Swann; *Music*: Stanley Wil- son; *Camera*: Jack Marta; *Editor*: Harold Minter; *Cast*: *ESTELITA RODRIGUEZ (ROSITA)*; Robert Rockwell (Kip Armitage III); Dorothy Patrick (Deborah); Thurston Hall (Horatio Hunington); Florence Bates (Nellie Chatfield); Dave Willock (Tommy Mayberry); Gordon Jones (Tex Barnet); Fritz Feld (Dr. Quincy); Anne O'Neal (Mrs. Ambercrombie); Nancho Galindo (Pico).

Rosita travels to be with her late brother's wartime friends. Thinking Rosita is a young child they have become her guardians. They are surprised to meet an attractive young woman.

BELLS OF SAN FERNANDO   Mexican/Native American   1947/Drama

Screen Guild; 80 min.; *Producer*: James S. Burket; *Director*: Terry Morse; *Screenplay*: Jack Dewitt/Renault Duncan; *Camera*: Robert Pettack; *Editor*: George McGuire; *Cast*: Donald Woods (Michael); *GLORIA WARREN (MARIA)*; *SHIRLEY O'HARA (NITA)*; Byron Foulger (Garcia); Paul Newlan (Gueyon); Anthony Warde (Mendoza); Monte Blue (Governor); Anthony Warde (Mendoza); Monte Blue (Governor); *Claire DuBrey (Manta)*; David Leonard (Padre); Gordon Clark (Enrico).

Mendoza is a cruel landlord who keeps the local population isolated in the San Fernando Valley in early California. He wants to marry Maria but she loves Michael. Mendoza also lusts after local Chula Indian maiden Nita. Nita also has eyes for Michael. When gold is found on church property things come to a conclusion with Michael defeating Mendoza and marrying Maria.

BENGAL BRIGADE   Indian   1954/Adventure

Universal; 84 min.; *Producer*: Ted Richmond; *Director*: Laslo Benedek; *Screenplay*: Richard Alan Simmons; *Music*: Joseph Gershenson; *Camera*: Maury Gertsman; *Editor*: Frank Gross; *Cast*: Rock Hudson (Capt. Jeffrey Claybourne); Arlene Dahl (Vivian Morrow); *URSULA THIESS (LAIAH)*; Torin Thatcher (Col. Morrow); Arnold Moss (Rajah Karam); Daniel O'Herlihy (Capt. Ronald Blaine); Harold Gordon (Hari Lai); Michael Ansara (Sgt. Major Puran Singh); Leonard Strong (Mahindra); Shepard Menken (Bulbir).

Story of rebellion against British rule in India. Laiah's unrequited love for Capt. Jeffrey Claybourne leads her to support the British against her own people.

BEYOND THE BLUE HORIZON   Island Exotic   1942/Drama

Paramount; 76 min.; *Assoc. Producer*: Monta Bell; *Director*: Alfred Santell; *Screenplay*: Frank Butler/Harry Tugend; *Camera*: Charles Boyle; *Editor*: Doane Harrison; *Cast*: *DOROTHY LAMOUR (TAMA)*; Richard Denning (Jakra); Jack Haley (Squidge); Helen Gilbert (Carol); Walter Abel (Thornton); Patricia Morison (Sylvia); Elizabeth Patterson (Mrs. Daly).

Tama travels to the United States to receive an inheritance left by her parents. When she arrives in America she meets Jakra, a lion tamer, as well as some greedy relatives who demand further proof of her parentage. Tama and Jakra return to Malaya to retrieve the proof she needs to claim her legacy.

BEYOND THE LIMIT   South American Indian   1983/Drama

20th Century-Fox; 104 min.; *Producer*: Richard F. Dalton; *Director*:
John MacKenzie; *Screenplay*: Christopher Hampton; *Music*: Stanley
Myers; *Camera*: Phil Meheux; *Editor*: Sutart Baird; *Cast*: Michael
Caine (Charley Fortnum); Richard Gere (Dr. Plarr); Bob Hoskins
(Colonel Perez); *ELPIDIA CARRILLO (CLARA)*; Joaquim de Almeida (Leon);
A. Martinez (Aquino); *Stephanie Cotsirilos (Maria)*: Domingo Ambirz
(Diego); Eric Valdez (Pablo).

    While searching for his father in Argentina, Dr. Plarr meets
Clara in a brothel. Plarr later discovers that his father has become a political prisoner and that Clara has married British Consul,
Charley Fortnum. Clara and Plarr discovers that his father was
murdered over a year ago and that Charley has found out about their
affair. Plarr is killed by Colonel Perez and Clara returns to
Charley.

BEYOND THE VALLEY OF DOLLS   Black   1970/Drama

20th Century-Fox; 109 min.; *Producer/Director*: Russ Meyer; *Screen-
play*: Roger Ebert; *Music*: Stu Phillips; *Camera*: Fred J. Koenekamp;
Cast: Dolly Read (Kelly MacNamara); Cynthia Myers (Casey Anderson);
MARCIA McBROOM (PETRONELLA DANFORTH); John LaZar (Ronnie/Z-man/
Barzell); Michael Blodgett (Lance Rocke); David Gurian (Harris
Allsworth); Phyllis Davis (Susan Lake); Harrison Page (Emerson
Thorne); Duncan McLeod (Porter Hall); Jim Iglehart (Randy Black);
Charles Napier (Baxter Wolfe); Henry Rowland (Otto); Edy Williams
(Ashley St. Ives).

    Petronella is a member of a female rock group who travels to
Hollywood looking for success. She becomes more involved with sex
and drugs than with rock and roll.

BHOWANI JUNCTION   Indian   1956/Drama

MGM; 110 min.; *Producer*: Pandro S. Berman; *Director*: George Cukor;
Screenplay: Sonya Levien/Ivan Moffat; *Music*: Miklos Rozsa; *Camera*:
F.A. Young; *Editors*: Frank Clarke/George Boemler; *Cast*: *AVA GARDNER
(VICTORIA JONES)*; Stewart Granger (Col. Rodney Savage); Bill Travers
(Patrick Taylor); Abraham Sofaer (Surabhal); Francis Matthews (Ranjit
Kasel); Marne Maitland (Govin Daswami); Peter Illing (Ghan Shyam);
Edward Chapman (Thomas Jones); *Freda Jackson (The Sadani)*; Lionel
Jeffries (Lt. Graham McDaniel); Alan Tilvern (Ted Dunphy).

    Victoria Jones, half English and half Indian, must face the
reality of her heritage as the British begin their withdrawal from
India. As an Englishwoman, she has been allowed certain privileges,
but feels threatened when the British leave. After she kills an
English officer who tries to rape her, she becomes involved with
Ranjit, an Indian, who helps her conceal her crime. Her crime and
her relationship with Ranjit force her to accept her Indian heritage.
She agrees to marry Ranjit. When she tries to convert to the Hindu

religion, she realizes that this is not what she wants. She returns
to Rodney Savage, the British colonel with whom she has fallen in
love.

THE BIG SKY   Native American--Blackfoot 1952/Adventure

RKO; 140 min.; *Producer/Director*: Howard Hawks; *Screenplay*: Dudley
Nichols; *Music*: Dimitri Tiomkin; *Camera*: Russell Harlan; *Editor*:
Christian Nyby; *Cast*: Kirk Douglas (Jim Deakins); Dewey Martin
(Boone); *ELIZABETH THREATT (TEAL EYE)*; Arthur Hunnicutt (Zeb); Buddy
Baer (Romaine); Steven Geray (Jourdonnais); Hank Worden (Poordevil);
Jim Davis (Streak); Henri Letondal (Labadie); Robert Hunter
(Chouquette); Booth Colman (Pascal); Paul Frees (McMasters); Frank
de Kova (Moleface); Guy Wilkerson (Longface).

    The story of the first voyage up the Missouri River in 1825.
Teal Eye is a Blackfoot woman being returned to her tribe by the men
on the expedition to insure that they will be able to trade amongst
the Blackfeet. In spite of obvious racial and sexual stereotyping
Teal Eye is an attractive, brave, and intelligent woman, an all too
rare film portrait of a Native American. Teal Eye is loved by Jim
Deakins but she loves Boone who refuses her because of his own
racism. In the end, Boone's love for Teal Eye overwhelms his bigotry
and he remains with her and her tribe.

THE BIG SOMBRERO   Mexican   1949/Western

Columbia; 77 min.; *Producer*: Armand Schaefer; *Director*: Frank
McDonald; *Screenplay*: Olive Cooper; *Music*: Mischa Bakaleinikoff;
Camera: William Bradford; *Editor*: Henry Batista; *Cast*: Gene Autry;
ELENA VERDUGO (ESTRELLITA ESTRADA); Stephen Dunne (James Garland);
George J. Lewis (Juan Vazcaro); Vera Marshe (Angie Burke); William
Edmunds (Luis Alvarado); Martin Garralaga (Felipe Gonzales); Neyle
Morrow (Tico); Champion.

    Estrellita is a wealthy ranch owner who is about to be married
to James Garland, her ranch manager, who wants to take over her ranch.
Working as a ranchhand, Gene observes the fraud that is taking place
and reveals it to Estrellita. A trap is set for Garland and the
police are soon on his trail.

BIRD OF PARADISE   Polynesian   1932/Adventure

RKO; 80 min.; *Producer/Director*: King Vidor; *Screenplay*: Wells Root/
Wanda Tuchock/Leonard Praskins; *Music*: Max Steiner; *Camera*: Clyde De
Vinna; *Editor*: Archie F. Marshel; *Cast*: *DOLORES DEL RIO (LUANA)*;
Joel McCrea (Johnny Baker); John Halliday (Mac); Creighton Chaney
(Thornton); Richard Gallagher (Chester); Bert Roach (Hector); Pukui
(The King); Agostino Borgalo (Medicine Man); *Sophie Ortego (Old
Native Woman)*.

    After Luana saves sailor Johnny Baker's life she returns to his

boat for a moonlight swim. Johnny is so taken with Luana that he
wants to remain with her despite the objections of the island witch
doctor. Johnny and Luana go to an island of their own where Luana is
soon speaking English and has learned civilized ways. The witch doctor, finding them, captures Luana and prepares her for sacrifice.
Johnny saves her with the help of his old shipmates, but is injured
in the process. As they plan to leave the island and bring Luana to
white civilization--with objections made by some of the crew as to
Luana's suitability as a wife--Luana decides that Johnny's fever is
caused by her leaving the island. She therefore sacrifices her life
to the gods to save his.

BIRD OF PARADISE   Polynesian   1951/Adventure

20th Century-Fox; 100 min.; *Producer/Director/Screenplay*: Delmer
Daves; *Music*: Daniele Amfitheatrof; *Camera*: Winton C. Hock; *Editor*:
James B. Clark; *Cast*: Louis Jordan (Andre Laurence); *DEBRA PAGET
(KALVA)*; Jeff Chandler (Tenga); Everett Sloane (The Beachcomber);
Maurice Schwartz (The Kahuna); Jack Elam (The Trader); Prince Lei
Lanie (Chief); Otto Waldis (Skipper); Alfred Zeisler (Van Hook); *Mary
Ann Ventura (Noanoa)*; David K. Bray (Chanter); Sam Monsarrat (Tenga's
friend).

    This remake is similar to the 1932 version. Andre Laurence
returns to the islands with his friend Tenga. He falls in love with
Tenga's sister Kalva. They romance and finally marry--much to the
dismay of the island witch doctors. When a volcano erupts Kalva
jumps into the volcano to save the islands.

THE BITTER TEA OF GENERAL YEN   Chinese   1933/Drama

Columbia; 89 min.; *Director*: Frank Capra; *Screenplay*: Edward Paramore;
Music: W. Frank Harling; *Camera*: C.C. Coleman; *Editor*: Edward Curtiss;
Cast: Barbara Stanwyck (Megan Davis); Nils Asther (General Yen); Gavin
Gordon (Dr. Robert Strike); Lucien Littlefield (Mr. Jackson); *TOSHIA
MORI (MAH-LI)*; Richard Loo (Captain Li); Clara Blandick (Mrs. Jackson);
Walter Connolly (Jones); Moy Ming (Dr. Lin); Robert Wayne (Rev.
Bostwick); Knute Erickson (Dr. Hansen); Ella Hall (Mrs. Hansen);
Arthur Millette (Mr. Pettis); Helen Jerome Eddy (Miss Reed); Martha
Mattox (Miss Avery); Jessie Arnold (Mrs. Blake); Emmett Corrigan
(Bishop Harkness).

    Mah-Li is mistress to General Yen, but loves Captain Li. For her
infidelity she is sentenced to death, but is saved by Megan Davis, the
hostage with whom General Yen has fallen in love. Mah-Li betrays
Megan, which leads General Yen to commit suicide.

BLACK BART   Mexican   1948/Western

Universal-International; 80 min.; *Producer*: Leonard Goldstein;
Director: George Sherman; *Screenplay*: Luci Ward/Jack Natteford/William
Bowers; *Music*: Frank Skinner; *Camera*: Irving Glassberg; *Editor*:

Russell Schoengarth; *Cast*: *YVONNE DE CARLO (LOLA MONTEZ)*; Dan Duryea (Charles E. Boles); Jeffrey Lynn (Lance Hardeen); Percy Kilbride (Jersey Brady); Lloyd Gough (Sheriff Gordon); Frank Lovejoy (Lorimer); John McIntire (Clark); Don Beddoe (J.T. Hall); Ray Walker (Mac Farland); *Soledad Jimenez (Teresa)*; Anne O'Neal (Mrs. Harmon); Chief Many Treaties (Indian).

Lola is a dancer interested in gold.

BLACK BELT JONES   Black   1974/Action

Warner Brothers; 87 min.; *Producers*: Fred Weintraub/Paul Heller; *Director*: Robert Clouse; *Screenplay*: Oscar Williams; *Music*: Luchi De Jesus; *Camera*: Kent Wakeford; *Editor*: Michael Kahn; *Cast*: Jim Kelly (Black Belt Jones); *GLORIA HENDRY (SYDNEY)*; Scatman Crothers (Pop); Alan Weeks (Toppy); Eric Laneuville (Quincy); Andre Phillipe (Don Steffano); Vincent Barbi (Big Tuna).

Sydney asks Black Belt Jones to help her father overcome a gang of thugs trying to take over his karate school.

BLACK CAESAR   Black   1973/Action

American International; 92 min.; *Producer/Director*: Larry Cohen; *Screenplay*: James Brown/Larry Cohen; *Music*: James Brown; *Camera*: Fenton Hamilton; *Editor*: George Folsey, Jr.; *Cast*: Fred Williamson (Tommy Gibbs); Phillip Rowe (Joe Washington); *GLORIA HENDRY (HELEN)*; Julius W. Harris (Mr. Gibbs); Val Avery (Cardoza); *Minnie Gentry (Mama Gibbs)*; Art Lund (John McKinney); D'Urville Martin (Rev. Rufas); William Wellman, Jr. (Alfred Coleman).

Helen, a nightclub singer, is the girlfriend of hoodlum Tommy Gibbs. Mama Gibbs is Tommy's distraught mother.

BLACK GIRL   Black   1972/Drama

Cinerama; 107 min.; *Producer*: Lee Savin; *Director*: Ossie Davis; *Screenplay*: Ms. J.E. Franklin; *Camera*: Glenwood J. Swanson; *Editor*: Graham Lee Mahin; *Cast*: Brock Peters (Earl); *LESLIE UGGAMS (NETTA)*; *Claudia McNeil (Mu' Dear)*; *Louise Stubbs (Mama Rosie)*; *Gloria Edwards (Norma)*; *Loretta Greene (Ruth Ann)*; *Peggy Pettitt (Billie Jean)*; *Ruby Dee (Netta's Mother)*; Kent Martin (Herbert).

Netta, the daughter of a mentally disturbed mute woman, has been taken in by Mama Rosie--to the neglect of her own daughters, Norma, Ruth Ann, and Billie Jean. Billie Jean wants to become a dancer but is ridiculed by her mother and sisters. Netta, who is in college, encourages Billie Jean to return to high school so that she can attend college and study dance there. Ruth Ann and Norma continue to ricicule Billie Jean and drive Netta out of the house. Rosie doesn't think Billie Jean should be encouraged to go to school, but Mu' Dear convinces Rosie that Netta is right.

BLACK GOLD   Native American   1947/Western

Allied Artists; 89 min.; *Producer*: Jeffrey Bernerd; *Director*: Phil
Karlson; *Screenplay*: Agnes Christine Johnston; *Music*: Edward J. Kay;
Camera: Harry Neumann; *Editor*: Roy Livingston; *Cast*: Anthony Quinn
(Charlie Eagle); *KATHERINE DE MILLE (SARAH)*; Ducky Louie (Davey);
Elyse Knox (Miss Fraser).

Charlie Eagle and Sarah adopt Davey after his father is murdered.
Charlie wants to breed one of his horses with a prized stallion but
needs money to do so. He leases his land to some oil investors to
obtain money. Oil is discovered on his land so he names his new colt
"Black Gold." He wants to enter Black Gold in the Kentucky Derby
with Davey as his jockey. Before he can realize his dream Charlie is
killed in an accident. Sarah takes Davey and Black Gold to the derby
anyway and Black Gold and Davey ride to victory.

BLACK GUNN   Black   1972/Action

Columbia; 94 min.; *Producers*: John Heyman/Norman Priggen; *Director*:
Robert Hartford-Davis; *Screenplay*: Franklin Coen; *Music*: Tony
Osborne; *Camera*: Richard H. Kline; *Editor*: Pat Somerset; *Cast*: Jim
Brown (Gunn); Martin Landau (Capelli); *BRENDA SYKES (JUDITH)*; Luciana
Paluzzi (Toni Lombardo); Vida Blue (Sam Green); Stephen McNally
(Laurento); Keefe Brasselle (Winman); Timothy Brown (Larry); William
Campbell (Rico); Bernie Casey (Seth).

Not enough information was available to describe this role
accurately.

BLACK MAMA, WHITE MAMA   Black   1973/Drama

American International; 87 min.; *Producers*: John Ashley/Eddie Romero;
Director: Eddie Romero; *Screenplay*: H.R. Christian; *Music*: Harry
Betis; *Camera*: Justo Paulino; *Editor*: Asagni V. Pastor; *Cast*: PAM
GRIER (LEE DANIELS); Margaret Markov (Karen Brent); Sid Haig (Ruben);
Lynn Borden (Densmore); Zaldy Zshornack (Ernesto); Laurie Burton
(Logan); Eddie Garcia (Capt. Cruz); *Alona Alegre (Juana)*; Dindo
Fernando (Rocco); Vic Diaz (Vic Cheng); Wendy Green (Ronda); Lotis M.
Key (Jeanette); Alfonso Carvajal (Galindo); Bruno Punzalah (Truck
Driver); Ricard Herrero (Luis); Jess Ramos (Alfredo).

Lee and Karen are imprisoned on a Latin American island. They
escape, but Karen is killed.

BLACK MOON   West Indian   1934/Mystery

Columbia; 68 min.; *Assoc. Producer*: Everett Riskin; *Director*: Roy
William Neill; *Screenplay*: Wells Root; *Camera*: Joseph August; *Editor*:
Richard Cahoon; *Cast*: Jack Holt (Stephen Lane); Fay Wray (Gail);
DOROTHY BURGESS (JUANITA LANE); Cora Sue Collins (Nancy Lane); Arnold
Korff (Dr. Perez); Clarence Muse (Lunch); Eleanor Wesselhoeft (Anna);

Mme. Sul-te-wan (Ruva); Lawrence Criner (Kala); Lumaden Hare
(Macklin).

Juanita was raised on a Caribbean island by Ruva who taught her
about voodoo. After Juanita marries she returns to the island and is
installed as high priestess of the voodoo cult. The natives begin a
revolt and threaten the lives of the white citizenry.

BLACK NARCISSUS   Indian   1947/Drama

Universal-International; 99 mn.; *Producer*: Michael Powell; *Directors*:
Michael Powell/Emeric Pressburger; *Screenplay*: Michael Powell;
Camera: Jack Cardiff; *Editor*: Reginald Mills; *Cast*: Deborah Kerr
(Sister Clodagh); Flora Robson (Sister Philippa); Jenny Laird (Sister
Honey); Judith Furse (Briony); Kathleen Byron (Ruth); Esmond Knight
(The Old General); Sabu (The Young General); *JEAN SIMMONS (KANCHI)*;
May Hallatt (Angu Ayah); David Farrar (Mr. Dean); Eddie Whaley, Jr.
(Joseph Anthony); Shaun Noble (Con); Nancy Roberts (Mother Dorothea);
Ley On (Phuba).

Kanchi goes to live and study at a newly organized convent. She
runs away with the Young General, who is also studying at the convent.

THE BLACK SCORPION   Mexican   1957/Science Fiction

Warner Brothers; 88 min.; *Producers*: Frank Melford/Jack Dietz;
Director: Edward Ludwig; *Screenplay*: David Duncan/Robert Blees;
Music: Paul Sawtell; *Camera*: Lionel Lindon; *Editor*: Richard Van Enger;
Cast: Richard Denning (Henry Scott); *MARA CORDAY (TERESA)*; Carlos
Rivas (Artur Ramos); Mario Navarro (Juanito); Carlos Muzquiz (Dr.
Velazco); Pascual Pena (Jose de la Cruz); *Fanny Schiller (Florentina)*;
Pedro Galvan (Father Delgado); Arturo Martinez (Major Cosio).

Teresa becomes involved with Henry Scott in stopping a giant
black scorpion, an atomic mutaion, from destroying Mexico.

BLACK SUNDAY   Arab--Palestinian   1977/Thriller

Paramount; 143 min.; *Producer*: Robert Evans; *Director*: John Franken-
heimer; *Screenplay*: Ernest Lehman/Kenneth Ross/Ivan Moffat; *Music*:
John Williams; *Camera*: John A. Alonzo; *Editor*: Tom Rolf; *Cast*: Robert
Shaw (Kabakov); Bruce Dern (Lander); *MARTHE KELLER (DAHLIA)*; Fritz
Weaver (Corley); Steve Keats (Moshevsky); Bekim Fehmiu (Fasil);
Michael V. Gazzo (Muzi); William Daniels (Pugh); Walter Gotell (Col.
Riaf).

Dahlia is a member of the Black September faction of the Pales-
tine Liberation Organization. She is involved in a terrorist plot to
blow up the Super Bowl. Israeli agents foil the plan.

BLACULA   Black   1972/Thriller

American International; 92 min.; *Producer*: Joseph T. Naar; *Director*:
William Crain; *Screenplay*: Joan Torres; *Music*: Gene Page; *Camera*:
John Stevens; *Editor*: Allan Jacobs; *Cast*: William Marshall (Blacula/
Mamuwalde); *VONETTA McGEE (TINA/LUVA)*; *Denise Nicholas (Michelle)*;
Thalmus Rasulala (Gordon Thomas); Gordon Pinsent (Lt. Peters); Charles
Macaulay (Dracula); *Emily Yancy (Nancy)*; Lance Taylor, Sr. (Swenson);
Ted Harris (Bobby); Rick Metzler (Billy); Jitu Cumbuka (Skillet);
Ketty Lester (Juanita Jones); Elisha Cook (Sam); Logan Field (Barnes).

    This Black Dracula begins with Blacula arriving in Los Angeles.
After assaulting several people he spots Tina, the reincarnation of
his long-dead wife. He pursues her and tells her of his plight; she
is sympathetic and understanding. The police are on his trail, and
although he has turned Tina into a vampire, she is destroyed. Blacula
is so distraught at this that he destroys himself by walking into the
blazing sunlight.

BLOOD ON THE SUN   Chinese   1945/War Drama

United Artists; 98 min.; *Producer*: William Cagney; *Director*: Frank
Lloyd; *Screenplay*: Lester Cole; *Music*: Miklos Rosza; *Camera*: Theodor
Sparkuhl; *Editors*: Truman Wood/Walter Hanneman; *Cast*: James Cagney
(Nick Condon); *SYLVIA SYDNEY (IRIS HILLIARD)*; Wallace Ford (Ollie
Hilliard); Rosemary De Camp (Edith Miller); Robert Armstrong (Colonel
Tojo); John Emery (Premier Tanaka); Leonard Strong (Higakata); Jack
Halloran (Secret Police Captain); Rhys Williams (Joseph Cassell);
Frank Puglia (Prince Tatsugi); Porter Hall (Arthur Bickett); James
Bell (Charlie Sprague).

    Iris Hilliard appears to be working for the Japanese, but is
really a spy for the Chinese government. American Nick Condon falls
in love with her although he is not sure where her loyalties lie.

BLUE HAWAII   Hawaiian   1961/Musical

Paramount; 101 min.; *Producer*: Hal Wallis; *Director*: Norman Taurog;
Screenplay: Hal Kanter; *Music*: Joseph J. Lilley; *Camera*: Charles Lang,
Jr.; *Editors*: Warren Low/Terry Morse; *Cast*: Elvis Presley (Chad
Gates); *JOAN BLACKMAN (MAILE DUVAL)*; Nancy Walters (Abigail Prentace);
Roland Winters (Fred Gates); Angela Lansbury (Sarah Lee Gates); John
Archer (Jack Kelman); Gregory Gay (Mr. Duval); Darlene Tompkins
(Patsy); Pamela Akert (Sandy); Christian Kay (Beverly); Jenny Maxwell
(Ellie Corbett); Frank Atienza (Ito O'Hara); Lani Kai (Carl); *Hilo
Hattie (Waihila)*.

    After his stint in the army, Chad becomes a travel guide, much
to the annoyance of his parents who want him to enter his father's
business. His mother, Sarah Lee, dislikes Maile, his girlfriend,
because she considers Maile a bad influence on Chad, chiefly because
she is half Hawaiian. Chad and Maile open a travel business in con-
junction with his father's pineapple business. When Chad and Maile

marry, Sarah Lee accepts the marriage, claiming that Maile is descended from Hawaiian royalty. Waihila is Maile's grandmother.

BOMBA AND THE HIDDEN CITY   Jungle Exotic   1950/Adventure

Monogram; 71 min.; *Producer*: Walter Mirisch; *Director*: Ford Beebe; *Screenplay*: Carroll Young; *Music*: Ozzie Caswell; *Camera*: William Sickner; *Editor*: Roy Livingston; *Cast*: Johnny Sheffield (Bomba); *SUE ENGLAND (LEAH)*; Paul Guilfoyle (Hassan); Damian O'Flynn (Dennis Johnson); Leon Belasco (Haschid); Charles La Torre (Abdullah); Smoki Whitfield (Hadji);

    Leah is a native princess whose throne was taken away by Hassan. Bomba helps to restore her to it.

BOMBA ON PANTHER ISLAND   Jungle Exotic   1950/Adventure

Monogram; 70 min.; *Producer*: Walter Mirisch; *Director/Screenplay*: Ford Beebe; *Camera*: William A. Sickner; *Cast*: Johnny Sheffield (Bomba); Allene Roberts (Judy Maitland); *LITA BARON (LOSANA)*; Bill Walker (Luke); Charles Irwin (Andy Barnes); Harry Lewis (Bob Maitland); Smoki Whitfield (Eli); Martin Wilkins (Moki).

    Bomba is tracking down a killer black panther when he meets Bob and Judy Maitland, who plan to settle in the jungle. Some native workers are killed by the panther. Losana loves Bomba, but he falls in love with Judy. Bob sets the jungle on fire to clear away some of the growth, and a major fire develops. Bomba kills the panther and retreats back into the jungle alone.

BOMBS OVER BURMA   Chinese   1942/War Drama

Producers Releasing Corp.; 62 min.; *Producers*: Alfred Stern/Arthur Alexander; *Director*: Joseph H. Lewis; *Screenplay*: Milton Raison/Joseph H. Lewis; *Camera*: Robert Cline; *Editor*: Charles Henkel, Jr.; *Cast*: *ANNA MAY WONG (LIN YING)*; Noel Madison (He-Hoi); Leslie Denison (Sir Roger Howe); Nedrick Young (Slim Jenkins); Dan Seymour (Pete Braganza); Frank Lackteen (Hallam); Judith Gibson (Lucy Dell); Dennis Moore (Tom Whitely); *Connie Leon (Ma Sing)*; Hayward Soo Hoo (Ling); Richard Loo (Col. Kim).

    Schoolteacher Lin Ying is working with the Chinese government in connection with convoys on the Burma road.

BOOK OF NUMBERS   Black   1973/Action

Avco Embassy Pictures; 80 min.; *Producer/Director*: Raymond St. Jacques; *Screenplay*: Larry Spiegel; *Music*: Al Schackman; *Camera*: Gayne Rescher; *Editor*: Irv Rosenblum; *Cast*: Raymond St. Jacques (Blue Boy Harris); *FREDA PAYNE (KELLY SIMMS)*; Philip Thomas (Dave Greene); Hope Clarke (Pigmean Goins); Willie Washington, Jr. (Makepeace Johnson);

Doug Finell (Eggy); Sterling St. Jacques (Kid Flick); C.L. Williams (Blip Slip); D'Urville Martin (Billy Bowlegs); Jerry Leon (Joe Gaines).

Kelly Simms is the girlfriend of numbers racketeer Dave Greene.

BOOLOO   Malaysian   1938/Adventure

Paramount; 61 min.; *Producer/Director*: Clyde E. Elliott; *Screenplay*: Robert E. Welsh; *Camera*: Carl Berger/Harry Sharp/Ben Wetzler; *Editor*: Ed Warren; *Cast*: Colin Tapley (Capt. Robert Rogers); Jayne Regan (Kate Jaye); Michio Ito (Sakai Chief); Herbert DeSouza (Rob DeSouza); Fred Pullen (Nah Laku); *MAMO CLARK (NATIVE GIRL)*; William Stack (Col. Stanley Jaye).

Mamo Clark is the token native girl in this production filmed in the jungle of Malaya.

THE BORDER   Mexican   1981/Drama

Universal/RKO Pictures; 108 min.; *Producer*: Edgar Bronfman, Jr.; *Director*: Tony Richardson; *Screenplay*: Derec Washburn/Walon Green/ David Freeman; *Music*: Ry Cooder; *Camera*: Ric Waite; *Editor*: Robert K. Lambert; *Cast*: Jack Nicholson (Charlie Smith); Harvey Keitel (Cat); Valerie Perrine (Marcy Smith); Warren Oates (Big Red); *ELPIDIA CARRILO (MARIA)*; Shannon Wilcox (Savannah); Manuel Viescas (Juan); Jeff Morris (J.J.); Dirk Blocker (Beef); Mike Gomez (Manuel); Lonny Chapman (Andy).

Charlie Smith, a border patrolman, helps Maria, an illegal alien, retrieve her baby which was stolen and given to a white family. Maria is nearly forced into prostitution until Charlie helps her by elimi-nating the thugs responsible for smuggling aliens into the United States. After the final shoot-out Charlie returns Maria's baby to her.

BORDER CAFE   Mexican   1937/Western

RKO; 67 min.; *Producer*: Robert Sisk; *Director*: Lew Landers; *Screen-play*: Lionel Houser; *Camera*: Nicholas Musurnea; *Editor*: Jack Hively; *Cast*: Harry Carey (Tex); John Beal (Keith Whitney); *ARMIDA (DOMINGA)*; George Irving (Senator Whitney); Leona Roberts (Mrs. Whitney); J. Carrol Naish (Rocky); Lee Patrick (Ellie); Paul Fix (Dolson); Max Wagner (Shakey); Walter Miller (Evans).

Dominga is a fiery cafe entertainer who becomes the romantic interest of wealthy Bostonian Keith Whitney.

BORDER INCIDENT   Mexican   1949/Western

MGM; 96 min.; *Producer*: Nicholas Nayfack; *Director*: Anthony Mann;
Screenplay: John C. Higgins; *Music*: Andre Previn; *Camera*: John Alton;
Editor: Conrad A. Nervig; *Cast*: Ricardo Montalban (Pablo Rodriguez);
George Murphy (Jack Bearnes); Howard da Silva (Owen Parkson); James
Mitchell (Juan Garcia); Arnold Moss (Zopilote); Alfonso Bedoya
(Cuchillo); *TERESA CELLI (MARIA)*; Charles McGraw (Jeff Amboy); Jose
Torvay (Pocoloco); John Ridgely (Mr. Neley); Arthur Hunnicutt (Clayton
Nordell); Sig Ruman (Hugo Wolfgang Ulrich); Otto Waldis (Fritz);
Harry Antrim (John Boyd); Tony Barr (Luis).

This is a story about aliens being smuggled illegally into California to work on farms and ranches.

BORDER RIVER   Mexican   1954/Western

Universal; 81 min.; *Producer*: Albert J. Cohen; *Director*: George
Sherman; *Screenplay*: William Sackheim/Louis Stevens; *Camera*: Albert J.
Cohen; *Cast*: Joel McCrea (Clete Mattson); *YVONNE DE CARLO (CARMELITA
CARJAS)*; Pedro Armendariz (General Calleja); Howard Petrie (Newlund);
Erika Nordin (Annina); Alfonso Bedoya (Captain Vargas); Ivan Triesault
(Baron Von Hollden); George J. Lewis (Sanchez); George Wallace
(Fletcher).

Carmelita Carjas, a cafe owner, is the girlfriend of General
Calleja, a renegade general. When she meets Clete Mattson--a confed-
erate major in town to purchase ammunition--she begins to change her
mind about the general and the way she has been living her life she
falls in love with Mattson.

BORDER ROMANCE   Mexican   1930/Western

Tiffany; 66 min.; *Producer*: Lester F. Scott, Jr.; *Director*: Richard
Thorpe; *Screenplay*: John Francis Natteford; *Music*: Al Short; *Camera*:
Harry Zech; *Editor*: Richard Cahoon; *Cast*:*ARMIDA (CONCHITA CORTEZ)*;
Don Terry (Bob Hamlin); Margerie Kane (Nina); Victor Potel (Slim);
Wesley Barry (Victor Hamlin); Nita Martan (Gloria); J. Frank Glendon
(Buck); Harry von Meter (Capt. of Rurales); William Costello (Lt. of
Rurales).

Bob and his brother, Victor, are horse trading in Mexico where
Bob meets and falls in love with Conchita. But he courts Gloria, the
girlfriend of the bandit Buck, to learn Buck's whereabouts. He convinces the heartbroken Conchita that he loves only her, captures Buck,
and claims the reward.

BOULEVARD NIGHTS   Mexican   1979/Drama

Columbia; 102 min.; *Producer*: Bill Beneson; *Director*: Michael Pressman; *Screenplay*: Desmond Nakano; *Music*: Lalo Schifrin; *Camera*: John
Bailey; *Editor*: Richard Halsey; *Cast*: Richard Yniguez (Raymond Avila);

Danny de la Paz (Chuco Avila); *MARTA DU BOIS ("SHADY" LANDEROS)*;
James Victor (Gil Moreno); *Betty Carvalho (Mrs. Avila)*; Carmen Zapata
(Mrs. Landeros); Victor Millan (Mr. Landeros); Gary Cervantes ("Big
Happy").

Shady loves ex-gang member Raymond Avila. She wants Raymond to
better himself in an office job instead of working as a garage
mechanic. They eventually marry, but the wedding is disrupted by
gang violence and Raymond's mother is killed. Raymond vows revenge
and Shady tries to dissuade him. Raymond's brother knows the dangers
if Raymond becomes involved, so Chuco goes after the gang alone. He
gets his mother's killer but is mortally wounded.

THE BRAVADOS   Mexican   1956/Western

20th Century-Fox; 99 min.; *Producer*: Herbert B. Swope; *Director*:
Henry King; *Screenplay*: Philip Yordan; *Music*: Lionel Newman; *Camera*:
Leon Shamroy; *Editor*: William Mace; *Cast*: Gregory Peck (Jim Douglas);
JOAN COLLINS (JOSEFA VELARDE); Stephen Boyd (Bill Zachary); Albert
Salmi (Ed Taylor); Henry Silva (Lujan); Kathleen Gallant (Emma);
Harry Coe (Tom); George Voskovec (Gus Steinmetz); Herbert Rudley
(Sheriff Eloy Sanchez); Lee Van Cleef (Alfonso Parral); Andrew Duggan
(Padre); Ken Scott (Primo); Gene Evans (Butler); Jack Mather (Quinn);
Joe De Rita (Simms); Robert Adler (Tony Mirabel); *Alicia del Lago
(Angela Lujan)*.

A revenge-oriented western with Jim Douglas seeking the outlaws
who raped and murdered his wife. Josefa Velarde provides romantic
interest.

THE BRAVE BULLS   Mexican   1951/Adventure

Columbia; 108 min.; *Producer/Driector*: Robert Rossen; *Screenplay*:
John Bright; *Camera*: Floyd Crosby/James Wong Howe; *Editor*: Henry
Batista; *Cast*: Mel Ferrer (Luis Bello); *MIROSLAVA (LINDA DE CALDERON)*;
Anthony Quinn (Raul Fuentes); Eugene Iglesias (Pepe Bello); Jose
Torvay (Eladio Gomez); *Charlita (Raquelita)*; Jose Luis Vasquez
"Mexicano" (Yank Delgado); Alfonso Alvirez (Loco Ruiz); Alfredo
Aguitar (Pancho Perez); Francisco Baldesas (Monkey Garcia); Felipe
Mota (Jackdaw).

Linda de Calderon is the mistress of bullfighter Luis Bello.

THE BRAVE ONE   Mexican   1957/Drama

Universal; 100 min.; *Producer*: Maurice King/Frank King; *Director*:
Irving Rapper; *Screenplay*: Harry Franklin/Merrill G. White; *Music*:
Victor Young; *Camera*: Jack Cardiff; *Editor*: Merrill G. White; *Cast*:
Michel Ray (Leonardo); Rodolfo Hoyos (Rafael Rosillo); *ELSA CARDENAS
(MARIA)*; Carlos Navarro (Don Alejandro); Joi Lansing (Marion); Fermin
Rivera (Fermin); George Trevino (Salvador); Carlos Fernandez (Manuel).

Maria is the sister of Leonardo, who raises a prize-winning bull and will not let the bull go into the ring to be fought.

THE BRIDES OF FU MANCHU   Chinese   1966/Mystery

Seven Arts Pictures; 94 min.; *Producer*: Harry Alan Towers; *Director*: Don Sharp; *Screenplay*: Peter Welbeck; *Music*: Philip Martell; *Camera*: Ernest Steward; *Editor*: Allan Morrison; *Cast*: Christopher Lee (Fu Manchu); Douglas Wilmer (Nayland Smith); Marie Versini (Marie Lentz); Heinze Drache (Franz Baumer); Howard Marion Crawford (Dr. Ronald Petrie); *TSAI CHIN (LIN TANG)*; Kenneth Fortescue (Sgt. Spicer).

Lin Tang is the daughter of the evil Fu Manchu. They plan to kidnap the daughters of twelve political/industrial figures in a plan to take over the world. Lin Tang enjoys tormenting the women. Their plan is foiled by Nayland Smith, who rescues the women.

THE BRIDGE OF SAN LUIS REY   Peruvian   1944/Adventure

United Artists; 85 min.; *Producer*: Benedict Bogeaus; *Director*: Rowland V. Lee; *Screenplay*: Howard Estabrook; *Music*: Dimitri Tiomkin; *Camera*: John Boyle; *Editor*: Harvey Manger; *Cast*: *LYNN BARI (MICHAELA)*; Akim Tamiroff (Uncle Pio); Francis Lederer (Manuel/Estaban); Nazimova (The Marquesa); Louis Calhern (The Viceroy); *Blanche Yurka (The Abbess)*; Donald Woods (Brother Juniper); *Emma Dunn (Dona Mercedes)*; Barton Hepburn (Don Rubio); *Joan Lorring (Pepita)*; Abner Biberman (Maita).

Michaela is a singer who rose from humble beginnings to become the Viceroy's favorite.

BRIGHT ROAD   Black   1953/Drama

MGM; 69 min.; *Producer*: Sol B. Fielding; *Director*: Gerald Mayer; *Screenplay*: Emmett Lavery; *Music*: David Rose; *Camera*: Alfred Gilks; *Editor*: Joseph Dervin; *Cast*: *DOROTHY DANDRIDGE (JANE RICHARDS)*; Philip Hepburn (C.T. Young); Harry Belafonte (School Principal); *Barbara Ann Sanders (Tanya)*; *Maidie Norman (Tanya's Mom)*; Robert Horton (Dr. Mitchell); Renee Beard (Booker T. Jones); Howard McNeely (Boyd); Robert McNeely (Lloyd).

Fourth-grade schoolteacher Jane Richards is in her first job. One of her students, C.T. Young, poses problems. Jane is determined to win C.T. over. She succeeds until his friend Tanya dies. When C.T. again rebels Jane persists in her attempts to socialize him. Eventually C.T. becomes a favored student when he saves his classmates from a swarm of bees.

Lita Baron, *The Broken Star* (UA, 1956)

BRING ME THE HEAD OF ALFREDO GARCIA   Mexican   1974/Drama

United Artists; 112 min.; *Producer*: Martin Baum; *Director*: Sam
Peckinpah; *Screenplay*: Gordon Dawson/Sam Peckinpah; *Music*: Jerry
Fielding; *Camera*: Alex Phillips, Jr.; *Editors*: Robee Roberts/Sergio
Ortega/Dennis E. Dolan; *Cast*: Warren Oates (Bennie); *ISELA VEGA
(ELITA)*; Gig Young (Quill); Robert Webber (Sappensly); Helmut Dantine
(Max).

Elita is the girlfriend of Bennie--a man trying to find Alfredo
Garcia in order to collect the bounty.

BROKEN ARROW   Native American--Apache   1950/Western

20th Century-Fox; 93 min.; *Producer*: Julian Blaustein; *Director*:
Delmer Daves; *Screenplay*: Michael Blankfort; *Music*: Alfred Newman;
Camera: Ernest Palmer; *Editor*: J. Watson Webb, Jr.; *Cast*: James
Stewart (Tom Jeffords); Jeff Chandler (Cochise); *DEBRA PAGET
(SONSEEAHRAY)*; Pasil Ruysdael (General Howard); Will Geer (Ben Slade);
Joyce MacKenzie (Terry); Arthur Hunnicutt (Duffield); Raymond Bramley
(Colonel Bernall); Jay Silverheels (Goklia); *Argentina Brunetti
(Nalikadeya)*; Jack Lee (Boucher); Robert Adler (Lonergan); Harry
Carter (Miner); Robert Griffin (Lowrie).

Sonseeahray is the daughter of Cochise. She falls in love with
Tom Jeffords, a scout sent to make peace with the Apaches. Sonseeahray and Jeffords marry, but Sonseeahray is murdered by white renegades. When Jeffords wants to seek revenge, Cochise convinces him
that the peace must be maintained even though Sonseeahray's life has
been sacrificed.

BROKEN LANCE   Native American   1954/Western

20th Century-Fox; 96 min.; *Producer*: Sol C. Siegel; *Director*: Edward
Dmytryk; *Screenplay*: Richard Murphy; *Music*: Leigh Harline; *Camera*:
Joseph McDonald/Anthony Newmann; *Editor*: Dorothy Spencer; *Cast*:
Spencer Tracy (Matt Devereaux); Robert Wagner (Joe Devereaux); Jean
Peters (Barbara); Richard Widmark (Ben); *KATY JURADO (SENORA
DEVEREAUX)*; Hugh O'Brian (Mike Devereaux); Eduard Franz (Two Moons);
Earl Holliman (Danny Devereaux); E.G. Marshall (The Governor); Carl
Benton Reid (Clem Lawton).

Senora Devereaux is the wife of cattle baron Matt Devereaux.
She is the mother of Joe, Matt's favorite son. Joe's older half-
brothers are upset at Matt's favoritism

THE BROKEN STAR   Mexican   1956/Western

United Artists; 81 min.; *Producer*: Howard W. Koch; *Director*: Lesley
Selander; *Screenplay*: John C. Higgins; *Music*: Paul Dunlap; *Camera*:
William Margulies; *Editor*: John F. Schreyer; *Cast*: Howard Duff (Frank
Smead); *LITA BARON (CONCHITA)*; Bill Williams (Bill Gentry); Henry

Calvin (Thornton Wills); Douglas Fowley (Hiram Charlton); Addison Richards (Wayne Forrester); Joel Ashley (Messen Pyke); John Pickar (Van Horn); William Phillips (Doc Mott); Dorothy Adams (Mrs. Trail); Joe Dominguez (Nachez).

Conchita, a singer, is the girlfriend of ex-lawman Frank Smead who stole some gold. Conchita is beaten up by a gang looking for the gold.

THE BROKEN WING   Mexican   1932/Western

Paramount; 71 min.; *Director*: Lloyd Corrigan; *Screenplay*: Gordon Jones/William Slavens McNutt; *Camera*: Henry Sharp; *Cast*: *LUPE VELEZ (LOLITA)*: Leo Carrillo (Captain Innocencio); Melvyn Douglas (Philip Marvin); George Babler (Luther Farley); Willard Robertson (Sylvester Cross); *Claire Dodd (Cecelia)*; *Soledad Jimenez (Maria)*; Arthur Stone (Justin Bailey); Julian Rivero (Bassilio); Pietro Soss (Pancho).

Lolita is loved by Mexican bandit Captain Innocencio, who steals dresses and jewels to give to her. She falls in love with an American flyer, Philip Marvin, who crashes near Lolita's home during a storm.

BROTHER JOHN   Black   1971/Drama

Columbia; 94 min.; *Producer*: Joel Glickman; *Director*: James Goldstone; *Screenplay*: Ernest Kinoy; *Music*: Quincy Jones; *Camera*: Gerald Perry Finnerman; *Editor*: Edward A. Biery; *Cast*: Sidney Poitier (John Kane); Will Geer (Doc Thomas); Bradford Dillman (Lloyd Thomas); *BEVERLY TODD (LOUISA MacGILL)*; Ramon Bieri (Orly Ball); Warren J. Kemmerling (George); P. Jay Sidney (Rev. MacGill); Charley Gray (Lincoln Kilpatrick); Richard Ward (Frank); Paul Winfield (Henry Birkardt).

Louisa MacGill is a schoolteacher who is attracted to mysterious childhood friend John Kane when he returns to his home town. Kane turns up at moments of crisis and then leaves as mysteriously as he arrived.

BROTHERS   Black   1977/Drama

Warner Brothers; 105 min.; *Producers*: Edward & Mildred Lewis; *Director*: Arthur Barron; *Screenplay*: Edward & Mildred Lewis; *Music*: Taj Mahal; *Camera*: John Morrill; *Editor*: William Dornisch; *Cast*: Bernie Casey (David Thomas); *VONETTA McGEE (PAULA JONES)*; Ron O'Neal (Walter Nance); Renny Roker (Lewis); Stu Gilliam (Robinson); John Lehne (Chief Guard McGee); Owen Pace (Joshua Thomas); Joseph Havener (Warden Leon).

In this fictionalization of an actual prison break-out and shoot-out at the Marin County courthouse, Paula Jones represents political activist Angela Davis.

BUCK AND THE PREACHER   Black   1972/Western

Columbia; 102 min.; *Producer*: Joel Glickman; *Director*: Sidney Poitier;
Screenplay: Ernest Kinoy; *Music*: Benny Carter; *Camera*: Alex Phillips;
Editor: Pembroke J. Herring; *Cast*: Sidney Poitier (Buck); Harry
Belafonte(The Preacher); *RUBY DEE (RUTH)*; Cameron Mitchell (Deshay);
Denny Miller (Floyd); Nita Talbot (Madam Esther); John Kelly
(Sheriff); Enrique Lucero (Indian Chief); Julie Robinson (Sinsie);
Tony Brubaker (Headman).

   Ruth is Buck's woman. Buck is involved with the protection of
former slaves.

THE BUDDY HOLLY STORY   Puerto Rican   1978/Musical

Columbia; 113 min.; *Producer*: Fred Bauer; *Director*: Steve Rash;
Screenplay: Robert Gittler; *Music*: Joe Renzetti; *Camera*: Stevan
Larner; *Editor*: David Blewitt; *Cast*: Gary Busey (Buddy Holly); Don
Stroud (Jesse); Charles Martin Smith (Ray Rob); Bill Jordan (Riley
Randolph); *MARIA RICHWINE (MARIA ELENA HOLLY)*; Conrad Janis (Ross
Turner); Albert Popwell (Eddie Foster); Amy Johnston (Jenny Lou);
Fred Travalena (Madman Mancuso); Dick O'Neil (Sol Zuckerman); *Gloria
Irricari (Mrs. Santiago)*.

   Maria Elena was Buddy Holly's wife.

BUFFALO BILL   Native American   1944/Western

20th Century-Fox; 90 min.; *Producer*: Harry A. Sherman; *Director*:
William A. Wellman; *Screenplay*: Aeneas MacKenzie/Clements Ripley/
Cecile Kramer; *Music*: David Buttolph; *Camera*: Leon Shamroy; *Editor*:
James B. Clark; *Cast*: Joel McCrea (Buffalo Bill); Maureen O'Hara
(Louisa Cody); *LINDA DARNELL (DAWN STARLIGHT)*; Thomas Mitchell (Ned
Buntline); Edgar Buchanan (Sgt. Chips); Anthony Quinn (Yellow Hand);
Moroni Olsen (Senator Frederici); Frank Fenton (Murdo Carvell); Matt
Briggs (Gen Blazier).

   Dawn Starlight is an Indian schoolteacher in love with the famous
Buffalo Bill.

THE BULLFIGHTER AND THE LADY   Mexican   1951/Drama

Republic; 87 min.; *Producer*: John Wayne; *Director*: Budd Boetticher;
Screenplay: James Edward Grant; *Music*: Victor Young; *Camera*: Jack
Draper; *Editor*: Richard L. Van Enger; *Cast*: Robert Stack (Chuck
Regan); *JOY PAGE (ANITA DE LA VEGA)*; Gilbert Roland (Manolo Estrada);
Virginia Grey (Lisbeth Flood); John Hubbard (Barney Flood); *Katy
Jurado (Chelo Estrada)*; Antonio Gomez (Antonio Gomez); Ismael Perez
(Panchito); Rodolfo Acosta (Juan); Ruben Padilla (Dr. Sierra); Dario
Ramirez (Pepe Mora).

   To impress Anita de la Vega, American Chuck Regan goes to Mexico
to become a bullfighter.

THE BULLFIGHTERS   Mexican   1945/Comedy

20th Century-Fox; *Producer*: William Girard; *Director*: Mal St. Clair;
Screenplay: W. Scott Darling; *Camera*: Norbert Brodine; *Editor*:
Stanley Rabjohn; *Cast*: Stanley Laurel (Stan); Oliver Hardy (Ollie);
Margo Woods (Tangerine); Richard Lane (Hot Shot Coleman); Carol
Andrews (Hattie Blake); *DIOSA COSTELLO (CONCHITA)*; Frank McCown (El
Brillante); Ralph Sanford (Muldoon); Irving Gump (Mr. Gump); Edward
Green (Vasso).

    Conchita sings "Bim Bam Boom" and does a fiery rhumba in a cafe.

BULLWHIP   Native American--Cheyenne   1958/Western

Allied Artists; 81 min.; *Producer*: Helen Ainsworth; *Director*: Harmon
Jones; *Screenplay*: Adele Buffington; *Music*: Leith Stevens; *Camera*:
John J. Martin; *Editor*: Thor Brooks; *Cast*: Guy Madison (Steve Dailey);
RHONDA FLEMING (CHEYENNE O'MALLEY); James Griffith (Slow Karp); Don
Beddoe (Judge Carr); Peter Adams (Parnell); Dan Sheridan (Podo); Burt
Nelson (Pine Hawk); Al Terr (Lem); Tim Graham (Pete); Hank Worden
(Tex); Wayne Mallory (Larry); Barbara Woodell (Mrs. Mason); Rush
Williams (Judd).

    According to the provisions of her father's will, Cheyenne must
marry to inherit control of a prosperous fur trading business. She
therefore marries Steve Dailey in name only. Cheyenne is headstrong
and ambitious, keeping her workers in line with a bullwhip. However,
Steve brings Cheyenne under his control and domination. She falls
in love with him and they finally consumate the marriage.

BUSTIN' LOOSE   Black   1981/Comedy

Universal; 94 min.; *Producers*: Richard Pryor/Michael S. Glick;
Director: Oz Scott; *Screenplay*: Roger L. Simon; *Music*: Mark Davis;
Camera: Dennis Dalzell; *Editor*: David Holden; *Cast*: Richard Pryor
(Joe Braxton); *CICELY TYSON (VIVIAN PERRY)*; Angel Ramirez (Julio);
Jimmy Hughes (Harold); Edwin DeLeon (Ernesto); Edwin Kinter (Anthony);
Tami Luchow (Linda); Janet Wong (Annie); Alphonso Alexander (Martin);
Kia Cooper (Samantha); Robert Christian (Donald).

    Vivian Perry teaches at a school for handicapped and emotionally
disturbed children. After petty criminal Joe Braxton is caught
stealing, he agrees to embark on a cross-country journey with Vivian
and her children in order to open a new school in Seattle. Donald,
Joe's probation officer and Vivian's boyfriend, follows them to make
sure Joe returns. Joe and Vivian fall in love as Joe begins to mend
his ways. When they arrive in Seattle, Donald is there to make sure
Joe returns, however, realizing that Joe has changed and that he and
Vivian are in love, Donald returns to the city alone.

CABIN IN THE SKY   Black   1943/Musical

MGM; 100 min.; *Producer*: Arthur Freed; *Director*: Vincente Minnelli;
Screenplay: Joseph Schrank; *Music*: George Stoll; *Camera*: Sidney
Wagner; *Editor*: Harold F. Kress; *Cast*: *LENA HORNE (GEORGIA BROWN)*;
ETHEL WATERS (PETUNIA JACKSON); Eddie "Rochester" Anderson (Little
Joe Jackson); Rex Ingram (Lucius Berry/Lucifer Jr.); Kenneth Spencer
(Rev. Green/Lord's General); Ernest Whitman (Jim Henry); Louis
Armstrong (Devil's Trumpeter); Oscar Polk (Deacon/Fleetfoot);
Butterfly McQueen (Lily); Duke Ellington.

Black musical in which Petunia tries to save the soul of her
wayward husband, Little Joe Jackson. The Lord's General and Lucifer,
Jr., are vying for Joe's soul. It looks as if all hope is lost when
Georgia, a seductive temptress, enters the picture. However, when
Petunia is shot she pleads for Joe's soul and gets him into heaven.

CAIRO   Arab--Egyptian   1963/Adventure

MGM; 92 min.; *Producer*: Ronald Kinnoch; *Director*: Wolf Rilla; *Screen-
play*: JoAnne Count; *Music*: Kenneth V. Jones; *Camera*: Desmond Dickin-
son; *Editor*: Bernard Gribble; *Cast*: George Sanders (The Major);
Richard Johnson (Ali); *FATEN HUMAMA (AMINA)*; John Meillon (Willy);
Eric Pohlmann (Nicodemus); Walter Rilla (Kuchuk); Ahmed Mazhar
(Kerim); Kamel El Shenawy (Ghattas).

Amina is a dancer involved in a jewel robbery at the Cairo
museum. The robbery is successful but Amina is caught with her lover,
who dies in her arms.

CAIRO ROAD   Arab--Egyptian   1950/Adventure

AB Pathe; 88 min.; *Director*: David MacDonald; *Screenplay*: Robert
Westerby; *Camera*: Oswald Morris; *Editor*: Peter Taylor; *Cast*: Eric
Portman (Col. Youssef Bey); Laurence Harvey (Lt. Mourad); Marie Mauban
(Marie); *CAMELIA (ANNA MICHELIS)*; Karel Stepanek (Edouardo Pavlis);
Harold Lang (Humble); Coco Asian (Lombardi); Abraham Sofaer (Coast-
guard Commandant).

Anna Michelis is involved with the police and a narcotics ring.

CALIFORNIA PASSAGE   Mexican   1950/Western

Republic; 90 min.; *Producer/Director*: Joseph Kane; *Screenplay*: James
Edward Grant; *Camera*: John MacBurnie; *Editor*: Arthur Roberts; *Cast*:
Forrest Tucker (Mike Prescott); Adele Mara (Beth Martin); *ESTELITA
RODRIGUEZ (MARIA SANCHEZ)*; Jim Davis (Linc Corey); Peter Miles
(Tommy Martin); Charles Kemper (Willy); Bill Williams (Bob Martin);
Rhys Williams (Norris); Paul Fix (Whalen).

Maria Sanchez sings "Second-Hand Romance" and "I'm Goin' Round
in Circles" while saloon owners Mike Prescott and Linc Corey vie for

the attentions of Beth Martin.

THE CALIFORNIA TRAIL   Mexican   1933/Western

Columbia; 65 min.; *Director*: Lambert Hillyer; *Screenplay*: Lambert
Hillyer; *Camera*: Ben Kline; *Cast*: Buck Jones (Santa Fe Stewart);
HELEN MACK (DOLORES); George Humbart (Mayor); Luis Alberni (Comman-
dante); Charles Stevens (Juan); Chris-Pin Martin (Pancho); Carlos
Villar (Governor); Bob Steele (Pedro).

     Dolores is the romantic interest of Santa Fe Stewart, a Robin
Hood-type who saves her town from the evil mayor.

THE CALIFORNIAN   Mexican   1937/Western

20th Century-Fox; 77 min.; *Producer*: Sol Lesser; *Director*: Gus Meins;
Screenplay: Gilbert Wright; *Camera*: Harry Newmann; *Editors*: Arthur
Hilton/Carl Pearson; *Cast*: Ricardo Cortez (Ramon Escobar); Marjorie
Weaver (Rosalia Miller); *KATHERINE DE MILLE (CHATA)*; Maurice Black
(Pancho); Morgan Wallace (Tod Barsto); Nigel de Bruller (Don Francisco
Escobar); George Regas (Ruiz); Pierre Watkin (Miller); James Farley
(Sheriff Stanton); Edward Keane (Marshall Morse).

     Not enough information was available to accurately describe this
role.

CALL HER SAVAGE   Native American   1932/Melodrama

20th Century-Fox; 88 min.; *Director*: John Francis Dillon; *Screenplay*:
Edwin Burke; *Camera*: Lee Garmes; *Cast*: *CLARA BOW (NASH)*; Monroe
Owsley (Lawrence Crosby); Gilbert Roland (Moonglow); Thelma Todd
(Bunny De Lan); Estelle Taylor (Ruth Springer); Willard Robertson
(Peter Springer); Weldon Heyburn (Ronasa); Arthur Hoyt (Attorney);
Hale Hamilton (Cyrus Randall).

     The wild Nash is the daughter of a white woman and Indian man--
who is, of course, a chief. She marries a man for vengeance and
leaves him in a fit of anger. Alone with her sick baby she is forced
to walk the streets. She eventually learns of her Indian heritage
and accepts it. She then marries a half-breed man to whom she has
been attracted all along.

CANCEL MY RESERVATION   Native American   1972/Comedy

Warner Brothers; 99 min.; *Producer*: Gordon Oliver; *Director*: Paul
Bogart; *Screenplay*: Arthur Marx/Robert Fisher; *Music*: Dominic
Frontiere; *Camera*: Russell L. Metty; *Editor*: Michael A. Hoey; *Cast*:
Bob Hope (Dan Bartlett); Eva Marie Saint (Sheila Bartlett); Ralph
Bellamy (John Ed); Anne Archer (Crazy Hollister); Keenan Wynn (Sheriff
Tom Riley); Chief Dan George (Chief Old Bear); Henry Darrow (Joe
Little Cloud); Doodles Weaver (Cactus Jones); *BETTY CARR (MARY LITTLE*

CLOUD).

Mary Little Cloud has information indicating that property belonging to John Ed really belongs to Indians. This knowledge leads to Mary's death. Dan Bartlett finds her body and is arrested for her murder, but he is eventually cleared.

CANNIBAL ATTACK   Jungle Exotic   1954/Adventure

Columbia; 69 min.; *Producer*: Sam Katzman; *Director*: Lee Sholem; *Screenplay*: Carrol Young; *Music*: Mischa Bakaleinikoff; *Camera*: Henry Freulich; *Editor*: Edwin Bryant; *Cast*: Johnny Weissmuller (Johnny Weissmuller); *JUDY WALSH (LUORA)*; David Bruce (Arnold King); Bruce Cowling (Rovak); Charles Evan (Commissioner); Steven Darrell (John King); Joseph A. Allen, Jr. (Jason).

Luora is stealing cobalt for a foreign government.

CAPRICORN ONE   Black   1978/Adventure

Warner Brothers; 127 min.; *Producer*: Paul N. Lazarus; *Director*: Peter Hyams; *Screenplay*: Peter Hyams; *Music*: Jerry Goldsmith; *Camera*: Bill Butler; *Editor*: James Mitchell; *Cast*: Elliott Gould (Robert Caulfield); Karen Black (Judy Drinkwater); Telly Savalas (Albain); James Brolin (Charles Brubaker); Brenda Vaccaro (Kay Brubaker); Sam Waterston (Peter Willis); O.J. Simpson (John Walker); *DENISE NICHOLAS (BETTY WALKER)*; Hal Holbrook (Dr. James Kelloway); David Huddleston (Hollis Peaker).

Betty Walker is the wife of astronaut John Walker.

CAPTAIN FROM CASTILE   Aztec Indian   1947/Adventure

20th Century-Fox; 140 min.; *Producer*: Lamar Trotti; *Director*: Henry King; *Screenplay*: Lamar Trotti; *Music*: Alfred Newman; *Camera*: Charles Clarke; *Editor*: Barbara McLean; *Cast*: Tyrone Power (Pedro De Vargas); *JEAN PETERS (CATANA)*; Cesar Romero (Cortez); Lee J. Cobb (Juan Garcia); John Sutton (Diego De Silva); Antonio Moreno (Don Francisco); Thomas Gomez (Father Bartolome); Alan Mowbray (Botello); Barbara Lawrence (Luisa); George Zucco (Marquis De Caravajal); Roy Roberts (Capt. Alvarado); Marc Lawrence (Cario); Robert Karnes (Manuel); Fred Libby (Soler).

Pedro De Vargas meets slave girl Catana while on an expedition with Cortez.

CAPTAIN JOHN SMITH AND POCAHONTAS Native American   1953/Drama

United Artists; 75 min.; *Producer*: Edward Small; *Director*: Lew Landers; *Screenplay*: Wisberg/Pollexfen; *Music*: Albert Glassner; *Camera*: Ellis Carter; *Editor*: Fred Feitshans; *Cast*: Anthony Dexter

(Captain John Smith); *JODY LAWRENCE (POCAHONTAS)*; Alan Hale, Jr.
(Fleming); Robert Clarke (Rolfe); Stuart Randall (Opechanco); James
Seay (Wingfield); Philip Van Zandt (Davis); Shepard Menken (Nanta-
ques); Douglas Dumbrille (Powhatan); Anthony Eustral (King James);
Henry Howland (Turnbull); Eric Colmar (Kemp); *Franchesca di Scaffa
(Mawhis)*; *Joan Nixon (Lacuma)*; William Cottrell (Macklin).

The story of the founding of Jamestown and the romance between
John Smith and Pocahontas. After Pocahontas saves John Smith from
being killed, they marry. When John Smith leaves for England he
leaves Pocahontas behind to marry John Rolfe.

CAPTAIN SINBAD   Arabian Nights   1963/Fantasy

MGM; 85 min.; *Producers*: Frank & Herman King; *Director*: Byron Haskin;
Screenplay: Samuel B. West/Harry Relis; *Music*: Michel Michelet;
Camera: Gunther Senftleben; *Editor*: Robert Swink/Eric Boyd-Perkins;
Cast: Guy Williams (Captain Sinbad); *HEIDI BRUHL (PRINCESS JANA)*;
Pedro Armendariz (El Kerim); Abraham Sofaer (Galgo); Bernie Hamilton
(Quintus); Helmut Schneider (Bendar); Margaret Jahnen (Lady-in-Wait-
ing); Rolf Wanka (The King); Walter Barnes (Rolf); James Dobson
(Iffritch); Maurice Marsac (Ahmed); Henry Brandon (Col. Kabar); John
Crawford (Aram).

While on Baristan, Sinbad falls in love with Princess Jana. Her
father, the King, is under the spell of El Kerim--who plans to take
over the kingdom and marry Jana. Sinbad destroys El Kerim and saves
Princess Jana.

CAPTAIN THUNDER   Mexican   1930/Western

Warner Brothers; 65 min.; *Director*: Alan Crosland; *Screenplay*: Gordon
Rigby/William K. Wells; *Camera*: James Van Trees; *Editor*: Arthur
Hilton; *Cast*: Victor Varconi (Captain Thunder); *FAY WRAY (YNEZ
DOMINGUEZ)*; Charles Judels (El Commandante Ruiz); Robert Elliot (Pete
Morgan); Don Alvarado (Juan Sebastian); *Natalie Moorehead (Bonita
Salazar)*; Bert Roach (Pablo); Robert E. Keane (Don Miguel Salazar);
John Sainpolis (Pedro Dominguez).

Ynez is in love with Juan but her father decides she will marry
Morgan, a wealthy rancher who is also a thief. Captain Thunder, who
will do anything to keep a promise, promises Morgan that he will ensure that the wedding is successful. Knowing of the love of Ynez and
Juan, and of Morgan's treachery, Captain Thunder kills Morgan after
the wedding ceremony, leaving Ynez a widow free to marry Juan.

CAPTIVE WILD WOMAN   Jungle Exotic   1943/Thriller

Universal; 61 min.; *Producer*: Ben Pivar; *Director*: Edward Dmytryk;
Screenplay: Henry Sucher/Griffin Jay; *Music*: H.J. Salter; *Camera*:
George Robinson; *Editor*: Milton Carruth; *Cast*: Evelyn Ankers (Beth
Colman); *ACQUANETTA (PAULA DUPREE)*; John Carradine (Dr. Walters);

Martha MacVicar (Dorothy Colman); Milburn Stone (Fred Mason); Lloyd
Corrigan (John Whipple); Vince Barnett (Curley Barret); Fay Helm
(Miss Strand).

Paula Dupree was transformed from an ape into a woman. She
works in a circus and falls for lion tamer John Whipple, who loves
another woman. This causes Paula to revert back to an ape and to
terrorize the circus.

CARAVAN   Gypsy   1934/Drama

20th Century-Fox; 101 min.; *Producer/Director*: Erik Charell; *Screen-
play*: Samson Raphaelson; *Music*: Werner Richard Heymann/Gus Kahn;
Camera: Ernest Palmer/Theodor Sparkuhl; *Cast*: Charles Boyer (Latzi);
Loretta Young (Countess Wilma); *JEAN PARKER (TINKA)*; Phillips Holmes
(Lt. von Tokay); Louise Fazenda (Miss Opita); Eugene Pallette (Gypsy
Chief); C. Aubrey Smith (Baron von Tokay); Charles Grapewin (Notary);
Noah Beery (Innkeeper); Dudley Digges (Administrator); Lionel Belmore
(Stationmaster).

   Tinka is the jealous girlfriend of Latzi—who has an eye for
Countess Wilma.

CARAVAN   Gypsy   1946/Drama

Eagle-Lion; 122 min.; *Producer*: Harold Huth; *Director*: Arthur Crab-
tree; *Screenplay*: Roland Pertwee; *Music*: Walford Hyden; *Camera*:
Stephen Dade; *Editor*: Charles Knott; *Cast*: Stewart Granger (Richard
Darrell); Anne Crawford (Oriana); *JEAN KENT (ROSAL)*; Dennis Price
(Sir Francis); Robert Helpmann (Wycroft); Gerald Hinze (Don Carlos);
Arthur Goullet (Suiza); Erin De Selfa (Singer in Cafe); H.R. Hignett
(Don Carlos' Butler); Peter Murray (Juan); Gypsy Petulengro (Paco);
Cecil Brook (Guitarist); Julian Somers (Manoel).

   Rosal, a cafe dancer living in Granada, meets and marries English
writer Richard Darrell. Oriana, Richard's girl back home also
marries. Years later Rosal is killed saving Richard's life, and
Oriana's husband also dies. Richard and Oriana are finally able to
marry.

CARMEN JONES   Black   1954/Drama

20th Century-Fox; 105 min.; *Producer/Director*: Otto Preminger; *Screen-
play*: Harry Kleiner; *Music*: Georges Bizet; *Camera*: Sam Leavitt;
Editor: Louis B. Loefler; *Cast*: *DOROTHY DANDRIDGE (CARMEN JONES)*;
Harry Belafonte (Joe); *Olga James (Cindy Lou)*; *Pearl Bailey (Frankie)*;
Diahann Carroll (Myrt); Roy Glenn (Rum); Nick Stewart (Dink); Joe
Adams (Husky); Brock Peters (Sgt. Brown); Sandy Lewis (T. Bone);
De Forest Covan (Trainer); *Mauri Lynn (Sally)*.

Dorothy Dandridge, *Carmen Jones* (20th Century Fox, 1954)

An updated, all-Black version of the opera *Carmen*. Carmen works in a parachute factory and Joe is a G.I. about to enter flying school.

CARNIVAL IN COSTA RICA   Latin American   1947/Musical

20th Century-Fox; 95 min.; *Producer*: William A. Bacher; *Director*: Gregory Ratoff; *Screenplay*: John Larkin/Samuel Hoffenstein/Elizabeth Reinhardt; *Music*: Ernesto Lecuona; *Camera*: Harry Jackson; *Editor*: William Reynolds; *Cast*: Dick Haymes (Jeff Stephens); *VERA ELLEN (LUISA MOLINA)*; Cesar Romero (Pepe Castro); Celeste Holm (Celeste); Anne Revere (Elsa Molina); J. Carrol Naish (Rica Molina); Pedro de Cordoba (Mr. Castro); *Barbara Whiting (Maria)*; Nestor Paiva (Father Rafael); Fritz Feld (Clerk); Tommy Ivo (Johnny Molina); *Mimi Agugia (Mrs. Castro); Anna Demetrio (Concha)*.

The families of Luisa Molina and Pepe Castro want them to marry, but because Pepe really loves Celeste, he tries to prove he is not worthy to marry Luisa. Luisa falls in love with American Jeff Stephens. After the fiesta's singing and dancing the families resign themselves to the inevitable.

CASBAH   Arab--Algerian   1948/Drama

Universal-International; 94 min.; *Producer*: Nat G. Goldstone; *Director*: John Berry; *Screenplay*: L. Bush-Fekete/Arnold Manoff; *Camera*: Irving Glassberg; *Editor*: Edward Curtiss; *Cast*: Tony Martin (Pepe LeMoko); *YVONNE DE CARLO (INEZ)*; Peter Lorre (Slimane); Marta Toren (Gaby); Thomas Gomez (Louvain); Hugo Haas (Omar); Douglas Dick (Carlo); *Katherine Dunham (Odette)*; Herbert Rudley (Claude); Virginia Gregg (Madeline); Gene Walker (Roland); Curt Conway (Maurice); Barry Bernard (Max); Andre Pola (Willem); Will Lee (Beggar); Katherine Dunham and her dancers.

Inez is in love with Pepe LeMoko but he has eyes only for Gaby.

CAT PEOPLE   Black   1982/Thriller

Universal/RKO; 118 min.; *Producer*: Charles Fries; *Director*: Paul Schrader; *Screenplay*: Alan Ormsby; *Music*: Giorgio Moroder/David Bowie; *Camera*: John Bailey; *Editors*: Bud Smith/Jacqueline Cambas; *Cast*: Nastassja Kinski (Irena Gallier); Malcolm McDowell (Paul Gallier); John Heard (Oliver); Annette O'Toole (Alice); *RUBY DEE (FEMALE)*; Ed Begley, Jr. (Joe); Scott Paulin (Bill); Frankie Faison (Detective Brandt); Ron Diamond (Detective Diamond).

Female is Paul Gallier's landlady. As his confidant she is aware of the true nature of Paul and his sister Irena as members of a secret cat society.

CATLOW   Mexican   1971/Western

MGM; 103 min.; *Producer*: Evan Lloyd; *Director*: Sam Wanamaker; *Screen-play*: Scot Finch/J.J. Griffith; *Music:* Roy Budd; *Camera*: Ted Scaife; *Editor*: Alan Killick; *Cast*: Yul Brynner (Catlow); Richard Crenna (Marshall Ben Cowan); Leonard Nimoy (Orville Miller); *DALIAH LAVI (ROSITA)*; Jo Ann Pflug (Christina); Jeff Corey (Merridew); Michael Delan (Rio); Julian Mateos (Recalde); David Ladd (Caxton); Bessie Love (Mrs. Frost); Bob Logan (Oley); John Clark (Keleher); Dan Van Husen (Dutch); Cass Martin (Sanchez).

After Catlow deserts her, Rosita hires a gang to go after him and steal the gold Catlow had stolen. The army captures Rosita and gang but they are then saved by Catlow posing as a marshall.

CATTLE QUEEN OF MONTANA   Native American   1954/Western

RKO; 88 min.; *Producer*: Benedict Bogeaus; *Director*: Allan Dwan; *Screenplay*: Howard Estabrook/Robert Blees; *Music*: Louis Forbes; *Camera*: John Alton; *Editor*: Carl Lodato; *Cast*: Barbara Stanwyck (Sierra Nevada Jones); Ronald Reagan (Farrell); Gene Evans (McCord); Lance Fuller (Colorados); Anthony Caruso (Natchakoa); Jack Elam (Yost); *YVETTE DUGAY (STARFIRE)*; Morris Ankrum (Pop Jones); Chubby Johnson (Nat); Myron Healey (Hank); Rod Redwing (Powhani).

Not enough information was available to describe this role accurately.

CATTLE TOWN   Mexican   1952/Western

Warner Brothers; 71 min.; *Producer*: Bryan Fox; *Director*: Noel Smith; *Screenplay*: Tom Blackburn; *Music*: William Lava; *Camera*: Ted McCord; *Editor*: Thomas Reilly; *Cast*: Dennis Morgan (Mike McGann); Philip Carey (Ben Curran); Amanda Blake (Marian); *RITA MORENO (QUELI)*; Paul Picerni (Pepe); Ray Teal (Judd Hastings); Jay Novello (Felipe Rojas); George O'Hanlon (Shiloh); Bob Wilke (Keeno); Sheb Wooley (Miller); Charles Meredith (Governor); Merv Griffin (Joe); A. Guy Teague (Easy).

Queli and Marian compete for the love of Mike McGann who has been sent to Texas to make peace between fighting ranchers. Marian wins his love.

CHANDU, THE MAGICIAN   Arab--Egyptian   1932/Mystery

20th Century-Fox; 75 min.; *Directors*: Marcel Varnel/William C. Menzies; *Screenplay*: Barry Conners/Philip Klein; *Camera*: James Wong Howe; *Editor*: Harold Schuster; *Cast*: Edmund Lowe (Chandu); *IRENE WARE (PRINCESS NADJI)*; Bela Lugosi (Roxor); Herbert Mundin (Albert Miggles); Henry B. Walthall (Robert Regent); Weldon Heyburn (Abdullah); Virginia Hammond (Dorothy); June Viasek (Betty Lou); Nestor Aber (Bobby).

The evil Roxor--who wants to rule the world--seeks the aid of Princess Nadji, the woman Chandu loves. She won't agree to help him so Roxor plans to destroy her. After Chandu saves her, Roxor kidnaps Nadji and Chandu. Chandu escapes and destroys Roxor.

CHANGE OF HABIT   Black   1970/Drama

Universal; 93 min.; *Producer*: Joe Connelly; *Director*: William Graham; *Screenplay*: James Lee/S.S. Schweitzer/Eric Bercovici; *Music*: William Goldenberg; *Camera*: Russell Metty; *Cast*: Elvis Presley (Dr. John Carpenter); Mary Tyler Moore (Sister Michelle); *BARBARA McNAIR (SISTER IRENE)*; Jane Elliot (Sister Barbara); Leora Dana (Mother Joseph); Edward Asner (Lt. Moretti); Robert Emhardt (The Banker); Regis Toomey (Father Gibbons); Doro Merande (Rose); Ruth McDevitt (Lily); Richard Carlson (Bishop Finley).

Sister Irene is one of three nuns who help Dr. John Carpenter in his ghetto community clinic.

CHANGE OF MIND   Black   1969/Drama

Cinerama; 98 min.; *Producers*: Seeleg Lester/Richard Weston; *Director*: Robert Stevens; *Screenplay*: Seeleg Lester/Richard Weston; *Music*: Duke Ellington; *Camera*: Arthur J. Ornitz; *Editor*: Donald ginsberg; *Cast*: Raymond St. Jacques (David Rowe); Susan Oliver (Margaret Rowe); *JANET MacLACHLAN (ELIZABETH DICKSON)*; Leslie Nielsen (Sheriff Webb).

The brain of a white man, David Rowe, is transferred into the body of a Black man. He is legally recognized as David Rowe but his wife and family have difficulty dealing with his new body. He turns to Elizabeth Dickson, the wife of the Black man whose body he now inhabits. She also rejects him. Meanwhile, an investigation of a murder with racial overtones is being conducted. As District Attorney, David Rowe solves the crime. Just as his wife and family begin to accept him, he decides to leave town.

THE CHARGE AT FEATHER RIVER Native American   1953/Western

Warner Brothers; 96 min.; *Producer*: David Weisbart; *Director*: Gordon Douglas; *Screenplay*: James R. Webb; *Camera*: Peverell Marley; *Editor*: Folmar Blangsted; *Cast*: Guy Madison (Miles Archer); Frank Lovejoy (Sgt. Baker); Helen Westcott (Anne McKeever); *VERA MILES (JENNIE Mc KEEVER)*; Dick Wesson (Cullen); Onslow Stevens (Grover Johnson); Ron Hagerthy (Johnny McKeever); Fred Carson (Chief Thunder Hawk).

Jenny, a white captive of the Cheyenne, has become acculturated into their society. Her sister, Anne, has not. Jenny and Anne are unwillingly rescued by their brother and a group of white men. Jenny's loyalties are with the Cheyenne and she rejects all attempts to bring her back to white society. When she manages to be cut loose (she is tied throughout the film because she wants to escape and return to the Cheyenne and the man she is going to marry) she is killed.

Anne wants to return to the Cheyenne only because she has been
sexually used and feels that she cannot return to white society.
Miles Archer loves her and convinces her to stay with him. [I listed
this film because it shows that by Jennie's association and loyalty
to the Cheyenne she becomes a woman of color and thus an outcast.]

CHARLIE CHAN IN EGYPT   Arab--Egyptian   1935/Mystery

20th Century-Fox; 72 min.; *Producer*: Edward T. Lowe; *Director*: Louis
King; *Screenplay*: Robert Ellis; *Music*: Sammy Kaylin; *Camera*: Daniel
B. Clark; *Editor*: Alfred DeGaetano; *Cast*: Warner Oland (Charlie Chan);
Pat Paterson (Carol Arnold); Thomas Beck (Tom Evans); *RITA CANSINO
[HAYWORTH] (NAYDA)*; Stepin Fetchit (Snowshoes); Frank Conroy (Profes-
sor Thurston); Nigel De Brulier (Edfu Ahmed); Paul Porcasi (Fouad
Soueida); Arthur Stone (Dragoman); James Eagles (Barry Arnold).

    This film provides an opportunity to see the young Rita Hayworth
as Nayda, a house servant.

CHATO'S LAND   Native American--Apache   1971/Western

United Artists; 100 min.; *Producer/Director*: Michael Winner; *Screen-
play*: Gerald Wilson; *Music*: Jerry Fielding; *Camera*: Robert Paynter;
Editor: Freddie Wilson; *Cast*: Charles Bronson (Pardon Chato); Jack
Palance (Quincey Whitmore); Richard Basehart (Nye Buell); James
Whitmore (Joshua Everette); Simon Oakland (Jubal Hooker); Ralph Waite
(Elias Hooker); Richard Jordon (Earl Hooker); *SONIA RANGAN (CHATO'S
WOMAN)*; Victor French (Martin Hall); William Watson (Harvey Lansing);
Roddy McMillan (Gavin Malechie); Paul Young (Brady Logan); Lee
Patterson (George Dunn).

    After killing a sheriff in self defense, Chato is hunted by a
posse. He manages to elude them and make them feel like they are
being pursued. The posse comes upon Chato's home where they rape his
wife (Chato's Woman). When they are finished they stake her out naked
to try and bring Chato out into the open. Chato manages to rescue his
wife after he is warned by his son but his Apache friend is burned
alive by the posse. Chato soon takes command of the situation and
eliminates the posse one by one.

CHE   Cuban   1969/Drama

20th Century-Fox; 96 min.; *Producer*: Sy Bartlett; *Director*: Richard
Fleischer; *Screenplay*: Michael Wilson/Sy Bartlett; *Music*: Lalo Schif-
rin; *Camera*: Charles Wheeler; *Editor*: Marion Rothman; *Cast*: Omar
Sharif (Ernesto "Che" Guevara); Jack Palance (Fidel Castro); Cesare
Danova (Ramon Valdez); Robert Loggia (Faustino Morales); Woody Strode
(Guillermo); *BARBARA LUNA (ANITA MARQUEZ)*; Frank Silvera (Goatherd);
Albert Paulsen (Capt. Vasquez); *Linda Marsh (Tania Guitterrez Bauer)*;
Tom Troupe (Felipe Munoz).

    Anita Marquez is a nurse for Che Guevara's/Fidel Castro's

revolutionary guerrillas.

CHEYENNE AUTUMN   Native American--Cheyenne   1964/Western

Warner Brothers; 159 min.; *Producer*: Bernard Smith; *Director*: John
Ford; *Screenplay*: James R. Webb; *Music*: Alex North; *Camera*: William
Clothier; *Editor*: Otho Lovering; *Cast*: Richard Widmark (Captain
Thomas Archer); Carroll Baker (Deborah Wright); James Stewart (Wyatt
Earp); Edward G. Robinson (Secretary of the Interior); Karl Malden
(Captain Wessels); Sal Mineo (Red Shirt); *DOLORES DEL RIO (SPANISH
WOMAN)*; Ricardo Montalban (Little Wolf); Gilbert Roland (Dull Knife);
Arthur Kennedy (Doc Holliday).

The story chronicles the Cheyenne's attempts to walk back to
their Wyoming homeland from Oklahoma. Spanish Woman is the mother of
Red Shirt, one of the men who wants to fight the whites.

CHIEF CRAZY HORSE   Native American--Sioux   1955/Western

Universal; 86 min.; *Producer*: William Alland; *Director*: George Sher-
man; *Screenplay*: Gerald Drayson Adams; *Music*: Frank Skinner; *Camera*:
Harold Lipstein; *Editor*: Al Clark; *Cast*: Victor Mature (Crazy Horse);
SUZAN BALL (BLACK SHAWL); John Lund (Major Twist); Ray Danton (Little
Big Man); Keith Larsen (Flying Hawk); James Millican (General Crook);
David Janssen (Lt. Cartwright); Robert Warwick (Spotted Tail); Paul
Guilfoyle (Worm).

This is the story of Chief Crazy Horse and the prophecy that
predicted his rise to power and his betrayal by one of his own people.
Black Shawl is the woman who becomes his wife.

CHILDREN OF SANCHEZ   Mexican   1978/Drama

Lone Star; 126 min.; *Producer/Director*: Hall Bartlett; *Screenplay*:
Cesare Zavattini/Hall bartlett; *Music*: Chuck Mangione; *Camera*: Gabriel
Figueroa; *Cast*: Anthony Quinn (Sanchez); *LUPITA FERRER (CONSUELO)*;
Dolores Del Rio (Grandma); Stathis Giallelis (Roberto); Duncan Quinn
(Manuel); *Lucia Mendez (Marta)*; *Katy Jurado (Chata)*.

A tale of poverty in Mexico and the machismo of the father,
Sanchez. His daughter Consuelo desperately tries to better herself
by working at a number of jobs in order to study to become a stewardess.

CHINA   Chinese   1943/War Drama

Paramount; 79 min.; *Producer*: Dick Blumenthal; *Director*: John Farrow;
Screenplay: Frank Butler; *Music*: Victor Young; *Camera*: Leo Tover;
Editor: Eda Warren; *Cast*: Loretta Young (Carolyn Brent); Alan Ladd
(Mr. Jones); William Bendix (Johnny Sparrow); Philip Ahn (1st
brother—Lin Cho); Richard Loo (2nd brother—Lin Yun); Sen Yung (3rd

brother Lin Yun); *Iris Wong (Kwan Su)*; *Marianne Quon (Tan Ying)*; *Irene Tso ("Donald Duck")*; *Barbara Jean Wong (Nanti)*.

Story of an American, Mr. Jones, helping a group of Chinese women university students and their teacher, Carolyn Brent, flee from the Japanese invaders.

CHINA CORSAIR   Eurasian   1951/Adventure

Columbia; 76 min.; *Producer*: Rudolph C. Flothow; *Director*: Ray Nazarro; *Screenplay*: Harold R. Greene; *Music*: Mischa Bakaleinikoff; *Camera*: Philip Tannura; *Editor*: Richard Fantl; *Cast*: Jon Hall (McMillen); *LISA FERRADAY (TAMARA)*; Ron Randell (Paul Lowell); Douglas Kennedy (Frenchie); Ernest Borgnine (Hu Chang); John Dehner (Pedro); *Morya Marco (Lotus)*; Philip Ahn (Wong San); Peter Mamakor (Juan); Weaver Levy (Kam).

Tamara's uncle has an antique collection that is sought by thieves. She is double-crossed by her boyfriend, Paul Lowell, who kills her uncle. McMillen attempts to help her, but she is shot and dies in his arms.

CHINA DOLL   Chinese   1958/War Drama

United Artists; 88 min.; *Producer/Director*: Frank Borzage; *Screenplay*: Kitty Buhler; *Music*: Henry Vars; *Camera*: William Clothier; *Editor*: Jack Murray; *Cast*: Victor Mature (Capt. Cliff Brandon); *LI LI HUA (SHU-JEN)*; Ward Bond (Father Cairns); Bob Mathias (Lt. Phil Gates); Johnny Desmond (Sgt. Steve Hill); Elaine Curtis (Alice Nichols); Stuart Whitman (Lt. Dan O'Neill); Anne McCrea (Mona Perkins); Danny Chang (Ellington); Ken Perry (Sgt. Ernie Fleming); *Tita Aragon (Shiao-Mee)*.

In China during World War II, Cliff Brandon drinks heavily. During one of his drunken sprees he purchases Shu-Jen as a housekeeper. Although he does not want her, she explains that her father needs the money to buy food, so he allows her to stay. They fall in love and Shu-Jen becomes pregnant. They marry and Shu-Jen gives birth to a daughter. While Cliff is away on a mission Shu-Jen is killed in a Japanese bomb attack. Out of his mind with grief, Cliff attacks the Japanese and is killed. Cliff's daughter, Shiao-Mee, is spared and years later travels to San Francisco to be with the family of Cliff's former crewmate.

CHINA GATE   Eurasian   1957/War Drama

20th Century-Fox; 96 min.; *Producer/Director/Screenplay*: Samuel Fuller; *Music*: Victor Young; *Camera*: Joseph Riroc; *Editor*: Gene Fowler, Jr.; *Cast*: Gene Barry (Brock); *ANGIE DICKINSON (LUCKY LEGS)*; Nat King Cole (Goldie); Paul DuBow (Captain Caument); Lee Van Cleef (Major Cham); George Givot (Corporal Pigalle); Gerald Milton (Private Andreades); Neyle Morrow (Leung); Marcel Dalio (Father Paul); Maurice

Marsac (Col. De Sars); Warren Hsieh (The Boy); Paul Busch (Corp. Kruger).

Lucky Legs is a French-Chinese woman living in Saigon in 1954 during the French occupation. Her American husband left her five years earlier, soon after the birth of their son, because the baby looks too Chinese. Since that time she has been living by her wits. She is called upon by the army, because of her connections, to help locate and destroy China Gate--the supply depot for the communists. She agrees, provided her son will be sent to America. She is reunited with her husband and they fall in love again as he begins to accept their son. When the sabotage is discovered, Lucky Legs sacrifices her life to ensure the success of the mission and her son's going to America.

CHINA GIRL   Chinese   1942/War Drama

20th Century-Fox; 95 min.; *Producer*: Ben Hecht; *Director*: Henry Hathaway; *Screenplay*: Ben Hecht; *Music*: Alfred Newman; *Camera*: Lee Garmes; *Editor*: James B. Clark; *Cast*: *GENE TIERNEY (MISS YOUNG)*; George Montgomery (Johnny Williams); Lynn Bari (Capt. Fifi); Alan Baxter (Jones); Victor McLaglen (Major Bull Weed); Sig Ruman (Janus); Bobby Blake (Chinese Boy); Ann Pennington (Entertainer); Philip Ahn (Dr. Young).

During World War II and the Japanese invasion of China, Miss Young falls in love with American Johnny Williams but delays a relationship with him because he is white and she is half Chinese. She leaves to teach at a Chinese school but he follows her. They acknowledge their love but soon after she is killed by Japanese bombers.

CHINA SKY   Chinese   1945/War Drama

RKO; 78 min.; *Producer*: Maurice Geraghty; *Director*: Ray Enright; *Screenplay*: Brenda Weisberg/Joseph Hoffman; *Music*: C. Bakaleinikoff; *Camera*: Nicholas Musuraca; *Editors*: Gene Milford/Marvin Coil; *Cast*: Randolph Scott (Dr. Gray Thompson); Ruth Warrick (Dr. Sara Durand); Ellen Drew (Louise Thompson); Anthony Quinn (Chen Ta); *CAROL THURSTON (SIU MEI)*; Richard Loo (Col. Yasuda); Ducky Louie (Little Goat); Philip Ahn (Dr. Kim); Benson Fong (Chung); Chin Kuang Chow (Charlie).

Story of Chinese guerrillas fighting the Japanese. Siu Mei is a nurse romantically involved with Dr. Kim.

CHOICE OF BULLETS   Native American   1972/Western

Warner Brothers; 93 min.; *Producer*: Harvey Matofsky; *Director*: William A. Graham; *Screenplay*: David Markson; *Music*: Richard Markwitz; *Camera*: Jordon Croneweth; *Editor*: Jim Benson; *Cast*: Cliff Potts (Billy); *XOCHITL (INDIAN GIRL)*; Harry Dean Stanton (Luke Todd); Don Willbanks (Sergeant); Woodrow Chambliss (Prospector).

Ex-gunfighter befriends a group of Indians who have been rounded
up by soldiers. Billy takes a special interest in Indian Girl but
the soldiers pressure him to move on. The soldiers massacre most of
the Indians and rape Indian Girl. Indian Girl and a few of the other
survivors escape but the soldiers pursue them. She meets with Billy
again and a romance develops. [This film was very difficult to
locate and there is little information available on it. The film was
re-released under other titles, FACE TO THE WIND, COUNT YOUR BULLETS,
CRY FOR ME BILLY, APACHE MASSACRE, for example.]

CHU CHIN CHOW   Arabian Nights   1934/Fantasy

Gaumont-British Release; 95 min.; *Director*: Walter Forde; *Screenplay*:
Sidney Gilliat/L.D. Peach/Edward Knoblock; *Music*: Frederic Norton;
Camera: B. Greenbaum; *Cast*: George Robey (Ali Baba); Fritz Kortner
(Abu Hasan); *ANNA MAY WONG (ZAHRAT)*; John Garrick (Nur-Al-Din);
Pearl Argyle (Marjanah); Jetsam (Abdullah); Denis Hoey (Rakham);
Sydney Fairbrother (Mahbabah); Laurence Hanray (Kasim Baba); Frank
Cochrane (Mustafa).

    Zahrat is an unfaithful and vengeful slave girl. Marjanah is
the romantic interest of Nur-Al-Din.

CIRCLE OF DEATH   Native American   1935/Western

Kent; 60 min.; *Producer*: Willis Kent; *Director*: J. Frank Glendon;
Screenplay: Roy Claire; *Camera*: James Diamond; *Cast*: Monte Montana
(Little Buffalo); Tove Linden (Mary Carr); Yakima Canutt (Yak); Henry
Hall (J.F. Henry); *PRINCESS AH-TEE-HA*; Chief Standing Bear; Ben
Corbett; Jack Carson; Dick Botiller; John Ince; J. Frank Glendon.

    Princess Ah-Tee-Ha is the local Indian maiden in this story of a
white man growing up among a band of Indians.

THE CISCO KID   Mexican   1931/Western

20th Century-Fox; 60 min.; *Director*: Irving Cummings; *Screenplay*:
Alfred A. Cohn; *Camera*: Barney McGill; *Editor*: Alex Troffe; *Cast*:
Warner Baxter (The Cisco Kid); Edmund Lowe (Sgt. Mickey Dunn);
CONCHITA MONTENEGRO (CARMENETTA); Nora Lane (Sally Benton); Frederick
Burt (Sheriff Tex Ransom); Willard Robertson (Enos Hankins); James
Bradbury, Jr. (Dixon); Jack Dillon (Bouse); Charles Stevens (Lopez);
Chris-Pin Martin (Gordito); Douglas Haig (Billy); Marilyn Knowlden
(Annie).

    Carmenetta is Cisco's current romantic interest.

THE CISCO KID RETURNS   Mexican   1945/Western

Mongram; 64 min.; *Producer*: Philip N. Krasne; *Director*: John P.
McCarthy; *Screenplay*: Betty Burbridge; *Camera*: Harry Neumann; *Editor*:

Marty Cohen; *Cast*: Duncan Renaldo (Cisco); Martin Garralaga (Pancho); *CECELIA CALLEJO (ROSITA)*; Roger Pryor (Harris); Anthony Warde (Conway); Fritz Leiber (Padre); Vicky Lane (Mrs. Page); Jan Wiley (Jeanette); *Eva Puig (Tia)*.

Cisco is charged with kidnapping and he quarrels with Rosita, his girlfriend. In the end he is cleared and makes up with Rosita.

CLAUDINE   Black   1974/Comedy

20th Century-Fox; 94 min.; *Producer*: Hannah Weinstein; *Director*: John Berry; *Screenplay*: Lester & Tina Pine; *Music*: Curtis Mayfield; *Camera*: Gayne Rescher; *Editor*: Luis San Andres; *Cast*: *DIAHANN CARROLL (CLAUDINE)*; James Earl Jones (Roop); Lawrence-Hilton Jacobs (Charles); *Tamu (Charlene)*; David Kruger (Paul); *Yvette Curtis (Patrice)*; Eric Jones (Francis); *Socorro Stephens (Lurlene)*; Adam Wade (Owen); Elisa Loti (Miss Kabak).

Claudine is a ghetto mother trying to raise her family and make ends meet. She begins seeing Roop, a sanitation worker, who helps the family by providing some needed provisions. These must be hidden when the welfare worker comes or Claudine's monthly check will be reduced. Claudine's family greets Roop with reactions ranging from love to indifference. When Roop begins to feel fenced in and responsible for her family he leaves, making Claudine miserable. But Roop soon realizes he loves Claudine and her family and comes back to marry her.

CLEOPATRA JONES   Black   1973/Action

Warner Brothers; 89 min.; *Producer*: William Tennant; *Director*: Jack Starrett; *Screenplay*: Max Julien/Sheldon Keller; *Music*: J.J. Johnson; *Camera*: David Walsh; *Editor*: Allan Jacobs; *Cast*: *TAMARA DOBSON (CLEOPATRA JONES)*; Bernie Casey (Reuben); Shelley Winters (Mommy); *Brenda Sykes (Tiffany)*; Antonio Fargas (Doodlebug); Bill McKinney (Purdy); Dan Frazer (Capt. Crawford); Stafford Morgan (Sgt. Kert); Mike Warren (Andy); Albert Popwell (Matthew); Carlo Kenyatta (Melvin); *Esther Rolle (Mrs. Johnson)*.

A female James Bond, Cleopatra Jones travels around the world to destroy the international narcotics trade.

CLEOPATRA JONES AND THE CASINO OF GOLD   Black   1975/Action

Warner Brothers; 96 min.; *Producer*: William Tennant; *Director*: Chuck Bail; *Screenplay*: William Tennant; *Music*: Dominic Frontiere; *Camera*: Alan Hume; *Editor*: Willy Kemplen; *Cast*: *TAMARA DOBSON (CLEOPATRA JONES)*; Stella Stevens (Dragon Lady); *Tonny (Mi Ling)*; Normen Fell (Stanley Nagel); Albert Popwell (Matthew Johnson).

Cleopatra Jones is on the trail of the Dragon Lady, the leader of an international narcotics ring.

CLUB HAVANA   Latin American   1945/Musical

PRC; 62 min.; *Producer*: Leon Fromkess; *Director*: Edgar G. Ulmer;
Screenplay: Raymond L. Schrock; *Camera*: Benjamin N. Kline; *Editor*:
Carl Pierson; *Cast*: Tom Neal (Bill Porter); Margaret Lindsay
(Rosalind); Don Douglas (Johnny Norton); *ISABELITA*; Dorothy Morris
(Lucy); Ernest Truex (Willy Kingston); Renie Riano (Mrs. Cavanaugh);
Gertrude Michael (Hetty); Eric Sinclair (Jimmy); Paul Cavanaugh
(Rogers).

     Isabelita sings "Tico Tico" and "Besame Mucho."

COBRA WOMAN   Island Exotic   1944/Thriller

Universal; 70 min.; *Producer*: George Waggner; *Director*: Robert
Siodmak; *Screenplay*: Gene Lewis/Richard Brooks; *Music*: Edward Ward;
Camera: George Robinson/W. Howard Greene; *Editor*: Charles Maynard;
Cast: *MARIA MONTEZ (TOLLEA/NADJA)*; Jon Hall (Ramu); Sabu (Kado); Lon
Chaney, Jr. (Hava); Edgar Barrier (Martok); *Mary Nash (Queen)*; Moroni
Olsen (MacDonald); *Lois Collier (Veeda)*; Samuel S. Hinds (Father
Paul); *Carmen D'Antonio (Dancer)*.

     Tollea is kidnapped on the eve of her wedding to Ramu and taken
back to her native island, now ruled by her evil twin sister Nadja.
Nadja uses snake superstition to intimidate the natives. Ramu and
Kado go after Tollea to rescue her. Although Tollea is entitled to
reign as high priestess instead of her sister, she prefers to leave
the island with Ramu after her sister has been defeated.

COFFY   Black   1973/Drama

American International; 91 min.; *Producer*: Robert A. Papazian;
Director/Screenplay: Jack Hill; *Music*: Roy Ayers; *Camera*: Paul Loh-
mann; *Editor*: Charles McCleeland; *Cast*: *PAM GRIER (COFFY)*; Booker
Bradshaw (Brunswick); Robert DoQui (King George); William Elliott
(Carter); Allan Arbus (Vitroni); Ruben Moreno (Ramos); John Perak
(Aleva); Sid Hale (Omar); Barry Cahill (McHenry).

     Coffy is a nurse with a mission--to wipe out drug peddling and
to kill pushers and pimps.

COLORADO TERRITORY   Native American--Pueblo   1949/Western

Warner Brothers; 94 min.; *Producer*: Anthony Veiller; *Director*: Raoul
Walsh; *Screenplay*: John Twist/Edmund H. North; *Music*: David Buttolph;
Camera: Sid Hickox; *Editor*: Owen Marks; *Cast*: Joel McCrea (Wes
McQueen); *VIRGINIA MAYO (COLORADO CARSON)*; Dorothy Malone (Julie Ann);
Henry Hull (Winslow); John Archer (Reno Blake); James Mitchell (Duke
Harris); Morris Ankrum (U.S. Marshal); Basil Ruysdael (Dave Rickard);
Frank Puglia (Brother Thomas); Ian Wolfe (Wallace); Harry Woods
(Pluthner).

Maria Montez, *Cobra Woman* (Universal, 1944)

Colorado, a half-breed of Pueblo descent, is a woman with a questionable reputation who is independent and free thinking. She is in love with Wes McQueen, an outlaw, who is in love with Julie Ann-- who reminds him of his dead girlfriend. Julie Ann is interested only in money and security and she betrays Wes to collect a reward. Wes realizes that he really loves Colorado, and they die together in a shoot-out.

COMANCHE   Mexican   1956/Western

United Artists; 87 min.; *Producer*: Carl Kreuger; *Director*: George Sherman; *Screenplay*: Carl Krueger; *Music*: Herschel Burke Gilbert; *Camera*: Jorge Stahl, Jr.; *Editor*: Charles L. Kimball; *Cast*: Dana Andrews (Read); Kent Smith (Quanah Parker); *LINDA CRISTAL (MARGARITA)*; Lowell Gilmore (Ward); Nestor Paiva (Paffer); Stacy Harris (Downey); Mike Mazurki (Flat Mouth); Henry Brandon (Black Cloud); Reed Sherman (French); John Litel (Gen. Miles).

Margarita is a captive of the Comanche who is rescued by Read.

COME BACK CHARLESTON BLUE   Black   1972/Action

Warner Brothers; 100 min.; *Producer*: Samuel Goldwyn, Jr.; *Director*: Mark Warren; *Screenplay*: Bontche Schweig/Peggy Elliott; *Music*: Donny Hathaway; *Camera*: Dick Kratina; *Editors*: Gerald Greenberg/George Bowers; *Cast*: Godfrey Cambridge (Gravedigger Jones); Raymond St. Jacques (Coffin Ed Johnson); Peter de Anda (Joe Painter); *JONELLE ALLEN (CAROL)*; Maxwell Glanville (Caspar Brown); *Minnie Gentry (Her Majesty)*; Dick Sabol (Jarema); Leonard Cimino (Frank Margo); Percy Rodrigues (Capt. Bryce); Toney Brealond (Drag Queen); Tim Pelt (Earl J.); Darryl Knibb (Douglas).

Carol is dating Joe Painter, an ambitious photographer who wants to take over the heroin market in Harlem.

CONFESSIONS OF AN OPIUM EATER   Chinese   1962/Drama

Allied Artists; 85 min.; *Producer/Director*: Albert Zugsmith; *Screenplay*: Robert Hill; *Music*: Albert Glasser; *Camera*: Joseph H. Biroc; *Editors*: Roy V. Livingston/Robert S. Eisen; *Cast*: Vincent Price (Gil De Quincey); *LINDA HO (RUBY LOW)*; Richard Loo (George Wah); *June Kim (Lotus)*; Philip Ahn (Ching Foon); Yvonne Moray (Child); *Caroline Kido (Lo Tsen)*; Terence De Marney (Scrawny Man); Gerald J. Ann (Fat Chinese); Vivianne Manka (Catatonic Girl); Victor Sen Yung (Wing Young); Ralph Ahn (Wah Chan); Arthur Wong (Kwai Tong); *Alicia Li (Ping Toy)*; John Mamo (Auctioneer).

Newspaperman George Wah attempts to break up a slave girl smuggling ring but is caught. He escapes with the help of Lotus, one of the slaves. Wah gets help from Gil De quincey, who joins up with Ruby Low, who is impersonating the tong leader she murdered. Lotus is recaptured and put on the auction block. Gil and Wah attempt to buy her but they are exposed. After an explosion, Wah and Lotus escape, but Gil and Ruby die in each other's arms.

CONQUEST OF COCHISE   Mexican   1953/Western

Columbia; 70 min.; *Producer*: Sam Katzman; *Director*: William Castle; *Screenplay*: Arthur Lewis; *Music*: Mischa Bakaleinikoff; *Camera*: Henry Frenlich; *Editor*: Al Clark; *Cast*: John Hodiak (Cochise); Robert Stack (Major Burke); *JOY PAGE (CONSUELO DE CORDOVA)*; Rico Alaniz (Felipe); Fortunio Bonanova (Mexican Minister); Edward Colman (Don Francisco de Cordova); Alex Montop (Garcia); Steven Ritch (Tukiwah); *Carol Thurston (Terua)*; Rod Redwing (Red Knife); Robert E. Griffin (Sam Maddock); Pappy del Vanda (Senora de Cordova); John Crawford (Bill Lawson).

Consuelo de Cordova is a Mexican aristocrat taken hostage by Cochise.

COOL BREEZE   Black   1972/Drama

MGM; 101 min.; *Producer*: Gene Corman; *Director/Screenplay*: Barry Pollack; *Music*: Solomon Burke; *Camera*: Andy Davis; *Editor*: Morton Tubor; *Cast*: Thalmus Rasulala (Sidney Lord Jones); *JUDY PACE (OBALESE EATON)*; Raymond St. Jacques (Bill Mercer); Jim Watkins (Travis Battle); Lincoln Kilpatrick (Lt. Brian Knowles); Sam Laws (Stretch Finian); *Margaret Avery (Lark)*; *Pamela Grier (Mona)*; *Paula Kelly (Martha Harris)*; Wally Taylor (John Battle); Rudy Challenger (Roy Harris); Stewart Bradley (Capt. Lloyd Harmon).

Obalese Eaton works in a massage parlor and is the girlfriend of Travis Battle who is involved in a million dollar jewel robbery. After the robbery Obalese and Travis head for Texas.

THE COOL WORLD   Black   1964/Drama

Cinema V; 105 min.; *Producer*: Frederick Wiseman; *Director*: Shirley Clarke; *Screenplay*: Shirley Clarke/Carl Lee; *Music*: Mal Waldron; *Camera*: Baird Bryant; *Editor*: Shirley Clarke; *Cast*: Hampton Clanton (Richard "Duke" Curtis); *YOLANDA RODRIGUEZ (LUANNE)*; Carl Lee (Priest); *Georgia Burke (Grandma)*; Bostic Felton (Rod); Charles Richardson (Beep Bop); Clarence Williams III (Blood).

The Royal Python gang members set up an apartment with Luanne, the girlfriend of the gang leader, Blood, as resident prostitute. Luanne falls in love with another gang member, Duke. Soon after Duke takes over leadership of the Pythons, Luannne vanishes and Duke is picked up by the police.

COOLEY HIGH   Black   1975/Comedy

American International; 107 min.; *Producer*: Steve Krantz; *Director*:
Michael Schultz; *Screenplay*: Eric Monte; *Music*: Freddie Perren;
Camera: Paul vom Brack; *Editor*: Christopher Holmes; *Cast*: Glynn
Turman (Robert "Preach" Morris); Lawrence-Hilton Jacobs (Larry
"Cochise" Jackson); Garrett Morris (Mr. Mason); *CYNTHIA DAVIS
(BRENDA)*; Corin Rogers (Pooter); Maurice Leon Havis (Willie); Joseph
Carter Wilson (Tyrone); Sherman Smith (Stone); Norman Gibson (Robert);
Maurice Marshall (Damon); Steven Williams (Jimmy Lee); Jackie Taylor
(Johnny Mae); *Christine Jones (Sandra)*; *Lynn Caridine (Dorothy)*.

    Preach is dating Sandra but is also attracted to Brenda. She
becomes attracted to him when she learns of his interest in poetry.

COPACABANA   Latin America   1947/Musical

United Artists; 80 min.; *Producer*: Sam Coslow; *Director*: Alfred E.
Green; *Screenplay*: Laslo Vadnay/Alan Doretz/Howard Harris; *Music*:
Edward Ward; *Camera*: Bert Glennon; *Editor*: Philip Cahn; *Cast*: Groucho
Marx (Lionel Devereaux); *CARMEN MIRANDA (CARMEN NOVARRO)*; Steve
Cochran (Steve Hunt); Gloria Jean (Anne); Ralph Sanford (Liggett);
Andy Russell; Andrew Tombes (Murphy); Louis Sobol, Earl Wilson, Abel
Green (Columnists).

    Groucho and Carmen are down on their luck so Groucho comes up
with the idea to have Carmen impersonate French entertainer Fifi at
the Copacabana, while doubling as Carmen Novarro. This keep Carmen
very busy rushing to change characters between sets. Steve falls for
Fifi, which causes even more complications. Things get worse when
the police think Groucho has killed Fifi. After it is revealed that
Fifi and Carmen are one and the same, Groucho and Carmen make a film
about it in Hollywood—while Steve begins romancing Anne.

CORNBREAD, EARL AND ME   Black   1975/Drama

American International; 94 min.; *Producer/Director*: Joe Manduke;
Screenplay: Leonard Lamesdorf; *Music*: Donald Byrd; *Camera*: Jules
Brenner; *Editor*: Aaron Stell; *Cast*: Moses Gunn (Blackwell); *ROSALIND
CASH (SARAH)*; Bernie Casey (Atkins); Keith Wilkes (Cornbread); *Madge
Sinclair (Leona)*; Lawrence Fishburne, III (Wilford); Tierre Turner
(Earl).

    Leona is the mother of Cornbread, a star basketball player slain
by the police by mistake. Sarah is the mother of his teammate and
friend Wilford. The plot concerns the aftermath and legal ramifica-
tions of Cornbread's death.

COTTON COMES TO HARLEM   Black   1970/Comedy

United Artists; 97 min.; *Producer*: Samuel Goldwyn, Jr.; *Director*:
Ossie Davis; *Screenplay*: Davis Perl; *Music*: Galt MacDermot; *Camera*:
Gerald Hirschfeld; *Cast*: Raymond St. Jacques (Coffin Ed Johnson);
Godfrey Cambridge (Gravedigger Jones); Calvin Lockhart (Rev. Deke
O'Malley); *JUDY PACE (IRIS)*; Redd Foxx (Uncle Budd); John Anderson
(Bryce); *Emily Yancy (Mabel)*; J.D. Cannon (Calhoun); *Mabel Robinson
(Billie)*; Dick Sabol (Jarema).

    Iris is the girlfriend of Rev. O'Malley--a man of questionable
integrity. Iris fights with Mabel, another woman entranced by
O'Malley. During the altercation Iris hits Mabel on the head and
tries to blame it on O'Malley. At the police station she tells the
police what she knows about O'Malley's illegal activities.

COUNTDOWN AT KUSINI   Black   1975/Adventure

Columbia; 99 min.; *Producers*: Ladi Ladibo/Ten International/Delta
Sigma Theta Sorority; *Director*: Ossie Davis; *Screenplay*: Ossie Davis/
Al Freeman, Jr.; *Music*: Manu Dibango; *Camera*: Andrew Laszlo; *Cast*:
RUBY DEE (LEAH MATANZIMA); Greg Morris (Red Salter); Ossie Davis
(Ernest Motapo); Jab Abu (Juma Bakari); Funso Adeolu (Marni/Yola);
Elsie Olusola (Mamouda); Michael Ebert (Charles Henderson); Thomas
Baptiste (John Okell); Tom Aldredge (Ben Amed).

    Leah is an agent working for revolutionary leader Ernest Motapo.
Jazz musician Red Salter is attracted to Leah and pursues her romantically. He soon recognizes what Leah and Ernest are struggling for
and begins to support their struggle for freedom. Ben Amed is hired
to assassinate Ernest.

CRIMINALS OF THE AIR   Mexican   1937/Drama

Columbia; 61 min.; *Producer*: Wallace MacDonald; *Director*: C.C.
Coleman, Jr.; *Screenplay*: Owen Francis; *Music*: Morris Stoloff;
Camera: George Meehan; *Cast*: Rosalind Keith (Nancy Rawlings); Charles
Quigley (Mark Owens); *RITA HAYWORTH (RITA)*; John Gallaudet (Ray
Patterson); Marc Lawrence (Blast Reardon); Patricia Farr (Mamie);
John Hamilton (Captain Walbee); Ralph Byrd (Williamson); Walter
Soderling (Camera-eye Condon); Russell Hicks (Kurt Feldon); John
Tyrrell (Bill Morris); Lester Dorr (Trigger).

    Rita is involved with smugglers on the Mexican border.

CRISIS   Latin American   1950/Drama

MGM; 95 min.; *Producer*: Arthur Freed; *Director/Screenplay*: Richard
Brooks; *Music*: Miklos Rozsa; *Camera*: Ray June; *Editor*: Robert J. Kern;
Cast: Cary Grant (Dr. Eugene Ferguson); Jose Ferrer (Raoul Farrago);
Paula Raymond (Helen Ferguson); *SIGNE HASSO (ISABEL FARRAGO)*; Ramon
Novarro (Col. Adragon); Antonio Moreno (Dr. Nierra); *Teresa Celli*

(Rosa); Leon Ames (Sam Proctor); Gilbert Roland (Gonzales).

Isabel Farrago is the wife of South American dictator Raoul Farrago, who has a brain tumor. Farrago kidnaps American Dr. Ferguson and his wife, so the doctor can perform the necessary surgery. Helen Ferguson is kidnapped by revolutionaries who send a letter to Dr. Ferguson telling him his wife will be killed if he performs the operation. Isabel intercepts the letter, so the surgery proceeds. However, Farrago dies of a hemmorrhage as revolutionaries break the army lines. Dr. Ferguson and his wife tend the wounded revolutionary leader.

CRY BLOOD APACHE   Native American--Apache   1971/Western

Golden Eagle International; 82 min.; *Producers*: Jody McCrea/Harold Roberts; *Director*: Jack Starrett; *Screenplay*: Sean MacGregor; *Music*: Elliot Kaplan; *Camera*: Bruce Scott; *Editor*: T. Robinson; *Cast*: Jody McCrea (Pitcalin); Dan Kemp (Vittorio); *MARIE GAHVA (JEMME)*; Don Henley (Benji); Rick Nervick (Billy); Robert Tessier (Two Card); Jack Starrett (Deacon); *Carolyn Stellar (Cochalla)*; Carroll Kemp (Old Indian); Barbara Sanford (Child); Andy Anza (Crippled Indian); Joel McCrea (The Older Pitcalin).

After watching the members of her family murdered, Jemme agrees to lead the men responsible to a hidden gold mine. Along the way she becomes attached to Pitcalin. As the group travels on members begin to be systematically killed off and suspicion falls upon Jemme and Pitcalin until it is realized that someone is stalking them. Vittorio, Jemme's brother, has been following them and eliminates all the murderers except Pitcalin. When Vittorio refuses Jemme's request to save Pitcalin's life, Jemme kills her brother.

CRY FOR HAPPY   Japanese   1960/Comedy

BLC/Columbia; 110 min.; *Producer*: William Goetz; *Director*: George Marshall; *Screenplay*: Irving Brecher; *Music*: George Duning; *Camera*: Burnett Guffrey; *Editor*: Chester W. Schaeffer; *Cast*: Glenn Ford (Andy Cyphers); Donald O'Connor (Murray Prince); *MIIKO TAKA (CHIYOKO)*; James Shigeta (Suzuki); *MIYOSHI UMEKI (HARUE)*; Michi Kobi (Hanakichi); Howard St. John (Admiral Bennett); Joe Flynn (McIntosh); Chet Douglas (Lank); Tsuruko Kobayashi (Koyuki); Harriet E. MacGibbon (Mrs. Bennett); Robert Kino (Endo); Bob Okazaki (Izumi); Harlan Warde (Chaplain); Nancy Kovack (Miss Cameron).

United States Navy men (Andy, Murray, and Lank) plan to set up a geisha house in Japan, thinking geishas are prostitutes. Harue and Chiyoko are two of the women who illustrate that geishas are very respectable.

CRY OF BATTLE   Filipino   1963/War Drama

Allied Artists; 99 min.; *Producer*: Joe Steinberg; *Director*: Irving
Lerner; *Screenplay*: Bernard Gordon; *Music*: Richard Markowitz; *Camera*:
Felipe Sacdalan; *Editor*: Verna Fields; *Cast*: Van Heflin (Joe Trent);
RITA MORENO (SISA); James MacArthur (David McVey); Leopoldo Salcedo
(Manuel Careo); Sidney Clute (C.L. Ryker); *Marilou Munoz (Pinang)*;
Oscar Roncal (Atug); Liza Moreno (Vera); Michael Parson (Capt. Davis);
Claude Wilson (Matchek); Vic Solyin (Capt. Garcia).

Sisa is a member of a group of Filipino guerrillas fighting the
Japanese in World War II. Among her acquaintances are Americans Joe
Trent and David McVey--who is at first appalled by her conduct and
life style but later comes to realize the necessity of the way she
lives. McVey eventually joins the guerrillas himself.

CRY THE BELOVED COUNTRY   Black   1951/Drama

Lopert Films; 105 min.; *Producer/Director*: Zoltan Korda; *Screenplay*:
Alan Paton; *Camera*: Robert Krasker; *Editor*: David Eady; *Cast*: Canada
Lee (Stephen Kumalo); Charles Carson (James Jarvis); Sidney Poitier
(Reverend Msimangu); Geoffrey Keen (Father Vincent); Joyce Carey
(Margaret Jarvis); Michael Goodlife (Martens); Lionel Ngakane
(Absalom); *RIBBON DHLAMINI (GERTRUDE)*; Edric Connor (John Kumalo);
Vivien Clinton (Mary); *Albertina Temba (Mrs. Kumalo)*.

Set in Johannesburg, South Africa, Stephen Kumalo travels to the
city looking for his son Absalom, who he finds in a reformatory and
his daughter Gertrude, who has become a prostitute.

CRY TOUGH   Puerto Rican   1959/Drama

United Artists; 83 min.; *Producer*: Harry Kleiner; *Director*: Paul
Stanley; *Screenplay*: Harry Kleiner; *Music*: Laurindo Almeida; *Camera*:
Philip Lathrop/Irving Glassberg; *Editor*: Frederic Knudtson; *Cast*:
John Saxon (Miguel Estrada); *LINDA CRISTAL (SARITA)*; Joseph Calleia
(Senor Estrada); Harry Townes (Carlos); Don Gordon (Incho); Perry
Lopez (Toro); Frank Puglia (Lavandero); *Penny Santon (Senora
Estrada)*; *Barbara Luna (Tina Estrada)*; Joe De Santis (Cortez); Arthur
Batanides (Alvears); Paul Clarke (Emilio); John Sebastian (Alberto);
Nira Monsour (Dolores).

Sarita is a dance hall hostess who will be deported to Puerto
Rico unless she marries a United States citizen. Miguel agrees to
marry her although he cannot fulfill her desire to become wealthy.
Eventually she leaves him because she can no longer stand poverty.

CUBA   Cuban   1979/Drama

United Artists; 122 min.; *Producers*: Alex Winitsky/Arlene Sellers;
Director: Richard Lester; *Screenplay*: Charles Wood; *Music*: Patrick
Williams; *Camera*: David Watkin; *Editor*: John Victor Smith; *Cast*:

Sean Connery (Robert Dapes); *BROOKE ADAMS (ALEXANDRA PULIDO)*; Jack
Weston (Gutman); Hector Elizondo (Ramirez); Denholm Elliott (Skinner);
Martin Balsam (Gen. Bello); Chris Sarandon (Juan Pulido); Alejandro
Rey (Faustino); *Lonette McKee (Therese)*; Danny De La Paz (Julio);
Louisa Moritz (Miss Wonderly).

Alexandra Pulido is a feminist businesswoman who enjoys capital-
ist comfort and is in love with Robert Dapes. She and Robert unwillingly become involved with revolutionaries on the eve of Castro's
revolution. When Dapes and other capitalists plan their exit from
Cuba, Alexandra discovers that she loves Cuba too much to leave.

CUBAN FIREBALL   Cuban   1951/Comedy

Republic; 78 min.; *Producer*: Sidney Picker; *Director*: William
Douglas; *Screenplay*: Charles E. Roberts/Jack Townley; *Camera*: Reggie
Lanning; *Editor*: Tony Martinelli; *Cast*: *ESTELITA RODRIGUEZ (ESTELITA)*;
Warren Douglas (Tommy Pomeroy); *Mimi Aguglia (Senora Martinez)*;
Leon Belasco (Hunvabi); Donald MacBride (Captain Brown); *Rosa Turich
(Maria)*; John Litel (Pomeroy Sr.); Tim Ryan (Bacon); Russ Vincent
(Ramon); Edward Gargan (Butler); Victoria Horne (Maid); Jack Kruschen
(Lefty); Pedro de Cordoba (Don Perez); Olan Soule (Jimmy); Tony Barr
(Estaban Martinez).

Estelita comes to Los Angeles to collect twenty million dollars.
To protect herself from fortune hunters she disguises herself as an
old woman. Through a series of misadventures she finally ends
romantically with Tommy Pomeroy.

THE CUBAN LOVE SONG   Cuban   1931/Drama

MGM; 86 min.; *Director*: W.S. Van Dyke; *Screenplay*: John Lynch; *Music*:
Herbert Stothart; *Camera*: Harold Rosson; *Editor*: Margaret Booth;
Cast: Lawrence Tibbett (Terry Burke); *LUPE VELEZ (NENITA)*; Ernest
Torrence (Romance); James Durante (O.O. Jones); Karen Morley
(Crystal); Louise Fazenda (Elvira); Hale Hamilton (John); *Mathilda
Comont (Aunt Rosa)*; Phillip Cooper (Terry, Jr.).

Nenita is a peanut vendor who falls in love with Terry Burke, an
American. Burke loves and leaves Nenita, but returns ten years later.
After his departure Nenita had given birth to Terry, Jr. Terry brings
his son home to the United States to meet his American sweetheart,
after Nenita conveniently dies.

CULT OF THE COBRA   Asian   1955/Thriller

Universal; 81 min.; *Producer*: Howard Pine; *Director*: Francis D. Lyon;
Screenplay: Jerry Davis/Cecil Maiden/Richard Collins; *Camera*: Russell
Metty; *Editor*: Milton Carruth; *Cast*: *FAITH DOMERGUE (LISA)*; Marshall
Thompson (Tom); Richard Long (Paul); David Janssen (Rico); Kathleen
Hughes (Julia Thompson); Jack Kelly (Carl Turner); William Reynolds
(Pete Norton); James Dobson (Corp. Nick Nommell); Edward C. Platt

(High Priest); Olan Soule (Air Force Doctor); Walter Coy (Police Inspector).

American soldiers discover a secret snake ceremony while on patrol. They return to the United States. Lisa, the Snake Goddess, follows them to make sure they don't reveal anything about the secret society. One by one the soldiers are killed off. When a giant cobra attacks the fiancee of one of the soldiers, the snake is killed and slowly turns back into Lisa.

CYCLONE RANGER   Mexican   1935/Western

Spectrum; 65 min.; *Producer*: Ray Kirkwood; *Director*: Bob Hill; *Screenplay*: Oliver Drake; *Camera*: Donald Keyes; *Cast*: Bill Cody (Pecos Kid); *NENA QUARTERO (NITA GARCIA)*; Eddie Gribbon (Duke); *Soledad Jiminez (Donna Castelar)*; Earl Hodgins (Pancho Gonzales); Zara Tazil (Martha); Donald Reed (Juan Castelar); Colin Chase (Luke Saunders); Budd Buster (Clem Ranking).

Nita Garcia is the romantic interest of the Pecos Kid.

THE DANCING PIRATE   Mexican   1936/Western

RKO; 85 min.; *Producer*: John Speaks; *Director*: Lloyd Corrigan; *Screenplay*: Ray Harris/Francis Faragoh/Jack Wagner/Boris Ingster; *Music/Lyrics*: Richard Rodgers/Lorenz Hart; *Camera*: William V. Skall; *Editor*: Archie Marshek; *Cast*: Charles Collins (Jonathan Pride); Frank Morgan (Alcalde); *STEFFI DUNA (SERAFINA)*; Luis Alberni (Pamfilo); Victor Varconi (Don Baltazzar); Jack LaRue (Chago); Alma Real (Bianca); William V. Mong (Tecolote); Mitchell Lewis (Pirate Chief); Cy Kendall (Pirate Cook); Julian Rivero (Shepart); Harold Waldridge (Orville); Vera Lewis (Orville's Mother).

Serafina falls in love with Jonathan Pride, a Boston dance instructor, who was shanghaied by pirates and taken to Mexico.

DANGEROUS MISSION   Native American   1954/Drama

RKO; 75 min.; *Producer*: Irwin Allen; *Director*: Louis King; *Screenplay*: Horace McCoy/W.R. Burnett/Charles Burnett; *Music*: Roy Webb; *Camera*: William Snyder; *Editor*: Gene Palmer; *Cast*: Victor Mature (Matt); Piper Laurie (Louise); William Bendix (Parker); Vincent Price (Adams); *BETTA ST. JOHN (MARY)*; Steve Darrell (Katoonai); Maria Dwyer (Mrs. Elster); Walter Reed (Dobson); Dennis Weaver (Pruitt); Harry Cheshire (Elster).

Mary works in the curio shop at a mountain vacation resort. She falls in love with Adams. At first he does not return her affection, and seems more interested in her co-worker, Louise. In fact, he is a hit man out to kill Louise, who witnessed a murder. During a hotel powwow Mary appears wearing a revealing Indian costume to entice

Adams and this time he succumbs. Soon his identity is revealed, and
he flees into the mountains with Mary, who is still ignorant of his
true nature. After a few nasty encounters she discovers he is not
the man she thought and is saved from him by Matt.

DANGEROUS TO KNOW   Chinese   1938/Drama

Paramount; 70 min.; *Director*: Robert Florey; *Screenplay*: William
Lipman/Robert Florey; *Camera*: Theodor Sparkuhl; *Editor*: Arthur
Schmidt; *Cast*: *ANNA MAY WONG (MME. LAN YING)*; Akim Tamiroff (Stephan
Recka); Gail Patrick (Margaret Van Kas); Lloyd Nolan (Inspector
Brandon); Harvey Stephens (Philip Easton); Anthony Quinn (Nicholas
Kusnoff); Roscoe Karns (Duncan); Porter Hall (Mayor Bradley); Barlowe
Borland (Butler); Hedda Hopper (Mrs. Carson; Hugh Sothern (Harvey
Greggson); Edward Pawley (John Ranee).

Mme. Lan Ying must compete for the attentions of gangster
Stephan Recka against socialite Margaret Van Kas. Mme. Lan Ying
proves herself by making Recka see that they are cut from the same
cloth and that his attempts at social climbing are futile. She and
Recka resign themselves to the fate that awaits them for being
criminals.

THE DARING CABALLERO   Mexican   1949/Western

United Artists; 60 min.; *Producer*: Philip N. Krasne; *Director*: Wallace
Fox; *Screenplay*: Betty Burbridge; *Music*: Albert Glasser; *Camera*:
Lester White; *Editor*: Marty Cohn; *Cast*: Duncan Renaldo (Cisco Kid);
Leo Carrillo (Pancho); *KIPPEE VALEZ (KIPPEE VALEZ)*; David Leonard
(Del Rio); Charles Halton; Pedro de Cordoba; Stephen Chase; Edmund
cobb; Frank Jaquet; Mickey Little.

Kippee Valez works in a bank. She helps Cisco and Pancho clear
the bank president, who has been framed for embezzlement by the mayor,
marshal, and deputy of the town.

DARK SANDS [See JERICHO]

DARKER THAN AMBER   Black   1970/Drama

National General Pictures; 97 min.; *Producers*: Walter Seltzer/Jack
Reeves; *Director*: Robert Clouse; *Screenplay*: Ed Waters; *Music*: John
Parker; *Camera*: Frank Phillips; *Editor*: Fred Chulack; *Cast*: Rod
Taylor (Travis McGee); Suzy Kendall (Vangie Merrimay); Theodore Bikel
(Meyer); Ahna Capri (Del); William Smith (Terry); Robert Phillips
(Griff); *JANET MacLACHLAN (NOREEN)*; Sherry Faber (Nina); James Booth
(Burk); Jane Russell (Alabama Tiger).

Noreen is a maid who provides a significant clue in a murder
case.

DARKTOWN STRUTTERS   Black   1975/Drama

New World Pictures; 90 min.; *Director*: William Witney; *Screenplay/ Camera*: George Armitage; *Editor*: Morton Tubor; *Cast*: TRINA PARKS *(SYREENA)*; *Edna Richardson (Carmen)*; *Bettye Sweet (Miranda)*; *Shirley Washington (Theda)*; Roger E. Mosley (Mellow); Christopher Joy (Wired); Stan Shaw (Rauchy); Norman Bartold (Commander Cross).

Syreena searches for her mother who has been kidnapped by Norman Bartold, who has been kidnapping Blacks in the area.

A DATE WITH JUDY   Latin American   1948/Musical

MGM; 113 min.; *Director*: Richard Thorpe; *Screenplay*: Dorothy Kingsley; *Camera*: Robert Surtees; *Cast*: Wallace Beery (Melvin Colner Foster); Jane Powell (Judy); Elizabeth Taylor (Carol); *CARMEN MIRANDA (ROSITA CONCHELLAS)*; Xavier Cugat; Robert Stack (Stephan); Scotty Beckett (Ogden "Oogie"); Selena Royle (Mrs. Foster); Leon Ames (Lucien T. Pringle).

Rosita Conchellas is secretly giving rhumba lessons to Melvin Foster. This gets him into trouble when his daughter, Judy, assumes they are having an affair. The situation is resolved at Melvin's wedding anniversary when he surprises his wife with his rhumba dancing.

DAUGHTER OF SHANGHAI   Chinese   1937/Drama

Paramount; 63 min.; *Director*: Robert Florey; *Screenplay*: Gladys Unger/Garnett Weston; *Camera*: Charles Schoenbaum; *Editor*: Ellsworth Hoagland; *Cast*: ANNA MAY WONG *(LAN YING LIN)*; Philip Ahn (Kim Lee); Charles Bickford (Otto Hartman); Larry Crabbe (Andrew Sleete); Cecil Cunningham (Mrs. Mary Hung); J. Carrol Naish (Frank Barden); Evelyn Brent (Olga Derey); Anthony Quinn (Harry Morgan); Gino Corrado (Interpreter); John Patterson (James Lang); Fred Kohler (Captain Guiner); Frank Sully (Jake Kelly).

After racketeers kill her American father, Lan Ying seeks revenge, posing as a cabaret singer.

DAUGHTER OF THE DRAGON   Chinese   1931/Mystery

Paramount; 70 min.; *Director*: Lloyd Corrigan; *Screenplay*:Lloyd Corrigan/Monte Kafferjohn; *Camera*: Victor Milner; *Cast*: ANNA MAY WONG *(LING MOY)*; Warner Oland (Fu Manchu); Sessue Hayakawa (Ah Kee); Bramwell Fletcher (Ronald Petrie); Frances Dade (Joan Marshall); Holmes Herbert (Sir John Petrie);Nella Walker (Lady Petrie); Nicholas Soussanin (Morloff); Lawrence Grant (Sir Basil); Harold Minjir (Rogers); E. Alyn Warren (Lu Chow); Harrington Reynolds (Hobbs); Tesu Komai (Lao); Ole Chan (The Amah).

The dying Fu Manchu urges his daughter, Ling Moy, to kill Sir

John Petrie and his son Ronald as an act of revenge. Ling Moy does her best but is thwarted by detective Ah Kee. Ronald falls in love with Ling Moy, but she does not respond to him. She plans to kill Ah Kee, who also loves her. Duty prevails and Ah Kee stops Ling Moy.

DAUGHTER OF THE WEST   Native American   1949/Western

Film Classics; 85 min.; *Producer*: Martin Mooney; *Director*: Harold Daniels; *Screenplay*: Raymond L. Shrock; *Music*: Victor Granadas; *Camera*: Henry Sharpe; *Editor*: Doug Bagler; *Cast*: MARTHA VICKERS *(LOLITA MORENO)*; Phil Reed (Navo); Donald Woods (Ralph Connors); *Marion Carney (Okeema)*; William Farnum (Father Vallejo); James Griffith (Jed Morgan); Luz Alba (Wateeka); Tony Barr (Yuba); Pedro de Cordova (Indian Chief); Tommy Cook (Ponca); Willow Bird (Medicine Man).

Lolita was brought up in a convent, unaware of her Indian heritage until she falls in love with full-blooded Navo. The two join forces to stop Connors and Morgan from swindling Indian mineral rights.

DEATH OF A GUNFIGHTER   Black   1969/Western

Universal; 94 min.; *Producer*: Richard E. Lyons; *Directors*: Allen Smithee (i.e., Robert Totten, Don Siegel); *Screenplay*: Joseph Jackson; *Music*: Oliver Nelson; *Camera*: Andrew Jackson; *Editor*: Robert F. Shugrue; *Cast*: Richard Widmark (Frank Patch); *LENA HORNE (CLAIRE QUINTANA)*; John Saxon (Lou Trinidad); Michael O'Connor (Lester Locke); Mercer Harris (Will Oxley); Kent Smith (Andy Oxley); Larry Gates (Mayor Chester Suyre); Morgan Woodward (Ivan Stanek); James O'Hara (Father Sweeney); Harry Carey (Rev. Rork); Jacqueline Scott (Laurie Mills); Dub Taylor (Doc Adams); Jimmy Lydon (Luke Mills).

Claire Quintana owns a saloon and brothel and is the mistress of the town sheriff, Frank Patch. The town is beginning to grow and prosper and the local townspeople decide to get rid of Sheriff Patch. He marries Claire but is soon killed by the mayor's council.

THE DECKS RAN RED   South Sea--Maori   1958/Adventure

MGM; 84 min.; *Producers*: Andrew & Virginia Stone; *Director/Screenplay*: Andrew Stone; *Music*: Virginia Stone; *Camera*: Meredith M. Nicholson; *Editor*: Virginia Stone; *Cast*: James Mason (Captain Edwin B. Rumill); *DOROTHY DANDRIDGE (MAHIA)*; Broderick Crawford (Henry Scott); Stuart Whitman (Leroy Martin); Katharine Bard (Joan Rumill); Jack Kruschen (Alex Cole); John Gallaudet ("Bull" Pringle); Barney Phillips (Karl Pope); David R. Cross (Mace); Hank Patterson (Mr. Moody).

Mahia is a cook on a steamer where a mutiny occurs. She aids Captain Rumill in overcoming the mutineers and saving the ship.

THE DEERSLAYER   Native American   1957/Western

20th Century-Fox; 76 min.; *Producer/Director*: Kurt Neumann; *Screen-
play*: Carrol Young/Kurt Neumann; *Music*: Paul Sawtell; *Camera*: Karl
Struss; *Editor*: Jodie Copelan; *Cast*: Lex Barker (The Deerslayer);
RITA MORENO (HATTY); Forrest Tucker (Harry Marsh); Cathy O'Donnell
(Judith); Jay C. Flippen (Old Tom Hutter); Carlos Rivas (Chingach-
gook); John Halloran (Old Warrior); Joseph Vitale (Huron Chief).

Hatty was stolen from Indians by Old Tom Hutter and raised as
his own daughter.

THE DESERT HAWK   Persian   1950/Adventure

Universal-International; 77 min.; *Producer*: Leonard Goldstein;
Director: Frederick de Cordova; *Screenplay*: Aubrey Wisberg/Jack
Pollexfen/Gerald Drayson; *Camera*: Russell Metty; *Editors*: Otto
Ludwig/Dan Nathan; *Cast*: *YVONNE DE CARLO (PRINCESS SHAHARAZADE)*;
Richard Greene (Omar); Jackie Gleason (Aladdin); George Macready
(Prince Murad); Rock Hudson (Capt. Ras); Carl Esmond (Kilbar);
Joe Besser (Sinbad); *Ann Pearce (Yasmin)*; *Lois Andrews (Maznah)*;
Marc Lawrence (Samad).

Omar is a Bedouin Robin Hood who poses as a prince in order to
marry Princess Shaharazade. After the marriage he runs away with her
dowry. She plans revenge, but after being together they fall in love.

DESERT LEGION   Arab   1953/Adventure

Universal; 85 min.; *Producer*: Ted Richmond; *Director*: Joseph Pevney;
Screenplay: Irving Wallace/Lewis Meltzer; *Music*: Frank Skinner;
Camera: John Seitz; *Editor*: Frank Gross; *Cast*: Alan Ladd (Paul
Lartal); Richard Conte (Crito); *ARLENE DAHL (MORJANA)*; Akim Tamiroff
(Pvt. Plevko); Oscar Beregi (Khalil); Leon Askin (Major Vasil);
Anthony Caruso (Lt. Messaoud); George J. Lewis (Lt. Lopez).

Morjana is the daughter of the leader of a hidden city. She
nurses Legionnaire Paul Lartal back to health after he is attacked by
revolutionaries.

DESERT SANDS   Arab   1955/Adventure

Untied Artists; 87 min.; *Producer*: Howard W. Koch; *Director*: Lesley
Sealander; *Screenplay*: Danny Arnold/George W. George/George F. Slavin;
Music: Paul Dunlap; *Camera*: Gordon Avil; *Editor*: John F. Schreyer;
Cast: Ralph Meeker (David Malcom); *MARIA ENGLISH (ZARA)*; J. Carrol
Naish (Diepel); John Smith (Rex Tyle); Ron Randell (Pete Havers);
John Carradine (Jola); Keith Larsen (El Zanal); Earl Victor (Gina);
Otto Waldis (Gabin); Peter Mamokos (Lucia); Albert Carrier (Ducco);
Mort Mills (Wolock); Philip Tongo (Sandy); Terence de Marney (Kramer).

Zara falls for Legionnaire David Malcom, who puts down an Arab rebellion.

DEVILS OF DARKNESS   Black & Gypsy   1965/Thriller

20th Century-Fox; 88 min.; *Producer*: Tom Blakeley; *Director*: Lance
Comfort; *Screenplay*: Lyn Fairhurst; *Music*: Bernie Fenton; *Editor*: Reg
Wyer; *Editor*: John Trumper; *Cast*: *TRACY REED (KAREN)*; William
Sylvester (Paul Baxter); Hubert Noel (Count Sinistre/Armond); *CAROLE
GRAY (TANIA)*; Diane Decker (Madeline Brown); Rona Anderson (Anne
Forest); Peter Illing (Insp. Malin); Geoffrey Kenion (Keith Forest);
Rod McLennan (Dave); *Marie Burke (Old Gypsy Woman)*.

Long ago Count Sinistre (a vampire) became attracted to and
wanted to marry gypsy Tania. So he killed her and raised her from
the dead. In contemporary times Paul is on the trail of Count
Sinistre for abducting Paul's model friend, Karen. Paul manages to
save Keren and destroy the Count in the process.

DEVIL'S PLAYGROUND   Latin American   1937/Drama

Columbia; 74 min.; *Director*: Erle C. Kenton; *Screenplay*: Liam
O'Flaherty/Jerome Chodorov/Dalton Trumbo; *Camera*: Lucien Ballard;
Editor: Viola Lawrence; *Cast*: Richard Dix (Jack Dorgan); *DOLORES DEL
RIO (CARMEN)*; Chester Morris (Robert Mason); George McKay (Red
Anderson); John Gallaudet (Jones); Pierre Watkins (Submarine Comman-
der); Ward Bond (Sidecar Wilson); Dan Rowan (Reilly); Francis McDonald
(Romano).

Carmen is married to skindiver Jack Dorgan, but is having an
affair with Robert Mason.

DIAMOND HEAD   Hawaiian   1962/Drama

Columbia; 107 min.; *Producer*: Jerry Bresler; *Director*: Guy Green;
Screenplay: Marguerite Roberts; *Music*: Johnny Williams; *Camera*: Sam
Leavitt; *Editor*: William A. Lyon; *Cast*: Charlton Heston (Richard
"King" Howland); Yvette Mimieux (Sloan); George Chakiris (Dr. Dean
Kahana); *FRANCE NUYEN (MEI CHEN)*; James Darren (Paul Kahana);
Aline MacMahon (Kaplolani); Elizabeth Allen (Laura Beckett); Vaughn
Taylor (Judge Blanding); Marc Marno (Bobbie Chen); Philip Ahn
(Emekona); Harold Fong (Coyama).

A film about racism in modern Hawaii. Sloan Howland falls in
love with Hawaiian Paul Kahana to the dismay of her family, but
especially her brother King Howland. King, however, has been quietly
keeping a Hawaiian mistress, Mei Chen, who is pregnant. Although
King will not acknowledge the child as his, he agrees to provide
support for Mei and her baby. During Sloan and Paul's engagement
party, King accidentally kills Paul, causing Sloan to leave home and
fall in love with Paul's half-brother, Dean. Mei Chen dies giving
birth to King's son. Sloan and Dean take the child because King still
refuses to acknowledge the boy. However, when King returns to his

isolated mansion he realizes the error of his ways and goes to
retrieve his son.

THE DIAMOND QUEEN   Asian   1953/Adventure

Warner Brothers; 80 min.; *Producer*: Frank Melford; *Director*: John
Brahm; *Screenplay*: Otto Englander; *Music*: Paul Sawtell; *Camera*:
Stanley Cortez; *Editor*: Francis V. Lyon: *Cast*: Fernando Lamas (Jean
Tavernier); *ARLENE DAHL (MAYA)*; Gilbert Roland (Baron Paul de
Cubannes); Sheldon Leonard (Great Mogul); Jay Novello (Gujar); Michael
Ansara (Jumia); Richard Hale (Gabriel Taveinier).

     Maya is the Queen of Nepal.

DIMENSION 5   Asian   1966/Science Fiction

United Pictures Corp.; *Producer*: Earle Lyons; *Director*: Franklin
Adreon; *Screenplay*: Arthur C. Pierce; *Music*: Paul Dunlap; *Camera*:
Alan Stenvold; *Editor*: Robert S. Eisen; *Cast*: Jeffrey Hunter (Justin
Power); *FRANCE NUYEN (KITTY TSU)*; Harold Sakata (Big Buddha); Donald
Woods (Cane); *Linda Ho (Nancy Ho)*; Robert Ito (Sato); David Chow
(Stoneface); Lee Kolima (Genghis).

     Super agent Justin Power and his assistant Kitty Tsu travel
ahead in time three weeks to prevent a communist organization (Dragon)
from blowng up Los Angeles. They are aided by Dragon agent Nancy Ho.
After a successful mission they return to enjoy the three weeks they
missed.

DIRTY DINGUS MAGEE   Native American   1970/Comedy

MGM; 97 min.; *Producer/Director*: Burt Kennedy; *Screenplay*: Tom
Waldman/Frank Waldman/Joseph Heller; *Music*: Billy Strange; *Camera*:
Harry Stradling; *Cast*: Frank Sinatra (Dingus Magee); George Kennedy
(Hoke Birdsill); Anne Jackson (Belle); Lois Nettleton (Prudence
Frost); Jack Elam (John Wesley Hardin); *MICHELE CAREY (ANNA HOTWATER)*;
John Dehner (General); Henry Jones (Rev. Green); Paul Fix (Chief
Crazy Blanket).

     Anna Hotwater is Dingus Magee's nymphomaniac mistress.

DOCTOR'S WIVES   Black   1971/Drama

Columbia; 95 min.; *Producer*: M.J. Frankovich; *Director*: George
Schaefer; *Screenplay*: Daniel Taradash; *Camera*: Charles B. Lang;
Editor: Carl Kress; *Cast*: Dyan Cannon (Lorrie Dellman); Richard
Crenna (Pete Brennan); Gene Hackman (Dave Randolph); Carroll
O'Connor (Joe Gray); Rachel Roberts (Della Randolph); Janice Rule
(Amy Brennan); *DIANA SANDS (HELEN STRAUGHN)*; Cara Williams (Maggie
Gray); Richard Anderson (D.A. Douglas); Ralph Bellamy (Jake Porter).

Helen Straughn, a widowed nurse, is having an affair with Dr.
Pete Brennan. Helen has a son who requires emergency neurosurgery.

DOMINO KID   Mexican   1957/Western

Columbia; 74 min.; *Producers*: Rory Calhoun/Victor M. Orsatti;
Director: Ray Nazarro; *Screenplay*: Kenneth Gamet/Hal Biller; *Music*:
Mischa Bakaleinikoff; *Camera*: Irving Lippman; *Editor*: Gene Havlick;
Cast: Rory Calhoun (Domino); Kristine Miller (Barbara Ellison);
Andrew Duggan (Wade Harrington); *YVETTE DUGAY (ROSITA)*; Peter Whitney
(Lafe Prentiss); Eugene Iglesias (Juan Cortez); Robert Burton
(Sheriff Travers); Bart Bradley (Pepe Garcias); James Griffith (Sam
Beal); Roy Barcroft (Ed Sandlin); Denver Pyle (Bill Dragger); Ray
Corrigan (Buck).

Rosita owns the cantina where she dances.

DOWN AMONG THE SHELTERING PALMS   Island Exotic   1953/Musical

20th Century-Fox; 86 min.; *Producer*: Fred Kohlmar; *Director*: Edmund
Goulding; *Screenplay*: Claude Binyon/Albert Lewis/Burt Styler; *Music*:
Lionel Newman; *Camera*: Leon Shamroy; *Editor*: Louis Loeffler; *Cast*:
William Lundigan (Captain Bill Willoby); Jane Greer (Diana Forrester);
MITZI GAYNOR (ROZOUILA); David Wayne (Lt. Carl O. Schmidt); Gloria
De Haven (Angela Toland); Gene Lockhart (Rev. Edgett); Jack Paar
(Lt. Mike Sloan); Alvin Greenman (Corp. Kolta); Billy Gilbert (King
Jilouili).

Rozouila, an island beauty, is one of the women vying for the
heart of Captain Bill Willoby.

DOWN ARGENTINE WAY   Latin American   1940/Musical

20th Century-Fox; 88 min.; *Producer*: Darryl F. Zanuck; *Director*:
Irving Cummings; *Screenplay*: Darrell Ware/Karl Tunberg; *Music*: Mack
Gordon/Harry Warren; *Camera*: Leon Shamroy/Ray Rennahan; *Cast*: Don
Ameche (Ricardo Quintano); Betty Grable (Glenda Crawford); *CARMEN
MIRANDA*; Charlotte Greenwood (Binnie Crawford); J. Carrol Naish
(Casiano); Henry Stephenson (Don Diego Quintano); Katharine Aldridge
(Helen Carson); Leonid Kinsky (Tito Aluna); Chris-Pin Martin (Este-
ban); Robert Conway (Jimmy Blake); Gregory Gaye (Sebastian); Bobby
Stone (Panchito).

Carmen Miranda plays herself, singing and dancing a few specialty
numbers.

DOWN LAREDO WAY   Gypsy   1953/Drama

Republic; 54 min.; *Producer*: Rudy Ralson; *Director*: William Witney;
Screenplay: Harold Mintor; *Camera*: John MacBurnie; *Editor*: Stanley
Wilson; *Cast*: Rex Allen; Slim Pickens; *DONA DRAKE (NARITA)*; Roy

Barcroft (Cooper); Marjorie Lord (Valerie); Judy Nugent (Taffy);
Percy Helton (Judge Sully); Clayton Moore (Chip Wells); Don Murray
(Joe).

Narita befriends Taffy after her father is killed in a circus
highwire accident.

DRAGON SEED   Chinese   1944/Drama

MGM; 148 min.; *Producer*: Pandro S. Berman; *Directors*: Jack Conway/
Harold S. Bucquet; *Screenplay*: Marguerite Roberts/Jane Murtin;
Music: Herbert Stothart; *Camera*: Sidney Wagner; *Editor*: Harold F.
Kress; *Cast*: *KATHARINE HEPBURN (JADE)*; Walter Huston (Ling Tan);
Aline MacMahon (Ling's Wife); Akim Tamiroff (Wu Lein); Turhan Bey
(Lao Er); Hurd Hatfield (Lao San); J. Carrol Naish (Japanese Kitchen
Overseer); *Agnes Moorehead (3rd Cousin's Wife)*; Henry Travers (3rd
Cousin); Robert Bice (Lao Ta); Robert Lewis (Captain Sato); *Frances
Rafferty (Orchid)*; *Jacqueline De Wit (Wife of Wu Lein)*; *Anna Demetrio
(Wu Sao)*; Clarence Lung (4th Cousin); Paul E. Burns (Neighbor Shen).

This story concerns the Chinese reaction to the Japanese occupation. Jade does her best to act as an independent woman despite the
social constraints of Chinese society. She becomes involved, with
her husband, in a rebel resistance movement. She even gives up her
baby in order to fight for her principles and the freedom of her
people.

DREAM WIFE   Middle Eastern   1953/Comedy

MGM; 99 min.; *Producer*: Dore Schary; *Director*: Sidney Sheldon;
Screenplay: Sidney Sheldon/Herbert Baker/Alfred Lewis Levitt; *Music*:
Conrad Salinger; *Camera*: Milton Krasner; *Editor*: George White; *Cast*:
Cary Grant (Clemson Reade); Deborah Kerr (Effie); Walter Pidgeon
(Walter McBride); *BETTA ST. JOHN (TARJI)*; Eduard Franz (Khan); Buddy
Baer (Vizier); Leo Treymayne (Ken Landwell); Donald Randolph (Ali);
Bruce Bennett (Charlie Elkwood); Richard Anderson (Henry Melvine);
Dan Tobin (Mr. Brown); *Movita (Rima)*; Gloria Holden (Mrs. Landwell);
June Clayworth (Mrs. Elkwood).

Clemson Reade's fiancee Effie is too independent for him so he
breaks his engagement to marry Tarji, a Middle Eastern woman brought
up to be totally dedicated to pleasing a man. Tarji comes to the
United States for the wedding and impresses all the men with her
dedication to pleasing Clem. She soon discovers the independence
American women have and begins becoming Americanized. Clem rapidly
becomes disillusioned and returns to Effie, who has learned some of
Tarji's ways.

DREAMS OF GLASS   Japanese   1970/Drama

Universal; 83 min.; *Producer/Director/Screenplay*: Robert Clouse;
Music: Ian Freebairn-Smith; *Camera*: Michael Murphy; *Cast*: John Denos

(Tom); *CAROLINE BARRETT (ANN)*; Joe Lo Presti (Tom's Father); Margaret Rich (Tom's Mother); Donald Elson (Ann's Father); *Pat Li (Ann's Mother)*; Paul Micale (Pucci).

Ann and Tom are young and in love but their families disapprove because of their racial differences. They continue a clandestine relationship and Tom promises to marry Ann.

DROP DEAD, DARLING   Asian   1966/Comedy
[ARRIVIDERCI, BABY!]

Paramount; 100 min.; *Producer/Director/Screenplay*: Ken Hughes; *Music*: Dennis Farnom; *Camera*: Denys Coop; *Editor*: John Shirley; *Cast*: Tony Curtis (Nick Johnson); Rosanna Schiaffino (Francesca de Rienzi); Lionel Jeffries (Parker); Zsa Zsa Gabor (Gigi); *NANCY KWAN (BABY)*; Fenella Fielding (Lady Fawcett); Anna Quayle (Aunt Miriam); Warren Mitchell (Count de Rienzi/Maximilian); Mischa Auer (Romeo).

Nick Johnson marries women for their money and then kills them. Between marriages he sees his girlfriend Baby. But when he marries Francesca de Rienzi, who has the same ideas about marriage and murder, he falls in love and settles down with her, while Baby happily marries a wealthy count.

DRUM   Black   1976/Drama

United Artists; 100 min.; *Producer*: Ralph Serpe; *Director*: Steve Carver; *Screenplay*: Norman Walker; *Music*: Charlie Smalls; *Camera*: Lucien Ballard; *Editor*: Carl Kress; *Cast*: Warren Oates (Hammond Maxwell); Isela Vega (Mariana); Ken Norton (Drum); *PAMELA GRIER (REGINE)*; Yaphet Kotto (Blaise); John Colicos (Bernard DeMarigny); Fiona Lewis (Augusta Chauvet); Royal Dano (Zeke); *Paula Kelly (Rachel)*; *Lillian Hayman (Lucretia Borgia)*; *Brenda Sykes (Calinda)*.

Sequel to MANDINGO. Regine is a slave.

DRUM BEAT   Native American--Modoc   1954/Western

Warner Brothers; 107 min.; *Director/Screenplay*: Delmer Daves; *Music*: Victor Young; *Camera*: J. Peverell Marley; *Editor*: Clarence Kolster; *Cast*: Alan Ladd (Johnny Mackay); Audrey Dalton (Nancy Meek); *MARISA PAVAN (TOBY)*; Robert Keith (Bill Satterwhite); Rodolfo Acosta (Scarface Charlie); Charles Bronson (Captain Jack); Warner Anderson (General Canby); Elisha Cook, Jr. (Crackel); Anthony Caruso (Manok); Richard Gaines (Dr. Thomas); Edgar Stehli (Jesse Grant); Hayden Roarke (General Grant).

Johnny Mackay is sent to make peace between the Modoc's and the United States government. Toby falls in love with Mackay but he loves Nancy Meek.

DRUMS OF TAHITI   Island Exotic   1953/Adventure

Columbia; 73 min.; *Producer*: Sam Katzman; *Director*: William Castle;
Screenplay: Douglas Heyes/Robert E. Kent; *Camera*: Lester H. White;
Editor: Jerome Thoms; *Cast*: Dennis O'Keefe (Mike Macklin); Patricia
Medina (Wanda Spencer); Francis L. Sullivan (Pierre Duvois); George
Keymas (Angelo); *SYLVIA LEWIS (MAWAII)*; Cicely Brown (Gay Knight);
Raymond Lawrence (Shoreham); *Frances Brandt (Island Queen)*.

    Mawaii is a dancer.

DRUMS OF THE CONGO   Black [African]   1942/Adventure

Universal; 70 min.; *Assoc. Producer*: Henry MacRae; *Director*: Christy
Cabanne; *Screenplay*: Paul Huston; *Camera*: George Robinson; *Editor*:
Maurice Wright; *Cast*: Ona Munson (Dr. Ann Montgomery); Stuart Erwin
(Congo Jack); Peggy Moran (Enid); Don Terry (Kirk); Richard Lane
(Cutlass); *DOROTHY DANDRIDGE (MALIMI)*; Jules Bledsoe (Kalu); Turhan
Bey (Juma); Ernest Whitman (King Malaba); Ed Stanley (Col. Robinson).

    Malimi is one of the local natives.

DUEL AT APACHE WELLS   Mexican   1957/Western

Republic; 69 min.; *Producer/Director*: Joe Kane; *Screenplay*: Bob
Williams; *Music*: Gerald Roberts; *Camera*: Jack Martin; *Editor*: Richard
L. Van Enger; *Cast*: ANNA MARIA ALBERGHETTI *(ANITA VALDEZ)*; Ben
Cooper (Johnny Shattuck); Jim Davis (Dean Cannary); Harry Shannon
(Wayne Shattuck); Francis J. McDonald (Hank); Bob Steele (Joe Dunn);
Frank Puglia (Senor Valdez); *Argentina Brunetti (Tia Maria)*; Ian
MacDonald (Marcus Wolf).

    Anita Valdez is the romantic interest of Johnny Shattuck. Her
father owns the local cantina.

DUEL IN THE SUN   Native American   1946/Western

Selznick; 138 min.; *Producer*: David O. Selznick; *Director*: King Vidor;
Screenplay: David O. Selznick; *Music*: Dimitri Tiomkin; *Camera*: Lee
Garmes/Hal Rosson/Ray Rennahan; *Editors*: Hal C. Kern/William Ziegler/
John D. Faure/Charles Freeman; *Cast*: JENNIFER JONES *(PEARL CHAVEZ)*;
Joseph Cotten (Jesse McCanles); Gregory Peck (Lewt McCanles); Lionel
Barrymore (Senator McCanles); Lillian Gish (Laura Belle McCanles);
Tilly Losch (Mrs. Chavez); Herbert Marshall (Scott Chavez); Charles
Bickford (Sam Pierce); Walter Huston (The Sin Killer); *Butterfly
McQueen (Vashti)*.

    Pearl Chavez must choose between becoming trash like her Indian
mother or being a good woman. After Scott Chavez kills his wife and
her lover, Pearl goes to live with her father's ex-sweetheart, Laura
Belle McCanles. Pearl falls in love with both of Laura Belle's sons,
the good Jesse, and the bad Lewt. Pearl is raped by Lewt and thereby

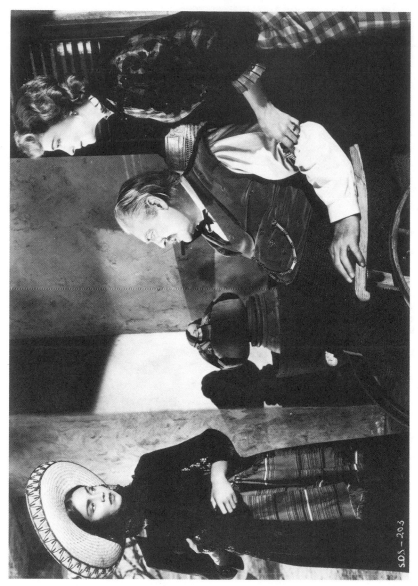

Jennifer Jones, *Duel in the Sun* (Selznick, 1946)

becomes his woman, rejected by Jesse. Pearl is consistently harassed
by Senator McCanles. The only person Pearl feels superior to is the
black maid, Vashti. Lewt becomes a fugitive from the law. Pearl
decides to avenge herself and she manages to kill Lewt but not before
he kills her. They die in each others arms.

DUEL ON THE MISSISSIPPI   Creole   1955/Drama

Columbia; 72 min.; *Director*: William Castle; *Screenplay*: Gerald
Drayson Adams; *Music*: Mischa Bakaleinikoff; *Camera*: Henry Freulich;
Editor: Edwin Bryant; *Cast*: Lex Barker (Andre Tulane); *PATRICIA
MEDINA (LILI SCARLET)*; Warren Stevens (Rene La Farge); John Dehner
(Jules Tulane); Ian Keith (Jacques Scarlet); Chris Alcaide (Anton);
John Mansfield (Louie); Celia Lovsky (Celeste Tulane); Lou Merrill
(Georges Gabriel); Mel Wells (Sheriff); Jean Del Val (Bidaut);
Baynes Barron (Gaspard).

Lili Scarlet, owner of a gambling ship, resents not being
accepted as an equal by southern aristorcracy. She encourages bayou
renegades to raid their sugar plantations. Jules Tulane, an aristocrat, becomes her bonded servant to save his father's plantation.
When the raids get out of hand, Jules helps Lili by fighting a duel
with Rene La Farge, leader of the renegades. When it is over, Lili
and Jules marry.

EAST IS WEST   Chinese   1930/Drama

Universal; 72 min.; *Producer*: Carl Laemmle, Jr.; *Director*: Monta Bell;
Screenplay: Winifred Eaton Reve/Tom Reed; *Camera*: Jerry Ash; *Editor*:
Harry Marker; *Cast*: *LUPE VALEZ (MING TONG)*; Lew Ayres (Billy Benson);
Edward G. Robinson (Charlie Yong); E. Allyn Warren (Lo Sang Kee);
Tetsu Komai (Hop Toy); Henry Kolker (Mr. Benson); Mary Forbes (Mrs.
Benson); Edgar Norton (Thomas); Charles Middleton (Dr. Fredericks).

Ming Tong is put on the auction block by her father but is rescued by Billy Benson and sent to the United States. She is taken in
by Lo Sang Kee, but soon he is forced to sell her to Charlie Yong, a
powerful Chinatown "king." Billy Benson kidnaps and once again saves
her; this time, however, he plans to marry her--much to the horror of
San Francisco society. At the end it is revealed that she was kidnapped from Americans when she was a baby and is really white.

EAST OF BORNEO   Jungle Exotic   1931/Adventure

Universal; 73 min.; *Producer*: Carl Laemmle, Jr.; *Director*: George
Melford; *Screenplay*: Edwin Knopf; *Camera*: George Robinson; *Cast*:
Rose Hobard (Linda Randolph); Charles Bickford (Dr. Allan Clark);
George Renavent (Prince Hashin); *LUPITA TOVAR (NIELA)*; Noble Johnson
(Osman).

Niela is the local native girl.

EAST OF SUMATRA   Island Exotic   1953/Adventure

Universal; 82 min.; *Producer*: Albert J. Cohen; *Director*: Budd
Boetticher; *Screenplay*: Frank Gill, Jr.; *Camera*: Clifford Stine;
Editor: Virgil Vogel; *Cast*: Jeff Chandler (Duke Mullane); Marilyn
Maxwell (Lory Hale); Anthony Quinn (Kiang); *SUZAN BALL (MINYORA)*;
Jay C. Flippen (MacLeod); John Sutton (Daniel Catlin); Scatman
Crothers (Baltimore); Eugene Iglesias (Paulo); Earl Holliman (Cupid);
Peter Graves (Cowboy); Anthony Eustrel (Clyde); James Craven (Drake);
Aram Katcher (Atib); John Warburton (Keith).

Minyora is to marry the chief's son, but she really loves Duke
Mullane. She performs an exotic dance.

EDGE OF THE CITY   Black   1957/Drama

MGM; 85 min.; *Producer*: David Susskind; *Director*: Martin Ritt;
Screenplay: Robert A. Aurthur; *Camera*: Joseph Brun; *Editor*: Sidney
Meyers; *Music*: Leonard Rosenman; *Cast*: John Cassavetes (Axel North);
Sidney Poitier (Tommy Tyler); Jack Warden (Charles Malik); Kathleen
Maguire (Ellen Wilson); *RUBY DEE (LUCY TYLER)*; Robert Simon (Mr.
Nordmann); Ruth White (Mrs. Nordmann); William A. Lee (David).

Lucy is married to Tommy, who becomes friendly with white co-
worker Axel North. Tommy is murdered when he defends Axel's job.

THE EDUCATION OF SONNY CARSON Black   1974/Drama

Paramount; 74 min.;*Producers*: Irwin Yablans/David Golden; *Director*:
Michael Campus; *Screenplay*: Fred Hudson; *Music*: Coleridge-Taylor
Perkinson; *Camera*: Ed Brown; *Editors*: Edward Warschilka/Harry Howard;
Cast: Rony Clanton (Sonny Carson); Don Gordon (Pigilani); *JOYCE
WALKER (VIRGINIA)*; Paul Benjamin (Popa); Thomas Hicks (Young Sonny);
Mary Alice (Moma); Ram John Holder (Preacher); Jerry Bell (Lil Boy).

Based on his autobiography, this is the story of Sonny Carson
who went from model student to gang leader and was unjustly sent to
prison. While he is in prison, his girlfriend, Virginia, becomes
addicted to heroin.

THE EIGER SANCTION   Black   1975/Action

Universal/Malpaso Company; 125 min.; *Producer*: Robert Daley;
Director: Clint Eastwood; *Music*: John Williams; *Camera*: John Cleare/
Jeff Schoolfield/Peter Pilafian/Pete White; *Editor*: Ferris Webster;
Cast: Clint Eastwood (Jonathan Hemlock); George Kennedy (Ben Bowman);
VONETTA McGEE (JEMIMA BROWN); Jack Cassidy (Miles Mellough); Heidi
Bruhl (Anna Montaigne); Thayer David (Dragon); Reiner Schoene
(Freytag); Michael Grimm (Meyer); Jean-Pierre Bernard (Montaigne);
Brenda Venus (George); Gregory Walcott (Pope).

Airline stewardess, Jemima Brown, is really a secret government agent sent to double cross ex-agent Jonathan Hemlock.

EL ALAMEIN   Arab   1953/War Drama

Columbia; 66 min.; *Producer*: Wallace MacDonald; *Director*: Fred F.
Sears; *Screenplay*: Herbert Purdum/George Worthington Yates; *Camera*:
Henry Freulich; *Editor*: Richard Fantl; *Cast*: Scott Brady (Banning);
Edward Ashley (Capt. Harbison); Robin Hughes (Sgt. Alf Law); *RITA
MORENA (JARA)*; Michael Pate (Sgt. McQueen); Peter Brocco (Selim);
Peter Mamakos (Corp. Singh Das); Ray Page (Nazi Pilot); Benny Rubin
(Egyptian Driver); Henry Rowland (Nazi Officer).

    Jara is the niece of an Arab aiding the Nazis.

EL CONDOR   Mexican   1970/Western

National General Pictures; 102 min.; *Producer*: Andre de Toth;
Director: John Guillermin; *Screenplay*: Larry Cohen; *Music*: Maurice
Jarre; *Camera*: Henri Persin; *Cast*: Jim Brown (Luke); Lee Van Cleef
(Jaroo); Patrick O'Neal (Chavez); Mariana Hill (Claudine); Iron Eyes
Cody (Santana); *IMOGEN HASSALL (DOLORES)*; Elisha Cook, Jr. (Old
Convict).

    Dolores is the romantic interest of Jaroo.

EL DORADO PASS   Mexican   1948/Western

Columbia; 56 min.; *Producer*: Colbert Clark; *Director*: Ray Nazarro;
Screenplay: Earle Snell; *Camera*: Rex Wimpy; *Editor*: Burton Kramer;
Cast: Charles Storrett (The Durango Kid); Smiley Burnette; *ELENA
VERDUGO (DOLORES)*; Steve Darrell (Page); Ted Mapes (Dodd); Rory
Mallison (Sheriff Tom Wright).

    Dolores and her father are the victims of a stagecoach robbery
and lose $20,000. The Durango Kid is falsely accused and must find
the real criminals.

ELEPHANT STAMPEDE   Jungle Exotic   1951/Adventure

Monogram; 70 min.; *Producer*: Walter Mirisch; *Director*: Ford Beebe;
Screenplay: Ford Beebe; *Camera*: William Sickner; *Editor*: William
Austin; *Cast*: Johnny Sheffield (Bomba); *DONNA MARTELL (LOLA)*; Edith
Evanson (Miss Banks); Martin Wilkins (Chief Nagala); John Kellogg
(Bob Warren); Myron Healey (Joe Collins); Leonard Madie (Andy Barnes);
Guy Kingsford (Mark Phillips).

    Lola is a native girl romanced by Bomba. Bomba is trying to save
a herd of elephants from being destroyed by greedy hunters.

ELLERY QUEEN'S PENTHOUSE MYSTERY   Chinese   1941/Mystery

Columbia; 69 min.; *Producer*: Larry Darmour; *Director*: James Hogan;
Screenplay: Eric Taylor; *Music*: Lee Zahler; *Camera*: James S. Brown,
Jr.; *Editor*: Dwight Caldwell; *Cast*: Ralph Bellamy (Ellery Queen);
Margaret Lindsay (Nikki Porter); Charley Grapewin (Inspector Queen);
ANNA MAY WONG (LOIS LING); James Burke (Sgt. Velie); Eduardo
Ciannelli (Count Brett); Ann Doran (Sheila Cobb); Noel Madison (Gordon
Cobb); Frank Albertson (Sanders); Charles Lane (Doc Prouty); Russell
Hicks (Walsh).

Lois Ling is involved with a group raising food for the poor of
China and inadvertently becomes involved in the robbery of valuable
gems.

EMPEROR JONES   Black   1933/Drama

United Artists; 80 min.; *Producers*: John Krimsky/Gifford Cochran;
Director: Dudley Murphy; *Screenplay*: DuBose Heyward; *Music*: Rosamond
Johnson; *Camera*: Ernest Haller; *Editor*: Grant Whytock; *Cast*: Paul
Robeson (Brutus Jones); Dudley Digges (Smithers); Frank Wilson (Jeff);
RUBY ELZY (DOLLY); *FREDI WASHINGTON (UNDINE)*; George Haymid Stamper
(Clem); *Jackie Mayble (Marcella)*; Blueboy O'Connor (Treasurer);
Brandon Evans (Carrington); Taylor Gordon (Stick-Man).

Dolly and Undine are Brutus Jones's wife and lover, respectively.

ENCHANTED ISLAND   Island Exotic   1958/Adventure

RKO; 94 min.; *Producer*: Benedict Bogeaus; *Director*: Allan Dwan;
Screenplay: James Leicester/Harold Jacob Smith; *Music*: Raul LaVista;
Camera: George Stahl; *Editor*: James Leicester; *Cast*: Dana Andrews
(Abner Bedford); *JANE POWELL (FAYAWAY)*; Don Dubbins (Tom); Arthur
Shields (Jimmy Dooley); Ted deCorsia (Captain Vangs); Friedrich
Ledebur (Kory Kory); Augustin Fernandez (Medicine Man); Les Hellman
(First Mate Moore).

Two sailors, Abner and Tom, escape from a tyrannical captain
and land on a nearby island inhabited by the cannibalistic Typee.
The Typee capture the men and plan to kill them, but the men are saved
by the chief's daughter, Fayaway. Fayaway and Abner marry. Problems
develop when Tom attempts to leave and is killed by the Typee. Abner
then kills the man responsible. Forced to flee he and Fayaway escape
to a ship in the harbor, but Fayaway is shot by a Typee arrow and
dies.

THE END OF THE RIVER   Brazilian   1947/Drama

Universal; 80 min.; *Producers*: Michael Powell/Emeric Pressburger;
Director: Derek Twist; *Screenplay*: Wolfgang Wilhelm; *Music*: Lambert
Williamson; *Camera*: Christopher G. Challis; *Editor*: Brereton Porter;
Cast: Sabu (Manoel); *BIBI FERREIRA (TERESA)*; Esmond Knight (Dantos);

Torin Thatcher (Lisboa); *Antoinette Cellier (Conceicaso)*; James
Hayter (Chico); Raymond Lovell (Porpino); Maurice Denham (Defense
Counsel); Eva Hudson (Maria Golsalves); Milo Sperber (Ze).

Manoel is an outlaw seeking revenge for the murder of his father
and brother and the rape/murder of his wife and mother. He travels
to another town and meets and marries Teresa. He gets into trouble
again and goes on trial. He is acquitted and he and Teresa settle
down on a farm and raise a family.

ENSIGN PULVER   Island Exotic   1964/Comedy

Warner Brothers; 104 min.; *Producer/Director*: Joshua Logan; *Screen-
play*: Joshua Logan/Peter Feibleman; *Music*: George Duning; *Camera*:
Charles Lawton; *Editor*: William Reynolds; *Cast*: Robert Walker, Jr.
(Ensign Pulver); Burl Ives (Capt. Morton); Walter Matthau (Doc);
Tommy Sands (Bruno); Millie Perkins (Scotty); Larry Hagman (Billings);
Al Freeman, Jr. (Taru); *DIANA SANDS (MILA)*.

Mila is the local island girl.

ENTER THE DRAGON   Chinese   1973/Action

Warner Brothers; 98 min.; *Producers*: Fred Weintraub/Paul Hiller;
Director: Robert Clouse; *Screenplay*: Michael Allin; *Camera*: Gilbert
Hubbs; *Editors*: Kurt Hirschler/George Watters; *Cast*: Bruce Lee (Lee);
John Saxon (Roper); Jim Kelly (Williams); Shih Kien (Han); Bob Wall
(Oharra); *AHNA CAPRI (TANIA)*; *ANGELA MAO-YING (SU-LIN)*.

Lee agrees to help uncover the illegal activities of Han, who
deals in white slavery and opium, to avenge the death of his sister
Su-Lin. Su-Lin was attacked by a group of Han's henchman and managed
to temporarily fight them off. When they had her surrounded she
killed herself rather than be taken prisoner. Lee arrives at Han's
island fortress and contacts agent Tania. With her help, and the
help of Roper, Lee manages to destroy Han and his crime syndicate.

ESCAPE FROM ZAHRAIN   Arab   1962/Adventure

Paramount; 93 min.; *Producer/Director*: Ronald Neame; *Screenplay*: Robin
Estridge; *Music*: Lyn Murray; *Camera*: Ellsworth Fredricks; *Editor*: Eda
Warren; *Cast*: Yul Brynner (Sharif); Sal Mineo (Ahmed); *MADLYN RHUE
(LAILA)*; Jack Warden (Huston); Tony Caruso (Tahar); Jay Novello
(Hassan); Leonard Strong (Ambulance Driver); James Mason (Johnson).

While en route to prison, revolutionary leader Sharif, with the
help of student leader Ahmed, manages to escape along with three other
men. They steal an ambulance, including nurse Laila, and begin a trek
across the desert. Laila and Ahmed fall in love but he is killed
before they reach their destination. When they reach safety Sharif
and Laila vow to return to overthrow the corrupt government.

Angela Mao, *Enter the Dragon* (Warner Brothers, 1973)

FABULOUS SENORITA   Cuban   1952/Comedy

Republic; 80 min.; *Director*: R.G. Springsteen; *Screenplay*: Charles E.
Roberts; *Music*: Stanley Wilson; *Camera*: Jack Marta; *Editor*: Tony
Martinelli; *Cast*: *ESTELITA RODRIGUEZ (ESTELITA)*; Robert Clarke
(Jerry Taylor); Nestor Paiva (Jose Rodriguez); Marvin Kaplan
(Clifford Van Kunkle); *Rita Moreno (Manuela Rodriguez)*; Leon Belasco
(Senor Gonzales); Tito Renaldo (Pedro Sanchez); Tom Powers (Delaney);
Emory Painell (Dean Bradshaw); Olin Howlin (Justice of the Peace);
Vito Scotti (Estaban).

Estelita is the daughter of businessman Jose Rodriguez. She is
romantically interested in college professor Jerry Taylor.

THE FACE OF FU MANCHU   Chinese   1965/Mystery

Warner-Pathe/Anglo; 94 min.; *Producer*: Harry Alan Towers; *Director*:
Don Sharp; *Screenplay*: Peter Welbeck; *Music*: Christopher Whelen;
Camera: Ernest Steward; *Editor*: John Trumper; *Cast*: Christopher Lee
(Fu Manchu); Nigel Green (Nayland Smith); Joachim Fuchsberger (Carl
Jansen); Karin Dor (Maria Muller); *TSAI CHIN (LIN TANG)*; Howard
Marion Crawford (Dr. Petrie); Walter Rilla (Professor Muller); Harry
Brogan (Professor Gaskell); James Robertson Justice (Sir Charles);
Poulet Tu (Lotus).

Fu Manchu is seeking a deadly poison that will help him dominate
the world. Lin Tang, his daughter, helps him recover some secret
documents which help him make a small amount of poison. Nayland
Smith discovers where they are hiding and tries to rid the world of
Fu Manchu and his daughter, but they escape.

FAIR WIND TO JAVA   Javanese   1953/Adventure

Republic; 92 min.; *Producer/Director*: Joseph Kane; *Screenplay*: Richard
Tregaskis; *Music*: Victor Young; *Camera*: Jack Marta; *Editor*: Richard
Van Enger; *Cast*: Fred MacMurray (Captain Boll); *VERA RALSTON (KIM
KIM)*: Robert Douglas (St. Ebenezer Palo Besar); Victor McLaglen
(O'Brien); John Russell (Flint); Buddy Baer (Kung); Claude Jarman,
Jr. (Chess).

Kim Kim is bought by Captain Boll.

THE FALCON IN MEXICO   Mexican   1944/Mystery

RKO; 70 min.; *Producer*: Maurice Gerahty; *Director*: William Berke;
Screenplay: George Worthington Yates/Gerald Gerahty; *Music*: C.
Bakaleinkoff; *Camera*: Frank Redman; *Editor*: Joseph Noriega; *Cast*: Tom
Conway (Falcon); *MONA MARIS (RAQUEL)*; Martha MacVicar (Barbara);
Nestor Paiva (Manuel); Mary Currier (Paula Dudley); *Cecillia Callejo
(Dolores)*; Emory Parnell (Winthrop Hughes); Fernando Alvarado
(Pancho); Pedro De Cordova (Sr. Ybarra).

Raquel is a dancer and Dolores is an artist's model. Both are connected with a supposedly dead artist and the murder of an art dealer.

THE FALCON'S ADVENTURE   Brazilian   1946/Mystery

RKO; 61 min.; *Producer*: Herman Schlom; *Director*: William Berke; *Screenplay*: Aubrey Wisberg; *Music*: Paul Sawtell; *Camera*: Harry Wild; *Editor*: Marvin Coil; *Cast*: Tom Conway (Falcon); *MADGE MEREDITH (LUISA BRAGANZA)*; Edward S. Brophy (Goldie); Robert Warwick (Sutton); Myrna Dell (Doris); Steve Brodie (Benny); Ian Wolfe (Denison); Carol Forman (Helen); Joseph Crehan (Inspector Cavanaugh).

Falcon rescues Luisa from kidnappers who want her father's secret formula for synthetic diamonds.

FAME   Black & Puerto Rican   1980/Musical

United Artists; 134 min.; *Producers*: David DeSilva/Alan Marshall; *Director*: Alan Parker; *Screenplay*: Christopher Gore; *Music*: Michael Gore; *Camera*: Michael Seresin; *Editor*: Gerry Hambling; *Cast*: Eddie Barth (Angelo); *IRENE CARA (COCO HERNANDEZ)*; Lee Curreri (Bruno Martelli); Laura Dean (Lisa Monroe); Antonio Franceschi (Hilary Van Doren); *Debbie Allen (Lydia)*; Boyd Gaines (Michael); Albert Hague (Shorofsky); Tresa Hughes (Naomi Finsecker); Steve Inwood (Francois Lafete); Maureen Teefy (Doris Finsecker); Paul McCrane (Montgomery MacNeil); Anne Meara (Mrs. Sherwood); Joanna Merlin (Miss Berg); Barry Miller (Raul Garcia/Ralph Garcy); Jim Moody (Farrell); Gene Anthony Ray (Leroy Johnson).

Coco Hernandez is one of the students at Manhattan's High school of the Performing Arts. Her naivete gets her into trouble when she believes a man she meets in a restaurant will get her into the movies. When she arrives at the job she finds he is a pornographic filmmaker. Lydia is the Black dance teacher.

FAMILY HONEYMOON   Black   1948/Comedy

Universal; 94 min.; *Producers*: John Beck/Z. Wayne Griffin; *Director*: Claude Binyon; *Screenplay*: Dane Lussier; *Music*: Milton Schwarzwald; *Camera*: William Daniels; *Editor*: Milton Carruth; *Cast*: Claudette Colbert (Katie Armstrong); Fred MacMurray (Grant Jordan); Rita Johnson (Minna Fenster); Lillian Bronson (Aunt Jo); William Daniels (Arch Armstrong); *HATTIE McDANIEL (PHYLLIS)*; Peter Miles (Abner); Gigi Perreau (Zoe); Chill Wills (Fred).

Phyllis is a maid.

FAR HORIZONS   Native American--Shoshoni   1955/Western

Paramount; 107 min.; *Producers*: William H. Pine/William C. Thomas;
Director: Rudolph Mate; *Screenplay*: Edmund H. North/Winston Miller;
Music: Hans Salter; *Camera*: Daniel L. Fapp; *Editor*: Frank Bracht;
Cast: Fred MacMurray (Merriweather Lewis); Charlton Heston (William
Clark); *DONNA REED (SACAJAWEA)*; Barbara Hale (Julia Hancock); William
Demarest (Sgt. Cass); Alan Reed (Charbonneau); Eduardo Noriega
(Cameahwait); Larry Pennell (Wild Eagle); Ralph Moody (Le Borgne);
Herbert Hayes (President Jefferson).

This is the story of the Lewis and Clark expedition and of the
Indian guide Sacajawea. When Lewis and Clark begin their exploration
of the Louisiana purchase they meet Sacajawea, a captive of the
Minitari, who wants to return to the Shoshoni. When Sacajawea saves
the expedition from attack, they decide to take her along. She falls
in love with Clark, who does not initially respond, but then admits
he loves her. However, once back in civilization, Sacajawea realizes
that they cannot be united because of racial prejudice and Clark's
prominent position in society. She returns to her tribe alone and
Clark returns to his white fiancee.

FATE IS THE HUNTER   Chinese   1964/Drama

20th Century-Fox; 106 min.; *Producer*: Aaron Rosenberg; *Director*:
Ralph Nelson; *Screenplay*: Harold Medford; *Music*: Jerry Goldsmith;
Camera: Milton Krasner; *Editor*: Robert Simpson; *Cast*: Glenn Ford
(McBane); *NANCY KWAN (SALLY FRASER)*; Rod Taylor (Captain Jack Savage);
Suzanne Pleshette (Martha Webster); Jane Russell (Guest Star); Wally
Cox (Bandy); Nehemiah Persoff (Ben Sawyer); Mark Stevens (Mickey
Doolan).

Following a plane crash which may have resulted from pilot
error, McBane investigates the pilot's friends. Sally Fraser was the
pilot's girlfriend and beneficiary of his will. McBane questions
Sally on her knowledge of the crash, but her reply is that it was
purely fate. McBane discovers that spilled coffee shorted out the
wires to make a proper reading.

FIESTA   Mexican   1947/Musical

MGM; 104 min.; *Producer*: Jack Cummings; *Director*: Richard Thorpe;
Screenplay: George Bruce/Lester Cole; *Music*: Johnny Green; *Camera*:
Sidney Wagner/Charles Rosher/Wilfred M. Cline; *Editor*: Blanche Sewell;
Cast: *ESTHER WILLIAMS (MARIA MORALES)*; Ricardo Montalban (Mario
Morales); Akim Tamiroff (Chato Vasquez); John Carroll (Jose "Pepe"
Ortega); *Mary Astor (Senora Morales)*; *Cyd Charisse (Conchita)*;
Fortunio Bonanova (Antonio Morales); Hugo Haas (Maximino Contreras).

Maria and Mario are twins whose father was a famous matador.
It is Maria, not Mario, who wants to follow in her father's footsteps
and become a matador. Mario is more interested in music, as is his
mother. Mario is scheduled to fight in front of a famous matador

but fails to show up. Maria disguises herself as Mario and takes his
place in the ring. Mario arrives in time to save Maria from the bull
when she lets her guard down.

55 DAYS AT PEKING   Chinese   1963/Drama

Allied Artists; 154 min.; *Producer*: Samuel Bronson; *Director*: Nicholas
Ray; *Screenplay*: Philip Yordan/Bernard Gordon; *Music*: Dimitri Tiomkin;
Camera: Jack Hildyard; *Editor*: Robert Lawrence; *Cast*: Charlton Heston
(Major Matt Lewis); Ava Gardner (Baroness Natalie Ivanoff); David
Niven (Sir Arthur Robertson); *FLORA ROBSON (THE DOWAGER EMPRESS TZU
HSI)*; John Ireland (Sgt. Harry); Harry Andrews (Father de Bearn);
Leo Genn (Gen. Jung-Lu); Robert Helpmann (Prince Tuan); Ichizo Itami
(Col. Shiba); Kurt Kasznar (Baron Sergei Ivanoff).

      Dowager Empress Tzu Hsi encourages the Boxers to revolt against
the foreigners controlling China. The British, determined to keep
their hold on China, refuse to leave. When the final assault comes
and the British appear doomed, the other imperialist nations return
to help. The British are then able to dispose of Empress Tzu Hsi
and the Boxers.

THE FIGHTER   Mexican   1952/Drama

United Artists; 78 min.; *Producer*: Alex Gottlieb; *Director*: Herbert
Kline; *Screenplay*: Abel Kandel; *Music*: Vincente Gomez; *Camera*: James
Wong Howe; *Editor*: Edward Mann; *Cast*: Richard Conte (Felipe); *VANESSA
BROWN (KATHY)*; Lee J. Cobb (Durango); Frank Silvera (Paulino); *Roberta
Haynes (Novis)*; Hugh Sanders (Roberts); Claire Carleton (Stella);
Martin Garralaga (Luis); Rodolfo Heyes, Jr. (Alvarado); *Argentina
Brunetti (Maria)*; *Margarita Padil (Elba)*; Paul Fierre (Jose); Rico
Alanis (Carlos).

      Felipe travels to El Paso to work with revolutionaries attempting
the overthrow of Diaz in Mexico. He meets and falls in love with
Kathy and reveals to her his reasons for fighting against Diaz.
Felipe becomes a prizefighter to raise money for the revolution. He
wins a match with a top contender and uses the money to buy guns for
the cause.

THE FIGHTING GRINGO   Mexican   1939/Western

RKO; 59 min.; *Producer*: Bert Gilroy; *Director*: David Howard; *Screen-
play*: Oliver Drake; *Camera*: Harry Wild; *Editor*: Frederic Knudison;
Cast: George O'Brien (Wade Barton); *LUPITA TOVAR (NITA)*; Lucio
Villegas (Don Allso); William Boyle (Ben Wallace); Glenn Strange
(Lance Potter); Slim Wittaker (Monty); Le Roy Mason (John Courtney);
Mary Field (Sandra Courtney).

      Nita is the love interest of gunfighter Wade Barton, who is more
of a problem solver than an outlaw.

THE FIGHTING RANGER   Mexican   1934/Western

Columbia; 60 min.; *Director*: George B. Seitz; *Screenplay*: Harry Hoyt;
Camera: Sid Wagner; *Editor*: Leon Barsha; *Cast*: Buck Jones (Jim);
DOROTHY REIVER (TONITA); Frank Rice (Thunder); Bradley Page (Cougar);
Ward Bond (Dave); Paddy O'Flynn (Bob); Moselle Brittone (Rose); Art
Mix (Kelso); Frank LaRue (Pegleg Barnes); John Wallace (Capt. Wilkes).

Jim is a ranger who is after outlaws. He leaves the rangers to
avenge the death of his brother. Tonita is the romantic interest.

THE FIREBRAND   Mexican   1962/Western

20th Century-Fox; 63 min.; *Producer/Director*: Maury Dexter; *Screenplay*: Harry Spalding; *Music*: Richard La Salle; *Camera*: Floyd Crosby;
Editor: Jodie Copelan; *Cast*: Valentin De Vargas (Joaquin Morieta);
Kent Taylor (Major Tim Bancroft); *LISA MONTELL (CLARITA VASCONCELOS)*;
Joe Raciti (Jack Garcia); Chubby Johnson (Tampico); Barbara Mansell
(Cassie); Allen Jaffe (Torres); Troy Melton (Walker).

Clarita is the sweetheart of Joaquin Morieta, a Robin Hood-type
hero fighting for justice in old California. After a confrontation
with the California rangers Clarita and Joaquin flee to safety in
Sonora, Mexico.

FIVE GATES TO HELL   Chinese   1959/War Drama

20th Century-Fox; 98 min.; *Producer/Director/Screenplay*: James Clavell;
Camera: Sam Leavitt; *Editor*: Harry Gerstad; *Cast*: Neville Brand (Chen
Pamok); Dolores Michaels (Athena); Patricia Owens (Joy); Ken Scott
(Dr. John Richter); *NOBU McCARTHY (CHIOKO)*; Benson Fong (Gung Sa);
John Morley (Dr. Jacques Minelle); Gerry Gaylor (Greta); *Greta Chi
(Yoette)*; Nancy Kulp (Susette); *Linda Wong (Ming Cha)*; Irish McCalla
(Sister Magdelana); Shirley Knight (Sister Maria).

Chioko, Yoette and Ming Cha are among a group of seven nurses
captured by Chinese guerrillas during the French Indo-Chinese War
and taken prisoner. Before they manage an escape they are raped and
brutalized by the guerrillas.

FIVE ON THE BLACK HAND SIDE   Black   1973/Drama

United Artists; 96 min.; *Producers*: Brock Peters/Michael Tolan;
Director: Oscar Williams; *Screenplay*: Charlie L. Russell; *Music*: H.B.
Barnum; *Camera*: Gene Polito; *Editor*: Michael Economou; *Cast*: *CLARICE
TAYLOR (MRS. BROOKS)*; Leonard Jackson (Mr. Brooks): *Virginia Capers
(Ruby)*; Glynn Turman (Gideon); D'Urville Martin (Booker T); *Bonnie
Banfield (Gail)*; Richard Williams (Preston); *Ja'Net Dubois (Stormy
Monday)*; Carl Mikal Franklin (Marvin); Sonny Jim (Sweetmeat).

Mrs. Brooks is an oppressed and obedient wife who finally
revolts against her tyrannical husband.

FLAME OF ARABY   Arab--Tunisian   1951/Adventure

Universal; 77 min.; *Producer*: Leonard Goldstein; *Director*: Charles
Lamont; *Screenplay*: Gerald Drayson Adams; *Camera*: Russell Metty;
Editor: Ted J. Kent; *Cast*: MAUREEN O"HARA (TANYA); Jeff Chandler
(Tamerlane); Maxwell Reed (Medina); *Susan Cabot (Clio)*; Lon Chaney
(Borka); Buddy Baer (Urkim); Richard Egan (Captain Fezil); Royal Dano
(Bogra); Dewey Martin (Yak); Neville Brand (Kral); Henry Brandon
(Mallik).

Tanya is trying to capture a wild black stallion to win a race
so she won't have to marry Borka or his brother, Urkim. Tamerlane
is also trying to capture the stallion. Tamerlane captures the
horse, wins the race, and claims Princess Tanya as his own.

THE FLAME OF LOVE   Chinese   1930/Drama

British International; 74 min.; *Director*: Richard Eichberg; *Screen-
play*: Moncton Hoffe; *Camera*: Henry Gartner; *Editor*: Emile De Rulle;
Cast: ANNA MAY WONG (HAI TANG); John Longden (Lt. Boris); George
Schnell (Grand Duke); Percy Standing (Col. Moravjev); Mona Goya
(Yvette); J. Leyon (Wang Hu).

Hai Tang is an actress who falls in love with Russian Lt. Boris.
Brought to the attention of the Grand Duke, he forces himself on her.
Her brother saves her, but he is condemned to death for interfering.
Hai Tang agrees to submit to the Grand Duke if he will release her
brother. Realizing that she loves Boris, the Grand Duke frees her
and her brother on the condition that she never see Lt. Boris again.

FLAMING FEATHER   Native American   1951/Western

Paramount; 79 min.; *Producer*: Nat Holt; *Director*: Ray Enright;
Screenplay: Gerald Drayson Adams; *Music*: Paul Sawtell; *Camera*: Ray
Rennahan; *Editor*: Elmo Billings; *Cast*: Sterling Hayden (Tex McCloud);
Forrest Tucker (Lt. Torn Blain); Barbara Rush (Nora Logan); Arleen
Whelan (Carolina); CAROL THURSTON (TURQUOISE); Edgar Buchanan (Sgt.
O'Rourke); Victor Jory (Lucky Lee); Richard Arlen (Showdown Calhoun);
Ian MacDonald (Tornbatone Jack); George Cleveland (Doc Rallon).

Turquoise gets even with Lucky Lee for jilting her by killing
him.

FLAMING STAR   Native American--Kiowa   1961/Western

20th Century-Fox; 101 min.; *Producer*: David Weisbart; *Director*: Don
Siegel; *Screenplay*: Clair Huffaker/Nunally Johnson; *Camera*: Charles
G. Clarke; *Editor*: Hugh S. Fowler; *Cast*: Elvis Presley (Pacer Burton);
Barbara Eden (Roslyn Pierce); Steve Forrest (Clint Burton); DOLORES
DEL RIO (NEDDY BURTON); John McIntire (Pa Burton); Rodolfo Acosta
(Buffalo Horn); Karl Swenson (Fred Pierce); Ford Rainey (Doc Phillips);
Richard Jaeckel (Angus Pierce); Anne Benton (Dorothy Howard).

Dolores Del Rio, *Flaming Star* (20th Century Fox, 1961)

When trouble breaks out between the Kiowa and the white settlers, Pacer and his mother, Neddy, experience divided loyalties. They try to make peace but fail when Neddy is killed by a white man. Pacer joins the Kiowa until his brother Clint is hurt. He changes sides, fights the Kiowa, and is killed.

FLAP   Native American   1970/Comedy

Warner Brothers; 106 min.; *Producer*: Jerry Adler; *Director*: Carol Reed; *Screenplay*: Clair Huffaker; *Music*: Marvin Hamlisch; *Camera*: Fred Koenekamp; *Editor*: Frank Bracht; *Cast*: Anthony Quinn (Flapping Eagle); Claude Akins (Lobo Jackson); Tony Bill (Eleven Snowflake); Victor Jory (Wounded Bear Mr. Smith); Don Collier (Mike Lyons); Shelly Winters (Dorothy Bluebell); *SUSANA MIRANDA (LOOKING DEER)*; Victor French (Rafferty); Rodolfo Acosta (Storekeep); Anthony Caruso (Silver Dollar); William Mims (Steve Gray).

Not enough information was available to accurately describe this role.

FLIGHT FROM ASHIYA   Arab--Algerian   1963/Adventure

United Artists; 102 min.; *Producer*: Harold Hecht; *Director*: Michael Anderson; *Screenplay*: Elliott Arnold/Waldo Salt; *Music*: Frank Cordell; *Camera*: Joseph MacDonald/Burnett Guffey; *Editor*: Gordon Pilkington; *Cast*: Yul Brynner (Sgt. Mike Takashima); Richard Widmark (Col. Glenn Stevenson); George Chakiris (Lt. John Gregg); Suzy Parker (Lucille Carroll); *DANIELE GAUBERT (LEILA)*; Eiko Taki (Tomiko); Joe de Reda (Sgt. Randy Smith); Mitsuhiro Sugiyama (Japanese Boy Charlie).

While on a flight to rescue a raft load of men from a sinking ship, three men recall events of their past. Takashima remembers his love for Leila, a woman he met in Manila. Their relationship was forbidden by her parents. As she was about to run away with him he accidentally killed her by blowing up the bridge she was crossing to reach him.

FLIGHT TO HONG KONG   Chinese   1956/Adventure

United Artists; 88 min.; *Producer/Director*: Joseph M. Newman; *Screenplay*: Leo Townsend/Edward G. O'Callaghan; *Music*: Albert Glasser; *Camera*: Ellis W. Carter; *Editor*: Ralph Dawson; *Cast*: Rory Calhoun (Tony Dumont); Barbara Rush (Pamela Vincent); Dolores Donlon (Jean Blake); *SOO YONG (MAMA LIN)*; Pat Conway (Nicco); Werner Klemperer (Bendesh); Mel Welles (Boris); Paul Picerni (Quisto); Aram Katcher (Lobero); Rhodes Reason (Bob Denham); Bob Hopkins (Cappy); Timothy Carey (Lagarto).

Mama Lin is the operator of a Macao nightclub.

FLOWER DRUM SONG   Chinese   1961/Musical

Universal; 133 min.; *Producer*: Ross Hunter; *Director*: Henry Koster;
Screenplay: Joseph Fields; *Music/Lyrics*: Richard Rodgers/Oscar
Hammerstein II; *Camera*: Russell Metty; *Editor*: Milton Carruim; *Cast*:
NANCY KWAN (LINDA LOW); James Shigeta (Wang Ta); *MIYOSHI UMEKI (MEI
LI)*; *Juanita Hall (Madame Liang)*; Jack Soo (Sammy Fong); Benson Fong
(Wang); Patrick Adiarte (Wang San); *Reiko Sato (Helen Chao)*; Kam
Tong (Doctor Li); Victor Sen Yung (Frankie Wing); *Soo Yong (Madame
Fong)*.

Set in contemporary San Francisco this musical focuses on the
tradition of arranged marriages among the Chinese. Wang Ta is an
Americanized Chinese. Mei Li is coming from China to marry him, but
he has other ideas. He is currently seeing Linda Low, a nightclub
singer and a gold digger. Linda is also seeing Sammy Fong, the owner
of the nightclub where she works. Sammy won't marry Linda so she is
trying to marry Wang Ta for his money. When Mei Li arrives, Wang Ta
begins to changes his mind about the marriage. Eventually he falls
in love with Mei Li and her traditonal upbringing. Linda Low finally
convinces Sammy to marry her and all ends happily.

FLYING DOWN TO RIO   Brazilian   1933/Musical

RKO; 89 min.; *Assoc. Producer*: Louis Brock; *Director*: Thornton
Freeland; *Screenplay*: H.W. Hanemann/Erwin Gelsey/Cyril Hume; *Music*:
Vincent Youmans; *Camera*: J. Roy Hunt; *Editor*: Jack Kitchin; *Cast*:
DOLORES DEL RIO (BELINHA DE REZENDE); Gene Raymond (Roger Bond);
Raul Roulien (Julio Rubeiro); Ginger Rogers (Honey Hale); Fred
Astaire (Fred Ayres); *Blanche Friderici (Dona Elena)*; Walter Walker
(Senor de Rezende).

Belinha, a Brazilian socialite, is engaged to Julio Rubreio.
She falls in love with American bandleader Roger Bond. Dona Elena,
her mother, tries to break up the relationship. However, Julio, who
realized that Belinha and Roger love each other, helps them to marry.

FOR LOVE OF IVY   Black   1968/Comedy

Cinerama; 102 min.; *Producer*: Edgar J. Scherick; *Director*: Daniel
Mann; *Screenplay*: Robert Alan Aurthur; *Music*: Quincy Jones; *Camera*:
Joseph Coffey; *Editor*: Patricia Jaffee; *Cast*: Sidney Poitier (Jack
Parks); *ABBEY LINCOLN (IVY MOORE)*; Beau Bridges (Tim Austin); Nan
Martin (Doris Austin); Lauri Peters (Gena Austin); Carroll O'Connor
(Frank Austin); Leon Bibb (Billy Talbot); Hugh Hurd (Jerry); Lon
Satten (Harry).

Ivy is a maid who is tired of domestic service and suburban
living. She wants to educate herself, move to the city, and improve
her life. Her white "family" has different ideas and they try to
involve her with a man in the hope that the relationship will satisfy
her and she will stay as their maid. The plan backfires when Ivy
falls in love with Jack Parks and moves to the city.

FORBIDDEN   Asian   1953/Drama

Universal; 84 min.; *Producer*: Ted Richmond; *Director*: Rudolph Mate;
Screenplay: William Sackheim/Gil Doud; *Music*: Frank Skinner; *Camera*:
William Daniels; *Editor*: Edward Curtiss; *Cast*: Tony Curtis (Eddie);
Joanne Dru (Christine); Lyle Bettger (Justin); Marvin Miller
(Chalmer); Victor Sen Yung (Allan); Peter J. Mamakos (Sam); *MAE TAI
SING (SOO LEE)*; Howard Chuman (Hon-Fai); Weaver Levy (Tang).

     Soo Lee works as a cigarette girl in a gambling joint in Macao.

FORT BOWIE   Native American--Apache   1958/Western

United Artists; 80 min.; *Producer*: Aubrey Schenck; *Director*: Howard
W. Koch; *Screenplay*: Carl E. Guthrie; *Music*: Les Baxter; *Camera*: Carl
E. Guthrie; *Editor*: John A. Bushelman; *Cast*: Ben Johnson (Captain
"Tomahawk" Thompson); Jan Harrison (Allison Garrett); Kent Taylor
(Colonel Garrett); *JANA DAVI (CHENZANA)*; Larry Chance (Victorio);
J. Ian Douglas (Major Wharton); Peter Mamakos (Sgt. Kukus); Jerry
Frank (Lt. Maywood);

     Major Wharton slaughters a band of peaceful Apaches. Since this
attack may lead to Apache retaliation, Captain Thompson is sent on a
mission to demand complete surrender from the Apaches. The Apaches
take Thompson prisoner but Chenzana helps him escape. They ride back
to the fort and with the help of fresh cavalry troops thwarts the
Apaches.

FORT MASSACRE   Native American--Paiute   1958/Western

United Artists; 80 min.; *Producer*: Walter M. Mirisch; *Director*: Joseph
M. Newman; *Screenplay*: Martin N. Goldsmith; *Camera*: Carl Guthrie;
Cast:Joel McCrea (Sgt. Vinson); Forrest Tucker (McGurney); *SUSAN
CABOT (PAIUTE GIRL)*; John Russell (Travis); Anthony Caruso (Pawnee);
Bob Osterloh (Schwabacker); Denver Pyle (Collins); George N. Neise
(Pendleton); Rayford Barnes (Moss); Guy Prescott (Tucker); Larry
Chance (Moving Cloud); Irving Bacon (Charlie); Claire Carleton
(Adele); Francis J. McDonald (Paiute Man); Walter Kray (Chief).

     Sgt. Vinson, an Indian-hating soldier, tries to provoke an
attack by traveling across Apache territory. The soldiers find themselves trapped in a deserted cliff dwelling where they meet an old
Paiute and his granddaughter. Sgt. Vinson kills an Apache after
the Paiute girl convinces the grandfather to get help for the trapped
soldiers. When the old man refuses, Vinson decides to kill the man
but is himself killed by one of his own soldiers.

FORT TI   Native American   1953/Western

Columbia; 73 min.; *Producer*: Sam Katzman; *Director*: William Castle;
Screenplay: Robert E. Kent; *Camera*: Lester R. White/Lothrop R. Worth;
Editor: William A. Lyon; *Cast*: George Montgomery (Capt. Pedediah Horn);

Joan Vohs (Fortune Mallory); Irving Bacon (Sgt. Monday Wash); James Seay (Mark Chesney); Ben Astar (Francois Leroy); *PHYLLIS FOWLER (RUNNING OTTER)*: Howard Petrie (Major Rogers); Cicely Brown (Bess Chesney).

In this film set in Fort Ticonderoga, Running Otter is married but lusts after Captain Horn. Fortune Mallory wins his love.

FORT YUMA   Native American--Apache   1955/Western

United Artists; 78 min.; *Producers*: Aubrey Schenck/Howard W. Koch; *Director*: Lesley Selander; *Screenplay*: Danny Arnold; *Music*: Paul Dunlap; *Camera*: Gordon Avil; *Editor*: John F. Schreyer; *Cast*: Peter Graves (Lt. Ben Keegan); Joan Vohs (Melanie Crowne); John Hudson (Sgt. Jonas); *JOAN TAYLOR (FRANCESCA)*; Addison Richards (Gen. Crooke); William Phillips (Sgt. Halleck); James Lilbann (Corp. Taylor); Abel Fernandez (Mangas).

In spite of himself, Indian-hating Lt. Ben Keegan falls in love with Francesca, whose brother, Sgt. Jonas, is a scout for the army.

FOXFIRE   Native American--Apache   1955/Drama

Universal; 91 min.; *Producer*: Aaron Rosenberg; *Director*: Joseph Pevney; *Screenplay*: Ketti Frings; *Music*: Frank Skinner; *Camera*: William Daniels; *Editor*: Ted J. Kent; *Cast*: Jane Russell (Amanda); Jeff Chandler (Jonathan Dartland); Dan Duryea (Hugh Slater); *MARA CORDAY (MARIA)*; Robert F. Simon (Ernest Tyson); Frieda Inescort (Mrs. Lawrence); Barton MacLane (Jim Mablett); Eddy Walker (Old Larky); *Celia Lovsky (Saba)*; *Beulah Archiletta (Indian Woman)*; Billy Wilkerson (Apache Chief).

Maria is a woman whom no man wants, because she is a half-breed and a tramp. Maria is constantly on the make for Dr. Hugh Slater who would rather have Amanda, Jonathan Dartland's wife. Saba is Jonathan Dartland's Apache mother. She is the tourist guide and attraction on the nearby reservation. Jonathan is ashamed of his mother and his Apache heritage, and does not want his wife to meet his mother. Saba, who dresses in buckskin and beaded headband, is not proud of her heritage either.

FOXHOLE IN CAIRO   Arab--Egyptian   1961/Adventure

Paramount; 79 min.; *Producers*: Steven Pallos/Donald Taylor; *Director*: John Moxey; *Screenplay*: Leonard Mosley/Donald Taylor; *Music*: Wolfram Roehrig/Douglas Gamley/Kenneth M. Jones; *Camera*: Desmond Dickinson; *Editor*: Oswald Hafenrichter; *Cast*: James Robertson Justice (Captain Robertson, D.S.O.); Adrian Hoven (John Eppler); Niall MacGinnis (Radek); Albert Lieven (Rommel); *GLORIA MESTRE (AMINA)*; Peter Van Eyck (Count Almaszy); Robert Urquhart (Major Wilson); Neil McCullum (Sandy); Fenella Fielding (Yvette); John Westbrook (Roger).

Amina is a cabaret dancer who helps German agent John Eppler spy on the British. However, the British know of Eppler's plans and are working to counteract his activities. Amina manages to drug and rob a British officer but is thwarted by Yvette, who kills Amina.

FOXY BROWN   Black   1974/Action

American International; 94 min.; *Producer*: Buzz Feltshans; *Director*: Jack Hill; *Screenplay*: Jack Hill; *Camera*: Brick Marquard; *Editor*: Chuck McCleeland; *Cast*: PAM GRIER *(FOXY BROWN)*; Antonio Fargas (Linx Brown); Peter Brown (Steve Elias); Terry Carter (Michael Anderson); Kathryn Loder (Katherine Wall); Harry Hotcombe (Judge Fenton); Sid Haig (Hays); *Juanita Brown (Claudia)*.

Foxy Brown goes after the mobsters, pimps, and pushers responsible for the deaths of her lover and kid brother.

FRIDAY FOSTER   Black   1975/Action

American International; 90 min.; *Producer/Director*: Arthur Marks; *Screenplay*: Orville Hampton; *Music*: Luchi de Jesus; *Camera*: Harry May; *Editor*: Stanley Frazen; *Cast*: PAM GRIER *(FRIDAY FOSTER)*; Yaphet Kotto (Colt Hawkins); Godfrey Cambridge (Ford Malotte); Thalmus Rasulala (Bleak Tart); *Eartha Kitt (Madame Rena)*; Ted Lange (Fancy Dexter); Jim Backus (Eros Griffith); Scatman Crothers (Rev. Noble Franklin).

Based on the comic strip "Friday Foster," about a model turned crime-solving photographer.

THE FUGITIVE   Mexican Indian   1947/Drama

RKO; 104 min.; *Producers*: John Ford/Merian C. Cooper; *Director*: John Ford; *Screenplay*: Dudley Nichols; *Music*: Richard Hageman; *Camera*: Gabriel Figueroa; *Editor*: Jack Murray; *Cast*: Henry Fonda (A Fugitive); *DOLORES DEL RIO (AN INDIAN WOMAN)*; Pedro Armendarez (Lt. of Police); J. Carrol Naish (Police Informer); Leo Carrillo (Chief of Police); Ward Bond (El Gringo); Robert Armstrong (Sgt. of Police); John Qualen (A Refugee Doctor); Fortunio Bonanova (The Governor's Cousin).

An Indian woman hides a fugitive priest from the law.

FUN IN ACAPULCO   Mexican   1963/Musical

Paramount; 100 min.; *Producer*: Hal Wallis; *Director*: Richard Thorpe; *Screenplay*: Allan Weiss; *Camera*: Daniel L. Fapp; *Editors*: Warren Low/ Stanley E. Johnson; *Cast*: Elvis Presley (Mike Windgren); Ursula Andress (Maggie Dauphine); *ELSA CARDENAS (DOLORES GOMEZ)*; Paul Lukas (Maximillian); Larry Domasin (Raoul Almeido); Alejandro Rey (Moreno); Robert Carricart (Jose); Teri Hope (Janice Harkins); Charles Evans (Mr. Harkins).

While living in Acapulco, Mike Windgren becomes involved with Maggie, a hotel social director, and Dolores, a lady bullfighter.

FURY OF THE CONGO   Jungle Exotic   1950/Adventure

Columbia; 69 min.; *Producer*: Sam Katzman; *Director*: William Berke; *Screenplay*: Carroll Young; *Camera*: Ira H. Morgan; *Editor*: Richard Fantl; *Cast*: Johnny Weissmuller (Jungle Jim); *SHERRY MORELAND (LETA);* William Henry (Ronald Cameron); Lyle Talbot (Grant); Joel Friedkin (Professor Dunham); George Eldredge (Baines); Rusty Wescoatt (Magruder); Paul Marion (Raadi); *Bianca Vischer (Mahara).*

Leta is the native girl in this Jungle Jim story.

FURY OF THE JUNGLE   Jungle Exotic   1934/Drama

Columbia; 68 min.; *Director*: Roy William Neill; *Screenplay*: Ethel Hill/Dore Schary; *Camera*: John Stumar; *Editor*: Ray Curtiss; *Cast*: Donald Cook (Allen); Peggy Shannon (Jean); Allan Dinehart (Taggart); Harold Huber (Frenchy); Dudley Digges (Parrish); *TOSHIA MORI (CHITA)*

Until Jean and her sick brother arrive, Chita is the only (and therefore the most popular) woman in the South American town of Malango. Soon all the men are after Jean, which makes Chita jealous, especially as it concerns her man, Taggart, a criminal. Chita betrays him to the law to get even for his interest in Jean.

THE GANG'S ALL HERE   Latin American   1943/Musical

20th Century-Fox; 103 min.; *Producer*: William LeBaron; *Director*: Busby Berkeley; *Screenplay*: Walter Bullock; *Music*: Alfred Newman/ Charles Henderson; *Camera*: Edward Cronjager; *Editor*: Ray Curtis; *Cast*: Alice Faye (Eadie); *CARMEN MIRANDA (ROSITA);* Phil Baker; Benny Goodman and Band; Eugene Pallette (Mr. Mason, Sr.); Charlotte Greenwood (Mrs. Peyton Potter); Edward Everett Horton (Peyton Potter); Tony DeMarco; James Ellison (Andy Mason); Sheila Ryan (Vivian); Dave Willock (Sgt. Casey).

Rosita sings and dances in this Busby Berkeley musical--the highlight is "The Lady in the Tutti Fruitti Hat."

GANJA AND HESS   Black   1973/Drama

Kelly-Jordan; 110 min.; *Producer*: Chiz Schultz; *Director*: Bill Gunn; *Screenplay*: Bill Gunn; *Music*: Sam Waymon; *Camera*: James E. Hinton; *Editor*: Victor Kanefsky; *Cast*: Duane Jones (Dr. Hess reen); *MARLENE CLARK (GANJA MEDA);* Bill Gunn (George Meda); Sam Waymon (Rev. Luther Williams); Leonard Jackson (Archie).

Carmen Miranda, *The Gang's All Here* (20th Century Fox, 1943)

Ganja begins a love affair with Dr. Hess Green—after he murders George Meda, her husband and Dr. Green's assistant.

THE GATLING GUN　　　　Native American—Apache　　　1972/Western

Ellman Enterprises; 93 min.; *Producer*: Oscar Nichols; *Director*: Robert Gordon; *Screenplay*: Joseph Van Winkle/Mark Hanna; *Camera*: Jacques Marquette; *Editor*: Edward Mann; *Cast*: Guy Stockwell (Lt. Malcolm); Woody Strode (Runner); *BARBARA LUNA (LEONA)*; Robert Fuller (Sneed); Patrick Wayne (Jim Boland); Pat Buttram (Tin Pot); John Carradine (Rev. Harper); Phil Harris (Boland); Judy Jordan (Martha Boland); Carlos Rivas (Two-Knife).

Leona is the illegitimate daughter of Apache chief Two-Knife. She is traveling with renegade soldiers and a stolen gatling gun. The soldiers want to sell the gun to the Apaches. When the Apaches attack to get the gun, Leona is killed and Two-Knife surrenders.

GAUCHOS OF EL DORADO　　　　Mexican　　　　1941/Western

Republic; 56 min.; *Assoc. Producer*: Louis Gray; *Director*: Les Orlebeck; *Screenplay*: Earle Snell; *Camera*: Reggie Lanning; *Editor*: Charles Craft; *Cast*: Bob Steele (Tucson); Tom Tyler (Stony); Rufe Davis (Lullaby); Lois Collier (Ellen); Duncan Renaldo (Gaucho); *ROSINA GALLI (ISABELLA)*; Norman Willis (Bart); Yakima Canutt (Snakes); William Ruhl (Tyndal).

One of the "Three Mesqueters" series. No information was available on the role of Isabella.

THE GAY AMIGO　　　　Mexican　　　　1949/Western

United Artists; 60 min.; *Producer*: Philip N. Krasne; *Director*: Wallace Fox; *Screenplay*: Doris Schroeder; *Music*: Albert Glasser; *Camera*: Ernest Miller; *Editor*: Martin Cohn; *Cast*: Duncan Renaldo (Cisco); Leo Carrillo (Pancho); *ARMIDA (ROSITA)*; Joe Sawyer (Sgt. McNulty); Clayton Moore (Lieutenant); Fred Kohler, Jr. (Brack); Walter Baldwin (Stoneham).

Rosita is a barmaid and Sgt. McNulty's girlfriend until Cisco begins to romance her.

THE GAY CABALLERO　　　　Mexican　　　　1932/Western

20th Century-Fox; 60 min.; *Director*: Alfred Werker; *Screenplay*: Barry Connors/Philip Klein; *Camera*: George Schneiderman; *Editor*: Al De Gaetano; *Cast*: George O'Brien (Ted Radcliffe); Victor McLaglen (Don Bob Harkness); *CONCHITA MONTENEGRO (ADELA MORALES)*; Linda Watkins (Ann Grey); C. Henry Gordon (Don Paco Morales); C. Robertson (Major Blount); Martin Garralaga (Manuel).

When Ted Radcliffe returns to his ranch, he finds that his assets have been stolen by evil cattle baron Paco Morales. Complicating matters, Ted falls in love with Paco's niece, Adela. Don Bob Harkness comes to Ted's aid in a Robin Hood-type manner. Soon Adela returns Ted's affections and the lovers are united.

THE GAY RANCHERO   Mexican   1948/Musical

Republic; 72 min.; *Producer*: Edward J. White; *Director*: William Witney; *Screenplay*: Sloan Nibley; *Camera*: Jack Marta; *Editor*: Tony Martinelli; *Cast*: Roy Rogers; Tito Guizar (Nicci Lopez); Jane Frazee (Betty Richards); Andy Devine (Cookie Bullfincher); *ESTELITA RODRIGUEZ (CONSUELO BELMONTE)*; George Meeker (Vance Brados); LeRoy Mason (Mike Ritter); Dennis Moore (Tex); Keith Richards (Slim); Betty Gagnon (Reception Clerk).

Consuelo Belmonte sings the title song.

GEORGE WASHINGTON SLEPT HERE   Black   1942/Comedy

Warner Brothers; 90 min.; *Producer*: Jerry Wald; *Director*: William Keighley; *Screenplay*: Everett Freeman; *Camera*: Ernie Haller; *Cast*: Jack Benny (Bill Fuller); Ann Sheridan (Connie); Charles Coburn (Uncle Stanley); Percy Kilbride (Mr. Kimber); *HATTIE McDANIEL (HESTER)*; William Tracy (Steve Eldridge); Joyce Reynolds (Madge).

Hester is a maid.

GEORGIA, GEORGIA   Black   1972/Drama

Cinerama; 91 min.; *Producer*: Jack Jordan; *Director*: Stig B. Jorkman; *Screenplay*: Maya Angelou; *Music*: Sven Olaf Waldorf; *Camera*: Andreas Bellis; *Editor*: Sten-Goran Camitz; *Cast*: *DIANA SANDS (GEORGIA MARTIN)*; *Minnie Gentry (Mrs. Alberta Anderson)*; Roger Furman (Herbert Thompson); Terry Whitmroe (Bobo); Dirk Benedict (Michael Winters).

Pop singer Georgia Martin prefers the company of white people to that of her own race. While she is touring Bobo asks her to help a group of Black defectors from the United States Army. She refuses, preferring to spend time with her new white lover, Michael Winters. **In retaliation Bobo tells Mrs. Alberta Anderson—Georgia's militant** maid/companion—of the affair. Angered by Georgia's neglecting her racial heritage, Alberta strangles her.

GERONIMO   Native American—Apache   1962/Western

United Artists; 101 min.; *Producer/Director*: Arnold Laven; *Screenplay*: Pat Fiedler; *Music*: Hugo Friedhofer; *Camera*: Alex Phillips; *Editor*: Marsh Hendry; *Cast*: Chuck Connors (Geronimo); *KAMALA DEVI (TEELA)*; Ross Martin (Mangus); Pat Conway (Maynard); Adam West (Delahay); Enid Jaynes (Huera); Lawrence Dobkin (Gen. Crook); Denver

Pyle (Senator Conrad); Armando Silvestre (Natchez); John Anderson
(Burns).

Geronimo and his followers, tiring of war, decide to settle down
to reservation life. Teela, the reservation schoolteacher, teaches
Geronimo to read and write so he can learn the benefits of white
civilization. Soon a government agent double-crosses the Apaches and
they go to war again. Teela and Geronimo fall in love, and she
travels with the warring band. In the face of annihilation they are
saved by a United States senator who rights the wrong committed
against them.

GHOST TOWN   Native American   1955/Western

United Artists; 77 min.; *Producer*: Howard W. Koch; *Director*: Allen
Miner; *Screenplay*: Jameson Brewer; *Music*: Paul Dunlap; *Camera*: Joseph
F. Biroc; *Editor*: Mike Pozen; *Cast*: Kent Taylor (Anse Conroy); John
Smith (Duff Dailey); Marian Carr (Barbara Leighton); John Doucette
(Doc Clawson); William Phillips (Kerry McCabe); *SERENA SLADE
(MAUREEN)*; Joel Ashley (Sgt. Dockery); Gilman H. Rankin (Simon Peter
Wheedle); Ed Hashim (Dull Knife); Gary Murray (Alex).

Half-breed Maureen wins Duff Dailey away from his gold-seeking
fiancee, Barbara Leighton.

GIANT   Mexican   1956/Drama

Warner Brothers; 198 min.; *Producers*: George Stevens/Henry Ginsberg;
Director: George Stevens; *Screenplay*: Fred Guiol/Ivan Moffat; *Camera*:
William C. Mellor; *Editors*: William Hornbeck/Philip W. Anderson/Fred
Bohanen; *Music*: Dimitri Tiomkin; *Cast*: Elizabeth Taylor (Leslie
Lynnton Benedict); Rock Hudson (Bick Benedict); James Dean (Jett Rink);
Mercedes McCambridge (Luz Benedict [the older]); Jane Withers (Vashti
Snythe); Chill Wills (Uncle Bawley Benedict); Dennis Hopper (Jordan
Benedict III); Carroll Baker (Luz Benedict [the younger]); *ELSA
CARDENAS (JUANA BENEDICT)*; Fran Bennett (Judy Benedict).

The epic tale of life on a Texas ranch. Conservative Bick Benedict marries liberal New Englander Leslie Lynnton and a life of love
and turmoil is the result. Their children grow up and both are dis-
appointments to their parents. Jordan becomes a doctor and marries
Juana against his father's wishes. Bick's conservatism and prejudice
are put to the test when he and Leslie take Juana into a restaurant
and are refused service because Juana is Mexican. Bick takes more
pride in his family and fights with the restaurant owner, now recog-
nizing the need for changes in social justice.

THE GIRL AND THE GAMBLER   Mexican   1939/Western

RKO; 63 min.; *Producer*: Cliff Reid; *Director*: Lew Landers; *Screenplay*: Joseph A. Fields/Clarence Upson Young; *Cast*: Leo Carrillo (El
Rayo); Tim Holt (Johnny Powell); *STEFFI DUNA (DOLORES)*; Donald

MacBride (Mike); Chris-Pin Martin (Pasqual); Edward Raquello
(Rodolfo); Paul Fix (Charlie); Julian Rivero (Pedro); Frank Puglia
(Gomez); Esther Muir (Madge); Paul Sutton (Manuelo).

Dolores is a cabaret dancer romantically involved with El Rayo.

THE GIRL FROM HAVANA   Cuban   1940/Western

Republic; 69 min.; *Producer*: Robert North; *Director*: Lew Landers;
Screenplay: Karl Brown; *Music*: Cy Feuer; *Camera*: Ernest Miller;
Editor: William Morgan; *Cast*: Dennis O'Keefe (Woody Davis); Claire
Carlton (Havana); Victor Jory (Tex Moore); *STEFFI DUNA (CHITA)*;
Gordon Jones (Tubby Waters).

Chita sings "Querido, Take Me Tonight," a Cuban song.

GIRL FROM MANDALAY   Madalayan   1936/Drama

Republic; 68 min.; *Producer*: Nat Levine; *Director*: Howard Bretherton;
Screenplay: Wellyn Totman/Endre Bohem; *Camera*: Ernest Miller/Jack
Marta; *Cast*: Conrad Nagel (John Foster); *KAY LINAKER (JEANIE)*;
Donald Cook (Kenneth Gringer); Esther Halston (Mary Trevor); Harry
Stubbs (Trevor); Reginald Barlow (Dr. Collins); George Regas
(Headman); David Clyde (Malone); Jack Santos (Oswald); John Bouer
(Mannering).

Jeanie is a cabaret singer who finds happiness when she marries
Englishman John Foster. Kenneth Grainger, one of Foster's friends,
treats Jeanie like a whore, which causes problems. Things are worked
out in the end.

THE GIRL FROM MEXICO   Mexican   1939/Comedy

RKO; 71 min.; *Producer*: Robert Sisk; *Director*: Leslie Goodwins;
Screenplay: Lionel Houser/Joseph A. Fields; *Music*: Roy Webb; *Camera*:
Jack MacKenzie; *Editor*: Desmond Marquette; *Cast*: *LUPE VALEZ
(CARMELITA)*; Donald Woods (Dennis); Leon Errol (Uncle Matt); Linda
Hayes (Elizabeth); Donald MacBride (Renner); Edward Raquello (Romano);
Elisabeth Risdon (Aunt Delia); Ward Bond (Mexican Pete).

Carmelita is discovered during a talent search and becomes a
radio star. Dennis is attracted to Carmelita and her mischief making.
When he and his fiancee separate he happily becomes engaged to
Carmelita. [See MEXICAN SPITFIRE.]

THE GIRL FROM RIO   Latin American   1939/Drama

Monogram; 63 min.; *Producer*: E.B. Derr; *Director*: Lambert Hillyer;
Screenplay: Milton Raison/John T. Neville; *Camera*: Paul Ivano; *Editor*:
Russell Schoengarth; *Cast*: *MOVITA (MARQUITA)*; Warren Hall (Steven);
Alan Baldwin (Carlos); Kay Linaker (Vicki); Clay Clement (Mitchell);

Adele Pearce (Annette); *Soledad Jiminez (Lola)*; Richard Tucker (Montgomery); Dennis Moore (Collins); Byron Foulger (Wilson).

Marquita goes to New York City to help clear her brother of a murder charge. Her American boyfriend, Steve, helps her. Marquita takes a job singing in a nightclub. The murder is solved and her brother is cleared.

A GIRL NAMED TAMIKO   Japanese   1962/Drama

Paramount; 110 min.; *Producers*: Hal Wallis/Joseph H. Hazen; *Director*: John Sturges; *Screenplay*: Edward Anhalt; *Music*: Elmer Bernstein; *Camera*: W. Wallace Kelly; *Editor*: Warren Low; *Cast*: Laurence Harvey (Ivan Kalin); *FRANCE NUYEN (TAMIKO)*; Martha Hyer (Fay Wilson); Gary Merrill (Max Wilson); Michael Wilding (Nigel Costairs); *Miyoshi Umeki (Eiko)*; Steve Brodie (James Hatten); John Mamo (Minya); Bob Okazaki (Kimitaka); Richard Loo (Otani); Lee Patrick (Mary Hatten).

Eiko lives with Ivan Kalin, a Russian/Chinese, until he begins dating American Fay Wilson. Eiko moves in with and eventually marries Ivan's friend Nigel Costairs. Ivan meets Tamiko, the daughter of a respected Japanese family. Ivan falls in love with Tamiko, but Fay manages to hold onto him with sexual favors and the promise of living in the United States. He decides to leave Tamiko for Fay and the United States. At the airport, however, he realizes how much he loves Tamiko and decides to stay in Japan.

GIRL OF THE RIO   Mexican   1932/Western

RKO; 80 min.; *Director*: Herbert Brenon; *Screenplay*: Elizabeth Meehan; *Camera*: Leo Tover; *Editor*: Artie Roberts; *Cast*: *DOLORES DEL RIO (DOLORES)*; Leo Carrillo (Don Jose Tostado); Norman Foster (Johnny Powell); Lucille Gleason (The Matron); Ralph Ince (O'Grady); Edna Murphy (Madge); Stanley Fields (Mike); Frank Compeau (Bill); Roberta Gale (Mabelle).

Dolores is a dancer who does everything she can to save Johnny Powell from being killed by the evil Don Jose Tostado.

THE GIRL WHO KNEW TOO MUCH   Chinese   1969/Drama

Commonwealth United; 95 min.; *Producer*: Earle Lyon; *Driector*: Francis D. Lyon; *Screenplay*: Charles Wallace; *Music*: Joe Green; *Camera*: Alan Stensvold; *Editor*: Terry O. Morse; *Cast*: Adam West (Johnny Cain); *NANCY KWAN (REVEL)*; Robert Alda (Allardice); Nehemiah Persoff (Lt. Crawford); Patricia Smith (Tricia); David Brian (Hal Dixon); Buddy Greco (Lucky); Diane Van Vila (Stripper).

Revel, the ex-mistress/girlfriend of slain gangster Grinaldi, is now secretary to ex-CIA agent Johnny Cain. Cain discovers that Revel is also going to be murdered and discovers that communists are plotting the destruction of the American economy. The plot fails, and

Revel and Cain become romantically involved.

GOLD OF THE SEVEN SAINTS   Native American   1961/Adventure

Warner Brothers; 88 min.; *Producer*: Leonard Freeman; *Director*: Gordon
Douglas; *Screenplay*: Leigh Brackett; *Music*: Howard Jackson; *Camera*:
Joseph Biroc; *Editor*: Folmar Blangsted; *Cast*: Clint Walker (Jim
Rainbolt); Roger Moore (Shaun Garrett); *LETICIA ROMAN (TITA)*; Robert
Middleton (Gondora); Chill Wills (Doc Gates); Gene Evans (McCracken);
Roberto Contrearas (Armanderez); Jack C. Williams (Amos); Arthur
Stewart (Ricca).

    Jim and Shaun find a fortune in gold nuggets, and soon McCracken
and his gang are after them. They manage to escape and join up with
Doc. They meet Gondora, an old friend of Jim's, and Tita, the orphan
he takes care of but is now willing to sell to the highest bidder.
In the end Tita remains with Gondora.

THE GOLDEN BLADE   Arabian Nights   1953/Fantasy

Universal; 81 min.; *Producer*: Richard Wilson; *Director*: Nathan Juran;
Screenplay: John Rich; *Music*: Joseph Gershenson; *Camera*: Maury
Gerisman; *Editor*: Ted J. Kent; *Cast*: Rock Hudson (Harun); *PIPER
LAURIE (PRINCESS KHAIRUZAN)*; Gene Evans (Hadi); *Kathleen Hughes
(Bakhamra)*; George Macready (Jafar); Steven Geray (Barcus); Edgar
Barrier (Caliph); Vic Romito (Sherkan).

    Princess Khairuzan, the daughter of the Caliph, masquerades as
a boy in the streets of Bagdad, where she meets and falls in love
with Harun. When Harun later shows up at the Caliph's palace, Princess Khairuzan enters him into a contest to marry her. However, he
loses the contest and she is fated to marry the evil Barcas--who is
plotting the overthrow of the Caliph. Harun saves Bagdad and the
Caliph, and Harun finally marries Princess Khairuzan.

GOLDEN EARRINGS   Gypsy   1947/War Adventure

Paramount; 95 min.; *Producer*: Harry Tugend; *Director*: Mitchell Leisen;
Screenplay: Frank Butler/Helen Deutsch/Abraham Polonsky; *Music*: Victor
Young; *Camera*: Daniel L. Fapp; *Editor*: Alma McCrorie; *Cast*: Ray
Milland (Colonel Ralph Denistoun); *MARLENE DIETRICH (LYDIA)*; Murvyn
Vye (Zoltan); Bruce Lester (Byrd); Dennis Hoey (Hoff); Quentin
Reynolds; Reinhold Schunzel (Professor Krosigk); Ivan Tiresault
(Major Reimann); Hermine Sterler (Greta Krosigk); Erick Feldary
(Zweig).

    Lydia helps Col. Ralph Denistoun escape the Nazis by disguising
him as a gypsy. He escapes to freedom and, when the war is over,
returns to her.

THE GOLDEN HORDE   Arabian Nights   1951/Fantasy

Universal; 75 min.; *Producers*: Robert Arthur/Howard Christie;
Director: George Sherman; *Screenplay*: Gerald Drayson Adams; *Music*:
Hans J. Salter; *Camera*: Russell Metty; *Editor*: Frank Gross; *Cast*: ANN
BLYTH *(PRINCESS SHALIMAR)*; David Farrar (Sir Guy); George MacCready
(Shaman); Harry Brandon (Jacki); Howard Petrie (Tuglik); Richard Egan
(Gill); Marvin Miller (Genghis Khan); Donald Randolph (Torga); Peggie
Castle (Lailee); Poodles Hanneford (Friar John); Leon Belasco
(Nazza); *Lucille Barkley (Azalah)*; *Karen Varga (Nima)*; Robert Hunter
(Herat).

    In this Arabian Nights adventure Princess Shalimar's city is
besieged by Ghenghis Khan and his hordes. To her rescue comes Englishman Sir Guy and his Crusaders. The barbarians are vanquished
and Princess Shalimar and Sir Guy live happily ever after.

THE GOLDEN STALLION   Mexican   1949/Musical

Republic; 67 min.; *Producer*: Edward J. White; *Director*: William
Witney; *Screenplay*: Sloan Nibley; *Music*: Nathan Scott; *Camera*: Jack
Marta; *Editor*: Tony Martinelli; *Cast*: Roy Rogers; Dale Evans (Stormy
Billings); *ESTELITA RODRIGUEZ (PEPITA VALEZ)*; Pat Brady (Sparrow
Biffle); Douglas Evans (Jeff Middleton); Frank Fenton (Sheriff);
Trigger; Greg McCure (Ben); Dale Van Sickel (Ed Hart).

    Not enough information was available to describe this role
accurately.

THE GOLDEN VOYAGE OF SINBAD   Arabian Nights   1974/Fantasy

Columbia; 105 min.; *Producers*: Charles H. Schneer/Ray Harryhausen;
Director: Gordon Hessler; *Screenplay*: Brian Clemens; *Music*: Miklos
Rozsa; *Camera*: Ted Moore; *Editor*: Roy Watts; *Cast*: John Phillip Law
(Sinbad); *CAROLINE MUNRO (MARGIANA)*; Tom Baker (Koura); Douglas
Wilmer (Vizier); Martin Shaw (Rachid); Gregoire Aslan (Hakim).

    Sinbad is after a golden tablet--a key to great wealth and power.
Margiana, the only woman on the voyage, provides romance for Sinbad.
Also after the tablet is Koura, who has a bag of tricks to keep
Sinbad occupied. But of course good conquers evil and Sinbad sails
home happily.

GONE ARE THE DAYS   Black   1963/Drama

A Hammer Brothers Presentation; 97 min.; *Producer/Director*: Nicholas
Webster; *Screenplay*: Ossie Davis; *Music*: Henry Cowen; *Camera*: Boris
Kaufman; *Editor*: Ralph Rosenblum; *Cast*: Ossie Davis (Purlie Victori-
ous); *RUBY DEE (LUTIEBELLE)*; Sorrell Booke (Capt. Cotchipee); Godfrey
Cambridge (Gitlow); *Hilda Haynes (Missy)*; Alan Alda (Charlie
Cotchipee); *Beah Richards (Idella)*; Charles Welch (Sheriff); Ralph
Roberts (Deputy).

Lutiebelle leaves her position as a maid to travel to Georgia with Purlie Victorious to open an integrated church. Lutiebelle poses as Purlie's deceased cousin to collect money being held in trust by Purlie's relatives. After plots and counterplots Purlie gets the money and opens the church.

GONE TO EARTH   Gypsy   1950/Drama
[THE WILD HEART]

Selznick-RKO; 110 min.; *Producers/Directors/Screenplay*: Michael Powell/Emeric Pressburger; *Music*: Brian Hasdale; *Camera*: Chris Challis; *Editor*: Reginald Mills; *Cast*: *JENNIFER JONES (HAZEL WOODUS)*; David Farrar (Jack Reddin); Cyril Cusack (Edward Marston); Sybil Thorndike (Mrs. Marston); Edward Chapman (Mr. James); Esmund Knight (Abel Woodus); Hugh Griffin (Andrew Vessons); Beatrice Varley (Aunt Prowde); George Cole (Albert); Frances Clare (Miss Amelia Clomber); Valentine Dunn (Martha); Richmond Nairne (Martha's Brother).

A child of the wilderness, Hazel Woodus is more comfortable in the company of her pet fox than with humans--until wealthy squire Jack Reddin begins to lust after her. She manages to escape his charms and marries the local minister who loves her soul and not her body. Reddin cannot stay away from her; he finally manages to seduce her and brings her to live in his home. Her husband retrieves her and she returns home with him mainly because Reddin abuses her fox. Their marriage begins to work when Reddin organizes a fox hunt and Hazel's fox is being chased. Hazel attempts to rescue the fox and Hazel and the fox are both killed by falling through a mine shaft.

GONE WITH THE WIND   Black   1939/Drama

MGM; 222 min.; *Producer*: David O. Selznick; *Director*: Victor Fleming; *Screenplay*: Sidney Howard; *Music*: Max Steiner; *Camera*: Ernest Haller/ Ray Rennahan; *Cast*: Vivien Leigh (Scarlett O'Hara); Clark Gable (Rhett Butler); Leslie Howard (Ashley Wilkes); Olivia de Havilland (Melanie Hamilton); *HATTIE McDANIEL (MAMMY)*; Thomas Mitchell (Gerald O'Hara); Barbara O'Neill (Ellen O'Hara); Carroll Nye (Frank Kennedy); Laura Hope Crews (Aunt Pittypat Hamilton); Harry Davenport (Dr. Meade); *Butterfly McQueen (Prissy)*; Ona Munson (Belle Watling); Rand Brooks (Charles Hamilton); Oscar Polk (Pork); Evelyn Keyes (Suellen); Everett Brown (Big Sam); Alicia Rhett (India Wilkes); Victor Jory (Jonas Wilkerson).

Mammy, Scarlett's maid, is like a second mother to her. Mammy remains loyal to the O'Hara family throughout the difficulties of the Civil War. Mammy is portrayed as wise and is a respected member of the household, despite the typical "Black mammy" stereotype. Prissy, on the other hand, is basically used for comic relief.

THE GOOD EARTH   Chinese   1937/Drama

MGM; 138 min.; *Producer*: Irving G. Thalberg; *Director*: Sidney

Franklin; *Screenplay*: Talbot Jennings/Tess Schlesinger; *Music*: Herbert
Stothart; *Camera*: Karl Freund; *Editor*: Basil Wrangell; *Cast*: Paul Muni
(Wang); *LUISE RAINER (O-LAN)*; Walter Connolly (Uncle); *Tilly Losch
(Lotus)*; Jesse Ralph (Cuckoo); Charley Grapewin (Old Father); Keye
Luke (Elder Son); Harold Huber (Cousin); Roland Got (Younger Son);
Soo Young (Old Mistress Aunt); Chingwah Lee (Ching); William Law
(Gateman); *Mary Wong (Little Bride)*; Charles Middleton (Banker);
Suzanna Kim (Little Fool).

O-lan is a slave sold into marriage to Wang Lung. O-lan makes
great sacrifices for her husband and family--helping in the fields
and managing to keep her family alive when famine comes. During a
revolution O-lan stumbles onto a bag of precious gems which her
husband then uses to give himself great wealth and power. To O-lan
he gives only two pearls. He soon takes Lotus, a teahouse dancer, as
his second wife. She is flirtatious and soon seduces Wang's son, who
is closer to her age. Wang believes Lotus loves him and gives her
the two pearls belonging to O-lan. When Wang finds out about their
affair he throws out both his son and Lotus. His son returns to the
house when his agricultural knowledge saves the family crops from a
plague of locust. Wang returns the pearls to O-lan on her deathbed,
realizing at last her worth and his love for her.

GRASSLANDS [See HEX]

GREASED LIGHTNING   Black   1977/Biography

Warner Brothers; 96 min.; *Producer*: Hannah Weinstein; *Director*:
Michael Schultz; *Screenplay*: Melvin Van Peebles/Leon Capetanos/
Kenneth Vose/Lawrence DuKore; *Music*: Fred Karlin; *Camera*: George
Bouillet; *Editors*: Bob Wyman/Christopher Holmes/Randy Roberts; *Cast*:
Richard Pryor (Wendell Scott); Beau Bridges (Hutch); *PAM GRIER (MARY
JONES)*; Cleavon Little (Peewee); Vincent Gardenia (Sheriff Cotton);
Richie Havens (Woodrow); Julian Bond (Russell); Earl Hindman (Beau
Wells); *Minnie Gentry (Wendell's Mother)*; Lucy Saroyan (Hutch's Wife).

Mary Jones is the patient wife of Wendell Scott, the first Black
race car driver.

THE GREAT LIE   Black   1941/Drama

Warner Brothers; 107 min.; *Producer*: Henry Blanke; *Director*: Edmund
Goulding; *Screenplay*: Lenore Coffe; *Camera*: Tony Gaudio; *Editor*:
Ralph Dawson; *Cast*: Bette Davis (Maggie); George Brent (Pete); Mary
Astor (Sandra); Lucile Watson (Aunt Ada); *HATTIE McDANIEL (VIOLET)*;
Grant Mitchell (Joshua Mason).

Violet is Maggie's loyal servant.

THE GREAT WHITE HOPE   ` Black   1970/Biography

20th Century-Fox; 103 min.; *Producer*: Lawrence Turman; *Director*:
Martin Ritt; *Screenplay*: Howard Sackler; *Camera*: Burnette Guffey;
Cast: James Earl Jones (Jack Jefferson); Jane Alexander (Eleanor
Bachman); *BEAH RICHARDS (MAMA TINY)*; Lou Gilbert (Goldie); Joel
Fluellen (Tick); *MARLENE WARFIELD (CLARA)*; Hal Holbrook (Cameron);
Chester Morris (Pop Weaver).

Clara is the common-law wife of Jack Jefferson--the first Black
heavyweight boxing champion of the world--who leaves her for Eleanor
Bachman, a white divorcee.

GREEN MANSIONS   Jungle Exotic   1959/Adventure

MGM; 104 min.; *Producer*: Edmund Grainger; *Director*: Mel Ferrer;
Screenplay: Dorothy Kingsley; *Music*: Bronislau Kaper; *Camera*: Joseph
Ruttenberg;*Editor*: Ferris Webster; *Cast*: *AUDREY HEPBURN (RIMA)*;
Anthony Perkins (Abel); Lee J. Cobb (Nuflo); Sessue Hayakawa (Runi);
Henry Silva (Kua-Ko); Nehemiah Persoff (Don Punta); Michael Pate
(Priest); *Estelle Hemsley (Cla-Cla)*.

Abel, fleeing a political upheaval in Venezuela, hides in the
jungle, where he finds the mysterious Rima. Village native Runi wants
Rima killed because his tribe thinks she is "The Daughter of Didi,"
an evil spirit haunting the forest. Abel falls in love with Rima and
tries to help her find her origins. They travel to her village and
find it has been burned down. Nuflo, who raised Rima, confesses that
an old woman in the village asked that he take care of Rima so he
brought her up as his own granddaughter. The native villagers
finally attack the forest where Rima lives and kill her before Abel
can save her.

GREENWICH VILLAGE   Latin American   1944/Musical

20th Century-Fox; 82 min.; *Producer*: William Le Baron; *Director*:
Walter Lang; *Screenplay*: Earl Baldwin/Walter Bullock; *Music*: Emil
Newman/Charles Robinson; *Camera*: Leon Shamroy/Harry Jackson; *Editor*:
Robert Simpson; *Cast*: *CARMEN MIRANDA (PRINCESS QUERIDA)*; Don Ameche
(Kenneth Harvey); William Bendix (Danny O'Mara); Vivian Blaine (Bonnie
Watson); Felix Bressart (Hofer); Tony & Sally De Marco.

Princess Querida works in a speakeasy as a fortune teller and
entertainer.

GUERILLA GIRL   Gypsy   1953/Adventure

United Artists; 80 min.; *Producer/Director*: John Christian; *Screen-
play*: John Byrne/Ben Parker; *Music*: Bernard Bossick; *Camera*: Sidney
Zucker; *Editor*: John Christian; *Cast*: Helmut Dantine (Demetri
Alexander); *MARIANNA (ZAIRA)*; Irene Champlin (Nina); Ray Julian
(Vanda); Michael Vale (Danov); Gerald Lee (Spiro); Charlotte Paul

(Lakme); Dora Weissman (Toula).

Zaira is a communist revolutionary in love with Greek official Demetri Alexander. Zaira warns Demetri of a revolutionary ambush, but they are killed and die in each other's arms.

GUN BATTLE AT MONTEREY   Mexican   1957/Western

Allied Artists; 67 min.; *Producer/Director*: Carl Hittleman; *Screenplay*: Jack Leonard/Lawrence Resner; *Music*: Robert Wiley; *Camera*: Harry Neumann; *Editor*: Harry Coswick; *Cast*: Sterling Hayden (Turner); *PAMELA DUNCAN (MARIA)*; Ted de Corsia (Reno); Mary Beth Hughes (Cleo); Lee Van Cleef (Kirby); Charles Canke (Mandy); Pat Comiskey (Frank); Byron Foulger (Carson); Mauritz Huge (Charley); I. Stanford Jolley (Idwall);

Maria saves the life of Turner after he is shot and left for dead.

GUN BROTHERS   Native American   1956/Western

United Artists; 79 min.; *Director*: Sidney Salkow; *Screenplay*: Gerald Drayson Adams/Richard Schayer; *Music*: Irving Gertz; *Camera*: Kenneth Peach; *Editor*: Arthur Hilton; *Cast*: Buster Crabbe (Chad); Ann Robinson (Rose Fargo); Neville Brand (Jubal); Michael Ansara (Shawnee); Walter Sande (Yellowstone); *LITA MILAN (MEE TEE SE)*; James Seay (Blackjack Silk); Roy Barcroft (Sheriff Jergen); Slim Pickens (Moose MacLain).

Mee Tee Se is misused by Shawnee and his gang.

GUN FEVER   Native American   1957/Western

United Artists; 82 min.; *Producers*: Harry Jackson/Sam Weston; *Director*: Mark Stevens; *Screenplay*: Stanley H. Silverman/Mark Stevens; *Music*: Paul Dunlap; *Camera*: Charles Van Enger; *Editor*: Lee Gilbert; *Cast*: Mark Stevens (Lucas); John Lupton (Simon); Larry Storch (Amigo); *JANA DAVI (TANANA)*; Aaron Saxon (Trench); Jerry Barclay (Singer); Norman Frederic (Whitman); Clegg Hoyt (Kane); Jean Innes (Martha); Russell Thorsen (Thomas); Michael Himm (Stableman); Iron Eyes Cody (Indian Chief).

Lucas Rand's parents are murdered by a renegade gang. He and his friend Simon seek revenge. Lucas has an affair with Tanana.

GUNMAN'S WALK   Native American   1958/Western

Columbia; 97 min.; *Producer*: Fred Kohlmar; *Director*: Phil Karlson; *Screenplay*: Frank Nugent; *Music*: George Duning; *Camera*: Charles Lawton; *Editor*: Jerome Thoms; *Cast*: Van Heflin (Lee Hackett); Tab Hunter (Ed Hackett); *KATHRYN GRANT (CLEE CHOUARD)*; James Darren (Davy

Hackett); Mickey Shaughnessy (Will Motely); Robert F. Simon (Harry
Brill); Edward Platt (Purcell Avery); Ray Teal (Jensen Sieverts);
Paul Birch (Bob Seikirk).

Lee Hackett brings up one son, Ed, in the tradition of "guns
speak louder than words," and virtually ignores his other son, Davy.
Davy, a law-abiding citizen, falls in love with Clee Chouard, the
victim of much racial discrimination. Ed goes bad by shooting two
men leading Lee to kill his son to prevent further bloodshed. Lee
is comforted by Davy and Clee.

GUNMEN FROM LAREDO   Native American   1959/Western

Columbia; 67 min.; *Producer/Director*: Wallace MacDonald; *Screenplay*:
Clark E. Reynolds; *Camera*: Irving Lippman; *Editor*: Al Clark; *Cast*:
Robert Knapp (Gil Reardon); *JANA DAVI (ROSITA)*; Walter Coy (Ben
Keefer); Paul Birch (Matt Crawford); Don C. Harvey (Dave Marlow);
Clarence Straight (Frank Bass); Jerry Barclay (Jordan Keefer);
Charles Horvath (Mangos Coloradas); Ron Hayes (Walt Keefer); Jean
Moorhead (Katy Reardon).

Gil Reardon seeks vengeance after his wife and foreman are
murdered by the Keefers of Laredo. He kills one of the murderers
but is framed by the Keefers and the dishonest sheriff of Laredo for
a murder he did not commit. He is sent to prison, but escapes. He
saves Rosita from a kidnapping and they travel to Laredo so Gil can
finish his mission. After disposing of the gang and the sheriff,
Rosita and Gil cross the border into Mexico.

GUNS OF THE MAGNIFICENT SEVEN   Mexican   1969/Western

United Artists; 106 min.; *Producer*: Vincent M. Fennelly; *Director*:
Paul Wendkos; *Screenplay*: Herman Hoffman; *Music*: Elmer Bernstein;
Camera: Antonio Macasoli; *Editor*: Walter Hannemann; *Cast*: George
Kennedy (Chris); James Whitmore (Levi Morgan); Monte Markham (Keno);
Bernie Casey (Cassie); Joe Don Baker (Slater); Scott Thomas (P.J.);
Reni Santoni (Max); Michael Ansara (Col. Diego); *WENDE WAGNER (TINA)*;
Frank Silvera (Lobero); Fernando Rey (Quintero); Tony Davis (Emiliano
Zapata).

The "magnificent seven" once again help the peasants of Mexico
overcome oppression. Tina is a peasant girl who falls in love with
P.J. In the final confrontation he is killed.

THE GURU   Indian   1968/Drama

20th Century-Fox; 112 min.; *Producer*: Ismail Merchant; *Director*:
James Ivory; *Screenplay*: Ruth Prawer Jhabvala/James Ivory; *Music*:
Ustad Vilayat Khan; *Camera*: Subrata Mitra; *Editor*: Prebhakar Supare;
Cast: Utpal Dutt (Ustad Zafar Khan); Michael York (Tom Pickle); Rita
Tushingham (Jenny); *APARNA SEN (GHAZALA)*; *Madhur Jaffrey (Begum
Sahiba)*; Zohra Seghal (Mustani); Nana Palsikar (The Guru's Guru);

Barry Foster (Chris).

Tom Pickle travels to India to study the sitar under guru Ustad
Zafar Khan. Begum Sahiba, Ustad's first wife, runs the house;
Ghazala, Ustad's second wife, lives in another town.

THE GYPSY AND THE GENTLEMAN   Gypsy   1958/Drama

Arthur Rank Presentation;107 min.; *Producer*: Maurice Cowan; *Director*:
Joseph Losey; *Screenplay*: Janet Green; *Music*: Hans May; *Camera*: Jack
Hildyard; *Editor*: Reginald Beck; *Cast*: *MELINA MERCOURI (BELLE)*; Keith
Michell (Sir Paul Deverill); Patrick McGoohan (Jess); June Laverick
(Sarah Deverill); Lyndon Brook (John Patterson); Flora Robson (Mrs.
Haggard); Clare Austin (Vanessa); Helen Haye (Lady Ayrton); Newton
Blick (Ruddock).

Sir Paul Deverill is about to marry for wealth when he falls in
love with Belle, a gypsy pickpocket, and marries her instead. Belle,
however, is also interested in money and is greatly distressed when
she realizes that Deverill has no money but many debts. Belle gives
all the money she gets her hands on to her gypsy lover, Jess. They
then plot to get money from Sarah, Deverill's sister, who is wealthy.
Sarah manages to avoid their plotting. When Deverill realizes what
is going on he kills Belle and himself.

GYPSY WILDCAT   Gypsy   1944/Drama

Universal; 75 min.; *Producer*: George Waggner; *Director*: Roy William
Neill; *Screenplay*: James Hogan/Gene Lewis/James M. Cain; *Music*:
Edward Ward; *Camera*: George Robinson; *Editor*: Russell Schoengarth;
Cast: *MARIA MONTEZ (CARLA)*; Jon Hall (Michael); Peter Coe (Tonio);
Nigel Bruce (High Sheriff); Leo Carrillo (Anube); Gale Sondergaard
(Rhoda); Douglas Dumbrille (Baron Tovar); Curt Bois (Valdi); Harry
Cording (Captain Marver).

Dancer Carla is kidnapped by the evil Baron Tovar. With
Michael's help she is restored to her proper position as a countess.

THE HALF-BREED   Native American   1952/Western

RKO; 81 min.; *Producer*: Herman Schlom; *Director*: Stuart Gilmore;
Screenplay: Harold Shumate/Richard Wormser; *Music*: Paul Entwell;
Camera: William V. Skall; *Editor*: Samuel E. Beetley; *Cast*: Robert
Young (Dan Craig); Janis Carter (Helen); Jack Buetel (Charlie Wolf);
Barton MacLane (Marshal); Reed Hadley (Crawford); Porter Hall
(Kraemer); *JUDY WALSH (NAH-LIN)*; Connie Gilchrist (Ma Joggins);
Sammy White (Willy Wayne); Damian O'Flynn (Captain Jackson); Frank
Wilcox (Sands).

As Nah-Lin watches the white townsfolk dancing, she is raped
and murdered by one of the town villains. When she fights to save

herself, he tells her that she is "just like and animal." Charlie
Wolf, her half-breed brother, seeks revenge on the town with an
attempted Indian uprising--which is averted when the attacker is
caught.

THE HALF-NAKED TRUTH   Latin American   1932/Comedy

RKO; 77 min.; *Director*: Gregory La Cava; *Screenplay*: Bartlett Cormack/
Corey Ford; *Camera*: Bert Glennon; *Editor*: C.L. Kimball; *Cast*: *LUPE
VELEZ (TERESITA)*; Lee Tracy (James Bates); Eugene Pallette (Achilles);
Frank Morgan (Farrell); Bob McKenzie (Col. Willikens); James Donlon
(Lou); Shirley Chambers (Gladys); Charles Dow Clark (The Sheriff).

    Teresita is masquerading as Princess Exotic, an escapee from a
Turkish harem. She is actually a member of a small carnival trying
to make it big. When it is discovered that she has a pet lion, the
princess becomes something of a celebrity.

HALLS OF ANGER   Black   1970/Drama

United Artists; 98 min.; *Producer*: Herbert Hirschman; *Director*: Paul
Bogart; *Screenplay*: John Shaner/Al Ramrus; *Music*: Dave Grusin;
Camera: Burnett Guffey; *Editor*: Bud Molin; *Cast*: Calvin Lockhart
(Quincy Davis); *JANET MacLACHLAN (LORRAINE NASH)*; James A. Watson,
Jr. (J.T. Watson); Jeff Bridges (Douglas Falk); Dewayne Jesse
(Lerone Johnson); Rob Reiner (Leaky Couloris).

    Lorraine Nash is a teacher at a racially troubled high school.
Quincy Davis, the vice principal, convinces her to stay at the
school.

HAMMER   Black   1972/Drama

United Artists; 91 min.; *Producer*: Al Adamson; *Director*: Bruce Clark;
Screenplay: Charles Johnson; *Music*: Solomon Burke; *Camera*: Bob
Steadman; *Editor*: George Folsey, Jr.; *Cast*: Fred Williamson (B.J.
Hammer); Bernie Hamilton (Davis); *VONETTA McGEE (LOIS)*; William
Smith (Brenner); Charles Lampkin (Big Sid); Elizabeth Harding (Rhoda);
Mel Stewart (The Professor); D'Urville Martin (Sonny); Stack Pierce
(Roughhouse).

    Lois becomes the lover of boxer B.J. Hammer. She is kidnapped
by thugs who want Hammer to throw a fight. They threaten to kill
Lois if Hammer does not cooperate. Hammer goes into the fight determined to win. Policeman Davis finds Lois. Hammer wins the fight and
he and Lois are reunited.

HARBOR LIGHTS   Puerto Rican   1963/Drama

20th Century-Fox; 68; *Producer/Director*: Maury Dexter; *Screenplay*:
Henry Cross; *Music*: Paul Sawtell; *Camera*: John Nicholaus, Jr.;

Editor: Jodie Copelan; *Cast*: Kent Taylor (Dan Crown); *MIRIAM COLON
(GINA)*; Jeff Morrow (Cardinal); Antonio Torres (Capt. Acosta); Jose
de San Antonio (Father Riva).

Gina Rosario helps Dan Crown find the murderer of Dan's brother
Alex. They discover that Alex was killed because of a diamond he
had smuggled into the country. Gina and the police arrive just in
time to save Don when the criminals who killed Alex descend on him.

HAREM GIRL   Arab   1952/Comedy

Columbia; 70 min.; *Producer*: Wallace MacDonald; *Director*: Edward
Bernds; *Screenplay*: Edward Bernds/Elwood Ullman; *Music*: Mischa
Bakaleinikoff; *Camera*: Lester White; *Editor*: Richard Fantl; *Cast*:
Joan Davis (Susie Perkins); *PEGGIE CASTLE (PRINCESS SHAREEN)*;
Arthur Blake (Abdul Nassib); Paul Marion (Majeed); Donald Randolph
(Jamal); Henry Brandon (Hassan); *Minerval Urecal (Aniseh)*; Peter
Brocco (Ameen); John Dehner (Khalil).

Jamal attempts to usurp Princess Shareen's throne in order to
steal the country's oil resources. Susie Perkins, the Princess's
secretary, helps save the day.

HARUM SCARUM   Arab   1965/Musical

MGM; 85 mn.; *Producer*: Sam Katzman; *Director*: Gene Nelson; *Screen-
play*: Gerald Drayson Adams; *Music*: Fred Karger; *Camera*: Fred H.
Jackman; *Editor*: Ben Lewis; *Cast*: Elvis Presley (Johnny Tyrone);
MARY ANN MOBLEY (PRINCESS SHALIMAR); *Fran Jeffries (Aishah)*; Michael
Ansara (Prince Dragna); Jay Novello (Zacha); Philip Reed (King
Toranshah); Theo Marcuse (Sinan); Billy Barty (Baba); Dick Harvey
(Mokar); Jack Costanzo (Julna); Larry Chance (Capt. Herat); *Barbara
Werle (Leilah)*; *Brenda Benet (Emerald)*.

In the Middle East to promote his latest film, Johnny Tyrone
meets Aishah, who invites him to her country, Lunarkarnd. While
there he meets Princess Shalimar, who is being passed off as a slave
girl by the evil Sinan so Prince Dragna will become king. Johnny
saves the day, marries Princess Shalimar, and takes her back to the
United States.

THE HATCHET MAN   Chinese   1932/Drama

First National; 74 min.; *Director*; William A. Wellman; *Screenplay*:
J.G. Alexander; *Camera*: Sid Hickox; *Editor*: Owen Marks; *Cast*: Edward
G. Robinson (Wong Low Get); *LORETTA YOUNG (TOYA SAN)*; Dudley Digges
(Nog Hong Fah); Leslie Fenton (Harry En Hai); Edmund Breese (Yu
Chang); Tully Marshall (Long Sen Yat); Noel Madison (Charles Kee);
Blanche Frederici (Mme. Si-Si); J. Carroll Naish (Sun Yat Sen);
Toshia Mori (Miss Ling); *Evelyn Selbie (Wah Li)*; Charles Middleton
(Kip Hop Fat); Ralph Ince (Malone); Otto Yamioka (Chung Ho).

Wong Low Get is the executioner for a tong. Wong must kill one of his closest friends, Sun Yat Sen, who has made Wong the benefici- ary of his will and asked him to take care of his daughter, Toya San, if he should die. Later Wong and Toya San marry, but Toya falls in love with Harry En Hai. Wong, discovering the affair, kills Harry but allows Toya Son to stay with him.

HAVANA ROSE   Latin American   1951/Comedy

Republic; 77 min.; *Producer*: Sidney Picker; *Director*: William Beaudine; *Screenplay*: Charles E. Roberts; *Camera*: Ellis W. Carter; *Editor*: Tony Martinelli; *Cast*: ESTELITA RODRIGUEZ (ESTELITA DeMARCO); Bill Williams (Tex Thompson); Hugh Herbert (Filbert Filmore); Florence Bates (Mrs. Filmore); Fortunio Bonanova (Ambassador DeMarco); Leon Belasco (Renaldi); Nacho Galiado (Carlo); Martin Garialaga (Philip); *Rosa Turich (Maria)*; Tom Kennedy (Hotel Detective); Manuel Paris (Rudolph); Bob Easton (Hotel Clerk).

Estelita is continually messing things up for her father who is trying to secure a five million dollar loan for his country. She runs away to Texas to be with rancher Tex Thompson the man she loves.

HAWAII CALLS   Hawaiian   1938/Drama

RKO; 72 min.; *Producer*: Sol Lesser; *Director*: Edward F. Cline; *Screenplay*: Wanda Tuchak; *Music*: Hugo Riesenfeld; *Camera*: Jack McKenzie; *Editor*: Arthur Hilton; *Cast*: Bobby Breen (Billy Coulter); Ned Sparks (Strigs); Irvin S. Cobb (Capt. O'Hare); Warren Hull (Commander Milburn); Gloria Holden (Mrs. Milburn); Juanita Quigley (Doris Milburn); *MAMO CLARK (HINA)*; Paul Lani (Pua); Raymond Page (Raymond Paige); Herbert Rawlinson (Harlow); Dora Clement (Mrs. Harlow).

Hina is the sister of Pua, who, along with orphan boy Billy, is a stowaway on a boat returning from San Francisco.

HAWIIAN NIGHTS   Hawaiian   1939/Drama

Universal; 65 min.; *Producer*: Max H. Golden; *Director*: Albert Rogell; *Screenplay*: Charles Grayson/Lee Loeb; *Music*: Charles Previn; *Camera*: Stanley Cortez; *Cast*: Johnny Downs (Ted Hartley); Constance Moore (Lonnie Lane); Mary Carlisle (Millie); Eddie Quillan (Ray Peters); Etienne Girardot (Alonzo Dilman); Samuel S. Hinds (Lane); *PRINCESS LUANA (LUANA)*; Thurston Hall (T.C. Hartley); Robert Emmett Keane (Fothering).

Luana is the token Hawaiian in this film.

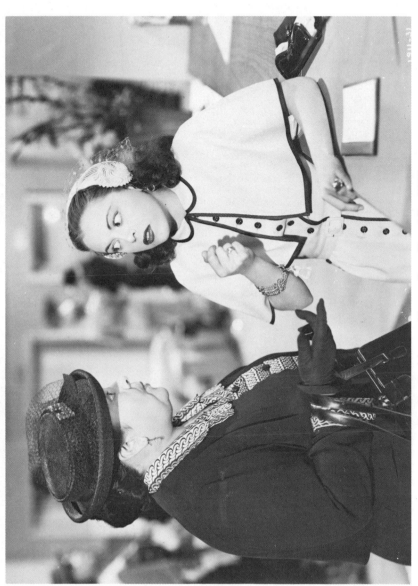

Estelita Rodriguez, *Havana Rose* (Republic, 1951)

THE HAWAIIANS   Hawaiian   1970/Drama

United Artists; 132 min.; *Producer*: Walter Mirisch; *Director*: Tom
Gries; *Screenplay*: James R. Webb; *Music*: Henry Mancini; *Camera*:
Philip Lathrop/Lucien Ballard; *Editor*: Ralph Winters; *Cast*: Charlton
Heston (Whip Hoxworth); *TINA CHEN (NYUK TSIN)*; *GERALDINE CHAPLIN
(PURITY HOXWORTH)*; John Phillip Law (Noel Hoxworth); Alec McCowen
(Micah Hale); Mako (Mun Ki); Don Knight (Milton Overpeck); *Miko
Mayama (Fumiko)*; *Virginia Ann Lee (Mei Li)*; *Naomi Stevens (Queen
Liliuokalani)*.

Purity persuades her husband, Whip Hoxworth, to hire Nyuk Tsin
and her husband, Mun Ki, to save Nyuk from a life of prostitution.
Nyuk is determined to feed her family and manages to grow vegetables
on Whip's miserable plantation. When water is found, Whip, with
Nyuk's help, introduces the pineapple to Hawaii. Meanwhile, Purity
is becoming more aware of her Hawaiin heritage and wants to raise
her son as a Hawaiian. Finally she leaves Whip. Nyuk accompanies
her dying husband to a leper colony. When she returns after his
death her children are prosperous and Whip is living with Fumiko. A
plague hits the island and Nyuk's plantation is ruined. Whip gives
her the money to rebuild. Her daughter, Mei Li, and his son, Noel,
marry.

THE HEART IS A LONEY HUNTER   Black   1968/Drama

Warner Brothers and Seven Arts; 124 min.; *Producers*: T.C. Ryan/Marc
Marson; *Director*: Robert Ellis Miller; *Screenplay*: Thomas C. Ryan;
Music: Dave Grusin; *Camera*: James Wong Howe; *Editor*: John F. Burnett;
Cast: Alan Arkin (Singer); Chuck McCann (Antonapoulos); Stacy Keach,
Jr. (Blount); Peter Mamakos (Spirmonedes); John O'Leary (Beaudine);
CICELY TYSON (PORTIA); Percy Rodrigues (Dr. Copeland); Sondra Locke
(Mick); Johnny Popwell (Willie); Sherri Vise (Dolores); Wayne Smith
(Harry).

In spite of her education, Portia is a servant married to a
field hand, much to the disappointment of her doctor father.

HEAVEN WITH A GUN   Native American--Hopi   1969/Western

MGM; 101 min.; *Producers*: Frank King/Maurice King; *Director*: Lee H.
Katzin; *Screenplay*: Richard Carr; *Music*: Johnny Mandel; *Camera*: Fred
Koenekamp; *Editor*: Dan Cahn; *Cast*: Glenn Ford (Jim Killian); Carolyn
Jones (Madge McCloud); *BARBARA HERSHEY (LELOOPA)*; John Anderson (Asa
Beck); David Carradine (Coke Beck); J.D. Cannon (Mace); Noah Beery
(Garvey); Harry Townes (Gus Sampson); William Bryant (Bart Patterson).

Leloopa is raped by Coke Beck. Jim Killian, the town minister
--and ex-gunfighter--beats Coke to avenge Leloopa's rape. Leloopa
falls in love with Killian, but he thinks of her as a daughter.

HELL'S HALF ACRE   Chinese   1954/Drama

Republic; 90 min.; *Producer/Director*: John H. Auer; *Screenplay*: Steve
Fisher; *Music*: R. Dale Butts; *Camera*: John L. Russell; *Editor*: Fred
Allen; *Cast*: Wendell Corey (Chet Chester); Evelyn Keyes (Dona
Williams); Elsa Lanchester (Lida O'Reilly); Marie Windsor (Rose);
NANCY GATES (SALLY LEE); Leonard Strong (Ippy); Jesse White (Tubby
Otis); Keye Luke (Chief Dan); Philip Ahn (Roger Kong); Robert Shield
(Frank); Clair Weidenaar (Jamison).

Sally Lee kills the man who blackmailed her boyfriend, Chet
Chester. Chester is tried for the murder. Dona Williams is trying
to prove that Chester is her long-lost husband. When Sally Lee is
murdered, Chester escapes from jail to confront the killer. He is
killed, which allows Dona Williams to remarry and to tell their son
that his father died a hero's death at Pearl Harbor.

HELP!   Asian   1965/Musical

United Artists; 90 min.; *Producer*: Walter Shenson; *Director*: Richard
Lester; *Screenplay*: Marc Behm/Charles Wood; *Music*: Ken Thorne;
Camera: David Watkin; *Editor*: John Victor Smith; *Cast*: John Lennon
(John); Paul McCartney (Paul); George Harrison (George); Ringo Starr
(Ringo); Leo McKern (Clang); *ELEANOR BRON (AHME)*; Victor Spinetti
(Professor Foot); Roy Kinnear (Algernon); Patrick Cargill (Super-
intendent); John Bluthal (Bhuta); Alfie Bass (Doorman); Warren
Mitchell (Abdul).

The Beatles become involved with Priestess Ahme after discovering
that Ringo has acquired the sacrificial ring of her cult. It at
first appears that Ahme is trying to murder Ringo to get the ring,
but she is later revealed as an ally and saves Ringo's life.

HER JUNGLE LOVE   Jungle Exotic   1938/Adventure

Paramount; 81 min.; *Producer*: George M. Arthur; *Director*: George
Archainbaud; *Screenplay*: Joseph Mancure March/Lillie Hayword/Eddie
Welch; *Music*: Gregory Stone; *Camera*: Ray Rennahan; *Editor*: Hugh
Bennett; *Cast*: *DOROTHY LAMOUR (TURA)*; Ray Milland (Bob Mitchell);
Lynne Overman (Jimmy Wallace); J. Carrol Naish (Juasa); Dorothy Howe
(Eleanor Martin); Jonathan Hale (J.C. Martin); Archie Twitchell (Roy
Atkins); Edward A. Earle (Capt. Avery).

Tura is the high priestess of a crocodile god who requires human
sacrifices. When white men Bob Mitchell and Jimmy Wallace crash on
her island, they begin to stir things up by introducing her to phono-
graph music and kissing.

A HERO AIN'T NOTHING BUT A SANDWICH   Black   1977/Drama

New World Pictures; 107 min.; *Producer*: Robert B. Radnitz; *Director*:
Ralph Nelson; *Screenplay*: Alice Childress; *Music*: Tom McIntosh;

Camera: Ralph Nelson; *Editor*: Fred Chulack; *Cast*: CICELY TYSON
(SWEETS); Paul Winfield (Butler); Larry B. Scott (Benjie); Helen
Martin (Mrs. Bell); Glynn Turman (Nigeria); David Groh (Cohen); Kevin
Hooks (Tiger); Kenneth Green (Jimmy Lee); Harold Sylvester (Doctor).

Sweets is the mother of Benjie, a 13-year-old heroin addict.

HEX [GRASSLANDS]   Native American   1972/Drama

20th Century-Fox; 92 min.; *Producer*: Clark Paylow; *Director*: Leo
Garen; *Screenplay*: Leo Garen/Steve Katz; *Music*: Charles Bernstein;
Camera: Charles Rosher, Jr.; *Editors*: Robert Belcher/Antranig
Mahakian; *Cast*: TINA HERAC [CHRISTINA RAINES] (ORIOLE); HILARIE
THOMPSON (ACACIA); Keith Carradine (Whizzer); Mike Combs (Golly);
Scott Glenn (Jimbang); Gary Busey (Giblets); Robert Walker (Chupo);
Doria Cook (China); Iggie Wolfington (Cuzak); Tom Jones (Elston);
Dan Haggerty (Brother Billy).

In this film set after World War I, Acacia and Oriole are taught
witchcraft by their father. When a group of motorcycle riders arrives
on their isolated farm, Oriole begins to practice her craft. Giblets
tries to assault Acacia but fails, and he is soon dead. Acacia tries
to stop Oriole but is unsuccessful. Oriole leaves the farm with
Whizzer. Acacia remains on the farm with Golly, who has fallen in
love with her.

HI, BEAUTIFUL   Black   1944/Comedy

Universal; 66 min.; *Producer*: Dick Irving Hyland; *Director*: Leslie
Goodwins; *Screenplay*: Dick Irving Hyland; *Music*: Frank Skinner;
Camera: Paul Ivano; *Editor*: Edward Curtiss; *Cast*: Martha O'Driscoll
(Patty Callahan); Noah Beery, Jr. (Jeff); HATTI McDANIEL (MILLIE);
Walter Catlett (Bisbee); Tim Ryan (Babcock); Florence Lake (Mrs.
Bisbee); Grady Sutton (Attendant); Lou Lubin (Husband); Virginia Sale
(Wife).

Millie is a maid.

HI GAUCHO   Latin American   1936/Drama

RKO; 59 min.; *Director*: Thomas Atkins; *Screenplay*: Adele Baffington;
Music: Albert Hay Malotte; *Camera*: Jack MacKenzie; *Cast*: John Carroll
(Lucio); STEFFI DUNA (INEZ); Rod la Rocque (Escurra); Montague Love
(Hillario); Ann Codee (Dona Vincenta); Tom Ricketts (Don Salvador);
Paul Porcast (Ortegas).

When Lucio saves Inez from a bandit she is initially put off by
the gaucho. She changes her mind once he kisses her. Her family
refuses to allow her to marry Lucio because a marriage has already
been arranged for her with the son of a wealthy family. Inez and
Lucio sneak away and decide to marry anyway and eventually her family

agrees.

HIAWATHA   Native American   1952/Drama

Monogram; 80 min.; *Producer*: Walter Mirisch; *Director*: Kurt Neumann;
Screenplay: Arthur Straun/Dan Ullman; *Music*: Marlin Ekiles; *Camera*:
Harry Neumann; *Editor*: Walter Ilamaemann; *Cast*: Vincent Edwards
(Hiawatha); *YVETTE DUGAY (MINNEHAHA)*; Keith Larsen (Pai Pel Keewis);
Gene Ingleins (Chibisbos); Armando Elivestre (Kwarind); Michael
Toland (Neyadji); Ian MacDonald (Megismogwea); *Katherine Kruery
(Nokomis)*; Morris Ankrum (Igaoo); Stephen Chase (Lekku); Stuart
Randall (Mudjekeewis); Richard Bartlett (Chunung); Michael Granger
(Ajawac); Robert Brice (Wabeek); Gene Peterson (Hikon); Henry Corden
(Ottobang).

    Based on the Longfellow poem "Hiawatha." Hiawatha is an Ojibway
who falls in love with Minnehaha--a woman of the rival Dacotahs.
Trouble is stirred up by Pai Pel Keewis. As the two tribes are about
to do battle Hiawatha saves the day. Minnehaha and Hiawatha marry,
but she must still face the antagonism of his tribe.

HICKEY & BOGGS   Black   1972/Drama

United Artists; 111 min.; *Producer*: Fouad Said; *Director*: Robert Culp;
Screenplay: Walter Hill; *Music*: Ted Ashford; *Camera*: Wilmer Butler;
Editor: David Berlatsky; *Cast*: Bill Cosby (Al Hickey); Robert Culp
(Frank Boggs); *ROSALIND CASH (NYONA)*; Carmen (Mary Jane); Robert
Mandan (Mr. Brill); Lester Fletcher (Rice); Vincent Gardenia
(Papadakis); Bill Hickman (Monte); Michael Moriarty (Ballard); Sil
Words (Mr. Leroy).

    Nyona is the estranged wife of private investigator Al Hickey.

HIGH NOON   Mexican   1952/Western

United Artists; 85 min.; *Producer*: Stanley Kramer; *Director*: Fred
Zinnemann; *Screenplay*: Carl Foreman; *Music*: Dimitri Tiomkin; *Camera*:
Floyd Crosby; *Editor*: Elmo Williams; *Cast*: Gary Cooper (Will Kane);
Thomas Mitchell (Jonas Henderson); Lloyd Bridges (Harvey Pell); *KATY
JURADO (HELEN RAMIREZ)*; Grace Kelly (Amy Kane); Otto Kruger (Percy
Mettrick); Lon Chaney (Martin Howe); Henry Morgan (William Fuller);
Ian MacDonald (Frank Miller); Even McVeagh (Mildred Fuller); Harry
Shannon (Cooper); Lee Van Cleef (Jack Colby); Robert Wilke (James
Pierce); Sheb Wooley (Ben Miller).

    Helen Ramirez is the former mistress of both outlaw Frank Miller
and Marshall Will Kane. She is now the owner of a saloon and store
and mistress of the town sheriff. Will Kane must once again face
Frank Miller. Helen is the only person in town who understands Kane's
position and why he must face Miller. She also makes Kane's Quaker
bride understand why he must stay and fight, thus convincing Amy to
stand by her man. Helen leaves town on the noon train which brings

Frank Miller into town.

HILLS OF UTAH   Native American   1951/Western

Columbia; 70 min.; *Producer*: Armand Schaefer; *Director*: John English; *Screenplay*: Gerald Geraghty; *Camera*: William Bradford; *Editor*: James Sweeney; *Cast*: Gene Autry; Pat Buttram (Dusty Cosgrove); Elaine Riley (Karen McQueen); *DONNA MARTELL (NOLA)*; Onslow Stevens (Jayde McQueen); Denver Pyle (Bowie French); William Fawcett (Washoe); Harry Lauter (Evan Fox); Kenne Duncan (Ingo Hubbard); Harry Harvey (Marshal Duffield).

Nola is a half-breed Indian girl.

HIS MAJESTY O'KEEFE   Island Exotic   1953/Adventure

Warner Brothers; 89 min.; *Producer*: Harold Hecht; *Director*: Byron Haskin; *Screenplay*: Borden Chase/James Hill; *Music*: Dimitri Tiomkin; *Camera*: Otto Heller; *Editor*: Manuel Del Campo; *Cast*: Burt Lancaster (Captain David O'Keefe); *JOAN RICE (DALABO)*; Andre Morell (Alfred Totins); Abraham Sofaer (Fatumak); Archie Savage (Boogulroo); Benson Fong (Mr. Chou); *Teresa Prendergast (Kakofel)*; Lloyd Berrell (Inifel); Charles Horvath (Bully).

During his visit to Polynesia, Captain David O'Keefe falls in love with Dalabo and makes arrangements with her while father to marry her. She is not sure she loves him and his egotistical ways, but she marries him anyway. He introduces her to white society, and although they encounter racism, O'Keefe's wealth causes people to overlook Dalabo's background. Dalabo soon begins to dress and act white until they return to the islands. Dalabo becomes disgusted by O'Keefe's lust for money and for another native woman. However, all ends well as O'Keefe becomes more native-like in his thinking, abandons his quest for wealth and power, and remains on the island with Dalabo.

HIT MAN   Black   1972/Drama

MGM; 93 min.; *Producer*: Gene Corman; *Director*: George Armitage; *Screenplay*: George Armitage; *Music*: H.B. Barnum; *Camera*: Andrew Davis; *Editor*: Morton Tubor; *Cast*: Bernie Casey (Tyrone Tackett); *PAMELA GRIER (GOZELDA)*; Lisa Moore (Laural Garfoot); Bhetty Waldron (Irvelle Way); Sam Laws (Sherwood Epps); *Candy All (Rochelle Tackett)*; Edmund Cambridge (Theotis Oliver); Don Diamond (Nano Zito); Bob Harris (Shag Merriweather).

Gozelda, the mistress of porno king, Nano Zito, is clawed to death by wild beasts. Rochelle is the niece of Tyrone Tackett, who is searching for his brother's murderer. His search leads him to Nano--who cast Rochelle in a rape scene in one of his films. Rochelle is soon murdered and Tyrone kills Zito and his gang.

HOLIDAY IN HAVANA   Cuban   1949/Musical

Columbia; 73 min.; *Producer*: Ted Richmond; *Director*: Jean Yarbrough;
Screenplay: Robert Lees/Frederic I. Rinaldo/Karen DeWolf; *Music*: Paul
Mertz; *Camera*: Vincent Farrar; *Editor*: Henry Batista; *Cast*: Desi
Arnaz (Carlos Estrada); *MARY HATCHER (LOLITA VALDEZ)*; Ann Doran
(Marge Henley); Stevan Geray (Lopez); *Minerva Urecal (Mama Valdez)*;
Sig Arno (Pepe).

   Lolita is a dancer romantically involved with bandleader Carlos.
They argue just before entering a contest that will bring fame to
both of them, but reconcile before going on with their act.

HOLIDAY INN   Black   1942/Musical

Paramount; 101 min.; *Producer/Director*: Mark Sandrich; *Screenplay*:
Claude Binyon; *Music*: Irving Berlin; *Camera*: David Abel; *Editor*:
Ellsworth Haagland; *Cast*: Bing Crosby (Jim Hardy); Fred Astaire (Ted
Hanover); Marjorie Reynolds (Linda Mason); Virginia Dale (Lillie
Dixon); Walter Abel (Danny Reid); *LOUISE BEAVERS (MAMIE)*.

   Mamie is Jim Hardy's maid. She gives advice and comfort to him,
but knows her place. She joins her employer in a musical number
about Abraham Lincoln freeing the slaves.

HONEYMOON   Mexican   1946/Comedy

RKO; 74 min.; *Producer*: Warren Duff; *Director*: William Keighley;
Screenplay: Michael Kanin; *Camera*: Edward Cronjager; *Editor*: Ralph
Dawson; *Cast*: Shirley Temple (Barbara); Franchot Tone (Flanner); Guy
Madison (Phil); *LINA ROMAY (RAQUEL)*; Gene Lockhart (Prescott); Grant
Mitchell (Chenshaw); *Corinna Mura (Senora Mendoza)*; Julio Villareal
(Senor Mendoza).

   American consul Flanner is engaged to Raquel, but his romance
in continually interrupted by Barbara and Phil who are in Mexico
trying to get married.

HONG KONG AFFAIR   Chinese   1958/Drama

Allied Artists; 79 min.; *Producers*: Paul F. Heard/J. Raymond Friedgen;
Director: Paul F. Heard; *Screenplay*: J. Raymond Friedgen/Helene
Turner/Herbert G. Luft/Paul F. Heard; *Music*: Louis Forbes; *Camera*:
S.T. Chow; *Editor*: Helene Turner; *Cast*: Jack Kelly (Steve Whelen);
MAY WYNN (CHU LAN); Richard Loo (Li Noon); Lo Lita Shek (Sou May);
Gerald Young (Louis Jordan); James Hudwon (Jim Long); Michael Bulmer
(Inspector Stuart).

   When Steve Whelen goes to Hong Kong to discover why his once
profitable tea business is in trouble he finds more than he bargained
for. He meets Chu Lan, the secretary of his lawyer, Louis Jordan,
who has been handling his business affairs and helping himself to

Steve's money while exporting opium. Chu Lan falls in love with
Steve and helps him bring Jordan to justice.

HONG KONG CONFIDENTIAL   Eurasian--Chinese   1958/Drama

United Artists; 67 min.; *Producer*: Robert E. Kent; *Director*: Edward L.
Cahn; *Screenplay*: Orville H. Hampton; *Music*: Paul Sawtell/Bert
Shefter; *Camera*: Kenneth Peach; *Editor*: Edward Mann; *Cast*: Gene Barry
(Casey Reed); Beverly Tyler (Fay Wells); *ALLISON HAYES (ELENA
MARTINE)*; Noel Drayton (Owen Howard); Ed Kemmer (Frank Paige);
Michael Pate (John Blanchard); Rico Alaniz (Fernando); W. Beal Wong
(Muto); Mel Prestige (Mao); King Calder (Dan Young).

Elena Martine is a suspect in the kidnapping of an Arab prince.
Elena and her boyfriend, Owen Howard, help to expose the real kid-
napper, Frank Paige.

HONKY   Black   1971/Drama

Jack H. Harris Enterprises; 89 min.; *Producers*: Will Chaney/Ron
Roth; *Director*: William A. Graham; *Screenplay*: Will Chaney; *Music*:
Quincy Jones; *Camera*: Ralph Woolsey; *Editor*: Jim Benson; *Cast*: BRENDA
SYKES (SHEILA SMITH); John Neilson (Wayne Divine); Mai Danziger
(Sharon); John Lasell (Archer Divine); William Marshall (Dr. Craig
Smith); *Amentha Dymally (Mrs. Smith)*; Marion Ross (Mrs. Divine).

Sheila and her white boyfriend, Wayne Divine, decide to leave
their parental and high school troubles behind and hitchhike to
California. Along the way they are terroized by a gang. Wayne is
beaten up and Sheila raped. They are left able only to look at each
other.

THE HORSE SOLDIERS   Black   1959/Western

United Artists; 119 min.; *Producer*: John Lee Mahin; *Director*: John
Ford; *Screenplay*: John Lee Mahin/Martin Rackin; *Music*: David Buttolph;
Camera: William H. Clothier; *Editor*: Jack Murray; *Cast*: John Wayne
(Colonel John Marlowe); William Holden (Major Hank Kendall); Constance
Towers (Hannah Kendall); *ALTHEA GIBSON (LUKEY)*; Hoot Gibson (Brown);
Anna Lee (Mrs. Buford); Russell Simpson (Sheriff Captain Henry
Goodboy).

Lukey is a maid to Hannah Kendall.

THE HORSEMEN   Afghan   1971/Adventure

Columbia; 109 min.; *Producer*: Edward Lewis; *Director*: John Franken-
heimer; *Screenplay*: Dalton Trumbo; *Music*; Georges Delarue; *Camera*:
Claude Renoir; *Editor*: Harold F. Kress; *Cast*: Omar Sharif (Uraz);
LEIGH TAYLOR-YOUNG (ZEREH); Jack Palance (Tursen); David De (Mukhi);
Peter Jeffrey (Hayatal); Mohammed Shams (Osman Bey); George Murcell

Jane Russell, *Hot Blood* (Columbia, 1956)

(Mizrar); Eric Pohlmann (Merchant of Kandahar).

After breaking his leg in a Buzkashi game, the feverish Uraz is nursed by Zereh. When Uraz recovers he realizes that Zereh is an untouchable and gives her to his servant, Mukhi. Zereh persuades Mukhi to kill Uraz so they can take his champion stallion, but Uraz takes them prisoner. Uraz eventually submits to his attraction to Zereh. They make love and then Uraz throws her out.

HOT BLOOD   Gypsy   1956/Drama

Columbia; 85 min.; *Producers*: Howard Welsch/Harry Tatelman; *Director*: Nicholas Ray; *Screenplay*: Jesse Lasky, Jr.; *Music*: Les Baxter; *Camera*: Ray June; *Editor*: Otto Ludwig; *Cast*: *JANE RUSSELL (ANNIE CALDASH)*; Cornel Wilde (Stephan Torino); Luther Adler (Marco Torino); Joseph Calleia (Papa Theordore); Makhail Rasumny (Old Johnny); *Nina Koshetz (Nita Johnny)*; *Helen Wescott (Velma)*; Jamie Russell (Xano); Wally Russell (Bimbo).

Marco Torino buys Annie Caldash as a bride for his brother Stephan, who is tricked into marrying Annie. Although Stephan prefers dancing to marriage, he eventually becomes a willing husband.

HOT PEPPER   South American   1933/Comedy

20th Century-Fox; 76 min;; *Director*: John G. Blystone; *Screenplay*: Barry Connors/Philip Klein; *Camera*: Charles Clarke; *Cast*: Edmund Lowe (Quirt); Victor McLaglen (Flagg); *LUPE VELEZ (PEPPER)*; El Brendel (Olsen); Boothe Howard (Trigger Thorne); Lilian Bond (Hortense); Gloria Ray (Lily).

Pepper is a singer and dancer best described as audacious/reckless/extraordinary. She is also the object of Quirt's and Flagg's desire.

HOTEL SAHARA   Arab--Egyptian   1951/Comedy

United Artists; 96 min.; *Producer*: George H. Brown; *Director*: Ken Annakin; *Screenplay*: Patrick Kirwan/George H. Brown; *Music*: Benjamin Frankel; *Camera*: David Harcourt; *Editor*: Alfred Roome; *Cast*: *YVONNE DE CARLO (YASMIN)*; Peter Ustinov (Emad); David Tomlinson (Captain Puffin Cheynie); Roland Culver (Major Randall); Albert Lieven (German Lieutenant); Bill Owen (Private Binns); Sydney Tafler (Corp. Puller); Tom Gil (Private O'Brien); Mireille Perrey (Madame Pallas); Ferdy Mayne (Yusef); Guido Lorraine (Italian Captain).

Yasmin saves her fiance Emad's desert hotel from destruction by cleverly adapting allegiance to the leaders of the various invading armies in Egypt during World War II.

HOUSE OF BAMBOO   Japanese   1955/Drama

20th Century-Fox; 102 min.; *Producer*: Buddy Adler; *Director*: Samuel
Fuller; *Screenplay*: Harry Kleiner; *Music*: Leigh Harline; *Camera*:
Joe MacDonald; *Editor*: James B. Clark; *Cast*: Robert Ryan (Sandy
Dawson); Robert Stack (Eddie Spanier); *SHIRLEY YAMAGUCHI (MARIKO)*;
Cameron Mitchell (Griff); Brad Dexter (Captain Hanson); Sessue
Hayakawa (Inspector Kita); Biff Elliot (Webber); Sandro Giglio
(Ceram); Harry Carey (John); Peter Gray (Willy).

Kimono girl Mariko is married to a man of questionable character.
After a gang of thieves kills her husband, Eddie Spanier convinces
her to continue as a kimono girl to help catch the murderers. She
is roughed up by Spanier and the murderer, Sandy Dawson. After the
criminals are caught, Spanier and Mariko declare their love for each
other.

HUMAN CARGO   Mexican   1936/Drama

20th Century-Fox; 66 min.; *Producer*: Sol M. Wurtzel; *Director*: Allan
Dwan; *Screenplay*: Jefferson Parker; *Music*: Sammy Kaylin; *Camera*:
Daniel B. Clark; *Editor*: Louis Loeffler; *Cast*: Claire Trevor (Bonnie
Brewster); Brian Donlevy (Packy Campbell); Alan Dinchart (Lionel
Crocker); Ralph Morgan (Attorney Carey); Helen Troy (Susie); *RITA
CANZINO [HAYWORTH] (CARMEN)*.

The story focuses on smuggling illegal aliens from Mexico.
Carmen is an alien who is killed during the operation.

THE HUNCHBACK OF NOTRE DAME   Gypsy   1939/Drama

RKO; 115 min.; *Producer*: Pandro S. Berman; *Director*: William
Dieterle; *Screenplay*: Sonya Levien; *Music*: Alfred Newman; *Camera*:
Joseph Walker; *Editors*: William Hamilton/Robert Wise; *Cast*: Charles
Laughton (Quasimodo); Sir Cedric Hardwicke (Frollo); Thomas Mitchell
(Cloping); *MAUREEN O'HARA (ESMERALDA)*; Edmund O'Brien (Gringoire);
Alan Marshall (Phoebus); Walter Hampden (Archbishop); Katherine
Alexander (Fleur's mother).

See next entry.

THE HUNCHBACK OF NOTRE DAME   Gypsy   1957/Drama

Allied Artists; 103 min.; *Producers*: Robert & Raymond Hakim;
Director: Jean Delanney; *Screenplay*: Jean Aurenche/Jacques Prevert;
Music: Georges Auric; *Camera*: Michael Kelber; *Editor*: Henri Taverns;
Cast: *GINA LOLLABRIDGIDA (ESMERALDA)*; Anthony Quinn (Quasimodo);
Jean Danet (Phoebus); Alain Cuny (Claude Frollo); Danielle Dumont
(Fleur de Lys); Jean Tissler (Louis XI).

Esmeralda is the gypsy loved by the deformed hunchback bell
ringer Quasimodo.

THE HURRICANE   Polynesian   1937/Adventure

United Artists; 108 min.; *Producer*: Samuel Goldwyn; *Directors*: John
Ford/Stuart Heisler; *Screenplay*: Dudley Nichols/Oliver P. Garrett;
Camera: Bert Glennon; *Editor*: Lloyd Nosler; *Cast*: *DOROTHY LAMOUR
(MARAMA)*; Jon Hall (Terangi); Mary Astor (Madame DeLaage); Thomas
Mitchell (Doctor Kersaint); C. Aubrey Smith (Father Paul); Raymond
Massey (Governor DeLaage); John Carradine (Warden); Jerome Cowan
(Captain Nagle); Chief Mehevi Al Kikume); *Mamo Clark (Hitia)*; *Movita
Castenada (Aral)*; *Flora Hayes (Mama Rua)*; *Mary Shaw (Marunga)*.

Marama is the wife of Terangi, who has been unjustly imprisoned
by the island's nasty governor. He escapes again and again but is
always brought back, which increases his sentence. He kills a sadis-
tic guard, but is saved by a hurricane which destroys almost everything and everyone except Marama and Terangi.

HURRICANE ISLAND   Native American   1951/Adventure

Columbia; 71 min.; *Producer*: Sam Katzman; *Director*: Lew Landers;
Screenplay: David Mathews; *Camera*: Lester White; *Editor*: Richard
Fantl; *Cast*: Jon Hall (Captain Carlos Montalvo); Marie Windsor (Jane
Bolton); Marc Lawrence (Angus Macready); Romo Vincent (Jose); Edgar
Barrier (Ponce de Leon); Karen Randle (Maria); *JO GILBERT (OKAHLA)*;
Nelson Leigh (Padre); Marshall Reed (Rolfe); Don Harvey (Valco); Rick
Vallin (Coba).

Okahla leads a tribe of Indians who guard a spring that may be
the legendary Fountain of Youth which Ponce de Leon seeks. Okahla
breaks the sacred trust by giving the injured Ponce de Leon water
from the spring. As a result, she dies and the spring dries up.

HURRICANE SMITH   Polynesian   1952/Adventure

Paramount; 90 min.; *Producer*: Nat Holt; *Director*: Jerry Hopper;
Screenplay: Frank Gruber; *Camera*: Ray Rennahan; *Editor*: Frank Bracht;
Cast: *YVONNE DE CARLO (LUANA)*; John Ireland (Hurricane Smith); James
Craig (Gorvahlsen); Forrest Tucker (Dan McGuire); Lyle Bettger
(Clobb); Richard Arlen (Brundage); Mike Kellin (Dicer); Murray
Matheson (Dr. Whitmore); Henry Brandon (Sam); Emile Meyer (Captain
Raikes); Stuart Randell (Matt Ward).

Hurricane Smith joins with singer/dancer Luana to protect his
fortune from theiving pirates. They fall in love.

HURRY SUNDOWN   Black   1967/Drama

Paramount; 146 min.; *Producer/Director*: Otto Preminger; *Screenplay*:
Thomas C. Ryan/Horton Foote; *Music*: Hugo Montenegro; *Camera*: Milton
Krasner/Loyal Griggs; *Editors*: Louis R. Loeffler/James D. Wells;
Cast: Michael Caine (Henry Warren); Jane Fonda (Julie Ann Warren);
John Phillip Law (Rad McDowell); *DIAHANN CARROLL (VIVIAN THURLOW)*;

Robert Hooks (Reeve Scott); Faye Dunaway (Lois McDowell); Burgess
Meredith (Judge Purcell); Jim Backus (Carter Sillens); Robert Reed
(Lars Finchley); *Beah Richards (Rose Scott)*; Rex Ingram (Professor
Thurlow); Madeleine Sherwood (Eula Purcell).

Vivian Thurlow is a schoolteacher and the daughter of the town's
most respected Black citizen. She helps Reeve Scott prove that he
owns his farmland so that Henry Warren cannot, with the help of the
local bigots, take it away from him. Henry dynamites a dam to flood
the land. However, his own son is caught in the flood and drowns.
By this time Reeve and Vivian have fallen in love and plan to rebuild
Reeve's farm.

HUSBANDS   Chinese   1970/Drama

Columbia; 138 min.; *Producer*: Al Ruban; *Director/Screenplay*: John
Cassavetes; *Camera*: Victor Kemper; *Editor*: Peter Tanner; *Cast*: Ben
Gazzara (Harry); Peter Falk (Archie); John Cassavetes (Gus); Jenny
Runacre (Mary Tynan); Jenny Lee Wright (Pearl Billingham); *NOELLE
KAO (JULIE)*; John Kullers (Red); Meta Shaw (Annie); Leola Harlow
(Leola); Delores Delmar (The Countess); Eleanor Zee (Mrs. Hines);
Claire Malis (Stuart's Wife).

While Harry, Gus, and Archie are on vacation from their wives,
Archie begins an affair with Julie in spite of the fact that she
speaks no English.

I LIVE FOR LOVE   Latin American   1935/Musical

Warner Brothers; 64 min.; *Producer*: Bryan Fox; *Director*: Busby
Berkeley; *Screenplay*: Jerry Wald/Julius J. Epstein/Robert Andrews;
Music: Allie Wrubel/Mort Dixon; *Camera*: George Barnes; *Editor*: Terry
Morse; *Cast*: *DOLORES DEL RIO (DONNA ALVAREZ)*; Everett Marshall (Roger
Kerry); Guy Kibbee (George Henderson); Allen Jenkins (Jim McNamara);
Berton Churchill (Howard Fabian); Hobart Cavanaugh (Townsend C.
Morgan); Don Alvarado (Rico Cesaro); Mary Treen (Clementine).

After initially disliking American singer Roger Kerry, Donna
Alvarez falls in love with him. She leaves her dancing partner and
lover, Rico, at the altar.

I PASSED FOR WHITE   Black   1960/Drama

Allied Artists; 91 min.; *Producer/Director/Screenplay*: Fred M. Wilcox;
Music: Johnny Williams; *Camera*: George Folsey; *Editor*: George White;
Cast: *SONYA WILDE (LILA BROWNELL)*; James Franciscus (Rick Leyton);
Pat Michon (Sally Roberts); Elizabeth Council (Mrs. Leyton); Griffin
Crafts (Mr. Leyton); Isabelle Cooley (Bertha); James Lydon (Jay); Lon
Ballantyne (Chuck Brownell); Freida Shaw (Gram); Thomas B. Henry (Dr.
Merrett).

Tired of racial prejudice, the light-skinned Bernice Lee decides
to pass. She moves to New York, changes her name to Lila Brownell,
and marries wealthy Rick Leyton. She does not tell Rick the truth
about her background, and lies pile up until she becomes pregnant and
gives birth. Her first concern is the color of the baby's skin,
rather than its poor health. The baby dies, and Rick accuses her of
having an affair with a Black man (who is really her brother).
Realizing that she can no longer live a life of lies, she returns
home to her family.

IF HE HOLLERS, LET HIM GO   Black   1968/Drama

Cinerama; 111 min.; *Producer/Director/Screenplay*: Charles Martin;
Music: Harry Sukman; *Camera*: William W. Spencer; *Editor*: Richard
Brockway; *Cast*: Dana Wynter (Ellen Whitlock); Raymond St. Jacques
(James Lake); Kevin McCarthy (Leslie Whitlock); *BARBARA McNAIR
(LILY)*; Arthur O'Connell (Prosecutor); John Russell (Sheriff); Ann
Prentiss (Thelma Wilson); Royal Dano (Carl Blair); Steve Sandor
(Harry); Susan Seaforth (Sally Blair).

Lily once had an affair with Lake, who recently escaped from
prison. Although she has since married, she agrees to help him
establish his innocence.

IMITATION OF LIFE   Black   1934/Melodrama

Universal; 116 min.; *Director*: John M. Stahl; *Screenplay*: William
Hurlburt; *Music*: Heinz Roemheld; *Camera*: Merritt Gerstad; *Editor*:
Philip Cahn/Maurice White; *Cast*: Claudette Colbert (Beatrice Pullman);
Warren William (Stephen Archer); Ned Sparks (Elmer); *LOUISE BEAVERS
(AUNT DELILAH)*; Baby Jane (Jessie Pullman at 3); Marilyn Knoylden
(Jessie at 8); Rochelle Hudson (Jessie at 18); *Sebie Hendricks (Peola
Johnson at 4) Dorothy Black (Peola at 9) FREDI WASHINGTON (PEOLA at
19)*; Alan Hale (Martin); Clarence Hummell Wilson (Landlord); Henry
Armetta (Painter).

Aunt Delilah goes into business with Beatrice Pullman, who turns
Delilah's pancakes into a booming enterprise, making them both
extremely wealthy. However, Delilah's problems are not solved by
wealth because her daughter, Peola, is a light-skinned Black woman
who has difficulty reconciling herself to being Black--especially
after growing up equal to Beatrice's daughter, Jessie. Peola and
Delilah have a falling out when Peola refuses to accept her Black
identity and starts to pass herself off as white and date white men.
Peola returns home when Delilah dies.

IMITATION OF LIFE   Black   1958/Melodrama

Universal; 125 min.; *Producer*: Ross Hunter; *Director*: Douglas Sirk;
Screenplay: Eleanore Griffin; *Music*: Frank Skinner; *Camera*: Russell
Metty; *Editor*: Milton Carruth; *Cast*: Lana Turner (Lora Meredith);
John Gavin (Steve Archer); *JUANITA MOORE (ANNIE JOHNSON)*; Sandra Dee

(Susie Meredith at 16): Terry Burnham (Susie at 6); *SUSAN KOHNER*
(SARAH JANE JOHNSON at 16); *Karen Dicker (Sarah Jane at 8)*; Dan
O'Herlihy (David Edwards); Robert Alda (Allen Loomis); Troy Donahue
(Frankie).

This remake of the 1934 film is basically the same, except for
names and professions.   In this version Lora Meredith (Beatrice
Pullman) is an actress who achieves success and wealth and Annie
Johnson (Aunt Delilah) is her loyal servant.

IMPACT   Chinese   1949/Drama

United Artists; 111 min.; *Producer*: Leo C. Popkin; *Director*: Arthur
Lubin; *Screenplay*: Dorothy Reid/Jay Dratler; *Camera*: Ernest Laslo;
Editor: Arthur Nadel; *Cast*: Brian Donlevy (Walter Williams); Ella
Raines (Marsha Peters); Charles Coburn (Lt. Quincy); Helen Walker
(Irene Williams); *ANNA MAY WONG (SU LIN)*; Mae Marsh (Mrs. Peters);
Tony Barrett (Jim Torrance); William Wright (Capt. Callahan); Philip
Ahn (Ah Sing); Art Baker (Eldredge); Erskine Sanford (Dr. Bender).

Su Lin works as a maid for golddigger Irene Williams, who plans
to murder her husband.

IN CALIENTE   Mexican   1935/Musical

Warner Brothers; 84 min.; *Director*: Lloyd Bacon; *Screenplay*: Jerry
Wald; *Camera*: Sol Polito/George Baines; *Editor*: Jimmy Gibbons; *Cast*:
DOLORES DEL RIO (RITA GOMEZ); Pat O'Brien (Larry MacArthur); Leo
Carillo (Jose Gomez); Edward Everett Horton (Harold Brandon); Glenda
Farrell (Clara).

Rita Gomez is furious when newspaper man Larry MacArthur criti-
cizes her dancing ability. Rita plans to get even, but soon she and
Larry are in love.

IN LOVE AND WAR   Eurasian   1958/War Drama

20th Century-Fox; 111 min.; *Producer*: Jerry Wald; *Director*: Philip
Dunne; *Screenplay*: Edward Anhalt; *Music*: Hugo Friedhofer; *Camera*: Leo
Tover; *Editor*: William Reynolds; *Cast*: Robert Wagner (Frankie
O'Neill); Dana Wynter (Sue Trumbell); Jeffrey Hunter (Nico Kantaylis);
Hope Lange (Andrea Lenaine); *FRANCE NUYEN (KALAI DUCANNE)*; Bradford
Dillman (Alan Newcombe); Sheree North (Lorraine); Mort Sahl (Danny
Krieger); Sebastian Cabot (D. Everett Styles); Steven Gant (Babe
Ricarno).

Alan Newcombe, a World War II marine, falls in love with nurse
Kalai Ducanne.

IN OLD AMARILLO   Mexican   1951/Musical

Republic; 67 min.; *Producer*: Edward J. White; *Director*: William
Whitney; *Screenplay*: Sloan Nibley; *Camera*: Jack Marta; *Editor*: Tony
Martinelli; *Cast*: Roy Rogers; *ESTELITA RODRIGUEZ (PEPITA)*; Penny
Edwards (Madge Adams); Pinky Lee (Pinky); Roy Barcroft (Clint
Burnside); Pierre Watkin (George B. Hills); Ken Howell (Phillip
Hills); Elizabeth Risdon (Granny Adams); Triggers; Bullet.

        Pepita, Pinky's girlfriend, is a singer.

THE INCIDENT   Black   1967/Drama

20th Century-Fox; 106 min.; *Producer*: Monroe Sachson; *Director*: Larry
Peerce; *Screenplay*: Nicholas E. Baehr; *Music*: Charles Fox; *Camera*:
Gerald Hirschfeld; *Editor*: Armond Lebowitz; *Cast*: Tony Musante (Joe
Ferrone); Martin Sheen (Artie Connors); Beau Bridges (PFC Felix
Teflinger); Brock Peters (Arnold Robinson); *RUBY DEE (JOAN ROBINSON)*;
Jack Gifford (Sam Beckerman); Thelma Ritter (Bertha Beckerman); Ed
McMahon (Bill Wilks); Diana Van Der Vlis (Helen Wilks).

        Joan Robinson and her husband are among the passengers terror-
ized by two punks on a New York subway.

INDIAN AGENT   Native American   1948/Western

RKO; 64 min.; *Producer*: Herman Schlom; *Director*: Lesley Selander;
Screenplay: Lesley Selander; *Camera*: J. Roy Hunt; *Editor*: Les
Millbrook; *Cast*: Tim Holt (Dave); Noah Beery, Jr. (Redfox); Richard
Martin (Chito); Nan Leslie (Ellen); Harry Woods (Carter); Richard
Powers (Hutchins); *CLAUDIA DRAKE (TURQUOISE)*; Robert Bray (Nichols);
Lee White (Inky); Bud Osborne (Sheriff); Iron Eyes Cody (Wovoka).

        Turquoise is the local Indian girl.

THE INDIAN FIGHTER   Native American   1955/Western

United Artists; 88 min.; *Producer*: William Schorr; *Director*: Andre
de Toth; *Screenplay*: Frank Davis/Ben Hecht; *Music*: Franz Waxman;
Camera: Wilfred M. Kline; *Editor*: Richard Cahoon; *Cast*: Kirk Douglas
(Johnny Hawks); *ELSA MARTINELLI (ONAHTI)*; Walter Abel (Capt. Trask);
Walter Matthau (Wes Todd); Diana Douglas (Susan Rogers); Eduard Franz
(Red Cloud); Lon Chaney (Chivington); Alan Hale (Will Crabtree);
Elisha Cook (Briggs); Harry Landers (Grey Wolf); Michael Winkelman
(Tommy Rogers).

        Johnny Hawks, leader of a wagon train, falls in love with Onahti.

INDIAN PAINT   Native American   1965/Western

Eagle American Film/Crown International; 91 min.; *Producer*: Gene
Gorec; *Director*: Norman Foster; *Screenplay*: Norman Foster; *Music*:

Marlin Skiles; *Camera*: Floyd Crosby; *Editors*: Robert Crawford, Sr./
George White; *Cast*: Johnny Crawford (Nishko); Jay Silverheels (Chief
Hevatanu); Pat Hogan (Sutamakis); Robert Crawford, Jr. (Wacopi);
George J. Lewis (Nopawallo); *JOAN HOLLMARK (AMATULA)*; Bill Blackwell
(Sutako); Robert Crawford, Sr. (Motopi); Al Doney (Lataso); *Cindy
Siler (Petala)*.

The story of a wild stallion and a young boy's initiation into
manhood. Nishko's mother, Amatula, is bitten by a snake, and he
makes a sacrifice to save her life.

THE IRON MISTRESS   Creole   1952/Adventure

Warner Brothers; 109 min.; *Producer*: Henry Blanke; *Director*: Gordon
Douglas; *Screenplay*: James R. Webb; *Music*: Max Steiner; *Camera*: John
Seitz; *Editor*: Alan Crosland; *Cast*: Alan Ladd (Jim Bowie); *VIRGINIA
MAYO (JUDALON DE BORNAY)*; Joseph Calleia (Juan Moreno); Phyllis Kirk
(Ursula de Veramendi); Alf Kjellin (Philippe de Cabanal); Douglas
Dick (Marcisse de Bornay).

Jim Bowie is led astray by Judalon de Bornay—a woman from the
wrong side of the tracks. This relationship inspires Bowie to design
a knife with which to protect himself. Eventually he decides that
the seedy side of life is not for him, and he marries Ursula de
Veramendi, the governor's daughter.

ISLAND IN THE SUN   West Indian   1957/Drama

20th Century-Fox; 123 min.; *Producer*: Darryl F. Zanuck; *Director*:
Robert Rossen; *Screenplay*: Alfred Hayes; *Music*: Malcolm Arnold;
Camera: F.A. Young; *Editor*: Reginald Beck; *Cast*: James Mason (Maxwell
Fleury); Joan Fontaine (Mavis); *DOROTHY DÀNDRIDGE (MARGOT SEATON)*;
JOAN COLLINS (JOCELYN); Michael Rennie (Hilary Carson); Diana Wynyard
(Mrs. Fleury); John Williams (Col. Whittingham); Stephan Boyd (Euan
Templeton); Patricia Owens (Sylvia); Basil Sydney (Julian Fleury);
John Justin (David Archer); Ronald Squire (The Governor); Hartley
Power (Bradshaw); Harry Belafonte (David Boyeur).

Margot Seaton and David Boyeur are lovers until Margot meets
David Archer, the governor's white assistant, and falls in love with
him. David also finds a white lover in Mavis, another of the governor's aides. Because of racism on the island Margot and Archer leave
to live in England, apparently a more racially tolerant country.
Boyeur and Mavis end their relationship because of racial problems.
Jocelyn and Euan Templeton fall in love and Jocelyn becomes pregnant.
Near disaster occurs when it is discovered that Jocelyn has a Black
heritage.

ISLAND OF BLUE DOLPHINS   Native American   1964/Adventure

Universal; 93 min.; *Producer*: Robert B. Radnitz; *Director*: James B.
Clark; *Screenplay*: Ted Sherdeman/Jane Klove; *Music*: Paul Sawtell;

Camera: Leo Tover; *Editor*: Ted J. Kent; *Cast*: *CELIA KAYE (KARANA)*;
Larry Domasin (Ramo); *Ann Daniel (Tutok)*; George Kennedy (Aleut
Captain); Carlos Romero (Chowig); Hal Jon Norman (Kimki); *Julie Payne
(Lurai)*; Junior (Rontou, the dog); Martin Garralaga (The Priest);
Alex Montoyo (Spanish Captain).

An unusual film which focuses on the life of a Native American
woman living alone on an island and managing her life for eighteen
years. Karana and her brother Ramo are marooned on an island after
the Aleut Captain massacres the rest of her tribe. When a pack of
wild dogs kills her brother, Karana makes a bow and arrow and wounds
the leader, Rontou but after a change of heart saves his life.
Several years later another tribe comes to the island, but Karana
refuses to leave. Years later Rontou dies and she adopts another dog,
Rontou-Aru (son of Rontou). When a missionary comes to the island
Karana and her animals decide to leave.

THE ISLAND OF DR. MOREAU   Panamanian   1977/Thriller

American International; 104 min.; *Producers*: John Temple-Smith/Skip
Steloff; *Director*: Don Taylor; *Screenplay*: John Herman Shaner/Al
Mamrus; *Music*: Laurence Rosenthal; *Camera*: Gerry Fisher; *Editor*:
Marion Rothman; *Cast*: Burt Lancaster (Dr. Moreau); Michael York
(Braddock); Nigel Davenport (Montgomery); *BARBARA CARRERA (MARIA)*;
Richard Basehart (Saver of the Law); Nick Cravet (M'Ling); The Great
John "L" (Boar Man); Bob Ozman (Bull Man); Fumio Demura (Hyena Man);
John Gillespie (Tiger Man).

Maria is an ex-prostitute now living as companion (non-sexual)
to the evil Dr. Moreau. Maria falls in love with Braddock, a shipwrecked sailor who is determined to stop Moreau from further experi-
mentation--especially when it comes to himself.

ISLAND OF LOST MEN   Chinese   1939/Drama

Paramount; 63 min.; *Producer*: Eugene Zukor; *Director*: Kurt Neumann;
Screenplay: William R. Lipman/Horace McCoy; *Camera*: Karl Struss;
Editor: Ellsworth Hoagland; *Cast*: *ANNA MAY WONG (KIM LING)*; J.
Carrol Naish (Gregory Prin); Eric Blore (Herbert); Ernest Truex
(Frobenius); Anthony Quinn (Chang Tai); William Haude (Hambly);
Broderick Crawford (Tex Ballister); Rudolf Forster (Professor Sen);
Richard Loo (General Ling).

Kim Ling is the daughter of General Ling who fled China when he
was falsely accused of a crime. Kim attempts to clear his name with
the help of Chang Tai. Together they fight the evil Gregory Prin and
succeed in clearing the General.

ISLAND OF LOST SOULS   Island/Jungle Exotic   1933/Thriller

Paramount; 74 min.; *Director*: Erle C. Kenton; *Screenplay*: Waldemar
Young/Philip Wylie; *Camera*: Karl Struss; *Cast*: Charles Laughton (Dr.

Moreau); Richard Arlen (Edward Parker); Leila Hyams (Ruth Walker);
Bela Lugosi (Sayer of the Law); *KATHLEEN BURKE (LOTA)*; Arthur Hohl
(Montgomery); Stanley Fields (Captain Davies); Robert Kortman (Hogan);
Tetsu Komai (M'Ling); Hans Steinke (Ouran); Harry Ekezian (Gola);
Rosemary Grimes (Samoan Girl); Paul Hurst (Captain Donahue); George
Irving (American Consul).

   Originally a panther Lota is the result of Dr. Moreau's experi-
ments transforming animals into humans. Dr. Moreau wants to mate
Lota with Edward Parker to create a new species of humans.

ISLE OF ESCAPE   Island Exotic   1930/Drama

Warner Brothers; 62 min.; *Director*: Howard Bretherton; *Screenplay*:
Lucien Hubbard/J. Grubb Alexander; *Cast*: Monte Blue (David Wade);
MYRNA LOY (MOIRA); Betty Compson (Stella Blackney); Noah Beery (Tom
Shane); Ivan Simpson (Judge); Jack Ackroyd (Hank); *Nina Quartero
(Loru)*; Duke Kahanamoku (Manua); Rose Dione (Ma Blackney).

   Moira is a loose woman on the island. Her goal is to go to bed
with David Wade, who snubs her. Loru is a servant.

IT HAPPENED OUT WEST   Mexican   1937/Western

20th Century-Fox; 70 min.; *Producer*: Sol Lesser; *Director*: Howard
Bretherton; *Screenplay*: Earl Snell/Harry Chandlee; *Music*: Harold Bell
Wright; *Camera*: Harry Neumann; *Editor*: Olive Hofman; *Cast*: Paul Kelly
(Dick Howe); Judith Allen (Anne Martin); Johnny Arthur (Thaddeus
Cruickshank); Leroy Mason (Burt Travis); *NINA COMPANA (MARIA)*; Steve
Clemento (Pedro); Frank Larve (Sheriff); Reginald Barlow (Middleton).

   Not enough information was available to describe this role
accurately.

JACK AHOY   Latin American   1935/Comedy

Gaumont British Production; 70 min.; *Director*: Walter Forde; *Screen-
play*: Sidney Gilliat/Leslie Arliss; *Music*: Henry M. Woods; *Cast*: Jack
Hulbert (Jack Ponsonby); Nancy O'Neil (Patricia); Alfred Drayton
(Admiral Fraser); *TAMARA DESNI (CONCHITA)*; Henry Peterson (Larios);
Sam Wilkinson (Dodger).

   Conchita is a vamp.

THE JACKIE ROBINSON STORY   Black   1950/Biography

Eagle Lion; 76 min.; *Producer*: Mort Briskin; *Director*: Alfred E.
Green; *Screenplay*: Lawrence Taylor/Arthur Mann; *Camera*: Ernest
Laszlo; *Editor*: Arthur H. Nadel; *Cast*: Jackie Robinson; *RUBY DEE (RAE
ROBINSON)*; Minor Watson (Branch Rickey); *Louise Beavers (Jackie's*

Mother); Richard Lane (Hopper); Harry Shannon (Charlie); Ben Lessy (Shorty); Bill Spaulding; Billy Wayne (Clyde Sukeforth); Joel Fluellen (Mack Robinson).

The story of Jackie Robinson, the first Black man to play in major-league baseball. Rai marries Jackie and gives him aid and comfort.

JAGUAR   Latin American   1956/Adventure

Republic; 66 min.; *Producers*: Mickey Rooney/Maurice Duke; *Director*: George Blair; *Screenplay*: John Fenton Murray/Benedict Freeman; *Music*: Van Alexander; *Camera*: Bud Thackery; *Editor*: Cliff Bell; *Cast*: Sabu (Juano); *CHIQUITA (RITA)*; Barton MacLane (Steve Bailey); Jonathan Hale (Dr. Powell); Touch Connors (Marty Lang); Fortunio Bonanova (Francisco Servente); Jay Novello (Tupi); Nacho Galindo (Garcia Solimos).

Rita is a dancer and the romantic interest of Juano.

JAPANESE WAR BRIDE   Japanese   1952/Drama

20th Century-Fox; 91 min.; *Producers*: Joseph Bernhard/Anson Bond; *Director*: King Vidor; *Screenplay*: Catherine Turney; *Music*: Emil Newmann; *Camera*: Lionel Lundon; *Editor*: Terry Morse; *Cast*: *SHIRLEY YAMAGUCHI (TAE SHIMIZU)*; Don Taylor (Jim Sterling); Cameron Mitchell (Art Sterling); Marie Windsor (Fran Sterling); James Bell (Ed Sterling); Louise Lorimer (Harriet Sterling); Philip Ahn (Eitaro Shimizu); Lane Nakano (Shiro Hasagawa); *May Takasugi (Emma Hasagawa)*; Sybil Merritt (Emily Shafer); Orley Lindgren (Ted Sterling); George Wallace (Woody Blacker); *Susie Matsumoto (Tae's Mother)*.

Tae Shimizu is the new bride of American Jim Sterling. She has difficulty dealing with racial prejudice and the vicious gossip her sister-in-law spreads about her.

JASSY   Gypsy   1947/Drama

Universal-International; 96 min.; *Producer*: Sydney Box; *Director*: Bernard Knowles; *Screenplay*: Dorothy & Campbell Christie/Geoffrey Kerr; *Music*: Louis Levy; *Camera*: Geoffrey Unsworth; *Editor*: Charles Knott; *Cast*: *MARGARET LOCKWOOD (JASSY WOODROFFE)*; Patricia Roc (Dilys Helmar); Basil Sydney (Nick Helmar); Dermot Walsh (Barney Hatton); Dennis Price (Christopher Hatton); Esma Cannon (Lindy); John Laurie (Woodroffe); Linden Travers (Mrs. Helman); Nora Swinburne (Mrs. Hatton); Grey Blake (Stephen Fennell).

Village girl Jassy is tormented because of her gypsy heritage. She is befriended by Christopher Hatton who brings her home and employs her as a servant. Jassy and Barney soon develop a relationship. This disturbs Mrs. Hatton, who sends Jassy away to school. There she becomes friendly with Dilys Helmar, the daughter of Squire

Nick Helmar. Dilys brings Jassy home and Jassy marries the Squire.
When Nick dies Jassy is accused of murder. She is saved by a servant
at her trial. She finally finds true love with Barney Hatton.

JAVA HEAD   Chinese   1935/Drama

First Division; 70 min.; *Producer*: Basil Dean; *Director*: J. Walter
Ruben; *Screenplay*: Martin Brown/Grodon Wellesley; *Music*: Ernest
Irving; *Camera*: Robert G. Martin; *Cast*: ANNA MAY WONG (TAOU YUEN);
Elizbeth Allan (Nettie Vollar); Edmund Gwenn (Jeremy Ammidon); John
Loder (Gerrit Ammidon); Herbert Lomas (Barzil Dunsack); George Curzon
(Edward Dunsack); John Marriner (John Stone); Gray Blake (Roger
Brevard); Roy Emerton (Broadrick); Amy Brandon Thomas (Rhoda); Frances
Carson (Kate).

    Taou Yuen is brought to an English fishing village to become the
wife of Gerrit Ammidon. Taou Yuen commits suicide so Gerrit can
marry an English girl.

JEREMIAH JOHNSON   Native American--Flathead   1972/Western

Warner Brothers; 108 min.; *Producer*: Joe Wizan; *Director*: Sydney
Pollack; *Screenplay*: John Milius/Edward Anhalt; *Music*: John Rubin-
stein; *Camera*: Andrew (Duke) Callaghan; *Editor*: Thomas Stanford;
Cast: Robert Redford (Jeremiah Johnson); Will Geer (Bear Claw);
Stefan Gierasch (Del Gue); DELLE BOLTON (SWAN); Allyn Ann McLerie
(Caleb's Mother); Charles Tyner (Robidoux); Josh Albee (Caleb);
Joaquin Martinez (Paints His Shirt Red); Paul Benedict (Reverend);
Matt Clark (Qualen); Richard Angarola (Lebeaux); Jack Colvin (Lt.
Mulvey).

    Ex-soldier Jeremiah Johnson decides to give up the comforts of
civilization and become a mountain man. He helps the Flathead Indians
against the thieving Blackfeet and is given the chief's virgin daughter as thanks. He moves on with Swan and his adopted white son and
builds a cabin for his family. Everything goes well until the United
States Cavalry hires Johnson to guide them to a band of starving
settlers. They cross a forbidden Crow burial ground against Johnson's
advice. The Crows kill Swan and the boy in retaliation. Johnson
leaves for Canada, killing every Crow he meets along the way, thereby
becoming a legend.

JERICHO   Black (African)   1939/Adventure
[DARK SANDS]

Record; 75 min.; *Producer*: Walter Futter; *Director*: Thornton Freeland;
Screenplay: Robert N. Lee/Peter Rurie; *Camera*: John W.W. Boyle;
Editor: E.B. Jarvis; *Cast*: Henry Wilcoxon (Captain Mack); Wallace
Ford (Mike Clancy); Paul Robeson (Jericho Jackson); PRINCESS KOUKA
(GARA); John Lauri (Hassan); James Carew (Major Barnes); Lawrence
Brown (Pvt. Face); Rufus Fenneli (Sgt. Gamey); Ike Hatch (Tag); Frank
Cram (Col. Lake); Frank Cockrane (Agouba).

Gara is the wife of Jericho Jackson. The film is set in Africa.

JOE KIDD   Mexican   1972/Western

Universal; 88 min.; *Producer*: Sidney Beckerman; *Director*: John Sturges; *Screenplay*: Elmore Leonard; *Music*: Lalo Schifrin; *Camera*: Bruce Surtees; *Editor*: Ferris Webster; *Cast*: Clint Eastwood (Joe Kidd); Robert Duvall (Frank Harlan); John Saxon (Luis Chama); Don Stroud (Lamarr); *STELLA GARCIA (HELEN SANCHEZ)*; James Wainwright (Mingo); Paul Koslo (Roy); Gregory Walcott (Sheriff Mitchell); Dick Van Patten (Hotel Manager); Lynne Marta (Elma); John Carter (Judge); Pepe Hern (Priest); Joaquin Martinez (Manolo).

Helen Sanchez is a member of Luis Chama's band of Mexican landowners who are fighting for their historic land claims against Frank Harlan and other white settlers. Helen is a fighter who knows how to handle a gun. Joe Kidd comes to the aid of the Mexicans and convinces Chama to fight in the courts instead of the streets.

THE JOE LOUIS STORY   Black   1953/Biography

United Artists; 87 min.; *Producer*: Sterling Silliphant; *Director*: Robert Gordon; *Screenplay*: Robert Sylvester; *Camera*: Joseph Brun; *Editor*: David Kummins; *Cast*: Coley Wallace (Joe Louis); Paul Stewart Tad McGeehan); *HILDA SIMMS (MARVA LOUIS)*; James Edwards (Chappie Blackburn); John Marley (Mannie Seamon); Dotts Johnson (Julian Black); *Evelyn Ellis (Mrs. Barrow)*.

Marva is the wife of fighter Joe Louis. She leaves him because he is unable to handle their relationship and boxing as well. Mrs. Barrow is Joe's mother.

JOE PANTHER   Native American--Seminole   1976/Adventure

Artist Creation; 110 min.; *Producer*: Stewart H. Beveridge; *Director*: Paul Krasny; *Screenplay*: Dale Eunson; *Music*: Fred Karlin; *Camera*: Robert L. Morrison; *Editors*: Mike Vejar/Millie Moore; *Cast*: Brian Keith (Capt. Harper); Ricardo Montalban (Turtle); Alan Feinstein (Rocky); Ray Tracey (Joe Panther); A. Martinez (Billy); Cliff Osmond (Rance); Robert W. Hoffman (George); Gem Thorpe Osceola (Tommy); *LOIS RED ELK (MOTHER); MONIKA RAMIREZ (JENNY)*.

Joe Panther is promised a job on a fishing boat if he proves himself by capturing an alligator from the Everglades. His mother and his girlfriend, Jenny give him love and support in pursuit of his goals.

JOURNEY THROUGH ROSEBUD   Native American--Sioux   1972/Drama

A GSF Production and Release; 93 min.; *Producer*: David Gil; *Director*: Tom Gries; *Screenplay*: Albert Ruben; *Music*: Johnny Mandel; *Camera*: Minervino Rojas; *Editor*: Patricia Finn Lewis; *Cast*: Robert Forster (Frank); Kristoffer Tabori (Danny); *VICTORIA RACIMO (SHIRLEY)*; Eddie Little Sky (Stanley Pike); Roy Jenson (Park Ranger); Wright King (Indian Agent); Larry Pennell (Sheriff); Robert Cornthwaite (Hearing Officer).

    Draft-resister Danny, searching for inner peace, travels to the Rosebud Sioux Reservation. He becomes friendly with Frank, an alcoholic Indian who is disillusioned with the struggle of reservation life. Danny is attracted to Shirley, Frank's estranged wife. When Frank finds out that Danny and Shirley have slept together, he goes on a drunken binge and kills himself. This leads Shirley and Frank's friends to reject Danny. As Danny leaves the reservation he is beaten up; he dutifully accepts his punishment.

THE JUNGLE   Indian   1952/Adventure

Lippert; 74 min.; *Producer*: T.R. Sundaram/William Berke; *Director*: William Berke; *Screenplay*: Carroll Young; *Music*: Dakshinamoorthy/G. Ramanathan; *Camera*: Clyde Vinna; *Editor*: L. Baler; *Cast*: Rod Cameron (Steve Bentley); Cesar Romero (Rama Singh); *MARIE WINDSOR (PRINCESS MARI)*; *Sulchana (The Aunt)*; M.N. Namblar (Mahaji); David Abraham (Prime Minister); Rama Krishna (Young Boy).

    Princess Mari is the ruler of Sunadar.

JUNGLE BOOK   Indian   1942/Adventure

United Artists; 115 min.; *Producer*: Alexander Korda; *Director*: Zoltan Korda; *Screenplay*: Laurence Stallings; *Music*: Miklos Rozsa; *Camera*: Leo Garmes/W. Howard Green; *Editor*: William Hornbeck; *Cast*: Sabu (Mowglie); Joseph Calleia (Buldeo); John Qualen (The Barber); Frank Puglia (The Pundit); *ROSEMARY DeCAMP (MESSUA)*; *PATRICIA O'ROURKE (MAHALA)*; Ralph Byrd (Durga); John Mather (Rao); Faith Brook (English Girl).

    Mowgli, lost to his mother, Messua, when he was a baby, was raised by wolves. Reunited with his people, he is befriended by Mahala and Messua. Realizing, however, that animals are better company, he destroys his family's village and returns to the jungle.

JUNGLE CAPTIVE   Jungle Exotic   1945/Thriller

Universal; 63 min.; *Assoc. Producer*: Morgan B. Cox; *Director*: Harold Young; *Screenplay*: M. Coates Webster/Dwight V. Babcock; *Music*: Paul Sawtell; *Camera*: Murray Gertsman; *Editor*: Fred R. Reitshans, Jr.; *Cast*: Otto Kruger (Dr. Stendahl); Amelita Ward (Ann Forrester); Phil Brown (Don Young); Jerome Cowan (Harrigan); Rondo Hation (Moloch);

VICKY LANE (PAULA, THE APE WOMAN).

Another in the series including CAPTIVE WILD WOMAN and JUNGLE WOMAN has Paula once again on the loose.

JUNGLE JIM   Jungle Exotic   1948/Adventure

Columbia; 73 min.; *Producer*: Sam Katzman; *Director*: William Berke; *Screenplay*: Carroll Young; *Music*: Mischa Bakaleinikoff; *Camera*: Lester White; *Editor*: Aaron Stell; *Cast*: Johnny Weissmuller (Jungle Jim); Virginia Grey (Hilary Parker); George Reeves (Bruse Edwards); *LITA BARON (ZIA)*; Rick Vallin (Kolu); Holmes Herbert (Commissioner Marsden); Tex Mooney (Chief Devil Doctor).

Zia is the local jungle girl.

JUNGLE MOON MEN   Egyptian   1955/Adventure

Columbia; 69 min.; *Producer*: Sam Katzman; *Director*: Dwight V. Babcock; *Screenplay*: Dwight V. Babcock/Jo Pagano; *Camera*: Henry Freulich; *Editor*: Henry Batista; *Cast*: Johnny Weissmuller; Jean Byron (Ellen Marston); *HELEN STANTON (OMA)*; Bill Henry (Bob Prentice); Myron Healey (Mark Santo); Billy Curtis (Damu); Michael Granger (Nolimo); Frank Sully (Max); Benjamin F. Chapman (Marro); Kenneth L. Smith (Link); Ed Hinton (Regan).

Oma is an Egyptian priestess who has discovered the secret of eternal life. She is now Queen of the Pygmies. She captures Bob Prentice to be her high priest. Johnny Weissmuller and writer Ellen Marston come searching for him and break into Oma's temple. Oma is destroyed when the rays of the sun hit her.

THE JUNGLE PRINCESS   Jungle Exotic   1936/Adventure

Paramount; 85 min.; *Producer*: E. Lloyd Sheldon; *Director*: William Thiele; *Screenplay*: Cyril Hume/Gerald Geraghty/Gouverneur Morris; *Music*: Frederic Hollander/Leo Rubin; *Camera*: Harry Fischbeck; *Editor*: Ellsworth Hoagland; *Cast*: *DOROTHY LAMOUR (ULAH)*; Ray Milland (Christopher Powell); Akim Tamiroff (Karen Nag); Lynne Overman (Frank); Molly Lamont (Ava); Mala (Nelon); Hugh Buckler (Col. Lane); Sally Martin (Ulah, as a child).

When Ulah was a baby her father was killed by a tiger. The tiger raised Ulah with her own cub. Ulah grows up with the tiger and other jungle animals as her friends. Chris Powell gets lost in the jungle and Ulah finds him. He teaches her English and they soon fall in love. The natives are afraid of Ulah and the tiger and plot to kill them. However, the jungle animals come to their rescue and destroy the natives and their village.

JUNGLE SIREN   Jungle Exotic   1942/Adventure

Producers Releasing Co.; 68 min.; *Director*: Sam Newfield; *Screenplay*:
George W. Sayre/Sam Robins; *Camera*: Jack Greenhalgh; *Editor*: Holbrook
N. Todd; *Cast*: *ANN CORIO (KUHLAYA)*; Buster Crabbe (Capt. Gary Hart);
Evelyn Wahl (Frau Anna); Paul Bryar (Sgt. Mike Jennings); Mil Kibbee
(Dr. Harrigan); Arno Frey (Herr Lukas); Jess Brooks (Chief Schlangi);
Manart Kippen (Major Renault); James Adamson (Johnny); Chimpanzee
(Greco).

Kuhlaya helps Captain Gary Hart combat German propaganda. She
also assists him with her knowledge of the bow and arrow.

JUNGLE WOMAN   Jungle Exotic   1944/Thriller

Universal; 54 min.; *Assoc. Producer*: Will Cowan; *Director*: Reginald
Le Borg; *Screenplay*: Henry Sucher/Edward Dein/Bernard Schubert;
Camera: Jack MacKenzie; *Editor*: Ray Snyder; *Cast*: *ACQUANETTA (PAULA
DUPREE)*; J. Carrol Naish (Dr. Carl Fletcher); Evelyn Ankers (Beth
Mason); Milburn Stone (Fred Mason); Lois Collier (Joan Fletcher);
Richard Davis (Bob Whitney); Eddie Hyans, Jr. (Willie); Samuel S.
Hinds (Coroner).

Sequel to CAPTIVE WILD WOMAN. Paula Dupree is in love again
and her jealousy causes her to regress into an ape.

KENNER   Indian   1969/Drama

MGM; 92 min.; *Producer*: Mary Phillips Murray; *Director*: Steve Sekely;
Screenplay: Harold Clemins/John R. Loring; *Music*: Piero Piccioni;
Camera: Dieter Liphardt; *Editor*: Richard Heermance; *Cast*: Jim Brown
(Roy Kenner); *MADLYN RHUE (ANASUYA)*; Robert Coote (Henderson); Ricky
Cordell (Saji); Charles Horvath (Tom Jordan); Prem Nath (Sandy);
Kuljit Singh (Young Sirh); Sulochana (Mother Superior); Ursula Prince
(Sister Katherine); Tony North (American Friend).

Anasuya meets Roy Kenner through her son, Saji, who is looking
for his father. Anasuya and Kenner fall in love, but Anasuya is
killed by a train. Kenner takes Saji back to the United States as
his son.

KILL A DRAGON   Chinese   1967/Adventure

United Artists; 91 min.; *Producer*: Hal Klein; *Director*: Michael Moore;
Screenplay: George Schenck/William Marks; *Music*: Philip Springer;
Camera: Emmanuel Rojos; *Editor*: John F. Schreyer; *Cast*: Jack Palance
(Rick); Fernando Lamas (Patrai); Aldo Ray (Vigo); *ALIZIA GUR (TISA)*;
Kam Tong (Win Lim); Don Knight (Ian); Hans Lee (Jimmie); *Judy Dan
(Chungyang)*.

Villagers on an island near Hong Kong claim the cargo aboard a wrecked ship. The owner of the cargo demands its return. The villagers enlist the aid of Rick who sympathizes with them and is romantically interested in Tisa.

KILLER SHARK   Mexican   1950/Adventure

Monogram; 74 min.; *Producer*: Lindsley Parson; *Director*: Budd Boetticher; *Screenplay*: Charles Lang; *Music*: Edward J. Kay; *Camera*: William Sickner; *Editor*: Leonard Herman; *Cast*: Roddy McDowall (Ted); *LAURETT LUEZ (MARIA)*; Roland Winters (White); Edward Norris (Ramon); Rick Vallin (Agapito); Douglas Fowley (Bracado); Nacho Galindo (Maestro); Ralf Harolde (Slattery); Dick Moore (Jonesy); Ted Hecht (Gano); Charles Lang (McCann); Robert Espinoza (Pinon); Julio Sebastian (Tony); Julian Rivero (Doctor).

Maria lives on the waterfront of a fishing village in southern California. She meets Ted who is a beginner in the fishing business.

KIM   Indian   1950/Adventure

MGM; 113 min.; *Producer*: Leon Gordon; *Director*: Victor Saville; *Screenplay*: Leon Gordon/Helen Deutsch/Richard Schayer; *Music*: Andre Previn; *Camera*: William Skall; *Editor*: George Boemler; *Cast*: Errol Flynn (Mahbub Ali, Red Beard); Dean Stockwell (Kim); Paul Lukas (Lama); Robert Douglas (Col. Creighton); Thomas Gomez (Emissary); Cecil Kellaway (Hurree Chunder); Arnold Moss (Lurgan Sahib); Reginald Owen (Father Victor); *LAURETTE LUEZ (LALULI)*; Richard Hale (Hassan Bey).

Laluli provides the romantic interest of Mahbub Ali.

THE KING AND I   Asian   1956/Musical

20th Century-Fox; 133 min.; *Producer*: Charles Brackett; *Director*: Walter Lang; *Screenplay*: Ernest Lehman; *Music/Lyrics*: Richard Rodgers/ Oscar Hammerstein II; *Camera*: Leon Shamroy; *Editor*: Robert Simpson; *Cast*: Deborah Kerr (Anna); Yul Brynner (The King); *RITA MORENO (TUPTIM)*; Martin Benson (Kralahome); *Terry Saunders (Lady Thiang)*; Rex Thompson (Louis Leonowens); Carlos Rivas (Lun Tha); Patrick Adiarte (Prince Chulalongkorn); Alan Mowbray (British Ambassador); Geoffrey Toone (Ramsey).

Schoolteacher Anna travels to Siam to become the teacher of the King's children. Tuptim was given to the King as a gift. She falls in love with someone else and plans to run away with him, however, the King finds out and wants them put to death. Anna convinces the King to allow the lovers their freedom.

KING OF CHINATOWN   Chinese   1939/Drama

Paramount; 60 min.; *Director*: Nick Grinde; *Screenplay*: Lillie Hayward/
Irving Reis; *Camera*: Leo Tover; *Editor*: Edna Warren; *Cast*: ANNA MAY
WONG (DR. MARY LING); Akim Tamiroff (Frank Baturin); J. Carrol Naish
(The Professor); Sidney Toler (Dr. Chang Ling); Philip Ahn (Robert
"Bob" Li); Anthony Quinn (Mike Gordon); Bernadene Hayes (Dolly
Warren); Roscoe Karns (Rep. Harrigan); Ray Mayer (Potatoes).

Dr. Mary Ling wrongly assumes that her father, Dr. Chang Ling,
shot Frank Baturin--a gangster terrorizing the local merchants. However, Baturin was double-crossed by the Professor. Dr. Mary Ling
operates to save Baturin's life. He recovers, while the district
attorney closes in on the criminals. Baturin is shot again but
before he dies he leaves all his money to Mary to use for her ambulance service.

THE KING OF COMEDY   Black   1982/Drama

20th Century-Fox; 109 min.; *Producer*: Arnon Milchan; *Director*: Martin
Scorsese; *Screenplay*: Paul D. Zimmerman; *Camera*: Fred Schuler;
Editor: Thelma Schoonmaker; *Cast*: Robert De Niro (Rupert Pupkin);
Jerry Lewis (Jerry Langford); DIAHNNE ABBOTT (RITA); Sandra Bernhard
(Masha); Ed Herlihy; Lou Brown (Band Leader); Shelley Hack (Cathy
Long).

Aspiring comedian Rupert Pupkin is in love with barmaid Rita,
who was Rupert's secret high school heartthrob. Rupert is somewhat
unstable so Rita is very cautious about becoming involved with him.

KING OF THE GYPSIES   Gypsy   1978/Drama

Paramount; 112 min.; *Producer*: Federico De Laurentiis; *Director*:
Frank Pierson; *Screenplay*: Frank Pierson; *Music*: David Grisman;
Camera: Paul Hirsch; *Editor*: Paul Hirsch; *Cast*: Sterling Hayden (King
Zharko Stepanowicz); *Shelley Winters (Queen Rachel)*; SUSAN SARANDON
(ROSE); Judd Hirsch (Groffo); Eric Roberts (Dave); *Brooke Shields
(Tita)*; Annette O'Toole (Sharon); Annie Potts (Persa); Michael V.
Gazzo (Spiro Giorgio); *Antonia Rey (Danitza Giorgio)*.

Queen Rachel is the aging queen of the gypsies. Rose is married
to Groffo who wants to be the new king and is willing to kill his son
Dave, the heir apparent. Tita is to be married to someone she does
not like.

KING OF THE WILD HORSES   Native American--Navajo   1934/Western

Columbia; 61 min.; *Director*: Earl Haley; *Screenplay*: Fred Myton;
Camera: Ben Kline; *Editor*: Clarence Kolster; *Cast*: Rex (Rex, the
Hero); Lady (Lady, the Heroine); Marquis (Marquis, the Villain);
William Janney (Red Wolf); DOROTHY APPLEBY (WANIMA); Wallace
MacDonald (Clint Rolling); Harry Semels (Big Man); Ford West

(Davidson); Art Mix (Cowboy).

Not enough information was available to describe this role accurately.

KINGS GO FORTH   Black   1958/Drama

United Artists; 109 min.; *Producer*: Frank Ross; *Director*: Delmer Daves; *Screenplay*: Merle Miller; *Music*: Elmer Bernstein; *Camera*: Daniel L. Fapp; *Editor*: William Murphy; *Cast*: Frank Sinatra (Sam Loggins); Tony Curtis (Britt Harris); *NATALIE WOOD (MONIQUE BLAIR)*; Leora Dana (Mrs. Blair); Karl Swenson (Colonel); Anne Codee (Mme. Brieux); Jackie Berthe (Jean Francoise).

Sam Loggins meets Monique Blair and is shocked to learn that she is half-Black. He falls in love with her nevertheless, but she does not respond to him. He introduces Monique to Britt Harris, a wealthy playboy who is interested in Monique only because she is Black and he has never had a Black girlfriend. Monique falls in love with Britt and is heartbroken when she learns that he was only using her. When Sam returns to Monique after the war, she realizes that he loves her and she begins to love him.

KINGS OF THE SUN   Mayan   1963/Adventure

United Artists; 107 min.; *Producer*: Lewis J. Rachmil; *Director*: J. Lee Thompson; *Screenplay*: Elliott Arnold/James R. Webb; *Music*: Elmer Bernstein; *Camera*: Joseph MacDonald; *Editor*: William Reynolds; *Cast*: Yul Brynner (Black Eagle); George Chakiris (Balam); *SHIRLEY ANNE FIELD (IXCHEL)*; Richard Basehart (Ah Min); Brad Dexter (Ah Haleb); Barry Morse (Ah Zok); Armando Silvestre (Isatai); Leo Gordon (Hunac Ceel); *Victoria Vettri (Ixzubin)*; Rudy Solari (Pitz); Ford Rainey (The Chief).

A group of Mayan Indians is forced to flee their land after an attack by Hunac Ceel. They travel by boat and land to an unidentified part of the United States. There they settle but are soon attacked by the local Indian tribe led by Chief Black Eagle. Black Eagle is wounded and taken prisoner. He is healed by Ixchel, the fiancee of Mayan leader Balam. After Balam saves Black Eagle from human sacrifice, the two tribes become friendly and mutually cooperative. Both men love Ixchel, and although she is supposed to marry Balam, she is not sure whether she really loves Black Eagle. When Hunac Ceel arrives to destroy the Mayans, the two tribes destroy him. Black Eagle is killed in battle, so Ixchel marries Balam.

KISMET   Arabian Nights   1930/Fantasy

Warner Brothers; 90 min.; *Director*: John Francis Dillon; *Screenplay*: Harold Estabrook; *Camera*: John Seitz; *Editor*: Al Hall; *Cast*: Otis Skinner (Hajj); *LORETTA YOUNG (MARSINAH ABDALLAH)*; David Manners (Caliph); *Mary Duncan (Zeleekha)*; Sidney Blackmer (Mansur); Ford

Sterling (Amru); Edmund Breese (Jawan); *Blanche Frederici (Narjis)*.

Marsinah Abdallah becomes betrothed to the caliph with the aid of her rogue father Hajj.

KISMET   Arabian Nights   1944/Fantasy

MGM; 100 min.; *Producer*: Everett Riskin; *Director*: William Dieterle; *Screenplay*: John Meehan; *Music*: Herbert Stothart; *Camera*: Charles Rosher; *Editor*: Ben Lewis; *Cast*: Ronald Colman (Hafiz); *MARLENE DIETRICH (JAMILLA)*; James Craig (Caliph); Edward Arnold (Grand Vizer); Hugh Herbert (Feisal); *Joy Ann Page (Marsinah)*; *Florence Bates (Karsha)*; Harry Davenport (Agha); Hobart Cavanaugh (Moulah).

Beggar/ersatz prince Hafiz marries his daughter Marsinah to the Caliph and keeps dancing girl Jamilla for himself.

KISMET   Arabian Nights   1955/Musical

MGM; 112 min.; *Producer*: Arthur Freed; *Director*: Vincente Minnelli; *Screenplay*: Charles Lederer/Luther Davis; *Music/Lyrics*: Robert Wright/ George Forrest; *Camera*: Joseph Ruttenberg; *Editor*: Adrienne Fazan; *Cast*: Howard Keel (The Poet); *ANN BLYTH (MARSINAH)*; *Dolores Gray (Lalume)*; Vic Damone (Caliph); Monty Woolley (Omar); Sebastian Cabot (Wazir); Jay C. Flippen (Jawan); Mike Mazurki (Chief Policeman); Jack Elam (Hassan-Ben).

Marsinah, the Poet's daughter, is loved by the Caliph's son. Lalume is the wife of the scheming Wazir who is planning to marry the Caliph's son to one of his associate's daughters. The Poet sets things aright: Marsinah marries the Caliph's son and the Poet gets the newly widowed Lalume.

THE KISSING BANDIT   Mexican   1948/Musical

MGM; 102 min.; *Producer*: Joe Pasternak; *Director*: Laslo Benedek; *Screenplay*: Isobel Lennart; *Music*: George Stoll; *Camera*: Robert Surtees; *Editor*: Adrienne Fazan; *Cast*: Frank Sinatra (Ricardo); *KATHRYN GRAYSON (TERESA)*; J. Carrol Naish (Chico); *Mildred Natwick (Isabella)*; *Sono Osato (Bianca)*; Clinton Sundbert (Colonel Gomez); Carleton Young (Count Belmonte); *Edna Skinner (Juanita)*; Henry Mirelez (Pepito).

In old California, Ricardo tries to take over as bandit leader of his dead father's gang by robbing men and kissing women. However, Ricardo cannot ride a horse, is unable to steal, and is afraid of women. While on a mission he meets Teresa, the Governor's daughter. He falls in love with her but is unable to kiss her. Teresa becomes upset at this and feels unattractive (she desperately wants to be kissed by the Kissing Bandit). Ricardo, posing as a tax collector, stays with the Governor, and Teresa falls in love with him. The Governor approves of the marriage of Teresa and Ricardo, and when the real tax collector arrives, he sends him on his way. Ricardo becomes the new tax collector.

THE KLANSMAN   Black   1974/Drama

Paramount; 112 min.; *Producer*: William Alexander; *Director*: Terence Young; *Screenplay*: Millard Kaufman/Samuel Fuller; *Music*: Dale O. Warren/Stu Gardner; *Camera*: Lloyd Ahern; *Editor*: Gene Micford; *Cast*: Lee Marvin (Sheriff Bascomb); Richard Burton (Breck Stancill); Cameron Mitchell (Butt Cut Cates); O.J. Simpson (Garth); *LOLA FALANA (LORETTA SYKES)*; David Huddleston (Mayor Hardy); Luciana Paluzzi (Trixie); Linda Evans (Nancy Poteet).

The story of the Ku Klux Klan's opposition to Black voter registration in the South.

KOREA PATROL   Korean   1951/War Drama

Eagle Lion Classics; 59 min.; *Producer*: Walter Shenson; *Director*: Max Nosseck; *Screenplay*: Kenneth G. Brown/Walter Shenson; *Music*: Alexander Gerens; *Camera*: Elmer Dyer; *Editor*: Norman Cerf; *Cast*: Richard Emory (Lt. Craig); Al Eben (Sgt. Abrams); Benson Fong (Kim); Li Sun (Ching); *TERI DUNA (NATIVE GIRL)*; Danny Davenport (Corp. Dykes); Weng Artarne (Murphy); Harold Fong (Lee); John V. Close (Capt. Greer).

Native Girl is picked up by United States Army Soldiers on their way to blow up a bridge held by the North Koreans.

LA CONGA NIGHTS   Latin American   1940/Musical

Universal; 60 min.; *Director*: Lew Landers; *Screenplay*: Jay Dratler/Harry Clark/Paul Gerard Smith; *Music*: Charles Previn; *Camera*: Elwood Bredell; *Editor*: Ted Kent; *Cast*: Hugh Herbert (Henry I. Dibble, Jr.); Dennis O'Keefe (Steve Collins); Constance Moore (Helen Curtiss); Ferike Boros (Mama O'Brien); Joe Brown, Jr. (Delancey O'Brien); *ARMIDA (CARLOTTA DE VERA)*; Eddie Quillan (Titus Endover); Sally Payne (Lucy Endover); Frank Orth (Dennis O'Brien).

Carlotta De Vera sings "La Cucaracha."

LADIES DAY   Latin American   1943/Comedy

RKO; 62 min.; *Producer*: Bert Gilroy; *Director*: Leslie Goodwins; *Screenplay*: Charles E. Roberts/Dane Lussier; *Camera*: Jack MacKenzie; *Editor*: Harry Marker; *Cast*: *LUPE VELEZ (PEPITA ZORITA)*; Eddie Albert (Wacky Waters); Patsy Kelly (Hazel); Max Baer (Hippo); Jerome Cowan (Updyke); Iris Adrian (Kitty); Joan Barclay (Joan); Cliff Clark (Dan); *Carmen Morales (Marianna)*; George Cleveland (Doc); Jack Briggs (Marty).

When baseball pitcher Wacky Waters falls in love with Pepita Zorita, the team's manager and players do their best to break up the romance because Wacky is useless when he is in love.

LADY OF THE TROPICS   Asian   1939/Drama

MGM; 91 min.; *Producer*: Sam Zimbalist; *Director*: Jack Conway; *Screenplay*: Ben Hecht; *Camera*: George Folsey; *Editor*: Elmo Vernon; *Cast*: Robert Taylor (Bill Carey); *HEDY LAMARR (MANON DeVARGNES)*; Joseph Schildkraut (Pierre Delaroch); Gloria Franklin (Nina); Ernest Cossart (Father Antoine); Mary Taylor (Dolly Harrison); Charles Trowbridge (Alfred Z. Harrison); Frederick Worlock (Col. Demassey); Paul Porcasi (Lamartine); *Margaret Paduin (Madame Kya)*: Cecil Cunningham (Countess Berichi); Natalie Moorhead (Mrs. Hazlitt).

Manon DeVargnes is the half-caste that Bill Carey loves and marries. Carey is unable to get his wife a passport so that she can leave Saigon, but he cannot find work in Saigon to support them. Local politician Pierre Delaroch offers help, but only because Manon is secretly meeting with him. Delaroch wants Manon all to himself and arranges for Carey to learn of their affair. Manon kills Delaroch and then kills herself.

LADY SINGS THE BLUES   Black   1972/Biography

Paramount; 144 min.; *Producer*: Jay Weston/James S. White; *Director*: Sidney J. Furie; *Screenplay*: Terence McCloy/Chris Clark/Suzanne De Passe; *Camera*: John Alonzo; *Editor*: Argyle Nelson; *Cast*: *DIANA ROSS (BILLIE HOLLIDAY)*; Billy Dee Williams (Louis McKay); Richard Pryor (Piano Man); James Callahan (Reg Hanley); Paul Hampton (Harry); Sid Melton (Jerry); *Virginia Capers (Mama Holliday)*; Yvonne Fair (Yvonne); Scatman Crothers (Big Ben); Robert L.Gordy (Hawk); Harry Caesar (Rapist).

Biography of blues singer Billie Holliday, her problems with men, and the drug addiction that led to her early death.

LAND RAIDERS   Mexican   1970/Western

Columbia; 100 min.; *Producer*: Charles H. Schneer; *Director*: Nathan Juran; *Screenplay*: Ken Pettus; *Music*: Bruno Nicolai; *Camera*: Wilkie Cooper; *Editor*: Archie Ludski; *Cast*: Telly Savalas (Vince Carden); George Maharis (Paul Cardenas); Arlene Dahl (Martha Carden); Janet Landgard (Kate Mayfield); *JOCELYN LANE (LUISA ROJAS)*; George Coulouris (Cardenas); Guy Rolfe (Tanner); Phil Brown (Mayfield); *Marcella St. Amant (Luisa Montoya)*.

Not enough information was available to accurately describe this role.

Marki Bey, *The Landlord* (UA, 1970)

THE LANDLORD   Black   1970/Comedy

United Artists; 113 min.; *Producer*: Norman Jewison; *Director*: Hal
Ashby; *Screenplay*: Bill Gunn; *Camera*: Gordon Willis; *Cast*: Beau
Bridges (Elger Enders); *DIANA SANDS (FANNY)*; Lee Grant (Mrs. Enders);
MARKI BEY (LANIE); *Pearl Bailey (Marge)*; Lou Gossett (Copee); Melvin
Steward (Professor Duboise); Susan Anspach (Susan).

Wealthy Elger Enders buys a ghetto apartment building to convert
into a swinging bachelor apartment for himself. However, he soon
becomes involved with the lives of his tenants: Marge, a fortune
teller; Fanny, with whom he has an affair; and the woman he loves,
Lanie. Complications arise when Fanny becomes pregnant. Elger
leaves Lanie to be with Fanny, but she wants to give the baby up for
adoption so Elger takes the child and returns to Lanie.

THE LASH   Mexican   1930/Adventure

Warner Brothers; 75 min.; *Director*: Frank Lloyd; *Screenplay*: Bradley
King; *Camera*: Ernst Haller; *Editor*: Harold Young; *Cast*: Richard
Barthelmess (Don Francisco Delfina); James Rennie (David Howard);
MARY ASTOR (ROSITA); *Marian Nixon (Dolores Delfino)*; Fred Kohler
(Peter Harkness); *Barbara Bedford (Lupe)*; Robert Edeson (Mariano
Delfino); Arthur Stone (Juan); *Mathilde Comot (Concha)*; Erville
Alderson (Judge Travers).

Don Francisco is a bandit/hero in old California. His close
friend is sheriff David Howard. David is in love with Francisco's
sister Dolores. Francisco loves Rosita and occasionally Lupe. The
friendship between David and Francisco becomes strained when things
become hot for the bandit Francisco. Francisco flees to Mexico with
the promise that Rosita will meet him there.

THE LAST COMMAND   Mexican   1955/Adventure

Republic; 110 min.; *Producer/Director*: Frank Lloyd; *Screenplay*: Warren
Duff; *Music*: Max Steiner; *Camera*: Jack Marta; *Editor*: Tony Martinelli;
Cast: Sterling Hayden (James Bowie); *ANNA MARIA ALBERGHETTI
(CONSUELA)*; Richard Carlson (William Travis); Arthur Hunnicutt (Davy
Crockett); Ernest Borgnine (Mike Radin); J. Carrol Naish (Santa Anna);
Ben Cooper (Jeb Lacey); John Russell (Lt. Dickinson); Virginia Grey
(Mrs. Dickinson); Jim Davis (Evans); Eduard Franz (Lorenzo de
Quesada); Slim Pickens (Abe).

Consuela is the daughter of a wealthy landowner who sides with
Texas against Mexican rule. She also has a romance with James Bowie,
leader of the rebellion against the Mexican government.

THE LAST HUNT   Native American   1956/Western

MGM; 108 min.; *Producer*: Dore Schary; *Director*: Richard Brooks;
Screenplay: Richard Brooks; *Music*: Daniele Amfitheatrof; *Camera*:
Russell Harlan; *Editor*: Ben Lewis; *Cast*: Robert Taylor (Charles

Gilson); Stewart Granger (Sandy McKenzie); Lloyd Nolan (Woodfoot);
DEBRA PAGET (INDIAN GIRL); Russ Tamblyn (Jimmy); Constance Ford (Peg);
Joe De Santis (Ed Black); Ainslie Pryor (1st Buffalo Hunter); Ralph
Moody (Indian Agent); Fred Graham (Bartender); Ed Lonehill (Spotted
Hand).

Charles Gilson gets a kick out of slaughtering buffalo and
Indians. After wiping out an impoverished family, he tries to make
love to the surviving Indian Girl. She is indifferent to him and
settles down with Sandy McKenzie after Gilson freezes to death.

THE LAST MOVIE   Peruvian   1971/Drama

Universal; 110 min.; *Producer*: Paul Lewis; *Director*: Dennis Hooper;
Screenplay: Stewart Stern; *Music*: Kris Kristofferson; *Camera*: Laszlo
Kovacs; *Editor*: Dennis Hopper; *Cast*: Dennis Hopper (Kansas); *STELLA
GARCIA (MARIA)*; Julie Adams (Mrs. Anderson); Tomas Milian (Priest);
Don Gordon (Neville Robey); Roy Engel (Mr. Anderson); Donna Baccala
(Miss Anderson); Samuel Fuller (Director); Poupee Bocar (Night Club
Singer).

Maria, a prostitute, becomes involved with Kansas, a crew member
of a film company shooting in the jungle.

THE LAST OF THE FAST GUNS   Mexican   1950/Western

Universal; 82 min.; *Producer*: Howard Christie; *Director*: George
Sherman; *Screenplay*: David P. Harmon; *Music*: Joseph Gershenson;
Camera: Alex Philips; *Editor*: Patrick McCormak; *Cast*: Jock Mahoney
(Brad Ellison); Gilbert Roland (Miles Lang); *LINDA CRISTAL (MARIA
O'REILLY)*; Fduard Franz (Padre Jose); Lorne Greene (Michael O'Reilly);
Carl Benton Reid (John Forbes); Edward C. Platt (Edward Forbes).

Not enough information was available to describe this role
accurately.

LAST OF THE PAGANS   Island Exotic   1936/Adventure

MGM; 70 min.; *Producer*: Philip Goldstone; *Director*: Richard Thorpe;
Screenplay: J.V. Farrow; *Music*: Nat Finston; *Camera*: Clyde De Vinna;
Editor: Martin G. Cohn; *Cast*: Mala (Taro); *LOTUS LONG (LILLEO)*; Tei
A. Tematus (Native Chief); *Rangapo A. Taipoo (Taro's Mother)*.

The usual South Sea island romance between Lilleo and her lover
Taro. The film climaxes with a hurricane.

THE LAST TIME I SAW ARCHIE   Asian   1961/Comedy

United Artists; 98 min.; *Producer/Director*: Jack Webb; *Screenplay*:
William Bowers; *Music*: Frank Comstock; *Camera*: Joseph MacDonald;
Editor: Robert Leeds; *Cast*: Robert Mitchum (Archie Hall); Jack Webb

(Bill Bowers); Martha Hyer (Peggy Kramer); *FRANCE NUYEN (CINDY)*;
Louis Nye (Pvt. Sam Beacham); James Lydon (Pvt. Billy Simpson); Del
Moore (Pvt. Frank Ostrow); Joe Flynn (Pvt. Russell Drexel); Richard
Arlen (Col. Martin); Don Knotts (Capt. Little); Robert Strauss
(Master Sgt. Stanley Erlenheim).

Toward the end of World War II, Archie Hall and Private Bill
Bowers spend their time on an Army Air Force base with Peggy and
Cindy--Archie's girl. The two men begin to suspect that Cindy is a
spy for Japan. However, she is in fact a lure to capture the real
spy who, when captured, helps Archie inadvertently become a hero.

LAUGHING AT LIFE   Latin American   1933/Adventure

Mascot; 71 min.; *Producer*: Nat Levine; *Director*: Ford Beebe; *Screen-
play*: Prescott Chaplin/Thomas Dugan; *Camera*: Ernie Miller/Tom
Galligan; *Editor*: Ray Snyder; *Cast*: Victor McLaglen (McHale);
CONCHITA MONTENEGRO (PANCHITA); William [Stage] Boyd (Mason); Lois
Wilson (Mrs. McHale); Henry B. Walthall (President Valenzuela); Regis
Toomey (Pat Collins); Ruth Hall (Alice Lawton); Ivan Lebedeff (Don
Flavio); Noah Beery (Hauseman); Tully Marshall (Stone).

Panchita is the companion of soldier of fortune McHale in South
America.

LAUGHING BOY   Native American   1934/Drama

MGM; 75 min.; *Director*: W.B. Van Dyke; *Screenplay*: John Colton/John
Lee Mahin; *Music*: Herbert Stothart; *Camera*: Lester White; *Editor*:
Blanche Sewell; *Cast*: Ramon Novarro (Laughing Boy); *LUPE VELEZ (SLIM
GIRL)*; William Dickenson (Hartshorne); Chief Thunderbird (Father);
Catalina Rambula (Mother); Tall Man's Boy (Wounded Face); F.A.
Armenta (Yellow Singer); Deer Spring (Squaw's Son); Pellican (Red
Man).

Slim Girl is a woman of easy virtue who enjoys spending time
with white men. She marries Laughing Boy, a man of her tribe, but
continues her sinful ways. When Laughing Boy learns of her white
lover, he aims to shoot him; instead, the arrow strikes Slim Girl.

LAW OF THE PAMPAS   Latin American   1939/Western

Paramount; 74 min.; *Producer*: Harry Sherman; *Director*: Nate Watt;
Screenplay: Harrison Jacobs; *Camera*: Russell Harian; *Editor*: Carroll
Lewis; *Cast*: William Boyd (Hopalong Cassidy); Russell Hayden (Lucky
Jenkins); *STEFFI DUNA (CHIQUITA)*; Sidney Toler (Fernando Rameriez);
Sidney Blackmer (Ralph Merritt); Pedro de Cordoba (Senor Jose Valdez);
Jojo La Sajio (Ernesto); Glenn Strange (Schultz); Eddie Dean (Naples);
Anna Demetrio (Dolores).

Hopalong Cassidy brings his brand of the west to the South American pampas, romancing Chiquita along the way.

THE LAWLESS   Mexican   1950/Drama

Paramount; 81 min.; *Producers*: William H. Pine/William C. Thomas; *Director*: Joseph Losey; *Screenplay*: Geoffrey Homes; *Music*: Mahlon Merrick; *Camera*: Roy Hunt; *Editor*: Howard Smith; *Cast*: Macdonald Carey (Larry Wilder); *GAIL RUSSELL (SUNNY GARCIA)*; John Sands (Joe Ferguson); Lee Patrick (Jan Dawson); John Hoyt (Ed Ferguson); Lalo Rios (Paul Rodriguez); Maurice Jara (Lopo Chavez); Walter Reed (Jim Wilson); Guy Anderson (Jonas Creel); *Argentina Brunetti (Mrs. Rodriguez)*.

The story of migrant farm workers in California and the racism they face. Sunny is one of these workers.

THE LEARNING TREE   Black   1969/Drama

Warner Brothers; 107 min.; *Producer/Director/Screenplay*: Gordon Parks; *Music*: Tom McIntosh; *Camera*: Burnett Guffey; *Editor*: George R. Rohrs; *Cast*: Kyle Johnson (Newt Winger); Alex Clarke (Marcus (Savage)); *ESTELLE EVANS (SARAH WINGER)*; Dana Elcar (Sheriff Kirky); *MIRA WATERS (ARCELLA JEFFERSON)*; Joel Fluellen (Uncle Rob); Malcom Atterbury (Silas Newhall); Richard Ward (Booker Savage); Russell Thorson (Judge Cavanaugh); Peggy Rea (Miss McClintock); Carole Lamond (Big Mabel).

The story of a Black family in Kansas during the 1920s. Sarah is a maid for the country judge. Her son Newt falls in love with Arcella Jefferson--who must leave town when she becomes pregnant by a wealthy white boy. The focus is on Newt, his witnessing of a robbery and murder, and the death of his mother. After the trial Newt leaves town to live with his aunt.

THE LEGEND OF NIGGER CHARLEY   Black &   1972/Western
                                Native American

Parmount; 98 min.; *Producer*: Larry G. Spangler; *Director*: Martin Goldman; *Screenplay*: Larry G. Spangler/Martin Goldman; *Music*: John Bennings; *Camera*: Peter Eco; *Editor*: Howard Kuperman; *Cast*: Fred Williamson (Nigger Charley); D'Urville Martin (Toby); Don Pedro Colley (Joshua); Gertrude Jeanette (Theo); *MARCIA McBROOM (JULIA)*; John Ryan (Houston); Alan Gifford (Hill Carter); Will Hussung (Dr. Sanders); *Tricia O'Neal (Sarah Lyons)*; Doug Rowe (Dewey Lyons); Joe Santos (Reverend); Keith Prentice (Niles); Bill Moor (Shadow).

Nigger Charley and Toby escape from Houston's plantation. They are hunted by Niles. Nigger Charley has a romance with Julia, who is also from the plantation. He almost has an affair with half-breed Sarah, who, with her husband Dewey, is being terrorized by the Reverend.

LEGEND OF THE LOST   Arab   1957/Adventure

United Artists; 109 min.; *Producer/Director*: Henry Hathaway; *Screen-play*: Ben Hecht; *Music*: A.F. Lavagnino; *Camera*: Jack Cardiff; *Editor*: Bert Bates; *Cast*: John Wayne (Joe January); *SOPHIA LOREN (DITA)*; Rossano Brazzi (Bonnard); Kurt Kasznar (Prefect Dukas).

Dita, a woman with a questionable reputation travels across the desert with Joe January and Bonnard searching for Bonnard's father's lost treasure. They find the treasure but Bonnard goes crazy. Joe is wounded in a fight with Bonnard. Joe and Dita are saved by a passing caravan and find that they are in love with each other.

LEO THE LAST   Black   1970/Drama

United Artists; 103 min.; *Producers*: Irwin Winkler/Robert Chartoff; *Director*: John Boorman; *Screenplay*: Bill Stair/John Boorman; *Music*: Fred Myrow; *Camera*: Peter Suschizky; *Cast*: Marcello Mastroianni (Leo); Billie Whitelaw (Margaret); Calvin Lockhart (Roscoe); *GLENNA FOSTER JONES (SALAMBO)*: Graham Crowden (Max); Gwen Frangcon Davies (Hilda); David de Keyser (David); Vladek Sheybal (Laslo).

When Leo, the last of a long line of European royalty, returns to his mansion in a London ghetto, he becomes aware of the plight of the poor people around him. He takes a personal interest in Salambo who is constantly harassed by men to the point almost of sexual assault. After her boy friend is sent to jail, a pimp tries to pressure her into prostitution. Leo decides to protect Salambo and help the poor of the neighborhood.

THE LEOPARD MAN   Latin American   1943/Thriller

RKO; 66 min.; *Producer*: Val Lewton; *Director*: Jacques Tourneur; *Screenplay*: Ardel Wray; *Music*: C. Bakaleinikoff; *Camera*: Robert de Grasse; *Editor*: Mark Robson; *Cast*: Dennis O'Keefe (Jerry Manning); *MARGO (CLO-CLO)*; Jean Brooks (Kiki Walker); *Isabel Jewell (Maria)*; James Bell (Dr. Galbraith); *Margaret Landry (Teresa Delgrade)*; Abner Biberman (Charlie How-come); Richard Martin (Raoul Belmonte); *Tula Parma (Consuelo Contreras)*; Ben Bard (Chief Robles); Ariel Heath (Eloise); *Fely Franquelli (Rosita)*.

Clo-Clo is a dancer in a town where a maniac disguised as a leopard is killing various inhabitants. Jerry Manning and Kiki Walker join forces and find the killer.

LET'S DO IT AGAIN   Black   1975/Comedy

Warner Brothers; 110 min.; *Producer*: Melville Tucker; *Director*: Sidney Poitier; *Screenplay*: Richard Wesley; *Music*: Curtis Mayfield; *Camera*: Donald M. Morgan; *Cast*: Sidney Poitier (Clyde Williams); Bill Cosby (Billy Foster); Calvin Lockhart (Biggie Smalls); John Amos (Kansas City Mack); *DENISE NICHOLAS (BETH FOSTER)*; Ossie Davis

(Elder Johnson); Jimmie Walker (Bootney Farnsworth); *Lee Chamberlain (Dee Dee Williams)*.

Beth Foster is the wife of Billy—who along with Clyde Williams is out to fix some fights and win big money.

THE LIBERATION OF L.B. JONES   Black   1969/Drama

Columbia; 102 min.; *Producer*: Ronald Lubin; *Director*: William Wyler; *Screenplay*: Stirling Silliphant/Jesse Hill Ford; *Music*: Elmer Bernstein; *Camera*: Robert Surtees; *Editor*: Carl Kress; *Cast*: Lee J. Cobb (Oman Hedgepath); Anthony Zerbe (Willie Joe Worth); Roscoe Lee Browne (Lord Byron Jones); *LOLA FALANA (EMMA JONES)*; Lee Majors (Steve Mundine); Barbara Hershey (Nella Mundine); Yaphet Kotto (Sonny Boy Mosby); Arch Johnson (Stanley Bumpas); Chill Wills (Mr. Ike); *Zara Cully (Mama Lavorn)*; Fayard Nicholas (Benny); Joe Attle (Henry); *Lauren Jones (Erleen); Brenda Sykes (Jelly)*.

Emma Jones is being divorced by her husband because of her affair with white policeman Joe Worth. Emma bears Worth's child and contests the divorce. Fearing a scandal, Worth beats Emma to convince her to drop the suit.

LT. ROBIN CRUSOE, U.S.N.   Island Exotic   1966/Comedy

Walt Disney; 114 min.; *Producers*: Bill Walsh/Ron Miller; *Director*: Byron Paul; *Screenplay*: Bill Walsh/Don DaBradi; *Music*: Bob Brunner; *Camera*: William Snyder; *Editor*: Cotton Warburton; *Cast*: Dick Van Dyke (Lt. Robin Crusoe); *NANCY KWAN (WEDNESDAY)*; Akim Tamiroff (Tanamashu); Arthur Malet (Umbrella Man); Tyler McVey (Captain); P.L. Renoudet (Pilot); Peter Duryea (Co-pilot); John Dennis (Crew Chief).

Lt. Robin Crusoe becomes marooned on an island and finds Wednesday. She is on the island because she would not marry the man her father chose for her. Soon other women arrive and Crusoe organizes the women seeking independence into an army. The women succeed in convincing the men that their native god approves of their new ways. Meanwhile, Wednesday has fallen in love with Crusoe and they dance together, which in her culture means they are married. Crusoe, who does not want to marry Wednesday, is rescued just in time by the Navy.

THE LIFE AND TIMES OF JUDGE ROY BEAN   Mexican   1972/Western

National General Pictures; 124 min.; *Producer*: John Foreman; *Director*: John Huston; *Screenplay*: John Milius; *Music*: Maurice Jarre; *Camera*: Richard Moore; *Editor*: Hugh S. Fowler; *Cast*: Paul Newman (Judge Roy Bean); Jacqueline Bisset (Rose Bean); Ava Gardner (Lily Langtry); Tab Hunter (Sam Dodd); John Huston (Grizzly Adams); Stacy Keach (Bad Bob); *VICTORIA PRINCIPAL (MARIA ELENA)*; Anthony Perkins (Rev. LaSalle); Roddy McDowall (Frank Gass); Ned Beatty (Tector Crites); Anthony Zerbe (Hustler); Jim Burk (Bart Jackson); Matt Clark

(Nick the Grub); Steve Kanaly (Whorehouse Lucky Jim).

Roy Bean goes to the outlaw town of Vinegaroon for refuge from rape and robbery charges. Instead of being welcomed he is nearly beaten to death. He is nursed by Maria Elena, who soon becomes his mistress. Bean plans to get revenge on the town and sets himself up as Judge Roy Bean. Maria Elena dies giving birth to Bean's child.

A LIFE IN THE BALANCE   Mexican   1955/Adventure

20th Century-Fox; 74 min.; *Producer*: Leonard Goldstein; *Director*: Harry Horner; *Screenplay*: Robert Presnell, Jr./Leo Townsend; *Music*: Raul Lavista; *Camera*: J. Gomez Urquiza; *Editor*: George Gittens; *Cast*: Ricardo Montalban (Antonio Gomez); *ANNE BANCROFT (MARIA IBINIA)*; Lee Marvin (The Murderer); Jose Perez (Paco Gomez); Rodolfo Acosta (Lt. Fernando); Carlos Muzquiz (Capt. Saldana); George Trevino (Sergeant); Jose Torvay (Andres Martinez).

Maria Ibinia and Antonio Gomez are lovers on the trail of the murderer.

LIMEHOUSE BLUES   Chinese   1934/Drama

Paramount; 65 min.; *Producer*: Arthur Hornblow, Jr.; *Director*: Alexander Hall; *Screenplay*: Arthur Phillips/Cyril Hume; *Music*: Sam Coslow; *Camera*: Harry Fischbeck; *Cast*: George Raft (Harry Young); Jean Parker (Toni); *ANNA MAY WONG (TU TUA)*; Kent Taylor (Eric Benton); Montagu Love (Pug Talbot); Billy Bevan (Herb); Louis Vincenot (Rhama); E. Alyn Warren (Ching Lee); Robert Loraine (Inspector Sheridan).

Tu Tua is involved with half caste Harry Young. When he leaves her for Toni, Tu Tua informs the police of Young's illegal activities. She then kills herself.

LITTLE BIG MAN   Native American--Cheyenne   1970/Western

National General Pictures; 147 min.; *Producer*: Stuart Miller; *Director*: Arthur Penn; *Screenplay*: Calder Willingham; *Music*: John Hammond; *Camera*: Harry Stradling, Jr.; *Editor*: Dede Allen; *Cast*: Dustin Hoffman (Jack Crabb); Faye Dunaway (Mrs. Pendrake); Martin Balsam (Allardyce T. Merriweather); Richard Mulligan (General George Armstrong Custer); Chief Dan George (Old Lodge Skins); Jeff Corey (Wild Bill Hickok); *AMY ECCLES (SUNSHINE)*; Jean Peters (Olga); Carole Androsky (Caroline); Robert Little Star (Little Horse); Cal Bellini (Younger Bear); Ruben Moreno (Shadow That Comes In Sight); Steve Snehmayne (Burns Red In The Sky).

(Sunshine is seen in only a small segment of this film.) Jack Crabb is living among the Cheyenne. He and Sunshine marry and have a child. They live an idyllic life until the cavalry attack their camp and kill Sunshine and her baby.

LITTLE EGYPT   Arab--Egyptian   1951/Drama

Universal; 81 min.; *Producer*: Jack Gross; *Director*: Frederick de
Cordova; *Screenplay*: Oscar Brodney/Doris Gilbert; *Camera*: Russell
Metty; *Editor*: Edward Curtiss; *Cast*: Mark Stevens (Wayne Cravat);
RHONDA FLEMING (IZORA); Nancy Guild (Sylvia Graydon); Charles Drake
(Oliver Doane); Tom D'Andrea (Max); Minor Watson (Cyrus Graydon);
Steven Geray (Pasha); Verna Felton (Mrs. Doane); Kathryn Givney
(Cynthia Graydon); John Litel (Shuster).

Cafe dancer Izora passes herself off as an Egyptian princess
and becomes an exotic/erotic dancer at the 1893 Chicago Exposition.
She is arrested for indecent exposure. Wayne Cravat, the man she
loves, is interested in Sylvia Graydon. At her trial her pretense is
revealed and she and Wayne finally get together.

THE LITTLE MINISTER   Gypsy   1934/Drama

RKO; 104 min.; *Producer*: Pandro S. Berman; *Director*: Richard Wallace;
Screenplay: Jane Murfin/Sarah Y. Mason/Victor Heerman; *Music*: Max
Steiner; *Camera*: Henry Gerrard; *Editor*: William Hamilton; *Cast*:
KATHARINE HEPBURN (BABBIE); John Beal (Gavin); Alan Hale (Rob Dow);
Donald Crisp (Dr. McQueen); Lumsden Hare (Thammas); Beryl Mercer
(Margaret); Billy Watson (Mican Dow); Dorothy Strickney (Jean); Mary
Gordon (Nanny); Frank Conroy (Lord Rintoul); Elly Malyon (Evalina);
Reginald Denny (Capt. Halliwell).

Babbie falls in love with the new minister, Gavin, of a small
Scottish village. The congregation becomes extremely irate when
Gavin returns Babbie's affections.

LITTLE TOKYO, U.S.A.   Japanese   1942/Drama

20th Century-Fox; 54 min.; *Producer*: Bryan Fox; *Director*: Otto Brower;
Screenplay: George Bricker; *Music*: Emil Newman; *Camera*: Joseph
MacDonald; *Editor*: Harry Reynolds; *Cast*: Preston Foster (Michael
Steele); Brenda Joyce (Maris Hanover); Harold Huber (Takimura); Don
Douglas (Hendricks); *JUNE DUPREZ (TERU)*; George E. Stone (Kingoro);
Abner Biberman (Satsuma); Charles Tannen (Marsten); Frank Orth
(Jerry); Edward Soohoo (Suma); Leonard Strong (Fujiama); J. Farrell
MacDonald (Capt. Wade).

Teru is in the United States working as a spy for the Japanese
prior to Pearl Harbor.

LIVING BETWEEN TWO WORLDS   Black   1963/Drama

Empire Films; 78 min.; *Producer*: Horace Johnson; *Director*: Robert
Johnson; *Screenplay*: Horace Johnson; *Music*: Gordon Zahler; *Camera*:
William Zsigmond; *Editor*: Gene Evans; *Cast*: *MAYE HENDERSON (MOM)*;
ANITA POREE (BUCKY); *MIMI DILLARD (HELEN)*; Horace Jackson (Harvey);
Irvin Mosley (Papa); Kyle Johnson (Larry); Derrick Lewis (Norman);

Geraldine West (Mrs. Peters).

Harvey is having difficulty choosing between the ministry and
becoming a jazz musician. His mother and sister, Bucky, support the
ministry. His fiancee, Helen, wants the jazz musician to emerge.
After Helen is raped by two white men, Harvey chooses the ministry.

LONE WOLF McQUADE   Mexican   1983/Action

Orion; 107 min.; *Producers*: Yoram Ben-Ami/Steve Carver; *Director*:
Steve Carver; *Screenplay*: B.J. Nelson; *Camera*: Roger Shearman;
Editor: Anthony Redman; *Music*: Francesco De Masi; *Cast*: Chuck Norris
(J.J. McQuade); David Carradine (Rawley Wilkes); *BARBARA CARRERA
(LOLA RICHARDSON)*; Leon Isaac Kennedy (Marcus Jackson); Robert
Beltran(Arcadio "Kayo" Ramos); L.Q. Jones (Dakota); Dana Kimmell
(Sally); R.J. Armstrong (Captain T. Tyler); Jorge Cervera (Jefe).

Widowed Lola Richardson is the lover of Rawley Wilkes until she
meets J.J. McQuade and decides to move in with him. Wilkes tries to
kill them, but McQuade's martial arts expertise saves them.

THE LONG DUEL   Indian   1967/Adventure

Paramount; 115 min.; *Producer/Director*: Ken Annakin; *Screenplay*:
Peter Yeldham; *Music*: Patrick John Scott; *Camera*: Jack Hildyard;
Editor: Bert Bates; *Cast*: Yul Brynner (Sultan); Trevor Howard (Freddy
Young); Harry Andrews (Superintendent Stafford); Andrew Keir
(Gungaram); Charlotte Rampling (June Stafford); *VIRGINIA NORTH
(CHAMPA)*; Laurence Naismith (McDougal); Maurice Denham (Governor);
Imogen Hassal (Tara); Paul Hardwick (Jamadar).

Another story of the British occupation of India. Champa is
tortured by the British to make her reveal the whereabouts of the
rebel leader sultan.

THE LONG ROPE   Mexican   1961/Drama

20th Century-Fox; 61 min.; *Producer*: Margia Dean; *Director*: William
Witney; *Screenplay*: Robert Hamner; *Camera*: Kay Norton; *Editor*: Peter
Johnson; *Cast*: Hugh Marlowe (Jonas Stone); Alan Hale (Sheriff John
Millard); Robert Wilke (Ben Matthews); *LISA MONTELL (ALICIA ALVAREZ)*;
Chris Robinson (Reb Gilroy); Jeffrey Morris (Will Matthews); David
Renard (Louis Ortega); *Madeleine Holmes (Senora Dana)*;
John Alonzo (Manuel Alvarez); Jack Powers (Luke Simms); Kathryn Harte
(Mrs. Creech).

Senora Dona Vega frames her son-in-law Manuel Alvarez for murder,
hoping he will be hanged, thus leaving her daughter, Alicia, free to
marry a local land baron who stole land from the Vega family. Jonas
Stone discovers that Senora Dona Vega is the real murderer.

THE LONG SHIPS   Arab--Moor   1964/Adventure

Columbia; 124 min.; *Producer*: Irving Allen; *Director*: Jack Cardiff;
Screenplay: Berkely Mather/Beverly Cross; *Music*: Dusan Radic; *Camera*:
Christopher Challis; *Editor*: Geoff Foot; *Cast*: Richard Widmark
(Rolfe); Sidney Poitier (El Mansuh); Russ Tamblyn (Orm); *ROSANNA
SCHIAFFINO (AMINAH)*; Beba Looncar (Gerda); Oscar Homolka (Krok);
Edward Judd (Sven); Clifford Evans (King Harald); Jeanne Moody
(Yiva); Colin Blakely (Rhykka); Gordon Jackson (Vahlin); David Lodge
(Olla); Paul Stassino (Raschid); Lionel Jeffreies (Aziz).

    An adventure about the Viking's search for the Golden Bell of
St. James. Their quest leads them to Morocco where they are captured
by El Mansuh. Aminah is El Mansuh's first wife. The Vikings manage
to overcome the Moors and El Mansuh and Aminah die.

LORD JIM   Asian   1965/Adventure

Columbia; 154 min.; *Producer/Director/Screenplay*: Richard Brooks;
Music: Bronislau Kaper; *Camera*: Frederick A. Young; *Editor*: Alan
Orbiston; *Cast*: Peter O'Toole (Jim); Paul Lukas (Stein); *DAHLIA LAVI
(THE GIRL)*: Eli Wallach (The General); Curt Jurgens (Cornelius);
James Mason (Gentleman Brown); Akim Tamiroff (Schamberg); Jack
Hawkins (Marlow); Ichizo Itami (Waris); Tatsuo Saito (Du-Ramin).

    Jim tries to remain anonymous in the Orient and falls in love
with a native girl. He leads her people to revolt, thereby becoming
their hero.

THE LOSERS   Asian   1970/War Drama

Fanfare Film Productions; *Producer*: Joe Solomon; *Director*: Jack
Starrett; *Screenplay*: Alan Caillou; *Camera*: Nonong Rasca; *Editor*:
James Moore; *Cast*: William Smith (Link Thomas); Bernie Hamilton (Capt.
Jackson); Adam Roarke (Duke); Houston Savage (Dirty Denny); Eugene
Cornelius (Speed); Paul Koslo (Limpy); John Garwood (Sgt. Winston);
ANA KORITA (KIM SUE); LILLIAN MARGAREJO (SURIYA); *Paraluman (Mama-
san)*; Paul Nuckles (Kowalski); Ronnie Ross (Lt. Hayworth); Armando
Lucero (Screw); Jact Starrett (Chet Davis); Fran Dinh Hy. (Charlie);
Alan Cailou (Albanian); Paquito Salcedo (Tac Houn); Von Deming
(Shillick); Hernan Robles (Inspector).

    Duke resumes his affair with Suriya when he returns to Vietnam
on a rescue mission. They are both killed when ambushed by the Viet
Cong. Kim Sue works in a brothel run by Mama-san.

LOST BOUNDARIES   Black   1949/Drama

Film Classics; 99 min.; *Producer*: Louis de Rochemont; *Director*:
Alfred Werker; *Screenplay*: Virginia Shaler/Eugene Ling; *Music*: Jack
Schaindlin; *Camera*: William J. Miller; *Editor*: David Kummins; *Cast*:
BEATRICE PEARSON (MARCIA CARTER); Mel Ferrer (Scott Carter); Richard

Hylton (Howard Carter); Susan Douglas (Shelley Carter); Canada Lee
(Lt. Thompson); Rev. Robert A. Dunn (Rev. John Taylor); Grace Coppin
(Mrs. Mitchell); Carleton Carpenter (Andy); Seth Arnold (Clint Adams);
Wendell Holmes (Mr. Mitchell).

Marcia Carter and her husband, Dr. Scott Carter, decide to pass
for white because of their light skin and their nonacceptance into
the Black community. In their white community they are totally
accepted as white and their children have no idea that they are Black.
At the outbreak of World War II Dr. Carter tries to enlist in the Navy
but is rejected as the truth about his background surfaces with
traumatic results.

LOST COMMAND   Arab   1966/Adventure

Columbia; 129 min.; *Producer/Director*: Mark Robson; *Screenplay*:
Nelson Gidding; *Music*: Franz Waxman; *Camera*: Robert Surtees; *Editor*:
Dorothy Spencer; *Cast*: Anthony Quinn (Lt. Col. Raspeguy); Alain Delon
(Capt. Esclavier); George Segal (Mahidi); Michele Morgan (Countess de
Clairefons); Maurice Roney (Capt. Boisfeuras); *CLAUDIA CARDINALE
(AICHA)*; Gregoire Aslan (Ben Saad); Jean-Claude Bercq (Lt. Orsini);
Syl Lamont (Sgt. Verte); Jacques Marin (The Mayor); Jean-Paul Moulinot
(De Guyot); Andres Monreal (Ahmed); Gordon Heath (Dia); Simono
(Sapinsky).

Aicha is a member of the Algerian underground fighting against
the French occupation. She is also involved with a smuggling ring.
She alternates between the virgin and the whore image so she becomes
involved with French Capt. Esclavier to obtain information on the
French occupation and to cover her smuggling activities. When Capt.
Esclavier finds he is being used, he beats Aicha.

LOST IN THE STARS   Black   1974/Musical

American Film Theater; 114 min.; *Producer*: Ely Landau; *Director*:
Daniel Mann; *Screenplay*: Alfred Hayes; *Music/Lyrics*: Kurt Weill/
Maxwell Anderson; *Camera*: Robert Hauser; *Editor*: Walt Hannemann;
Cast: Brock Peters (Stephan Kumalo); *MELBA MOORE (IRINA)*; Raymond
St. Jacques (John Kumalo); Clifton Davis (Absalom); Paul Rogers
(James Jarvis); *Pauline Meyers (Grace)*; *Paula Kelly (Rose)*.

Musical version of CRY, THE BELOVED COUNTRY. Irina is a poor
ghetto woman in Johannesburg, South Africa.

THE LOST MAN   Black   1969/Drama

Universal; 105 min.; *Producers*: Edward Muhl/Melville Tucker;
Director: Robert Alan Aurthur; *Screenplay*: Robert Alan Aurthur;
Music: Quincy Jones; *Camera*: Gerald Finnerman; *Editor*: Edward Mann;
Cast: Sidney Poitier (Jason Higgs); Joanna Shimkus (Cathy Ellis); Al
Freeman, Jr. (Dennis Laurence); Michael Tolan (Hamilton); Leon Bibb
(Eddie Moxy); *BEVERLY TODD (SALLY)*; Richard Dysart (Barnes).

Sally aids fugitive Jason Higgs.

THE LOST VOLCANO   Jungle Exotic   1950/Adventure

Mongram; 75 min.; *Producer*: Walter Mirisch; *Director/Screenplay*:
Ford Beebe; *Camera*: Marcel Le Picard; *Editor*: Richard Heermance;
Cast: Johnny Sheffield (Bomba); Donald Woods (Paul Gordon); Marjorie
Lord (Ruth Gordon); John Ridgely (Barton); *ELENA VERDUGO (NONA)*;
Tommy Ivo (David); Don Harvey (Higgins); Grandon Rhodes (Charles
Langley); robert Lewis (Daniel).

Nona is a native girl.

LOVE IS·A MANY SPLENDORED THING   Eurasian   1955/Drama

20th Century-Fox; 102 min.; *Producer*: Buddy Adler; *Director*: Henry
King; *Screenplay*: John Patrick; *Music*: Alfred Newman; *Camera*: Leon
Shamroy; *Editor*: William Reynolds; *Cast*: William Holden (Mark
Elliott); *JENNIFER JONES (HAN SUYIN)*; Torin Thatcher (Mr. Palmer-
Jones); Isobel Elsom (Adeline Palmer-Jones); Virginia Gregg (Ann
Richards); Richard Loo (Robert Hung); *Soo Yong (Nora Hung)*; Philip
Ahn (Third Uncle); Jorja Curtright (Suzanne); *Donna Martell
(Suchen)*; *Candace Lee (Oh-no)*; Kam Tong (Dr. Sen).

Eurasian doctor Han Suyin reluctantly becomes involved with news
reporter Mark Elliott--who is white and married. As their love grows,
Mark plans to leave his wife. However, she will not give him a
divorce. Because of racism and her relationship with Mark, Han Suyin
loses her job and considers returning to China, presently involved in
its Marxist revolution. Mark takes an assignment in Korea and is
killed, leaving Han Suyin to face the world alone.

THE LOVES OF CARMEN   Gypsy   1948/Drama

Columbia; 99 min.; *Producer/Director*: Charles Vidor; *Screenplay*:
Helen Deutsch; *Music*: Mario Castelnuovo-Tedesco; *Camera*: William
Snyder; *Editor*: Charles Nelson; *Cast*: *RITA HAYWORTH (CARMEN)*; Glenn
Ford (Don Jose); Ron Randell (Andres); Victor Jory (Garcia); Luther
Adler (Dancaire); Arnold Moss (Colonel); Joseph Buloff(Remendado);
Margaret Wycherly (Old Crone); Bernard Nedeli (Pablo); John Baragrey
(Lucas); Philip Van Zandt (Sergeant).

[Based on the opera *Carmen.*] Don Jose falls in love with Carmen.
After killing his Colonel, he and Carmen take off into the mountains
where he becomes an outlaw. Jealous of Carmen's marriage to Garcia,
the leader of the outlaw band, Don Jose kills him and becomes leader
in his place. Carmen then becomes involved with wealthy bullfighter
Lucas. Jose's jealousy getting the better of him, he goes into town
to confront Carmen and begs her to return with him. She refuses, so
he stabs her just as the police show up and kill him. They die in
each other's arms.

MA AND PA KETTLE AT WAIKIKI   Hawaiian   1955/Comedy

Universal; 79 min.; *Producer*: Leonard Goldstein; *Director*: Lee Sholem; *Screenplay*: Jack Henley/Harry Clork/Elwood Ullman; *Music*: Joseph Gershenson; *Camera*: Clifford Stine; *Editor*: Virgil Vogel; *Cast*: Marjorie Main (Ma Kettle); Percy Kilbride (Pa Kettle); Lori Nelson Rosie Kettle); Byron Palmer (Bob Baxter); Russell Johnson (Eddie Nelson); *HILO HATTIE (MAMA LOTUS)*; Loring Smith (Rodney Kettle); Lowell Gilmore (Robert Coates); Mabel Albertson (Mrs. Andrews); Fay Roope (Fulton Andrews); Oliver Blake (Geoduck); Teddy Hart (Crowbar); Esther Dale (Birdie Hicks).

    Mama Lotus and her husband are the Hawaiian equivalents of Ma and Pa Kettle.

THE MACK   Black   1973/Drama

Cinerama; 110 min.; *Producer*: Harvey Bernard; *Director*: Michael Campus; *Screenplay*: Robert J. Poole; *Music*: Willie Hutch; *Camera*: Ralph Woolsey; *Editor*: Frank C. Decot; *Cast*: Max Julian (Goldie); Don Gordon (Hank); Richard Pryor (Slim); *CAROL SPEED (LULU)*; Roger E. Mosley (Olinga); Dick Williams (Pretty Tony); *Juanita Moore (Mother)*.

    Goldie is a Black pimp; Lulu is one of his hookers. Goldie's mother is killed by the police.

MACKENNA'S GOLD   Native American--Apache   1969/Western

Columbia; 128 min.; *Producers*: Carl Foreman/Dimitri Tiomkin; *Director*: J. Lee Thompson; *Screenplay*: Carl Foreman; *Music*: Quincy Jones; *Camera*: Joseph MacDonald; *Editor*: Bill Lenny; *Cast*: Gregory Peck (Mackenna); Omar Sharif (Colorado); Telly Savalas (Sgt. Tibbs); Camilla Sparv (Inga); Keenan Wynn (Sanchez); *JULIE NEWMAR (HESH-KE)*; Ted Cassidy (Hachita); Eduardo Ciannelli (Prairie Dog); Dick Peabody (Avila); Rudy Diaz (Besh); Robert Phillips (Monkey); *Shelly Morrison (The Pima Squaw)*; J. Robert Porter (Young Englishman); John Garfield, Jr. (Adams' Boy).

    Hesh-ke is a renegade Apache searching for lost gold.

MACUMBA LOVE   Brazilian   1960/Thriller

United Artists; 86 min.; *Producer/Director*: Douglas Fowley; *Screenplay*: Norman Graham; *Music*: Enrico; *Camera*: Rudolfo Icsey; *Cast*: Walter Reed (Weils); *ZIVA RODANN (VENUS DE VIASA)*; June Wilkinson (Sarah); William Wellman, Jr. (Sarah's Husband); *Ruth De Souza (Mama Rataloy)*.

    American writer Weils goes to a South American island to expose the use of voodoo and human sacrifice. While there he is attracted to Venus de Viasa who does not like his snooping around. Venus is under the spell of Madame Rataloy, the Voodoo Queen. Things climax

when Weils' daughter and her husband arrive. Venus, under the
control of Mama Rataloy, is about to kill Weils' son-in-law when the
police arrive. Mama Rataloy is killed and Venus is freed from her
spell.

MAD ABOUT LOVE   Mexican   1954/Comedy

Universal; 81 min.; *Producer*: John W. Rogers; *Director*: Jesse Hibbs;
Screenplay: Geoffrey Homes; *Camera*: George Robinson; *Editor*: Frank
Gross; *Cast*: Joel McCrea (Del Rockwell); Mari Blanchard (Aldis Spain);
Race Gentry (Ti); Murvyn Vye (Jennings); Irving Bacon (Doc); John
Pickard (Duke); Ewing Mitchell (Sheriff); *PILAR DEL REY (JUANITA)*;
William J. Williams (Graves).

     Not enough information was available to describe this role
accurately.

THE MAD DOCTOR OF MARKET STREET   Island Exotic   1942/Thriller

Universal; 61 min.; *Producer*: Paul Malvern; *Director*: Joseph H. Lewis;
Screenplay: Al Martin; *Camera*: Jerry Ash; *Editor*: Ralph Dixon; *Cast*:
Lionel Atwill (Dr. Benson); Una Merkel (Aunt Margaret); Nat Pendleton
(Red); Claire Dodd (Patricia); Richard Davies (Jim); Anne Nagel (Mrs.
Wm. Saunders); *ROSINA GALLI (TANAO)*; John Eldredge (Dwight); Ray
Mala (Barab); Noble Johnson (Elon); Al Kikuhme (Halo); Milton Kibbee
(Hadley).

     Tanao is the local native girl.

MADAME BUTTERFLY   Japanese   1932/Drama

Paramount; 86 min.; *Producer*: B.P. Schulberg; *Director*: Marion
Gering; *Screenplay*: Josephine Lovett/Joseph Moncure March; *Music*:
Puccini, adapted by W. Frank Harling; *Camera*: David Abel; *Cast*:
SYLVIA SIDNEY (CHO-CHO-SAN); Cary Grant (Lt. Pinkerton); Charles
Ruggles (Lt. Barton); Sandor Kallay (Goro); Irving Pichel (Yomadori);
Helen Jerome Eddy (Cho-Cho's Mother); Edmund Breese (Cho-Cho's
Grandfather); Judith Vosselli (Mme. Goro); *Dorothy Libaire (Peach
Blossom)*; *Louise Carter (Suzuki)*; Sheila Terry (Mrs. Pinkerton).

     Based on Puccini's opera *Madame Butterfly*. The story of Cho-Cho-
San, a geisha who falls in love with American Lt. Pinkerton, bears
his child, and kills herself because he loves a white woman.

MADONNA OF THE SEVEN MOONS   Gypsy   1946/Drama

Universal; 88 min.; *Producer*: R.E. Dearing; *Director*: Arthur Crabtree;
Screenplay: Roland Pertwee; *Music*: Louis Levy; *Camera*: Jack Cox;
Cast: *PHYLLIS CALVERT (MADALENA LABARDI/ROSANNA)*; Patricia Roc
(Angela Labardi); Stewart Granger (Nino); Peter Glenville (Sandru);
John Stuart (Giuseppe); Reginal Tate (Ackroyd); Peter Murray Hill

(Logan); Dalcie Gray (Nesta); Alan Haines (Evelyn); Hilda Bayley (Mrs. Fiske); Evelyn Darvell (Millie); Nancy Price (Madonna Barucci); Jean Kent (Vittoria); Amy Veness (Tessa).

Every seven years Madalena Labardi, a refined, quiet married woman, is transformed into the flashy, fiery Rosanna, who has an affair with gypsy Nino.

THE MAGIC CARPET   Arabian Nights   1951/Fantasy

Columbia; 82 min.; *Producer*: Sam Katzman; *Director*: Lew Landers; *Screenplay*: David Mathews; *Camera*: Ellis W. Carter; *Editor*: Edwin Bryant; *Cast*: *LUCILLE BALL (NAIAH)*; John Agar (Ramoth); *PATRICIA MEDINA (LIDA)*; George Tobias (Gazi); Raymond Burr (Boreg); Gregory Gay (Ali); Rick Vallin (Abdul); *Jo Gilbert (Maras)*; William Fawcett (Ahkmid); Perry Sheehan (Copah); *Doretta Johnson (Tanya)*; *Linda Williams (Estar)*; *Eileen Howe (Varnah)*; *Winona Smith (Ziela)*.

Both Naiah and Lida have eyes for Ramoth--who is really the heir to the Caliph's throne. After Ramoth overcomes Boreg, who usurped the throne, Ramoth chooses Lida as his wife.

THE MAGIC GARDEN   Black [African]   1952/Comedy

Swan Films/Trans Lux; 63 min.; *Producer/Director*: Donald Swanson; *Screenplay*: Ferdinand Webb/Donald Swanson/C. Pennington-Richards; *Music*: Ralph Trewhela; *Camera*: C. Pennington-Richards; *Editor*: Gerald Ehrlich; *Cast*: Tommy Ramokgopa (The Thief); *DOLLY RATHEBE (LILI)*; Harriet Qubeka (Mrs. Sakabona); David Mnkwanazi (Lucas Ranku); Victor Cwai (John); Grinsell Nogauza (Mr. Shabulala); Lucas Khosa (Isaac Wela); Linda Madikisa (Mrs. Wela); Jonathan Mzamo (The Priest); Willard Cele (The Pennywhistle Player).

Lili is a poor widow with four children.

THE MAGNIFICENT SEVEN   Mexican   1960/Western

United Artists; 126 min.; *Producer*: Walter Mirisch; *Director*: John Sturges; *Screenplay*: William Roberts; *Music*: Elmer Bernstein; *Camera*: Charles Lang; *Editor*: Ferris Webster; *Cast*: Yul Brynner (Chris); Eli Wallach (Calvera); Steve McQueen (Vin); Horst Buchholz (Chico); Charles Bronson (O'Reilly); Robert Vaughn (Lee); Brad Dexter (Harry Luck); James Coburn (Britt); Vladimir Sokoloff (Old Man); *ROSENDA MONTEROS (PETRA)*; Jorge Martinez De Hoyos (Hilario); Whit Bissell (Chamlee); Val Avery (Henry); Bing Russell (Robert); Rico Alaniz (Sotero); Robert Wilke (Wallace).

Petra falls in love with would-be gunslinger Chico and convinces him that living in a Mexican village with her would be a better way of life.

MAHOGANY   Black   1975/Drama

Paramount; *Producer*: Rob Cohen/Jack Ballard; *Director*: Berry Gordy;
Screenplay: John Byrum; *Music*: Michael Masser; *Camera*: David Watkin;
Editor: Peter Zinner; *Cast*: DIANA ROSS *(TRACY)*; Bill Dee Williams
(Brian); Anthony Perkins (Sean); Jean-Pierre Aumont (Christian
Rosetti); *Beah Richards (Florence)*; Nina Foch (Mrs. Evans); Marisa
Mell (Carlotta Gavina); Lenard Norris (Will).

Tracy rises from poverty to become a top fashion model. She
gives up career to return to Brian, a grassroots politician.

THE MAIN ATTRACTION   Asian   1963/Drama

MGM; 90 min.; *Producer*: John Patrick; *Director*: Daniel Petrie;
Screenplay: Daniel Petrie/John Patrick; *Music*: Andrew Adorian;
Camera: Geoffrey Unsworth; *Editor*: Geoffrey Foot; *Cast*: Pat Boone
(Eddie); NANCY KWAN *(TESSIE)*; Mai Zetterling (Gina); Yvonne Mitchell
(Elenora); Kieron Moore (Ricco); John Le Mesurier (Bozo); Carl
Duering (Bus Driver); Warren Mitchell (Proprietor).

Tessie is a circus bareback rider, who becomes involved with
drifter Eddie. After an accident Eddie flees the circus, fearing he
many be accused of murder. However, he realizes that he loves
Tessie and must face the truth. When he returns he finds that the
man did not die.

THE MAIN CHANCE   Black   1966/Drama

Merton Park-Embassy; 61 min.; *Producer*: Jack Greenwood; *Director*:
John Knight; *Screenplay*: Richard Harris; *Music*: Bernard Ebbinghouse;
Camera: James Wilson; *Editor*: Derek Holding; *Cast*: Gregoire Aslan
(Potter); Edward De Souza (Michael Blake); TRACY REED *(CHRISTINE)*;
Stanley Meadows (Joe Hayes); Jack Smethurst (Ross); Bernard Stone
(Miller); Will Stampe (Carter); Julian Strange (Butler); Joyce
Barbour (Madame Rozanne).

Christine is a secretary who becomes involved with diamond
smuggling.

MALAYA   Malaysian   1950/Adventure

MGM; 98 min.; *Producer*: Edwin H. Knopf; *Director*: Richard Thorpe;
Screenplay: Frank Fenton; *Music*: Bronislau Kaper; *Camera*: George
Folsey; *Editor*: Ben Lewis; *Cast*: Spencer Tracy (Carnahan); James
Stewart (John Royer); VALENTINA CORTESA *(LUANA)*; Sydney Greenstreet
(The Dutchman); John Hodiak (Kellar); Lionel Barrymore (John
Manchester); Gilbert Roland (Romano); Roland Winters (Bruno Gruber);
Richard Loo (Col. Genichi Tomura); Ian MacDonald (Carlos Tassuma);
Tom Helmore (Matisson).

Luana is the romantic interest of Carahan who is trying to

sabotage Japanese interests in Malaya.

MAN AND BOY   Black & Mexican   1972/Western

A.J. Cornelius Crean Films; 98 min.; *Producer*: Marvin Miller;
Director: E.W. Swackhamer; *Screenplay*: Harry Essex/Oscar Saul; *Music*:
J.J. Johnson; *Camera*: Arnold Rich; *Editor*: John A. Martinelli; *Cast*:
Bill Cosby (Caleb Revers); *GLORIA FOSTER (IVY REVERS)*; Leif Erickson
(Sheriff Mossman); George Spell (Billy Revers); Douglas Turner Ward
(Lee Christmas); John Anderson (Stretch); Henry Silva (Caine); Dub
Taylor (Atkins); *Shelley Morrison (Rosita)*: Yaphet Kotto (Nate
Hodges).

Ivy is the wife of Caleb Revers, a landowner in post-Civil War
Arizona. Rosita is the wife of a Seminole who provides shelter for
Caleb and his son, Billy, while they are searching for their stolen
horse.

A MAN CALLED ADAM   Black   1966/Drama

Avco Embassy; 103 min.; *Producers*: Ike Jones/James Waters; *Director*:
Leo Penn; *Screenplay*: Les Pine/Tina Rome; *Music*: Benny Carter;
Camera: Jack Priestly; *Editor*: Carl Lerner; *Cast*: Sammy Davis, Jr.
(Adam Johnson); Ossie Davis (Nelson Davis); *CICELY TYSON (CLAUDIA
FERGUSON)*; Louis Armstrong (Willie "Street Daddy" Ferguson); Frank
Sinatra, Jr. (Vincent); Peter Lawford (Manny); Mel Torme; *Lola
Falana (Theo)*; *Jeanette Du Bois (Martha)*; Johnny Brown (Les); George
Rhodes (Leroy); Michael Silva (George); Michael Lipton (Bobby Gales).

Hot-headed trumpet player Adam Johnson falls in love with civil
rights activist Claudia Ferguson. As Claudia begins to understand
Adam she helps him overcome his hot temper and heavy drinking. Their
relationship sours while Adam is playing a series of one-night engage-
ments in the South, and Claudia leaves Adam. Adam's attempts to play
the trumpet end tragically when he collapses on stage and dies.

A MAN CALLED HORSE   Native American--Sioux   1970/Western

Cinema Center; 114 min.; *Producer*: Sandy Howard; *Director*: Elliot
Silverstein; *Screenplay*: Jack DeWitt; *Music*: Leonard Rosenman;
Camera: Robert Hauser; *Editor*: Philip Anderson; *Cast*: Richard Harris
(Lord John Morgan); *DAME JUDITH ANDERSON (BUFFALO COW HEAD)*; Jean
Gascon (Batise); Manu Tupou (Yellow Hand); *CORINNA TSOPEI (RUNNING
DEER)*; Dub Taylor (Joe); William Jordan (Bent); James Gammon (Ed);
Edward Little Sky (Black Eagle); *Lina Marin (Thorn Rose)*; *Tamara
Garina (Elk Woman)*; Michael Baseleon (He-Wolf). [Running Deer and
Buffalo Cow Head are the major women characters in this supposedly
authentic Native American film; however, neither actress is Native
American.]

Running Deer is the virgin Indian princess who falls for the
white hero. Buffalo Cow Head is an old Indian shrew. Neither

character does much to enhance the image of Native American women.

MAN-EATER OF KUMAON   Indian   1948/Adventure

Universal-International; 80 min.; *Producers*: Monty Shaff/Frank P.
Rosenberg; *Director*: Byron Haskin; *Screenplay*: Jeanne Bartlett/Lewis
Meltzer; *Music*: Hans J. Salter; *Camera*: William C. Mellor; *Editor*:
George Arthur; *Cast*: Sabu (Narain); Wendell Corey (Dr. John Collins);
JOANNE PAGE (LALI); Morris Carnovsky (Ganga Ram); *Argentina Brunetti
(Sita)*; James Moss (Panwah); Ted Hecht (Native Doctor); John Mansfield
(Bearer); Eddie Das (Ox-cart Driver); Charles Wagenheim (Panwah's
Father).

     An evil tiger on the loose in the jungle causes Lali, Narain's
wife, to lose her child. She is then unable to conceive another.

MAN FROM DEL RIO   Mexican   1956/Western

United Artists; 82 min.; *Producer*: Robert L. Jacks; *Director*: Harry
Horner; *Screenplay*: Richard Carr; *Music*: Frederick Steiner; *Camera*:
Stanley Cortez; *Editor*: Robert Golden; *Cast*: Anthony Quinn (Dave
Robles); *KATY JURADO (ESTELLA)*; Peter Whitney (Ed Bannister); Douglas
Fowley (Doc Adams); John Lurch (Bill Dawson); Whit Bissell (Breezy
Morgan); Douglas Spencer (Jack Tillman); Guinn "Big Boy" Williams
(Fred Jasper); Marc Hamilton (George Dawson).

     Estella is the girlfriend of gunslinger Dave Robles.

THE MAN IN THE MIDDLE   Asian   1964/Drama

20th Century-Fox; 94 min.; *Producer*: Walter Seltzer; *Director*: Guy
Hamilton; *Screenplay*: Keith Waterhouse/Willis Hall; *Music*: John Barry;
Camera: Wilkie Cooper; *Editor*: John Bloom; *Cast*: Robert Mitchum (Lt.
Col. Barney Adams); *FRANCE NUYEN (KATE DAURAY)*; Barry Sullivan (Gen.
Kempton); Trevor Howard (Major Kensington); Keenan Wynn (Lt.
Winston); Sam Wanamaker (Major Kaufman); Alexander Knox (Co. Burton);
Gary Cockrell (Lt. Morse).

     Kate Dauray is a nurse and provides minor romantic interst for
Lt. Col. Barney Adams.

THE MAN WHO WOULD BE KING   Indian   1975/Adventure

Allied Artists; 129 min.; *Producer*: John Foreman; *Director*: John
Huston; *Screenplay*: Gladys Hill/John Huston; *Music*: Maurice Jarre;
Camera: Oswald Morris; *Editor*: Russell Lloyd; *Cast*: Sean Connery
(Daniel Dravot); Michael Caine (Peachy Carnehan); Christopher Plummer
(Rudyard Kipling); Saeed Jaffrey (Billy Fish); Karroum Ben Bouih
(Kafu-Selim); Jack May (District Commissioner); Doghmi Larbi (Ootah);
SHARIKA CAINE (ROXANNE).

Based on Rudyard Kipling's story of two British soldiers
finding a secret tribal people with great wealth. Because of Daniel
Dravot's resemblance to Alexander the Great his is installed as their
leader and Roxanne is the exotic tribal beauty chosen by Dravot to be
his bride. But the thought of marrying a "god" is too much for her
and her unwillingness reveals that he is only human after all.

MANDINGO   Black   1975/Drama

Paramount; 127 min.; *Producer*: Dino De Laurentiis; *Director*: Richard
Fleischer; *Screenplay*: Norman Wexler; *Music*: Maurice Jarre; *Camera*:
Richard H. Kline; *Editor*: Frank Bracht; *Cast*: James Mason (Maxwell);
Susan George (Blanche); Perry King (Hammond); Richard Ward
(Agamemnon); *BRENDA SYKES (ELLEN)*; Ken Norton (Mede); *Lillian Hayman
(Lucrezia Borgia)*; Roy Poole (Doc Redfield); Ji-Tu Cumbuka (Cicero).

This story of slavery in the old South focuses on Hammond, the
son of a wealthy plantation owner who marries Blanche but is disap-
pointed in her because she is not a virgin on their wedding night.
He buys Black slave Ellen and falls in love with her. However, because of the racial barrier, he is only able to keep her as a slave
and will not acknowledge the children she bears him.

THE MARINES ARE COMING   Mexican   1935/Drama

Mascot Production; 70 min.; *Producer*: Nat Levine; *Director*: David
Howard; *Screenplay*: James Gruen; *Music*: Gus Edwards; *Camera*: Ernie
Miller/William Nobles; *Editor*: Thomas Scott; *Cast*: William Haines
(Bill Traylor); Esther Ralston (Dorothy); Conrad Nagel (Captain
Benton); *ARMIDA (ROSITA)*; Edgar Kennedy (Buck Martin); Hale Hamilton
(Colonel Gilroy); George Regas (The Torch).

Rosita is a singer/dancer who uses men to get her way.

MARK OF THE GORILLA   Jungle Exotic   1950/Adventure

Columbia; 68 min.; *Producer*: Sam Katzman; *Director*: William Berke;
Screenplay: Carroll Young; *Camera*: Ira S. Morgan; *Editor*: Henry
Batista; *Cast*: Johnny Weissmuller (Jungle Jim); Trudy Marshall
(Barbara Bentley); *SUZANNE DALBERT (NYOBI)*; Onslow Stevens (Brandt);
Robert Purcell (Kramer).

Nyobi is the queen of a country whose gold was stolen by thieves.
Jungle Jim helps her to find the culprits and retrieve the gold.

MARK OF THE HAWK   Black [African]   1958/Drama

Universal; 83 min.; *Producer*: Lloyd Young; *Director*: Michael Audlay;
Screenplay: M. Kean Carmichael; *Music*: Malyas Seiber; *Camera*: Edwin
Hillier; *Editor*: Edward Jarvis; *Cast*: *EARTHA KITT (RENEE)*; Sidney
Poitier Obara); Juano Hernandez (Amugu); John McIntire (Craig); Helen

Horton (Barbara); Marne Maitland (Sundar Lal); Gerard Heinz (Governor General); Patrick Allen (Gregory); Clifton Macklin (Kanda); Earl Cameron (Prosecutor); Ewen Solon (Inspector); David Goh (Ming Tao).

Renee is a highly educated woman married to Obara, a representative of the workers. Obara is torn between duty to his job and his desire to become a terrorist like his brother to work to rid Africa of white domination.

MARK OF THE RENEGADE   Mexican   1951/Adventure

Universal-International; 81 min.; *Producer*: Jack Gross; *Director*: Hugo Fregonese; *Screenplay*: Louis Soloman/Robert H. Andrews; *Music*: Frank Skinner; *Camera*: Charles P. Boyle; *Editor*: Frank Gross; *Cast*: Ricardo Montalban (Marcos); *CYD CHARISSE (MANUELLA)*; J. Carrol Naish (Luis); Gilbert Roland (Don Pedro Garcia); *Andrea King (Anita Gonzales)*; George Tobias (Baroosa); Antonio Moreno (Jose De Vasquez); *Georgia Backus (Duenna Conception)*; Robert Warwick (Col. Vega); Armando Silvestre (Miguel De Gandara); *Bridget Carr (Rosa)*; Alberto Morin (Cervera).

Manuella is the romantic interest of renegade Marcos.

THE MARK OF ZORRO   Mexican   1940/Adventure

20th Century-Fox; 93 min.; *Director*: Rouben Mamoulian; *Screenplay*: John Taintonfoote; *Music*: Alfred Neumann; *Camera*: Arthur Miller; *Editor*: Robert Bischoff; *Cast*: Tyrone Power (Diego Vega); *LINDA DARNELL (LOLITA QUINTERO)*; Basil Rathbone (Estaban Pasquale); *Gale Sondergaard (Inez Quintero)*; Eugene Pallette (Fray Felipe); J. Edward Bromberg (Don Luis Quintero); Montagu Love (Don Alejandro Vega); *Janet Beecher (Senora Isabella Vega)*; Robert Lowery (Rodrigo); Chris-Pin Martin (Turnkey).

Lolita Quintero doesn't care much for the foppish Diego Vega, but becomes very enamored of Zorro, not realizing they are the same person. Eventually Zorro and Lolita are married.

MARLOWE   Latin American   1969/Mystery

MGM; 95 min.; *Producer*: Gabriel Katzka; *Director*: Paul Bogart; *Screenplay*: Stirling Silliphant; *Music*: Peter Matz; *Camera*: William H. Daniels; *Editor*: Gene Ruggiero; *Cast*: James Garner (Philip Marlowe); Gayle Hunnicutt (Mavis Wald); Carroll O'Connor (Lt. Christy French); *RITA MORENO (DOLORES GONZALES)*; Sharon Farrell (Orfamay Quest); William Daniels (Crowell); Jackie Coogan (Hicks); H.M. Wynant (Steelgrave); Paul Stevens (Dr. Lagardie); Bruce Lee (Wong); Corinne Camacho (Julie).

Dolores is a stripper involved in a murder/ Philip Marlowe is on the case, and when he is wounded Dolores takes care of him. Marlowe discovers that Dr. Lagardie is involved in the murder and is also involved with Dolores. Dolores is killed by Dr. Lagardie, who then commits suicide.

MAROC 7 Tahitian & Black 1968/Adventure

Paramount; 92 min.; *Producers*: John Gale/Leslie Phillips; *Director*: Gerry O'Hara; *Screenplay*: David Osborn; *Music*: Kenneth V. Jones; *Camera*: Kenneth Talbot; *Editor*: John Jympson; *Cast*: Gene Barry (Simon Grant); Elsa Martinelli (Claudia); Cyd Charisse (Louise Henderson); *ALEXANDRA STEWART (MICHELE CRAIG)*; *Tracy Reed (Vivienne)*; Leslie Phillips (Raymond Love); Denholm Elliott (Insp. Barrada); Eric Barker (Professor Bannen); Maggie London (Suzie).

Michele Craig is assistant to police inspector, Barrada. Barrada is hunting jewel thieves who are planning to steal an ancient Arab medallion. The thieves are posing as fashion photographers to find the medallion. While they are taking pictures they find the medallion. Claudia takes it from Simon, only to be killed by Michele. She takes the medallion and flees home to Tahiti.

THE MASK OF FU MANCHU Chinese 1932/Mystery

MGM; 72 min.; *Directors*: Charles Brabin/Charles Vidor; *Screenplay*: John Willard/Edgar Woolf/Irene Kuhn; *Camera*: Tony Gaudio; *Editor*: Ben Lewis; *Cast*: Boris Karloff (Dr. Fu Manchu); Lewis Stone (Nayland Smith); Karen Morley (Sheila Barton); Charles Starrett (Terrence Granville); *MYRNA LOY (FAH LO SEE)*; Jean Hersholt (Professor Von Berg); Lawrence Grant (Sir Lionel Barton); David Torrence (McLeod).

Fah Lo See is the daughter of Fu Manchu. She is helping him locate the sword and mask of Genghis Khan so he can reincarnate himself as the great Khan and take over the world. He is foiled by Nayland Smith.

THE MASKED RIDER Mexican 1941/Adventure

Universal; 58 min.; *Assoc. Producer*: Will Cowan; *Director*: Ford Beebe; *Screenplay*:; Sherman Lowe/Victor McLeod; *Camera*: Charles Van Enger; *Cast*: Johnny Mack Brown (Larry); Fuzzy Knight (Patches); Nell O'Day (Jean); Grant Withers (Douglas); *VIRGINIA CARROLL (MARGERITA)*; Guy D'Ennery (Don Sebastian); *Carmelia Cansino (Carmencita)*; Roy Barcroft (Luke); Dick Botiller (Pablo); Al Haskell (Jose); Rico De Montez (Manuel).

Margerita is the romantic interest of Larry.

MASSACRE Native American 1933/Drama

First National; 70 min.; *Director*: Alan Crosland; *Screenplay*: Ralph Block/Sheridan Gibney; *Camera*: George Barnes; *Editors*: Terry Morse; *Cast*: Richard Barthelmess (Joe Thunder Horse); *ANN DVORAK (LYDIA)*;

Dudley Digges (Quisenberry); Claire Dodd (Norma); Henry O'Neill
(Dickinson); Robert Barrat (Dawson); Arthur Hohl (Dr. Turner); Sidney
Toler (Shanks); Clarence Muse (Sam); William V. Mong (Grandy); Agnes
Narcha (Jennie).

Lydia is a well-educated, determined woman fighting for reform
on her reservation. In the process she transforms Joe Thunder Horse
from a "cigar store"-type Indian to one who truly cares about the
plight of his people.

THE MASTER GUNFIGHTER   Mexican   1975/Western

Taylor-Laughlin Distributing Corp.; 120 min.; *Producer*: Philip P.
Parslow; *Director*: Frank Laughlin; *Music*: Lalo Schifrin; *Camera*: Jack
A. Marta; *Editors*: William Reynolds/Danford Greene; *Cast*: Tom Laughlin
(Finley); Ron O'Neal (Paulo); GeoAnne Sosa (Chorika); *BARBARA CARRERA
(EULA)*.

Eula is the wife of Finley, a gunfighter who settles his scores
with a gun and sword. Eula's family killed a group of Indians.
Finley avenges the Indians by killing the Mexicans.

THE McMASTERS   Native American   1970/Western

Chevron Pictures; 97 min.; *Producer*: Monroe Sachson; *Director*: Alf
Kjellin; *Screenplay*: Harold Jacob Smith; *Music*: Coleridge-Taylor
Perkinson; *Camera*: Lester Shorr; *Cast*: Burl Ives (McMasters); Brock
Peters (Benjie); David Carradine (White Feather); *NANCY KWAN (ROBIN)*;
Jack Palance (Kolby); John Carradine (Preacher); L.Q. Jones (Russell);
R.G. Armstrong (Watson); Dane Clark (Spencer).

After the Civil War, Benjie comes home and is made an equal
partner in the home of his former owner, McMaster. When they join
forces with the local Indian band he is given Robin as a bride. She
is at first unwilling, but after he rapes her they come to a mutual
understanding and fall in love.

A MEDAL FOR BENNY   Paisanos (Spanish/Indian)   1945/Comedy

Paramount; 77 min.; *Producer*: Paul Jones; *Director*: Irving Pichel;
Screenplay: Frank Butler; *Music*: Victor Young; *Camera*: Lionel Lindon;
Editor: Arthur Schmidt; *Cast*: *DOROTHY LAMOUR (LOLITA SIERRA)*; Arturo
De Cordova (Joe Morales); J. Carrol Naish (Charley Martini); Mikhail
Resumny (Raphael Catalina); Fernando Alvarado (Chito Sierra); Charles
Dingle (Zalk Mibbs); Frank McHugh (Edgar Lovekin); *Rosita Moreno
(Toodles Castro)*; Grant Mitchell (Mayor); Douglas Dumbrille (General).

Lolita Sierra has always been Benny Martini's girl, but with
Benny in the army Joe Morales has been trying to win Lolita's heart.
When Benny is killed in action and becomes a hero Lolita feels a new
sense of loyalty to the deceased Benny. But Joe persists and wins
Lolita in the end.

Ethel Waters, *Member of the Wedding* (Paramount, 1952)

MELINDA   Black   1972/Drama

MGM; 109 min.; *Producer*: Pervis Atkins; *Director*: Hugh A. Robertson;
Screenplay: Lonne Elder III; *Music*: Jerry Butler/Jerry Peters;
Camera: Wilmer C. Butler; *Editor*: Paul L. Evans; *Cast*: Calvin Lockhart
(Frankie J. Parker); *ROSALIND CASH (TERRY DAVIS); VONETTA McGEE
(MELINDA)*; Paul Stevens (Mitch); Rockne Tarkington (Tank); Ross Hagen
(Gregg Van); Renny Roker (Dennis Smith); Judyann Elder (Gloria); Jim
Kelly (Charles Atkins); Jan Tice (Marcia).

Frankie J. Parker meets Melinda and goes to bed with her. However, she is soon murdered by the syndicate because of tapes she made
while mistress to the syndicate boss. Frankie sets out to solve her
murder. Helping him is his ex-mistress, Terry Davis, who masquerades
as Melinda to get the tapes. She is kidnapped by the gang and held
hostage until Frankie manages to save her and dispose of the syndicate boss.

MEMBER OF THE WEDDING   Black   1952/Drama

Paramount; 91 min.; *Producer*: Stanley Kramer; *Director*: Fred
Zinnemann; *Screenplay*: Edna Anhalt/Edward Anhalt; *Camera*: Hal Mohr;
Editor: William Lyon; *Cast*: *ETHEL WATERS (BERENICE SADIE BROWN)*; Julie
Harris (Frankie Addams); Brandon de Wilde (John Henry); Arthur Franz
(Jarvis); Nancy Gates (Janice); William Hansen (Mr. Addams); James
Edwards (Henry Camden Brown); Harry Bolden (T.T. Williams).

Berenice is the housekeeper. She is also closest to the
family's daughter, Frankie, who is having difficulty dealing with
her brother's marriage and with adolescence.

MEN OF THE NORTH   Canadian Indian   1930/Adventure

MGM; 80 min.; *Producer/Director*: Hal Roach; *Screenplay*:Willard Mack;
Camera: Roy Binger; *Editor*: Thomas Held; *Cast*: Gilbert Roland (Louis);
Barbara Leonard (Nedra); Robert Greaves, Jr. (Priest); *NINA QUARTERO
(WOOLIE-WOOLIE)*; Arnold Korff (John Ruskin); Robert Elliott (Sgt.
Mooney); George Davis (Corp. Smith).

Not enough information was available to describe this role
accurately.

A MESSAGE TO GARCIA   Cuban   1936/Drama

20th Century-Fox; 110 min.; *Producer*: Darryl F. Zanuck; *Director*:
George Marshall; *Screenplay*: W.P. Lipscomb/Gene Fowler; *Music*: Louis
Silvers; *Camera*: Rudolph Mate; *Editor*: Herbert Levy; *Cast*: Wallace
Beery (Sgt. Dory); *BARBARA STANWYCK (SENORITA RAPHAELITA MODEROS)*;
John Boles (Lt. Rowan); Alan Hale (Dr. Krug); Herbert Mundin (Henry
Piper); Mona Barrie (Spanish Spy); Enrique Acosta (General Garcia);
Juan Torena (Luis Maderos); Martin Garralaga (Rodriguez); *Glanca
Vischer (Chiquita)*.

Sgt. Dory has been sent to Cuba to inform the leaders of the revolution against Spanish rule that they have United States support. Sgt. Dory meets Senorita Raphaelita Moderos, the daughter of a deceased Cuban patriot. Raphaelita helps Sgt. Dory complete his mission.

MEXICALI ROSE   Mexican   1939/Musical

Republic; 58 min.; *Producer*: Harry Gray; *Director*: George Sherman; *Screenplay*: Gerald Geraghty; *Camera*: William Nobles; *Editor*: Tony Martinelli; *Cast*: Gene Autry (Gene); Smiley Burnette (Frog); Noah Beery (Valdez); *LUANA WALTERS (ANITA LOREDO)*; William Farnuto (Padre Dominic); LeRoy Mason (Blythe); Wally Albright (Tommy); *Kathryn Frye (Chalita)*; Roy Barcroft (McEltroy); Dick Botiller (Manuel); Vic Demourelle (Hollister); John Beach (Brown); Henry Otho (Alcalde); Champion.

Anita runs a mission for children and receives help from Gene Autry.

MEXICAN HAYRIDE   Mexican   1948/Comedy

Universal; 77 min.; *Director*: Charles T. Barton; *Screenplay*: Oscar Brodney/John Grant; *Music*: Walter Scharf; *Camera*: Charles Van Enger; *Editor*: Frank Gross; *Cast*: Bud Abbott (Harry Lambert); Lou Costello (Joe Bascom); Virginia Grey (Montana); *LUVA MALINA (DAGMAR)*; John Hubbard (David Winthrop); Pedro de Cordoba (Senor Martinez); Fritz Feld (Prof. Ganzmeyer).

Dagmar is a sinister woman who uses Joe Bascom to trick people out of their money. She sings "Is It Yes, Or Is It No?"

MEXICAN SPITFIRE   Mexican   1940/Comedy

RKO; 67 min.; *Producer*: Cliff Reid; *Director*: Leslie Goodwins; *Screenplay*: Joseph A. Fields/Charles E. Roberts; *Music*: Paul Sawtell; *Camera*: Jack MacKenzie; *Editor*: Desmond Marquette; *Cast*: *LUPE VALEZ (CARMELITA)*; Leon Errol (Uncle Matt/Lord Epping); Donald Woods (Dennis); Linda Hayes (Elizabeth); Elisabeth Risdon (Aunt Della); Cecil Kellaway (Chumley); Charles Coleman (Butler).

Carmelita and Dennis return from their Mexican honeymoon to discover that Dennis' Aunt Della strongly disapproves of the marriage. Also on hand are Elizabeth (his ex-fiancee), who sets out to break up their marriage, and Uncle Matt, who approves of the union. Elizabeth manages to humiliate Carmelita, who, along with Uncle Matt, makes a mess of a business dinner between Dennis and Lord Epping. Carmelita and Uncle Matt leave for Mexico so Carmelita can get a divorce. There they meet Lord Epping and set things right. When they arrive back in New York Dennis is having a bachelor party on the eve of his wedding to Elizabeth. Carmelita informs Dennis that their divorce is not legal and that they are still married--to their mutual delight.

In the morning guests arrive for the wedding and Carmelita and
Elizabeth get into a fight which turns into a pie-throwing free-for-
all.

MEXICAN SPITFIRE AT SEA   Mexican   1942/Comedy

RKO; 73 min.; *Producer*: Cliff Reid; *Director*: Leslie Goodwins;
Screenplay: Jerry Cady/Charles Roberts; *Camera*: Jack MacKenzie;
Editor: Theron Warth; *Cast*: *LUPE VELEZ (CARMELITA)*; Leon Errol
(Uncle Matt/Lord Epping); Charles "Buddy" Rogers (Dennis); Zasu
Pitts (Miss Pepper); Elisabeth Risdon (Aunt Della); Florence Bates
(Mrs. Baldwin); Marion Martin (Fifi); Lydia Bilbrook (Lady Epping);
Eddie Dunn (Mr. Skinner); Harry Holman (Mr. Baldwin); Marten Lamont
(Purser).

Uncle Matt is trying to win Lord Epping's advertising account
and eliminate a business rival in the process. So Uncle Matt imper-
sonates Lord Epping, adding much confusion to this comic situation.

MEXICAN SPITFIRE OUT WEST   Mexican   1940/Comedy

RKO; 76 min.; *Producer*: Cliff Reid; *Director*: Leslie Goodwins;
Screenplay: Charles E. Roberts/Jack Townley; *Music*: Roy Webb; *Camera*:
Jack MacKenzie; *Editor*: Desmond Marquette; *Cast*: *LUPE VELEZ
(CARMELITA LINDSAY)*; Leon Errol (Matthew Lindsay/Lord Epping); Donald
Woods (Dennis Lindsay); Elisabeth Risdon (Aunt Della); Cecil Kellaway
(Chumley); Linda Hayes (Elizabeth); Lydia Bilbrook (Lady Epping);
Eddie Dunn (Skinner); Paul Everton (Dignitary); Charles Coleman
(Roberts); Grant Withers (Withers).

Carmelita and Uncle Matt become involved in identity swapping.

MEXICAN SPITFIRE SEES A GHOST   Mexican   1942/Comedy

RKO; 70 min.; *Producer* : Cliff Reid; *Director* : Leslie Goodwins;
Screenplay : Charles E. Roberts/Monte Brice; *Camera* : Russell Metty;
Editor: Theron Warth; *Cast* : Leon Errol (Uncle Matt/Lord Epping/
Hubbell); *LUPE VELEZ (CARMELITA)*: Charles "Buddy" Rogers (Dennis
Lindsay); Elisabeth Risdon (Aunt Della); Donald McBride (Percy Fitz-
Patten); Minna Gombell (Edith Fitz-Patten); Don Barclay (Fingers
O'Toole); John Maguire (Luders); Lillian Randolph (Hyacinth); Mantan
Moreland (Lightnin); Harry Tyler (Bascombe).

This time Carmelita is involved in haunted house shenanigans.

MEXICAN SPITFIRE'S BABY   Mexican   1941/Comedy

RKO; 70 min.; *Producer*: Cliff Reid; *Director*: Leslie Goodwins;
Screenplay: Jerry Cady/Charles E. Roberts; *Camera*: Jack MacKenzie;
Editor: Theron Warth; *Cast*: *LUPE VELEZ (CARMELITA)*; Leon Errol (Uncle
Matt/Lord Epping); Charles "Buddy" Rogers (Dennis); Zasu Pitts (Miss

Pepper); Elisabeth Risdon (Aunt Della); Fritz Feld (Pierre); Marion Martin (Fifi); Lloyd Corrigan (Chumley); Lydia Bilbrook (Lady Epping).

Carmelita adopts a French war baby along with Fifi, an attractive blonde who tends to disrupt Carmelita's wedded bliss.

MEXICAN SPITFIRE'S BLESSED EVENT   Mexican   1943/Comedy

RKO; 63 min.; *Producer*: Bert Gilroy; *Director*: Leslie Goodwins; *Music*: C. Bakaleinikoff; *Camera*: Jack MacKenzie; *Editor*: Harry Marker; *Cast*: *LUPE VELEZ (CARMELITA)*; Leon Errol (Uncle Matt); Elisabeth Risdon (Aunt Della); Walter Reed (Dennis); Lydia Bilbrook (Lady Epping); Hugh Beaumont; Aileen Carlyle; Alan Carney; Wally Brown; Ruth Lee; George Rogers; Don Kramer.

Carmelita and her husband have a baby.

MEXICAN SPITFIRE'S ELEPHANT   Mexican   1942/Comedy

RKO; 63 min.; *Producer*: Bert Gilroy; *Director*: Leslie Goodwins; *Screenplay*: Charles E. Roberts; *Music*: C. Bakaleinikoff; *Camera*: Jack MacKenzie; *Editor*: Harry Marker; *Cast*: *LUPE VELEZ (CARMELITA)*; Leon Errol (Uncle Matt/Lord Epping); Elisabeth Risdon (Aunt Della); Walter Reed (Dennis); Lydia Bilbrook (Lady Epping); Marion Martin (Diana); Lyle Talbot (Reddy); Luis Alberni (Luigi); George Cleveland (Chief Inspector); Marten Lamont (Arnold); Jack Briggs (Operative).

The elephant of the title is a trinket with a valuable diamond inside smuggled into the United States. Carmelita also sings and dances in two musical numbers.

MEXICANA   Mexican   1945/Comedy

Republic; 83 min.; *Producer/Director*: Alfred Santell; *Screenplay*: Frank Gill, Jr.; *Music*: Walter Scharf; *Camera*: Jack Marta; *Editor*: Arthur Roberts; *Cast*: Tito Guizar ("Pepe" Villarreal); Constance Moore (Alison Calvert); Leo Carrillo (Esteban (Guzman); *ESTELITA RODRIGUEZ (LUPITA)*; Howard Freeman (Beagle); Steven Geray (Laredo); Jean Stevens (Bunny).

Singer/dancer Lupita is romantically interested in Latin singing idol "Pepe," who pretends to be married to Alison Calvert so he can get all the amourous women off his back. Lupita sings a number called "Lupita."

MILDRED PIERCE   Black   1945/Melodrama

Warner Brothers; 111 min.; *Producer*: Jerry Wald; *Director*: Michael Curtiz; *Screenplay*: Ronald MacDougall/Catherine Turney; *Music*: Max Steiner; *Camera*: Ernest Haller; *Cast*: Joan Crawford (Mildred Pierce);

Ann Blyth (Veda Pierce); Jack Carson (Wally Fay); Zachary Scott (Monty Beragon); Eve Arden (Ida); Bruce Bennett (Bert Pierce); JoAnn Marlowe (Kay Pierce); *BUTTERFLY McQUEEN (LOTTIE)*.

Lottie is Mildred's maid. Veda humiliates her mother by giving Lottie Mildred's waitress uniform.

MIRACLE IN HARLEM   Black   1949/Drama

Herald Pictures/Screen Guild; 69 min.; *Producer*: Jack Goldberg; *Director*: Jack Kemp; *Screenplay*: Vincent Valentini; *Music*: John Gluskin; *Camera*: Don Melkames; *Cast*: *SHEILA GUYSE (JULIE WESTON)*; Stepin Fetchit (Swifty); *Hilda Offley (Aunt Hattie)*; William Greaves (Bert Hallam); *Sybyl Lewis (Alice Adams)*; Creighton Thompson (Rev. Jackson); Kenneth Freeman (Jim Marshall); Jack Carter (Philip Manley); Lawrence Carter (Albert Marshall).

All-Black film centers on Aunt Hattie and her foster daughter, Sheila, who are swindled out of their candy store. When the syndicate boss winds up dead Sheila is a prime suspect. She is eventually cleared.

THE MIRACLE WORKER   Black   1962/Drama

United Artists; 107 min.; *Producer*: Fred Coe; *Director*: Arthur Penn; *Screenplay*: William Gibson; *Music*: Laurence Rosenthal; *Camera*: Jack Horton; *Editor*: Aram Avakian; *Cast*: Anne Bancroft (Annie Sullivan); Patty Duke (Helen Keller); Victor Jory (Capt. Keller); Inga Swenson (Kate Keller); Andrew Prine (James Keller); Kathleen Comegys (Aunt Eve); *BEAH RICHARDS (VINEY)*; Jack Hollander (Mr. Anagnos).

Viney is a servant in the Keller household.

MR. BLANDINGS BUILDS HIS DREAM HOUSE   Black   1948/Drama

RKO; 94 min.; *Producers/Screenplay*: Norman Panama/Melvin Frank; *Director*: H.C. Potter; *Camera*: James Wong Howe; *Editor*: Harry Marker; *Cast*: Cary Grant (Jim Blandings); Myrna Loy (Muriel Blandings); Melvyn Douglas (Bill Cole); Sharyn Moffett (Joan Blandings); Connie Marshall (Betsy Blandings); *LOUISE BEAVERS (GUSSIE)*; Henry Simms (Reginald Denny).

Gussie is the Blandings' housekeeper who manages to provide Jim Blandings with an advertising slogan which saves the account of an important client. This enables the family to leave their overcrowded apartment and move to a house in the country.

MR. ROBINSON CRUSOE   Island Exotic   1932/Adventure

United Artists; 76 min.; *Producer*: Douglas Fairbanks; *Director*: Edward Sutherland; *Screenplay*: Tom Geraghty; *Music*: Alfred Newman; *Camera*:

Max Dupont; *Editor*: Robert Kern; *Cast*: Douglas Fairbanks (Steve Drexel); William Farnum (William Belmont); Earle Browne (Professor Carmichael); *MARIA ALBA (SATURDAY)*.

Steve Drexel bets that he can live on a desert island as Robinson Crusoe did. He and his dog, Rooney, begin life on a deserted island. He finds a man Friday, and also a woman whom he names Saturday, who only grunts. When the ship comes to retrieve Drexel, Saturday stows away on the boat. On their arrival in New York City, Drexel makes Saturday a Broadway star.

MOHAWK   Native American--Mohawk   1956/Western

20th Century-Fox; 79 min.; *Producer*: Edward L. Alperson; *Director*: Kurt Neumann; *Screenplay*: Maurice Geraghty/Milton Krims; *Music*: Edward L. Alperson, Jr.; *Camera*: Karl Struss; *Editor*: William B. Murphy; *Cast*: Scott Brady (Jonathan Adams); *RITA GAM (ONIDA)*; Neville Brand (Rokhawah); Lori Nelson (Cynthia Stanhope); Allison Hayes (Greta); John Hoyt (Butler); Vera Vague (Aunt Agatha); Rhys Williams (Clem Jones); Ted De Corsia (Kowanen); *Mae Clarke (Minikah)*; John Hudson (Capt. Langley); Tommy Cook (Keoga); Michael Granger (Priest).

Indian princess Onida loves artist Jonathan Adams but she is in competition with Cynthia Stanhope and Greta. When trouble breaks out between the Mohawks and whites, Adams chooses Onida. Minikah is the wife of the peace-loving Chief Kowanen.

THE MOON AND SIXPENCE   Tahitian   1942/Drama

United Artists; 89 min.; *Producer*: Loew Lewin; *Director/Screenplay*: Albert Lewin; *Music*: Dmitri Tiomkin; *Camera*: John F. Seitz; *Editor*: Richard L. Van; *Cast*: George Sanders (Charles Strickland); Herbert Marshall (Geoffrey Wolfe); Steve Geray (Dick Stroeve); Doris Dudley (Blanche Stroeve); Eric Blore (Capt. Nichols); *ELENA VERDUGO (ATA)*; Molly Lamont (Mrs. Strickland).

Ata becomes the last wife of artist Charles Stricklan as he is about to die and make a name for himself.

MOONLIGHT IN HAWAII   Hawaiian   1941/Comedy

Universal; 60 min.; *Assoc. Producer*: Ken Goldsmith; *Director*: Charles Lamont; *Screenplay*: Morton Grant/James Gow/Erna Lazarus; *Music*: Charles Previn; *Camera*: Stanley Cortez; *Editor*: Arthur Hilton; *Cast*: Jane Frazee (Toby); Leon Errol (Spencer); Mischa Auer (Clipper); Johnny Downs (Pete); Sunnie O'Dea (Gloria); *MARIA MONTEZ (ILANI)*; Marjorie Gateson (Mrs. Floto); Richard Carle (Lawton); Elaine Morey (Doris).

Ilani is the main feature of the film's only musical production number, "Aloha Low Down."

MORALS OF MARCUS   Arab--Syrian   1936/Drama

Gaumont-British; 72 min.; *Producer*: Julius Hagen; *Director*: Miles
Mander; *Screenplay*: Guy Bolton/Miles Mander; *Camera*: Sidney Blythe;
Editor: Miles Mander; *Cast*: *LUPE VELEZ (CARLOTTA)*; Ian Hunter (Sir
Marcus Ordeyne); Adrianne Allen (Judith); Noel Madison (Tony
Pasquale).

To escape a forced marriage to a sultan, Carlotta stows away
on a ship bound for England from Syria. She is protected by Sir
Marcus, who falls in love with her and wants to marry her. Thinking
that Sir Marcus only feels pity for her, she runs away to become a
cabaret singer in Paris. Sir Marcus sets out to find her and bring
her back.

THE MOUNTAIN MEN   Native American--Blackfoot   1980/Western

Columbia; 105 min.; *Producer*: Martin Shafer/Andrew Scheinman;
Director: Richard Lang; *Screenplay*: Fraser Clarke Heston; *Music*:
Michel Legrand; *Camera*: Michael Hugo; *Editor*: Eva Ruggiero; *Cast*:
Charlton Heston (Bill Tyler); Brian Keith (Henry Frapp); *VICTORIA
RACIMO (RUNNING MOON)*; Stephen Macht (Heavy Eagle); John Glover
(Nathan Wyeth); Seymour Cassel (La Bont); David Ackroyd (Medicine
Wolf); Cal Bellini (Cross Otter); Bill Lucking (Jim Walker); Ken
Ruta (Fontenelle); Victor Jory (Iron Belly); Danny Zapien (Blackfoot
Chief); Tim Haldeman (Whiskey Clerk).

One of the most recent films to degrade Indian women, the film
portrays Indian women as whores, as women who enjoy physical abuse,
and as happy slaves to men. Running Moon latches on to Bill Tyler
and refuses to return to her people because she loves him. When her
Indian ex-husband arrives, she is trampled by his horse and dragged
back to his home where he beats and sexually abuses her. When she
finally kills him it is to save Tyler's life. They ride off together.

THE MOUNTAIN ROAD   Chinese   1960/Adventure

Columbia; 102 min.; *Producer*: William Goetz; *Director*: Daniel Mann;
Screenplay: Alfred Hayes; *Music*: Jerome Moross; *Camera*: Burnett
Guffey; *Editor*: Edward Curtiss; *Cast*: James Stewart (Major Baldwin);
LISA LU (MADMAME SUE-MEI HUNG); Glenn Corbett (Collins); Henry/Harry
Morgan (Michaelson); Frank Silvera (General Kwan); James Best
(Niergaard); Rudy Bond (Miller); Mike Kellin (Prince); Frank Maxwell
(Bullo); Eddie Firestone (Lewis); Alan Baxter (General Loomis); Leo
Chen (Col. Li).

Madame Sue-Mei Hung is the widow of a general, now traveling
with United States Army Major Baldwin through war-torn China.
Baldwin is attracted to Sue-Mei but she does not understand his
indifference to the plight of her people. When some of his men are
killed he orders the destruction of an entire village to punish the
murderers, thereby killing hundreds of innocent women and children.
This act causes him to lose any chance of winning Sue-Mei's love,

but he does realize his mistake.

THE MUMMY   Arab--Egyptian   1932/Thriller

Universal; 78 min.; *Producer*: Stanley Bergermann; *Director*: Karl
Freund; *Screenplay*: John L. Balderson; *Camera*: Charles Stumar; *Cast*:
Boris Karloff (Im-Ho-Tep); *ZITA JOHANN (HELEN GROSVENOR)*; David
Manners (Frank Whemple); Edward Van Sloan (Professor Muller);
Bramwell Fletcher (Norton); Henry Victor (Marion); Noble Johnson
(Nubian); Arthur Byron (Sir Joseph Whemple).

Helen Grosvenor is the half-Egyptian descendant of ancient
Egyptian Princess Ananka. When archeologists find the Princess'
grave they unknowingly unleash Im-Ho-Tep--the man who loved Ananka--
now an evil mummy. Soon (Im-Ho-Tep is transformed into a man with
the help of tanna leaves. Realizing that Helen is her descendant he
sets out to restore Ananka to life. Helen becomes increasingly under
his spell, but is saved from him before she is completely consumed
by Ananka's spirit.

MUTINY ON THE BOUNTY   Tahitian   1935/Adventure

MGM; 132 min.; *Producer*: Irving Thalberg; *Director*: Frank Lloyd;
Camera: Arthur Edeson; *Editor*: Margaret Booth; *Cast*: Clark Gable
(Fletcher Christian); Charles Laughton (Capt. Bligh); Franchot Tone
(Byam); Dudley Digges (Bachus); Henry Stephenson (Sir Joseph Banks);
Donald Crisp (Burkitt); Eddie Quillan (Ellison); Francis Lister
(Capt. Nelson); Spring Byington (Mrs. Byam); *MARIA CASTANEDA/MOVITA
(TEHANI)*; *Mamo Clark (Maimiti)*; Robert Livingston (Young); Douglas
Walton (Stewart); Ian Wolfe (Samuel).

While in Tahiti Roger Byam--Fletcher Christian's friend--spends
his time with Tehani and arranges shore leave for Christian, who has
been forbidden to leave the ship by Capt. Bligh. While ashore
Christian falls in love with the island chief's granddaughter,
Maimiti. When it is time to leave, Christian promises to return.
Conditions become abominable on the ship and Christian leads a mutiny.
Returning to Tahiti, he marries Maimiti and Byam marries Tehani.
Soon the British arrive and the mutineers must leave. They settle
down to a life in exile on Pitcairn's island.

MUTINY ON THE BOUNTY   Tahitian   1962/Adventure

MGM; 179 min.; *Producer*: Aaron Rosenberg; *Director*: Lewis Milestone;
Screenplay: Charles Lederer; *Music*: Bronislau Kaper; *Camera*: Robert L.
Surtees; *Editor*: John McSweeney, Jr.; *Cast*: Marlon Brando (Fletcher
Christian); Trevor Howard (Capt. Bligh); Richard Harris (John Mills);
Hugh Griffith (Smith); Richard Haydn (Brown); *TARITA (MAIMITI)*;
Percy Herbert (Quintal); Duncan Lamont (Williams); Gordon Jackson
(Birkett); Chips Rafferty (Byrne); Noel Purcell (McCoy).

Remake of the 1935 version.

MY BLUE HEAVEN   Black   1950/Musical

20th Century-Fox; 96 min.; *Producer*: Sol C. Siegel; *Director*: Henry
Koster; *Screenplay*: Lamar Trotti/Claude Binyon; *Music*: Alfred Newman;
Camera: Arthur E. Arling; *Editor*: James B. Clark; *Cast*: Betty Grable
(Kitty Moran); Dan Dailey (Jack Moran); David Wayne (Walter Pringle);
Jane Wyatt (Janet Pringle); Mitzi Gaynor (Gloria Adams); Una Merkel
(Miss Gilbert); *LOUISE BEAVERS (SELMA)*; Laura Pierpont (Mrs. Johnson).

     Selma is the maid.

MY BROTHER, THE OUTLAW [See MY OUTLAW BROTHER]

MY DARLING CLEMENTINE   Native American--Apache   1946/Western

20th Century-Fox; 97 min.; *Producer*: Samuel G. Engel; *Director*: John
Ford; *Screenplay*: Samuel G. Engel/Winston Miller; *Music*: Cyril J.
Mockridge; *Camera*: Joseph MacDonald; *Editor*: Dorothy Spencer; *Cast*:
Henry Fonda (Wyatt Earp); *LINDA DARNELL (CHIHAUHAU)*; Victor Mature
(Doc Holliday); Walter Brennan (Old Man Clanton); Tim Holt (Virgil
Earp); Ward Bond (Morgan Earp); Cathy Downs (Clementine Carter);
Alan Mowbray (Granville Thorndyke); John Ireland (Billy Clanton);
Grant Withers (Ike Clanton); Roy Roberts (Mayor).

     Chihauhau is the mistress of Doc Holliday. When Clementine,
Doc's former love, arrives, Chihauhau feels she is being abandoned,
although Wyatt Earp and Clementine become romantically involved. For
spite Chihauhau goes to bed with Doc and Wyatt's rival, Billy Clanton.
Billy shoots Chihauhau and Holliday is unable to save her life.

MY FAVORITE BRUNETTE   Latin American   1947/Comedy

Paramount; 87 min.; *Producer*: Daniel Dare; *Director*: Elliott Nugent;
Screenplay: Edmund Beleia/Jack Rose; *Camera*: Lionel Linden; *Editor*:
Ellsworth Heagland; *Cast*: Bob Hope (Ronnie Jackson); *DOROTHY LAMOUR
(CARLOTTA MONTAY)*; Peter Lorre (Kismet); Lon Chaney (Willie); John
Hoyt (Dr. Lundau); Charles Dingle (Major Simon Montague); Reginald
Denny (James Collins); Frank Puglia (Baron Montay); Ann Doran (Miss
Rogers).

     Carlotta Montay is in trouble and she mistakenly thinks baby
photographer Ronnie Jackson is a private detective. Ronnie bungles
his attempts to help Carlotta, resulting in her disappearance and his
arrest for murder. As he is about to be executed Carlotta appears
and saves him.

MY GEISHA   Japanese   1962/Comedy

Paramount; 120 min.; *Producer*: Steve Parker; *Director*: Jack Cardiff;
Screenplay: Norman Krasna; *Music*: Franz Waxman; *Camera*: Shunichiro
Nakao; *Editor*: Archie Marshek; *Cast*: Shirley MacLaine (Lucy Dell/Yoko

Mori); Yves Montand (Paul Robaix); Edward G. Robinson (Sam Lewis); Bob Cummings (Bob Moore); *YOKO TANI (KAZUMI ITO)*; Tatsuo Saito (Kenichi Takata); Alex Gerry (Leonard Lewis); Nobuo Chiba (Shig); Ichiro Hayakawa (Hisaka Amatsu).

Lucy Dell follows her husband to Japan, disguising herself as a geisha to get a part in his new movie. Kazumi Ito helps her transform her into Yoko Mori. Eventually her husband finds out but they do not reveal the truth to the public.

MY OUTLAW BROTHER   Mexican   1951/Western
[MY BROTHER, THE OUTLAW]

United Artists; 82 min.; *Producer*: Benedict Bogeaus; *Director*: Elliott Nugent; *Screenplay*: Gene Fowler, Jr.; *Camera*: Jose Ortiz Ramos; *Editor*: George Crone; *Cast*: Mickey Rooney (Denny O'More); *WANDA HENDRIX (CARMEL ALVARADO)*; Robert Preston (Joe Warnder); Robert Stack (Patrick O'More); Carlos Muzquiz (El Captian); Fernando Waggner (Burger); Jose Torvay (Ortiz); Elliott Nugent (Ranger Captain).

Carmel Alvarado is loved by both Danny O'More and his brother Patrick.

THE MYSTERIOUS DESPERADO   Mexican   1949/Western

RKO; 61 min.; *Producer*: Herman Schlom; *Director*: Lesley Selander; *Screenplay*: Norman Houston; *Music*: Paul Sawtell; *Camera*: Nicholas Musuraca; *Cast*: Tim Holt (Tim); Richard Martin (Chito); *MOVITA CASTANEDA (LUISA)*; Edward Norris (Ramon); Frank Wilcox (Stevens); William Tannen (Barton); Robert B. Williams (Whittaker); Kenneth MacDonald (Sheriff); Frank Lackteen (Pedro).

Ramon is heir to some land but is being framed for murder by thieves who want the land. Tim and Chito help him out and pave the way for him to marry his girlfriend, Luisa.

THE MYSTERIOUS MR. MOTO   Japanese   1938/Mystery

20th Century-Fox; 62 min.; *Producer*: Sol M. Wurtzel; *Director*: Norman Foster; *Screenplay*: Philip MacDonald/Norman Foster; *Music*: Samuel Kaylin; *Camera*: Virgil Miller; *Editor*: Norman Colbert; *Cast*: Peter Lorre (Kentaro Moto); Henry Wilcoxon (Anton Darvak); Ann Richman (Mary Maguire); Erik Rhodes (David Scott-Frensham); Harlod Huber (Ernst Litmar); *KAREN SORRELL (LOTUS LIU)*; Leon Ames (Paul Brissac); Forrester Harvey (George Higgins); Fredrik Vogeding (Gottfried Brujo); Lester Matthews (Sir Charles Murchison); John Rogers (Sniffy).

Lotus Liu is Mr. Moto's assistant.

THE MYSTERIOUS MR. WONG   Chinese   1935/Mystery

Monogram; 60 min.; *Producer*: George Yohalem; *Director*: William Nigh;
Screenplay: Nina Howatt; *Camera*: Harry Neumann; *Editor*: Jack Ogilvie
Cast: Bela Lugosi (Mr. Wong); Wallace Ford (Jason Barton); Arline
Judge (Peg); Fred Warren (Tsung); *LOTUS WONG (MOONFLOWER)*; Robert
Emmet O'Connor (McGillicuddy); Edward Peil (Jen Yu); Luke Chan (Chan
Fu); Lee Shumway (Brandon).

     Moonflower is kept prisoner by the evil Mr. Wong. She is freed
when Mr. Wong is captured.

THE NAKED DAWN   Mexican   1955/Western

Universal; 82 min.; *Producer*: James O. Radford; *Director*: Edgar C.
Ulmer; *Screenplay*: Nina & Herman Schneider; *Music*: Herschel Burke
Gilbert; *Camera*: Frederick Gately; *Editor*: Dan Milner; *Cast*: Arthur
Kennedy (Santiago); Eugene Iglesias (Manuel); *BETTA ST. JOHN (MARIA)*;
Roy Engel (Guntz); *Charlita (Tita)*.

     Maria is the unhappy wife of Manuel, a poor farmer. When out-
law Santiago arrives at their home Maria falls in love with him.
Santiago has enlisted Manuel's help in recovering stolen money, but
soon Manuel is thinking about killing Santiago and keeping all the
money and Maria. However, the law intervenes and Santiago is killed,
allowing Maria and Manuel to keep the money and start a new life
together.

NAKED PARADISE   Hawaiian   1957/Adventure

American International; 68 min.; *Producer/Director*: Roger Corman;
Screenplay: Charles B. Griffith; *Music*: Ronald Stein; *Camera*: Floyd
Crosby; *Editor*: Charles Gross, Jr.; *Cast*: Richard Denning (Duke);
Beverly Garland (Max); *LISA MONTELL (KEENA)*; Leslie Bradley (Zac);
Richard Miller (Mitch); Jonathan Haze (Stony).

     Keena is the local native girl.

NANCY GOES TO RIO   Latin American   1950/Musical

MGM; 99 min.; *Producer*: Joe Pasternak; *Director*: Robert Z. Leonard;
Screenplay: Sidney Sheldon; *Music*: George Stoll; *Camera*: Ray June;
Editor: Adrienne Fazan; *Cast*: Ann Sothern (Frances Elliott); Jane
Powell (Nancy Barklay); Barry Sullivan (Paul Berten); *CARMEN MIRANDA
(MARINA RODRIGUEZ)*; Louis Calhern (Gregory Elliott); Scotty Beckett
(Scotty Sheldon); Fortunio Bonanova (Ricardo Domingos); Glenn Anders
(Arthur Barrett); Nelia Walker (Mrs. Harrison); Hans Conried
(Alfredo); Frank Fontaine (Masher).

     Marina Rodriguez is involved in the shenanigans of the plot but
is mostly relegated to song and dance.

NAVAJO   Native American--Navajo   1952/Drama

Lippert; 70 min.; *Producer*: Hall Bartlett; *Director/Screenplay*:
Norman Foster; *Music*: Keith Stevens; *Camera*: Virgil E. Miller;
Editor: Lloyd Nosler; *Cast*: Francis Lee Teller (Son of the Hunter);
John Mitchell (Grey Singer); *MRS. TELLER (Mother)*; Billy Draper
(Ute Guide); Hall Bartlett (Indian School Council).

Set on a Navajo reservation, the plot concerns the intrusion of
the government authorities on Navajo lives when officials come to
take Son of the Hunter away from his mother and the reservation and
send him to a government boarding school.

NAVY WIFE   Japanese   1956/Drama

Allied Artists; 82 min.; *Producer*: Walter Wanger; *Director*: Edward L.
Bernds; *Screenplay*: Kay Lenard; *Music*: Hans Salter; *Camera*: Wilfrid
Cline; *Editor*: Richard Cahoon; *Cast*: Joan Bennett (Peg Blain); Gary
Merrill (Jack Blain); *SHIRLEY YAMAGUCHI (AKASHI)*; Maurice Manson
(Capt. Arwin); Judy Nugent (Debby Blain); Teru Shimada (Mayor
Yoshida); Robert Nichols (Oscar); John Craven (Dr. Carter); Tom
Komuro (Ohara); Shizue Nakamura (Mitsuko).

Akashi is a geisha.

NEVADA SMITH   Cajun & Native American--Kiowa   1966/Western

Paramount; 128 min.; *Producer/Director*: Henry Hathaway; *Screenplay*:
John Michael Hayes; *Music*: Alfred Newman; *Camera*: Lucien Ballard;
Editor: Frank Bracht; *Cast*: Steve McQueen (Max Sand/Nevada Smith);
Karl Malden (Tom Fitch); Brian Keith (Jonas Cord); Arthur Kennedy
(Bill Bowdre); *SUZANNE PLESHETTE (PILAR)*; Raf Vallone (Father
Zaccardi); *JANET MARGOLIN (NEESA)*; Howard Da Silva (Warden); Pat
Hingle (Big Foot); Martin Landau (Jesse Coe).

Halfbreed Max Sand seeks revenge on the men who tortured and
murdered his parents. He kills one of the men in a knife fight in
which he is also wounded. His injuries are tended by Kiowa Neesa.
He is then sent to the same prison in Louisiana as another of the
killers. In prison he falls in love with Cajun Pilar, who is an
inmate of a nearby women's prison. He befriends the killer, Bowdre,
and the three escape from prison. Pilar dies from a snake bite, and
Max kills Bowdre. Max finally finds the last of the murderers, Tom
Fitch, but cannot bring himself to kill him. Regretting his previous
actions, Max begins a new life as Nevada Smith.

NEVER THE TWAIN SHALL MEET   Polynesian   1931/Drama

Metro; 79 min.; *Director*: W.S. Van Dyke; *Screenplay*: Edwin Justin
Mayer; *Music*: Arthur Freed; *Camera*: Merritt B. Gerstad; *Editor*: Ben
Lewis; *Cast*: Leslie Howard (Dan); *CONCHITA MONTENEGRO (TAMEA)*   C.
Aubrey Smith (Mr. Pritchard); Karen Morley (Maisie); Mitchell Lewis

(Larrieau); Hale Hamilton (Mellenger); Clyde Cook (Porter); Joan
Standing (Julia).

Wealthy Dan takes Tamea into his San Francisco home as a favor
to a deceased friend. He soon falls in love with her. Abandoning
his home and white fiancee, he travels with Tamea to Polynesia. Soon
he begins to drink heavily and their world turns sour. Julia, still
in love with Dan, arrives and persuades him to return home with her.

THE NEW CENTURIONS   Black   1972/Drama

Columbia; 103 min.; *Producers*: Irwin Winkler/Robert Chartoff;
Director: Richard Fleischer; *Screenplay*: Stirling Silliphant; *Music*:
Quincy Jones; *Camera*: Ralph Woolsey; *Editor*: Robert C. Jones; *Cast*:
George C. Scott (Sgt. Kilvinski); Stacy Keach (Roy Fehler); Jane
Alexander (Dorothy Fehler); Scott Wilson (Gus); *ROSALIND CASH
(LORRIE)*; Erik Estrada (Sergio); Clifton James (Whitey); Richard
Kalk (Milton); James Sikking (Sgt. Anders).

Lorrie is a nurse who takes care of wounded police officer Roy
Fehler. Later Roy investigates a burglary at Lorrie's apartment and
makes a pass at her. She rebuffs him because he is both drunk and
married. After Roy is beaten up trying to arrest a prostitute, he
returns to Lorrie's apartment and she takes care of him. They fall
in love and are extremely happy until Roy is killed on a routine
investigation.

A NIGHT IN PARADISE   Persian   1946/Fantasy

Universal; 84 min.; *Producer*: Walter Wanger; *Director*: Arthur Lubin;
Screenplay: Ernest Pascal; *Music*: Frank Skinner; *Camera*: Hal Mohr/W.
Howard Greene; *Editor*: Milton Carruth; *Cast*: *MERLE OBERON (DELARAI)*;
Turhan Bey (Aesop); Thomas Gomez (King Croesus); Gale Sondergaard
(ATtossa); Ray Collins (Leonides).

Delarai is the Queen of Persia and the betrothed of King Croesus
of Lydia. She is in love with Aesop, who is trying to prevent a war
and to keep King Croesus from finding out about his romance with
Delarai. Attossa is a sorceress who wants Croesus for herself.

NIGHT OF THE QUARTER MOON   Black   1959/Drama

MGM; 96 min.; *Producer*: Albert Zugsmith; *Director*: Hugo Haas; *Screen-
play*: Frank Davis/Franklin Coen; *Camera*: Ellis Carter; *Editor*: Ben
Lewis; *Cast*: *JULIE LONDON (GINNY NELSON)*; John Drew Barrymore
(Roderick/Chuck/Nelson); Nat "King" Cole (Cy Robbin); Anna Kashfi
(Maria Robbin); Dean Jones (Lexington Nelson); Agnes Moorhead
(Cornelia Nelson); Cathy Crosby (The Singer); Ray Anthony (Hotel
Manager); Jackie Coogan (Sgt. Bragen).

When Chuck and Ginny plan to marry, she explains to him that she
is one-quarter Black. They marry anyway and return to Chuck's home

town. The truth about Ginny's ancestry is soon revealed, and Chuck's parents pressure him into having the marriage annulled. Ginny's sympathetic lawyer manages to counter every move by the opposition until Chuck finally comes to his senses and admits that he loves Ginny and knew of her background.

NIGHTHAWKS   Middle Eastern   1981/Thriller

Universal; 99 min.; *Producer*: Martin Poll; *Director*: Bruce Malmuth; *Screenplay*: David Shaber; *Music*: Keith Emerson; *Camera*: James A. Conter; *Editor*: Christopher Holmes; *Cast*: Sylvester Stallone (Deke DaSilva); Billy Dee Williams (Matthew Fox); Lindsay Wagner (Irene); *PERSIS KHAMBATTA (SHAKKA)*; Nigel Davenport (Inspector Peter Hartman); Rutger Hauer (Wulfgar); Hilarie Thompson (Pam); Joe Spinell (Lt. Munafo); Walter Mathews (Commissioner).

Shakka is a terrorist working with Wulfgar in New York City. The police kill her.

NINE HOURS TO RAMA   Indian   1963/Thriller

20th Century-Fox; 125 min.; *Producer/Director*: Mark Robson; *Screenplay*: Nelson Gidding; *Music*: Malcolm Arnold; *Camera*: Arthur Ibbetson; *Editor*: Ernest Walter; *Cast*: Horst Buchholz (Nathuram Godse); Jose Ferrer (Superintendent Das); *VALERIE GEARSON (RANI MEHTA)*; Don Borisenko (Narayan Apte); Robert Morley (P.K. Mussad); Diane Baker (Sheila); Harry Andrews (General Singh); J.S. Casshyap (Mahatma Gandhi); Jairaj (G.D. Birla); David Abraham (Detective Manda).

Nathuram Godse becomes involved with the political faction opposed to Mahatma Gandhi and his policy of nonviolence. He falls in love with married Rani Mehta, a follower of Gandhi. Their relationship is unsuccessful because of their opposite viewpoints. Later Natu is assigned to assassinate Gandhi. Rani discovers the plan but cannot prevent the assassination.

NINE LIVES OF ELFEGO BACA   Mexican   1959/Drama

Walt Disney Productions; 79 min.; *Producer*: James Pratt; *Director/ Screenplay*: Norman Foster; *Music*: Buddy Baker; *Camera*: William Snyder; *Editor*: Edward Sampson, Jr.; *Cast*: Robert Loggia (Elfego Baca); Robert Simon (Deputy Ed Morgan); *LISA MONTELL (ANITA CHAVEZ)*; Nestor Paiva (Justice of the Peace); Leonard Strong (Zangana Martinez); Charles Maxwell (Dice Smith); Linc Foster (Jim Spears); Rico Alaniz (El Sinverguenza); Emmet Lynn (Grubstake Charlie).

Anita Chavez shelters Elfego Baca after he is beaten up trying to arrest a drunk. He falls in love with Anita, but she marries someone else, leaving Elfego to study law.

NO WAY OUT   Black   1950/Drama

20th Century-Fox; 106 min.; *Producer*: Darryl Zanuck; *Director/Screenplay*: Joseph Mankiewicz; *Music*: Alfred Newman; *Camera*: Milton Krasner; *Editor*: Barbara McLean; *Cast*: Sidney Poitier (Dr. Luther Brooks); Richard Widmark (Ray Biddle); Linda Darnell (Edie Johnson); Stephen McNally (Dr. Daniel Wharton); *MILDRED JOANNE SMITH (CORA BROOKS)*; *Ruby Dee (Connie)*; Dots Johnson (Lefty); Don Hicks (Johnny Biddle); Ken Christy (Officer Kowalski); Harry Bellaver (George Biddle).

Dr. Luther Brooks has jsut begun practicing medicine when he becomes involved in a case that precipitates racial violence. His only support comes from his wife, Cora, and the rest of his family.

NOBODY'S PERFECT   Japanese   1968/Adventure

Universal; 103 min.; *Producer*: Howard Christie; *Director*: Alan Rafkin; *Screenplay*: John D.F. Black; *Music*: Irving Gertz; *Camera*: Robert Wyckoff; *Editor*: Gene Palmer; *Cast*: Doug McClure (Doc Willoughby); *NANCY KWAN (TOMIKO MOMOYAMA)*; James Whitmore (Mike Riley); David Hartman (Boats McCafferty); Gary Vinson (Walt Purdy); James Shigeta (Toshi O'Hara); Steve Carlson (Johnny Crane); George Furth (Hamner); Keye Luke (Gondai-San).

On a previous liberty in Japan, Doc Willoughby and his cohorts stole a smiling Buddha from a Japanese village. Upon his return to Japan, Doc meets Tomiko (Tommy), a villager. He learns that the village has been very unlucky since the idol was stolen. After several unsuccessful episodes the statue is returned and Willoughby wins Tommy's love.

NORMAN. . .IS THAT YOU?   Black   1976/Comedy

MGM; 92 min.; *Producer/Director*: George Schlatter; *Screenplay*: Ron Clark/Sam Bobrick/George Schlatter; *Music*: William Goldstein; *Camera*: Gayne Rescher; *Editor*: George Folsey, Jr.; *Cast*: Redd Foxx (Ben Chambers); *PEARL BAILEY (BEATRICE CHAMBERS)* Dennis Dugan (Garson Hobart); Michael Warren (Norman Chanbers); *Tamara Dobson (Audrey)*; *Vernee Watson (Melody)*; Jayne Meadows (Adele, Garson's Mother).

Beatrice is shocked to learn that her son Norman is gay. Ben, Norman's father, sets Norman up with hooker Audrey to try and lure him away from his male lover. When the plan proves unsuccessful, Ben sleeps with Audrey himself. Melody, a friend of Norman's, seduces him, but Norman remains gay. When Norman announces that he is joining the Navy, Beatrice and Ben resolve their personal differences and take Garson, Norman's white lover, home to live with them, hoping Norman will eventually return to them.

NORTHERN PATROL   Canadian Indian   1953/Adventure

Allied Artists; 62 min.; *Producer*: Lindley Parsons; *Director*: Rex

Balley; *Screenplay*: Warren Douglas; *Camera*: William Sickner; *Editor*:
Leonard W. Herman; *Cast*: Kirby Grant (Col. Rod Webb); Chinock the
dog; Marion Carr (Quebec Kid); Bill Phipps (Frank Stevens); *CLAUDIA
DRAKE (OWEENA)*; Dale Van Sickel (Jason); Gloria Talbot (Meg Stevens);
Richard Walsh (Ralph Gregg); Emmett Lynn (Old Timer); Frank Lackteen
(Dancing Horse); Frank Sully (Bartender).

Oweena is the local Indian maid.

NORTHWEST MOUNTED POLICE   Canadian Indian   1940/Western

Paramount; 125 min.; *Producer/Director*: Cecil B. DeMille; *Screenplay*:
Alan LeMay/Jesse Lasky, Jr.; *Music*: Victor Young; *Camera*: Victory
Milner/W. Howard Green; *Cast*: Gary Cooper (Dusty Rivers); Madeleine
Carroll (April Logan); *PAULETTE GODDARD (LOUVETTE CORBEAU)*; Preston
Foster (Sgt. Jim Brett); Robert Preston (Ronnie Logan); George
Bancroft (Jacques Corbeau); Lynne Overman (Tod McDuff); Akim Tamiroff
(Dan Duroc); Walter Hampden (Big Bear); Lon Chaney, Jr. (Shorty);
Montague Love (Inspector Cabot).

Louvette Corbeau is a nasty fur-stealing, knife-wielding trader
who manages to destroy her love for mountie Ronnie Logan when she
lures him away from his post and begins the major uprising by the
oppressed Metis which became known as the Northwest Rebellion.

NOTHING BUT A MAN   Black   1963/Drama

Cinema V; 92 min.; *Producers*: Michael Roemer/Robert Young/Robert
Rubin; *Director*: Michael Roemer; *Screenplay*: Michael Romer/Robert
Young; *Camera*: Robert Young; *Editor*: Luke Bennett; *Cast*: Ivan Dixon
(Duff Anderson); *ABBEY LINCOLN (JOSIE DAWSON)*; *Gloria Foster (Lee)*;
Julius Harris (Will Anderson); Martin Priest (Driver); Leonard Parker
(Frankie); Yaphet Kotto (Jocko); Stanley Greene (Rev. Dawson); Helen
Lounck (Effie Simms); *Helene Arrindell (Doris)*.

Josie is a minister's daughter who marries (against her father's
wishes) the irresponsible Duff Anderson, who is unable to keep a job
and refuses to take care of his illegitimate son, whom Josie wants to
take in. Frustrated at losing his job, Duff abandons his pregnant
wife and returns to his dying father. Watching his father die, he
begins to realize that he must change his life. He retrieves his son
and returns to Josie.

OKEFENOKEE   Native American--Seminole   1959/Drama

Grand National; 76 min.; *Producer*: Aaron A. Daches; *Director*: Roul
Haig; *Screenplay*: Jesse Abbott; *Cast*: Peter Coe (Chick); Peggy Maley
(Owner of Swampside Dive); Henry Brandon (Gang Leader); *SERENA SANDE
(INDIAN GIRL)*; Walter Klavun (Drunk).

After being raped, Indian Girl must, according to tribal custom,

walk in the Everglades looking into the sun until she is blind. She
is stopped from doing this by her fiance.

OKLAHOMA TERRITORY   Native American--Cherokee   1960/Western

United Artists; 67 min.; *Producer*: Robert E. Kent; *Director*: Edward L.
Cahn; *Screenplay*: Orville H. Hampton; *Music*: Albert Glasser; *Camera*:
Walter Strenge; *Editor*: Grant Whytock; *Cast*: Bill Williams (Temple
Houston); *GLORIA TALBOTT (RUTH RED HAWK)*; Ted de Corsia (Buffalo
Horn); Walter Sande (Rosslyn); John Cliff (Larkin); Grant Richards
(Bigelow); Grandon Rhodes (Blackwell); X. Brands (Running Cloud);
Walter Baldwin (Ward Harian).

     Ruth Red Hawk is the daughter of Buffalo Horn, chief of the
Cherokees, who are being swindled out of their land.

THE OKLAHOMAN   Native American--Cherokee   1957/Western

Allied Artists; 80 min.; *Producer*: Walter Mirisch; *Director*: Francis
D. Lyon; *Screenplay*: Daniel B. Ullman; *Music*: Hans Salter; *Camera*:
Carl Guthrie; *Editor*: George White; *Cast*: Joel McCrea (John Brighton);
Barbara Hale (Anne Barnes); Brad Dexter (Cass Dobie); *GLORIA TALBOTT
(MARIA SMITH)*; Verna Felton (Mrs. Waynebrook); Douglas Dick (Mel
Dobie); Michael Pate (Charlie Smith); Anthony Caruso (Hawk); Esther
Dale (Mrs. Fitzgerald); Adam Williams (Randell).

     Maria Smith tries to assimilate into white society. John
Brighton takes her into his home to care for his daughter. She loves
him, but he thinks of her only as a sister. After John saves her
from being raped, Maria realizes that he loves Anne Barnes, a white
woman, and so she leaves town.

OLD DRACULA   Black   1976/Comedy

American International; 89 min.; *Producer*: Jack H. Wiener; *Director*:
Clive Donner; *Screenplay*: Jeremy Lloyd; *Caemra*: Tony Richmond; *Cast*:
David Niven (Count Dracula); *TERESA GRAVES (COUNTESS VAMPIRA)*; Peter
Bayliss (Maltravers); Jennie Linden (Angela); Nicky Henson (Marc).

     The Count tries to revive his dead wife, Countess Vampira. She
receives an infusion of blood from a Black woman and when she comes
to life she is Black. Count Dracula himself eventually turns Black.

OLD LOS ANGELES   Mexican   1948/Western

Republic; 82 min.; *Producer/Director*: Joseph Kane; *Screenplay*: Gerard
Adams/Clements Ripley; *Music*: Morton Scott; *Camera*: William Bradford;
Cast: William Elliott (Bill Stockton); John Carroll (Johnny Morrell);
Catherine McLeod (Marie Marlowe); Joseph Schildkraut (Luis Savarin);
Andy Devine (Sam Bowie); *ESTELITA RODRIGUEZ (ESTILITA DEL REY)*;
Virginia Brissac (Senora Del Rey); Grant Withers (Marshal Luckner);

Tito Renaldo (Tonio Del Rey); Roy Barcroft (Clyborne); Henry Bardon
(Larry Stockton).

Estilita Del Rey is in love with Johnny Morrell—who killed
Larry Stockton, Bill Stockton's brother, on orders from Luis Savarin.

OMAR KHAYYAM   Arab   1957/Drama

Paramount; 101 min.; *Producer*: Frank Freeman, Jr.; *Director*: William
Dieterle; *Screenplay*: Barre Lyndon; *Music*: Victor Young; *Camera*:
Ernest Laszlo; *Editor*: Everett Douglass; *Cast*: Cornel Wilde (Omar);
Michael Rennie (Hasani); *DEBRA PAGET (SHARAIN)*; Raymond Massey (The
Shah); John Derek (Malik); *Yma Sumac (Karina)*; *Margaret Hayes
(Zarada)*; *Joan Taylor (Yaffa)*; Sebastian Cabot (Nizam); Perry Lopez
(Prince Ahmud); Morris Ankrum (Imam Mowaftak); Abraham Sofaer
(Tutush); Edward Platt (Jayhan).

Sharain is betrothed to the Shah for political reasons. Omar
loves Sharain. Zarada is the Shah's first wife. Yaffa is Omar's
devoted slave and personal companion.

THE OMEGA MAN   Black   1971/Science Fiction

Warner Brothers; 98 min.; *Producer*: Walter Seltzer; *Director*: Boris
Sagal; *Screenplay*: John William Corrigton/Joyce Corrington; *Music*:
Ron Granier; *Camera*: Russell Metty; *Editor*: William Ziegler; *Cast*:
Cast: Charlton Heston (Robert Neville); Anthony Zerbe (Matthias);
ROSALIND CASH (LISA); Paul Koslo (Dutch); Lincoln Kilpatrick
(Zachary); Eric Laneuville (Richie); Jill Giraldi (Little Girl); Anna
Aries (Woman in Cemetery Crypt); Brian Tochi (Tommy).

A bacteriological war has nearly eliminated civilization and
left the survivors blood-sucking mutants. Dr. Robert Neville, who is
unaffected by the bacteria, hides from the mutants. After he meets
Lisa he develops a cure for the disease, using his own blood as the
basis for the serum. He falls in love with Lisa, but he is killed by
one of the mutants. Neville leaves the precious serum with Lisa.

ON THE BORDER   Mexican   1930/Adventure

Warner Brothers; 47 min.; *Director*: William McGann; *Screenplay*:
Lillie Hayward; *Camera*: William Rees; *Cast*: Rin-Tin-Tin (Rinty);
ARMIDA (PEPITA); David B. Litel (Dave); Philo McCullough (Farrell);
Bruce Covington (Don Jose); Walter Miller (Border Patrol Commission-
er); William Irving (Dusty).

Pepita is the daughter of a poor rancher. She and her dog, Rinty,
help border patrolmen Dave and Dusty capture a gang of smugglers who
are trying to buy her father's ranch as a headquarters for their
smuggling operation.

ON THE ISLE OF SAMOA   Samoan   1950/Adventure

Columbia; 65 min.; *Producer*: Wallace MacDonald; *Director*: William
Burke; *Screenplay*: Brenda Weisberg; *Music*: Mischa Bakaleinikoff;
Camera: William Bradford; *Editor*: Aaron Stell; *Cast*: Jon Hall
(Kenneth Crandall); *SUSAN CABOT (MOANA)*; Raymond Greenleaf (Peter
Appleton); Henry Marco (Karaki); Al Kikume (Chief Tiboti); *Rose
Turich (Waini)*; Leon Lontoc (Laki); Neyle Morrow (Mutu); *Jacqueline
deWit (Papita)*; Ben Welden (Nick Leach).

Kenneth Crandall is running from a mistaken accusation of murder
when his plane crashes on a tropical island. He falls in love with
Moana, the daughter of the chief. As he spends more time on the
island, Crandall realizes that he must clear his name in society so
that he can return to Moana and live on the island a free man.

ON THE OLD SPANISH TRAIL   Mexican   1947/Musical

Republic; 75 min.; *Producer*: Edward J. White; *Director*: William
Witney; *Screenplay*: Sloan Nibley; *Music*: Morton Scott; *Camera*: Jack
Marta; *Editor*: Tony Martinelli; *Cast*: Roy Rogers; Tito Guizar (Ricco);
Jane Frazee (Candy Martin); *ESTELITA RODRIGUEZ (LOLA)*; Charles McGraw
(Harry Blaisdell); Fred Graham (Marco the Great); Steve Darrell (Al);
Marshall Reed (Gus); Wheaton Chambers (Silas MacIntyre); The Sons of
the Pioneers; Trigger.

Lola is interested in Ricco, who has eyes only for Candy Martin.
The only thing Lola and Ricco do together is sing.

ONE-EYED JACKS   Mexican   1960/Western

Paramount; 141 min.; *Producer*: Frank P. Rosenberg; *Director*: Marlon
Brando; *Screenplay*: Guy Trosper/Calder Willingham; *Music*: Hugo
Friedhofer; *Camera*: Charles Lang; *Editor*: Archie Marshek; *Cast*:
Marlon Brando (Rio); Karl Malden (Dad Longworth); *PINA PELLICER
(LOUISA)*; *KATY JURADO (MARIA)*; Ben Johnson (Bob Amory); Slim Pickens
(Lon); Larry Duran (Modesto); Sam Gilman (Harvey); Timothy Carey
(Howard Tetley); Miriam Colon (Redhead); Elisha Cook (Bank Teller);
Rodolfo Acosta (Ruales Leader).

Rio spends five years in prison because he was betrayed by Dad
Longworth, his accomplice in a bank robbery. Escaping, he heads for
Monterey, intending to rob a bank. He finds Dad Longworth now a
sheriff and a respected member of the town, living with his Mexican
wife, Maria, and her daughter, Louisa. There is a great deal of
animosity between Rio and Dad. Dad strikes at Rio first. However,
Rio and Louisa fall in love and Louisa becomes pregnant. Rio's
cohorts rob the bank. Dad arrests Rio but Louisa helps him to escape.
Rio kills Dad and promises to send for Louisa.

100 RIFLES   Native American--Yaqui   1969/Western

20th Century-Fox; 110 min.; *Producer*: Marvin Schwartz; *Director*: Tom
Gries; *Screenplay*: Clair Huffaker/Tom Gries; *Music*: Jerry Goldsmith;
Camera: Cecilio Paniagua; *Editor*: Robert Simson; *Cast*: Jim Brown
(Lydecker); *RAQUEL WELCH (SARITA)*; Burt Reynolds (Yaqui Joe);
Fernando Lamas (General Verdugo); Dan O'Herlihy (Grimes); Hans
Gudegast (Von Klemme); Michael Forest (Humara); Aldo Sambrell (Sgt.
Paletes); Soledad Miranda (Girl in Hotel); Alberto Dalbes (Padre
Francisco); Carlos Bravo (Lopez).

As Lydecker is hunting down bank robber Yaqui Joe, he becomes
involved in the Yaqui fight against Mexican oppression. Sarita is
deeply committed to the struggle and is willing to die for her people.
She falls in love with Lyedecker who eventually helps the Yaquis in
their struggle.

ONE MILE FROM HEAVEN   Black   1937/Drama

20th Century-Fox; *Producer*: Sol M. Wurtzel; *Director*: Allan Dwan;
Screenplay: Lou Brestow/John Patrick; *Music*: Samuel Kaylin; *Camera*:
Sidney Wagner; *Editor*: Fred Allen; *Cast*: Claire Trevor (Lucy/Tex/
Warren); Bill Robinson (Officer Joe); Sally Blane (Barbara Harrison);
Douglas Fowley (Jim Tabor); *FREDI WASHINGTON (FLORA JACKSON)*; Joan
Carrol (Sunny); Ralf Harolde (Maxie McGrath); John Eldredge (Jerry
Harison); Paul McVey (Johnny).

Flora Jackson has been raising a white child as her own. The
Child's mother is a wealthy society woman who is being blackmailed.
When everything is straightened out, Flora becomes the child's nurse.

ONE MORE TRAIN TO ROB   Chinese   1971/Western

Universal; 108 min.; *Producer*: Robert Arthur; *Director*: Andrew V.
McLaglen; *Screenplay*: Don Tait/Dick Nelson; *Music*: David Shire;
Camera: Alric Edens; *Editor*: Robert Simpson; *Cast*: George Peppard
(Harker Fleet); Diana Muldaur (Katy); John Vernon (Timothy X. Nolan);
FRANCE NUYEN (AH TOY); Steve Sandor (Jim Gant); Soon-Taik Oh (Yung);
Richard Loo (Mr. Chang); C.K. Yang (Wong); John Doucette (Sheriff
Monte); Robert Donner (Sheriff Adams).

Ah Toy is imprisoned in a brothel and is saved by Harker Fleet,
who is trying to win the confidence of the Chinese community in order
to seal a gold shipment from them. Harker returns her to her fiance,
Yung, and then they rescue Mr. Chang, another captive, who knows where
the gold is hidden. The community trusts Harker with the gold, and
he has a change of heart and makes sure the gold gets to its proper
destination.

ONE POTATO, TWO POTATO   Black   1964/Drama

Cinema V; 92 min.; *Producer*: Sam Weston; *Director*: Larry Peerce;

Jane Russell, *The Outlaw* (RKO, 1943)

Screenplay: Raphael Hayes/Orville H. Hampton; *Music*: Gerald Fried; *Camera*: Andrew Laszlo; *Editor*: Robert Fritch; *Cast*: Barbara Barrie (Julie Cullen Richards); Bernie Hamilton (Frank Richards); Richard Mulligan (Joe Cullen); Harry Bellaver (Judge Powell); *VINETTE CARROLL (MARTHA RICHARDS)*; Marti Mericka (Ellen Mary); Robert Earl Jones (William Richards); *Faith Richards (Ann Richards)*.

Trouble begins for Julie Cullen when she marries Black Frank Richards. Mrs. Richards accepts Julie immediately but Mr. Richards does so only after they have a child. Then Julie's ex-husband, Joe, turns up to claim their child, Ellen. In spite of the good home Frank and Julie provide, the court awards custody to Joe.

OREGON PASSAGE   Native American   1958/Western

Allied Artists; 80 min.; *Producer*: Lindsley Parsons; *Director*: Paul Landres; *Screenplay*: Jack DeWitt; *Camera*: Ellis Carter; *Editor*: Maury Wright; *Cast*: John Ericson (Lt. Niles Ord); Lola Albright (Sylvia Dane); *TONI GERRY (LITTLE DEER)*; Edward Platt (Roland Dane); Judith Ames (Marion); H.M. Wynat (Black Eagle); Jon Shepodd (Lt. Baird Dobson); Walter Barnes (Sgt. Jed Ershick); Paul Fierro (Nato).

Little Deer is a captive of the Shoshoni, who comes from the north--we know this because Lt. Niles Ord declares that she is lighter than her captors. Little Deer uses various charms to induce Niles to fall in love with her. She eventually succeeds in her mission. She also helps Niles to capture Black Eagle.

THE OREGON TRAIL   Native American   1959/Western

20th Century-Fox; 82 min.; *Producer*: Richard Einfeld; *Director*: Gene Fowler, Jr.; *Screenplay*: Gene Fowler, Jr./Louis Vittes; *Music*: Paul Dunlap; *Camera*: Kay Norton; *Editor*: Betty Steinberg; *Cast*: Fred Mac-Murray (Neal Harris); William Bishop (Capt. George Wayne); Nina Shipman (Prudence Cooper); *GLORIA TALBOTT (SHONA HASTINGS)*; Henry Hull (Seton); John Carradine (Zachariah Garrison) John Dierkes (Gabe Hastings); Elizabeth Patterson (Maria Cooper).

Shona Hastings helps Neal Harris escape from her tribe. When her tribe attacks the fort she proudly declares, "It is because of this that I renounce my people."

THE ORGANIZATION   Black   1971/Drama

United Artists; 107 min.; *Producer*: Walter Mirisch; *Director*: Don Medford; *Screenplay*: James R. Webb; *Music*: Gile Melle; *Camera*: Joseph Biroc; *Editor*: Ferris Webster; *Cast*: Sidney Poitier (Lt. Virgil Tibbs); *BARBARA McNAIR (VALERIE TIBBS)*; Sheree North (Gloria Morgan); Gerald S. O'Loughlin (Lt. Jack Pecora); Raul Julia (Juan Mendoza); Ron O'Neal (Joe Peralex); Lani Miyazaki (Annie Sekido).

Valerie is married to police lieutenant Virgil Tibbs.

OUR MAN FLINT   Asian   1966/Action

20th Century-Fox; 107 min.; *Producer*: Saul David; *Director*: Daniel
Mann; *Screenplay*: Hal Fimberg/Ben Starr; *Music*: Jerry Goldsmith;
Camera: Daniel L. Fappl; *Editor*: William Reynolds; *Cast*: James Coburn
(Derek Flint); Lee J. Cobb (Cramden); Gila Golan (Gila); Edward
Mulhare (Malcolm Rodney); Benson Fong (Dr. Schneider); Gianna Serra
(Gina); Sgrio Valdis (Anna); *HELEN FUNAI (SAKITO)*; Shelby Grant
(Leslie); Michael St. Clair (Grumer).

　　Sakito is one of the four women secret agent Derek Flint lives
with.

OUTCAST OF THE ISLANDS   Island Exotic   1952/Adventure

British Lion; 102 min.; *Producer/Director*: Carol Reed; *Screenplay*:
W.E.C. Fairchild/Bert Bates; *Camera*: John Wilcox; *Editor*: Brian
Easdale; *Cast*: Ralph Richardson (Capt.Lingard); Trevor Howard
(Willems); Robert Mcrley (Almayer); *KERIMA (AISSA)*; Wendy Hiller (Mrs.
Alayer); George Coulouris (Babalatchi); Wilfrid Hyde-White (Vinck);
Frederick Valk (Hudig); Betty Ann Davies (Mrs. Williams); Dharma
Emmanuel (Ali); Peter Illing (Alagappan).

　　Willems is accused of stealing from his boss and is fired. He
is saved by his friend Capt. Lindgard, who raised him. He meets
Aissa and falls in love with her. She was sent to learn Capt.
Lindgard's secret of the river. Willems betrays Lindgard. When
confronted he leaves Aissa and Lindgard alone in the jungle.

THE OUTLAW   Mexican   1943/Western

RKO; 117 min.; *Producer*: Howard Hughes; *Directors*: Howard Hawks/
Howard Hughes; *Screenplay*: Jules Furthman; *Music*: Victor Young;
Camera: Gregg Toland; *Editor*: Walter Grissell; *Cast*: Jack Beutel
(Billy the Kid); *JANE RUSSELL (RIO)*; Thomas Mitchell (Pat Garrett);
Walter Huston (Doc Holliday); *Mimi Aguglia (Guadalupe)*; Joe Sawyer
(Charley); Gene Rizzi (Stranger); Frank Darien (Shorty); *Nina
Quartaro (Chita)*.

　　Half-breed Rio is the romantic interest of Billy the Kid.

OUTLAW EXPRESS   Mexican   1938/Musical

Universal; 56 min.; *Assoc. Producer*: Paul Malvern; *Director*: George
Waggner; *Screenplay*: Norton S. Parker; *Camera*: Harry Neumann; *Cast*:
Bob Baker (Bob Bradley); *CECILIA CALLEJO (LORITA)*; Don Barclay (Andy);
LeRoy Mason (Summers); *Nina Campana (Lupe)*; Forrest Taylor (Ferguson);
Martin Garralaga (Don Ricardo); Carleton Young (Ramon); Carlyle Moore,
Jr. (Bill Cody); Jack Kirk (Phelps).

　　Bob Bradley romances and sings to Lorita.

THE OUTLAW JOSEY WALES   Native American--Navajo   1976/Western

Columbia/Warner Brothers; 134 min.; *Producers*: Jim Fargo/John G.
Wilson; *Director*: Clint Eastwood; *Screenplay*: Phil Kaufman/Sonia
Chernus; *Music*; Jerry Fielding; *Camera*: Bruce Surtees; *Editor*: Ferris
Webster; *Cast*: Clint Eastwood (Josey Wales); Chief Dan George (Lone
Watie); Sondra Locke (Laura Lee); Bill McKinney (Terrill); John
Vernon (Fletcher); Paula Trueman (Grandma Sarah); Sam Bottoms (Jamie);
GERALDINE KEAMS (LITTLE MOONLIGHT); Woodrow Parfrey (Carpetbagger);
Joyce Jameson (Rose).

After Little Moonlight is saved by Josey Wales from a gang rape,
she joins his gang. She proves useful by thwarting Josey's capture.

OUTPOST IN MOROCCO   Arab   1949/Adventure

United Artists; 92 min.; *Producer*: Samuel Bischoff; *Director*: Robert
Florey; *Screenplay*: Charles Grayson/Paul de Sante-Colombe; *Music*:
Michel Michelet; *Camera*: Lucien Andriot; *Editor*: George Arthur; *Cast*:
George Raft (Capt. Paul Gerard); *MARIE WINDSOR (CARA)*; Akim Tamiroff
(Lt. Glyak); John Litel (Col. Pascal); Eduard Franz (Emir of Bel-
Rashad); Erno Verebes (Bamboule); Crane Whitley (Caid Osman); Damian
O'Flynn (Commandant Fronval).

While escorting Cara to her father's desert home, Capt. Paul
Gerard falls in love with her. Her family is fighting against French
occupation forces and is planning a revolt. After a French garrison
is destroyed, the occupation forces retaliate by kidnapping Cara, who
still loves Gerard. Gerard returns her to her father who is planning
another attack. Cara tries to warn the French and is killed.

PAGAN LOVE SONG   Island Exotic   1950/Musical

MGM; 76 min.; *Producer*: Arthur Freed; *Director*: Robert Alton; *Screen-
play*: Robert Nathan/Jerry Davis; *Music*: Harry Warren; *Camera*: Charles
Rosher; *Editor*: Adrienne Fazan; *Cast*: Esther Williams (Mimi Bennett);
Howard Keel (Hazard Endicott); Minna Gombell (Kate Bennett); Charles
Mauu (Tavae); *RITA MORENO (TEURU)*; Philip Costa (Manu); Dione Leilani
(Tani).

Teuru is one of the island's native girls.

THE PALOMINO   Mexican   1950/Drama

Columbia; 72 min.; *Producer*: Robert Cohn; *Director*: Ray Nazarro;
Screenplay: Tom Kilpatrick; *Camera*: Vincent Farrar; *Editor*: Aaron
Stell; *Cast*: Jerome Courtland (Steve Norris); *BEVERLY TYLER (MARIA
GUEVARA)*; Joseph Calleia (Miguel Gonzales); Roy Roberts (Ben Lane);
Gordon Jones (Bill); Robert Osterloh (Sam); Tom Trout (Williams);
Harry Garcia (Johnny); Trevor Bardette (Brown); Juan Duval (Manuel).

Maria Guevara is the owner of a once-prominent palomino horse

ranch. She plans to restore the ranch to its original grandeur with
her prize-winning palomino colt.

PALS OF THE GOLDEN WEST   Mexican   1951/Musical

Republic; 68 min.; *Producer*: Edward J. White; *Director*: William
Whitney; *Screenplay*: Albert Demond/Eric Taylor; *Music*: Stanley Wilson;
Camera: Jack Marta; *Editor*: Harold Minter; *Cast*: Roy Rogers; Dale
Evans (Cathy Marsh); *ESTELITA RODRIGUEZ (ELENA MADERA)*; Pinky Lee
(Pinky); Anthony Caruso (Jim Bradford); Roy Barcroft (Ward Sloan);
Eduardo Jiminez (Pancho); Ken Terrell (Tony); Emmett Vogan (Col.
Wells); Maurice Jara (Lopez); The Roy Rogers Riders; Trigger; Bullet.

     Elena Madera is a newspaperwoman.

PAN AMERICANA   Latin American   1945/Musical

RKO; 84 min.; *Producer/Dreictor*: John H. Auer; *Screenplay*: Lawrence
Kimball; *Music*: C. Bakaleinikoff; *Camera*: Frank Redman; *Editor*: Harry
Marker; *Cast*: Philip Terry (Dan); Audrey Long (JoAnne); Robert
Benchley (Charlie); Eve Arden (Hoppy); Ernest Truex (Uncle Rudy);
Marc Cramer (Jerry); *ISABELITA (LUPITA)*.

     This film was a showcase for Latin American entertainers with a
minor plot--JoAnne is a magazine writer traveling south of the border
to write about Latin American performers--to hold it all together.

PARADISE ISLE   Island Exotic   1937/Adventure

Monogram; 73 min.; *Producer*: Dorothy Reid; *Director*: Arthur Greville;
Screenplay: Marion Orth; *Camera*: Gilbert Warrenton; *Editor*: Russell
Schoengarth; *Cast*: *MOVITA (HA)*; Warren Hull (Kennedy); George Pilita
(Tono); William Davidson (Hoener); John St. Polis (Coxon); Pierre
Watkin (Steinmeyer); Kenneth Harlan (Johnson); Russell Simpson
(Baxter).

     Ha loves blind painter Kennedy. His sight restored, Kennedy
returns to white society. He soon realizes his mistake and returns
to Ha and the island.

PARDON MY SARONG   Island Exotic   1942/Comedy

Universal; 84 min.; *Assoc. Producer*: Alex Gottlieb; *Director*: Erle C.
Kenton; *Screenplay*: True Boardman/Nat Perrin/John Grant; *Music*:
Charles Previn; *Camera*: Milton Krasner; *Editor*: Arthur Hilton; *Cast*:
Bud Abbott (Algey Shaw); Lou Costello (Wellington Phlug); Virginia
Bruce (Joan Marshall); Robert Paige (Tommy Layton); Lionel Atwill
(Varnoff); Leif Erikson (Whoba); *NAN WYNN (LUANA)*; William Demarest
(Detective Kendall); Samuel S. Hinds (Chief Kolua); Marie McDonald
(Ferna); *Elaine Morey (Amo)*.

Abbott and Costello hijinks has native girl Luana singing "Lovely Luana" and "Vingo Jingo."

PARIS BLUES   Black   1961/Drama

United Artists; 98 min.; *Producer*: Sam Shaw; *Director*: Martin Ritt; *Screenplay*: Jack Sher/Irene Kamp/Walter Bernstein; *Music*: Duke Ellington; *Camera*: Christian Matras; *Editor*: Roger Dwyre; *Cast*: Paul Newman (Ram Bowen); Joanne Woodward (Lillian Corning); Sidney Poitier (Eddie Cook); Louis Armstrong (Wild Man Moore); *DIAHANN CARROLL (CONNIE LAMPSON)*; Serge Reggiani (Michael Duvigne); Barbara Laage (Marie Seoul); Andre Luguet (Rene Bernard); Marie Versini (Nichole).

While vacationing in Paris, Connie Lampson and Lillian Corning meet two American jazzmen, Eddie Cook and Ram Bowen. Both couples hit it off and Eddie and Connie decide to marry and return to the United States. Ram wants to be a composer and chooses to remain in Paris. Lillian returns home alone.

PASSION   Mexican   1954/Drama

RKO; 84 min.; *Producer*: Benedict Bogeaus; *Director*: Allan Dwan; *Screenplay*: Beatrice A. Dresher; *Music*: Louis Forbes; *Camera*: John Alton; *Editor*: Carl Lodato; *Cast*: Cornel Wilde (Juan Obreon); *YVONNE DE CARLO (TONYA/ROSE)*; Raymond Burr (Rodriguez); Lon Chaney (Castro); Rodolfo Acosta (Sandro); John Qualen (Gaspar); Anthony Caruso (Munoz); Frank de Kova (Martinez); Peter Coe (Colfie); John Dierkes (Escobar).

Tonya and Rose are twins. Rose is married to Juan Obreon. When she is murdered Tonya and Juan join forces to bring the killer to justice.

PASSPORT HUSBAND   Latin American   1938/Drama

20th Century-Fox; 72 min.; *Producer*: Sol M. Wurtzel; *Director*: James Tinling; *Screenplay*: Karen De Wolf/Robert Chapin; *Music*: Samuel Kaylin; *Camera*: Edward Snyder; *Editor*: Nick De Maggio; *Cast*: Stuart Erwin (Henry Cabot); Pauline Moore (Mary Jane Clayton); Douglas Fowley (Tiger Martin); *JOAN WOODBURY (CONCHITA MONTEZ)*; Robert Lowery (Ted Markson); Harold Huber (Blackie Bennett); Edward S. Brophy (Spike); Paul McVey (H.C. Walton).

Henry Cabot marries Conchita Montez to save her from deportation. After he inherits a million dollars, he tricks Conchita into divorcing him so he will be free to marry his true love.

A PATCH OF BLUE   Black   1965/Drama

MGM; 105 min.; *Producer*: Pandro S. Berman; *Director/Screenplay*: Guy Green; *Music*: Jerry Goldsmith; *Camera*: Robert Burks; *Editor*: Rita Roland; *Cast*: Sidney Poitier (Gordon Ralfe); Shelley Winters (Rose

Ann D'Arcey); Elizabeth Hartman (Selina D'Arcey); Wallace Ford (Ole
Pa); Ivan Dixon (Mark Ralfe); *ELISABETH FRASER (SADIE)*; John Qualen
(Mr. Faber); Kelly Flynn (Yanek Faber).

Blind Selina D'Arcey lives a sheltered and mundane life until
the day she meets Gordon Ralfe in the park. They become friends, but
their friendship is hindered not only because of color but also
because Selina's mother, Rose Ann, and her friend, Sadie, want to
open a whorehouse with Selma as the main attraction. Gordon takes
her away from them and enrolls her in a school for the blind.

PAWNEE   Native Aemrican--Pawnee   1957/Western

Republic; 79 min.; *Producers*: Jack J. Gross/Philip N. Krasne;
Director: George Waggner; *Screenplay*: George Waggner/Louis Vittes/
Endre Bohem; *Music*: Paul Sawtell; *Camera*: Hal McAlpin; *Editor*:
Kenneth G. Crane; *Cast*: George Montgomery (Paul); Bill Williams
(Matt); Lola Albright (Meg); Francis J. McDonald (Tip); Robert E.
Griffin (Doc); Dabbs Greer (Brewster); Kathleen Freeman (Mrs.
Carter); *CHARLOTTE AUSTIN (DANCING FAWN)*; Ralph Moody (Wise Eagle);
Anne Barton (Mrs. Brewster); Raymond Hatton (Obie Dilks); Charles
Horvath (Crazy Fox); Robert Nash (Carter).

Dancing Fawn loves Paul, an adopted white member of her tribe.
Paul, however, falls in love with Meq.

THE PEARL   Mexican Indian   1948/Drama

RKO; 77 min.; *Producer*: Oscar Daneingers; *Director*: Emilio Fernandez;
Screenplay: John Steinbeck/Jack Wagner/Emilio Fernandez; *Music*;
Antonio Diaz Conde; *Camera*: Gabriel Figueroa; *Editor*: Gloria
Schoemann; *Cast*: Pedro Armendariz (Kino); *MARIA ELENA MARQUES
(JUANA)*; Fernando Wagner (Buyer of Pearls); Charles Rooner (Village
Doctor); Alfonso Bedoyo (Baby's Godfather); Juan Garcia (Sapo).

A poor Indian couple find a pearl and hope that this will improve their life. Various attempts to take the pearl end with Kino
killing two men. He and Juana flee their village with the law in
pursuit. Their baby is killed and Kino kills the murderer of the
baby. When they return to their village, they throw the pearl into
the sea and return to the simple life.

PEARL OF THE SOUTH PACIFIC   Island Exotic   1955/Adventure

RKO; 85 min.; *Producer*: Benedict Bogeaus; *Director*: Alan Dwan;
Screenplay: Jesse Lasky, Jr.; *Music*: Louis Forbes; *Camera*: John Alton;
Editor: James Leicester; *Cast*: Virginia Mayo (Rita Delaine); Dennis
Morgan (Dan Merrill); David Farrar (Bully Hayes); Murvyn Vye
(Halemano); Lance Fuller (George); Basil Raysdael (Michael); *LISA
MONTELL (MOMU)*.

Momu is the jealous island woman who burns Rita Delaine's

clothes. Rita then has to run around in a sarong.

PERSONAL BEST   Native American   1982/Drama

Columbia; 127 min.; *Producer/Director/Screenplay* : Robert Towne;
Music : Jack Nitzsche/Jill Fraser; *Camera* : Michael Chapman; *Editors* :
Ned Humphreys/Jere Huggins/Jacqueline Cambas/Walt Mulconery; *Cast* :
MARIEL HEMINGWAY (CHRIS CAHILL) ; Scott Glenn (Terry Tingloff);
Patrice Donnelly (Tory Skinner); Kenny Moore (Denny Stites); Jim
Moody (Roscoe Travis); Kari Gosswiller (Penny Brill); Jodi Anderson
(Nadia "Pooch" Anderson); Maren Seidler (Tanya).

   In this film focusing on sports and a love affair between Chris
and Tory, mention is made of Chris' American Indian background. At
one point Tory says to Chris, "Don't give me the silent Indian bit."

PHANTOM OF CHINATOWN   Chinese   1941/Mystery

Monarch; 62 min.; *Producer* : Paul Malvern; *Director* : Phil Rosen;
Screenplay : Joseph West; *Camera* : Fred Jackman; *Editor* : Jack Ogilvie;
Cast : Keye Luke (Jimmy Wong); *LOTUS LONG (WIN LEN)* ; Grant Withers
(Street); Paul McVey (Grady); Charles Miller (Dr. Benton); Virginia
Carpenter (Louise Benton); Charles Fraser (John Dilson).

   Win Len is a secretary to an archeologist who is murdered. She
helps detective Jimmy Wong to find the killer.

PHANTOM RAIDERS   Panamanian   1940/Adventure

MGM; 70 min.; *Producer* : Frederick Stephani; *Director* : Jacques
Tourneur; *Screenplay* : William R. Lipman; *Camera* : Clyde De Vinno;
Cast : Walter Pidgeon (Nick Carter); Florence Rice (Cora Banes);
Joseph Schildkraut (Al Taurez); Donald Meek (Bartholomew); John
Carroll (John Ramsell, Jr.); *STEFFI DUNA (DOLORES)* ; Cecil Kellaway
(Franklin Morris); Matthew Boulton (John Ramsell, Sr.); Alex Craig
(Andy Macmillan); Thomas Rose (Dr. Grisson); Dwight Frye (Eddie
Anders).

   Dolores is the local native girl who lusts after Nick Carter.

PHARAOH'S CURSE   Egyptian   1957/Thriller

United Artists; 66 min.; *Producers* : Aubrey Schenck/Howard W. Koch;
Director : Lee Sholem; *Screenplay* : Richard Landau; *Music* : Lee Baxter;
Camera : William Margulies; *Editor* : George A. Gitten; *Cast* : Mark Dan
(Capt. Storm); *ZIVA RODANN (SIMIRA)* ; Diane Brewster (Sylvia Quentin);
George Neise (Robert Quentin); Ben Wright (Walter Andrews); Guy
Prescot (Dr. Michael Faraday); Terence de Marney (Sgt. Smollett);
Kurt Katch (Hans Brecht); Robert Forti (Claude Beauchamp).

   Simira is a menacing reincarnation of an Egyptian cat goddess.

A PIECE OF THE ACTION   Black   1977/Drama

Warner Brothers; 134 min.; *Producer*: Melville Tucker; *Director*:
Sidney Poitier; *Screenplay*: Charles Blackwell; *Music*: Curtis Mayfield;
Camera: Donald H. Morgan; *Editor*: Pembroke J. Herring; *Cast*: Sidney
Poitier (Manny Durrell); Bill Cosby (Dave Anderson); James Earl Jones
(Joshua Burke); *DENISE NICHOLAS (LILA FRENCH)*; Hope Clarke (Sarah
Thomas); *Tracy Reed (Nikki McLean)*; Titos Vandis (Bruno); *Frances
Foster (Bea Quitman)*; Jason Evers (Ty Shorter); Marc Lawrence
(Louie); *Ja'net DuBois (Nellie Bond)*.

      Con men Manny Durrell and Dave Anderson are blackmailed by for-
mer police officer Joshua Burke into actively helping a community
center for Black youths run by Lila French. Nikki McLean is Manny's
romantic interest.

PINKY   Black   1949/Drama

20th Century-Fox; 102 min.; *Producer*: Darryl F. Zanuck; *Director*:
Elia Kazan; *Screenplay*: Philip Dunne/Dudley Nichols; *Camera*: Joe
MacDonald; *Editor*: Harmon Jones; *Cast*: *JEANNE CRAIN (PINKY)*; Ethel
Barrymore (Miss Em); *ETHEL WATERS (GRANNY)*; William Lundigan (Dr.
Thomas Adams); Basil Ruysdael (Judge Walker); Kenny Washington (Dr.
Canady); *Nina Mae McKinney (Rozelia)*; Griff Barnett (Dr. Joe);
Frederick O'Neal (Jake Walters).

      Pinky is the story of a light-skinned Black woman. While
studying nursing in the north she passes for white and has a romance
with a white doctor. When the relationship becomes serious she
returns home, where she has difficulty adjusting to the racism
Blacks experience. She begins to nurse a wealthy white woman, Miss
Em, who is at first hostile but eventually comes to love Pinky. When
Miss Em dies she leaves her estate to Pinky. Miss Em's relatives are
furious and challenge the will. Meanwhile, Dr. Tom Adams arrives to
take Pinky back north. Although shocked to learn she is Black, he
tries to convince Pinky to forget about the lawsuit, return north
with him, and pass for white. In the end Pinky wins the inheritance,
says goodbye to her doctor/lover, and opens a nursing school for
young Black women.

THE PIRATE   Latin American   1948/Musical

MGM; 102 min.; *Producer*: Arthur Freed; *Director*: Vincente Minnelli;
Screenplay: Albert Hackett; *Music*: Lennie Hayton; *Camera*: Henry
Stradling; *Editor*: Blanche Sewell; *Cast*: Gene Kelly (Serafin); *JUDY
GARLAND (MANUELA)*; Walter Slezak (Don Pedro Vargas); Gladys Cooper
(The Advocate); Reginald Owen (The Viceroy).

      Manuella is about to enter into an arranged marriage when she
meets and falls in love with Serafin, the leader of a group of
traveling entertainers.

PIRATES OF MONTEREY   Mexican   1947/Adventure

Universal; 77 min.; *Producer*: Paul Malvern; *Director*: Alfred Werker;
Screenplay: Sam Hellman/Margaret Buell Wilder; *Music*: Milton Rosen;
Camera: Hal Mohr; *Editor*: Russell Schoengarth; *Cast*: *MARIA MONTEZ
(MARGUERITA)*; Rod Cameron (Philip Kent); Mikhail Rasumny (Pio);
Philip Reed (Lt. Carlo Otega); Gilbert Roland (Major De Roja); *Gale
Sondergaard (Senorita de Sola)*; *Tamara Shyne (Filomena)*; Robert
Warwick (Governor); Michael Ralfetto (Sgt. Gomara).

    In old California, Marguerita is suspected of being a Spanish
royalist by Philip Kent--who is smuggling rifles to defend against
the royalists. She and Philip soon fall in love. She is already
engaged to his best friend, Capt. Carlo Otega, but Carlo frees her so
she can marry Kent. Marguerita and Kent are captured by the royalists
but escape to freedom.

PIRATES OF TRIPOLI   Arab--Libyan   1955/Adventure

Columbia; 70 min.; *Producer*: Sam Katzman; *Director*: Felix Feist;
Screenplay: Allen March; *Music*: Mischa Bakaleinikoff; *Camera*: Henry
Freulich; *Editor*: Edwin Bryant; *Cast*: Paul Henreid (Edri-Al-Gadrian);
PATRICIA MEDINA (KARJAN); Paul Newland (Hammid Khassan); John Miljan
(Malek); Mark Hanna (Ben Ali); Jean Del Val (Abu Tala); *Lillian Bond
(Sono)*; Mel Welles (Tomidi); Louis G. Mercier (The Cat); Karl Davis
(Assassin).

    Princess Karjan's country has been taken over by the evil Malek.
Karjan goes to the pirate Edri-Al-Gadrian for help in regaining her
throne.

PLAYMATES   Mexican   1941/Comedy

RKO; 94 min.; *Producer/Director*: David Butler; *Screenplay*: James V.
Kern; *Music*: James Van Heusen; *Camera*: Frank Redman; *Editor*: Irene
Mora; *Cast*: Kay Kyser; John Barrymore; *LUPE VELEZ (CARMEN DEL TORO)*;
Ginny Simms (Ginny); May Robson (Grandma); Patsy Kelly (Lulu Monahan);
Peter Lind Hayes (Peter Lindsey); George Cleveland (Mr. Pennypacker);
Alice fleming (Mrs. Pennypacker).

    Carmen del Toro is a bullfighter who attempts to woo Kay Kyser
to help out her lover, John Barrymore.

POPI   Puerto Rican   1969/Comedy

United Artists; 113 min.; *Producer*: Herbert B. Leonard; *Director*:
Pete Scoppa/Don Moody; *Screenplay*: Tina and Lester Pine; *Music*:
Dominic Frontiere; *Camera*: Ross Lowell; *Editor*: Anthony Ciccolini;
Cast: Alan Arkin (Popi); *RITA MORENO (LUPE)*; Miguel Alejandro
(Junior); Ruben Figueroa (Luis); John Harkins (Harmon); Joan Tompkins
(Miss Musto); Anthony Holland (Pickett); Arny Freeman (Diaz); Barbara
Dana (Receptionist); *Antonia Rey (Mrs. Cruz)*; *Gladys Velez (Silvia)*.

Before Popi will marry Lupe he wants to be sure his sons will
have a good future. He devises a scam whereby his sons will be mistaken for Cuban refugees and will be adopted by wealthy parents.
However, his sons want to be with him in spite of his poverty, and
they return to Popi and Lupe.

PORGY AND BESS   Black   1959/Musical

Columbia; 146 min.; *Producer*: Samuel Goldwyn; *Director*: Otto
Preminger; *Screenplay*: N. Richard Nash; *Music*: George Gershwin;
Camera: Leon Shamroy; *Editor*: Daniel Mandell; *Cast*: Sidney Poitier
(Porgy); *DOROTHY DANDRIDGE (BESS)*; Sammy Davis, Jr. (Sportin' Life);
Pearl Bailey (Maria); Brock Peters (Crown); Leslie Scott (Jake);
Diahann Carroll (Clara); *Ruth Attaway (Serena)* ; Clarence Muse
(Peter); *Everdine Wilson (Annie)*.

Porgy is in love with Bess, so when her lover, Crown, runs away
after killing someone Porgy offers Bess a place to stay. Bess soon
finds herself attracted to Porgy's kindness and affection. They are
very happy together until Crown returns and drags Bess off. When she
returns to Porgy she is bruised and battered and promises never to
leave him again. Crown returns and leaves again, and everyone thinks
he is dead. Porgy and Bess adopt a child, only to have Crown return
again. This time, however, Porgy kills him. The police take Porgy
away only to identify the body. Meanwhile Sportin' Life convinces
Bess that Porgy will never return to her and takes her to New York.
Porgy returns to find that Bess has left him. He vows to follow her
to New York and bring her home.

PRINCESS OF THE NILE   Arabian Nights   1954/Fantasy

United Artists; 71 min.; *Producer*: Robert L. Jacks; *Director*: Harmon
Jones; *Screenplay*: Gerald Drayson Adams; *Music*: Lionel Newman;
Camera: Lloyd Ahern; *Editor*: George G. Hens; *Cast*: *DEBRA PATET
(TAURA, THE DANCER)*; Jeffrey Hunter (Prince Haidi); Michael Rennie
(Rama Khan); *Dona Drake (Mirva)*; Wally Cassel (Goghi); Edgar Barrier
(Shaman); Michael Ansara (Capt. Krai); Jack Elam (Basra); Lester
Sharpe (Baba); Lee Van Cleef (Hakar); Billy Curtis (Tut); Robert
Roark (Capt. Hussein).

Taura is the daughter of the deposed ruler of Halwan. She
enlists the aid of Prince Haidi to help her free her father and liber-
ate her city from the evil Rama Khan. When Rama Khan treatens to
destroy the city she promises to marry him. Prince Haidi and various
local ruffians prevent the marriage by overthrowing Rama Khan, leaving
Prince Haidi to marry Taura.

PRISONER OF THE CASBAH   Arabian Nights   1953/Fantasy

Columbia; 78 min.; *Producer*: Sam Katzman; *Director*: Richard Bare;
Screenplay: De Vallon Scott; *Camera*: Henry Freulich; *Editor*: Charles
Nelson; *Cast*: *GLORIA GRAHAME (PRINCESS NADJA)*; Cesar Romero (Firouz);

Turhan Bey (Ahmed); Nestor Paiva (Marouf); Paul E. Newlan (Thief #1); *Lucille Barkley (Soura)*; Philip Van Zandt (Selim); Frank Richards (Theif #2); John Parrish (Thief #3); Wade Crosby (Yogoub); *Gloria Saunders (Zeida)*; Eddy Fields (Abdulla); *Mimi Bonel (Slave Girl)*.

Ahmed saves Princess Nadja from the clutches of the evil grand vizier, Firouz.

THE PROFESSIONALS   Mexican   1966/Adventure

Columbia; 117 min.; *Producer/Director/Screenplay*: Richard Brooks; *Music*: Maurice Jarre; *Camera*: Conrad Hall; *Editor*: Peter Zinner; *Cast*: Burt Lancaster (Bill Dolworth); Lee Marvin (Henry Rico Fardan); Robert Ryan (Hans Ehrengard); Jack Palance (Capt. Jesus Raza); *CLAUDIA CARDINALE (MARIA GRANT)*; Ralph Bellamy (J. W. Grant); Woody Strode (Jacob Sharp); Joe De Santis (Oretaga); Rafael Bertrand (Fierro); Jorge Martinez de Hoyos (Padilla); *Maria Gomez (Chiquita)*.

Four professional soldiers are hired to return Maria, the wife of wealthy J.W. Grant, who was kidnapped by guerrilla-bandit Raza. However, Maria does not want to return to Grant as she loves Raza. The four soldiers take her back anyway so they can get their money. When Raza shows up to claim Maria the soldiers allow them to escape.

THE PURPLE PLAIN   Burmese   1954/Drama

General Film; 100 min.; *Director*: Robert Parrish; *Screenplay*: Erich Ambler; *Music*: John Veale; *Camera*: Geoffrey Unsworth; *Editor*: Clive Donner; *Cast*: Gregory Peck (Forrester); *WIN MIN THAN (ANNA)*; Bernard Lee (Dr. Harris); Maurice Denham (Blore); Ram Gopal (Mr. Phang); Brenda de Banzie (Miss McNab); Lyndon Brook (Carrington); Anthony Bushell (Aldridge).

Anna gives aid and comfort to pilot Forrester who is under mental stress. When he crashes in the jungle he remembers conversations with Anna and they give him the strength to save himself and the life of another airman. He then returns to Anna.

PUTNEY SWOPE   Black   1969/Comedy

Contemporary/Cinema V; 85 min.; *Producer*: Ronald Sullivan; *Director*: Robert Downey; *Screenplay*: Robert Downey; *Music*: Charley Cuva; *Camera*: Gerald Cotts; *Editor*: Burt Smith; *Cast*: Arnold Johnson (Putney Swope); Antonio Fargas (The Arab); *LAURA GREENE (MRS. SWOPE)*; Eric Krupnik (Marc Focus); Pepi Hermine (President of the United States); Ruth Hermine (First Lady); Larry Wolfe (Mr. Borman Six).

Mrs. Swope is the wife of Putney. When her husband becomes chairman of the board of an advertising agency, he promptly fires the white employees and replaces them with Black militants. Mrs. Swope has a white maid whom she mistreats.

THE QUIET AMERICAN   Vietnamese   1958/Drama

United Artists; 120 min.; *Director/Screenplay*: Joseph L. Mankiewicz; *Music*: Mario Nascimbene; *Camera*: Robert Kraslino; *Editor*: William Hornbeck; *Cast*: Audie Murphy (The American); Michael Redgrave (Fowler); Claude Dauphin (Inspector Vigot); *GIORGIA MOLL (PHUONG)*; *Kerima (Miss Hei)*; Bruce Cabot (Bill Granger); Fred Sadoff (Dominguez); Richard Loo (Mister Heng); Peter Trent (Eliot Wilkins); Clinton Andersen (Joe Morton).

Phuong is the mistress of English journalist Thomas Fowler. She is also loved by an American. When Fowler lies to Phuong about divorcing his wife she turns to the American. Fowler is enraged by this and by what he feels is bungling by the American. He consorts with the communists to have the American killed. Phuong hates and rejects him, and he learns that the American did not bungle anything.

THE QUIET GUN   Native American   1957/Western

20th Century-Fox; 77 min.; *Producer*: Earle E. Lyon; *Director*: William Claxton; *Screenplay*: Eric Norden; *Music*: Paul Dunlap; *Camera*: John Mescall; *Editor*: Robert Fritch; *Cast*: Forrest Tucker (Carl); *MARA CORDAY (IRENE)*; Jim Davis (Ralph); Kathleen Crowley (Teresa); Lee Van Cleef (Sadler); Tom Brown (Reilly); Lewis Martin (Hardy); Hank Worden (Sampson); Gerald Milton (Lesser); Everett Glass (Judge); Edith Evanson (Mrs. Merric).

Irene lives with rancher Carl and his wife. When his wife is away a scandal arises. Carl kills attorney Hardy and is himself lynched by the townsfolk. The scandal was a set-up by Sadler and Reilly to take over Carl's ranch.

RAGTIME   Black   1981/Drama

Columbia-EMI-Warner; *Producer*: Dino De Laurentiis; *Director*: Milos Forman; *Screenplay*: Michael Weller; *Music*: Randy Newman; *Camera*: Miroslav Ondricek; *Editors*: Anne V. Coates/Antony Gibbs/Stanley Warnow; *Cast*: James Cagney (New York Police Commissioner Rheinlander Waldo); Brad Dourif (Younger Brother); Moses Gunn (Booker T. Washington); Elizabeth McGovern (Evelyn Nesbit); Kenneth McMillan (Willie Conklin); Mary Steenburgen (Mother); *DEBBIE ALLEN (SARAH)*; Howard E. Rollins (Coalhouse Walker, Jr.); Mandy Patinkin (Tateh); James Olson (Father); Donald O'Connor (Evelyn's Dance Instructor); Pat O'Brien (Delmas); Jeff DeMunn (Houdini); Robert Joy (Harry K. Thaw); Norman Mailer (Stanford White).

Sarah abandons her newborn baby, which is found by Mother who takes Sarah and her baby into her home. Soon Coalhouse Walker, Jr., arrives, confident enough to marry Sarah and take care of their baby. However, racial problems develop and Sarah is clubbed to death by a policeman. Eventually Coalhouse is killed also.

THE RAIDERS   Mexican   1952/Western

Universal; 83 min.; *Producer*: William Alland; *Director*: Lesley
Selander; *Screenplay*: Polly James/Lillie Hayward; *Music*: Joseph
Gershenson; *Camera*: Carl Guthrie; *Editor*: Paul Weatherwax; *Cast*:
Richard Conte (Jan Morrell); *VIVECA LINDFORS (ELENA ORTEGA)*; Barbara
Britton (Elizabeth Ainsworth); Hugh O'Brian (Hank Purvis); Richard
Martin (Felipe Ortega); Palmer Lee (Marty Smith); William Reynolds
(Frank Morrell); William Bishop (Marshall Bill Henderson); Morris
Ankrum (Thomas Ainsworth); Dennis Weaver (Dick Logan); Margaret Field
(Mary Morrell); John Kellogg (Welch).

Ranch owner Jan Morrell joins forces with once wealthy landowner
Felipe Ortega and his sister, Elena, to stop a group of claim jumpers
from taking over their land. A romance develops between Jan and
Elena.

RAIDERS OF THE DESERT   Arab   1941/Adventure

Universal; 60 min.; *Assoc. Producer*: Ben Pivar; *Director*: John
Rawlins; *Screenplay*: Maurice Tombragel/Victor I. McLeod; *Cast*: Richard
Arlen (Dick Manning); Andy Devine (Andy McCoy); Linda Hayes (Alice
Evans); Lewis Howard (Abdullah Ibn el Azora el Karim); George Carleton
(Jones); Turhan Bey (Hassen Mohammed); *MARIA MONTEZ (ZALEIKA)*; John
Harmon (Ahmed); Ralf Harolde (Sheik Talifah); Neyle Marx (Moviow,
Zeid).

Not enough information was available to describe this role
accurately.

RAINBOW ISLAND   Island Exotic   1944/Musical

Paramount; 97 min.; *Assoc. Producer*: E.D. Leshin; *Director*: Ralph
Murphy; *Screenplay*: Walter DeLeon,/Arthur Phillips; *Music*: Roy Webb;
Camera: Karl Struss; *Cast*: DOROTHY LAMOUR (LONA); Eddie Bracken (Toby
Smith); Gil Lamb (Pete Jenkins); Barry Sullivan (Ken Masters);
Forrest Orr (Dr. Curtis); Marc Lawrence (Alcoa); *Anne Revere (Queen
Okalana)*; *Olga San Juan (Miki)*; *Elena Verdugo (Moana)*.

Lona is the main attraction for three shipwrecked sailors on a
South Pacific island. Lona sings "Beloved."

RAINBOW ON THE RIVER   Black   1936/Drama

RKO; 100 min.; *Producer*: Sol Lessor; *Director*: Kurt Newmann; *Screen-
play*: Earl Snell/Will Hurlbert; *Music*: Dr. Hugo Riesenfeld; *Camera*:
Charles Schoenbaum; *Editor*: Robert Crandall; *Cast*: Bobby Breen
(Phillip); May Robson (Mrs. Aimsworth); Charles Butterworth (Barrett);
LOUISE BEAVERS (TOINETTE); Alan Mowbray (Ralph Layton); Benita Hume
(Julia Layton); Henry O'Neill (Father Josef); Marilyn Knowlden
(Lucille Layton); Lillian Yarbo (Seline); Stymie Beard (Lilybell).

Toinette brings up orphaned Phillip until Father Josef discovers he is the grandson of a wealthy New York woman. Phillip goes to New York but runs away because of a vicious aunt. When Mrs. Aimsworth learns why he ran away she sends for Toinette to come to New York and take care of the boy.

THE RAINS CAME   Indian   1939/Drama

20th Century-Fox; 103 min.; *Producer*: Darryl F. Zanuck; *Director*: Clarence Brown; *Screenplay*: Philip Dunne/Julien Josephson; *Music*: Alfred Newman; *Camera*: Arthur Miller; *Editor*: Barbara McLean; *Cast*: Myrna Loy (Lady Edwina Esketh); Tyrone Power (Major Rama Safti); George Brent (Tom Ransome); Brenda Joyce (Fern Simon); Nigel Bruce (Lord Albert Esketh); *MARIA OUSPENSKAYA (MAHARANI)*; Joseph Shildkraut (Mr. Bannerjee); Mary Nash (Miss MacDaid); Jane Darwell (Aunt Phoebe Smiley); Marjorie Rambeau (Mrs. Simon); Henry Travers (Reverend Homer Smiley); H.B. Warner (Mararajah).

Story of colonial India with Maharani as the mother of Major Rama Safti who is romantically involved with Lady Edwina Esketh.

A RAISIN IN THE SUN   Black   1961/Drama

Columbia; 128 min.; *Producers*: David Suskind/Phillip Rose; *Director*: Daniel Petrie; *Screenplay*. Lorraine Hansberry; *Music*: Laurence Rosenthal; *Camera*: Charles Lawton; *Editor*: William A. Lyon; *Cast*: Sidney Poitier (Walter Lee Younger); *CLAUDIA McNEIL (LENA YOUNGER)*; *RUBY DEE (RUTH YOUNGER)*; *Diana Sands (Beneatha Younger)*; Ivan Dixon (Asagai); John Fiedler (Mark Linder); Louis Gossett (George Murchison); Stephen Perry (Travis Younger); Joel Fluellen (Bobo); Roy Glenn (Willie Harris).

Lena, the matriarch of a Chicago ghetto family, must decide how to spend her dead husband's $10,000 insurance settlement. Lena decides to use a portion of the money as down payment on a house in a white neighborhood. The rest she will give to her daughter Beneatha for medical school. This upsets her son Walter Lee who wants to invest the money in a liquor store so he can become a businessman instead of a chauffeur. Ruth, Walter Lee's wife, intervenes and suggests that Walter can have some of the money for his liquor store, with the understanding that the rest is for Beneatha's education. Walter, however, uses all the remaining money for the store, only to be swindled out of it. To recoup their losses Walter decides to accept a financial offer from a group of white neighbors who don't want the Younger family in their neighborhood. The rest of the family is opposed to this and convince Walter that this would be a step in the wrong direction. They all decide to move into their new home and face the problems that may result.

RAMONA   Native American   1936/Drama

20th Century-Fox; 90 min.; *Producer*: Sol M. Wurtzel; *Director*: Henry

King; *Screenplay*: Lamar Trotti; *Music*: Alfred Newman; *Camera*: William
Skall/Chester Lyons; *Editor*: Alfred De Gaetano; *Cast*: LORETTA YOUNG
(RAMONA); Don Ameche (Alessandro); Kent Taylor (Felipe Moreno);
Pauline Frederic (Sonora Moreno); Jane Darwell (Aunt R. Hyar);
Katherine De Mille (Margarita); Victor Killian (Father Gaspara);
John Carradine (Jim Farrar); J. Carrol Naish (Juan Can); Pedro de
Cordoba (Father Salvierderra); Charles Waldron (Dr. Weaver); Clair
Du Brey (Marda); Russell Simpson (Scroggs); William Benedict (Joseph
Hyar); Robert Spindola (Paquito); Chief Thunder Cloud (Pablo).

Ramona is a half-breed brought up by a wealthy family. Problems
develop when the son, Felipe Moreno, declares his love for Ramona.
The family is forced to reveal her parentage to destroy the romance.
But Ramona admits that she really loves Alessandro, an Indian employee
of the home, and she is now free to marry him.

RAW EDGE   Native American   1956/Western

Universal; 76 min.; *Producer*: Albert Zugsmith; *Director*: John Sher-
wood; *Screenplay*: Harry Essox/Robert Hill; *Camera*: Irving Glassberg;
Editor: Russell Schoengarth; *Cast*: Rory Calhoun (Tex Kirby); Yvonne
De Carlo (Hannah Montgomery); *MARA CORDAY (PACA)*; Rex Reason (John
Randolph); Neville Brand (Pop Penny); Emile Myer (Tarp Penny); Herbert
Rudley (Gerald Montgomery); Bob Wilke (Sile Doty).

Paca seeks revenge on Gerald Montgomery, the murderer of her
husband.

REBELLION   Mexican   1936/Drama

Crescent; 60 min.; *Producer*: E.B. Derr; *Director*: Lynn Shores;
Screenplay: John T. Neville; *Camera*: Arthur Martinelli; *Editor*: Donald
Barratt; *Cast*: Tom Keene (Carroll); *RITA CANSINO [HAYWORTH] (PAULA)*;
Duncan Renaldo (Ricardo); William Royle (Harris); Gino Carrado(Pablo);
Roger Gray (Halsing); *Lita Cortez (Lolita)*; Robert McKenzie (Taylor);
Allan Cavan (Kito); Jack Cortez (Halde).

Paula's father was murdered by land thieves in California.
Carroll was sent to California to ensure the rights of Mexican landowners. He helps Paula fight the thieves.

RED WAGON   Gypsy   1935/Drama

First Division; 97 min.; *Director*: Paul L. Stein; *Screenplay*: Edward
Knoblock/Robert Burford/Arthur Woods; *Music*: London Symphony Orches-
tra; *Camera*: Jack Cox; *Editor*: Leslie Norman; *Cast*: Charles Bickford
(Joe Prince); Jimmy Hanley (Joe as a boy); *RAQUEL TORRES (SHEBA)*;
Greta Nissen (Zara); Don Alvarado (Davey Heron); Anthony Bushell
(Toby); Paul Graetz (Schultz); Amy Veness (Petal); Frank Pettingell
(McGinty); Alexander Fields (Cronk).

Joe Prince marries Sheba in a gypsy ceremony. He really loves

Mara Corday, *Raw Edge* (Universal, 1956)

Zara and eventually returns to her.

THE RED, WHITE AND BLACK [See SOUL SOLDIER]

THE RENEGADE RANGER   Mexican   1938/Western

RKO; 60 min.; *Producer*: Bert Gilroy; *Director*: David Howard; *Screen-play*: Bennett Cohen; *Camera*: Harry Wild; *Editor*: Frederick Knudtson; *Cast*: George O'Brien (Capt. Jack Steele); *RITA HAYWORTH (JUDITH ALVAREZ)*; Ray Whitley (Happy); Tim Holt (Larry); Lucio Villegas (Juan); William Royle (Sanderson); *Cecilia Callejo (Tonia)*; Neal Hart (Sheriff Rawlings); Monte Montague (Monty); Bob Kortman (Idaho); Charles Stevens (Manuell).

Judith Alvarez is a Mexican outlaw charged with a murder she did not commit. Capt. Jack Steele sets out to find the real culprits and marries Judith.

THE RETURN OF A MAN CALLED HORSE   Native American   1976/Western

United Artists; 125 min.; *Producer*: Therry Morse, Jr.; *Director*: Irvin Kershner; *Screenplay*: Jack De Witt; *Music*: Laurence Rosenthal; *Camera*: Owen Rolzman; *Editor*: Michael Kahn; *Cast*: Richard Harris (John Morgan); *GALE SONDERGAARD (ELK WOMAN)*; Geoffrey Lewis (Zenas Morro); Bill Lucking (Tom Gryce); Jorge Luke (Running Bull); Claudio Brook (Chemin d'Fer); Enrique Lucero (Rayan); Jorge Russek (Black-smith); *Ana De Sade (Moon Star)*; Pedro Damien (Standing Bear); Huberto Lopez-Pineda (Thin Dog).

Elk Woman is one of the few survivors of an attack on her tribe by a rival band. John Morgan returns from England to help the tribe once again. (See A MAN CALLED HORSE.)

RETURN OF CHANDU   Indian   1935/Mystery

Principal Pictures; 76 min.; *Director*: Ray Taylor; *Screenplay*: Barry Barringer; *Camera*: John Hickson; *Editor*: Lou Sackin; *Cast*: Bela Lugosi (Chandu); *MARIA ALBA (PRINCESS ELAINE)*; Clara Kimball Young (Mrs. Chandler); Dean Benton (Robert); Josef Swickard (Chief Yogi); Wilfred Lucas (Yogi's aide).

Princess Elaine has many enemies so she seeks the help of Chandu the Magician.

RETURN TO PARADISE   Island Exotic   1953/Adventure

United Artists; 109 min.; *Producers*: Theron Warth/Robert Wise/Mark Robson; *Director*: Mark Robson; *Screenplay*: Charles Kaufman; *Music*: Dimitri Tiomkin; *Camera*: Winton Hoch; *Editor*: Daniel Mandell; *Cast*: Gary Cooper (Mr. Morgan); *ROBERTA HAYNES (MAEVA)*; Barry Jones (Pastor

Corbett); *Moira MacDonald (Turia)*; John Hudson (Harry Faber); Va'a
(Rori at age 9); Hans Kruse (Rori at 21); *Mamea Matamua (Tanga)*;
Herbert Ah Sue (Kura).

Mr. Morgan, a soldier of fortune, finds himself on an island
paradise. He falls in love with Maeva. When she dies giving birth
to his daughter, Mr. Morgan decides to leave the island. Years later
he returns to the island and the love of his daughter, Turia.

THE REVENGE OF GENERAL LING   Chinese   1938/Drama

Gaumont British; 71 min.; *Producer*: Premier Stafford; *Director*:
Ladislaus Vajda/John Stafford; *Screenplay*: Akos Tolnay; *Camera*: Joe
Doakes; *Cast*: Griffith Jones (John Fenton); Inkijinoff (General Ling);
ADRIANNE RENN (TAI); Alan Napier (The Governor); Anthony Eustrel (See
Long); Jino Soneya (Yuan); Hugh McDermott (Tracy); Gibson Gowland
(Mike).

Unbeknownst to Tai, her philanthropist husband, Wong, is really
the infamous warlord General Ling, trying to rid China of British
domination. John Fenton, a British agent on the trail of the General,
soon falls in love with Tai who refuses his advances. When the
identity of Ling is revealed Tai changes her attitude toward Fenton.

REVENGE OF THE NINJA   Japanese   1983/Action

Cannon; 90 min.; *Producers*: Menahem Golan/Yoram Globus; *Director*: Sam
Firstenberg; *Screenplay*: James R. Silke; *Music*: Rob Walsh; *Camera*:
David Gurfinkel; *Editor*: Mark Helfrich; *Cast*: Sho Kosugi (Cho Osaki);
Keith Vitali (Dave Hatcher); Virgil Frye (Lt. Dime); Arthur Roberts
(Braden); Mario Gallo (Caifano); *GRACE OSHITA (GRANDMOTHER)*; Ashley
Ferrare (Cathy); Kane Kosugi (Kane Osaki); John La Motta (Joe);
Melvin C. Hampton (Detective Rios); Joe Pagliuso (Alberto).

Cho Osaki's Grandmother and his son Kane are the only survivors
of a Ninja assassination attack on his family. Cho, also a Ninja,
travels to the United States to eliminate the murderers of his family.

RHYTHM OF THE ISLANDS   Island Exotic   1943/Musical

Universal; 60 min.; *Assoc. Producer*: Bernard W. Burton; *Director*: Roy
William Neill; *Screenplay*: Oscar Brodney/M.M. Musselman; *Music*:
Charles Previn; *Camera*: George Robinson; *Editor*: Paul Landers; *Cast*:
Allan Jones (Tommy); Jane Frazee (Joan Holton); Andy Devine (Eddie);
Ernest Truex (Mr. Holton); Marjorie Gateson (Mrs. Holton); Mary
Wickes (Susie Dugan); *ACQUANETTA (LUANI)*; Nestor Paiva (Nataro); John
Maxwell (Marco); Maceo Anderson (Abercrombie).

Luani is the local island girl.

RIDE A CROOKED TRAIL   Creole   1958/Western

Universal; 87 min.; *Producer*: Howard Pine; *Director*: Jesse Hibbs;
Screenplay: Borden Chase; *Music*: Joseph Gershenson; *Camera*: Harold
Lipstein; *Editor*: Edward Curtiss; *Cast*: Audie Murphy (Joe Maybe);
GIA SCALA (TESSA); Walter Matthau (Judge Kyle); Henry Silva (Sam
Teeler); Joanna Moore (Little Brandy); Eddie Little (Jimmy); Mary
Field (Mrs. Curtis); Leo Gordon (Sam Mason); Mort Mills (Pecos);
Frank Chase (Deputy Ben); Bill Walker (Jackson); Ned Wever (Attorney
Clark); Richard Cutting (Mr. Curtis).

Tessa alone is aware that the new sheriff is really renegade Joe
Maybe, in town to rob the bank. Tessa's boyfriend, Sam Teeler, is
also planning to rob the bank, so he and Joe join forces. Tessa and
Joe pretend they are married and set up housekeeping. The judge who
hired Joe asks them to care for Jimmy, an orphaned boy. Eventually
Joe and Tessa fall in love with each other and also with Jimmy. When
Teeler robs the bank Joe goes after him, killing most of his gang and
finally capturing Teeler. On his return Joe tells the judge the
truth and offers to resign, but the judge tells him that he deserves
the sheriff's job.

THE RIDE BACK   Mexican   1957/Western

United Artists; 79 min.; *Producer*: William Conrad; *Director*: Allen H.
Miner; *Screenplay*: Antony Ellis; *Music*: Frank de Vol; *Camera*: Joseph
Biroc; *Editor*: Michael Luciano; *Cast*: Anthony Quinn (Kallen); William
Conrad (Hamish); George Trevino (Guard); *LITA MILAN (ELENA)*; Victor
Milan (Padre); Ellen Hope Monroe (Child); Joe Dominguez (Luis); Louis
Towers (Boy).

Elena is the girlfriend of an outlaw.

RIDE 'EM COWBOY   Native American & Black   1957/Comedy

Untied Artists; 86 min.; *Producer*: Alex Gottlieb; *Director*; Arthur
Lubin; *Screenplay*: True Boardman/John Grant; *Music*: Charles Previn;
Camera: John Boyle; *Editor*: Phil Kahn; *Cast*: Bud Abbott (Duke); Lou
Costello (Willoughby); Dick Foran (Robert "Bronco Bob" Mitchell);
Anne Gwynne (Anne Shaw); Johnny Mack Brown (Alabam Brewster); Samuel
S. Hinds (Sam Shaw); Douglass Dumbrille (Jake Rainwater); *JODY
GILBERT (MOONBEAM)*; *Ella Fitzgerald (Ruby)*.

Willoughby accidentally shoots an arrow into the tipi of an un-
married woman and, according to tribal custom, must marry the woman
who lives there. He is delighted when an attractive, shapely woman
emerges from the tipi, but is told that her sister, Moonbeam, is the
owner of the tipi. Lou gets all excited until Moonbeam appears,
unattractive and overweight. Lou immediately runs away and for the
rest of the film Moonbeam's tribe chases after Lou trying to force
him into marriage.

RIDE ON, VAQUERO   Mexican   1941/Western

20th Century-Fox; 64 min.; *Producer*: Sol M. Wurtzel; *Director*: Herbert
I. Leeds; *Screenplay*: Samuel G. Engel; *Camera*: Lucien Andriot;
Editor: Louis Loeffler; *Cast*: Cesar Romero (Cisco Kid); Mary Beth
Hughes (Sally); LYNNE ROBERTS (MARGUERITA); Chris-Pin Martin
(Gordito); Robert Lowery (Carlos); Ben Carter (Watchman); William
Demarest (Barney); Robert Shaw (Cavalry Officer); Edwin Maxwell
(Clark); Paul Sutton (Sleepy).

　　Marguerita is Cisco's romantic interest.

RIDE OUT FOR REVENGE   Native American--Cheyenne   1957/Western

United Artists; 79 min.; *Producer*: Norman Retchin; *Director*: Bernard
Girard; *Screenplay*: Norman Retchin; *Music*: Leith Stevens; *Camera*:
Floyd Crosby; *Editor*: Leon Barsha; *Cast*: Rory Calhoun (Marshall Tate);
Gloria Grahame (Amy Forter); Lloyd Bridges (Capt. George); JOANNE
GILBERT (PRETTY WILLOW); Frank DeKova (Yellow Wolf); Vince Edwards
(Little Wolf); Michael Winkelman (Billy); Richard Shannon (Gervin);
Cyril Delevanti (Preacher).

　　The story concerns the Cheyenne's removal to Oklahoma from their
native land in Dakota. One of the Cheyenne chiefs refuses to move
and is murdered by Capt. George. Little Wolf agrees with his deceased
father and now seeks revenge on white men. Capt. George seeks the
help of the town sheriff, Tate, who is in love with Pretty Willow,
Little wolf's sister, to get the Cheyenne to cooperate. However,
Capt. George ambushes Little Wolf and Tate kills him. Tate joins
Pretty Willow and the caravan to Oklahoma.

RIDE THE PINK HORSE   Mexican Indian   1947/Drama

Universal International; 101 min.; *Producer*: Joan Harrison; *Director*:
Robert Montgomery; *Screenplay*: Ben Hecht/Charles Lederer; *Music*:
Skinner; *Camera*: Russell Metty; *Editor*: Ralph Dawson; *Cast*: Robert
Montgomery (Gagin); Thomas Gomez (Pancho); WANDA HENDRIX (PILA); Art
Smith (Frank Hugo); Andrea King (Marjorie); Richard Gaines (Jonathan);
Martin Garralaga (Barkeeper); Ritz Conde (Carlo); Iris Flores
(Maria); Edward Earle (Locke); Harold Goodwin (Red).

　　During the fiesta in San Pablo, Pila meets Gagin and, sensing
that he is a doomed man, gives him an Indian charm to ward off evil
spirits. Gagin has some evidence on the mob which he wants to pass
on to the FBI. He soon involves Pila in the situation which leads to
her being mistreated by the gangsters until FBI agents arrive just in
time. Gagin and Pila say goodbye to each other. Pila becomes something of a celebrity among the children of her village.

RIDE THE WILD SURF   Hawaiian   1964/Comedy

Columbia; 101 min.; *Producers*: Jo & Art Napoleon; *Director*: Don

Taylor; *Screenplay*: Jo & Art Napoleon; *Camera*: Joseph Biroc; *Editor*:
Eda Warren/Howard A. Smith; *Cast*: SUSAN HART (LILLY); Fabian (Jody
Wallis); Shelley Fabares (Brie Matthews); Tab Hunter (Steamer);
Barbara Eden (Augie Poole); Peter Brown (Chase Colton); Anthony Hayes
(Frank Decker); James Mitchum (Eskimo); Catherine McLeod (Mrs. Kilua);
Murray Rose (Swag).

Lilly falls in love with surfer Steamer. Her mother objects
because Lilly's Hawaiian father was a surf bum who abandoned the
family. Lilly displays her native heritage when she does the hula
for Steamer. Eventually Lilly's mom realizes that Steamer is not
like her husband and accepts him warmly into the family.

RIDER ON A DEAD HORSE   Chinese   1962/Western

Allied Artists; 72 min.; *Producer*: Kenneth Altose; *Director*: Herbert
L. Strock; *Screenplay*: Stephen Longstreet; *Music* : Frank Phillips;
Camera: Melvin Shapiro; *Cast*: John Vivyan (Hayden); Bruce Gordon
(Barney Senn); Kevin Hagen (Jake Fry); LISA LU (MING); Charles
Lampkin (Taylor).

Ming lives on a settlement in Arizona and nurses the wounded
prospector Hayden in the hope that she can convince him to take her
to San Francisco. Hayden, found gold and buried it, takes Ming with
him to locate the gold. Senn, Hayden's partner and the man who shot
him, convinces bounty hunter Jake Fry that Hayden killed their partner
Taylor so Fry takes off after Ming and Hayden. Fry locks Hayden in
jail and forces Ming to take him to the gold. Hayden escapes from
jail saves Ming from Fry who has dynamited the gold and destroyed it.
This causes Senn to go crazy and attack Ming. Hayden kills Senn,
and Hayden and Ming leave together.

RIMFIRE   Mexican   1949/Western

Screen Guild; 61 min.; *Producer*: Ron Ormond; *Director*: B. Reeves
Eason; *Screenplay*: Arthur St. Clair/Frank Wisbar/Ron Ormond; *Camera*:
Ernest Miller; *Editor*: Hugh Winn; *Cast*: James Millican (Capt. Tom
Harvey); Mary Beth Hughes (Polly); Reed Hadley (The Abilene Kid);
Henry Hull (Editor Greeley); Fuzzy Knight (Porky); Victor Killian
(Sheriff Jordan); Chris-Pin Martin (Chico): MARGIA DEAN (LOLITA);
Jason Robards (Banker Elkins); John Cason (Blazer); George Cleveland
(Judge Gardner); Ray Bennett (Barney).

Not enough information was available to describe this role
accurately.

RIO CONCHOS   Native American   1964/Western

20th Century-Fox; *Producer*: David Weisbart; *Director*: Gordon Douglas;
Screenplay: Joseph Landon/Clair Huffaker; *Music*: Jerry Goldsmith;
Camera: Joe MacDonald; *Editor*: Joseph Silver; *Cast*: Richard Boone
(Lassiter); Stuart Whitman (Capt. Haven); Tony Franciosa (Rodriguez);

WENDY WICKER (SALLY); Warner Anderson (Col. Wagner); Edmund O'Brien (Pardee); Jim Brown (Franklyn); Rodolfo Acosta (Bloodshirt); Barry Kelley (Croupier); Vito Scotti (Bandit).

Post-Civil War story tells of Pradee, who is still fighting the war, and of his attempts to build an Apache army by supplying the Apache with stolen rifles. Capt. Haven and Sgt. Franklyn are sent to stop him. They meet up with Lassiter, who owns some of the rifles, and with Mexican bandit Rodriguez who seems to be in Pardee's employ. On their journey they meet Sally, who helps them locate Pardee. Lassiter wants to kill her because he hates Indians because his family was killed by them. They finally meet up with Pardee who is about to hand over the guns to Bloodshirt, the man who killed Lassiter's family. They are taken prisoner and tortured but Sally helps them escape. Lassiter and Franklyn sacrifice their lives by torching the camp and killing everyone except Sally and Capt. Haven.

THE RIVER NIGER   Black   1976/Drama

Columbia; 105 min.; *Producers*: Sidney Beckerman/Isaac L. Jones; *Director*: Krishna Shah; *Screenplay*: Joseph A. Walker; *Camera*: Michael Margulies; *Editor*: Irving Lerner; *Cast*: CICELY TYSON *(MATTIE WILLIAMS)*; James Earl Jones (Johnny Williams); Lou Gossett (Dr. Dudley Stanton); Glynn Turman (Jeff Williams); Roger E. Mosley (Big Mo Hayes); *Jonelle Allen (Ann Vanderguild)*; *Hilday Haynes (Wilhemina Geneva Brown)*; Theodore Wilson (Chips); Charles Weldon (Skeeter); Ralph Wilcox (Al); *Shirley Jo Finney (Gail)*; Ed Crick (White Police Lieutenant); Tony Burton (Black Policeman).

On the day of her son Jeff's return from the Air Force, Mattie learns she has cancer. Several years earlier she had had cancer but recovered. This time, however, it is terminal. Wilhemina is Jeff's grandmother and Ann Vanderguild is a South African friend of his.

RIVER'S END   Canadian Indian   1940/Western

Warner Brothers; 69 min.; *Assoc. Producer*: William Jacobs; *Director*: Ray Enright; *Screenplay*: Barry Trivers/Bertram Milhauser; *Camera*: Arthur L. Todd; *Editor*: Clarence Kolster; *Cast*: Dennis Morgan (John Keith/Sgt. Conniston); Elizabeth Earl (Linda); George Tobias (Andy); Victor Jory (Talbot); James Stephenson (McDowell); *STEFFI DUNA (CHEETA)*; Edward Pawley (Crandall); John Ridgely (Jeffers); Frank Wilcox (Kentish).

Not enough information was available to describe this role accurately.

ROAD TO BALI   Balinese   1952/Comedy

Paramount; 91 min.; *Producer*: Harry Tugend; *Director*: Hal Walker; *Screenplay*: Frank Butler/Hal Kanter/William Morrow; *Music*: Joseph J. Lilley; *Camera*: George Barnes; *Editor*: Archie Marshek; *Cast*: Bob Hope

(Harold Gridley); Bing Crosby (George Cochran); *DOROTHY LAMOUR
(LALAH)*; Murvyn Vye (Ken Arok); Peter Coe (Gung); Ralph Moody (Bhoma
Da); Leon Askin (Ramayana); Bernie Gozier (Bo Kassar); Herman Cantor
(Priest).

Harold Gridley and George Cochran arrive on Bali and meet
Princess Lalah. She is searching for a sunken treasure which belongs
to her but which is also being sought by the nasty Ken Arok. Harold
and George manage to overcome all obstacles and find the treasure.

ROAD TO MOROCCO   Arab   1942/Comedy

Paramount; 81 min.; *Assoc. Producer*: Paul Jones; *Director*: David
Butler; *Screenplay*: Frank Butler/Don Harman; *Music*: Victor Young;
Camera: William C. Mellor; *Editor*: Irene Morra; *Cast*: Bing Crosby
(Jeff Peters); Bob Hope (Turkey Jackson/Aunt Lucy); *DOROTHY LAMOUR
(PRINCESS SHALMAR)*; Anthony Quinn (Mullay Kasim); *Dona Drake
(Mihirmah)*; Mikhail Rasumny (Ahmed Fey); Vladimir Sokoloff (Hyder
Khan); George Givot (Neh Joaal); Andrew Tombes (Oso Bucco); Leon
Belasco (Yusef).

Peters and Turkey Jackson both fall in love with Princess
Shalmar, who is trying to escape the clutches of the evil Mullay
Kasim. Jeff Peters wins the love of Princess Shalmar, and Turkey
Jackson becomes involved with Mihirmah.

ROAD TO RIO   Latin American   1947/Comedy

Paramount; 100 min.; *Producer*: Daniel Dare; *Director*: Norman Z.
McLeod; *Screenplay*: Edmund Beloin/Jack Rose; *Music*: Robert Emmett
Dolan; *Camera*: Ernest Laszlo; *Editor*: Ellsworth Hoagland; *Cast*: Bing
Crosby (Scat Sweeney); Bob Hope (Hot Lips Barton); *DOROTHY LAMOUR
(LUCIA MARIA DE ANDRADE)*; *Gail Sondergaard (Catherine Vail)*; Frank
Faylen (Harry); Joseph Vitale (Tony); Frank Puglia (Rodrigues);
Nestor Paiva (Cardoso); Robert Barrat (Johnson).

Lucia Maria is being hypnotized by her wicked Aunt Catherine who
wants her to marry the man of Catherine's choosing. Scat Sweeney and
Hot Lips Barton are impoverished musicians who meet and fall in love
with Lucia and manage to break her aunt's spell. Scat Sweeney wins
Lucia's love.

ROAD TO SINGAPORE   Asian   1940/Comedy

Paramount; 84 min.; *Producer*: Harlan Thompson; *Director*: Victor
Schertzinger; *Screenplay*: Don Hartman/Frank Butler; *Music*: Victor
Young; *Camera*: William C. Mellor; *Editor*: Paul Weatherwax; *Cast*:
Bing Crosby (Josh Mallon); *DOROTHY LAMOUR (MIMA)*; Bob Hope (Ace
Lannigan); Charles Coburn (Joshua Mallon IV); Judith Barrett (Gloria
Wycott); Anthony Quinn (Caesar); Jerry Colonna (Achilles Bombanassa);
Johnny Arthur (Timothy); Pierre Watkin (Morgan Wycott).

Josh Mallon and Ace Lannigan land on a south sea island and both fall in love with Mima who is trying to escape villain Caesar. Mima chooses Josh as her lover, but his rich fiancee shows up and takes him away. Ace remains with Mima (who, although she doesn't love him, won't allow him to marry another island beauty) until Josh comes to his senses and returns to Mima.

THE ROBIN HOOD OF EL DORADO   Mexican   1936/Biography

MGM; 86 min.; *Producer*: John W. Considine, Jr.; *Director*: William A. Wellman; *Screenplay*: William A. Wellman/Joseph Calleia/Melvin Levy; *Music*: Herbert Stothart; *Camera*: Chester Lyons; *Editor*: Robert J. Kern; *Cast*: Warner Baxter (Joaquin Murrieta); Ann Loring (Juanita de la Cuesta); Bruce Cabot (Bill Warren); *MARGO (ROSITA)*; J. Carrol Naish (Three Fingered Jack); *Soledad Jimenez (Madre Murrieta)*; Carlos de Valdez (Jose Murrieta).

Based on the biography of Joaquin Murrieta who was thrown off his land by white claim jumpers. His wife, Rosita, was attacked and murdered. This led Murrieta to become a notorious outlaw who went after the men who destroyed his life.

ROCK ISLAND TRAIL   Native American   1950/Western

Republic; 90 min.; *Producer*: Paul Malvern; *Director*: Joseph Kane; *Screenplay*: James Edward Grant; *Camera*: Jack Marta; *Editor*: Arthur Roberts; *Cast*: Forrest Tucker (Reed Loomis); Adele Mara (Constance Strong); *ADRIAN BOOTH (ALEETA)*; Bruce Cabot (Kirby Morrow); Chill Wills (Hogger); Barbra Fuller (Annabelle); Grant Withers (David Strong); Jeff Corey (Abe Lincoln); Roy Barcroft (Barnes); Pierre Watkin (Major); Valentine Perkins (Annette).

Aleeta is the granddaughter of Keokak, a tribal chief who becomes a peacemaker between white men and the tribes of the west. She develops an attraction to Reed Loomis who marries Constance Strong.

ROMANCE OF THE RIO GRANDE   Mexican   1940/Western

20th Century-Fox; 73 min.; *Producer*: Sol M. Wurtzel; *Director*: Herbert I. Leeds; *Screenplay*: Harold Buchman/Samuel G. Engel; *Cast*: Cesar Romero (Cisco Kid); *PATRICIA MORISON (ROSITA)*; *LYNNE ROBERTS (MARIA)*; Ricardo Cortez (Ricardo); Chris-Pin Martin (Gordito); Aldrich Bowker (Padre); Joseph McDonald (Carlos Hernandez); Pedro de Cordoba (Don Fernando); *Inez Palange (Mama Lopez)*; Raphael Bennett (Carver); Trevor Bardette (Manuel).

Rosita and Ricardo are up to no good. Maria, a singer is the heroine of this Cisco Kid adventure.

ROOTIN' TOOTIN' RHYTHM   Mexican   1937/Musical

Republic; 60 min.; *Director*: Mark V. Wright; *Screenplay*: Jack
Natteford; *Camera*: William Nobles; *Editor*: Tony Martinelli; *Cast*:
Gene Autry (Gene); Smiley Burnette (Frog); *ARMIDA (ROSA)*; Monte Blue
(Stafford); Al Clause and the Outlaws; Hal Taliaferro (Buffalo); Ann
Pendleton (Mary); Max Hoffman, Jr. (Kid); Charles King (Jim); Frankie
Marvin (Hank); *Nina Campana (Inez)*; Champion.

Not enough information was available to describe this role
accurately.

ROSE OF CIMARRON   Native American--Cherokee   1952/Western

20th Century-Fox; 74 min.; *Producer*: Edward L. Alperson; *Director*:
Harry Keller; *Screenplay*: Maurice Geraghty; *Music*: Raoul Kraoshaak;
Camera: Karl Struss; *Editor*: Arthur Roberts; *Cast*: *MALA POWERS (ROSE
OF CIMARRON)*; Jack Buetel (Marshal Hollister); Bill Williams (George
Newcomb); Jim Davis (Willie Whitewater); Dick Curtis (Clem Dawley);
Lillian Bronson (Emmy Anders); Monte Blue (Lone Eagle); Bob Steele
(Rio).

Rose was brought up by Cherokees. Outlaws kill her Indian foster parents and she seeks revenge on the three killers. Rose, who
can shoot and ride like a man, receives help from Marshal Hollister.
After the last outlaw is taken care of, Marshal and Rose are able to
pursue their romance.

ROSE OF THE RANCHO   Mexican   1936/Western

Paramount; 83 min.; *Producer*: William Le Baron; *Director*: Marion
Gering; *Screenplay*: Arthur Sheekman/Nat Perrin/Frank Partos/Charles
Brackett; *Music*: Ralph Rainger/Leo Robin; *Camera*: Leo Tover; *Editor*:
Hugh Bennett; *Cast*: John Boles (Jim Kearney); *GLADYS SWARTHOUT
(ROSITA CASTRO, DON CARLOS)*; Charles Bickford (Joe Kincaid); Willie
Howard (Pancho Spiegelgass); Herb Williams (Phineas P. Jones); Grace
Bradley (Flossie); H.B. Warner (Don Pascual Castro); *Charlotte
Granville (Dona Petrona)*; Don Alvarado (Don Luis); Minor Watson
(Jonathan Hill).

Well-bred Rosita Castro disguises herself as Don Carlos and
leads a band of Mexican vigilantes against land grabbers.

ROSE OF THE RIO GRANDE   Mexican   1938/Western

Monogram; 61 min.; *Producer*: George E. Kann; *Director*: William Nigh;
Screenplay: Ralph Beffinson; *Music*: Hugo Reisenfeld; *Camera*: Gill
Warrenton; *Cast*: *MOVITA (ROSITA)*; John Carroll (El Gato); Antonio
Moreno (Lugo); *Lina Basquette (Anita)*; Don Alvarado (Don Jose);
George Cleveland (Pedro); Duncan Renaldo (Sebastian); Gino Corrado
(Castro); Martin Garralaga (Luis); *Rose Turich (Maria)*.

Rosita is the romantic interest of El Gato.

ROGUE OF THE RIO GRANDE   Mexican   1930/Western

World Wide; 65 min.; *Producer*: George W. Weeks; *Director*: William
Nigh/Spencer Gordon Bennett; *Screenplay*: Oliver Drake; *Cast*: Jose
Bohr (El Malo); *MYRNA LOY (CARMELITA)*; Raymond Hatton (Pedro); William
Burt (Tango Dancer); Florence Dudley (Big Bertha); *Carmelita
Geraghty (Dolores)*; Walter Miller (Sheriff Rankim).

Bandit El Malo robs the mayor's safe. Carmelita is his dancer
girlfriend, Pedro is his accomplice, and Dolores is his girlfriend.
After much confusion, singing, and dancing, they all escape across
the border.

RUMBA   Cuban   1935/Musical

Paramount; 77 min.; *Producer*: William Le Baron; *Director*: Marion
Gering; *Screenplay*: Howard J. Green; *Music*: Ralph Rainger; *Camera*:
Ted Tetzlaff; *Cast*: George Raft (Joe Martin); Carole Lombard (Diana
Harrison); Lynn Overman (Flash); *MARGO (CAMELITA)*; Monroe Owsley
(Hobart Fletcher); Iris Adrian (Goldie Allen); Samuel S. Hinds (Henry
B. Harrison); Virginia Hammond (Mrs. Harrison); Gail Patrick (Patsy).

Carmelita and her dancing partner, Joe Martin, introduce the
rumba to the world. After gangsters threaten to kill her, she refuses
to dance with Joe. Heiress Diana Harrison goes on in her place, and
Carmelita loses Joe to Diana.

RUN OF THE ARROW   Native American--Sioux   1957/Western

Universal; 85 min.; *Producer/Director/Screenplay*: Samuel Fuller;
Music: Victor Young; *Camera*: Joseph Biroc; *Editor*: Gene Fowler, Jr.;
Cast: Rod Steiger (O'Mera); *SARITA MONTEIL (YELLOW MOCCASIN)*; Brian
Keith (Capt. Clark); Ralph Meeker (Lt. Driscoll); Jay C. Flippen
(Walking Coyote); Charles Bronson (Blue Buffalo); Olive Carey (Mrs.
O'Mera); H.M. Wynant (Crazy Wolf); Neyle Morrow (Red Cloud); Tim
McCoy (General Allen).

Yellow Moccasin becomes the wife of ex-confederate soldier O'Mera
when he joins the Sioux in their fight against the whites.

SAADIA   Arab--Moroccan   1953/Adventure

MGM; 81 min.; *Producer/Director/Screenplay*: Albert Lewin; *Music*:
Bronislau Kaper; *Camera*: Christopher Challis; *Editor*: Harold F. Kress;
Cast: Cornel Wilde (Si Lahssen); Mel Ferrer (Henrik); *RITA GAM
(SAADIA)*; Michel Simon (Bou Rezza); Cyril Cusack (Khadir); *Wanda
Rotha (Fatima)*; Marcel Poncin (Moha); Anthony Marlowe (Capt. Sabert);
Helena Vallier (Zoubida); Mahjoub Ben Brahim (Ahmed); Jacques

Dafilho (Bandit Leader).

Fatima is a sorceress influencing Saadia. When a spell is put on her she is saved by Henrik. She feels gratitude toward him, but not love. She loves Si Lahssen.

SADDLE LEGION   Mexican   1951/Western

RKO; 61 min.; *Producer*: Herman Schlom; *Director*: Leslie Selander; *Screenplay*: Ed Earl Repp; *Camera*: J. Roy Hunt; *Editor*: Desmond Marquette; *Cast*: Tim Holt (Dave Saunders); Dorothy Malone (Dr. Ann Rollins); Robert Livingston (Regan); Mauritz Hugo (Kelso); James Bush (Gabe); *MOVITA CASTANEDA (MERCEDES)*; Cliff Clark (Warren); Stanley Andrews (Chief Layton); George Lewis (Rurales Captain); Dick Foote (Sandy); Bob Wilke (Hooker).

Mercedes is a dancer in a saloon south of the border.

SALT OF THE EARTH   Mexican   1954/Drama

Independent Production; 94 min.; *Producer*: Paul Jarrico; *Director*: Herbert Biberman; *Screenplay*: Michael Wilson; *Music*: Sol Kaplan; *Camera*: Leonard Stark/Stanley Meredith; *Editor*: Ed Spiegel/Joan Laird; *Cast*: *ROSAURA REVUELTAS (ESPERANZA QUINTERO)*; Will Geer (Sheriff); David Wolfe (Barton); Mervin Williams (Hartwell); David Sarvis (Alexander).

The story of Mexican miners in New Mexico. The miners live under the most oppressive conditions and suffer from severe mining accidents. A strike is called and the women workers take over. Esperanza Quintero is the wife of the strike leader.

SAN ANTONE   Mexican   1953/Western

Republic; 90 min.; *Producer/Director*: Joseph Kane; *Screenplay*: Steve Fisher; *Music*: R. Dale Butts; *Camera*: Bud Trackery; *Editor*: Tony Martinelli; *Cast*: Rod Cameron (Carl Miller); Arleen Whalen (Julia Allerby); Forrest Tucker (Brian Culver); *KATY JURADO (MISTANIA FIGUEROA)*; Rodolfo Acosta (Chino Figueroa); Roy Roberts (John Chisum); Bob Steele (Bob); Harry Carey, Jr. (Dobe); James Liburn (Jim); Andrew Brennan (Ike); Richard Hale (Abraham Lincoln); Martin Garralaga (Mexian); *Argentina Brunetti (Mexican Woman)*.

Mistania Figueroa loves Carl Miller; she joins him on a cattle drive.

SANCTUARY   Black   1961/Drama

20th Century-Fox; 90 min.; *Producer*: Richard D. Zanuck; *Director*: Tony Richardson; *Screenplay*: James Poe; *Music*: Alex North; *Camera*: Ellsworth Fredricks; *Editor*: Robert Simpson; *Cast*: Lee Remick (Temple

Drake); Yves Montand (Candy Man); Bradford Dillman (Gowan Stevens); Harry Townes (Ira Bobbitt); *ODETTA (NANCY MANNIGOC)*; Howard St. John (Governor Drake); Jean Carson (Norma); Reta Shaw (Miss Reba); Strother Martin (Dog Boy); William Mims (Lee); Marge Redmond (Flossie); Jean Bartel (Swede); Hope DuBois (Mamie).

Based on William Faulkner's *Sanctuary* and *Requiem for a Nun*, which tell the story of Temple Drake, the daughter of a Mississippi judge who becomes a prostitute in a New Orleans brothel. When Candy Man, the man who started her as a prostitute, is presumed killed, Temple takes her maid, Nancy, and returns home. She marries Gowan Stevens and has a child. When Candy Man suddenly turns up she plans to leave her husband and return to her former profession. Nancy, seeing her doom, kills Temple's infant child to return her to her senses. Temple confesses everything to her father, hoping he will spare Nancy's life. He does not, and Nancy must pay for her crime.

THE SAND PEBBLES   Chinese   1966/War Drama

20th Century-Fox; 179 min.; *Producer/Director*: Robert Wise; *Screenplay*: Robert W. Anderson; *Music*: Jerry Goldsmith; *Camera*: Joseph MacDonald; *Editor*: William Reynolds; *Cast*: Steve McQueen (Jake Holman); Richard Attenborough (Frenchy Burgoyne); Richard Crenna (Capt. Collins); Candice Bergen (Shirley Eckert); *MARAYAT ANDRIANE (MAILY)*; Mako (Po-han); Larry Gates (Jameson); Charles Robinson (Ensign Bordelles); Simon Oakland (Stawski); Ford Rainey (Harris); Joseph Turkel (Bronson); Gavin MacLeod (Crosley); Richard Loo (Major Chin).

Maily, a well-educated woman, has been sold into forced prostitution, during political turmoil in 1926 China. Frenchy Burgoyne, a sailor, is in love with her. He eventually manages to buy her freedom and takes her as his common-law wife because they are unable to legally wed. Maily becomes pregnant but Frenchy dies of pneumonia. Frenchy's friend, Jake, visits her but is caught by the Chinese and beaten up. They kill Maily and blame Jake who is eventually killed in a battle.

SANDERS OF THE RIVER   Black [African]   1935/Drama

United Artists; 80 min.; *Producer*: Alexander Korda; *Director*: Zoltan Korda; *Screenplay*: Lajos Biro/Jeffrey Dell; *Music*: Muir Mathieson; *Camera*: Bernard Brown; *Editor*: Charles Crighton; *Cast*: Paul Robeson (Bosambo); Leslie Banks (Sanders); *NINA MAE McKINNEY (LILONGO)*; Robert Cochrane (Tibbeta); Martin Walker (Ferguson); Richard Grey (Hamilton); Tony Wane (Mofolaba); Marquis de Portago (Farini); Eric Maturin (Smith); Allan Jeayes (Father O'Leary); Charles Carson (Governor of the Territory).

Lilongo portrays an African tribal woman--a rarity in feature films. However, she is seen simply as a nagging wife.

SANTA FE PASSAGE   Native American   1955/Western

Republic; 91 min.; *Producer*: Sidney Picker; *Director*: William Witney;
Screenplay: Lillie Hayward; *Music*: R. Dale Butts; *Camera*: Bud
Thackery; *Editor*: Tony Martinelli; *Cast*: John Payne (Kirby Randolph);
FAITH DOMERGUE (AURELIE ST. CLAIR); Rod Cameron (Jess Griswold); Slim
Pickens (Sam Beckman); *Irene Tedrew (Ptweaquin)*; George Keymas
(Satank); Leo Gordon (Tuss McLawery); Anthony Caruso (Chavez).

Kirby Randolph falls in love with Aurelie St. Clair, one of the
passengers on the wagon train he is leading. Also vying for her
affections is Jess Griswold. Problems develop when Kirby learns she
is part Indian, since he hates Indians. After an Indian attack Jess
allows Aurelie and Kirby to flee to safety when he realizes that they
love each other.

THE SANTA FE TRAIL   Mexican   1930/Western

Paramount; 80 min.; *Director*: Otto Brower/Edwin H. Knopf; *Screenplay*:
Sam Mintz; *Camera*: David Abel; *Editor*: Verna Willis; *Cast*: Richard
Arlen (Stan Hollister); *ROSITA MORENO (MARIA CASTINADO)*; Eugene
Pallette ("Doc" Brady); Mitzi Green (Emily); Junior Durkin ("Old
Timer"); Hooper Atchley (Marc Collard); Luis Alberni (Juan Castinado);
Lee Shumway (Slaven); Standing Bear (Chief Sutanek); Blue Cloud
(Eagle Feather); Yowlache (Brown Bear); Jack Byron (Webber).

Stan Hollister is in charge of transporting a flock of sheep.
He crosses the Spanish Acres range belonging to Juan Castinado. Here
he meets and falls in love with Juan's daughter, Maria. After some
problems with thieves Maria and Stan are united.

SANTIAGO   Cuban   1956/Adventure

Warner Brothers; 92 min.; *Producer*: Martin Rackin; *Director*: Gordon
Douglas; *Screenplay*: Martin Rackin/John Twist; *Music*: David Buttolph;
Camera: John Seitz; *Editor*: Owen Marks; *Cast*: Alan Ladd (Cash Adams);
ROSSANA PODESTA (ISABELLA); Lloyd Nolan (Clay Pike); Chill Wills
(Sidewheel); Paul Fix (Trasker); L.Q. Jones (Digger); Frank de Kova
(Jingo); George J. Lewis (Pablo); Royal Dano (Lobo); Don Blackman
(Sam); Francisco Ruiz (Juanito); Clegg Hoyt (Dutch); Ernest Sarracino
(Josef Marti).

Isabella is the romantic interest of rival gun runners, Cash
Adams and Clay Pike, in Cuba prior to the Spanish-American war.

SARATOGA TRUNK   Creole & Black   1945/Drama

Warner Brothers; 135 min.; *Producer*: Hal B. Wallis; *Director*: Sam
Wood; *Screenplay*: Casey Robinson/Edna Ferber; *Music*: Max Steiner;
Camera: Ernest Haller; *Editor*: Ralph Dawson; *Cast*: Gary Cooper
(Col. Clint Maroon); *INGRID BERGMAN (CLIO DULAINE) Flora Robson
(Angelique Buiton)*; Jerry Austin (Cupidon); John Warburton (Bartholomew

Van Steed); Florence Bates (Mrs. Coventry Bellop); Curt Bois
(Augustin Haussy); John Abbott (Roscoe Bean); Ethel Griffies (Mme.
Clarissa Van Steed); Marla Shelton (Mrs. Porcelain).

Illegitimate Clio Dulaine returns to New Orleans from Paris to
seek revenge on her father's snobbish family. She succeeds in
conning them out of $10,000 and then begins her search for a million-
aire husband. Meanwhile, she has been flirting with Texas gambler
Clint Maroon, who becomes fed up with her conniving ways. After she
finally lands a millionaire, Clint is injured and Clio realizes she
loves him and goes to his side, leaving a fortune behind. Angelique
is her maid/companion--actress Flora Robson in blackface.

SARUMBA   Cuban   1950/Musical

Eagle Lion; 65 min.; *Producers*: Marion Gering/Julian Roffman/George
P. Quigley; *Director*: Marion Gering; *Screenplay*: Jay Victor; *Camera*:
Don Malkames; *Cast*: Michael Whalen (Senor Valdez); *DORIS DOWLING
(HILDITA)*; Tommy Wonder (Joe Thomas); *Dolores Tatum (Maria)*; Rodriguez
Molina (Rodriguez); Sheila Garret (Helen); Manuel Folgoso (The
Beggar); Red Davis ("La Paloma" Manager); Laurette Campeau (Laurie).

Maria and Hildita are out-of-work entertainers when they meet Joe
Thomas, who convinces Hildita to leave her sister and team up with
him. They get a start but things are foiled by Senor Valdez, who
lusts after Hildita, and by the police, who are searching for Joe (who
had jumped ship). Things work out in the end with Joe and Hildita
doing the sarumba--a combination of the rumba and samba--and Senor
Valdez chasing after Maria.

SATAN NEVER SLEEPS   Chinese   1962/Drama

20th Century-Fox; 126 min.; *Producer/Director*: Leo McCarey; *Screen-
play*: Claude Binyon/Leo McCarey; *Music*: Richard Rodney Bennett;
Camera: Oswald Morris; *Editor*: Gordon Pilkington; *Cast*: William Holden
(Father O'Banion); Clifton Webb (Father Bovard); *FRANCE NUYEN (SIU
LAN)*; Athene Seyler (Sister Agnes); Martin Benson (Kuznietsky); Edith
Sharpe (Sister Theresa); Robert Lee (Chung Ren); Weaver Lee (Ho San);
Marie Yang (Ho San's Mother); Andy Ho (Ho San's Father); *Lin Chien
(Sister Mary)*; Anthony Chinn (Ho San's Driver).

Set in China at the time of the communist revolution. Siu Lan
falls in love with a priest, Father O'Banion, who is on his way to
take over a mission from Father Bovard. She follows him to the mission, much to his dismay. When the communists takes over the mission,
Siu Lan is raped by Colonel Ho San--a former member of the mission.
Father Bovard, unaware that she has been raped, forces Siu Lan to
leave the mission because of her love for Father O'Banion. She returns because she is pregnant. She gives birth to Ho San's son, and
he begins to have doubts about communism. Communist advisers arrive
to see how Ho San is doing as commander in the area and they are not
pleased. His parents are murdered by soldiers and Ho San renounces
communism. He then helps Siu Lan and the priests escape. However,

France Nuyen, *Satan Never Sleeps* (20th Century Fox, 1962)

the communists are on their trail, and Father Bovard sacrifices his life so the rest may escape. Ho San and Siu Lan are married when they reach safety.

THE SAVAGE   Native American--Sioux   1953/Western

Paramount; 95 min.; *Producer*: Mel Epstein; *Director*: George Marshall; *Screenplay*: Sydney Boehm; *Camera*: John F. Seitz; *Editor*: Arthur Schmidt; *Cast*: Charlton Heston (Warbonnet); Susan Morrow (Tally Hathersall); Peter Hanson (Lt. Weston Hathersall); *JOAN TAYLOR (LUTA)*; Richard Rober (Capt. Arnold Vaugant); Donald Porter (Running Dog); Ted De Corsia (Iron Breast); Ian MacDonald (Yellow Eagle); Milburn Stone (Corp. Martin); *Angela Calrk (Pehangi)*; Orley Lindgren ("Whopper" Aherne); Larry Tolan (Long Mane).

    Luta and Tally Hathersall compete for the affections of Warbonnet, a white man brought up by the Sioux.

SAVAGE DRUMS   Island Exotic   1951/Adventure

Lippert; 70 min.; *Producer/Director*: William Berke; *Screenplay*: Fenton Earnshaw; *Camera*: Jack Greenhalgh; *Editor*: Carl Pierson; *Cast*: Sabu (Tipe); *LITA BARON (SARI)*; H.G. Warner (Maou); Sid Melton (Jimmy); Steven Geray (Chang); Bob Easton (Max); *Margia Dean (Tania)*; Francis Pierlot (Aruna); Paul Marion (Rata); Ray Kinney (Rami); John Mansfield (John); Edward Clark (Tabuana); Harold Fong (Officer); Nick Thompson (Spy).

    Tipe and Sari prevent a communist take-over of their island.

THE SAVAGE GUNS   Mexican   1962/Western

MGM; 85 min.; *Producer*: Jimmy Sangster; *Director*: Michael Carreras; *Screenplay*: Edmund Morris; *Music*: Anton Garcia; *Camera*: Alfredo Fraile; *Editor*: David Hawkins/Pedro del Rey; *Cast*: Richard Basehart (Steve Fallon); Don Taylor (Mike Summers); Alex Nicol (Danny Post); Jose Nicol (Ortega); *PAQUITA RICO (FRANCHEA)*; *MARIA GRANADA (JUANA)*; Fernando Rey (Don Hernan); Felix Fernandez (Paco).

    After being wounded, gunman Steve Fallon recuperates at the ranch of Mike Summers. He becomes attracted to Mike's sister-in-law, Juana. He also becomes involved with the Summers' attempts to save their ranch from the evil, land-grabbing Ortega. Mike and Fallon manage to get rid of Ortega and Fallon settles down with Juana.

SAVAGE SISTERS   Black & Asian   1974/Drama

American International; 89 min.; *Producers*: John Ashley/Eddie Romero; *Director*: Eddie Romero; *Screenplay*: H. Franco Moon/Harry Corner; *Camera*: Justo Paulino; *Editor*: Isagani V. Pastor; *Cast*: *GLORIA HENDRY (LYNN JACKSON)*; Cheri Caffaro (Jo Turner); *ROSANA ORTIZ (MEI LING)*;

John Ashley (W.P. Billingsley).

Lynn Jackson and Mei Ling join Jo Turner in trying to overthrow an island republic.

SAYONARA   Japanese   1957/Drama

Warner Brothers; 147 min.; *Producer*: William Goetz; *Director*: Joshua Logan; *Screenplay*: Paul Osborn; *Music*: Franz Waxman; *Camera*: Ellsworth Fredericks; *Editor*: Arthur P. Schmidt/Philip W. Anderson; *Cast*: Marlon Brando (Major Lloyd Gruver); Red Buttons (Joe Kelly); Ricardo Montalban (Nakamura); *MIIKO TAKA (HANA-OGI)*; *MIYOSHI UMEKI (KATSUMI)*; Patricia Owens (Eileen Webster); James Garner (Capt. Mike Bailey); Martha Scott (Mrs. Webster); Kent Smith (General Webster); Douglas Watson (Colonel Crawford); Reiko Kuba (Fumiko-san); Soo Yong (Terukosan); Harlan Warde (Consul).

Major Lloyd Gruver bears intense racial hatred for the Japanese until he meets and falls in love with Hana-ogi. His friend, Joe Kelly, falls in love with Katsumi and wants to marry her and return to the United States. However, the army will not allow this so Joe and Katsumi commit suicide. Gruver and Hana-ogi realize that prejudice will doom their love and they part.

SCARED STIFF   Cuban   1953/Comedy

Paramount; 106 min.; *Producer*: Hal Wallis; *Director*: George Marshall; *Screenplay*: Herbert Baker/Walter De Leon; *Music*: Joseph J. Lilley; *Camera*: Ernest Laszlo; *Editor*: Warren Low; *Cast*: Dean Martin (Larry Todd); Jerry Lewis (Myron Mertz); Lizabeth Scott (Mary Carroll); *CARMEN MIRANDA (CARMELITA CASTINA)*; George Dolenz (Mr. Cortega); Dorothy Malone (Rosie); William Ching (Tony Warren); Paul Marion (Cairsso Twins); Jack Lambert (Zombie).

Carmelita Castina is an entertainer. Myron Mertz does an imitation of her, complete with costume and head-dress.

SCREAM BLACULA SCREAM   Black   1973/Thriller

American International; 96 min.; *Producer*: Joseph T. Naar; *Director*: Bob Keljan; *Screenplay*: Joan Torres/Raymond Koenig/Maurice Jules; *Camera*: Isadore Manofsky; *Editor*: Fabian; *Cast*: William Marshall (Mamuwalde/Blacula); *PAM GRIER (LISA)*; Don Mitchell (Justin); Richard Lawson (Willis); Lynn Moody (Denny); Beverly Gill (Maggie).

Lisa is a voodoo priestess enlisted by vampire Blacula to help him return to his own time.

THE SEARCHERS   Native American--Comanche   1956/Western

Warner Brothers; 119 min.; *Producer*: C.V. Whitney; *Director*: John

Rita Moreno, *Seven Cities of Gold* (20th Century Fox, 1955)

Ford; *Screenplay*: Frank S. Nugent; *Music*: Max Steiner; *Camera*: Alfred Gilks; *Editor*: Jack Murray; *Cast*: John Wayne (Ethan Edwards); Jeffrey Hunter (Martin Pawley); Vera Miles (Laurie Jorgensen); Ward Bond (Capt. Reverend Samuel Clayton); Natalie Wood (Debbie Edwards); John Qualen (Lars Jorgensen); Olive Carey (Mrs. Jorgensen); Henry Brandon (Chief Scar); *BEULAH ARCHULETTA (LOOK)*; Ken Curtis (Charlie McCorry); Harry Carey, Jr. (Brad Jorgensen).

Ethan and Martin are trading among a band of Comanche. In the process Martin unknowingly makes a trade for a wife, Look--who is unattractive and overweight. When Ethan and Martin leave the tribe, Look follows. Martin tries to explain to her that he does not want her, but she does not understand English. When Martin storms off to bed Look follows him and goes to sleep next to him. Martin promptly kicks her out of bed, and she rolls down a hill. Ethan is hysterical with laughter; no consideration is given to the possibility that Look may have injured herself. She is then roughed up by Martin and Ethan. Look is murdered by the cavalry after Martin and Ethan kick her out.

SENOR AMERICANO   Mexican   1930/Drama

Universal; 71 min.; *Director*: Harry J. Brown; *Screenplay*: Bennett Cohen; *Camera*: Ted McCord; *Editor*: Fred Allen; *Cast*: Ken Maynard (Michael Banning); *KATHRYN CRAWFORD (CARMELITA)*; Gino Corrado (Ramirez); J.P. McGowan (Maddox); Frank Beale (Don Manuel); Frank Yaconelli (Manana); Tarzan.

Carmelita sings and provides the romantic interest for Michael Banning, who helps her rich, landowning father against thieves.

SERENADE   Mexican   1956/Musical

Warner Brothers; 121 min.; *Producer*: Henry Blanke; *Director*: Anthony Mann; *Screenplay*: Ivan Goff/Ben Roberts/John Twist; *Music*: Nicholas Brodazky/Sammy Cahn; *Camera*: J. Peverell Marley; *Editor*: William Ziegler; *Cast*: Mario Lanza (Damon Vincenti); Joan Fontaine (Kendall Hale); *SARITA MONTIEL (JUANA MONTEZ)*; Vincent Price (Charles Winthrop); Joseph Calleia (Maestro Marcalello); Harry Bellaver (Monte); Silvio Minciotti (Lardelli); Edward Platt (Carter); Frank Publia (Manuel); Frank Yaconelli (Giuseppe).

Damon Vincenti is a gifted singer from a humble background who leaves Juana Montez, the woman who loves him, in favor of wealthy socialite Kendall Hale. After he reaches stardom, Kendall abandons him, leaving him in despair. Juana returns to him and puts him on the road to recovery. He makes a comeback and is a star once more, with Juana at his side.

SEVEN CITIES OF GOLD   Native American   1955/Adventure

20th Century-Fox; 103 min.; *Producers*: Robert D. Webb/Barbara McLean; *Director*: Robert D. Webb; *Screenplay*: Richard L. Breen/John C.

Higgens; *Music*: Hugo Friedhofer; *Camera*: Lucien Ballard; *Editor*: Hugh S. Fowler; *Cast*: Richard Egan (Jose); Anthony Quinn (Capt. Portola); Michael Rennie (Father Serra); Jeffrey Hunter (Matuwir); *RITA MORENO (ULA)*; Eduardo Noriega (Galnez); Leslie Bradley (Juan Coronel); John Doucette (Lt. Faces); Victor Juncos (Pilot Vila); Julio Villareal (Schrichak); Miguel Inclan (Dr. Pratt); Carlos Musquiz (Father Vizcaino).

Ula is the sister of Chief Matuwir who opposes the Catholic settlement of California. She has a tragic romance with Jose, a soldier on the expedition.

7TH DAWN   Eurasian   1964/Adventure

United Artists; 123 min.; *Producer*: Charles K. Feldman; *Director*: Lewis Gilbert; *Screenplay*: Karl Tunberg; *Music*: Riz Ortolani; *Camera*: Frederick Young; *Editor*: John Shirley; *Cast*: William Holden (Ferris); Susannah York (Candace); *CAPUCINE (DHANA)*; Tetsuro Tamba (Ng); Michael Goodliffe (Trumpey); Allan Cuthbertson (Cavendish); Maurice Denham (Tarlton); Sidney Tafler (C.P.O.); *Beulah Quo (Ah Ming)*.

As a guerrilla, Dhana fought the Japanese in Malaysia during **World War II. She is now a schoolteacher and the mistress of Ferris,** who was also a member of the guerrilla band. Communist revolutionaries led by Ng, another member of the same guerrilla band, are trying to free Malaya from British rule. Dhana becomes involved with the communists but soon changes her mind. She is set up by Ng and sentenced to death by the British. Ferris' attempts to save Dhana are thwarted. By the time the dying Ng confesses the truth Dhana has already been executed. Ferris leaves Malaya.

THE 7TH VOYAGE OF SINBAD   Arabian Nights   1958/Fantasy

Columbia; 89 min.; *Producer*: Charles H. Schneer; *Director*: Nathan Juran; *Screenplay*: Kenneth Kolb; *Music*: Bernard Herrmann; *Camera*: Wilkie Cooper; *Editor*: Edwin Bryant/Jerome Thoms; *Cast*: Kerwin Mathews (Sinbad, Prince of Bagdad); *KATHRYN GRANT (PARISA, THE PRINCESS)*; Richard Eyer (The Genii); Torin Thatcher (Sokurah, the Magician); Alec Mango (The Caliph); Danny Green (Karim); Harold Kasket (Sultan); Alfred Brown (Harifa); Nanade Herrera (Sadi); Nino Falanga (Suant Sailor).

Sinbad saves magician Sokurah from a cyclops but leaves his magic lamp behind. Sinbad refuses to return for it so Sokurah shrinks Princess Parisa to three inches. Sinbad must seek out the cure for Parisa and in doing so has several magical adventures before forcing Sokurah to return the Princess to normal size.

SHADOW OF THE HAWK   Native American   1976/Thriller

Columbia-Warner; *Producer*: John Kemeny; *Director*: George McCowan; *Screenplay*: Norman Thaddeus Vane/Herbert J. Wright; *Music*: Robert

McMullin; *Camera*: John Holbrook/Reginald Morris; *Editor*: O. Nicholas
Brown; *Cast*: Jan-Michael Vincent (Mike); Marilyn Hassett (Maureen);
Chief Dan George (Old Man Hawk); Pia Shandel (Faye); *MARIANNE JONES
(DSONOQUA)*; Jacques Hubert (Andak).

Dsonoqua is an evil sorceress who is destroying Old Man Hawk
with supernatural powers. Old Man Hawk and his grandson Mike destroy
Dsonoqua.

SHADOWS   Black   1960/Drama

Lion International; 81 min.; *Producer*: Maurice McEndree; *Director*:
John Cassavetes; *Screenplay*: This was filmed without a script as a
series of improvisations; *Music*: Charles Mingus; *Camera*: Seymour
Cassel; *Editor*: Len Appelson/Maurice McEndree; *Cast*: *LELIA GOLDONI
(LELIA)*; Ben Carruthers (Ben); Hugh Hurd (Hugh); Anthony Ray (Tony);
Rupert Crosse (Rupe); Tom Allen (Tom); Dennis Sallas (Dennis); David
Pokitellow (David).

Lelia can pass for white and does when she meets Tony, who
seduces her. Tony leaves her when he finds out she is Black. Later
he tries to renew contact with her, but she is seeing a Black man.

SHAFT   Black   1971/Action

MGM; 100 min.; *Producer*: Joel Freeman; *Director*: Gordon Parks, Sr.;
Screenplay: John D.F. Black/Ernest Tidyman; *Music*: Isaac Hayes;
Camera: Urs Furrer; *Editor*: Hugh A. Robertson; *Cast*: Richard Roundtree
(John Shaft); Moses Gunn (Bumby Jones); Charles Cioffi (Lt. Vic
Androzzi); Christopher St. John (Ben Buford); *GWENN MITCHELL (ELLIE
MOORE)*; Lawrence Pressman (Tom Hannon); Victor Arnold (Charlie); Rex
Robbins (Rollie); *Sherri Brewer (Marcy)*.

Shaft is a private investigator who saves Bumby Jones's kidnapped
daughter from Black gangsters.

SHAFT IN AFRICA   Black   1973/Action

MGM; 112 min.; *Producer*: Roger Lewis; *Director*: John Guillermin;
Screenplay: Stirling Silliphant; *Music*: Johnny Pate; *Camera*: Marcel
Grignon; *Editor*: Max Benedict; *Cast*: Richard Roundtree (John Shaft);
Frank Finlay (Steve Dexter); *VONETTA McGEE (ALEMA)*; Neda Arneric
(Jazar); Debebe Eshetu (Wassa); Cy Grant (Emir); Spiros Focas
(Sassari).

Shaft is involved in breaking up a slave-market ring. Alema,
Emir's daughter, becomes romantically involved with Shaft. Jazar is
the nymphomaniac mistress to slave-ringleader Steve Dexter.

SHANGHAI EXPRESS   Chinese   1932/Drama

Paramount; 84 min.; *Director*: Josef von Sternberg; *Screenplay*: Jules
Furthman; *Camera*: Lee Garmes; *Cast*: Marlene Dietrich (Shanghai Lily);
Clive Brook (Capt. Donald Harvey); *ANNA MAY WONG (HUI FEI)*; Warner
Oland (Henry Chang); Eugene Pallette (Sam Salt); Lawrence Grant (Rev.
Carmichael); Louise Closser Hale (Mrs. Haggerty).

Hui Fei is a woman of questionable moral character traveling on
the Shanghai express. When the train is held up by revolutionaries
Hui Fei kills the leader, thus saving Shanghai Lily from having to be
his woman in order to save the life of the man she loves, Capt.
Donald Harvey.

THE SHANGHAI GESTURE   Chinese   1941/Drama

Untied Artists; 90 min.; *Producer*: Arthur Pressburger; *Director/
Screenplay*: Josef von Sternberg; *Camera*: Paul Ivano; *Editor*: Sam
Winston; *Cast*: *GENE TIERNEY (POPPY)*; Walter Huston (Sir Guy
Chatteris); Victor Mature (Dr. Omar); *ONA MUNSON (MADAME GIN SLING)*;
Phyllis Brooks (Chorus Girl); Albert Basserman (The Commissioner).

Madame Gin Sling is the operator of a gambling casino. When
Sir Guy Chatteris tries to close her down and buy the property she
vindictively goes after his daughter Poppy and leads her into a life
of sin—despite the fact that Poppy is also her daughther. When
Poppy disobeys Gin Sling she kills her.

SHE   Arab   1965/Fantasy

Warner-Pathe; 105 min.; *Producer*: Michael Carreras; *Director*: Robert
Day; *Screenplay*: David T. Chandler; *Music*: James Bernard; *Camera*:
Harry Waxman; *Editor*: James Needs/Eric Boyd-Perkins; *Cast*: John
Richardson (Leo Vincey); *URSULA ANDRESS (AYESHA)*; Peter Cushing (Major
Holly); *ROSENDA MONTEROS (USTANE)*; Bernard Cribbins (Job); Christopher
Lee (Billali); Andre Morell (Haumeid); John Maxim (Captain of the
Guard).

Ustane, a half-caste, is the hand maiden of Ayesha, Queen of
Kuma. Ustane loves Leo whom she tricked into finding Ayesha. Leo
falls in love with Ayesha and sacrifices Ustane's life so he can have
Ayesha.

SHEBA BABY   Black   1975/Drama

American International; 90 min.; *Producer*: David Sheldon; *Director/
Screenplay*: William Girdier; *Camera*: Henry Asman/Jack Davies; *Cast*:
PAM GRIER (SHEBA); **Austin Stoker (Brick)**; **D'Urville Martin (Pilot)**;
Rudy Challenger (Andy); Dick Merrifield (Shark).

Sheba is a private investigator who helps her father in his
fight against the mob.

THE SHOPWORN ANGEL   Black   1938/Drama

MGM; 85 min.; *Producer*: Joseph L. Mankiewicz; *Director*: H.C. Potter;
Screenplay: Walter Salt; *Camera*: Joseph Ruttenberg; *Editor*: W. Don
Hayes; *Cast*: Margaret Sullavan (Daisy Heath); James Stewart (Bill
Pettigrew); Walter Pidgeon (Sam Bailey); *HATTIE McDANIEL (MARTHA)*;
Nat Pendleton ("Dice"); Alan Curtis ("Thin Lips"); Sam Leven
("Leer"); Eleanor Lynn (Sally); Charles D. Brown (McGonigle).

   Martha is actress Daisy Heath's servant.

A SHOT IN THE DARK   Black   1964/Comedy

United Artists; 101 min.; *Producer/Director*: Blake Edwards; *Screen-
play*: Blake Edwards/William Peter Blatty; *Music*: Henry Mancini;
Camera: Christopher Challis; *Editor*: Ralph E. Winters; *Cast*: Peter
Sellers (Insp. Jacques Clouseau); Elke Sommer (Maria Gambrelli);
George Sanders (Benjamin Ballon); Herbert Lom (Chief Insp. Charles
Dreyfus); *TRACY REED (DOMINIQUE BALLON)*; Graham Stark (Hercule
Lajoy).

   Clouseau tries to solve the murder of Dominique Ballon's maid,
which leads to several other murders.

SHOW BOAT   Black   1936/Musical

Universal; 113 min.; *Producer*: Carl Laemmle, Jr.; *Director*: James
Whale; *Screenplay*: Oscar Hammerstein II/Jerome Kern; *Music/Lyrics*:
Jerome Kern/Oscar Hammerstein II; *Camera*: John Mescall; *Editors*: Ted
Kent/Bernard W. Burton; *Cast*: Irene Dunne (Magnolia Hawks); Allan
Jones (Gaylord Ravenal); Charles Winninger (Cap'n Andy Hawks); Helen
Westley (Parthy Henry); *HELEN MORGAN (JULIE)*; Paul Robeson (Joe);
Donald Cook (Steve); Sammy White (Frank Schultz); Queenie Smith
(Ellie); J. Farrell MacDonald (Windy); *Hattie McDaniel (Queenie)*.

   Julie LaVerne is the star on the Show Boat, a traveling riverboat variety show, until an ex-lover informs the sheriff that Julie
has Negro blood but is married to Steve, a white man. Because their
marriage is against the law, Steve cuts Julie in order to swallow
some of her blood and be able to claim that he too has Negro blood.
Nevertheless, Steve and Julie are forced to leave the riverboat to
escape imprisonment. Julie goes to work in a theater in Chicago but
quits in favor of her best friend, Magnolia Hawks, who becomes a star.
Queenie provides comic relief and words of wisdom.

SHOW BOAT   Black   1951/Musical

MGM; 107 min.; *Producer*: Arthur Freed; *Director*: George Sidney;
Screenplay: John Lee Mahin; *Music/Lyrics*: Jerome Kern/Oscar Hammer-
stein II; *Camera*: Charles Rosher; *Editor*: John Dunning; *Cast*:
Kathryn Grayson (Magnolia Hawks); *AVA GARDNER (JULIE LAVERNE)*; Howard
Keel (Gaylord Ravenal); Joe E. Brown (Capt. Andy Hawks); Marge

Champion (Ellie May Shipley); Gower Champion (Frank Schultz); Robert
Sterling (Stephen Baker); Agnes Moorehead (Parthy Hawks); William
Warfield (Joe).

Remake of the 1936 film.

SINBAD AND THE EYE OF THE TIGER   Arabian Nights   1977/Fantasy

Columbia; 112 min.; *Producers*: Charles H. Schneer/Ray Harryhausen;
Director: Sam Wanamaker; *Screenplay*: Beverly Cross; *Music*: Roy Budd;
Camera: Ted Moore; *Editor*: Roy Watts; *Cast*: Patrick Wayne (Sinbad);
TARYN POWER (DIANE); Margaret Whiting (Zenobia); *Jane Seymour
(Farah)*; Patrick Troughton (Melanthius); Kurt Christian (Rafi); Nadim
Sawaiha (Hassan); Damien Thomas (Kassim); Bruno Barnabe (Balsora);
Bernard Kay (Zahid); Salami Coker (Maroof); David Sterne (Aboo-Seer).

So her son can remain Caliph, evil stepmother Farah turns Prince
Kassim into a baboon. Sinbad, who wants to marry Diane, Kassim's
sister, begins to restore things to normalcy through magical adventures.

SINBAD THE SAILOR   Arabian Nights   1947/Fantasy

RKO; 117 min.; *Producer*: Stephen Ames; *Director*: Richard Wallace;
Screenplay: John Twist; *Music*: C. Bakaleinikoff; *Camera*: George
Barnes; *Editor*: Frank Doyle; *Cast*: Douglas Fairbanks, Jr. (Sinbad);
MAUREEN O'HARA (SHIREEN); Anthony Quinn (Emir); Walter Slezak (Melik);
George Tobias (Abba); *Jane Greer (Pirouze)*; Mike Maxurki (Yusuf);
Sheldon Leonard (Auctioneer); Alan Napier (Aga); John Miljan (Moga);
Barry Mitchell (Maulin).

Shireen is the woman with whom Sinbad falls in love on his
voyage searching for Alexander the Great's treasure.

SINCE YOU WENT AWAY   Black   1944/Drama

United Artists; 140 min.; *Producer*: David O. Selznick; *Director*: John
Cromwell; *Screenplay*: David O. Selznick; *Music*: Max Steiner; *Camera*:
Stanley Cortez; *Editor*: Hal C. Kern; *Cast*: Claudette Colbert (Anne
Hilton); Jennifer Jones (Jane Hilton); Shirley Temple (Bridget
Hilton); Joseph Cotten (Lt. Tony Willett); Lionel Barrymore (Clergy-
man); Robert Walker (Corp. Bill Smollett); Monty Woolley (Col.
Smollett); *HATTIE McDANIEL (FIDELIA)*; Jackie Moran (Johnny Mahoney);
Lloyd Corrigan (Mr. Mahoney).

Fidelia, the Hilton's maid, takes another job so she can help
out the family when they experience financial difficulties while Mr.
Hilton is away at war.

SINGER NOT THE SONG   Mexican   1960/Drama

Rank; 132 min.; *Producer/Director*: Roy Baker; *Screenplay*: Nigel
Balchin; *Music*: Philip Green; *Camera*: Otto Heller; *Editor*: Roger
Cherrill; *Cast*: John Mills (Father Keogh); Dirk Bogarde (Anacleto);
MYLENE DEMONGEOT (LOCHA); John Bentley (Police Captain); Laurence
Naismith (Old Uncle); Eric Pohlmann (Presidente); Nyal Florenz (Vito);
Roger Delgado (De Cortinez); Laurence Payne (Pablo); Leslie French
(Father Gomez); *Selma Vaz Dias (Chela)*; Lee Montague (Pepe);

Locha falls in love with Father Keogh, the priest who brings
religion back to her village after its takeover by Anacleto, a bandit
leader. Locha is caught in the middle of the many conflicts between
the two men. Anacleto becomes Locha's friend only to hold her as
hostage against the priest so that Father Keogh will restore him to
his control over the town. This ploy fails and Anacleto is taken to
prison. He escapes, and in the shoot-out that follows, Anacleto and
Father Keogh are killed.

SIREN OF BAGDAD   Arabian Nights   1953/Fantasy

Columbia; 72 min.; *Producer*: Sam Katzman; *Director*: Richard Quine;
Screenplay: Robert E. Kent; *Camera*: Henry Freulich; *Editor*: Jerome
Thomas; *Cast*: Paul Henreid (Kazah); *PATRICIA MEDINA (ZENDI)*; Hans
Conried (Ben Ali); Charlie Lung (Sultan El Malid); *Laurette Luez
(Orena)*; *Anne Dore (Leda)*; George Keymas (Soradin); Michael Fox
(Telar); Karl Davis (Morab).

Zendi, daughter of a deposed sultan, becomes involved with
magician Kazah.

SIX LESSONS FROM MADAME LA ZONGA   Latin American   1941/Comedy

Universal; 62 min.; *Assoc. Producer*: Joseph G. Sanford; *Director*:
John Rawlins; *Screenplay*: Stanley Crea Rubin/Marion Orth/Larry Rhine/
Ben Chapman; *Cast*: *LUPE VELEZ (MADAME LA ZONGA)*; Leon Errol (Senor
Alvarez); *Helen Parrish (Rosita)*; Charles Lang (Steve); William
Frawley (Beheegan); Eddie Quillan (Skat); Guinn "Big Boy" Williams
(Alvin); Shemp Howard (Gabby); Frank Mitchell (Maxwell).

Madame La Zonga, a nightclub owner, is in financial difficulty
and receives assistance from Senor Alvarez.

SKIN GAME   Black   1971/Comedy

Warner Brothers; 102 min.; *Producer*: Harry Keller; *Director*: Paul
Bogart; *Screenplay*: Pierre Marton; *Camera*: Fred Koenekamp; *Editor*:
Walter Thompson; *Cast*: James Garner (Quincy Drew); Lou Gossett (Jason
O'Rourke); Susan Clark (Ginger); *BRENDA SYKES (NAOMI)*; Edward Asner
(Plunkett); Andrew Duggan (Calloway); Henry Jones (Sam); Neva
Patterson (Mrs. Claggart); George Tyne (Bonner); Parley Baer (Mr.

Claggart); Royal Dano (John Brown).

Quincy Drew and Jason O'Rourke are running a scam whereby Quincy sells Jason on the slave market and then steals him back. On one of their excursions Jason falls in love with another slave, Naomi, and wants Quincy to buy her. Things go wrong and Jason and Naomi are set to work on a plantation. Quincy finally shows up and they escape into Mexico where Naomi and Jason decide to settle down.

SLAVE GIRL   Arab   1947/Drama

Universal-International; 80 min.; *Producer*: Michael Fessler; *Director*: Charles Lamont; *Screenplay*: Michael Fessler; *Music*: Milton Rosen; *Camera*: George Robinson; *Editor*: Frank Gross; *Cast*: *YVONNE DE CARLO (FRANCESCA)*; George Brent (Matt Claiborne); Broderick Crawford (Chips Jackson); Albert Dekker (Pasha); *Lois Collier (Aleta)*; Andy Devine (Ben); Carl Esmond (El Hamid); Arthur Treacher (Liverpool); Philip Van Zandt (Yusef); Dan Seymour (Tolok Taureg); Trevor Bardette (Cafe Proprietor).

Chips Jackson and Matt Claiborne are sent to negotiate the release of United States seamen being held for ransom. Chips manages to buy slave girl Aleta while Matt falls for Francesca, a dancing girl. Matt loses all his money to her. Francesca plans to give the money to her boyfriend, El Hamid, to finance the revolution. However, he is not really interested in her and gives her to an evil desert chieftain. Francesca, managing to escape, goes to Matt and helps him save the day.

SLAVES   Black   1969/Drama

Warner-Pathe; 110 min.; *Producer*: Philip Langner; *Director*: Dan Eriksen; *Screenplay*: Herbert J. Biberman/John O. Killen/Alida Sherman; *Music*: Bobby Scott; *Camera*: Joseph Brun; *Editor*: Sidney Meyers; *Cast*: Stephen Boyd (Nathan Mackay); *DIONNE WARWICK (CASSY)*; Ossie Davis (Luke); Robert Kya-Hill (Jericho); *Barbara Ann Teer (Esther)*; David Huddleston (Holland); Shepperd Strudwick (Arthur Stillwell); Nancy Coleman (Mrs. Stillwell); *ADLINE KING (EMMELINE)*; Gale Sondergaard (New Orleans Lady).

Cassy, a slave, is Nathan Mackay's mistress. Emmeline, also a slave, is the object of Nathan's lust. With help from the other slaves, Cassy and Emmeline escape from Nathan's plantation.

SMOOTH AS SILK   Black   1946/Drama

Universal; 65 min.; *Producer*: Howard Welsch; *Director*: Charles Barton; *Screenplay*: Dane Lussier/Kerry Shaw; *Music*: Ernest Gold; *Camera*: Woody Bredell; *Editor*: Ray Snyder; *Cast*: Kent Taylor (Mark Fenton); Virginia Grey (Paula); Jane Adams (Susan); Milburn Stone (John Kimble); John Litel (Stephen Elliott); Danny Morton (Dick Elliott); Charles Trowbridge (Fletcher Holliday); *TERESA HARRIS (LOUISE)*; Harry

Cheshire (Wolcott).

Louise is a maid.

SNOW DOG   Canadian Indian   1950/Adventure

Monogram; 63 min.; *Producer*: Lindsley Parsons; *Director*: Frank
McDonald; *Screenplay*: Bill Raynor; *Camera*: William Sickner; *Editor*:
Ace Herman; *Cast*: Kirby Grant (Rod); Elena Verdugo (Andree); Rick
Vallin (Louis); Milburn Stone (Dr. McKenzie); Richard Karlan (Biroff);
JANE ADRIAN (RED FEATHER); Hal Gerard (Antoine); Richard Avonds
(Phillippe); Duke York (Duprez); Guy Zanette (Baptiste); Chinook the
Dog.

Red Feather is one of the natives that Mountie Rod and Chinook
encounter while searching for Dr. McKenzie.

SOMBRERO   Mexican & Gypsy   1953/Comedy

MGM; 103 min.; *Producer*: Jack Cummings; *Director*: Norman Foster;
Screenplay: Josefina Nigglie/Norman Foster; *Music*: Leo Arnaud; *Camera*:
Ray June; *Editor*: Cotton Warburton; *Cast*: Ricardo Montalban (Pepe
Gonzales); *PIER ANGELI (EUFEMIA CALDERON)*; Vittorio Glassman
(Alejandro Castillo); *YVONNE DE CARLO (MARIA)*; CYD CHARISSE (LOLA DE
TORRANO)*; Rick Jason (Ruben); Nina Foch (Elena Cantu); Kurt Kasznar
(Father Zacaya); Walter Hampden (Don Carlos Castillo); Thomas Gomez
(Don Homero Calderon); Jose Greco (Gitanillio de Torrano); John Abbott
(Don Daniel); Andres Soler (Little Doctor).

Eufemia Calderon and Pepe Gonzales, members of a rival village,
fall in love and must reconcile their families to their getting
married.

Wealthy aristocrat Alejandro Castillo falls in love with Maria,
a woman from the wrong side of the tracks. He is dying and wants to
marry Maria, but she convinces him he should marry Elena Cantu. After
Alejandro dies his father discovers the truth and brings Maria to live
in his house.

Lola de Torrano is the sister of bullfighter Gitanillio who does
not want her to marry. He breaks up her romances until he is killed
by a bull as he attempts to kill Ruben, her lover. She and Ruben
marry, but she is plagued by guilt. This gives her the opportunity
to dance as she exorcises a gypsy curse.

SOMETHING FOR THE BOYS   Latin American   1944/Musical

20th Century-Fox; 85 min.; *Producer*: Irving Starr; *Director*: Lewis
Seiler; *Screenplay*: Robert Ellis/Helen Logan/Frank Gabrielson; *Music*:
Cole Porter/Jimmy McHugh/Harold Adamson; *Camera*: Ernest Palmer;
Editor: Robert Simpson; *Cast*: CARMEN MIRANDA (CHIQUITA HART)*; Michael
O'Shea (Staff Sgt. Rocky Fulton); Vivian Blaine (Blossom Hart); Phil

Silvers (Harry Hart); Sheila Ryan (Melanie Walker); Perry Como (Sgt. Laddie Green); Glenn Langan (Lt. Ashley Crothers); Roger Clark (Lt.); Cara Williams (Secretary).

Chiquita Hart, Harry Hart, and Blossom Hart inherit an old mansion and turn it into a war-wives home, with much singing and dancing.

THE SON-DAUGHTER   Chinese   1932/Drama

MGM; 79 min.; *Director*: Clarence Brown; *Screenplay*: John Goodrich/ Claudine West; *Music*: Herbert Stothart; *Camera*: Oliver T. Marsh; *Editor*: Margaret Booth; *Cast*: Ramon Novarro (Tom Lee); *HELEN HAYES (LIEN WHA)*; Lewis Stone (Dr. Tong); Warner Oland (Fen Sha); Ralph Morgan (Fang Fou Hy); *Louise Closser Hale (Toy Yah)*; H.B. Warner (Sin Kai).

Lien Wha watched as her father and lover were butchered. She becomes the unwilling bride of the murderous Fen Sha. Lien Wha gets her revenge when she strangles Fen Sha with his pigtail. Fleeing to San Francisco she helps Dr. Tong and his daughter Toy Yah--who is in love with Tom Lee. Lien Wha auctions herself as a wife to the highest bidder to help finance the revolution in her homeland.

SON OF A GUNFIGHTER   Mexican   1966/Western

MGM; 92 min.; *Producer*: Lester Welch; *Director*: Paul Landres; *Screenplay*: Clarke Reynolds; *Music*: Frank Barber; *Camera*: Manuel Berenguer; *Editor*: Sherman Rose; *Cast*: Russ Tamblyn (Johnny); Kieron Moore (Deputy Fenton); James Philbrook (James Ketchum); Fernando Rey (Don Fortuna); *MARIA GRANADA (PILAR)*; Aldo Sambrell (Morales); Antonio Casas (Pecos); Barta Barri (Esteban); Ralph Browne (Sheriff); Andy Anza (Fuentes).

Johnny, an expert with a gun, helps stop a stagecoach robbery. The same outlaws later attempt to rob Don Fortuna's ranch; Johnny is on hand to help but is wounded in the attack. He falls in love with Pilar, Don Fortuna's daughter. Johnny, however, leaves the ranch to hunt down James Ketchum, the leader of the outlaws, who may be responsible for the death of his mother. When Johnny catches up with Ketchum, Ketchum refuses to draw his gun because Johnny is his son. The two reconcile and return to Don Fortuna's ranch. During a shoot-out with Mexican bandits Ketchum is killed. Johnny is finally ready to settle down and marry Pilar.

SON OF BELLE STARR   Mexican   1953/Western

Allied Artists; 70 min.; *Producer*: Peter Scully; *Director*: Frank McDonald; *Screenplay*: D.D. Beaucham/William Raynor; *Camera*: Harry Neumann; *Editor*: Bruce Schoengarth; *Cast*: Keith Larson (The Kid); *DONA DRAKE (DOLORES)*; Peggie Castle (Clara Wren); Regis Toomey (Tom Wren); James Seay (Clark); Myron Healey (Sheriff); Frank Puglia

(Manuel); Robert Keys (Bart Wren); Stanford Jolley (Rocky); Paul McGuire (Pinkly); Lane Bradford (Beacher); Mike Ragan (Earl); Joe Dominguez (Pablo); Alex Montoya (Mexican).

Dolores betrays the Kid to get the reward money.

SON OF SINBAD   Arabian Nights   1955/Fantasy

RKO; 88 min.; *Producer*: Robert Sparks; *Director*: Ted Tetzlaff; *Screenplay*: Aubrey Wisberg/Roland Green/Jack Pollexfen; *Music*: Victor Young; *Camera*: Frederic Knudtson; *Editor*: William Snyder; *Cast*: Dale Robertson (Sinbad); *SALLY FORREST (AMEER)*; *LILI ST. CLAIR (NERISSA)*; Vincent Price (Omar); *MARI BLANCHARD (KRISTINA)*; Leon Askin (Khalif); Jay Novello (Jiddah); Raymond Greenleaf (Simon).

Sinbad is sent to find the secret of fire so as to defeat Tamerline. Kristina has the secret locked in her subconscious and Sinbad must unlock it. Ameer is the slave girl who helps him. Nerissa is one of the harem beauties that Sinbad sneaks in to visit.

SONG OF INDIA   Indian   1949/Adventure

Columbia; 77 min.; *Producer/Director*: Albert S. Rogell; *Screenplay*: Art Arthur/Kenneth Perkins; *Music*: M.W. Stoloff; *Camera*: Henry Freulich; *Editor*: Charles Nelson; *Cast*: Sabu (Ramdar); *GAIL RUSSELL (PRINCESS TARA)*; Turhan Bey (Gopal, Maharajah of Hakwar); Anthony Caruso (Major Doraj); *Aminta Dyne (Aunt Shayla)*; Fritz Leiber (Nanaram); Trevor Bardette (Rewa); Robert H. Barrat (Maharajah of Ranjat); David Bond (Ranjit Singh); Rodric Redwing (Kumari); Ted Hecht (Numtai).

Princess Tara, a photographer, is the fiancee of Gopal. While on a jungle safari they meet Ramdar, who lives in the jungle and wants to protect the animals living there. Gopal is a hunter and wants to kill animals. Ramdar takes Tara to photograph ancient ruins in the jungle. Gopal, thinking that Tara has been kidnapped, seeks revenge on Ramdar but is killed by a tiger. Ramdar is really the last in a royal family so he and Tara marry.

SONG OF SCHEHERAZADE   Arab--Moroccan   1947/Musical

Universal; 106 min.; *Producer*: Edward Kaufman; *Director/Screenplay*: Walter Reisch; *Music*: Miklos Rosza; *Camera*: Hal Mohr; *Editor*: Frank Gross; *Cast*: *YVONNE DE CARLO (CARA)*; Brian Donlevy (Captain); Jean Pierre Aumont (Rimsky-Korsakoff); Eve Arden (Madame de Talavera); Philip Reed (Prince Mischetsky); Charles Kullman (Dr. Klin); John Qualen (Lorenzo); Richard Lane (Lieutenant); Terry Kilburn (Lorin); George Dolenz (Pierre); Elena Verdugo (Fioretta); Robert Kendall (Hassan).

Cara is the dancer for whom Rimsky-Korsakoff wrote "The Song of Scheherazade." This is the story of their romance beginning when

Rimsky-Korsakoff arrives in Morocco with the Russian navy.

SONG OF THE ISLANDS   Island Exotic   1942/Musical

20th Century-Fox; 75 min.; *Producer*: William Le Baron; *Director*:
Walter Lang; *Screenplay*: Joseph Schrank/Robert Pirosh/Robert Ellis/
Helen Logan; *Music*: Harry Owens/Mack Gordon; *Camera*: Ernest Palmer;
Editor: Robert Simpson; *Cast*: Betty Grable (Eileen O'Brien); Victor
Mature (Jefferson Harper); Jack Oakie (Rusty Smith); Thomas Mitchell
(Dennis O'Brien); George Barbier (Harper); *HILO HATTIE (PALOLA)*;
Billy Gilbert (Palola's father).

     Palola and Eileen O'Brien sing "Sing Me a Song of the Islands."

THE SOUL OF NIGGER CHARLEY   Black   1973/Western

Paramount; 109 min.; *Producer/Director/Screenplay*: Larry G. Spangler;
Music: Don Costa;   *Camera*: Richard C. Gloaner; *Editor*: Howard
Kuperman; *Cast*: Fred Williamson (Charley); D'Urville Martin (Toby);
DENISE NICHOLAS (ELENA); Pedro Armendariz, Jr. (Sandoval); Kirk
Calloway (Marcellus); George Allen (Ode); Kevin Hagen (Col.
Blanchard).

     Elena is in love with Charley, who is helping to free slaves.

SOUL SOLDIER   Black   1972/Western
[THE RED, WHITE AND BLACK]

Fanfare Films; 84 min.; *Producers*: James M. Northern/Stuart Z.
Hirschman; *Director*: John Cardos; *Screenplay*: Marlene Weed; *Music*:
Tom McIntosh; *Camera*: Lewis J. Guinn; *Editor*: Lewis J. Guinn/Morton
Tubor; *Cast*: Rafer Johnson (Pvt. Armstrong); Lincoln Kilpatrick (Sgt.
Hatch); Robert DoQui (Trooper Eli Brown); *JANEE MICHELL (JULIE)*;
Cesar Romero (Col. Grierson); Barbara Hale (Mrs. Grierson); Isaac
Fields (1st Sgt. Robertson); Otis Taylor (Pvt. Adams); *Isabel
Sanford (Isabel)*; Robert Dix (Walking Horse); Bobby Clark (Kayitah);
Steve Drexel (Capt. Carpenter); Byrd Holland (The Sutler); Bill
Collins (Pvt. Washington).

     Story of the Tenth Cavalry, the only all-Black regiment of the
United States Army. Julie, the camp seamstress, is loved by fun-
loving Eli Brown and the arrogant Sgt. Hatch. Julie marries Brown,
but when he leaves on a mission she is easily seduced by Hatch.
When Brown finds out about the affair, he wants to kill Hatch. However, Julie's love and her remorse over the incident help him reconcile with her.

SOUNDER   Black   1972/Drama

20th Century-Fox; 105 min.; *Producer*: Robert B. Radnitz; *Director*:
Martin Ritt; *Screenplay*: Lonne Elder III; *Music*: Taj Mahal; *Camera*:

John Alonzo; *Editor*: J. Sid Levin; *Cast*: *CICELY TYSON (REBECCA MORGAN)*; Paul Winfield (Nathan Lee Morgan); Kevin Hooks (David Lee Morgan); Carmen Mathews (Mrs. Boatwright); Taj Mahal (Ike); James Best (Sheriff Young); Yvonne Jarrell (Josie Harriet); *Janet MacLachlan (Camille Johnson)*; Teddy Airhard (Mr. Perkins); Judge William Thomas Bennett (The Judge); Inez Durham (Court Clerk).

Rebecca, mother of three children and wife to Nathan Lee, takes in laundry to help her sharecropper family. When Nathan is sent to prison for stealing food, Rebecca becomes the sole provider. David Lee sets out to see his father and comes across an all-Black school run by Camille Johnson. Miss Johnson takes him in and he soon becomes aware of Black pride and culture. He returns home to continue working the land. Because Nathan is released from prison early, David can return to Miss Johnson's school.

SOUTH OF MONTEREY   Mexican   1946/Western

Monogram; 63 min.; *Producer*: Scott R. Dunlap; *Director*: William Nigh; *Screenplay*: Charles S. Belden; *Music*: Edward J. Kay; *Camera*: Harry Neumann; *Editor*: Fred McGuire; *Cast*: Gilbert Roland (Cisco Kid); Martin Garralaga (Police Arturo); Frank Yaconelli (Baby); *MARJORIE RIORDAN (MARIA)*; *IRIS FLORES (CARMELITA)*; George J. Lewis (Carlos Mandreno); Harry Woods (Senor Bennet).

The Cisco Kid helps Maria get out of a forced marriage to Senor Bennet arranged by her brother Arturo. Maria loves Carlos, who is imprisoned on false charges. Cisco helps Carlos clear his name so Carlos and Maria can marry.

SOUTH OF PAGO PAGO   Island Exotic   1940/Adventure

Untied Artists; 96 min.; *Producer*: Edward Small; *Director*: Alfred E. Green; *Screenplay*: George Bruce/Kenneth Gamet; *Music*: Edward Ward; *Camera*: John Mescall; *Editor*: Ray Curtis; *Cast*: Victor McLaglen (Bucko Larson); Jon Hall (Kehane); Frances Farmer (Ruby Taylor); *OLYMPE BRADNA (MALIA)*; Gene Lockhart (Lindsay); Douglas Dumbrille (Williams); Francis Fort (Foster); Ben Welden (Grimes); Abner Biberman (Ferro); Pedro De Cordoba (Chief); *Ruby Robles (Luna)*; Robert Stone (Hano); *Nellie Duran (Laulau)*.

Melia marries Kehane after the death of Ruby Taylor, his white wife.

SOUTH OF TAHITI   Polynesian   1941/Adventure

Universal; 78 min.; *Assoc. Producer/Director*: George Waggner; *Screenplay*: Gerald Geraghty; *Music*: Charles Previn; *Camera*: Elwood Bredell; *Cast*: Brian Donlevy (Bob); Broderick Crawford (Chuck); *MARIA MONTEZ (MELAHI)*; Andy Devine (Moose); Henry Wilcoxon (Capt. Larkin); H.B. Warner (High Chief); *Armida (Tutara)*; Abner Biberman (Tahawa); Ignacio Saenz (Kuana); Frank Lackteen (Besar); Barbara

Pepper (Julie); *Belle Mitchell (Taupa)*.

    Shipwrecked sailor Bob falls in love with and marries island
girl Melahi.

SOUTH OF THE BORDER   Mexican   1939/Adventure

Republic; 71 min.; *Producer*:·William Berke; *Director*: George Sherman;
Screenplay: Betty Burbridge/Gerald Geraghty; *Camera*: William Nobles;
Editor: Lester Orlebeck; *Cast*: Gene Autry (Gene); Smiley Burnette
(Frog); June Storey (Lois); *LUPITA TOVAR (DOLORES)*; Mary Lee (Patsy);
Duncan Renaldo (Andreo); Frank Reicher (Don Diego); Alan Edwards
(Saunders); Claire DuBrey (Duenna); Dick Botiller (Pablo); William
Farnum (Padre); Selmer Jackson (Consul); *Sheila Darcy (Rosita)*; Rex
Lease (Flint); The Checkerboard Band; Champion.

    Dolores gets Gene involved in a Mexican revolution.

SOUTH OF THE RIO GRANDE   Mexican   1945/Western

Monogram; 67 min.; *Producer*: Glen Cook; *Director*: Lambert Hillyer;
Screenplay: Victor Hammond/Ralph Bettinson; *Music*: Edward J. Ray;
Camera: William Austin; *Cast*: Duncan Renaldo (Cisco); Martin
Garralaga (Pancho); *ARMIDA (PEPITA)*; George J. Lewis (Sanchez);
Lillian Moller (Dolores); Charles Stevens (Sebastian); Francis
McDonald (Torres); Pedro Regan (Luis); *Soledad Jimenez (Mama Maria)*;
Tito Renaldo (Manuel).

    Pepita is a nightclub entertainer in this Cisco Kid tale.

SOUTH PACIFIC   South Sea   1958/Musical

Magna Theatre Corp.; 171 min.; *Producer*: Buddy Adler; *Director*: Joshua
Logan; *Screenplay*: Paul Osborn; *Music/Lyrics*: Richard Rodgers/Oscar
Hamemrstein II; *Camera*: Leon Shamroy; *Editor*: Robert Simpson; *Cast*:
Rossano Brazzi (Emile DeBecque); Mitzi Gaynor (Nellie Forbush); John
Kerr (Lt. Cable); Ray Walston (Luther Billis); *Juanita Hall (Bloody
Mary)*; *FRANCE NUYEN (LIAT)*; Russ Brown (Capt. Brackett); Jack Mullaney
(Professor); Ken Clark (Stewpot).

    This musical deals with racism in the South Pacific. Nellie
**Forbush falls in love with Emile DeBecque but is disturbed to meet
his children by his deceased Polynesian wife. Lt. Cable falls in love**
with Liat but is unable to overcome racial barriers and marry her.
Eventually Nellie accepts the situation and agrees to marry Emile.

SOUTH PACIFIC TRAIL   Mexican   1952/Western

Republic; 60 min.; *Producer*: Edward J. White; *Director*: William
Whitney; *Screenplay*: Arthur Orloff; *Music*: Jack Elliott/Aaron Gonzales/
Rex Allen; *Camera*: John MacBurnie; *Editor*: Harold Minter; *Cast*: Rex

Allen; Kiki; *ESTELITA RODRIGUEZ (LITA ALVAREZ)*; Slim Pickens; Nestor Paiva (Carlos Alvarez); Roy Barcroft (Link Felton); Douglas Evans (Rodney Brewster); Joe McGuinn (Ace); Forrest Taylor (Conductor).

Not enough information was available to describe this role accurately.

SPARKLE   Black   1976/Musical

Warner Brothers; 99 min.; *Producer*: Howard Rosenman; *Director*: Sam O'Steen; *Screenplay*: Joel Schumacher; *Music*: Curtis Mayfield; *Camera*: Bruce Surtees; *Editor*: Gordon Scott; *Cast*: Philip M. Thomas (Stix); *IRENE CARA (SPARKLE)*; *LONETTE McKEE (SISTER)*; *DWAN SMITH (DELORES)*; *Mary Alice (Effie)*.

Sparkle, Sister, and Delores are sisters who form a singing group and escape the Harlem ghetto.

THE SPLIT   Black   1968/Drama

MGM; 90 min.; *Producers*: Irwin Winkler/Robert Chartoff; *Director*: Gordon Flemyng; *Screenplay*: Robert Sabaroff; *Camera*: Burnett Guffey; *Editor*: Rita Roland; *Cast*: Jim Brown (McClain); *DIAHANN CARROLL (ELLIE McCLAIN)*; Julie Harris (Gladys); Ernest Borgnine (Bert Clinger); Gene Hackman (Lt. Walter Brill); Jack Klugman (Harry Kifka); Warren Oates (Marty Gough); James Whitmore (Herb Sutro); Donald Sutherland (Dave Negli); Jackie Joseph (Jackie); Harry Hickox (Detective); Joyce Jameson (Jennifer).

Ellie McClain agrees to hide stolen money for her ex-husband, provided this will be his last job. Ellie's landlord, Herb Sutro, attempts to rape Ellie and winds up murdering her and taking the money.

SPOILERS OF THE NORTH   Native American   1947/Drama

Republic; 66 min.; *Assoc. Producer*: Donald H. Brown; *Director*: Richard Sale; *Screenplay*: Milton M. Raison; *Music*: Mort Glickman; *Camera*: Alfred Keller; *Editor*: William Thompson; *Cast*: Paul Kelly (Matt Garraway); *ADRIAN BOOTH (JANE KOSTER)*; Evelyn Ankers (Laura Reed); James A. Millican (Bill Garraway); Roy Barcroft.

This is the story of two brothers operating an Alaskan salmon fishery. Matt, the evil brother, is romancing both Jane and Laura, who agrees to marry him. Matt uses illegal methods to increase salmon output. Jane helps him and he murders her boyfriend when he discovers they are violating Indian fishing quotas. When Jane learns about Laura she murders Matt and is sent to prison. Laura and Bill, the good brother, marry.

THE SQUAW MAN   Native American   1931/Drama

MGM/Paramount; 107 min.; *Producer/Director*: Cecil B. DeMille; *Screenplay*: Lucien Hubbard/Lenor Coffee; *Camera*: Harold Rosson; *Editor*: Anne Bauchens; *Cast*: Warner Baxter (Jim Wynn); *LUPE VELEZ (NATURICH)*; Eleanor Boardman (Diana); Paul Cavanagh (Lord Henry Kerhill); Lawrence Grant (General Stafford); Roland Young (Sir John Applegate); Charles Bickford (Cash Hawkins); Desmond Roberts (Hardwick); Mitchell Lewis (Tabywanna).

Jim Wynn rescues Naturich and she in turn saves his life. They wed, although he loves Diana, the woman he left behind in England. Naturich bears him a child. She also kills one of her husband's enemies. Diana arrives from England. When the sheriff discovers that Naturich killed Cash Hawkins, she commits suicide, leaving Wynn free to marry Diana and return to England with his child.

STAY AWAY, JOE   Native American   1968/Musical

MGM; 101 min.; *Producer*: Douglas Laurence; *Director*: Peter Tewksbury; *Screenplay*: Burt Kennedy/Michael A. Hoey; *Music*: Jack Marshall; *Camera*: Fred Koenekamp; *Editor*: George W. Brooks; *Cast*: Elvis Presley (Joe Lightcloud); Burgess Meredith (Charlie Lightcloud); Joan Blondell (Glenda Callahan); *KATY JURADO (ANNIE LIGHTCLOUD)*; Thomas Gomez (Grandpa); Henry Jones (Hy Slager); L.Q. Jones (Bronc Hoverty); Quentin Dean (Mamie Callahan); Anne Seymour (Mrs. Hawkins); Angus Duncan (Lorne Hawkins); *Susan Trustman (Mary Lightcloud)*; *Maurishka (Connie Shortgun)*; Buck Kartalian (Bull Shortgun); *Jennifer Peak (Little Deer)*.

Annie Lightcloud is Joe's stepmother. She feels that no matter what Joe does it will eventually lead to trouble. Mary (Joe's half sister) and Annie try to impress the family of Mary's white boyfriend.

STILETTO   Black   1969/Drama

Avco Embassy; 98 min.; *Producer*: Norman Rosemont; *Director*: Bernard L. Kowalski; *Screenplay*: A.J. Russell; *Music*: Sid Ramin; *Camera*: Jack Priestley; *Editor*: Frank Mazzola/Stuart Chasmar; *Cast*: Alex Cord (Count Cesare Cardinali); Britt Ekland (Illena); Patrick O'Neal (George Baker); Joseph Wiseman (Emilio Matteo); *BARBARA McNAIR (AHN DESSJE)*; John Dehner (Frank Simpson); Titos Vandia (Tonio); Eduardo Ciannelli (Don Andrea); Roy Scheider (Bennett); Lincoln Kilpatrick (Hannibal Smith).

Ahn Dessje is the girlfriend of Cesare Cardinali, a mafia hit man whom the mafia wants dead. This association costs Ahn her life.

STORM OVER THE ANDES   Latin American   1935/Adventure

Universal; 82 min.; *Producer*: Carl Laemmle; *Director*: Christy Cabanne; *Screenplay*: Albert De Mond/Frank Wead/Even Green; *Camera*: Charles

Stunar; *Editor*: Maurice E. White; *Cast*: Jack Holt (Bob Kent);
Antonio Moreno (Major Tovar); *MONA BARRIE (THERESA)*; *Juanita Quigley
(Pepita)*; Gene Lockhart (Cracker); Grant Withers (Mitchell); Barry
Norton (Diaz); George Lewis (Garcia); June Gittelson (Big Woman).

Bob Kent pursues Theresa, not knowing that she is Major Tovar's
wife. He picks Pepita up at a fiesta.

STORMY WEATHER   Black   1943/Musical

20th Century-Fox; 77 min.; *Producer*: William Le Baron; *Director*:
Andrew Stone; *Screenplay*: Frederick Jackson/Ted Koehler; *Music*:
Fanchon; *Camera*: Leon Shamroy; *Editor*: James B. Clark; *Cast*: *LENA
HORNE (SELINA ROGERS)*; Bill Robinson (Corky); Cab Calloway and his
band; Fats Waller (Fats); Nicholas Brothers; Katherine Dunham and
her troupe; *Ada Brown (Ada)*; Dooley Wilson (Gabe); The Tramp Band;
Babe Wallace (Chick Bailey); Ernest Whitman (Jim Europe); Zuttie
Singleton (Zuttie); *Mae E. Johnson (Mae)*.

All-Black musical has Selina Rogers and Corky paired romantically. Selina is a major star who gives Corky a part in her show.

THE STORY OF DR. WASSELL   Asian   1944/War Drama

Paramount; 140 min.; *Producer/Director*: Cecil B. DeMille; *Screenplay*:
Alan Le May/Charles Bennett; *Music*: Victor Young; *Camera*: Victor
Milner; *Editor*: Anne Bauchens; *Cast*: Gary Cooper (Dr. Corydon M.
Wassell); Laraine Day (Madelein Day); Signe Hasso (Bettina); *CAROL
THURSTON (TREMARTINI)*; Dennis O'Keefe (Benjamin "Hoppy" Hopkins);
Carl Esmond (Lt. Dirk Van Daal); Stanley Ridges (Cdr. William B.
Goggins); Renny McEvoy (Joe Leinwerber); Elliott Reid (William
Anderson); Melvin Francis.

The story of World War II's heroic Dr. Wassell. Tremartini is a
Javanese nurse marooned with Benjamin "Hoppy" Hopkins in a jungle
full of Japanese invaders.

THE STRANGE VENGEANCE OF ROSALIE   Native American   1972/Drama

20th Century-Fox; 107 min.; *Producer*: John Kohn; *Director*: Jack
Starrett; *Screenplay*: Anthony Greville-Bell/John Kohn; *Music*: John
Cameron; *Camera*: Ray Parslow; *Editor*: Thom Noble; *Cast*: *BONNIE
BEDELIA (ROSALIE)*; Ken Howard (Virgil); Anthony Zerbe (Fry).

Virgil picks up hitchhiker Rosalie and takes her back to her
dead grandfather's shack. She is attracted to Virgil so she slashes
his tires so he cannot leave her. When that fails she breaks his leg.
Virgil tries to escape but fails. Fry, an Indian biker, arrives
looking for her grandfather's gold. Tricking Fry into thinking some
worthless gems are real, Virgil and Rosalie flee the shack. Fry is
soon on their trail. Rosalie slashes Fry's throat. When the police
arrive she tells them Virgil murdered her boyfriend Fry.

STRANGE VOYAGE   Mexican   1946/Drama

Monogram; 63 min.; *Producer*: Louis B. Appleton, Jr.; *Director*: Irving
Allen; *Screenplay*: Andrew Holt; *Editor*: Jack Greenhalgh, Jr.; *Cast*:
Eddie Albert (Chris Thompson); Forrest Taylor (Skipper); Ray Teal
(Capt. Andrews); *ELENA VERDUGO (CARMELITA)*; Bobby Cooper (Jimmy);
Matt Willis ("The Hammer"); Martin Garralaga (Manuel); Daniel Herry
(Ben).

    Not enough information was available to describe this role
accurately.

STRICTLY DYNAMITE   Latin American   1934/Comedy

RKO; 71 min.; *Producer*: Pandro S. Berman; *Director*: Elliott Nugent;
Screenplay: Maurice Watkins/Ralph Spence; *Music*: Jimmy Durante/Burton
Lane/Harold Adamson/Irving Kahal/Sammy Fain; *Camera*: Edward Cronjager;
Editor: George Crone; *Cast*: Jimmy Durante (Moxie Slaight); *LUPE*
VELEZ (VERA); Norman Foster (Nick Montgomery); William Gargan (George
Ross); Marian Nixon (Sylvia Montgomery); Eugene Pallette (Sourwood
Sam); Minna Gombell (Miss LeSeur); Sterling Holloway (Fleming).

    Vera, temperamental radio star, is the partner of a radio
comedian rapidly running out of jokes and trying to find some new
entertainment for his show.

STUDY IN SCARLET   Chinese   1933/Mystery

World Wide; 70 min.; *Director*: Edwin L. Marin; *Screenplay*: Robert
Florey; *Camera*: Arthur Edeson; *Editor*: Rose Loewinger; *Cast*: Reginald
Owen (Sherlock Holmes); *ANNA MAY WONG (MRS. PYKE)*; June Clyde (Eileen
Forrester); Allan Dinehart (Thaddeus Merrydew); John Warburton (John
Stanford); Warburton Gamble (Dr. Watson); J.M. Kerrigan (Jabez
Wilson); Alan Mowbray (Insp. Lestrade); Doris Lloyd (Mrs. Murphy);
Billy Bevan (Will Swallow); Cecil Reynolds (Baker); Wyndham Standing
(Captain Pyke); Tetsu Komai (Ah Yet).

    Mrs. Pyke becomes involved with Sherlock Holmes and Dr. Watson.

SUDAN   Arab--Egyptian   1945/Adventure

Universal; 76 min.; *Producer*: Paul Malvern; *Director*: John Rawlins;
Screenplay: Edmund L. Hartman; *Music*: Milton Rosen; *Camera*: George
Robinson; *Editor*: Milton Carruth; *Cast*: *MARIA MONTEZ (NAILA)*; Jon
Hall (Merab); Turhan Bey (Herua); Andy Devine (Nebka); George Zucco
(Horadef); Robert Warwick (Naatet); Phil Van Zandt (Setna); Harry
Cording (Uba); George Lynn (Bata); Charles Arnt (Khafra).

    Naila, the Queen of the Sudan, falls in love with Merab, the
leader of the slave rebellion. Merab is accused of murdering Naila's
father so she must sentence him to death. Naila discovers just in
time that the real murderer is the royal chamberlain. When every-

thing is settled Naila and Merab marry.

SUNSET IN THE WEST   Mexican   1950/Musical

Republic; 67 min.; *Producer*: Edward J. White; *Director*: William
Whitney; *Screenplay*: Gerald Geraghty; *Camera*: Jack Marta; *Editor*: Tony
Martinelli; *Cast*: Roy Rogers; *ESTELITA RODRIGUEZ (CARMELITA)*; Penny
Edwards (Dixie Osborne); Gordon Jones (Splinters); Will Wright
(Sheriff Osborne); Pierre Watkin (Mac Knight); Charles La Torre (Nick
Corella); William J. Tannen (John Kimball); Gaylord Pendleton (Walter
Kimball); Paul E. Burns ("Blink" Adams); Dorothy Ann White (Dot);
Trigger; Fox Willing and the Riders of the Purple Sage.

　　　Carmelita is a singer in a Mexican cafe.

SUPER FLY   Black   1972/Drama

Warner Brothers; 98 min.; *Producer*: Sig Shore; *Driector*: Gordon
Parks; *Screenplay*: Phillip Fenty; *Music*: Curtis Mayfield; *Camera*:
James Signorelli; *Editor*: Bob Brady; *Cast*: Ron O'Neal (Youngblood
Priest); Carl Lee (Eddie); *SHEILA FRAZIER (GEORGIA)*; Julius W. Harris
(Soatter); Charles McGregor (Fat Freddie); Nat Adams (Dealer); Polly
Niles (Cynthia); Yvonne DeLaine (Mrs. Freddie); "K.C." (Pimp); Jim
Richardson (Junkie); Sig Shore (Deputy Commissioner).

　　　Georgia is the girlfriend of cocaine dealer Youngblood Priest.
Youngblood wants to make one final score so he and Georgia can retire
to a life of luxury. He succeeds.

SUPER FLY, TNT   Black   1973/Drama

Paramount; 87 min.; *Producer*: Sig Shore; *Director*: Ron O'Neal; *Screen-
play*: Alex Haley; *Music*: Osibisa; *Camera*: Robert Gaffney; *Editor*: Bob
Brady; *Cast*: Ron O'Neal (Priest); Roscoe Lee Browne (Dr. Lamine Sonko);
SHEILA FRAZIER (GEORGIA); Robert Guillaume (Jordan Gaines); Jacques
Sernas (Matty Smith); William Berger (Lefeure).

　　　Sequel to SUPER FLY shows the relationship between Georgia and
Priest after his big score.

SURRENDER-HELL   Filipino   1959/War Drama

Warner-Pathe; 85 min.; *Producer*: Edmund Holdman; *Director*: John
Barnwell; *Screenplay*: John Barnwell; *Music*: Francisco Buencamino, Jr.;
Camera: Miguel Accion; *Editors*: Hugo Grimaldi/Gerardo DeLeon/Harry
Kaye; *Cast*: Keith Andes (Col. Donald D. Blackburn); *SUSAN CABOT
(DELLA)*; *Paraluman (Pilar)*; Nestor de Villa (Major Bulao).

　　　Della escapes the invading Japanese with American Army Lt.
Donald Blackburn. He comes down with malaria and Della helps him
recover. Afterward, Della stays with her parents and Blackburn joins

with a group of guerrillas led by Pilar. He organizes a group and
assists General MacArthur. Pilar falls in love with Blackburn, but
she dies in his arms.

SUSANNA PASS   Mexican   1949/Musical

Republic; 67 min.; *Producer*: Edward J. White; *Director*: William
Witney; *Screenplay*: Sloan Nibley/John K. Butler; *Camera*: Reggie
Lanning; *Editor*: Tony Martinelli; *Cast*: Roy Rogers; Dale Evans (Kay/
Doc/Parker); *ESTELITA RODRIGUEZ (RITA)*; Martin Garralaga (Carlos
Mendoza); Robert Emmett Kean (Martin Masters); Lucien Littlefield
(Russell Masters); Douglas Fowley (Del Roberts); David Sharpe (Vince);
Robert Bice (Bob Oliver); Fox Willing and the Riders of the Purple
Sage; Trigger.

    Rita does a comic specialty number, "Two Gun Rita."

SWAMP FIRE   Cajun   1946/Drama

Paramount; 68 min.; *Producers*: William Pine/William Thomas; *Director*:
William Pine; *Screenplay*: Geoffrey Homes; *Camera*: Fred Jackman, Jr.;
Editor: Howard Smith; *Cast*: Johnny Weissmuller (Johnny Duval);
Virginia Grey (Janet Hilton); Buster Crabbe (Mike Kalavich); *CAROL
THURSTON (TONI ROUSSEAU)*; Edwin Maxwell (Capt. Moise); Pedro De
Cordoba (Tim Rousseau); Pierre Watkin (Mr. Hilton); Marcelle Corday
(Grandmere Rousseau).

    Johnny Duval guides boats down the Mississippi in the bayou
country of Louisiana. He loves Cajun native Toni Rousseau. He meets
Janet Hilton, a member of a powerful Louisiana family, who tries to
entice him into marriage with the promise of wealth and power. When
Johnny has an accident, Janet keeps Toni from seeing him. After he
recovers he sees that Janet's family is responsible for the oppression
of the Cajuns, and he returns to Toni.

SWING HIGH, SWING LOW   Panama   1937/Drama

Paramount; 96 min.; *Producer*: Arthur Hornblow; *Director*: Mitchell
Leisen; *Screenplay*: Virginia Van Upp/Oscar Hammerstein; *Music*: Boris
Morros; *Camera*: Ted Tetzlaff; *Editor*: Eda Warren; *Cast*: Carole Lombard
(Maggie King); Fred MacMurray (Skid Johnson); Charles Butterworth
(Harry); Jean Dixon (Ella); *DOROTHY LAMOUR (ANITA ALVAREZ)*; Harvey
Stephens (Havery Howell); Cecil Cunningham (Murphy); Charles Judles
(Tony); Cahrles Arnt (Georgie).

    Anita Alvarez is a vamp who sings one song.

SWORD OF ALI BABA   Arabian Nights   1965/Fantasy

Universal; 81 min.; *Producer*: Howard Christie; *Director*: Virgil Vogel;
Screenplay: Edmund Morrison; *Music*: Frank Skinner; *Camera*: William

Margulies; *Editor*: Gene Palmer; *Cast*: Peter Mann (Ali Baba); *JOCELYN LANE (AMARA)*; Peter Whitney (Abou); Gavin McLeod (Hulagu Khan); Frank Puglia (Prince Cassim); Frank McGrath (Pindar); Greg Morris (Yusuf); Frank De Kova (Baba).

Low-budget, trashy remake of ALI BABA AND THE FORTY THIEVES, including some of the same footage.

SWORD OF THE AVENGER   Filipino   1948/Adventure

Eagle-Lion; 76 min.; *Producer/Director*: Sidney Salkow; *Screenplay*: Julius Evans; *Music*: Eddison von Offenfield; *Camera*: Clyde DeVinna; *Editor*: Mel Thorsen; *Cast*: Ramon Del Gado (Roberto Balagtas); *SIGRID GURIE (MARA LOUISA)*; Ralph Morgan (Don Adolfo); Duncan Renaldo (Fernando); Leonard Strong (Ming Ting); David Leonard (Ignacio); Tim Huntley (Rodrigo).

Roberto and Mara, members of a group of Filipino patriots, are engaged to be married. On the eve of their wedding Roberto is betrayed by Rodrigo, who wants Mara for himself. When Roberto is taken to prison Mara assumes leadership of the group. Rodrigo takes charge of the prison and makes sure no one finds Roberto. After many years of abuse Roberto escapes and finds a hidden treasure. He returns as a wealthy Spanish nobleman and is reunited with Mara. Rodrigo finally gets what he deserves.

SYNANON   Black   1965/Drama

Columbia; 107 min.; *Producer/Director*: Richard Quine; *Screenplay*: Ian Bernard/S. Lee Pogostin; *Music*: Neal Hefti; *Camera*: Harry Stradling; *Editor*: David Wages; *Cast*: Chuck Connors (Ben); Stella Stevens (Joaney); Alex Cord (Zankie Albo); Richard Conte (Reid); *EARTHA KITT (BETTY COLEMAN)*; Edmond O'Brien (Chuck Dederich); Barbara Luna (Mary).

Betty Coleman is a member of Synanon, a drug rehabilitation center.

TAHITI NIGHTS   Tahitian   1944/Musical

Columbia; 63 min.; *Producer*: Sam White; *Director*: Will Jason; *Screenplay*: Lillie Hayward; *Camera*: Benjamin Kline; *Editor*: Jerome Thoms; *Cast*: *JINX FALKENBURG (LUANA)*; David O'Brien (Jack); *Florence Bates (Queen Liliha)*; *Mary Treep (Mata)*; Eddie Bruce (Chopstick); Pedro De Cordoba (Tonga); *Hilo Hattie (Temata)*; Carole Mathews (Betty Lou); Cy Kendal (Chief Enciza).

Bandleader Jack arrives on a Tahitian island and soon finds himself engaged to Luana.

TAKE A GIANT STEP   Black   1960/Drama

United Artists; 100 min.; *Producer*: Julius J. Epstein; *Director*:
Philip Leacock; *Screenplay*: Louis Peterson/Julius Epstein; *Music*:
Jack Marshals; *Camera*: Arthur Arling; *Editor*: Frank Gross; *Cast*:
Johnny Nash (Spencer Scott); *Estelle Hemsley (Grandma)*; *RUBY DEE
(CHRISTINE)*; Frederick O'Neal (Lem Scott); *Pauline Meyers (Violet)*;
Ellen Holly (Carol); *Beah Richards (May Scott)*.

       Spencer, a confused teenager, has difficulty relating to his
white friends but is unable to adjust to the Black community. Grandma
tries to comfort him, but help comes from the family maid, Christine,
who manages to show love and (sexual) affection and understanding.

TAMAHINE   Polynesian   1963/Comedy

MGM; 95 min.; *Producer*: John Bryan; *Director*: Philip Leacock; *Screen-
play*: Denis Cannan; *Music*: Malcolm Arnold; *Camera*: Geoffrey Unsworth;
Editor: Peter Tanner; *Cast*: *NANCY KWAN (TAMAHINE)*; John Fraser
(Richard); Dennis Price (Poole); Coral Browne (Madam Becque); Dick
Bentley (Storekeeper); Derek Nimmo (Clove); Justine Lord (Diana);
Michael Gough (Cartwright); Allan Cuthbertson (Housemaster).

       After her English father dies, Tamahine is sent to England to
live with her father's cousin, Charles Poole. Her Polynesian manners
disrupt the school where Poole is headmaster. Richard, Poole's son,
falls in love with Tamahine. Poole himself becomes so enamored of
Tamahine that he leaves the headmastership to his son and goes to
Polynesia.

TAMMY AND THE BACHELOR   Black   1957/Comedy

Universal; 87 min.; *Producer*: Ross Hunter; *Director*: Joseph Pevney;
Screenplay: Oscar Brodney; *Music*: Frank Skinner; *Camera*: Arthur E.
Arling; *Editor*: Ted J. Kent; *Cast*: Debbie Reynolds (Tammy); Leslie
Nielsen (Peter Brent); Walter Brennan (Grandpa); Mala Powers
(Barbara); Sidney Blackmer (Professor Brent); Mildred Natwick (Aunt
Renie); Fay Wray (Mrs. Brent); *LOUISE BEAVERS (OSIA)*; Philip Ober
(Alfred Bissie); Craig HIll (Ernie); April Kent (Tina).

       When Tammy goes to live with a wealthy southern family, Osia,
the maid, becomes her close friend and helps her win the heart of
Peter Brent.

TARZAN AND THE LEOPARD WOMAN   Jungle Exotic   1946/Adventure

RKO; 72 min.; *Producer*: Sol Lesser; *Director*: Kurt Neumann; *Screen-
play*: Carroll Young; *Camera*: Karl Struss; *Editor*: Robert O. Crandall;
Cast: Johnny Weissmuller (Tarzan); Brenda Joyce (Jane); Johnny
Sheffield (Boy); *ACQUANETTA (LEA)*; Edgar Barrier (Lazar); Tommy Cook
(Kimba); Dennis Hoey (Commissioner); Anthony Caruso (Mongo); George J.
Lewis (Corporal).

       Tarzan is on the trail of men dressed as leopards who attack and

loot caravans. These leopard men are members of a tribal cult. Lea
is the queen and she and her brother are the leaders. They are
fighting encroachment of their land by white settlers. The film's
sympathy is with the white settlers, not the natives.

TARZAN AND THE MERMAIDS   Jungle Exotic   1948/Adventure

RKO; 68 min.; *Producer*: Sol Lesser; *Director*: Robert Florey; *Screen-
play*: Carroll Young; *Camera*: Jack Draper/Gabriel Figueroa/Raul
Martinez Solares; *Editor*: Merrill White; *Cast*: Johnny Weissmuller
(Tarzan); Brenda Joyce (Jane); Johnny Sheffield (Boy); *LINDA
CHRISTIAN (MARA)*; George Zucco (Palanth); John Laurenz (Benji);
Fernando Wagner (Varga); Edward Ashley (Commissioner); *Andrea Palma
(Luana)*; Gustavo Rojo (Tike).

Mara is a young woman who escapes from her island so she won't
have to marry an evil pearl trader. She is recaptured, but Tarzan
saves her and reunites her with her true love.

TARZAN AND THE SLAVE GIRL   Jungle Exotic   1950/Adventure

RKO; 74 min.; *Producer*: Sol Lesser; *Director*: Lee Sholem; *Screenplay*:
Hans Jacoby/Arnold Belgard; *Music*: Paul Sawtell; *Camera*: Russell
Harlan; *Editor*: Christian Nyby; *Cast*: Lex Barker (Tarzan); Vanessa
Brown (Jane); Robert Alda (Neil); *DENISE DARCEL (LOLA)*; Hurd Hatfield
(The Prince); Arthur Shields (Randini Doctor); Robert Warwick (High
Priest); Anthony Caruso (Sengo); Tito Renaldo (Chief's Son); Mary
Ellen Kay (Moana).

This Tarzan story focuses on tribal women who are taken away to
be slaves to an evil prince living in the jungle. Lola is a doctor's
assistant who is after Tarzan. While Tarzan and the doctor are
investigating the kidnappings Lola and Jane live together--until they
too are kidnapped. Tarzan saves the day in the end.

TARZAN GOES TO INDIA   Indian   1962/Adventure

MGM; 86 min.; *Producer*: Sy Weintraub; *Director*: John Guillermin;
Screenplay: Robert Hardy Andrews/John Guillermin; *Music*: Ken Jones;
Camera: Paul Beeson; *Editor*: Max Benedict; *Cast*: Jock Mahoney
(Tarzan); Jai (The Elephant Boy); Mark Dana (O'Hara); *SIMI (PRINCESS
KAMARA)*; Leo Gordon (Bryce); Feroz Khan (Rama); Murad (Maharajah);
Jagdish Raaj (Raaj); Aaron Joseph (Driver); Abas Khan (Pilot);
Pehelwan Ameer (Mooty); G. Raghaven (Chakra); K.S. Tripathi (Conser-
vation Officer).

Tarzan is in India to help Princess Kamara and her Maharajah
father save a herd of elephants from being killed.

TARZAN TRIUMPHS   Jungle Exotic   1943/Adventure

RKO; 76 min.; *Producer*: Sol Lesser; *Director*: William Thiele; *Screen-play*: Roy Chansler/Carroll Young; *Camera*: Harry Wild; *Editor*: Hal Kern; *Cast*: Johnny Weissmuller (Tarzan); Johnny Sheffield (Boy); *FRANCES GIFFORD (ZANDRA)*; Stanley Ridges (Col. Von Reichart); Sig Ruman (Sergeant); Pedro de Cordoba (Patriarch); Philip Van Zandt (Bausch).

    Zandra, a girl from a hidden jungle city, becomes involved with Tarzan and Nazis.

TARZAN'S DEADLY SILENCE   Black [African]   1970/Adventure

National General Pictures; 88 min.; *Producer*: Leon Benson; *Director*: Robert L. Friend; *Screenplay*: Lee Erwin/Jack A. Rubinson/John Considine; *Music*: Walter Greene; *Camera*: Abraham Vialla/Gabriel Torres; *Editor*: Edward M. Abroms; *Cast*: Ron Ely (Tarzan); Manuel Padilla, Jr. (Jai); Jock Mahoney (The Colonel); Woody Strode (Marshak); *NICHELLE NICHOLS (RUANA)*; Gregorio Acosta (Chico); Rudolph Charles (Officer); Robert DoQui (Metusa).

    Not enough information was available to describe this role accurately.

TARZAN'S PERIL   Black [African]   1951/Adventure

RKO; 79 min.; *Producer*: Sol Lesser; *Director*: Byron Haskin; *Screen-play*: Samuel Newman/Francis Swann; *Cast*: Lex Barker (Tarzan); Virginia Huston (Jane); George MacReady (Gun-runner); Douglas Fowley (His Accomplice); Glenn Anders (Gun Smuggler); *DOROTHY DANDRIDGE (JUNGLE QUEEN)*; Frederic O'Neal (Evil Chieftan).

    Tarzan becomes involved with the Jungle Queen.

TARZAN'S THREE CHALLENGES   Thai   1963/Adventure

MGM; 92 min.; *Producer*: Sy Weintraub; *Director*: Robert Day; *Screen-play*: Berne Giler/Robert Day; *Music*: Joseph Horovitz; *Camera*: Ted Scaife; *Editor*: Fred Burnley; *Cast*: Jock Mahoney (Tarzan); Woody Strode (Khan/Tarim); *TSURUKO KOBAYASHI (CHO-SAN)*; Earl Cameron (Mang); Salah Jamal (Hani); Anthony Chinn (Tor); Robert Hu (Nari); Christopher Carlos (Sechung); Ricky Der (Kashi): Hungry (The Baby Elephant).

    Tarzan goes to Thailand to escort Kashi to his throne. Cho-San, Kashi's nurse, travels with them.

TAZA, SON OF COCHISE   Native American--Apache   1953/Western

Universal; 79 min.; *Producer*: Ross Hunter; *Director*: Douglas Sirk; *Screenplay*: George Zuckerman; *Music*: Frank Skinner; *Camera*: Russell

Metty; *Editor*: Milton Carruth; *Cast*: Rock Hudson (Taza); *BARBARA
RUSH (OONA)*; Gregg Palmer (Captain Burnett); Bart Roberts (Naiche);
Morris Ankrum (Grey Eagle); Eugene Iglesias (Chato); Richard H.
Cutting (Cy Hagen); Ian MacDonald (Geronimo); Joe Sawyer (Sgt. Hamma);
Lance Fuller (Lt. Willis); Brad Jackson (Lt. Richards); Robert Burton
(General Crook); Charles Horvath (Locha); James van Horn (Skinya);
Robert Hoy (Lobo); Dan White (Charlie); Jeff Chandler as the dying
Cochise.

Oona is in love with Taza, the leader of his tribe. Taza has
decided to follow in his father's footsteps and maintain peace with
the United States government. Taza soon begins wearing a U.S.
Cavalry uniform, much to the disgust of those of his people who want
to fight the army. Oona's father is one of those people and when he
discovers Oona is in love with Taza he beats her. Eventually Taza's
way proves to be the better one. The malcontents are overcome and
Taza and Oona marry.

THE TEAHOUSE OF THE AUGUST MOON   Japanese   1956/Comedy

MGM; 123 min.; *Producer*: Jack Cummings; *Director*: Daniel Mann;
Screenplay: John Patrick; *Music*: Saul Chaplin; *Camera*: John Alton;
Editor: Harold F. Kress; *Cast*: Marlon Brando (Sakini); Glenn Ford
(Capt. Fisby); *MACHIKO KYO (LOTUS BLOSSOM)*; Eddie Albert (Capt.
McLean); Paul Ford (Col. Purdy); Jun Negami (Mr. Seiko); *Nijiko
Kiyokawa (Miss Higa Jiga)*; *Mitsuko Sawamura (Little Girl)*; Henry/
Harry Morgan (Sgt. Gregovich); Schichizo Takeda (Ancient Man);
Kichizaemon Saramaru (Mr. Hokaida).

Lotus Blossom is a geisha.

TELL THEM WILLIE BOY IS HERE Native American--Paiute 1969/Western

Universal; 98 min.; *Producer*: Philip A. Waxman; *Director*: Abraham
Polon   *Screenplay*: Abraham Polonsky; *Music*: Dave Grusin; *Camera*:
Conrad Hall; *Editor*: Melvin Shapiro; *Cast*: Robert Redford (Christopher
Cooper); *KATHARINE ROSS (LOLA)*; Robert Blake (Willie Boy); Susan Clark
(Elizabeth Arnold); Barry Sullivan (Ray Calvert); Charles McGraw
(Frank Wilson); Charles Aidman (Benby); John Vernon (Hacker); Shelley
Novack (Finney); Ned Romero (Tom); John Day (Sam Wood); Lee De Broux
(Meathead).

Lola's attempts to assimilate into white society are thwarted
when Willie Boy returns to town and she becomes involved with him.
He accidentally kills her father, who was trying to end the romance.
Lola is portrayed as a subservient woman who will follow her man any-
where, feels unworthy of his love, and makes the ultimate sacrifice
of taking her own life because she feels she is slowing down Willie's
escape.

TEMPLE OF THE SWINGING DOLL   Latin American   1960/Adventure

20th Century-Fox; 48 min.; *Producer* : Herbert Swope, Jr.; *Director* :
Paul Wendkos; *Screenplay* : Jerry Devine; *Music* : Lionel Newman; *Camera* :
Wilfred M. Cline; *Editor* : Fred Feitshans; *Cast* : David Hedison (Victor
Sebastion); Luciana Paluzzi (Simone Genet); *VIVECA LINDFORS (MADAME
ZAPOTE)*; John Emery (Norman Kingsley); Clu Gulager (Larry Dane);
Sterling Holloway (Hayden); Rodolfo Hoyos (Rios); Joan Tabor (Mona);
Casey Adams (Randy).

Madame Zapote, the leader of native revolutionaries, is being
hounded by secret agent Victor Sebastion. When he finally manages
to capture a group of revolutionaries, Madame Zapote kills herself by
jumping into a sacrificial fire.

TEN DAYS TO TULARA   Central American   1958/Adventure

United Artists; 77 min.; *Producers* : George Sherman/Clarence Eurist;
Director : George Sherman; *Screenplay* : Laurence Mascott; *Music* : Lon
Adomain; *Camera* : Alex Phillips; *Editor* : Carlos Savage; *Cast* : Sterling
Hayden (Scotty McBride); *GRACE RAYNOR (TERESA)*; Rodolfo Hoyos (Cesar);
Carlos Muzquiz (Dario); Tony Caravajal (Francisco); Juan Garcia
(Piranha); Rafael Alcayde (Colonel); Felix Gonzales (Marco); Jose
Pulido (Captain).

Scotty McBride's son is held hostage by Cesar, who is wanted by
the police for a gold robbery. To free his son Scotty agrees to fly
Cesar and the gold to safety. He meets and falls in love with Cesar's
daughter Teresa. Scotty manages to alert the police. Cesar and his
gang are trapped.

TEN TALL MEN   Arab   1951/Adventure

Columbia; 97 min.; *Producer*: Harold Hecht; *Director*: Willis Goldbeck;
Screenplay: Roland Kibbee/Frank Davis; *Music*: Morris Stoloff; *Camera*:
William Snyder; *Editor*: William Lyon; *Cast*: Burt Lancaster (Sgt. Mike
Kincaid); *JODY LAWRENCE (MAHLA)*; Gilbert Roland (Cpl. Luis Delgado);
Kieron Moore (Cpl. Pierre Molier); George Tobias (Londos); John
Dehner (Jardine); Nick Dennis (Mouse); Mike Mazur (Roshko); Gerald
Mohr (Caid Hussin); Ian MacDonald (Lustig); Marie Blanchard (Marie De
Latour).

Mahla is a sheik's daughter who is kidnapped by legionnaires
because her father is planning a revolt against French occupation.

TEN WANTED MEN   Mexican   1955/Western

Columbia; 80 min.; *Producer*: Harry Joe Brown; *Director*: Bruce Humber-
stone; *Screenplay*: Kenneth Gamet; *Music*: Paul Sawtell; *Camera*:
Wilfred M. Cline; *Editor*: Gene Havlick; *Cast*: Randolph Scott (John
Stewart); Jocelyn Brando (Corine Michaels); Richard Boone (Wick
Campbell); *DONNA MARTELL (MARIA SEGURA)*; Skip Homeier (Howie Stewart);
Clem Bevans (Tod Grinnel); Lee Gordon (Frank Scavo); Minor Watson

(Jason Carr); Lester Matthews (Adam Stewart); Tom Powers (Green); Dennis Weaver (Sheriff Clyde Gibbons); Lee Van Cleef (Al Drucker); Louis Jean Heydt (Tom Baines); Alfonso Bedoya (Hernando).

Maria is the niece of the evil Wick Campbell. When Campbell's attentions become too romantic, Maria goes to live with John Stewart to be near his nephew, Howie Stewart. After all the gunfights, Maria and Howie marry.

TERMINAL ISLAND   Black   1973/Drama

Dimension Pictures; 88 min.; *Producer*: Charles S. Swartz; *Director*: Stephanie Rothman; *Screenplay*: Jim Barnett/Charles S. Swartz/ Stephanie Rothman; *Music*: Michael Andres; *Camera*: Daniel Lacambre; *Editor*: John O'Connor; *Cast*: Phyllis Davis (Joy Lang); Don Marshall (A.J. Thomas); *ENA HARTMAN (CARMEN SIMS)*; Marta Kristen (Lee Phillips); Barbara Leigh (Bunny Campbell); Sean David Kenney (Bobby Farr); Geoffrey Deuel (Chino); Tom Selleck (Dr. Millford); Ford Clay (Cornell); Clyde Ventura (Julian Dylan).

Carmen Sims is sent to an island prison where she is one of four women prisoners. The men treat the women as slaves, using them for household and sexual purposes. Carmen and the other women and some male rebels overthrow the ruler and transform the island into a peaceful prison.

TERROR IN THE CITY   Black   1966/Drama

Allied Artists; 90 min.; *Producers*: Allen Baron/Merrill Brody/Dorothy E. Reed; *Director/Screenplay*: Allen Baron; *Music*: Robert Mersey; *Camera*: Donald Malkames; *Editor*: Ralph Rosenblum; *Cast*: Lee Grant (Suzy); Richard Bray (Brill); Michael Higgins (Carl); Roberto Marsach (Paco); Robert Allen (Brill's Father); Sylvia Miles (Rose); Jaime Charlamagne (Rick); Robert Earl Jones (Farmer); *RUTH ATTAWAY (WIFE)*.

A farm couple help Brill learn the meaning of self-respect after he runs away from home.

TERROR OF THE TONGS   Chinese   1960/Drama

Columbia; 79 min.; *Producer*: Kenneth Hyman; *Director*: John Peverall; *Screenplay*: Jimmy Sangster; *Music*: James Bernard; *Camera*: Arthur Grant; *Editor*: Jim Needs; *Cast*: Geoffrey Toone (Jackson); Christopher Lee (Chung King); *YVONNE MONLAUR (LEE)*; Brian Worth (Harcourt); Richard Leech (Inspector Dean); Marne Maitland (Beggar); Marie Burke (Maya); Roger Delgado (Wang How); Charles Loyd Pack (Doctor); Ewen Solon (Tang How); Tom Gill (Beamish); Barbara Brown (Helena); Bandana Das Gupta (Anna).

Lee is the slave to Wang How, a Tong collector in a secret society headed by the evil Chung King. Lee becomes involved with Jackson, who tries to break up the society following the murder of his

daughter by the Tongs. Chung King plans to kill Jackson in a ceremony. Lee tries to warn him but is killed by the executioner's
hatchet. Lee's last words provide the clue Jackson needs to end the
terror of the Tongs.

THE TEXAN   Mexican   1930/Western

Paramount;   min.; *Director*: John Cromwell; *Screenplay*: Daniel N.
Rubin; *Camera*: Victor Milner; *Editor*: Verna Willis; *Cast*: Gary
Cooper (Enrique/"Quico"/The Llano Kid); *FAY WRAY (CONSUELO)*; *Emma
Dunn (Senora Ibarra)*; Oscar Apfel (Thacker); James Marcus (John
Brown); Donald Reed (Nick Ibarra); *Soledad Jiminez (The Duenna)*; Veda
Buckland (Mary, the Nurse); Cesar Vanoni (Pasquale); Edwin J. Brady
(Henry); Enrique Acosta (Sicto); Romualdo Tirado (Cabman); Russel
Columbo (Singing Cowboy).

     The Llano Kid manages a series of disguises to keep from being
caught by the law. While in a South American port he becomes involved
with Senora Ibarra and passes himself off as her long-lost son. He
falls in love with her niece, Consuelo. As he becomes more involved
with the family he decides to go straight and clear his name with the
law.

TEXAS ACROSS THE RIVER   Native American   1966/Western

Universal; 101 mn.; *Producer*: Harry Keller; *Director*: Michael Gordon;
Screenplay: Wells Root/Harold Greene/Ben Starr; *Music*: De Vol; *Camera*:
Russell Metty; *Editor*: Gene Milford; *Cast*: Dean Martin (Sam Hollis);
Alain Delon (Don Andrea Baldasar); Rosemary Forsyth (Phoebe Ann
Naylor); Joey Bishop (Kronk); *TINA MARQUAND (LONETTA)*; Peter Graves
(Capt. Stimpson); Michael Ansara (Chief Iron Jacket); Linden Chiles
(Yellow Knife); Andrew Prine (Lt. Sibley); Stuart Anderson (Yancy);
Roy Barcroft (Morton); George Wallace (Willet); Don Beddoe (Mr.
Naylor); Kelly Thordsen (Turkey Shoot Boss).

     Don Andrea Baldasar is to marry Phoebe Ann Naylor, but the
wedding is interrupted by news of the death of one of Phoebe's former
suitors. Don Andrea is accused of murder and flees, joining up with
a gun runner, Sam, and his Indian companion, Kronk. On their way to
Texas Don Andrea saves Lonetta's life and she joins the group. Don
Andrea is reunited with Phoebe but realizes that Sam is in love with
Don Andrea. She and Phoebe have a fight over Don Andrea while Don
Andrea and Sam attempt to have a duel over Phoebe. All turns out
well in the end when Don Andrea realizes he loves Lonetta, Sam and
Phoebe get together, and they all strike oil.

THANK GOD IT'S FRIDAY   Black & Mexican   1978/Musical

Columbia; 100 min.; *Producer*: Rob Cohen; *Director*: Robert Klane;
Screenplay: Barry Armyan Bernstein; *Camera*: James Crabe; *Editor*:
Richard Halsey; *Cast*: Valerie Landsburg (Frannie); Terri Nunn
(Jeannie); *CHICK VENNERA (MARY GOMEZ)*; *DONNA SUMMER (NICOLE SIMS)*;

Ray Vitte (Bobby Speed); Mark Lonow (Dave); Andrea Howard (Sue); Jeff Goldblum (Tony); Robin Menker (Maddy); Debra Winger (Jennifer); John Friedrich (Ken); Paul Jabara (Carl); Marya Small (Jackie).

Story follows the adventures of Mary Gomez and Nichole Sims one night in a disco. Nichole Sims is a singer whose star is on the ascent.

THANK YOU, MR. MOTO   Chinese   1938/Mystery

20th Century-Fox; 67 min.; *Producer*: Sol M. Wurtzel; *Director*: Norman Foster; *Screenplay*: Willis Cooper/Norman Foster; *Camera*: Virgil Miller; *Editor*: Irene Mora/Nick DiMaggio; *Cast*: Peter Lorre (Mr. Moto); Thomas Beck (Tom Nelson); *PAULINE FREDERICK (MME. CHUNG)*; Jayne Regan (Eleanor Joyce); Sidney Blackmer (Herr Kroeger); Sig Rumann (Colonel Tchernov); John Carradine (Periera); William Von Brincken (Schneider); Nedda Harrigan (Mme. Tchernov); Philip Ahn (Prince Chung); John Bleiter (Ivan).

Mme. Chung is a mother killed trying to save the honor of her house.

THAT CERTAIN FEELING   Black   1956/Comedy

Paramount; 102 min.; *Producers/Directors/Screenplay*: Norman Panama/ Melvin Frank; *Camera*: Loyal Griggs; *Editor*: Tom McAdoo; *Cast*: Bob Hope (Francis X. Dignan); Eva Marie Saint (Dunreath Henry); George Sanders (Larry Larkin); *PEARL BAILEY (GUSSIE)*; David Lewis (Joe Wicks); Al Capp; Jerry Mathers (Norman Taylor).

Gussie is maid to cartoonist Larry Larkin. When not doing household chores she sings "That Certain Feeling," "Zing Went the Strings of My Heart," and "Hit the Road to Dreamland," and plays matchmaker for Francis Dignan and Dunreath Henry.

THAT NIGHT IN RIO   Latin American   1941/Musical

20th Century-Fox; 94 min.; *Assoc. Producer*: Fred Kohlmar; *Director*: Irving Cummings; *Screenplay*: George Seaton/Bess Meredyth/Hal Long; *Music*: Mack Gordon/Harry Warren; *Camera*: Leon Shamroy/Ray Rennahan; *Editor*: Walter Thompson; *Cast*: Alice Faye (Baroness); Don Ameche (Larry Martin/Baron Negreti); *CARMEN MIRANDA (CARMEN)*; S.Z. Sakall (Penna); J. Carrol Naish (Machado); Curt Bois (Salles); Leonid Kinskey (Pierre); Frank Puglia (Pedro); Lillian Porter (Luiza); *Maria Montez (Inez)*; George Renauent (Ambassador); Edward Conrad (Alfonso); Fortunio Bonanova (Pereira).

Carmen does some singing.

THEY CALL ME MR. TIBBS   Black   1970/Drama

United Artists; 108 min.; *Producer*: Herbert Hirschman; *Director*:
Gordon Douglas; *Screenplay*: Alan R. Trustman/James R. Webb; *Music*:
Quincy Jones; *Camera*: Gerald Finnerman; *Cast*: Sidney Poitier (Virgil
Tibbs); Martin Landau (Rev. Logan Sharpe); *BARBARA McNAIR (VALERIE
TIBBS)*; Anthony Zerbe (Rice Weedon); Jeff Corey (Capt. Marden); David
Sheiner (Herbert Kenenr); Juano Hernandez (Mealie); Norma Crane
(Marge Garfield); Edward Asner (Woody Garfield); Ted Gehring (Sgt.
Deutsch); Beverly Todd (Puff); Linda Towne (Joy Sturges); George
Spell (Andrew); Wanda Spell (Ginger).

     Valerie is the wife of San Francisco police detective Virgil
Tibbs.

THIEF OF BAGDAD   Arabian Nights   1940/Fantasy

United Artists; 106 min.; *Producer*: Alexander Korda; *Directors*: Ludwig
Berger/Michael Powell/Tom Whelan; *Screenplay*: Lajos Biro; *Music*: Muir
Mathieson; *Camera*: George Perinal/Osmand Borradaile; *Editors*: William
Hornbeck/Charles Crichton; *Cast*: Conrad Veidt (Jaffar); Sabu (Abu);
JUNE DUPREZ (PRINCESS); John Justin (Ahmad); Rex Ingram (Djinni);
Miles Malleson (Sultan); Myrton Selten (The Old King); *Mary Morris
(Halima)*; Bruce Winston (The Merchant); Hay Petrie (Astrologer).

     Ahmad, royal heir to the throne, is overthrown by evil wazir
Jaffar. Ahmad tries to reclaim his throne and the hand of the Princess
of Basra, who is now under the spell of Jaffar. Ahmad manages to
accomplish all his tasks with the aid of beggar/thief Abu and assorted
magical encounters.

THE THIEF OF BAGDAD   Arabian Nights   1978/Fantasy

Columbia; 102 min.; *Producer*: Aida Young; *Director*: Clive Donner;
Screenplay: A.J. Carothers; *Music*: John Cameron; *Camera*: Denis
Lewiston; *Editor*: Peter Tanner; *Cast*: Roddy McDowall (Hasan); Peter
Ustinov (Caliph); Terence Stamp (Wazir Jaudur); Kabir Bedi (Prince
Taj); Frank Finlay (Abu Bakar); *MARINA VLADY (PERIZADAH)*; *PAVLA
USTINOV (PRINCESS YASMINE)*; Daniel Emilfork (Genie); Ian Holm (Gate-
keeper); Ahmed El-Shenawi (Kanishka).

     Princess Yasmine is the Caliph's daughter. She falls in love
with Prince Taj who must compete with evil wazir Jaudur to win her
hand by bringing her the most precious thing in the world. With the
help of genie Hasan, and a magic carpet Taj manages to vanquish
Jaudur. Perizadah is Yasmine's chaperone.

THIEF OF DAMASCUS   Arabian Nights   1952/Fantasy

Columbia; 78 min.; *Producer*: Sam Katzman; *Director*: Will Jason;
Screenplay: Robert E. Kent; *Music*: Mischa Bakaleinikoff; *Cmaera*: Ellis
W. Carter; *Editor*: William Lyon; *Cast*: Paul Henreid (Abu Andar); John

Sutton (Khalid); Jeff Donnell (Sheherazade); *ELENA VERDUGO (NEELA)*; *Helen Gilbert (Princess Zafir)*; Lon Chaney (Sinbad); Edward Colmans (Sultan Raadah); Philip Van Zandt ((Ali Baba).

Abu Andar saves the sultan's city and daughter, Neela, winning her love in the process.

THINK FAST, MR. MOTO   Chinese   1937/Mystery

20th Century-Fox; 65 min.; *Producer*: Sol M. Wurtzel; *Director*: Norman Foster; *Screenplay*: Howard Ellis Smith/Norman Foster; *Music*: Samuel Kaylin; *Camera*: Harry Jackson; *Editor*: Alex Troffey; *Cast*: Peter Lorre (Mr. Moto); Virginia Field (Gloria Danton); Thomas Beck (Bob Hitchings); Sig Rumann (Nicholas Marloff); Murray Kinnell (Joseph Wilkie); John Rogers (Carson); *LOTUS LONG (LELA LIU)*; George Cooper (Muggs Blake); J. Carrol Naish (Adram).

Lela Liu is Mr. Moto's assistant.

13 FRIGHTENED GIRLS   Chinese   1963/Thriller

Columbia; 89 min.; *Producer/Director*: William Castle; *Screenplay*: Robert Dillon; *Music*: Van Alexander; *Camera*: Gordon Avil; *Editor*: Edwin Bryant; *Cast*: Murray Hamilton (Wally Sanders); Kathy Dunn (Candace Hull); *LYNNE SUE MOON (MAI-LING)*; Joyce Taylor (Soldier); *Judy Pace (Liberia)*; Hugh Marlowe (John Hughes); Khigh Dhiegh (Kang); Charlie Briggs (Mike); Norma Varden (Miss Pittford); Garth Benton (Peter Van Hagen); *Maria Cristina Servero (Argentina)*; Janet Mary Prance (Australia); Penny Anne Mills (Canada); Alexandra Bastedo (England); Ariane Gloser (France); Illona Schutze (Germany); Anna Baj (Italy); *Aiko Sakamoto (Japan)*; *Luz Gloria Hervias (Mexico)*; Gina Trikonis (Russia); Marie-Louise Bielke (Sweden); *Ignacia Farias Luque (Venezuela)*.

Mai-Ling, the daughter of a Chinese ambassador, is a major character in this film.

THIRTEEN WOMEN   Indian   1932/Thriller

RKO; 73 min.; *Producer*: David O. Selznick; *Director*: George Archinbaud; *Screenplay*: Bartlett Cormack; *Music*: Max Steiner; *Camera*: Leo Tover; *Editor*: Charles L. Kimball; *Cast*: Ricardo Cortez (Sgt. Clive); Irene Dunne (Laura); *MYRNA LOY (URSULA GEORGI)*; Jill Esmond (Jo); Florence Eldredge (Grace); Kay Johnson (Helen); Julie Haydon (Mary); Harriet Hagman (May Rasob); Mary Duncan (June Rasob); Peg Entwistle (Hazel); Elsie Prescott (Nan); Wally Albright (Bobby); C. Henry Gordon (Swami Yagadachi); Edward Pawley (Burns); Blanche Friderici (Teacher).

Ursula Georgi was tormented by a sorority during her school days because she was a half-caste. Years later she seeks revenge by murdering members of the sorority one by one. As she is about to kill Laura, she is killed.

THIS REBEL BREED   Mexican   1959/Drama

Warner Brothers; 87 min.; *Producer*: William Rowland; *Director*:
Richard L. Bare; *Screenplay*: Morris Lee Green; *Music*: David Rose;
Camera: Monroe Askins; *Editor*: Tony Martinelli; *Cast*: RITA MORENO
(LOLA); Mark Damon (Frank); Gerald Mohr (Lt. Brooks); Jay Novello
(Papa); Eugene Martin (Rudy); Tom Gilson (Muscles); Richard Rust
(Buck); Douglas Hume (Don); Richard Laurier (Manuel); Don Eitner
(Jimmy); Diane Cannon (Wiggles); Kenny Miller (Winnie).

    Frank Serrano is a police officer who is having a hard time
adjusting to undercover police work because he is half Black/half
Mexican. His white partner, Don Walters, has an easier time infil-
trating a white youth gang to break up a drug ring. Frank eventually
becomes involved with Lola, who is involved with a member of a rival
white gang, Jimmy Wallace. Wallace is murdered and Lola's brother is
the prime suspect. During a confrontation between gang members, Don
and Frank reveal themselves and arrest the murderer of Jimmy Wallace.

THOMASINE AND BUSHROD   Black   1974/Western

Columbia; 95 min.; *Producer*: Harvey Bernhard; *Director*: Gordon Parks,
Jr.; *Screenplay*: Max Julien; *Music*: Coleridge-Taylor Perkinson;
Camera: Lucien Ballard; *Editor*: Frank C. Decont; *Cast*: Max Julien
(Bushrod); *VONETTA McGEE (THOMASINE)*; George Murdock (Sheriff
Bogardie); Glynn Turman (Jomo); *Juanita Moore (Pecolia)*; Joel Fluellen
(Nathaniel); Jackson D. Kane (Adolph Smith); Bud Conlan (Mr. Tyler);
Kip Allen (Jenkius); Ben Zeller (Scruggs); Herb Robins (Dodson).

    Once-prosperous bounty hunter Thomasine is now a laundress.
When she rebuffs a man, she ends up in prison. When she is released
she joins forces with her former lover, Bushrod, who is wanted by the
police. They become Robin Hood-type heros to Mexicans, Indians, and
others. Thomasine becomes pregnant and for a short time the two are
happy. Then the police find and kill both Thomasine and Bushrod.

A THOUSAND AND ONE NIGHTS   Arabian Nights   1945/Fantasy

Columbia; 93 min.; *Producer*: Samuel Bischoff; *Director*: Alfred E.
Green; *Screenplay*: Wilfrid H. Pettitt/Richard English/Jack Henley;
Music: M.W. Stoloff; *Camera*: Ray Rennahan; *Editor*: Gene Havlick;
Cast: Cornel Wilde (Aladdin); *EVELYN KEYES (THE GENIE)*; Phil Silvers
(Abdullah); *ADELE JERGENS (PRINCESS ARMINA)*; Dusty Anderson (Novira);
Dennis Hoey (Sultan Kamal Al-Kir); Philip Van Zandt (Prince Hadji/
Grand Wazir Abu-Hassan); Gus Schilling (Jafar); Nestor Paiva (Kahim);
Rex Ingram (Giant); Richard Hale (Kohr, the Sorcerer).

    Aladdin falls in love with Princess Armina, the Sultan's daugh-
ter. However, Aladdin's genie is extremely jealous and has no intention of helping him win the princess.

THREE IN THE ATTIC   Black   1968/Comedy

American International; 90 min.; *Producer/Director*: Richard Wilson;
Screenplay: Stephen Yafa; *Music*: Chad Stuart; *Camera*: J. Burgi
Contner; *Editor*: Richard C. Meyer; *Cast*: Christopher Jones (Paxton
Quigley); Yvette Mimieux (Tobey Clinton); *JUDY PACE (EULICE)*; Maggie
Thrett (Jan); Nan Martin (Dean Nazarin); Reva Rose (Selma); John Beck
(Jake); Richard Derr (Mr. Clinton); Eve McVeagh (Mrs. Clinton); Honey
Alden (Flo); Thomas F. Ahearne (Wilfred).

     Eulice is one of three women with whom Paxton Quigley is having
simultaneous affairs. When the other women, Tobey and Jan, find out,
they and Eulice plan to teach Paxton a lesson. They lock him in an
attic with the intention of destroying his sexual appetite. Eulice
and Jan eventually relent but Tobey insists they keep the pressure on
in spite of his hunger strike. He is finally released and realizes
that one woman is enough and that woman is Tobey.

THREE WARRIORS   Native American   1977/Drama

Fantasy Films; 109 min.; *Producers/Screenplay*: Saul Zaentz/Sy Gomberg;
Director: Kieth Merrill; *Camera*: Bruce Surtees; *Cast*: McKee "Kiko" Red
Wing (Michael); Charles White Eagle (Grandfather); Randy Quaid
Quentin Hammond); *LOIS RED ELK (MOTHER)*.

     Story focuses on city-raised Michael, whose mother takes him
home to the reservation to see his dying grandfather. Michael is at
first disgusted at reservation life and the old Indian customs, but
soon comes to appreciate his heritage.

THUNDER ISLAND   Latin American   1965/Adventure

20th Century-Fox; 65 min.; *Producer/Director*: Jack Leewood; *Screen-
play*: Don Devlin/Jack Nicholson; *Music*: Paul Sawtell; *Camera*: John
Nickolaus; *Editor*: Jodie Copelan; *Cast*: Gene Nelson (Billy Poole);
Fay Spain (Helen Dodge); Brian Kelly (Vincent Dodge); *MIRIAM COLON
(ANITA CHAVEZ)*; Art Dedard (Ramon Aloa); Antonio Torres Martino (Col.
Cepeda); Esther Sandoval (Rena); Jose De San Anton (Antonio Perez);
Evelyn Kaufman (Jo Dodge); Stephanie Rifkinson (Linda Perez).

     Billy Poole enlists the help of Anita Chaves in assassinating a
South American dictator. They gain access to the island where the
dictator is living but fail in the assassination attempt. Believing
he was betrayed, Billy kills Anita.

TIARA TAHITI   Tahitian   1963/Adventure

Zenith International; 100 min.; *Producer*: Ivan Foxwell; *Director*:
William T. Kotcheff; *Screenplay*: Geoffrey Cotterell/Ivan Foxwell;
Music: Philip Green; *Camera*: Otto Heller; *Editor*: Anthony Gibb; *Cast*:
James Mason (Capt. Brett Aimsley); John Mills (Lt. Col. Clifford
Southey); *ROSENDA MONTEROS (BELLE ANNIE)*; Herbert Lom (Chong Sing);

Claude Dauphin (Henri Farengue); Jacques Marin (Desmoulins); Libby
Morris (Adele Franklin); Madge Ryan (Millie Brooks); Gary Cockrell
(Joey); Peter Barkworth (Lt. David Harper); Roy Kinnear (Capt. Tom
Enderby).

Belle Annie is the romantic interest of Capt. Brett Aimsley.

...tick...tick...tick...   Black   1969/Drama

MGM; 97 min.; *Producers*: Ralph Nelson/James Lee Barrett; *Director*:
Ralph Nelson; *Screenplay*: James Lee Barrett; *Music*: Jerry Styner;
Camera: Loyal Griggs; *Editor*: Alex Beaton; *Cast*: Jim Brown (Jimmy
Price); George Kennedy (John Little); Fredric March (Mayor Jeff
Parks); Lynn Carlin (Julia Little); Don Stroud (Bengy Springer);
JANET MacLACHLAN (MARY PRICE); Richard Elkins (Bradford Wilkes);
Clifton James (D.J. Rankin); Bob Random (John Braddock); Mills Watson
(Deputy Joe Warren).

Jimmy Price, the first Black sheriff in a small southern town,
faces extreme prejudice. His pregnant wife, Mary, gives him love
and support and encourages him to accept help from the former white
sheriff, John Little, when a murder occurs.

TIGER SHARK   Mexican   1932/Drama

First National Prod.; 80 min.; *Director*: Howard Hawks; *Screenplay*:
Wells Root; *Camera*: Tony Gaudio; *Editor*: Thomas Pratt; *Cast*: Edward
G. Robinson (Mike Mascarena); *ZITA JOHANN (QUITA)*; Richard Arlen
(Pipes Boley); Leila Bennett (Lady Barber); Vince Barnett (Engineer);
J. Carrol Naish (The Man); William Riccia (Manuel).

Quita marries Mike Mascarena because her father is dead and she
has no means of support. She falls in love with Pipes Boley, Mike's
best friend. When Mike discovers they are lovers, he attempts to
kill them but he dies instead.

TO THE ENDS OF THE EARTH   Asian   1948/Drama

Columbia; 109 min.; *Producer*: Sidney Buchman; *Director*: Robert
Stevenson; *Screenplay*: Jay Richard Kennedy; *Music*: M.W. Stoloff;
Camrea: Burnett Guffey; *Editor*: William Lyon; *Cast*: Dick Powell
(Michael Barrows); Signe Hasso (Ann Grant); *MAYLIA (SHU PAN WU)*;
Ludwig Donath (Nicholas Sokim); Vladimir Sokoloff (Lum Chi Chow);
Edgar Barrier (Grieg); John Hoyt (Bennett); Marcel Journet (Commis-
sioner Larissier); Luis Van Rooten (Alberto Berado); Fritz Leiber
(Binda Sha); Vernon Steele (Commissioner Hadley); Peter Virgo
(Mahmoud).

Shu Pan Wu is American Ann Grant's traveling companion.

TOKYO ROSE   Japanese   1945/Drama

Paramount; 70 min.; *Producers*: William Pine/William Thomas; *Director*:
Lew Landers; *Screenplay*: Geoffrey Homes; *Music*: Rudy Schrager;
Camera: Fred Jackman, Jr.; *Editors*: Howard Smith/Henry Adams; *Cast*:
LOTUS LONG (TOKYO ROSE); Byron Barr (Peter Sherman); Osa Massen
(Greta Swanson); Don Douglas (Timothy O'Brien); Richard Loo (Colonel
Suzuki); Keye Luke (Charlie Otani); Grace Lem (Soon Hee); Leslie
Fong (Wong); H.T. Tsiang (Chung Yu); Larry Young (Jack Martin);
William Challee (Mike Kovak).

Tokyo Rose's propaganda causes an American soldier to kill himself. His friend, Peter Sherman, promises to avenge his death by
killing Rose. He poses as a newspaperman and with the aid of others
manages to capture Rose. She is killed trying to escape.

TOMAHAWK   Native American   1951/Western

Universal; 82 min.; *Producer*: Leonard Goldstein; *Director*: George
Sherman; *Screenplay*: Silvia Richards; *Music*: Hans J. Salter; *Camera*:
Charles P. Boyle; *Editor*: Danny B. Landres; *Cast*: Van Heflin (Bridger);
Yvonne De Carlo (Julie Madden); Alex Nicol (Lt. Rob Dancy); Preston
Foster (Col. Carrington; Jack Oakie (Sol Beckworth); Tom Tully (Dan
Castello); John War Eagle (Red Cloud); Rock Hudson (Burt Hanna);
SUSAN CABOT (MONAHSEEIAH); Arthur Space (Capt. Fetterman); Russell
Conway (Major Horton); Ann Doran (Mrs. Carrington); Stuart Randall
(Sgt. Newell).

Monahseeiah is one of the survivors of a massacre of her family
by Lt. Rob Dancy.

TOMAHAWK TRAIL   Native American--Apache   1957/Western

United Artists; 61 min.; *Producer*: Howard W. Koch; *Director*: Leslie
Selander; *Screenplay*: David Chandler; *Music*: Les Baxter; *Camera*:
William Margulies; *Editors*: John F. Schreyer/John A. Bushelman; *Cast*:
Chuck Connors (Sgt. Wade McCoy); John Smith (Pvt. Reynolds); Susan
Cummings (Ellen Carter); LISA MONTELL (TULA); George Neise (Lt.
Jonathan Davenport); Robert Knapp (Pvt. Barrow); Eddie Little (Johnny
Dogwood); Frederick Ford (Pvt. Macy); Dean Stanton (Pvt. Miller).

Tula is a chief's daughter who befriends Ellen Carter.

TOPAZ   Cuban   1969/Thriller

Universal; 125 min.; *Producer/Director*: Alfred Hitchcock; *Screenplay*:
Samuel Taylor; *Music*: Maurice Jarre; *Camera*: Jack Hildyard; *Editor*:
William H. Ziegler; *Cast*: Frederick Stafford (Andre Devereaux); Dany
Robin (Nicole Devereaux); John Vernon (Rico Parra); KARIN DOR (JUANITA
DE CARDOBA); Michel Piccoli (Jacques Granville); Philippe Noiret
(Henry Jarre); Roscoe Lee Browne (Philippe Dubois); Per-Axel Arosenius
(Boris Kusenov); John Forsythe (Michael Nordstrom).

Juanita is a member of the Cuban underground and mistress to French agent Andre Devereaux. After one of Juanita's comrades is caught, she is killed by Rico, head of the Cuban delegation and one-time protector of Juanita.

THE TORCH   Mexican   1950/Adventure

Eagle-Lion; 90 min.; *Producer*: Bert Granet; *Director*: Emilio Fernandez; *Screenplay*: Emilio Fernandez/Indigo de Martino Norieg; *Music*: Antonio Diaz Conde; *Camera*: Gabriel Figueroa; *Editor*: Charles L. Kimball; *Cast*: *PAULETTE GODDARD (MARIA DOLORES)*; Pedro Armendarez (Jose Juan Rejes); Gilbert Roland (Father Sierra); Walter Reed (Dr. Robert Stanley); Julio Villareal (Don Carlos Penafiel); Carlos Musquiz (Fidel Bernal); Margarito Luna (Capt. Bocanegra); Jose I. Torvay (Capt. Quinones); Garcia Pena (Don Apolinio); *Antonia Kaneem (Adelita)*.

Revolutionary leader Jose Juan Rejes takes over the town of Cholula and soon has the local aristocracy handing over money for the revolution. He meets and falls in love with Maria Dolores who is about to marry an American, Dr. Robert Stanley. He pursues her but she rejects him, especially because of his humble origins. When a flu epidemic hits Cholula, Maria Dolores takes an interest in the sufferings of the peasants around her and begins to understand Jose. When the Federals attack on the day she is to marry Dr. Stanley, Juan and his followers leave the village and Maria decides to travel with them.

TOUGHEST MAN ALIVE   Latin American   1955/Adventure

Allied Artists; 70 min.; *Producer*: William F. Broidy; *Director*: Sidney Salkow; *Screenplay*: Steve Fisher; *Music*: Edward J. Kay; *Camera*: John Martin; *Editor*: Chandler House; *Cast*: Dane Clark (Lee); *LITA MILAN (LIDA)*; Anthony Caruso (Gore); Ross Elliott (York); Myrna Dell (Nancy); Thomas B. Henry (Dolphin); Paul Levitt (Don); John Eldredge (Ingo Widmer); Dehl Berti (Salvador); Richard Karlan (Morgan); Syd Saylor (Proprietor); Jonathan Seymour (Agency Chief); Don Mathers (Bank Manager).

Revolutionary Lida poses as a cafe singer while she raises arms for the revolution.

TRAIL TO MEXICO   Mexican   1946/Western

Monogram; 56 min.; *Producer/Director/Screenplay*: Oliver Drake; *Music*: Frank Sanucci; *Camera*: James Brown; *Editor*: Ralph Dixon; *Cast*: Jimmy Wakely; Lee "Lasses" White (Lasses); Brad Slaven (Texas Kid); Julian Rivero (Don Roberto Lopez); *DELORES CASTELLI (CHINITA)*; *DORA DEL RIO (DOLORES)*; Terry Frost (Bart Thomas); Forrest Matthews (Fred Jackson); Dee Cooper (Mack); Wheaton Chambers (Padre); The Saddle Pals; The Guadalajara Trio.

The Texas Kid forces Jimmy to exchange identities so the Kid will have access to a gold shipment. After the Kid kills a man during the robbery, Jimmy is arrested but released by Bart Thomas who thinks Jimmy is really the Texas Kid. Jimmy becomes involved with the Thomas gang in order to clear his name. In the interim he meets Chinita and her guardian Dolores. Chinita is able to identify the Kid and all turns out well when the final showdown takes place.

THE TREASURE OF PANCHO VILLA   Mexican   1955/Adventure

RKO; 96 min.; *Producer*: Edmund Grainger; *Director*: George Sherman; *Screenplay*: Niven Busch; *Music*: Leith Stevens; *Camera*: William Snyder; *Editor*: Harry Marker; *Cast*: Rory Calhoun (Tom Bryan); Shelley Winters (Ruth Harris); Gilbert Roland (Juan Castro); Joseph Calleia (Pablo Morales); Carlos Mosquiz (Commandant); *FANNY SCHILLER (MARIA MORALES)*; Tony Carvajal (Farolito); Pasquel Pena (Ricardo).

The story of a gold shipment being sent to Pancho Villa to help with the revolution. Maria Morales and her husband, Pablo, are members of the Villistas but Pablo wants to keep the gold for himself.

TRICK BABY   Black   1973/Drama

Universal; 89 min.; *Producer*: Marshal Backlar; *Director*: Larry Yust; *Screenplay*: T. Raewyn/A. Neuberg/Larry Yust; *Music*: James Bond; *Camera*: Isidore Mankofsky; *Editor*: Peter Parasheles; *Cast*: Kiel Martin (White Folks); Mel Stewart (Blue Howard); Beverly Ballard (Susan); *VERNEE WATSON (CLEO HOWARD)*; Donald Symington (Morrison); Don Fellows (Phillips); Tom Anderson (Felix the Fixer); Clebert Ford (Josephus); Fuddle Bagley (Percy).

Blue Howard's wife, Cleo, unintentionally informs the mafia of her husband's whereabouts, which leads to his death.

TRIUMPHS OF A MAN CALLED HORSE Native American--Sioux/Crow 1982/
                                                             Western

Redwing Productions; 89 min.; *Producer*: Derek Gibson; *Director*: John Hough; *Screenplay*: Ken Blackwell/Carlos Aured; *Music*: Georges Garvarentz; *Camera*: John Alcott/John Cabrera; *Editor*: Roy Watts; *Cast*: Richard Harris (John Morgan, Man Called Horse); Michael Beck (Koda); *ANA DE SADE (REDWING)*; Vaughn Armstrong (Capt. Cummings); Buck Taylor (Sgt. Bridges); Sebastian Ligarde (Pvt. Mullins); *Anne Seymour (Elk Woman)*; Miguel Angel Fuentes (Big Bear); Regino Herrera (Eye of the Bull); Lauturo Murua (Perkins).

Koda, son of Man Called Horse, is falsely arrested by the United States cavalry. Sgt. Bridges tries to kill Koda but he manages to escape. He meets Redwing, the survivor of a cavalry led massacre. They hide out in the cave of a Sioux witch, Elk Woman. Soon Redwing and Koda are terrorizing prospectors who are trespassing onto Indian territory. The prospectors soon leave and peace is restored to the territory.

TROPIC FURY   Latin American   1939/Adventure

Universal; 62 min.; *Producer*: Ben Pivar; *Director*: Christy Cabanne;
Screenplay: Michael Simmons; *Camera*: Jerry Ash; *Cast*: Richard Arlen
(Dan Burton); Andy Devine (Tiny Andrews); Beverly Roberts (Judith
Adams); Lou Merrill (Scipio); *LUPITA TOVAR (MARIA)*; Samuel Hinds (J.
P. Waterford); Charles Trowbridge (Dr. Taylor); Leonard Mudie
(Gallon); Adia Kuznetzoff (Soldedad); Noble Johnson (Hannibal); Frank
Mitchell (Amando); Milburne Stone (Thomas Snell).

     Maria is the local native girl with a heart of gold.

TROPIC HOLIDAY   Mexican   1938/Musical

Paramount; 78 min.; *Producer*: Arthur Hornblow; *Director*: Theodore
Reed; *Screenplay*: Don Hartman/Frank Butler/John C. Moffitt/Duke
Atteberry; *Music*: Augustin Lara; *Camera*: Ted Tetzloff; *Editor*: Archie
Marshek; *Cast*: *DOROTHY LAMOUR (MANUELA)*; Bob Burns (Breck Jones);
Martha Raye (Midge Miller); Ray Milland (Ken Warren); Binnie Barnes
(Marilyn Joyce); Tito Guizai (Ramon); Pepito (Chico); Chris-Pin
Martin (Pancho); *Elviria Rios (Rosa)*; Michael Visaroft (Felipe);
Bobbie Moya (Pepito); Roberto Soto (Roberto); Frank Publia (Co-
Pilot); Jesus Topete (Pedro).

     Singer Manuela becomes involved with writer Ken Warren.
Marily Joyce arrives to save Ken from Manuela's charms, only to fall
for Ramon.

TROPIC ZONE   Latin American   1952/Comedy

Paramount; 89 min.; *Producers*: William H. Pine/William C. Thomas;
Director: Lewis R. Foster; *Screenplay*: Lewis R. Foster; *Music*: Lucien
Callilet; *Camera*: Lionel Lindon; *Editor*: Howard Smith; *Cast*: Ronald
Reagan (Dan McCloud); Rhonda Fleming (Flanders White); *ESTELITA
RODRIGUEZ (ELENA)*; Noah Beery (Tapathula Sam); Grant Withers (Bert
Nelson); *Argentina Brunetti (Tia Feliciana)*; Maurice Jara (Marcarle);
Rico Alane (Capt. Basilla).

     Elena is a cafe singer and dancer chasing after Dan McCloud.

TROPICAL HEAT WAVE   Cuban   1952/Musical

Republic; 74 min.; *Producer*: Sidney Picker; *Director*: R.G. Springsteen;
Screenplay: Arthur J. Horman; *Camera*: John MacBurnie; *Editor*: Harold
Minter; *Cast*: *ESTELITA RODRIGUEZ (ESTELITA)*; Robert Hutton (Statford
Carver); Grant Withers (Norman James); Kristine Miller (Sylvia
Enwright); Edwin Max (Moore); Lou Lubin (Frost); Martin Garralaga
(Ignacio Ortega); Earl Lee (Dean Enwright); Leenie Bremen (Stoner);
Jack Kruschen (Stickey Langley).

Estelita is a singer who works in her uncle's nightclub. Professor Statford Carver meets and falls in love with her there.

TROUBLE IN TEXAS   Mexican   1937/Western

Grand National; 64 min.; *Producer*: Edward F. Finney; *Director*: Robert N. Bradbury; *Screenplay*: Robert Emmett; *Music*: Frank Sanucci; *Camera*: Gus Peterson; *Editor*: Fred Bain; *Cast*: Tex Ritter (Tex); *RITA CANSINO [HAYWORTH] (CARMEN)*; Earl Dwire (Barker); Yakima Canutt (Squint); Dick Palmer (Duke); Hal Price (G-Man); Fred Parker (Sheriff); Horace Murphy (Lucky); Charles King (Pinto); Tom Cooper (Announcer).

Not enough information was available to describe this role accurately.

TRUMPET BLOWS   Mexican   1934/Drama

Paramount; 68 min.; *Director*: Stephen Roberts; *Screenplay*: Bartlett Cormack; *Camera*: Harry Rischback; *Editor*: Ellsworth Hoagland; *Cast*: George Raft (Manuel Montez); Adolphe Menjou (Pancho Gomez/Senor Montez); *FRANCES DRAKE (CHULITA)*; Sidney Toler (Pepi Sancho); Edward Ellis (Carmela Ramirez); Douglas Wood (Senor Ramirez); *Katherine De Mille (Lupe)*; Francis McDonald (Vega); Morgan Wallace (Police Inspector).

Chulita is loved by Manuel Montez, a bullfighter educated in the United States who can't quite make the grade. She is also loved by Pancho Gomez, a reformed bandit. Manuel and Pancho continually try to outdo each other to impress and win the love of Chulita. In the end Manuel wins Chulita's heart, but Pancho is still around.

TULSA   Native American--Cherokee   1949/Adventure

Eagle-Lion; 90 min.; *Producer*: Walter Wanger; *Director*: Stuart Heisler; *Screenplay*: Frank Nugent/Curtis Kenyon; *Music*: Charles Previn; *Camera*: Winton Hoch; *Editor*: Terrell Moore; *Cast*: *SUSAN HAYWORTH (CHEROKEE)*; Robert Preston (Brad Brady); Pedro Armendariz (Redbird); Lloyd Gough (Bruce Tanner); Chill Wills (Pinny Jimpson); Edward Begley ("Crude" Johnny Brady); Jimmy Conlin (Hemer Triplette); Roland Jack (Cowboy); Harry Shannon (Neise Lansing).

After her father dies, Cherokee gives up her cattle ranch to go into the oil business. Redbird--a full-blooded Indian--lends her money to get started and Brad Brady helps her locate oil. Cherokee strikes oil and builds an empire with Brad. Her oil business leads to water pollution. When Redbird's cattle die from drinking tainted water, he goes wild and sets her oil fields on fire.

THE TUTTLES OF TAHITI   Tahitian   1942/Comedy

RKO; 92 min.; *Producer*: Sol Lesser; *Director*: Charles Vidor; *Screen-play*: S. Lewis Meltzer/Robert Carson; *Camera*: Nicholas Musuraca; *Editor*: Fredric Knudtson; *Cast*: Charles Laughton (Jonas Tuttle); Jon Hall (Chester Tuttle); *PEGGY DRAKE (TAMARA)*; Victor Francen (Dr. Blondin); Gene Reynolds (Ru); Florence Bates (Emily Taio); Curt Bois (Jensen).

The Tuttle family is trying to refurbish the family fortune by pearl diving in Tahiti. But something always manages to stop them from gaining a fortune. Tamara is the romantic interest of the Tuttle son, Chester.

TWILIGHT IN THE SIERRAS   Cuban   1950/Musical

Republic; 67 min.; *Producer*: Edward J. White; *Director*: William Witney; *Screenplay*: Sloan Nigley; *Music*: Stanley Wilson; *Camera*: John MacBurnie; *Editor*: Toni Martinelli; *Cast*: Roy Rogers; Dale Evans (Pat Callahan); *ESTELITA RODRIGUEZ (LOLA CHAVEZ)*; Pat Brady (Sparrow Biffle); Russ Vincent (Ricardo Chavez); George Meeker (Mat Brunner); Fred Kohler, Jr. (Mason); Edward Keane (Judge Wiggins); House Peters, Jr. (Williams); Trigger.

Singer Lola Chavez is visiting Pat Callahan and Roy Rogers.

TWILIGHT ON THE RIO GRANDE   Mexican   1947/Musical

Republic; 71 min.; *Assoc. Producer*: Armand Schaefer; *Director*: Frank McDonald; *Screenplay*: Dorrell & Stuart McGowan; *Camera*: William Bradford; *Editor*: Harry Keller; *Cast*: Gene Autry; Sterling Holloway (Pokie); *ADELE MARA (ELENA)*; Bob Steele (Dusty); Charles Evans (Blackstone); Martin Garralaga (Mucho); Howard J. Negley (Jake).

Elena is a singer in a Mexican saloon, El Molino Verde. She is attracted to Gene's partner Dusty. They become involved with smug-glers, but all turns out well in the end after a few songs by Gene.

TWO GENTLEMEN SHARING   Jamaican   1969/Drama

American International; 106 min.; *Producer*: J. Barry Kulick; *Director*: Ted Kotcheff; *Screenplay*: Evan Jones; *Music*: Stanley Myers; *Camera*: Billy Williams; *Cast*: Robin Phillips (Roddy); Judy Geeson (Jane); Hal Frederick; *ESTHER ANDERSON (CAROLINE)*; Norman Rossington (Phil); Hilary Dwyer (Ethel); Rachel Kempson (Mrs. Ashby-Kydd); Daisy Mae Williams (Amanda).

Story concerns roommates Roddy, who is white, and Andrew, a Jamaican. Roddy begins dating Jane, who has a Black stepfather. Andrew dates Caroline, who is also from Jamaica. The apartment sharing does not work out because the landlords are racists who do not want Andrew and Caroline there. Roddy is unable to accept Jane's stepfather. Andrew and Caroline return to Jamaica.

TYPHOON   Island Exotic   1940/Adventure

Paramount; 71 min.; *Producer*: Anthony Veiller; *Director*: Louis King;
Screenplay: Allen Riuken; *Music*: Frederic Hollander; *Camera*: William
Mellor; *Editor*: Alma Maerorie; *Cast*: *DOROTHY LAMOUR (LEA)*; Robert
Preston (Johnny Potter); Lynne Overman (Skipper Joe); J. Carrol Naish
(Makaike); Chief Thunder Cloud (Kehi); Frank Reicher (The Doctor);
John Rogers (The Barkeep).

Dea is the sole inhabitant of a south sea island. She manages
to build a home, make clothing, and learn a language all by herself.
Eventually Johnny, a white man, shows up and they fall in love. Soon
a native chieftain arrives with vengeance on his mind because of the
theft of black pearls from his island. A typhoon hits the island
but Dea and Johnny survive and live happily ever after.

UNCONQUERED   Native American--Seneca   1947/Western

Paramount; 146 min.; *Producer/Director*: Cecil B. De Mille; *Screen-
play*: Charles Bennett/Frederic M. Frank/Jesse Lasky, Jr.; *Music*:
Victor Young; *Camera*: Ray Rennahan; *Editor*: Anne Bauchens; *Cast*: Gary
Cooper (Capt. Christopher Holden); Paulette Goddard (Abigail Martha
Hale); Howard Da Silva (Martin Garth); Boris Karloff (Guyasuta, Chief
of the Senecas); Cecil Kellaway (Jeremy Love); Ward Bond (John
Fraser); *KATHERINE DE MILLE (HANNAH)*; Henry Wilcoxon (Capt. Steele);
Sir C. Aubrey Smith (Lord Chief Justice); Victor Varconi (Capt.
Simeon Ecuyer); Virginia Grey (Diana); Porter Hall (Leach).

Hannah is married to Martin Garth who wants her only because
she is the Chief's daughter.

UNDER A TEXAS MOON   Mexican   1930/Western

Warner Brothers; 70 min.; *Director*: Michael Curtiz; *Screenplay*:
Gordon Rigby; *Camera*: Bill Rees; *Cast*: Frank Fay (Don Carlos);
RAQUEL TORRES (RAQUELLA); *Myrna Loy (Lolita Romero)*; *Armida
(Dolores)*; Noah Beery (Jed Parker); Georgie Stone (Pedro); George
Cooper (Philipe); Fred Kohler (Bad Man of Pool); Betty Boyd (Girl of
the Pool); Charles Sellon (Jose Romero): Jack Curtis (Buch Johnson);
Sam Appel (Pancho Gonzales).

Raquella, Lolita Romero, and Dolores are the romantic interests
of desperado Don Carlos.

UNDER FIRE   Nicaraguan   1983/Thriller

Orion; 127 min.; *Producer*: Jonathan Taplin; *Director*: Roger Spottiswoode; *Screenplay*: Ron Shelton/Clayton Frohman; *Music*: Jerry Gold-

Alma Martinez, *Under Fire* (Orion, 1983)

smith; *Camera*: John Alcott; *Editor*: Mark Conte; *Cast*: Nick Nolte
(Russell Price); Gene Hackman (Alex Grazier); Joanna Cassidy (Claire
Stryder); Jean-Louis Trintignant (Marcel Jazy); Ed Harris (Oates);
Richard Masur (Hub Kittle); Hamilton Camp (Regis Seydor); *ALMA
MARTINEZ (ISELA)*; Holly Palance (Journalist).

Isela is a member of the Sandinista revolution against Somoza
in 1979. She convinces journalist Russell Price to photograph fallen
leader Rafael as if he were alive. Price commits himself to the
Sandinista revolution and takes the photograph.

UNDER STRANGE FLAGS   Mexican   1937/Adventure

Crescent Production; 70 min.; *Director*: I.V. Willat; *Screenplay*: Mary
Ireland; *Camera*: Arthur Martinelli; *Cast*: Tom Keene (Tom Kenyon);
LANA WALTERS (DOLORES de VARGAS); Bud Buster (Tequilla); Maurice
Black (Pancho Villa); Roy D'Arcy (Morales); Paul Sutton (General
Barrance); Paul Barrell (Denny); Donald Reed (Garcia); Jane Wolfe
(Mrs. Kenyon).

Another adventure about Pancho Villa. This time American Tom
Kenyon and Dolores deVargas are supporting Villa. Dolores' brother
is supporting the local army leader, General Barrance (who is only
after Tequilla and Dolores' silver mine). General Barrance is finally
outdone by Tom, and the silver mine is saved.

UNDER THE TONTO RIM   Mexican   1947/Western

RKO; 61 min.; *Producer*: Herman Schlom; *Director*: Lew Landers; *Screen-
play*: Norman Houston; *Camera*: Paul Sawtell; *Editor*: Lyle Boyer; *Cast*:
Tim Holt (Brad); Nan Leslie (Lucy); Richard Martin (Chito); *CAROL
FORMAN (JUANITA)*; Tony Barrett (Patton); Harry Harvey (Sheriff);
Jason Robards (Capt. McLean); Robert Clarke (Hooker); Jay Norris
(Andy); Lex Barker (Joe); Steve Savage (Curly).

Brad runs a stagecoach and is seeking the Tonto gang for robbery. He sets a trap to catch the gang but Juanita almost gives him
away. He manages to hold off the gang until the posse arrives.

THE UNFORGIVEN   Native American--Kiowa   1960/Western

United Artists; 120 min.; *Producer*: James Hill; *Director*: John Huston;
Screenplay: Ben Maddow; *Music*: Dimitri Tiomkin; *Camera*: Franz Planer;
Editor: Hugh Russell Lloyd; *Cast*: Burt Lancaster (Ben Zachary);
AUDREY HEPBURN (RACHEL ZACHARY); Audie Murphy (Cash Zachary); John
Saxon (Johnny Portugal); Charles Bickford (Zeb Rawlins); Lillian Gish
(Mattilda Zachary); Albert Salmi (Charlie Rawlins); Joseph Wiseman
(Abe Kelsey); June Walker (Hagar Rawlins); Kipp Hamilton (Georgia
Rawlins); Arnold Merritt (Jude Rawlins); Carlos Rivas (Lost Bird);
Doug McClure (Andy Zachary).

As a baby, Rachel Zachary was kidnapped by whites from the

Kiowas. Years later the Kiowas find the adult Rachel and want her
returned to her natural family. Her white family refuses, and conflict ensues. Rachel murders her blood brother and marries her
adopted brother.

UP IN THE CELLAR   Black   1970/Comedy

American International; 92 min.; *Producers*: James H. Nicholson/Samuel
Z. Arkoff; *Director*: Theodore Flicker; *Screenplay*: Theodore Flicker;
Music: Don Randi; *Camera*: Earl Rath; *Editor*: Richard Halsey; *Cast*:
Wes Stein (Colin Slade); Joan Collins (Pat Camber); Larry Hagman
(Maurice Camber); Nira Barab (Tracy Camber); *JUDY PACE (HARLENE
JONES)*; David Arkin (Hugo Cain); Joan Darling (Madame Krigo).

    This campus comedy has Colin Slade seeking revenge against
college president Maurice Camber by seducing his wife, daughter, and
secretary. Harlene Jones is Maurice Camber's Black secretary and
also his sweetheart. To seduce her Colin pretends that he is Black
and then reveals that he is white. When the hijinks are over Harlene
is delighted for now she can consummate her love with Maurice, who
divorces his wife to be with her.

UPTIGHT   Black   1968/Drama

Paramount; 104 min.; *Producer/Director*: Jules Dassin; *Screenplay*:
Jules Dassin/Ruby Dee/Julian Mayfield; *Music*: Booker T. Jones;
Camera: Boris Kaufman; *Editor*: Robert Lawrence; *Cast*: Raymond St.
Jacques (B G); *RUBY DEE (LAURIE)*; Frank Silvera (Kyle); Julain May-
field (Tank Williams); Roscoe Lee Browne (Clarence); *Janet MacLachlan
(Jennie)*; Max Julien (Johnny Wells); *Juanita Moore (Mama Wells)*;
Michael Baseleon (Teddy); Robert DoQui (Street Speaker); Ketty Lester
(Alma); Dick Williams (Corbin).

    Laurie becomes a prostitute to support her children. Jennie is
Jennie is B G's girlfriend.

THE VEILS OF BAGDAD   Arabian Nights   1953/Fantasy

Universal; 82 min.; *Producer*: Albert J. Cohen; *Director*: George
Sherman; *Screenplay*: William R. Cox; *Music*: Joseph Gershenson;
Camera: Russell Metty; *Editor*: Paul Weatherwax; *Cast*: Victor Mature
(Antar); *MARI BLANCHARD (SELENA)*; *VIRGINIA FIELD (ROSANNA)*; Guy Rolfe
(Kasseim); James Arness (Targut); Palmer Lee (Oaman); Nick Cravet
(Ahmed); Ludwig Donath (Kaffar); Dave Sharpe (Ben Ali); Jackie
Loughery (Handmaiden); Leon Askin (Pascha Hamman); Howard Petrie
(Karsh); Charles Arnt (Zapolya); Glenn Strange (Mik-Kel); Sammy Stein
(Abdullah); Bobby Blake (Beggar Boy).

    Selena, a dancer in a Bagdad tavern, is trying to find the men
responsible for the death of her father, a tribal chieftain.

Audrey Hepburn, *The Unforgiven* (UA, 1960)

THE VENGEANCE OF FU MANCHU   Chinese   1968/Mystery

Warner Brothers-Seven Arts; 89 min.; *Producer*: Harry Alan; *Director*:
Jerry Summers; *Screenplay*: Peter Welbeck; *Music*: Malcolm Lockyer;
Camera: John Von Kotze; *Editor*: Allan Morrison; *Cast*: Christopher Lee
(Fu Manchu); Tony Ferrer (Inspector Ramos); *TSAI CHIN (LIN TANG)*;
Douglas Wilmer (Nayland Smith); Wolfgang Kieling (Dr. Liberson);
Susanne Roquette (Maria Liberson); Howard Marion Crawford (Dr.
Petrie); Noel Trevarthen (Mark Weston); Horst Frank (Rudy Moss); Peter
Carsten (Kurt); Maria Rohm (Ingrid); *Mona Chong (Jasmin)*.

      Ling Tang assists her father, Fu Manchu, in organizing an inter-
national crime syndicate. They also plot the demise of Nayland Smith.
Fu Manchu's schemes do not work out, but he promises to return.

VERA CRUZ   Mexican   1954/Adventure

Untied Artists; 94 min.; *Producer*: James Hill; *Director*: Robert
Aldrich; *Screenplay*: Roland Kibbee/James R. Webb; *Music*: Hugo
Friedhofer; *Camera*: Ernest Laszlo; *Editor*: Alan Crosland, Jr.; *Cast*:
Gary Cooper (Benjamin Trane); Burt Lancaster (Joe Erin); Denise
Darcel (Countess Marie Duvarre); Cesar Romero (Marquis de Labordere);
SARITA MONTIEL (NINA); George Macready (Emperor Maximilian); Ernest
Borgnine (Donnegan); Henry Brandon (Danette); Charles Bronson
(Pittsburgh); Morris Ankrum(General Aguilar); James McCallion (Little-
Bit); Jack Lambert (Charlie).

      In Maximilian's Mexico, Benjamin Trane becomes enamored of Nina,
although devoting much of his attention to the Countess Marie Duvarre.
Nina keeps the pressure on Trane and he soon succumbs to her charms.

VILLA RIDES   Mexican   1968/Adventure

Paramount; 125 min.; *Producer*: Ted Richmond; *Director*: Buzz Kulik;
Screenplay: Robert Towne/Sam Peckinpah; *Music*: Maurice Jarre; *Camera*:
Jack Hildyard; *Editor*: David Bretherton; *Cast*: Yul Brynner (Pancho
Villa); Robert Mitchum (Lee Arnold); *GRAZIA BUCCELLA (FINA GONZALEZ)*;
Charles Bronson (Fierro); Robert Viharo (Urbina); Frank Wolff (Capt.
Ramirez); Herbert Lom (General Huerta); Alexander Knox (President
Madero); *Diana Lorys (Emilita)*; Robert Carricart (Luis Gonzalez);
Fernando Rey (Fuentes).

      In this story about Pancho Villa, Fina is Lee Arnold's romantic
interest.

THE VIRGIN ISLAND   West Indian   1958/Drama

British Lion Release; 94 min.; *Producers*: Leon Close/Grahame Thorpe;
Director: Pat Jackson; *Screenplay*: Philip Rush; *Music*: Clifton Parker;
Camera: Freddie Francis; *Editor*: Gordon Pilkington; *Cast*: John
Cassavetes (Evan); Virginia Maskell (Tina); Sidney Poitier (Marcus);
Isabel Dean (Mrs. Lomax); Colin Gordon (The Commissioner); Howard

Marion Crawford (Prescott); *RUBY DEE (RUTH)*; Gladys Boot (Mrs. Carruthers).

Islanders Marcus and Ruth befriend newlyweds Evan and Tina and wind up falling in love themselves.

VIRGIN SACRIFICE   Guatemalan   1959/Thriller

RCIP; NA min.; *Producer*: Joseph F. Horn; *Director*: Fernando Wagner; *Screenplay*: V.J. Rheyms; *Music*: Paul Sawtell; *Camera*: Walter Reuter; *Camera*: Edward Mann; *Cast*: David Da Lie (Samson); Antonio Gutierrez (Tumic); *ANGELICA MORALES (MORENA)*; Fernando Wagner (Fernando); *Linda Cordova (Girl Sacrifice)*; Philip Pearl (Indian); Hamdy Sayed (Indian).

While hunting jaguars in the Guatemalan jungle, Samson is mauled by a jaguar and taken to the home of his friend Fernando. While recovering he falls in love with Morena, Fernando's daughter. Morena is desired by Tumic who wishes to sacrifice her to the Tiger God. Tumic kidnaps Morena, but she is saved by Samson as she is about to be sacrificed. Tumic is killed.

THE VIRGIN SOLDIERS   Malaysian   1969/War Drama

Columbia; 96 min.; *Producers*: Leslie Gilliat/Ned Sherrin; *Director*: John Dexter; *Screenplay*: John Hopkins; *Music*: Peter Greenwell; *Camera*: Ken Higgins; *Editor*: Thelma Connell; *Cast*: Lynn Redgrave (Phillipa Raskin); Hywel Bennet (Private Brigg); Nigel Davenport (Sgt. Driscoll); Nigel Patrick (R.S.M. Raskin); *TSAI CHIN (JUICY LUCY)*; Rachel Kempson (Mrs. Raskin); Jack Shepherd (Sgt. Wellbeloved); Michael Gwynn (Lt. Col. Bromley-Pickering); Christopher Timothy (Cpt. Brook).

Pvt. Brigg is one of the soldiers who succumbs to the local prostitute, Juicy Lucy.

VIVA VILLA   Mexican   1934/Adventure

MGM; 115 min.; *Producer*: David O. Selznick; *Director*: Jack Conway; *Screenplay*: Ben Hecht; *Camera*: James Wong Howe/Charles G. Clarke; *Editor*: Robert J. Kern; *Cast*: Wallace Beery (Pancho Villa); *FAY WRAY (TERESA)*; Leo Carrillo (Diego); Donald Cook (Don Felipe); Stuart Erwin (Johnny); George E. Stone (Chavito); Joseph Schildkraut (Pascal); Henry B. Walthall (Madero); *Katherine De Mille (Rosita)*; David Durand (Bugle Boy).

Another story about Pancho Villa. Teresa is a sympathetic aristocrat whom Villa assaults and then murders.

Tsai Chin, *The Virgin Soldiers* (Columbia, 1969)

VIVA ZAPATA   Mexican   1952/Adventure

20th Century-Fox; 113 min.; *Producer*: Darry F. Zanuck; *Director*:
Elia Kazan; *Screenplay*: John Steinbeck; *Music*: Alex North; *Camera*:
Joe MacDonald; *Editor*: Barbara McLean; *Cast*: Marlon Brando (Zapata);
JEAN PETERS (JOSEFA); Anthony Quinn (Enfemio); Joseph Wiseman
(Fernando); Arnold Moss (Don Nacio); Alan Reed (Pancho Villa); *Margo
(Soldadera)*; Lou Gilbert (Pablo); Harold Gordon (Madero); *Mildred
Dunnock (Senora Espejo)*; Frank Silvera (Huerta).

The story of Emiliano Zapata and his fight for the Indians of
Mexico against the Mexican/Spanish oppressors. Josefa is the woman
he loves and eventually marries.

VOODOO TIGER   Jungle Exotic   1952/Adventure

Columbia; 67 min.; *Producer*: Sam Katzman; *Director*: Spencer G.
Bennett; *Screenplay*: Samuel Newman; *Camera*: William Whitney; *Editor*:
Gene Havlick; *Cast*: Johnny Weissmuller (Jungle Jim); Jean Byron
(Phyllis Bruce); James Seay (Abel Peterson); *JEANNE DEAN (SHALIMAR)*;
Charles Horvath (Wombulu); Robert Bray (Major Bill Green); Michael
Fox (Carl Werner); Rick Vallin (Sgt. Bono); John Cason (Jerry
Masters); Paul Hoffmon (Michael Kovacs).

Shalimar is the leader of a dance troupe traveling through the
jungle.

VOODOO WOMAN   Jungle Exotic   1957/Thriller

American-International; 77 min.; *Producer*: Alex Gordon; *Director*:
Edward L. Cahn; *Screenplay*: Russell Bender/V.L. Voss; *Music*: Darrell
Calker; *Camera*: Frederic E. West; *Editor*: Ronald Sinclair; *Cast*:
Tom Conway (Dr. Roland Gerard); Maria English (Marilyn Blanchard);
JEAN DAVIS (NATIVE GIRL); Touch Connors (Ted Bronson); Lance Fuller
(Rick/Harry); Mary Ellen Kay (Susan); Paul Durov (Marcel); Martin
Wilkins (Chaka); Norman Willis (Harry West); Otto Greene (Bobo);
Emmett E. Smith (Gandor); Paul Blaisdell (Monster).

In a village that practices voodoo, Dr. Roland Gerard is a mad
scientist who lusts after Native Girl, who is pure of heart.

WALK LIKE A DRAGON   Chinese   1960/Drama

Paramount; 95 min.; *Producer/Director/Screenplay*: James Clavell;
Music: Paul Dunlap; *Camera*: Loyal Griggs; *Editor*: Howard Smith; *Cast*:
Jack Lord (Linc Bartlett); *NOBU McCARTHY (KIM SUNG)*; James Shigeta
(Cheng); Mel Torme (The Deacon); Josephine Hutchinson (Ma Bartlett);
Rudolph Acosta (Sheriff Margusiez); Benson Fong (Wu); Michael Pate
(Will Allen); Lilyan Chauvin (Mme. Lill Raide); Don Kennedy (Masters);
Donald Barry (Cabot); Natalie Trundy (Susan).

Kim Sung is about to be sold into prostitution when Linc
Bartlett buys her and sets her free. She has no place to go so Linc
takes her to his home town. Returning to the town at that time is
Cheng, who is going to work with Linc's uncle. Both men fall in love
with Kim. Cheng decides he will challenge Linc to a gunfight to win
KIm. But the prejudiced town arranges the fight so he will kill the
Deacon, the local gunfighter. The town then puts Cheng on trial for
murder. Linc points out that the law is for all colors and Cheng is
freed. Meanwhile, Kim realizes the power of racial prejudice and
decides to marry Cheng.

WALK ON THE WILD SIDE   Mexican & Black   1962/Drama

Columbia; 114 min.; *Producer*: Charles K. Feldman; *Director*: Edward
Dmytryk; *Screenplay*: John Fante/Edmund Morris; *Music*: Elmer Bernstein;
Camera: Joseph MacDonald; *Editor*: Harry Gerstad; *Cast*: Laurence
Harvey (Dove Likkhorn); Capucine (Hallie); Jane Fonda (Kitty Twist);
ANNE BAXTER (TERESINA VIDAVERRI); Barbara Stanwyck (Jo Courtney);
Joanna Moore (Miss Precious); Richard Rust (Oliver); Karl Swenson
(Schmidt); Donald Barry (Dockery); *Juanita Moore (Mama)*; John
Anderson (Preacher); Ken Lynch (Frank Bonito); Todd Armstrong (Lt.
Omar Stroud).

Teresina Vidaverri, a lonely widow who owns a diner, falls in
love with Dove Likkhorn a farmer who has come to Louisiana searching
for his lost lover, Hallie. Dove finds Hallie in a bordello run by
Jo Courtney, a lesbian who loves Hallie. Jo's jealousy causes Dove
to be beaten up and taken to Teresina's diner. Hallie finds out and
goes to the diner. Jo once again interferes, this time accidentally
causing Hallie to be killed.

WALK THE PROUD LAND   Native American--Apache   1956/Western

Universal; 88 min.; *Producer*: Aaron Rosenberg; *Director*: Jesse Hibbs;
Screenplay: Gil Doud/Jack Sher; *Music*: Joseph Gershenson; *Camera*:
Harold Lipstein; *Editor*: Sherman A. Todd; *Cast*: Audie Murphy (John
Clum); *ANNE BANCROFT (TIANAY)*; Pat Crowley (Mary Dennison); Charles
Drake (Tom Sweeney); Tommy Rall (Tagligo); Robert Warwick (Eskimin-
zin); Jay Silverheels (Geronimo); Eugene Mazzola (Tono); Anthony
Caruso (Disalin); Victor Millan (Santos); Ainslie Pryor (Capt.
Larsen); Eugene Iglesias (Chato); Morris Ankrum (General Wade);
Maurice Jara (Alchise); Frank Chase (Stone); Ed Hinton (Naylor);
Marty Carrizosa (Pica).

Widow Tianay wants to marry Indian agent John Clum. She does
not mind that he already has a wife.

WALLS OF GOLD   Latin American   1933/Adventure

20th Century-Fox; 74 min.; *Director*: Kenneth MacKenna; *Screenplay*:
Lester Cole; *Camera*: George Schneiderman; *Cast*: Sally Eilers (Jeanie
Satterlee); Norman Foster (Barnes Ritchie); Ralph Morgan (J. Gordon

Ritchie); *ROSITA MORENO (CARLA MONTEREZ)*; Rochelle Hudson (Joan Street); Frederic Santley (Tony Van Raalte); Marjorie Gateson (Cassie Street); Mary Mason (Honey Satterlee); Margaret Seddon (Mrs. Satterlee).

Not enough information was available to describe this role accurately.

WAR ARROW   Native American--Seminole   1953/Western

Universal; 78 min.; *Producer*: John W. Rogers; *Director*: George Sherman; *Screenplay*: John Michael Hayes; *Camera*: William Daniels; *Editor*: Frank Gross; *Cast*: Maureen O'Hara (Elaine Corwin); Jeff Chandler (Major Howell Brady); John McIntire (Col. Jackson Meade); *SUZAN BALL (AVIS)*; Noah Beery (Sgt. Augustus Wilks); Charles Drake (Sgt. Luke Schermerhorn); Henry Brandon (Maygro); Dennis Weaver (Pino); Jay Silverheels (Santanta).

Major Howell Brady brings Seminole Indians to Texas to fight the Kiowa Indians. Avis is the daughter of the chief of the Seminole. She wants to improve her standard of living.

WAR DRUMS   Native American--Apache   1957/Western

United Artists; 75 min.; *Producer*: Howard W. Koch; *Director*: Reginald Le Borg; *Screenplay*: Gerald Drayson Adams; *Music*: Les Baxter; *Camera*: William Margulies; *Editor*: John A. Bushelman; *Cast*: Lex Barker (Mangas Coloradas); *JOAN TAYLOR (RIVA)*; Ben Johnson (Luke Fargo); Larry Chance (Ponce); Richard Cutting (Judge Bolton); James Parnell (Arizona); John Pickard (Sheriff Ballard); John Colicos (Chino); Tom Monroe (Dutch Herman); Jill Jarmyn (Nona); *Jeanne Carmen (Yellow Moon)*; Mauritz Hugo (Clay Staub); Ward Ellis (Delgadito); Fred Sherman (Dr. Gordon); Paul Fierro (Fiero).

Riva is a brave woman riding with her Apache husband.

WAR PAINT   Native American   1953/Western

United Artists; 85 min.; *Producer*: Howard W. Koch; *Director*: Lesley Selander; *Screenplay*: Richard Alan Simmons/Martin Berkeley; *Music*: Emil Newman/Arthur Lang; *Camera*: Gordon Avil; *Editor*: John F. Schreyer; *Cast*: Robert Stack (Lt. Billings); *JOAN TAYLOR (WANIMA)*; Charles McGraw (Sgt. Clarke); Keith Larsen (Tasik); Peter Graves (Tolson); Robert Wilke (Grady); Walter Reed (Allison); John Doucette (Charnotsky); Douglas Kennedy (Clancy); Charles Nolte (Corp. Hamilton); James Parnell (Martin); Paul Richards (Perkins); William Pullen (Jeb); Richard Cutting (Kirby).

Wanima is the chief's daughter. She leads a band of stranded soldiers who are seeking water and a peace council with her father.

A WARM DECEMBER   Black [African]   1973/Drama

National General; 103 min.; *Producer*: Melville Tucker; *Director*:
Sidney Poitier; *Screenplay*: Lawrence Roman; *Music*: Coleridge-Taylor
Perkinson; *Camera*: Paul Beeson; *Editor*: Pembroke Herring/Peter Pitt;
Cast: Sidney Poitier (Matt Younger); *ESTHER ANDERSON (CATHERINE)*;
Yvette Curtis (Stefanie); George Baker (Henry Barlow); Johnny Sekka
(Myomo); Earl Cameron (George Oswanda); Hilary Crane (Marsha Barlow).

   While living in London, Catherine meets and falls in love with
American Matt Younger. She then learns that she is dying from sickle
cell anemia.

WAY OF A GAUCHO   Argentine   1952/Adventure

20th Century-Fox; 90 min.; *Producer/Screenplay*: Philip Dunne;
Director: Jacques Tourneur; *Music*: Sol Kaplan; *Camera*: Harry Jackson;
Editor: Robert Fritch; *Cast*: Rory Calhoun (Martin); *GENE TIERNEY
(TERESA)*; Richard Boone (Salinas); Hugh Marlowe (Miguel); Everett
Sloane (Falcon); Enrique Chaico (Father Fernandez); Jorge Villoldo
(Valverde); Roland Dumas (Julio);

   Teresa meets and falls in love with outlaw gaucho Martin. As
the story develops she changes from an aristocratic lady to an Indian
woman living with the outlaw gauchos. When Martin and Teresa attempt
to get married they are thwarted in the process. They consummate
their love anyway and Teresa becomes pregnant. Martin then turns
himself in so he and Teresa can be married and live a respectable
life.

WE WERE STRANGERS   Cuban   1948/Drama

Columbia; 106 min.; *Producer*: S.P. Eagle; *Director*: John Huston;
Screenplay: Peter Viertel/John Huston; *Music*: George Antheil; *Camera*:
Russell Metty; *Editor*: Al Clark; *Cast*: *JENNIFER JONES (CHINA VALDES)*;
John Garfield (Tony Fenner); Pedro Armendariz (Armando Ariete);
Gilbert Roland (Guillermo); Ramon Novarro (Chief); Wally Cassell
(Miguel); David Bond (Ramon); Jose Perez (Toto); Morris Ankrum (Bank
Manager); Tito Rinaldo (Manolo).

   During political repression in Cuba in the 1930s, China Valdes
watches as her brother is murdered by the chief of the secret police.
She becomes involved with underground revolutionaries and helps
secure false identity papers for American revolutionary Tony Fenner.
An elaborate plot to assassinate the country's rulers is unsuccessful
and only one leader is killed. Tony Fenner tries to escape but dies
in China's arms during a battle with police.

WEEK-END IN HAVANA   Cuban   1941/Comedy

20th Century-Fox; 80 min.; *Producer*: William Le Baron; *Director*:
Walter Lang; *Screenplay*: Karl Tunberg/Darrell Ware; *Music*: Mack

Gordon/Harry Warren/James V. Monaco; *Camera*: Ernest Palmer; *Editor*: Allen McNeil; *Cast*: Alice Faye (Nan Spencer); *CARMEN MIRANDA (ROSITA RIVAS)*; John Payne (Jay Williams); Cesar Romero (Monte Blanca); Cobina Wright, Jr. (Terry McCracken); George Barbier (Walter McCracken); Sheldon Leonard (Boris); Leonid Kinskey (Rafael); Bill Gilbert (Arbolado); Hal K. Dawson (Mr. Marks).

Rosita Rivas sings and dances the final production number, "The Nango."

WEIRD WOMAN   Island Exotic   1944/Thriller

Universal; 63 min.; *Producer*: Oliver Drake; *Director*: Reginald Le Borg; *Screenplay*: Brenda Weisberg; *Music*: Paul Sawtell; *Camera*: Virgil Miller; *Editor*: Milton Carruth; *Cast*: Lon Chaney, Jr. (Norman Reed); *ANNE GWYNNE (PAULA REED)*; Evelyn Ankers (Ilona Carr); Ralph Morgan (Prof. Millard Sawtelle); Lois Collier (Margaret); Elizabeth Russell (Evelyn Sawtelle); Elisabeth Risdon (Grace Gunnison); Harry Hayden (Professor Septimus Carr); Phil Brown (David Jennings); Jackie Lou Harding (Student); Hianna Kaapa (Larava).

Paula Reed grew up believing in voodoo. Her new husband brings home his ex-girlfriend who exploits Paula's beliefs and seeks vengeance through various voodoo methods. Paula has the strength to turn the tables on Ilona and keep her marriage intact.

WELCOME TO THE CLUB   Japanese & Black   1972/Drama

Columbia; 88 min.; *Producer/Director*: Walter Shenson; *Screenplay*: Clement Biddle; *Music*: Ken Thorne; *Camera*: Mikael Salomon; *Editor*: Jim Connock; *Cast*: Brian Foley (Lt. Andrew Oxblood); Jack Warden (Gen. Strapp); Andy Jarrell (Robert E. Lee Fairfax); Kevin O'Connor (Harrison W. Morve); *FRANCESCA TU (HOGAN)*; David Toguri (Hideki Ikada); Al Mancini (PFC Marcantonio); Art Wallace (Col. Boonocuore); Louis Quinn (Capt. Sigmus); Lionel Murton (Col. Ames); *Marsha Hunt (Leah Wheat)*; *Joyce Wilford (Shawna O'Shay)*; Lon Satton (Marshall Bowles).

Hogan is the housekeeper for American Army officers--who, except for Lt. Oxblood, are extremely racist. Hogan is attracted to Lt. Oxblood, but he ignores her. Depressed, she goes to bed with Marshall Bowles. Shawna O'Shay, Leah Wheat, and Marshall are members of a Black singing group playing at the base. The singers suffer the same racial intolerance as Hogan. When Oxblood discovers that Hogan and Marshall are lovers he hits Marshall. Oxblood then realizes his own deep-seated racial attitude.

THE WELL   Black   1951/Drama

United Artists; 89 min.; *Producers*: Leo C. Popkin/Clarence Green; *Directors*: Leo C. Popkin/Russell Rouse; *Screenplay*: Clarence Green/ Russell Rouse; *Music*: Dimitri Tiomkin; *Camera*: Ernest Laszlo; *Editor*:

Rita Moreno, *West Side Story* (UA, 1961)

Chester Schaeffer; *Cast*: *Gwendolyn Laster (Carolyn)*; Richard Rober
(Ben Kellogg); *MAIDIE NORMAN (MRS. CRAWFORD)*; George Hamilton (Grandfather); Ernest Anderson (Mr. Crawford); Dick Simmons (Mickey).

Mrs. Crawford at first assumes her missing daughter, Carolyn,
has been kidnapped by a white man. This stirs up racial tension.
When Carolyn is found trapped in a well the town pulls together to
save her.

WEST OF THE PECOS   Black & Mexican   1934/Western

RKO; 70 min.; *Director*: Phil Rosen; *Screenplay*: Milton Krims/John
Twist; *Camera*: James Van Trees; *Editor*: Archie Marshek; *Cast*: Richard
Dix (Pecos Smith); Martha Sleeper (Terrill); Samuel Hinds (Colonel
Lambeth); Fred Kohler (Breen Sawtell); Sleep-n-Eat (Jonah); *MARIA
ALBA (DOLORES)*; *Louise Beavers (Mauree)*.

Dolores flirts with Terrill, a woman disguised as a man.

WEST SIDE STORY   Puerto Rican   1961/Musical

United Artists; 155 min.; *Producer*: Robert Wise; *Director*: Jerome
Robbins/Robert Wise; *Screenplay*: Ernest Lehman; *Music/Lyrics*: Leonard
Bernstein/Stephen Sordheim; *Camera*: Daniel Fapp; *Editor*: Thomas
Stanford; *Cast*: *NATALIE WOOD (MARIA)*; Richard Beymer (Tony); Russ
Tamblyn (Riff); *RITA MORENO (ANITA)*; George Chakiris (Bernardo);
Tucker Smith (Ice); Tony Mordente (Action); Eliot Feld (Baby John);
David Winters (A-Rab); Burt Michaels (Snowboy); Sue Oakes (Anybodys);
Gina Trikonis (Graziella); Carole D'Andrea (Velma); Joe De Vega
(Chino); Jay Norman (Pepe); Simon Oakland (Lt. Schrank); Bill Bramley
(Officer Krupke); Ned Glass (Doc).

Maria attends her first dance in the United States and falls in
love with Tony, unaware that he is from a rival gang. Her brother,
Bernardo, takes her home immediately but Tony finds her and they
continue seeing each other. Maria finds out that the two gangs are
planning a rumble and she begs Tony to stop the fight. Tony tries
to stop the fight but after Riff, his best friend, is killed, Tony
kills Bernardo, Maria's brother. Maria and Tony plan to leave the
city together. When Anita, Bernardo's lover and Maria's friend, is
harassed by the Jets, she lies and tells them that Chino has killed
Maria. When Tony hears that Maria is dead, he goes looking for Chino
so Chino can kill him also. Tony finds Maria instead but as the
lovers are about to embrace, Chino appears and kills Tony.

WEST TO GLORY   Mexican   1947/Adventure

PRC; 61 min.; *Producer*: Jerry Thomas; *Director*: Ray Taylor; *Screen-
play*: Elmer Clifton/Robert B. Churchill; *Camera*: Milford Anderson;
Editor: Hugh Winn; *Cast*: Eddie Dean; Roscoe Ates (Soapy); *DOLORES
CASTLE (MARIA)*; Gregg Barton (Barrett); Jimmy Martin (Cory); Zon
Murray (Avery); Harry Vejor (Don Lopez).

Dolores works for the Mexican government trying to get back the stolen Lopez diamond.

WHAT EVER HAPPENED TO BABY JANE   Black   1962/Thriller

Warner Brothers; 132 min.; *Producer/Driector*: Robert Aldrich; *Screenplay*: Lukas Heller; *Music*: Frank DeVol; *Camera*: Ernest Haller; *Editor*: Michael Luciano; *Cast*: Bette Davis (Jane Hudson); Joan Crawford (Blanche Hudson); Victor Buono (Edwin Flagg); Anna Lee (Mrs. Bates); *MAIDIE NORMAN (ELVIRA STITT)*; Marjorie Bennett (Mrs. Flagg); Dave Willock (Ray Hudson); Anne Barton (Cora Hudson); Barbara D. Merrill (Liza Bates).

Elvira is the maid to two crazy sisters, Jane and Blanche. When Elvira becomes suspicious of the goings on in the house, Jane murders her with a hammer.

WHEN WERE YOU BORN?   Chinese   1938/Comedy

Warner Brothers; 65 min.; *Director*: William McGann; *Screenplay*: Anthony Coldeway; *Camera*: L. Wm. O'Connell; *Editor*: Doug Gould; *Cast*: Margaret Lindsay (Doris Kane); *ANNA MAY WONG (MARY LEE LING)*; Lola Lane (Nira Kenton); Anthony Averill (Larry Camp); Charles Wilson (Inspector Gregg); Frank Jaquet (Sgt. Kelly); Eric Stanley (Shields); James Stephenson (Phillip Corey); Jeffrey Lynn (Davis); Leonard Mudic (Fred Gow); Maurice Cass (Dr. Merton); Jack Moore (Asst. District Attorney).

Mary Lee Ling is an astrologer who helps the police track down a murderer by charting horoscopes.

WHITE CARGO   Jungle Exotic   1942/Drama

MGM; 90 min.; *Producer*: Victor Saville; *Director*: Richard Thorpe; *Screenplay*: Leon Gordon; *Camera*: Harry Stradling; *Editor*: Frederick Y. Smith; *Cast*: *HEDY LAMARR (TONDELAYO)*; Walter Pidgeon (Harry Witzell); Frank Morgan (The Doctor); Richard Carlson (Langford); Reginald Owen (Skipper); Henry O'Neill (Reverend Roberts); Bramwell Fletcher (Wilbour Ashley); Clyde Cook (Ted); Leigh Whipper (Jim Fish); Oscar Polk (Umeela).

Tondelayo, the jungle beauty, hopes to seduce Langford and make herself wealthy. Magistrate Harry Witzell forbids Tondelayo to see Langford, so Langford marries her out of spite (and lust). Tondelayo soon develops a desire for Witzell but he rebuffs her. Tondelayo decides to poison Langford but Witzell catches her and makes her drink the poison.

WHITE FEATHER   Native American--Cheyenne   1955/Western

20th Century-Fox; 102 min.; *Producer*: Robert L. Jacks; *Director*:

Hedy Lamarr, *White Heat* (MGM, 1942)

Robert Webb; *Screenplay*: Delmar Daves/Leo Townsend; *Music*: Hugo
Friedhofer; *Camera*: Lucien Ballard; *Editor*: George Gittens; *Cast*:
Robert Wagner (Josh Tanner); John Lund (Col. Lindsay); *DEBRA PAGET
(APPEARING DAY)*; Jeffrey Hunter (Little Dog); Hugh O'Brian (American
Horse); Eduard Franz (CHief Broken Hand); Noah Beery (Lt. Ferguson);
Virginia Leith (Ann Magruder); Emile Meyer (Magruder); Milburn Stone
(Commissioner Trenton).

Appearing Day is the daughter of Chief Broken Hand. She falls
in love with white man Josh Tanner and leaves her people to be with
him.

WHITE HEAT   Island Exotic   1934/Drama

Seven Seas Corp.; 60 min.; *Director*: Lois Weber; *Screenplay*: Lois
Weber/James Bodrero; *Camera*: Alvin Wyckoff/Frank Titus; *Cast*: Virginia
Cherrill (Lucille Cheney); *MONA MARIS (LEILANI)*; Hardie Albright
(Chandler Morris); David Newell (William Hawks); Arthur Clayton
(Armia); Robert Stevenson (Mac); Whitney de Rahm (Hale); Naomie
Childers (Mrs. Cheney); Nani Palsa (Adam); Kolimau Kamai (Lono);
Kamaunani Achi (Mrs. Hale); Peter Lee Hyun (Soong); Nohill Naumu
(Leilani's Father).

Leilani is the native mistress of plantation owner William Hawks.
Hawks leaves Leilani to marry white Lucille Cheney, who rapidly becomes bored with her life on the plantation. Lucille almost has an
affair with a native but becomes involved with a former lover instead.
Hawks returns to Leilani.

THE WHITE ORCHID   Mexican   1954/Adventure

Untied Artists; 81 min.; *Producer/Director*: Reginald Le Borg; *Screen-
play*: Reginald Le Borg/David Duncan; *Music*: Antonio Diaz; *Camera*:
Gilbert Warrenton; *Editor*: Jose W. Bustos; *Cast*: William Lundigan
(Robert Burton); Peggie Castle (Kathryn Williams); Armando Silvestre
(Juan Cervantes); *ROSENDA MONTEROS (LUPITA)*; Alejandro de Montenegro
(Miguel); Miguel A. Gallardo (Pedro); Jorge Trevino (Arturo).

Lupita is in love with Juan Cervantes, who loves Kathryn
Williams, who loves Robert Burton.

WHITE SAVAGE   Island Exotic   1943/Adventure

Universal; 75 min.; *Producer*: George Waggner; *Director*: Arthur Lubin;
Screenplay: Richard Brooks; *Music*: Charles Previn; *Camera*: William
Snyder/Lester White; *Editor*: Russell Schoengarth; *Cast*: Jon Hall
(Kaloe); *MARIA MONTEZ (PRINCESS TAHIA)*; Sabu (Orano); Don Terry
(Chris); Turhan Bey (Tamara); Thomas Gomez (Miller); Sidney Toler
Wong); Paul Guifoyle (Erik); Constance Purdy (Blossom).

Princess Tahia is the ruler of a small island where Kaloe wants
permission to fish. Orano plays cupid for Tahia and Kaloe while

Kaloe fights the evil Miller who wants to rob the island of its
wealth.

THE WHITE SQUAW   Native American--Sioux   1956/Western

Columbia; 73 min.; *Producer*: Wallace MacDonald; *Director*: Ray
Nazarro; *Screenplay*: Les Savage, Jr.; *Camera*: Henry Freulich; *Editor*:
Edwin Bryant; *Cast*: David Brian (Sigrod Swanson); *MAY WYNN (EETAY-
O-WAHNEE)*; William Bishop (Bob Garth); Nancy Hale (Kerry Arnold);
William Leslie (Thor Swanson); Myron Healey (Eric Swanson); Robert
C. Ross (Knute Swanson); Frank de Kova (Yellow Elk); George Keymas
(Yotah); Roy Roberts (Purvis).

Cattleman Bob Garth comes to the aid of Eetay-O-Wahnee when
evil Sigrod Swanson tries to drive her people off their land.

WHO'S BEEN SLEEPING IN MY BED   Japanese   1963/Comedy

Paramount; 103 min.; *Producer*: Jack Rose; *Director*: Daniel Mann;
Screenplay: Jack Rose; *Music*: George Duning; *Camera*: Joseph Rutten-
berg; *Editor*: George Tomasini; *Cast*: Dean Martin (Jason Steel);
Elizabeth Montgomery (Melissa Morris); Carol Burnett (Stella Irving);
Martin Balsam (Sanford Kaufman); Jill St. John (Toby Tobler);
Richard Conte (Leonard Ashley); Macha Meril (Jacqueline Edwards);
Louis Nye (Harry Tobler); *YOKO TANI (ISAMI HIROTI)*; Jack Soo (Yoshimi
Hiroti); Dianne Foster (Mona Kaufman); Eliott Reid (Tom Edwards).

Jason Steel portrays a sympathetic and problem-solving doctor
on a television series. The wives of his friends cannot distinguish
between the actor and the character he plays so they call upon him
for comfort and attention. Isami Hiroti wants to be a traditional
Japanese wife but her husband is more modern. She waits upon Jason
in traditional Japanese fashion.

THE WILBY CONSPIRACY   Indian   1975/Adventure

United Artists; 101 min.; *Producer*: Martin Baum; *Director*: Ralph
Nelson; *Screenplay*: Rod Amateau/Harold Nebenzai; *Camera*: John
Coquillon; *Editor*: Ernest Walter; *Cast*: Sidney Poitier (Shack Twala);
Michael Caine (Keogh); Nicol Williamson (Horn); Prunella Gee (Rina);
PERSIS KHAMBATTA (PERSIS RAY); Saeed Jaffrey (Mukeriee); Ryk De Graf
(Wilby).

Persis Ray is a dental assistant in South Africa.

THE WILD AFFAIR   Chinese   1965/Comedy

Goldstone Film Enterprises; 87 min.; *Producer*: Richard L. Patterson;
Director: John Krish; *Screenplay*: John Krish; *Music*: Martin Slavin;
Camera: Arthur Ibbetson; *Editor*: Russell Lloyd; *Cast*: *NANCY KWAN
(MARJORIE LEE)*; Terry-Thomas (Godfrey Deane); Jimmy Logan (Craig);

Bud Flanagan (Sgt. Bletch); Gladys Morgan (Mrs. Tovey); Betty Marsden (Mavis Cook); Paul Whitsun Jones (Tiny Hearst); Donald Churchill (Andy).

Marjorie Lee is engaged to marry Andy but decides to have a final fling before the wedding. She attends an office party with the intention of being seduced. When her boss makes a pass at her, she begins to have doubts, but continues having fun at the party without sex. She is finally reunited with Andy.

THE WILD HEART [See GONE TO EARTH]

THE WILD NORTH   Native American--Chippewa   1952/Western

MGM; 97 min.; *Producer*: Steven Ames; *Director*: Andrew Marton; *play*: Frank Fenton; *Music*: Bronislau Kaper; *Camera*: Robert Surtees; *Editor*: John Dunning; *Cast*: Stewart Granger (Jules Vincent); *CYD CHARISSE (INDIAN GIRL)*; Wendell Corey (Constable Pedley); Morgan Faley (Father Simon); J.M. Kerrigan (Callahan); Howard Petrie (Brody); Housley Stevenson (Old Man); Lewis Martin (Sergeant); John War Eagle (Indian Chief); Clancy Cooper (Sloan); Ray Teal (Ruger).

The Indian Girl is a singer in a saloon. She returns home with **Jules Vincent. After the death of a man they were traveling with,** he flees north, leaving her behind to take care of his home until he returns.

THE WIND CANNOT READ   Japanese   1958/Drama

Rank; 115 min.; *Producers*: Betty E. Box/Ralph Thomas; *Director*: Ralph Thomas; *Screenplay*: Richard Mason; *Music*: Angelo Lavagnino; *Camera*: Ernest Steward; *Editor*: Frederick Wilson; *Cast*: Dick Borgarde (Flt. Lt. Michael Quinn); *YOKO TANI (SUZUKI SAN)*; Ronald Lewis (Officer Peter Munroe); Anthony Bushnell (Brigadier); Henry Okawa (Lt. Nakamura); Marn Maitland (Bahadur); Michael Medwin (Officer Lamb); Richard Leech (Hobson).

Suzuki San teaches Japanese to American flyer Michael Quinn. They fall in love and marry. He goes off to battle and is taken prisoner. Escaping he returns to Suzuki who is dying following neurosurgery.

WINDWALKER   Native American--Cheyenne   1980/Western

Pacific International Enterprises; 106 min.; *Producers*: Arthur R. Dubs/Thomas E. Ballard; *Director*: Kieth Merrill; *Screenplay*: Ray Goldrup; *Music*: Merrill Jensen; *Camera*: Reed Smoot; *Editor*: Janice Hampton/Peter L. McCrea/Stephen L. Johnson; *Cast*: Trevor Howard (Windwalker); Nick Ramus (Smiling Wolf/Twin Brother); James Remar (Young Windwalker); *SERENE HEDIN (TASHINA)*; *Dusty Iron Wing McCrea (Dancing Moon)*; *Silvana Gallardo (Little Feather)*; *Fredelia Smith*

(Tashina's Mother); Billy Drago (Crow Scout); Rudy Diaz (Crow Eyes); Harold Goss (Coyote/Crow Hair); Roy J. Cohoe (Wounded Crow); Emerson John (Spotted Deer); Jason Stevens (Horse That Follows).

An unusual, positive film about Native Americans, but lacking in the portrayal of women. Tashina, the major woman character, is killed early in the film. The other women do show some spunk, especially when one is attacked by a potential rapist and she beats him senseless.

WINGS OF THE HAWK   Mexican   1953/Adventure

Universal; 81 min.; *Producer*: Aaron Rosenberg; *Director*: Budd Boetticher; *Screenplay*: James E. Moser; *Music*: Frank Skinner; *Camera*: Clifford Stine; *Editor*: Russell Schoengarth; *Cast*: Van Heflin (Irish Gallagher); *JULIA ADAMS (RAQUEL)*; Rodolfo Acosta (Arturo); George Dolenz (Colonel Ruiz); Pedro Gonzales (Tomas); Antonio Moreno (Father Perez); Noah Beery, Jr. (Orozco); Paul Fierro (Carlos); *Abbe Lane (Elena)*; *Nancy Westbrook (Lita)*; Ricardo Acosta (Arturo).

Raquel is a Mexican bandit/revolutionary fighting injsutice toward her people. She and Irish Gallagher become romantically involved and she tries to enlist his help in fighting the forces of evil. Raquel is an interesting character, dedicated to her cause and willing to die for it.

WINGS OF THE MORNING   Gypsy   1937/Comedy

20th Century-Fox; 87 min.; *Producer*: Robert X. Kane; *Director*: Harold Schuster; *Screenplay*: Tom Geraghty; *Music*: Arthur Benjamin; *Camera*: Henry Imus/Jack Cardiff; *Cast*: *ANNABELLA (MARIE)*; Henry Fonda (Kerry); John McCormack; Leslie Banks (Lord Clontarf); D.J. Williams (Mairik); Philip Sydney Frost (Valentine); Stewart Rome (Sir Valentine); *Irene Vanbrugh (Marie)*; Harry Tate (Paddy); Helen Haye (Jenepher); Teddy Underdown (Don Diego); Mark Daly (Jimmy); Sam Livesey (Angelo).

In the prologue, Marie marries a wealthy Irishman, Lord Clontarf. She is scorned by his family and when he dies accidentally she returns to her own people. The story then skips to Marie's granddaughter, who is disguised as a boy. She meets Kerry, a member of the family that rejected her grandmother. When Kerry discovers the Marie is a woman they fall in love. The remainder of the story focuses on their race horse winning the grand derby.

WINTERHAWK   Native American--Blackfoot   1976/Western

Howco International Pictures; 98 min.; *Producer/Director/Screenplay*: Charles B. Pierce; *Music*: Lee Holdridge; *Camera*: Jim Roberson; *Editor*: Tom Boutross; *Cast*: Michael Dante (Winterhawk); Leif Erickson (Elkhorn Guthrie); Woody Strode (Big Rude); Denver Pyle (Arkansas); *SACHEEN LITTLEFEATHER (PALE FLOWER)*; Elisha Cook, Jr. (Will Finley); L.Q. Jones (Gates); Arthur Hunnicutt (McCluskey); Dawn Wells

(Clayanna); Chuck Pierce, Jr. (Cotton); Dennis Fimple (Scobie); Seamon Glass (Big Smith); Jimmy Glen (Little Smith); Gilbert Lucero (Crow); Ace Powell (Red Calf).

Pale Flower is the wife of Elkhorn Guthrie who is helping Chief Winterhawk fight a smallpox epidemic. While Guthrie is away from home two men come to his cabin and rape and murder Pale Flower. They steal furs bearing her special brand. This brand helps Elkhorn track down the rapists/murderers and bring them to justice.

THE WIZ   Black   1978/Musical

Motown-Universal; 133 min.; *Producer*: Rob Cohen; *Director*: Sidney Lumet; *Screenplay*: Joel Schumacher; *Music*: Quincy Jones; *Camera*: Oswald Morris; *Editor*: Dede Allen; *Cast*: *DIANA ROSS (DOROTHY)*; Michael Jackson (Scarecrow); Nipsey Russell (Tinman); *Lena Horne (Glinda the Good)*; Richard Pryor (The Wiz); Ted Ross (Lion); *Mabel King (Evillene)*; *Theresa Merritt (Aunt Em)*; *Thelma Carpenter (Miss One)*.

A Black musical version of THE WIZARD OF OZ. This time Dorothy is a Harlem schoolteacher transported to magical Oz.

THE WIZARD OF BAGDAD   Arabian Nights   1961/Fantasy

20th Century-Fox; 92 min.; *Producer*: Sam Katzman; *Director*: George Sherman; *Screenplay*: Jesse L. Lasky, Jr./Pat Silver; *Music*: David Saxon; *Camera*: Ellis W. Carter; *Editor*: Saul A. Goodkind; *Cast*: Dick Shawn (Genie Ali Mahmud); *DIANE BAKER (PRINCESS YASEMEEN)*; Barry Coe (Prince Husan); John Van Dreelan (Jullnar); Robert F. Simon (Shamadin); Vaughn Taylor (Norodeen); Michael David (Meroki); Stanley Adams (Kuetch); William Edmonson (Asmodeus); *Leslie Wenner (Yasemeen as a child)*; Michael Burns (Young Prince Husan); Don Beddoe (Raschid); *Kim Hamilton (Teegra)*.

Alcoholic genie Ali Mahmud is assigned to ensure that Princess Yasemeen and Prince Husan marry. While Ali is intoxicated, the evil Jullnar takes over, planning to marry Yasemeen himself and kill Husan. Husan escapes to the desert and becomes leader of desert warriors. After a few years Hussan, the warriors, and Ali return to destroy Jullnar. Husan and Yasemeen marry.

WOLF CALL   Native American   1939/Western

Monogram; 70 min.; *Producer*: Paul Malvern; *Director*: George Waggner; *Screenplay*: Joseph West; *Camera*: Fred Jackman; *Editor*: Carl Pierson; *Cast*: John Carroll (Michael Vance); *MOVITA (TOWANAH)*; Peter George Lynn (Father Devliln); Guy Usher (Vance, Sr.); Holmes Herbert (Winton); Polly Ann Young (Natalie); George Cleveland (Dr. MacTavish); John Kelly (Bull Nelson); Wheeler Oakman (Carson); John Sheehan (Grogan); Charles Irwin (Police Sgt.).

Michael Vance, sent to report on his father's radium mine in the north country, finds love with Towanah. He also discovers the treachery of Carson, who is trying to sell the mine to a conglomerate. Vance is helped by Smokey, a dog who lives among the wolves, to overcome Carson's schemes.

THE WOLF MAN   Gypsy   1941/Thriller

Universal; 71 min.; *Producer/Director*: George Waggner; *Screenplay*: Curtis Siodmak; *Camera*: Joe Valentine; *Editor*: Ted Kent; *Cast*: Claude Rains (Sir John Talbott); Warren William (Dr. Lloyd); Lon Chaney, Jr. (Lawrence (The Wolf Man) Talbott); Ralph Bellaby (Cpt. Paul Montford); *MARIA OUSPENSKAYA (MALEVA)*; Bela Lugosi (Bela); Patric Knowles (Frank Andrews); Forrester Harvey (Twiddle); Fay Helm (Jenny); Evelyn Ankers (Gwenn Conliffe); J.M. Kerrigan (Charles Conliffe).

Maleva, the mother of a fortune teller, understands Larry Talbott's plight because it was her werewolf son who bit Larry, thus causing him to become a werewolf. Maleva helps Larry throughout the film.

WOMAN HUNT   Chinese   1962/Mystery

20th Century-Fox; 60 min.; *Producer/Director*: Maury Dexter; *Screenplay*: Edward J. Lasko/Russ Bender; *Music*: Henry Vars; *Camera*: Floyd Crosby; *Editors*; Jodie Copelan/Carl Pierson; *Cast*: Steven Piccaro (Hal Weston); *LISA LU (LI SHENG)*; Barry Kroeger (Petrie/Osgood); Bob Okazaki (Dr. Sheng); Ann Carroll (Janet Oberon); Tom Daly (Mr. Davalos); Ivan Bonar (Jacobs).

Hal Weston enlists the aid of Li Sheng in finding his ex-wife. He discovers that Nora was murdered and discovers that her murderer was Petrie. Li Sheng's father, Dr. Sheng, did plastic surgery on Petrie to make him look like Osgood--who in turn kills Petrie. Osgood is killed in a fight with Weston. Weston and Li Sheng become romantically involved.

A WOMAN'S DEVOTION   Mexican   1956/Mystery

Republic; 88 min.; *Producer*: John Bash; *Director*: Paul Henreid; *Screenplay*: Robert Hill; *Music*: Les Baxter; *Camera*: Jorge Stahl, Jr.; *Editor*: Richard L. Van Enger; *Cast*: Ralph Meeker (Trevor Stevenson); Janice Rule (Stella); Paul Henreid (Capt. Henrique Monteros); *ROSENDA MONTEROS (MARIA)*; *Fanny Schiller (Senora Reidl)*; Jose Torvay (Gomez); Yerye Beirute (Amigo Herrera); Tony Carbajal (Sergeant); Jamie Gonzalez (Roberto); Carlos Requelme (Chief of Police).

Maria is a maid who is murdered.

WOMEN IN THE NIGHT   Chinese   1948/Drama

Film Classics; 90 min.; *Producer*: Lewis K. Ansell; *Director*: William
Rowland; *Screenplay*: Robert S. Clair/Edwin Westry; *Editor*: Dan Milner;
Cast: Tala Birell (Yvette Aubert); William Henry (Major Van Arnheim);
Richard Loo (Col. Von Meyer); Bernadine Hayes (Frau Thaler); *FRANCES
CHUNG (LI LING)*; Benson Fong (Chang); Kathy Frye (Helen James); Helen
Mowery (Sheila Hallett); Philip Ahn (Prof. Kunioshi); Iris Flores
(Maria Gonzales).

The story is based on actual accounts of women who became prisoners of the Nazis in Shanghai before the fall of Japan. The women
are forced to entertain Nazi and Japanese dignitaries in the officers
club but they also manage to work for the Chinese underground. They
are finally saved by Major Van Arnheim.

WONDER BAR   Latin American   1934/Musical

Warner Brothers; 84 min.; *Producer*: Robert Lord; *Director*: Lloyd
Bacon; *Screenplay*: Earl Baldwin; *Music*: Leo F. Forbstein; *Camera*:
Sol Polito; *Editor*: George Amy; *Cast*: Al Jolson (Al Wonder); *DOLORES
DEL RIO (INEZ)*; Ricardo Cortez (Harry); Kay Francis (Liane Renaud);
Dick Powell (Tommy); Guy B. Kibbee (Henry Simpson); Hugh Herbert
(Corey Pratt); Robert Barrat (Capt. Von Ferring); Ruth Donnelly (Ella
Simpson).

Inez is the main attraction in Al Wonder's nightclub. She is
loved by Al and bandleader Tommy, but she loves her dancing partner
Harry who is loved by Liane Renaud.

THE WORLD OF SUZIE WONG   Chinese   1960/Drama

Paramount; 129 min.; *Producer*: Ray Stark; *Director*: Richard Quine;
Screenplay: John Patrick; *Music*: George Duning; *Camera*: Geoffrey
Unsworth; *Editor*: Bert Bates; *Cast*: William Holden (Robert Lomax);
NANCY KWAN (SUZIE WONG); Sylvia Sims (Kay); Michael Wilding (Ben);
Laurence Naismith (O'Neill); *Jacqui Chan (Gwenny Lee)*; Andy Ho (Ah
Tong); Bernard Cribbins (Otis); *Yvonne Shima (Minnie Ho)*; *Lier Hwang
(Wednesday Lu)*; Lionel Blair (Dancing Sailor).

Suzie Wong is a prostitute in Hong Kong who falls in love with
American artist Robert Lomax. At first Robert is interested in Suzie
only as a model but he eventually falls in love with her. In spite
of the racist attitudes of his white friends he decides to marry
Suzie.

THE WRATH OF GOD   Central American Indian   1972/Western

MGM; 111 min.; *Director/Screenplay*: Ralph Nelson; *Music*: Lalo
Schifrin; *Camera*: Alex Phillips, Jr.; *Editors*: J. Terry Williams/
Richard Bracken/Albert Wilson; *Cast*: Robert Mitchum (Van Horn); Frank
Langella (Tomas De La Plata); *Rita Hayworth (Senora De La Plata)*;

John Colicos (Col. Santilla); Victor Buono (Jennings); Ken Hutchison (Emmet Keogh); *PAULA PRITCHETT (CHELA)*; Gregory Sierra (Jurado); Frank Ramirez (Moreno); Enrique Lucero (Nacho); Jorge Russer (Cordona); Chano Urueta (Antonio); Jose Luis Parades (Pablito); *Aurora Clavel (Senora Moreno)*; Victor Eberg (Delgado).

During a revolution in a Central American country, mute Chela is saved by Emmet Keogh from rape. Keogh becomes involved with the deranged Tomas De La Plata and Senora De La Plata, his mother. Tomas is killed by the Senora because his madness has progressed beyond hope. As Keogh is about to be killed Chela regains her voice.

THE WRECKING CREW   Asian   1968/Thriller

Columbia; 105 min.; *Producer*: Irving Allen; *Director*: Phil Karlson; *Screenplay*: William McGivern; *Music*: Hugo Montenegro; *Camera*: Sam Leavitt; *Editor*: Maury Winetrobe; *Cast*: Dean Martin (Matt Helm); Elke Sommer (Linka Karensky); Sharon Tate (Freya Carlson); *NANCY KWAN (YU-RANG)*; Nigel Green (Count Massimo Contini); Tina Louise (Lola Medina); John Larch (MacDonald); John Brascia (Karl); Weaver Levy (Kim); Wilhelm von Homburg (Gregory); Bill Saito (Ching); Fuji (Toki); Pepper Martin (Frankie).

Yu-Rang is out to trap secret agent Matt Helm and kill him. Matt is saved by a timely interruption and Yu-Rang is killed in an explosion.

THE YAKUZA   Japanese   1975/Thriller

Warner Brothers; 112 min.; *Producer/Director*: Sidney Pollack; *Screenplay*: Paul Schrader/Robert Towne; *Music*: Dave Grusin; *Camera*: Okazaki Kozo; *Editor*: Frederic Steinkamp; *Cast*: Robert Mitchum (Harry Kilmer); Takakura (Ken); Brian Keith (George Tanner); Herb Edelman (Wheat); Richard Jordan (Dusty); *KISHI KEIKO (EIKO)*; Okada Eiji (Tono); James Shiqeta (Goro); Kyosuke Mashida (Kato).

During World War II, Harry Kilmer became responsible for Eiko and gave her financial support she needed to open a business and help her family. Kilmer returns to Japan to eliminate the Yakuza (Japanese gangsters) and is reunited with Eiko.

YANKEE DON   Mexican   1931/Western

Talmadge/Capitol; 60 min.; *Producer*: Richard Talmadge; *Director*: Noel Mason; *Screenplay*: Frances Jackson; *Cast*: Richard Talmadge; *LUPITA TOVAR*; Julian Rivero; Sam Appel; Wayne Whitman; Alma Reat; Victor Stanford. [Character names not available.]

Richard Talmadge becomes involved with Lupita Tovar whose father's ranch is being bothered by outlaws.

THE YEAR OF THE HORSE   Chinese   1966/Drama

Myriad Productions; 58 min.; *Producers*: Mildred Dienstag/Therese
Orkin; *Director/Screenplay*: Irving Sunasky; *Camera*: Morton L. Heilig;
Cast: Gabriel Mason (Michael Farrow); Bradley Joe (Richard Han, Jr.);
Alvin Lum (Richard Han, Sr.); *MARY MON TOY (MRS. RICHARD HAN, SR.)*;
Lorraine Wong (Tina Han); Mr. Thom, Mrs. Thom (Grandparents); *Mary
Hui (Stewardess)*; Peter Wong (Bachelor); Dick Hanover (Veterinarian).

Richard Han, Jr. befriends a hansom cab driver, Michael Farrow,
and his horse, Molly. When Molly dies Michael becomes extremely
despondent. His parents and other residents of Chinatown raise money
to buy him another horse.

THE YELLOW TOMAHAWK   Native American   1954/Western

United Artists; 82 min.; *Producer*: Howard W. Koch; *Director*: Lesley
Selander; *Screenplay*: Richard Alan Simons; *Music*: Les Baxter; *Camera*:
Gordon Avil; *Editor*: John F. Schreyer; *Cast*: Rory Calhoun (Adam);
Peggie Castle (Katherine); Noah Beery (Tonio); Warner Anderson (Major
Ives); Peter Graves (Sawyer); Lee Van Cleef (Fire Knife); Dan Riss
(Sgt. Bandini); *RITA MORENO (HONEY BEAR)*; Walter Reed (Keats); Adam
Williams (Corp. Maddock); Ned Glass (Willy).

Honey Bear is Tonio's girlfriend.

YELLOWSTONE KELLY   Native American--Arapaho   1959/Western

Warner Brothers; 91 min.; *Director*: Gordon Douglas; *Screenplay*: Burt
Kennedy; *Music*: Howard Jackson; *Camera*: Carl Guthrie; *Editor*: William
Ziegler; *Cast*: Clint Walker (Yellowstone Kelly); Edward Byrnes (Anse
Harper); John Russell (Chief Gall); Ray Danton (Sayapi); *ANDRA
MARTIN (WAHLEEAH)*; Claude Akins (Sergeant); Rhodes Reason (Major
Towns); Gary Vinson (Lieutenant); Warren Oates (Corporal).

Sioux Indians capture Yellowstone Kelly and Anse Harper. Kelly
must save the life of a female captive, Wahleeah, or die. She lives,
and Kelly and Harper leave the camp. Soon Wahleeah escapes by
stealing a horse and arrives at Kelly's place. She is still very
sick, so when the Sioux find her they allow her to remain until she
is well. However, she wants to return to her Arapaho people. Kelly
does not want to help her, but Harper, who has fallen in love with
her, does. He is killed in the process. In the meantime she and
Kelly fall in love. Wahleeah saves Kelly's life during a confrontation with the Sioux, after which they ride off into the mountains
together. [This film makes a point of using the word "squaw" and the
derogatory connotations that the word has in referring to Inidan
women.]

YOLANDA AND THE THIEF   Latin American   1945/Musical

MGM; 108 min.; *Producer*: Arthur Freed; *Director*: Vincent Minnelli;

Screenplay: Irving Brecher; *Camera*: Charles Rosher; *Editor*: George White; *Cast*: Fred Astaire (Johnny Parkson Riggs); *LUCILLE BREMER (YOLANDA AQUAVIVA)*; Frank Morgan (Victor Budlow Trout); *Mildred Natwick (Amarilla Aquaviva)*.

Heiress Yolanda Aquaviva becomes the target for con men Johnny Parkson Riggs and Victor Budlow Trout. Riggs poses as Yolanda's guardian angel in order to steal her fortune. However, Riggs falls in love with Yolanda and soon confesses that he was about to swindle her. After an initial period of rejection Yolanda admits her love and her Aunt Amarilla approves of Riggs a a suitable husband.

YOU CAN'T WIN THEM ALL   Turkish   1970/Adventure

Columbia; 97 min.; *Producer*: Gene Corman; *Director*: Peter Collinson; *Screenplay*: Leo V. Gordon; *Music*: Herbert Rehbein; *Camera*: Ken Higgins; *Editor*: Raymond Poulton; *Cast*: Tony Curtis (Adam Dyer); Charles Bronson (Josh Corey); *MICHELE MERCIER (AILA)*; Gregoire Aslan (Osman Bey); Fikret Hakan (Col. Elei); Salih Guney (Capt. Enver); Patrick Magee (General).

Aila is the companion to the daughters of Turkish governor Osman Bey—who has hired two mercenaries, Josh Corey and Adam Dyer, to accompany them to the safety of Samyina. Soon Aila and Josha and Adam join forces to steal jewels which are also on the excursion. Revolutionaries overtake the caravan and the jewels are lost. The three manage to trade a valuable copy of the *Koran* for freedom and continue on their way.

YOU ONLY LIVE TWICE   Asian   1967/Thriller

United Artists; 116 min.; *Producers*: Harry Saltzman/Albert R. Broccoli; *Director*: Lewis Gilbert; *Screenplay*: Roald Dahl; *Music*: John Barry; *Camera*: Freddie Young; *Editor*: Thelma Connell; *Cast*: Sean Connery (James Bond); Akiko Wakabayashi (Aki); Tetsuro Tamba (Tiger Tanaka); *MIE HAMA (KISSY SUZUKI)*; Teru Shimada (Osato); Karin Dor (Helga Brandt); Lois Maxwell (Miss Moneypenney); Desmond Llewelyn (Q); Charles Gray (Henderson); *Tsai Chin (Chinese Girl)*; Bernard Lee (M); Donald Pleasence (Blofeld).

In this James Bond film, Bond marries Kissy Suzuki, a member of the Japanese secret service. Of course the marriage is a pretense to help them capture or destroy the villians, which they do before making their escape.

YOU WERE NEVER LOVELIER   Latin American   1942/Musical

Columbia; 97 min.; *Producer*: Louis F. Edelman; *Director*: William A. Seiter; *Screenplay*: Delmar Daves/Michael Fessler/Ernest Pagano; *Music*: Leigh Harline; *Camera*: Ted Tetzlaff; *Editor*: William Lyon; *Cast*: Fred Astaire (Robert Davis); *RITA HAYWORTH (MARIA ACUNA)*; Adolphe Menjou (Edouardo Acuna); *Leslie Brooks (Cecy Acuna)*; *Adele*

Mara (Lita Acuna); Xavier Cugat; *Isabel Elsom (Maria Elsom)*; Gus
Schilling (Fernando); *Barbara Brown (Delfina Acuna)*; Larry Parks
(Tony); *Lina Romay (Band Singer)*.

Maria Acuna has no interest in romance, which distresses her
lovesick younger sisters who cannot marry until Maria is married.
Her father decides to pretend that she has a secret admirer who is
sending her letters and flowers. Robert Davis delivers one of the
poems so she assumes that he is her secret admirer. To prevent Maria
from discovering the truth, her father hires Robert to court his
daughter with the plan that eventually Robert will prove himself to
be a scoundrel. Of course Maria and Robert fall in love and Dad
soon finds that he approves of Robert as a suitable husband for his
daughter.

YOUNGBLOOD   Black   1978/Drama

American International; 90 min.; *Producers*: Nick Grillo/Alan Riche;
Director: Noel Nosseck; *Screenplay*: Paul Carter Harrison; *Camera*:
Robbie Greenberg; *Editor*: Frank Morriss; *Cast*: Lawrence-Hilton Jacobs
(Rommel); Bryan O'Dell (Youngblood); *REN WOODS (SYBIL)*; Tony Allen
(Hustler); Vince Cannon (Corelli); Art Evans (Junkie); Jeff Hollis
(Basketball Pusher); Dave Pendleton (Reggie); Ron Trice (Bummie);
Sheila Wilis (Joan).

Sybil is the girlfriend of would-be streetgang member Youngblood.
Sybil is also a heroin addict. Joan is the wife of Vietnam veteran
Rommel, who teaches Youngblood the ropes of streetgang life.

ZOOT SUIT   Mexican   1982/Musical Drama

Universal; 103 min.; *Producer*: Peter Burrell; *Director/Screenplay*:
Luis Valdez; *Music*: Daniel Valdez/Shorty Rogers; *Camera*: David Meyers;
Editor: Jacqueline Cambas; *Cast*: Daniel Valdez (Henry Reyna); Edward
James Olmos (El Pachuco); Charles Aidman (George); Tyne Daly (Alice);
John Anderson (Judge); Abel Franco (Enrique); Mike Gomez (Joey);
ALMA ROSE MARTINEZ (LUPE); Frank McCarthy (Press); *Lupe Ontiveros
(Dolores)*; Ed Peck (Lt. Edwards); Robert Phalen (D.A.); Tony Plana
(Rudy); *Rose Portillo (Della)*; Marco Rodriguez (Smiley); Kelly Ward
(Tommy).

This film is based on the zoot suit riots in 1942 Los Angeles
and an unsolved murder. Henry Reyna and his friends are arrested
for the murder. Henry's girlfriend, Lupe, speaks out in his defense
and is sent to a reformatory. After an unfair trial, Henry is sent
to prison. Through the diligence of newspaperwoman Alice, Henry is
acquitted and he and Lupe are reunited.

ZORRO THE GAY BLADE   Mexican   1981/Comedy

20th Century-Fox; 93 min.; *Producers*: George Hamilton/C.O. Erickson;

Director: Peter Medak; *Screenplay*: Hal Dresner; *Camera*: John A. Alonzo; *Editor*: Hillary Jane Kranze; *Cast*: George Hamilton (Don Diego Vega/Bunny Wigglesworth); Lauren Hutton (Charlotte Taylor Wilson); *BRENDA VACCARO (FLORINDA)*; Ron Leibman (Esteban); Donovan Scott (Paco); James Booth (Velasquez); *Helen Burns (Consuela)*; Clive Revill (Garcia); *Carolyn Seymour (Dolores)*; Eduardo Alcaraz (Don Jose).

Florinda, the childhood sweetheart of Don Diego Vega, is now married to the evil Esteban. Don Diego and his twin brother, Bunny, alternate impersonating the legendary Zorro (who was their father). They steal a valuable diamond necklace from Florinda in order to give the money to the poor.

Natalie Wood, *West Side Story* (UA, 1961)

ACTRESS INDEX

Note: This index includes only actresses playing minority roles.

Abbott, Diahnne
THE KING OF COMEDY

Acquanetta
ARABIAN NIGHTS
CAPTIVE WILD WOMAN
JUNGLE WOMAN
RHYTHM OF THE ISLANDS
TARZAN AND THE LEOPARD WOMAN

Adams, Brooke
CUBA

Adams, Julia
WINGS OF THE HAWK

Adrian, Jane
SNOW DOG

Princess Ah-Tee-Ha
CIRCLE OF DEATH

Alba, Maria
MR. ROBINSON CRUSOE
RETURN OF CHANDU
WEST OF THE PECOS

Alberghetti, Anna Maria
DUEL AT APACHE WELLS
THE LAST COMMAND

Aldana, Vida
BEAUTY AND THE BANDIT

Allen, Debbie
FAME
RAGTIME

Allen, Jonelle
COME BACK CHARLESTON BLUE
THE RIVER NIGER

Anderson, Esther
TWO GENTLEMEN SHARING
A WARM DECEMBER

Anderson, Dame Judith
A MAN CALLED HORSE

Ando, Eiko
THE BARBARIAN AND THE GEISHA

Andress, Ursula
SHE

Andriane, Marayat
THE SAND PEBBLES

Annabella
WINGS OF THE MORNING

Appleby, Dorothy
KING OF THE WILD HORSES

Archuletta, Beulah
FOXFIRE
THE SEARCHERS

Armida
BORDER CAFE
BORDER ROMANCE
THE GAY AMIGO
LA CONGA NIGHTS
THE MARINES ARE COMING
ON THE BORDER
ROOTIN' TOOTIN' RHYTHM
SOUTH OF TAHITI
SOUTH OF THE RIO GRANDE
UNDER A TEXAS MOON

Astor, Mary
THE LASH

Attaway, Ruth
PORGY AND BESS
TERROR IN THE ICTY

Aubert, Lenore
ACTION IN ARABIA

Austin, Charlotte
PAWNEE

Bailey, Pearl
ALL THE FINE YOUNG CANNIBALS
CARMEN JONES
THE LANDLORD
NORMAN...IS THAT YOU?
PORGY AND BESS
THAT CERTAIN FEELING

Baker, Diane
THE WIZARD OF BAGDAD

Ball Lucille
THE MAGIC CARPET

Ball Suzan
CHIEF CRAZY HORSE
EAST OF SUMATRA
WAR ARROW

Bancroft, Anne
A LIFE IN THE BALANCE
WALK THE PROUD LAND

Bari, Lynn
THE BRIDGE OF SAN LUIS REY

Baron, Lita
BOMBA ON PANTHER ISLAND
THE BROKEN STAR
JUNGLE JIM
SAVAGE DRUMS

Barrett, Caroline
DREAMS OF GLASS

Barrie, Mona
STORM OVER THE ANDES

Baxter, Anne
WALK ON THE WILD SIDE

Beavers, Louise
ALL THE FINE YOUNG CANNIBALS

HOLIDAY INN
IMITATION OF LIFE (1938)
THE JACKIE ROBINSON STORY
MR. BLANDINGS BUILDS HIS DREAM HOUSE
MY BLUE HEAVEN
RAINBOW ON THE RIVER
TAMMY AND THE BACHELOR
WEST OF THE PECOS

Bedelia, Bonnie
THE STRANGE VENGEANCE OF ROSALIE

Bedford, Barbara
THE LASH

Bergman, Ingrid
SARATOGA TRUNK

Bey, Marki
THE LANDLORD

Blackman, Joan
BLUE HAWAII

Blanchard, Mari
SON OF SINBAD
THE VEILS OF BAGDAD

Blyth, Ann
THE GOLDEN HORDE
KISMET (1955)

Bolton, Delle
JEREMIAH JOHNSON

Booth, Adrian
ROCK ISLAND TRAIL
SPOILERS OF THE NORTH

Bow, Clara
CALL HER SAVAGE

Bradna, Olympe
SOUTH OF PAGO-PAGO

Bremer, Lucille
YOLANDA AND THE THIEF

Britton, Barbara
BANDIT QUEEN

Bron, Eleanor
HELP!

Brown, Vanessa
THE FIGHTER

Bruhl, Heidi
CAPTAIN SINBAD

Brunetti, Argentina
THE APPALOOSA
BROKEN ARROW
THE LAWLESS
MAN-EATER OF KUMAON
SAN ANTONE
TROPIC ZONE

Bucella, Grazia
VILLA RIDES

Bujold, Genevieve
ALEX AND THE GYPSY

Burgess, Dorothy
BLACK MOON

Burke, Kathleen
ISLAND OF LOST SOULS

Cabot, Susan
BATTLE AT APACHE PASS
FLAME OF ARABY
FORT MASSACRE
ON THE ISLE OF SAMOA
SURRENDER-HELL
TOMAHAWK

Caine, Sharika
THE MAN WHO WOULD BE KING

Callejo, Cecila
THE CISCO KID RETURNS
THE FALCON IN MEXICO
OUTLAW EXPRESS
THE RENEGADE RANGER

Calvert, Phyllis
MADONNA OF THE SEVEN MOONS

Camelia
CAIRO ROAD

Cansino, Carmelia
THE MASKED RIDER

Cansino, Rita
See Hayworth, Rita

Capri, Ahna
ENTER THE DRAGON

Capucine
ARABIAN ADVENTURE
7TH DAWN

Cara, Irene
AARON LOVES ANGELA
FAME
SPARKLE

Cardenas, Elsa
FUN IN ACAPULCO
GIANT

Cardinale, Claudia
LOST COMMAND
THE PROFESSIONALS

Carey, Michele
DIRTY DINGUS MAGEE

Carr, Betty
CANCEL MY RESERVATION

Carrera, Barbara
THE ISLAND OF DR. MOREAU
LONE WOLF McQUADE
THE MASTER GUNFIGHTER

Carrilo, Elpidia
BEYOND THE LIMIT
THE BORDER

Carroll, Diahann
CARMEN JONES
CLAUDINE
HURRY SUNDOWN
PARIS BLUES
PORGY AND BESS
THE SPLIT

Carroll, Vinette
ONE POTATO, TWO POTATO

Carroll, Virginia
THE MASKED RIDER

Cash, Rosalind
AMAZING GRACE
CORNBREAD, EARL AND ME

HICKEY & BOGGS
MELINDA
THE NEW CENTURIONS
THE OMEGA MAN

Castaneda, Movita
APACHE AMBUSH
DREAM WIFE
THE GIRL FROM RIO
THE HURRICANE
MUTINY ON THE BOUNTY (1935)
THE MYSTERIOUS DESPERADO
PARADISE ISLE
ROSE OF THE RIO GRANDE
SADDLE LEGION
WOLF CALL

Castelli, Delores
TRAIL TO MEXICO

Castle, Dolores
WEST TO GLORY

Castle, Peggie
HAREM GIRL

Celli, Teresa
BORDER INCIDENT
CRISIS

Chaplin, Geraldine
THE HAWAIIANS

Charisse, Cyd
FIESTA
MARK OF THE RENEGADE
SOMBRERO
THE WILD NORTH

Charlita
BELA LUGOSI MEETS A BROOKLYN
     GORILLA
THE BRAVE BULLS
THE NAKED DAWN

Chen, Tina
ALICE'S RESTAURANT
THE HAWAIIANS

Chen, Tsai
THE BRIDES OF FU MANCHU
THE FACE OF FU MANCHU
THE VENGEANCE OF FU MANCHU
THE VIRGIN SOLDIERS
YOU ONLY LIVE TWICE

Chiquita
JAGUAR

Christian, Linda
TARZAN AND THE MERMAIDS

Chung, Frances
WOMEN IN THE NIGHT

Clark, Mamo
BOOLOO
HAWAII CALLS
THE HURRICANE
MUTINY ON THE BOUNTY (1935)

Clark, Marlene
GANJA AND HESS

Collins, Joan
THE BRAVADOS
ISLAND IN THE SUN

Colon, Miriam
THE APPALOOSA
HARBOR LIGHTS
THUNDER ISLAND

Comer, Anjanette
THE APPALOOSA

Compana, Nina
IT HAPPENED OUT WEST

Corday, Mara
THE BLACK SCORPION
FOXFIRE
THE QUIET GUN
RAW EDGE

Corio, Ann
JUNGLE SIREN

Cortesa, Valentina
MALAYA

Costello, Diosa
THE BULLFIGHTERS

Crain, Jeanne
PINKY

Crawford, Kathryn
SENOR AMERICANO

Cristal, Linda
COMANCHE
CRY TOUGH
THE LAST OF THE FAST GUNS

Dahl, Arlene
DESERT LEGION
THE DIAMOND QUEEN

Dandridge, Dorothy
BAHAMA PASSAGE
BRIGHT ROAD
CARMEN JONES
THE DECKS RAN RED
DRUMS OF THE CONGO
ISLAND IN THE SUN
PORGY AND BESS
TARZAN'S PERIL

Darcel, Denise
TARZAN AND THE SLAVE GIRL

Darnell, Linda
ANNA AND THE KING OF SIAM
BUFFALO BILL
THE MARK OF ZORRO
MY DARLING CLEMENTINE

Davi, Jana
FORT BOWIE
GUN FEVER
GUNMEN FROM LAREDO

Davis, Cynthia
COOLEY HIGH

Davis, Jean
VOODOO WOMAN

Dean, Jeanne
VOODOO TIGER

Dean, Margia
AMBUSH AT CIMARRON PASS
RIMFIRE

DeCamp, Rosemary
JUNGLE BOOK

DeCarlo, Yvonne
BAND OF ANGELS
BLACK BART
BORDER RIVER

CASBAH
THE DESERT HAWK
HOTEL SAHARA
HURRICANE SMITH
PASSION
SLAVE GIRL
SOMBRERO
SONG OF SCHEHERAZADE

Dee, Ruby
THE BALCONY
BLACK GIRL
BUCK AND THE PREACHER
CAT PEOPLE
COUNTDOWN AT KUSINI
EDGE OF THE CITY
GONE ARE THE DAYS
THE INCIDENT
THE JACKIE ROBINSON STORY
NO WAY OUT
A RAISIN IN THE SUN
TAKE A GIANT STEP
UPTIGHT
THE VIRGIN ISLAND

Del Ray, Pilar
MAD ABOUT LOVE

Del Rio, Dolores
BIRD OF PARADISE
CHEYENNE AUTUMN
DEVIL'S PLAYGROUND
FLAMING STAR
FLYING DOWN TO RIO
THE FUGITIVE
GIRL OF THE RIO
I LIVE FOR LOVE
IN CALIENTE
WONDER BAR

Del Rio, Dora
TRAIL TO MEXICO

DeMille, Katherine
ALOMA OF THE SOUTH SEAS
BLACK GOLD
THE CALIFORNIAN
TRUMPET BLOWS
UNCONQUERED
VIVA VILLA

DeSade, Ana
RETURN OF A MAN CALLED HORSE
TRIUMPHS OF A MAN CALLED HORSE

Desni, Tamara
JACK AHOY

Devi, Kamal
GERONIMO

Dhlamini, Ribbon
CRY THE BELOVED COUNTRY

Dickinson, Angie
CHINA GATE

Dietrich, Marlene
GOLDEN EARRINGS
KISMET

Dillard, Mimi
LIVING BETWEEN TWO WORLDS

Dobson, Tamara
CLEOPATRA JONES
CLEOPATRA JONES AND THE CASINO
    OF GOLD
NORMAN...IS THAT YOU?

Domergue, Faith
CULT OF THE COBRA
SANTA FE PASSAGE

Dor, Karin
TOPAZ

Dowling, Doris
SARUMBA

Drake Claudia
INDIAN AGENT
NORTHERN PATROL

Drake, Dona
ALOMA OF THE SOUTH SEAS
DOWN LAREDO WAY
PRINCESS OF THE NILE
ROAD TO MOROCCO
SON OF BELLE STARR

Drake, Frances
TRUMPET BLOWS

Drake, Peggy
THE TUTTLES OF TAHITI

DuBois, Ja'Net
FIVE ON THE BLACK HAND SIDE
A MAN CALLED ADAM

A PIECE OF THE ACTION

DuBois, Marta
BOULEVARD NIGHTS

Dugay, Yvette
CATTLE QUEEN OF MONTANA
DOMINO KID
HIAWATHA

Duna, Steffi
THE DANCING PIRATE
THE GIRL AND THE GAMBLER
THE GIRL FROM HAVANA
HI GAUCHO
LAW OF THE PAMPAS
PHANTOM RAIDERS
RIVER'S END

Duna, Teri
KOREA PATROL

Duncan, Pamela
GUN BATTLE AT MONTEREY

Duprez, June
LITTLE TOKYO, U.S.A.
THIEF OF BAGDAD

Dvorak, Ann
MASSACRE

Eccles, Amy
LITTLE BIG MAN

Elzy, Ruby
EMPEROR JONES

England, Sue
BOMBA AND THE HIDDEN CITY

English, Maria
DESERT SANDS

Evans, Estelle
THE LEARNING TREE

Falana, Lola
THE KLANSMAN
THE LIBERATION OF L.B. JONES
A MAN CALLED ADAM

Falkenburg, Jinx
TAHITI NIGHTS

Ferraday, Lisa
CHINA CORSAIR

Ferreira, Bibi
THE END OF THE RIVER

Ferrer, Lupita
CHILDREN OF SANCHEZ

Field, Shirley Anne
KINGS OF THE SUN

Field, Virginia
THE VEILS OF BAGDAD

Fleming, Rhonda
BACKTRACK
BULLWHIP
LITTLE EGYPT

Flores, Iris
RIDE THE PINK HORSE
SOUTH OF MONTEREY

Forman, Carol
UNDER THE TONTO RIM

Forrest, Sally
SON OF SINBAD

Foster, Gloria
MAN AND BOY
NOTHING BUT A MAN

Fowler, Phyllis
FORT TI

Fraser, Elisabeth
A PATCH OF BLUE

Frazier, Sheila
SUPER FLY
SUPER FLY, TNT

Frederick, Pauline
THANK YOU, MR. MOTO

Funai, Helen
OUR MAN FLINT

Gahva, Marie
CRY BLOOD APACHE

Galli, Rosina
GAUCHOS OF EL DORADO
THE MAD DOCTOR OF MARKET STREET

Gam, Rita
MOHAWK
SAADIA

Garcia, Stella
JOE KIDD
THE LAST MOVIE

Gardner, Ava
BHOWANI JUNCTION
SHOW BOAT

Garland, Judy
THE PIRATE

Gates, Nancy
HELL'S HALF ACRE

Gaubert, Daniele
FLIGHT FROM ASHIYA

Gaynor, Mitzi
DOWN AMONG THE SHELTERING PALMS

Gearson, Valerie
NINE HOURS TO RAMA

Gerry, Toni
OREGON PASSAGE

Gibson, Althea
THE HORSE SOLDIERS

Gifford, Frances
TARZAN TRIUMPHS

Gilbert, Joanne
HURRICANE ISLAND
RIDE OUT FOR REVENGE

Gilbert, Jody
RIDE 'EM COWBOY

Goddard, Paulette
BABES IN BAGDAD
NORTHWEST MOUNTED POLICE
THE TORCH

Goldoni, Lelia
SHADOWS

Grahame, Gloria
PRISONERS OF THE CASBAH

Granada, Maria
THE SAVAGE GUNS
SON OF A GUNFIGHTER

Grant, Kathryn
GUNMAN'S WALK
THE 7TH VOYAGE OF SINBAD

Graves, Teresa
OLD DRACULA

Gray, Carole
DEVIL'S OF DARKNESS

Grayson, Kathryn
THE KISSING BANDIT

Greene, Laura
PUTNEY SWOPE

Grier, Pam
BLACK MAMA, WHITE MAMA
COFFY
COOL BREEZE
DRUM
FOXY BROWN
FRIDAY FOSTER
GREASED LIGHTNING
HIT MAN
SCREAM BLACULA SCREAM
SHEBA BABY

Gur, Alizia
KILL A DRAGON

Gurie, Sigrid
ADVENTURES OF MARCO POLO
SWORD OF THE AVENGER

Guyse, Sheila
MIRACLE IN HARLEM

Gwynne, Anne
WEIRD WOMAN

Hama, Mie
YOU ONLY LIVE TWICE

Harris, Teresa
SMOOTH AS SILK

Hart, Susan
RIDE THE WILD SURF

Harman, Ena
TERMINAL ISLAND

Hassall, Imogen
EL CONDOR
THE LONG DUEL

Hasso, Signe
CRISIS

Hatcher, Mary
HOLIDAY IN HAVANA

Hattie, Hilo
BLUE HAWAII
MA AND PA KETTLE AT WAIKIKI
SONG OF THE ISLANDS
TAHITI NIGHTS

Hayes, Allison
HONG KONG CONFIDENTIAL

Hayes, Helen
THE SON-DAUGHTER

Haynes, Roberta
RETURN TO PARADISE

Hayward, Susan
TULSA

Hayworth (Cansino), Rita
CHARLIE CHAN IN EGYPT
CRIMINALS OF THE AIR
HUMAN CARGO
THE LOVES OF CARMEN
REBELLION
THE RENEGADE RANGER
TROUBLE IN TEXAS
THE WRATH OF GOD
YOU WERE NEVER LOVELIER

Hedin, Serene
WINDWALKER

Hemingway, Mariel
PERSONAL BEST

Henderson, Maye
LIVING BETWEEN TWO WORLDS

Hendrix, Wanda
MY OUTLAW BROTHER
RIDE THE PINK HORSE

Hendry, Gloria
BLACK BELT JONES
BLACK CAESAR
SAVAGE SISTERS

Hepburn, Audrey
GREEN MANSIONS
THE UNFORGIVEN

Hepburn, Katharine
DRAGON SEED
THE LITTLE MINISTER

Hernandez, Teri
THE ADVENTURES OF FRONTIER
    FREMONT

Hershey, Barbara
HEAVEN WITH A GUN

Ho, Linda
CONFESSIONS OF AN OPIUM EATER
DIMENSION 5

Hollmark, Joan
INDIAN PAINT

Horne, Lena
CABIN IN THE SKY
DEATH OF A GUNFIGHTER
STORMY WEATHER
THE WIZ

Hovic, Louise
ALI BABA GOES TO TOWN

Hua, Li Li
CHINA DOLL

Humama, Faten
CAIRO

Isabelita
CLUB HAVANA
PAN AMERICANA

Jergens, Adele
A THOUSAND AND ONE NIGHTS

Jimenez, Soledad
BLACK BART
THE BROKEN WING
CYCLONE RANGER
THE ROBIN HOOD OF EL DORADO

Johann, Zita
THE MUMMY
TIGER SHARK

Johnson, Beverly
ASHANTI

Jones, Glenna Foster
LEO THE LAST

Jones, Jennifer
DUEL IN THE SUN
GONE TO EARTH
LOVE IS A MANY SPLENDORED THING
WE WERE STRANGERS

Jones, Marianne
SHADOW OF THE HAWK

Jurado, Katy
ARROWHEAD
THE BADLANDERS
BROKEN LANCE
THE BULLFIGHTER AND THE LADY
CHILDREN OF SANCHEZ
HIGH NOON
MAN FROM DEL RIO
ONE-EYED JACKS
SAN ANTONE
STAY AWAY, JOE

Kaye, Celia
ISLAND OF BLUE DOLPHINS

Keams, Geraldine
THE OUTLAW JOSEY WALES

Keiko, Kishi
THE YAKUZA

Keller, Marthe
BLACK SUNDAY

Kelly, Paula
COOL BREEZE
DRUM
LOST IN THE STARS

Kent, Jean
CARAVAN

Kerima
OUTCAST OF THE ISLANDS

Keyes, Evelyn
A THOUSAND AND ONE NIGHTS

Khambatta, Persis
NIGHTHAWKS
THE WILBY CONSPIRACY

Kim, June
CONFESSIONS OF AN OPIUM EATER

King, Aldine
SLAVES

Kitt, Eartha
ANNA LUCASTA
MARK OF THE HAWK

Kobayashi, Tsuruko
TARZAN'S THREE CHALLENGES

Kohner, Susuan
IMITATION OF LIFE (1958)

Korita, Ana
THE LOSERS

Princess Kouka
JERICHO

Kwan, Nancy
DROP DEAD, DARLING
FATE IS THE HUNTER
FLOWER DRUM SONG
THE GIRL WHO KNEW TOO MUCH
LT. ROBIN CRUSOE, U.S.N.
THE MAIN ATTRACTION
THE McMASTERS
NOBODY'S PERFECT
TAMAHINE
THE WILD AFFAIR
THE WORLD OF SUZIE WONG
THE WRECKING CREW

Kyo, Machiko
THE TEAHOUSE OF THE AUGUST MOON

Lamarr, Hedy
LADY OF THE TROPICS
WHITE CARGO

Lamour, Dorothy
ALOMA OF THE SOUTH SEAS
BEYOND THE BLUE HORIZON
HER JUNGLE LOVE
THE HURRICANE
THE JUNGLE PRINCESS
A MEDAL FOR BENNY
MY FAVORITE BRUNETTE
RAINBOW ISLAND
ROAD TO BALI
ROAD TO MOROCCO
ROAD TO RIO
ROAD TO SINGAPORE
SWING HIGH, SWING LOW
TROPIC HOLIDAY
TYPHOON

Lane, Jocelyn
LAND RAIDERS
SWORD OF ALI BABA

Lane Vicky
JUNGLE CAPTIVE

Lang, June
ALI BABA GOES TO TOWN

Laurie, Piper
THE GOLDEN BLADE

Lavi, Daliah
CATLOW
LORD JIM

Lawrence, Jody
CAPTAIN JOHN SMITH AND POCAHONTAS
TEN TALL MEN

Lawson, Linda
APACHE RIFLES

Lazo, Lilla
AFFAIR IN HAVANA

Lewis, Sylvia
DRUMS OF TAHITI

Linaker, Kay
GIRL FROM MANDALAY

Lincoln, Abbey
FOR LOVE OF IVY
NOTHING BUT A MAN

Lindfors, Viveca
THE RAIDERS
TEMPLE OF THE SWINGING DOLL

Littlefeather, Sacheen
WINTERHAWK

Lockwood, Margaret
JASSY

Lollabridgida, Gina
THE HUNCHBACK OF NOTRE DAME

London, Julie
NIGHT OF THE QUARTER MOON

Long, Lotus
LAST OF THE PAGANS
THE MYSTERIOUS MR. WONG
PHANTOM OF CHINATOWN
THINK FAST, MR. MOTO
TOKYO ROSE

Loren, Sophia
ARABESQUE
LEGEND OF THE LOST

Losch, Tilly
DUEL IN THE SUN
THE GOOD EARTH

Loy, Myrna
THE BARBARIAN
ISLE OF ESCAPE
THE MASK OF FU MANCHU
ROGUE OF THE RIO GRANDE
THIRTEEN WOMEN
UNDER A TEXAS MOON

Lu, Lisa
THE MOUNTAIN ROAD
RIDER ON A DEAD HORSE
WOMAN HUNT

Princess Luana
HAWAIIAN NIGHTS

Luez, Laurett
KILLER SHARK

Luna, Barbara
CHE
CRY TOUGH
THE GATLING GUN

Lupino, Ida
BACKTRACK

Mabley, Moms
AMAZING GRACE

MacDonald, Moira
RETURN TO PARADISE

Mack, Helen
THE CALIFORNIA

MacLachlan, Janet
CHANGE OF MIND
DARKER THAN AMBER
HALLS OF ANGER
SOUNDER
...tick...tick...tick...
UPTIGHT

Malina, Luva
MEXICAN HAYRIDE

Mao-Ying, Angela
ENTER THE DRAGON

Mara, Adele
TWILIGHT ON THE RIO GRANDE
YOU WERE NEVER LOVELIER

Margarejo, Lillian
THE LOSERS

Margo
BEHIND THE RISING SUN
THE LEOPARD MAN
THE ROBIN HOOD OF EL DORADO
RUMBA
VIVA ZAPATA

Margolin, Janet
NEVADA SMITH

Marianna
GUERILLA GIRL

Maris, Mona
THE ARIZONA KID
THE FALCON IN MEXICO
WHITE HEAT

Marquand, Tina
TEXAS ACROSS THE RIVER

Marques, Maria Elena
ACROSS THE WIDE MISSOURI
AMBUSH AT TOMAHAWK GAP
THE PEARL

Martell, Donna
ELEPHANT STAMPEDE
HILLS OF UTAH
LOVE IS A MANY SPLENDORED THING
TEN WANTED MEN

Martin, Andra
YELLOWSTONE KELLY

Martinelli, Elsa
THE INDIAN FIGHTER

Martinez, Alma
UNDER FIRE
ZOOT SUIT

Maylia
TO THE ENDS OF THE EARTH

Mayo, Virginia
COLORADO TERRITORY
THE IRON MISTRESS

McBroom, Marcia
BEYOND THE VALLEY OF THE DOLLS
THE LEGEND OF NIGGER CHARLEY

McCarthy, Nobu
FIVE GATES TO HELL
WALK LIKE A DRAGON

McDaniel, Hattie
FAMILY HONEYMOON
GEORGE WASHINGTON SLEPT HERE
GONE WITH THE WIND
THE GREAT LIE
HI, BEAUTIFUL
THE SHOPWORN ANGEL
SHOWBOAT
SINCE YOU WENT AWAY

McGee, Vonetta
BLACULA
BROTHERS
THE EIGER SANCTION
HAMMER
MELINDA
SHAFT IN AFRICA
THOMASINE AND BUSHROD

McKinney, Nina Mae
PINKY
SANDERS OF THE RIVER

McNair, Barbara
CHANGE OF HABIT
IF HE HOLLERS, LET HIM GO!
THE ORGANIZATION
STILETTO
THEY CALL ME MR. TIBBS

McNeil, Claudia
BLACK GIRL
A RAISIN IN THE SUN

McQueen, Butterfly
AMAZING GRACE
CABIN IN THE SKY
DUEL IN THE SUN
GONE WITH THE WIND
MILDRED PIERCE

Medina, Patricia
ALADDIN AND HIS LAMP
THE BEAST OF HOLLOW MOUNTAIN
DUEL ON THE MISSISSIPPI
THE MAGIC CARPET
PIRATES OF TRIPOLI
SIREN OF BAGDAD

Mercier, Michele
YOU CAN'T WIN THEM ALL

Mercouri, Melina
THE GYPSY AND THE GENTLEMAN

Meredith, Madge
THE FALCON'S ADVENTURE

Mestre, Gloria
FOXHOLE IN CAIRO

Michell, Janee
SOUL SOLDIER

Milan, Lita
BAYOU
GUN BROTHERS
THE RIDE BACK
TOUGHEST MAN ALIVE

Miles, Vera
THE CHARGE AT FEATHER RIVER

Miranda, Carmen
COPACABANA
A DATE WITH JUDY
DOWN ARGENTINE WAY
THE GANG'S ALL HERE
GREENWICH VILLAGE
NANCY GOES TO RIO
SCARED STIFF
SOMETHING FOR THE BOYS
THAT NIGHT IN RIO
WEEK-END IN HAVANA

Miranda, Susana
FLAP

Miroslava
THE BRAVE BULLS

Mitchell, Gwenn
SHAFT

Mobley, Mary Ann
HARUM SCARUM

Moll, Giorgia
THE QUIET AMERICAN

Monlaur, Yvonne
TERROR OF THE TONGS

Montell, Lisa
THE FIREBRAND
THE LONG ROPE
NAKED PARADISE
NINE LIVES OF ELFEGO BACA
PEARL OF THE SOUTH PACIFIC
TOMAHAWK TRAIL

Montenegro, Conchita
THE CISCO KID
THE GAY CABALLERO
LAUGHING AT LIFE
NEVER THE TWAIN SHALL MEET

Monteros, Rosenda
THE MAGNIFICENT SEVEN

SHE
TIARA TAHITI
THE WHITE ORCHID
A WOMAN'S DEVOTION

Montez, Maria
ALI BABA AND THE FORTY THIEVES
ARABIAN NIGHTS
COBRA WOMAN
GYPSY WILDCAT
MOONLIGHT IN HAWAII
PIRATES OF MONTEREY
RAIDERS OF THE DESERT
SOUTH OF TAHITI
SUDAN
THAT NIGHT IN RIO
WHITE SAVAGE

Montiel, Sarita
RUN OF THE ARROW
SERENADE
VERA CRUZ

Moon, Lynne Sue
13 FRIGHTENED GIRLS

Moore, Juanita
ABBY
IMITATION OF LIFE (1958)
THE MACK
THOMASINE AND BUSHROD
UPTIGHT
WALK ON THE WILD SIDE

Mooer, Melba
LOST IN THE STARS

Morales, Angelica
VIRGIN SACRIFICE

Moreland, Sherry
FURY OF THE CONGO

Moreno, Rita
CATTLE TOWN
CRY OF BATTLE
THE DEERSLAYER
EL ALAMEIN
THE KING AND I
MARLOWE
PAGAN LOVE SONG
POPI
SEVEN CITIES OF GOLD
THIS REBEL BREED
WEST SIDE STORY

THE YELLOW TOMAHAWK

Moreno, Rosita
A MEDAL FOR BENNY
THE SANTA FE TRAIL
WALLS OF GOLD

Morgan, Helen
SHOW BOAT

Mori, Toshia
THE BITTER TEA OF GENERAL YEN
FURY OF THE JUNGLE
THE HATCHET MAN

Morison, Patricia
ROMANCE OF THE RIO GRANDE

Morrison, Shelley
MAN AND BOY

Movita
(See Castaneda, Movita)

Munro, Caroline
THE GOLDEN VOYAGE OF SINBAD

Munson, Ona
THE SHANGHAI GESTURE

Murcelo, Karmin
BODERLINE

Newmar, Julie
MACKENNA'S GOLD

Nicholas, Denise
BLACULA
CAPRICORN ONE
LET'S DO IT AGAIN
A PIECE OF THE ACTION
THE SOUL OF NIGGER CHARLEY

Nichols, Nichelle
TARZAN'S DEADLY SILENCE

Norman, Maidie
BRIGHT ROAD
THE WELL
WHAT EVER HAPPENED TO BABY JANE

North, Virginia
THE LONG DUEL

Nuyen, France
BATTLE FOR THE PLANET OF THE APES
DIAMOND HEAD
DIMENSION 5
A GIRL NAMED TAMIKO
IN LOVE AND WAR
THE LAST TIME I SAW ARCHIE
THE MAN IN THE MIDDLE
ONE MORE TRAIN TO ROB
SATAN NEVER SLEEPS
SOUTH PACIFIC

Oberon, Merle
A NIGHT IN PARADISE

Odetta
SANCTUARY

O'Hara, Maureen
BAGDAD
FLAME OF ARABY
THE HUNCHBACK OF NOTRE DAME
SINBAD THE SAILOR

O'Hara, Shirley
BELLS OF SAN FERNANDO

O'Neal, Tricia
THE LEGEND OF NIGGER CHARLEY

Ortiz, Rosana
SAVAGE SISTERS

Oshita, Grace
REVENGE OF THE NINJA

Ouspenskaya, Maria
THE RAINS CAME
THE WOLF MAN

Pace, Judy
COOL BREEZE
COTTON COMES TO HARLEM
THREE IN THE ATTIC
UP IN THE CELLAR

Page, Joanne
MAN-EATER OF KUMAON

Page, Joy
THE BULLFIGHTER AND THE LADY

CONQUEST OF COCHISE
KISMET (1944)

Paget, Debra
BIRD OF PARADISE
BROKEN ARROW
THE LAST HUNT
OMAR KHAYYAM
PRINCESS OF THE NILE
WHITE FEATHER

Parker, Jean
THE BARRIER
CARAVAN

Parks, Trina
DARKTOWN STRUTTERS

Paul, Eugenia
APACHE WARRIOR

Pavan, Marisa
DRUM BEAT

Payne, Freda
BOOK OF NUMBERS

Pearson, Beatrice
LOST BOUNDARIES

Pellicer, Pina
ONE-EYED JACKS

Peters, Jean
APACHE
CAPTAIN FROM CASTILE
VIVA ZAPATA

Pleshette, Suzanne
NEVADA SMITH

Podesta, Rossana
SANTIAGO

Poree, Anita
LIVING BETWEEN TWO WORLDS

Powell, Jane
ENCHANTED ISLAND

Power, Taryn
SINBAD AND THE EYE OF THE TIGER

Powers, Mala
ROSE OF CIMARRON

Principal, Victoria
THE LIFE AND TIMES OF JUDGE ROY BEAN

Quartero, Nina
CYCLONE RANGER
ISLE OF ESCAPE
MEN OF THE NORTH
THE OUTLAW

Quigley, Juanita
STORM OVER THE ANDES

Racimo, Victoria
JOURNEY THROUGH ROSEBUD
THE MOUNTAIN MEN

Rainer, Luise
THE GOOD EARTH

Raines, Christina
HEX

Ralston, Vera
FAIR WIND TO JAVA

Rangan, Sonia
CHATO'S LAND

Rathebe, Dolly
THE MAGIC GARDEN

Raynor, Grace
TEN DAYS TO TULARA

Red Elk, Lois
THREE WARRIORS

Reed, Donna
FAR HORIZONS

Reed, Tracy
DEVIL'S OF DARKNESS
THE MAIN CHANCE
MAROC 7
A PIECE OF THE ACTION
A SHOT IN THE DARK

Reiver, Dorothy
THE FIGHTING RANGER

Renn, Adrianne
THE REVENGE OF GENERAL LING

Revueltas, Rosaura
SALT OF THE EARTH

Rhue, Madlyn
ESCAPE FROM ZAHRAIN
KENNER

Rice, Joan
HIS MAJESTY O'KEEFE

Richards, Beah
GONE ARE THE DAYS
THE GREAT WHITE HOPE
HURRY SUNDOWN
MAHOGANY
THE MIRACLE WORKER
TAKE A GIANT STEP

Richwine, Maria
THE BUDDY HOLLY STORY

Rico, Paquita
THE SAVAGE GUNS

Riordan, Marjorie
SOUTH OF MONTEREY

Roberts, Lynne
RIDE ON, VAQUERO
ROMANCE OF THE RIO GRANDE

Robson, Flora
55 DAYS AT PEKING
SARATOGA TRUNK

Rodann, Ziva
MACUMBA LOVE
PHAROAH'S CURSE

Rodriguez, Estelita
ALONG THE NAVAJO TRAIL
BELLE OF OLD MEXICO
CALIFORNIA PASSAGE
CUBAN FIREBALL
FABULOUS SENORITA
THE GAY RANCHERO
THE GOLDEN STALLION
HAVANA ROSE
IN OLD AMARILLO
MEXICANA
OLD LOS ANGELES
ON THE OLD SPANISH TRAIL

PALS OF THE GOLDEN WEST
SOUTH PACIFIC TRAIL
SUNSET IN THE WEST
SUSANNA PASS
TROPIC ZONE
TROPICAL HEAT WAVE
TWILIGHT IN THE SIERRAS

Rodriguez, Yolanda
THE COOL WORLD

Roman, Leticia
GOLD OF THE SEVEN SAINTS

Romay, Lina
HONEYMOON

Ross, Diana
LADY SINGS THE BLUES
MAHOGANY
THE WIZ

Ross, Katharine
TELL THEM WILLIE BOY IS HERE

Rush, Barbara
TAZA, SON OF COCHISE

Russell, Gail
THE LAWLESS
SONG OF INDIA

Russell, Jane
HOT BLOOD
THE OUTLAW

St. Clair, Lili
SON OF SINBAD

St. John, Betta
ALL THE BROTHERS WERE VALIANT
DANGEROUS MISSION
DREAM WIFE
THE NAKED DAWN

Samms, Emma
ARABIAN ADVENTURE

Sande, Serena
OKEFENOKEE

Sands, Diana
AN AFFAIR OF THE SKIN

DOCTORS' WIVES
ENSIGN PULVER
GEORGIA, GEORGIA
THE LANDLORD
A RAISIN IN THE SUN

Sanford, Isabel
SOUL SOLDIER

Sarandon, Susan
KING OF THE GYPSIES

Scala, Gia
RIDE A CROOKED TRAIL

Schiaffino, Rosanna
THE LONG SHIPS

Schiller, Fanny
THE TREASURE OF PANCHO VILLA

Sen, Aparna
THE GURU

Sidney, Sylvia
BEHOLD MY WIFE
BLOOD ON THE SUN
MADAME BUTTERFLY

Simi
TARZAN GOES TO INDIA

Simmons, Jean
BLACK NARCISSUS

Simms, Hilda
THE JOE LOUIS STORY

Sing, Mae Tai
FORBIDDEN

Slade, Serena
GHOST TOWN

Smith, Mildred Joanne
NO WAY OUT

Sondergaard, Gale
ANNA AND THE KING OF SIAM
THE MARK OF ZORRO
PIRATES OF MONTEREY
THE RETURN OF A MAN CALLED HORSE
ROAD TO RIO

Sorrell, Kare
THE MYSTERIOUS MR. MOTO

Speed, Carol
ABBY
THE MACK

Stanton, Helen
JUNGLE MOON MEN

Stanwyck, Barbara
A MESSAGE TO GARCIA

Stewart, Alexandra
MAROC 7

Stewart, Elaine
THE ADVENTURES OF HAJJI BABA

Sulchano
THE JUNGLE

Summers, Donna
THANK GOD IT'S FRIDAY

Swarthout, Gladys
ROSE OF THE RANCHO

Sykes, Brenda
BLACK GUNN
CLEOPATRA JONES
DRUM
HONKY
THE LIBERATION OF L.B. JONES
MANDINGO
SKIN GAME

Taka, Miiko
CRY FOR HAPPY
SAYONARA

Talbott, Gloria
ARIZONA RAIDERS
OKLAHOMA TERRITORY
THE OKLAHOMAN
THE OREGON TRAIL

Tani, Yoko
MY GEISHA
WHO'S BEEN SLEEPING IN MY BED
THE WIND CANNOT READ

Tarita
MUTINY ON THE BOUNTY (1962)

Taylor, Clarice
FIVE ON THE BLACK HAND SIDE

Taylor, Joan
APACHE WOMAN
FORT YUMA
OMAR KHAYYAM
THE SAVAGE
WAR DRUMS
WAR PAINT

Taylor-Young, Leigh
THE ADVENTURERS
THE HORSEMEN

Mrs. Teller
NAVAJO

Than, Win Min
THE PURPLE PLAIN

Thiess, Ursula
THE AMERICANO
BENGAL BRIGADE

Thompson, Hilarie
HEX

Threatt, Elizabeth
THE BIG SKY

Thurston, Carol
APACHE CHIEF
ARCTIC MANHUNT
CHINA SKY
CONQUEST OF COCHISE
FLAMING FEATHER
THE STORY OF DR. WASSELL
SWAMP FIRE

Tierney, Gene
CHINA GIRL
THE SHANGHAI GESTURE
WAY OF A GAUCHO

Todd, Beverly
BROTHER JOHN
THE LOST MAN

Torres, Raquel
RED WAGON
UNDER A TEXAS MOON

Tovar, Lupita
EAST OF BORNEO
THE FIGHTING GRINGO
SOUTH OF THE BORDER
TROPIC FURY
YANKEE DON

Toy, Mary Mon
THE YEAR OF THE HORSE

Tsopei, Corinna
A MAN CALLED HORSE

Tu, Francesca
WELCOME TO THE CLUB

Tyler, Beverly
THE PALOMINO

Tyson, Cicely
BUSTIN' LOOSE
THE HEART IS A LONELY HUNTER
A HERO AIN'T NOTHING BUT A SANDWICH
A MAN CALLED ADAM
THE RIVER NIGER
SOUNDER

Uggams, Leslie
BLACK GIRL

Umeki, Miyoshi
CRY FOR HAPPY
FLOWER DRUM SONG
A GIRL NAMED TAMIKO
SAYONARA

Ustinov, Paula
THE THIEF OF BAGDAD

Vaccaro, Brenda
ZORRO THE GAY BLADE

Valez, Kippee
THE DARING CABALLERO

Vega, Isela
BRING ME THE HEAD OF ALFREDO GARCIA

Velez, Lupe
THE BROKEN WING
THE CUBAN LOVE SONG

EAST IS WEST
THE GIRL FROM MEXICO
THE HALF-NAKED TRUTH
HOT PEPPER
LADIES DAY
LAUGHING BOY
MEXICAN SPITFIRE
MEXICAN SPITFIRE AT SEA
MEXICAN SPITFIRE OUT WEST
MEXICAN SPITFIRE'S BABY
MEXICAN SPITFIRE'S BLESSED EVENT
MEXICAN SPITFIRE'S ELEPHANT
MORALS OF MARCUS
PLAYMATES
SIX LESSONS FROM MADAME LA ZONGA
THE SQUAW MAN
STRICTLY DYNAMITE

Vennera, Chick
THANK GOD IT'S FRIDAY

Venus, Brenda
AGAINST A CROOKED SKY

Vera-Ellen
CARNIVAL IN COSTA RICA

Verdugo, Elena
THE BIG SOMBRERO
EL DORADO PASS
THE LOST VOLCANO
THE MOON AND SIXPENCE
RAINBOW ISLAND
STRANGE VOYAGE
THIEF OF DAMASCUS

Vickers, Martha
DAUGHTER OF THE WEST

Vlady, Marina
THE THIEF OF BAGHDAD

Wagner, Wende
GUNS OF THE MAGNIFICENT SEVEN

Walker, Joyce
THE EDUCATION OF SONNY CARSON

Walsh, Judy
CANNIBAL ATTACK
THE HALF-BREED

Walters, Lana
MEXICALI ROSE
UNDER STRANGE FLAGS

Ware, Irene
CHANDU, THE MAGICIAN

Warfield, Marlene
THE GREAT WHITE HOPE

Warren, Gloria
BELLS OF SAN FERNANDO

Warwick, Dionne
SLAVES

Washington, Fredi
EMPEROR JONES
IMITATION OF LIFE (1934)
ONE MILE FROM HEAVEN

Waters, Ethel
CABIN IN THE SKY
MEMBER OF THE WEDDING
PINKY

Waters, Mira
THE LEARNING TREE

Watson, Vernee
TRICK BABY

Welch, Raquel
BANDOLERO!
100 RIFLES

Wicker, Wendy
RIO CONCHOS

Wilde, Sonya
I PASSED FOR WHITE

Wilford, Joyce
WELCOME TO THE CLUB

Williams, Esther
FIESTA

Windsor, Marie
THE JUNGLE
OUTPOST IN MOROCCO

Wong, Anna May
BOMBS OVER BURMA
CHU CHIN CHOW

DANGEROUS TO KNOW
DAUGHTER OF SHANGHAI
DAUGHTER OF THE DRAGON
ELLERY QUEEN'S PENTHOUSE
    MYSTERY
THE FLAME OF LOVE
IMPACT
ISLAND OF LOST MEN
JAVA HEAD
KING OF CHINATOWN
LIMEHOUSE BLUES
SHANGHAI EXPRESS
STUDY IN SCARLET
WHEN WERE YOU BORN?

Wong, Iris
BEHIND THE RISING SUN
CHINA

Wood, Natalie
KINGS GO FORTH
WEST SIDE STORY

Woodbury, Joan
PASSPORT HUSBAND

Woods, Ren
YOUNGBLOOD

Wray, Fay
CAPTAIN THUNDER
THE TEXAN
VIVA VILLA

Wynn, May
HONG KONG AFFAIR
THE WHITE SQUAW

Wynn, Nan
PARDON MY SARONG

Xochitl
CHOICE OF BULLETS

Yamaguchi, Shirley
HOUSE OF BAMBOO
JAPANESE WAR BRIDE
NAVY WIFE

Yong, Soo
FLIGHT TO HONG KONG

LOVE IS A MANY SPLENDORED THING

Young, Loretta
THE HATCHET MAN
KISMET
RAMONA

DIRECTOR INDEX

Adreon, Franklin
DIMENSION 5

Aldrich, Robert
APACHE
VERA CRUZ
WHAT EVER HAPPENED TO BABY JANE

Allen, Irving
STRANGE VOYAGE

Alton, Robert
PAGAN LOVE SONG

Ander, Michael
ALL THE FINE YOUNG CANNIBALS

Anderson, Michael
FLIGHT FROM ASHIYA

Annakin, Ken
HOTEL SAHARA
THE LONG DUEL
PAPER TIGER

Archainbaud, George
HER JUNGLE LOVE
THIRTEEN WOMEN

Armitage, George
HIT MAN

Arnold, Jack
BLACK EYE

Ashby, Hal
THE LANDLORD

Atkins, Thomas
HI GAUCHO

Audlay, Michael
MARK OF THE HAWK

Auer, John H.
HELL'S HALF ACRE

PAN AMERICANA

Aurthur, Robert Alan
THE LOST MAN

Babcock, Dwight V.
JUNGLE MOON MEN

Bacon, Lloyd
IN CALIENTE
WONDER BAR

Bail, Chuck
CLEOPATRA JONES AND THE CASINO OF
GOLD

Baker, Roy
SINGER NOT THE SONG

Balley, Rex
NORTHERN PATROL

Bare, Richard
PRISONERS OF THE CASBAH
THIS REBEL BREED

Barnwell, John
SURRENDER-HELL

Baron, Allen
TERROR IN THE CITY

Barron, Arthur
BROTHERS

Bartlett, Hall
CHILDREN OF SANCHEZ

Barton, Charles T.
MEXICAN HAYRIDE
SMOOTH AS SILK

Beaudine, William
BELA LUGOSI MEETS A BROOKLYN GORILLA

HAVANA ROSE

Beebe, Ford
BOMBA AND THE HIDDEN CITY
BOMBA ON PANTHER ISLAND
ELEPHANT STAMPEDE
LAUGHING AT LIFE
THE LOST VOLCANO
THE MASKED RIDER

Bell, Monta
EAST IS WEST

Bellamy, Earl
AGAINST A CROOKED SKY
BACKTRACK

Benedek, Laslo
AFFAIR IN HAVANA
BENGAL BRIGADE
THE KISSING BANDIT

Bennett, Spencer G.
ROUGE OF THE RIO GRANDE
VOODOO TIGER

Berger, Ludwing
THIEF OF BAGDAD

Berke, William
BANDIT QUEEN
THE FALCON IN MEXICO
THE FALCON'S ADVENTURE
FURY OF THE CONGO
THE JUNGLE
JUNGLE JIM
MARK OF THE GORILLA
SAVAGE DRUMS

Berkeley, Busby
THE GANG'S ALL HERE
I LIVE FOR LOVE

Bernads, Edward L.
HAREM GIRL
NAVY WIFE

Berry, John
CASBAH
CLAUDINE

Biberman, Herbert
SALT OF THE EARTH

Binyon, Claude
FAMILY HONEYMOON

Blair, George
JAGUAR

Blystone, John G.
HOT PEPPER

Boetticher, Budd
THE BULLFIGHTER AND THE LADY
EAST OF SUMATRA
KILLER SHARK
WINGS OF THE HAWK

Bogart, Paul
CANCEL MY RESERVATION
HALLS OF ANGER
MARLOWE
SKIN GAME

Boorman, John
LEO THE LAST

Borzage, Frank
CHINA DOLL

Brabin, Charles
THE MASK OF FU MANCHU

Bradbury, Robert N.
TROUBLE IN TEXAS

Brahm, John
THE DIAMOND QUEEN

Brando, Marlon
ONE-EYED JACKS

Brannon, Fred C.
WILD HORSE AMBUSH

Brenon, Herbert
GIRL OF THE RIO

Bretherton, Howard
GIRL FROM MANDALAY
ISLE OF ESCAPE

Brooks, Richard
CRISIS
THE LAST HUNT
LORD JIM
THE PROFESSIONALS

Brower, Otto
LITTLE TOKYO, U.S.A.
THE SANTA FE TRAIL

Brown, Clarence
THE RAINS CAME
THE SON-DAUGHTER

Brown, Henry J.
SENOR AMERICANO

Burke, William
ON THE ISLE OF SAMOA

Butler, David
ALI BABA GOES TO TOWN
PLAYMATES

Cabanne, Christy
DRUMS OF THE CONGO
STORM OVER THE ANDES
TROPIC FURY

Cahn, Edward L.
HONG KONG CONFIDENTIAL
OKLAHOMA TERRITORY
VOODOO WOMAN

Campus, Michael
THE EDUCATION OF SONNY CARSON
THE MACK

Capra, Frank
THE BITTER TEA OF GENERAL YEN

Cardiff, Jack
THE LONG SHIPS
MY GEISHA

Cardos, John
SOUL SOLDIER

Carreras, Michael
THE SAVAGE GUNS

Carver, Steve
LONE WOLF McQUADE

Cassavetes, John
HUSBANDS
SHADOWS

Castle, William
THE AMERICANO
CONQUEST OF COCHISE
DRUMS OF TAHITI
DUEL ON THE MISSISSIPPI
FORT TI
13 FRIGHTENED GIRLS

Charell, Erik
CARAVAN

Christian, John
GUERILLA GIRL

Clark, Bruce
HAMMER

Clark, James B.
ISLAND OF BLUE DOLPHINS
VILLA!

Clarke, Shirley
THE COOL WORLD

Clavell, James
FIVE GATES TO HELL
WALK LIKE A DRAGON

Claxton, William
THE QUIET GUN

Cline, Edward F.
HAWAII CALLS

Clouse, Robert
BLACK BELT JONES
DARKER THAN AMBER
ENTER THE DRAGON

Cohen, Larry
BLACK CAESAR
HELL UP IN HARLEM

Coleman, C.C., Jr.
CRIMINALS OF THE AIR

Collinson, Peter
YOU CAN'T WIN THEM ALL

Comfort, Lance
DEVILS OF DARKNESS

Connor, Kevin
ARABIAN ADVENTURE

Conway, Jack
DRAGON SEED
LADY OF THE TROPICS
VIVA VILLA

Copelan, Jodie
AMBUSH AT CIMARRON PASS

Corman, Roger
APACHE WOMAN
NAKED PARADISE

Corrigan, Lloyd
THE BROKEN WING
THE DANCING PIRATE
DAUGHTER OF THE DRAGON

Crabtree, Arthur
CARAVAN
MADONNA OF THE SEVEN MOONS

Crain, William
BLACULA

Cromwell, John
ANNA AND THE KING OF SIAM
SINCE YOU WENT AWAY
THE TEXAN

Crosland, Alan
CAPTAIN THUNDER
MASSACRE

Cukor, George
BHOWANI JUNCTION

Culp, Robert
HICKEY & BOGGS

Cummings, Irving
THE CISCO KID
DOWN ARGENTINE WAY
THAT NIGHT IN RIO

Curtiz, Michael
MILDRED PIERCE
UNDER A TEXAS MOON

Daniels, Harold
BAYOU
DAUGHTER OF THE WEST

Dassin, Jules
UPTIGHT

Daves, Delmer
THE BADLANDERS
BIRD OF PARADISE
BROKEN ARROW
DRUM BEAT
KINGS GO FORTH

Davis, Ossie
BLACK GIRL
COTTON COMES TO HARLEM
COUNTDOWN AT KUSINI

Day, Robert
SHE
TARZAN'S THREE CHALLENGES

de Cordova, Frederick
THE DESERT HAWK
LITTLE EGYPT

Delanney, Jean
THE HUNCHBACK OF NOTRE DAME

DeMille, Cecil B.
NORTHWEST MOUNTED POLICE
THE SQUAW MAN
THE STORY OF DR. WASSELL
UNCONQUERED

de Toth, Andre
THE INDIAN FIGHTER

Dexter, John
THE VIRGIN SOLDIERS

Dexter, Maury
THE FIREBRAND
HARBOR LIGHTS
WOMAN HUNT

Dieterle, William
THE HUNCHBACK OF NOTRE DAME
KISMET
OMAR KHAYYAM

Dillon, John Francis
CALL HER SAVAGE
KISMET

Dmytryk, Edward
BEHIND THE RISING SUN
BROKEN LANCE

CAPTIVE WILD WOMEN
WALK ON THE WILD SIDE

Donen, Stanley
ARABESQUE

Donner, Clive
OLD DRACULA
THE THIEF OF BAGDAD

Douglas, Gordon
THE CHARGE AT FEATHER RIVER
GOLD OF THE SEVEN SAINTS
THE IRON MISTRESS
RIO CONCHOS
SANTIAGO
THEY CALL ME MR. TIBBS
YELLOWSTONE KELLY

Douglas, William
CUBAN FIREBALL

Downey, Robert
PUTNEY SWOPE

Drake, Oliver
TRAIL TO MEXICO

Dunne, Philip
IN LOVE AND WAR

Dwan, Allan
CATTLE QUEEN OF MONTANA
ENCHANTED ISLAND
HUMAN CARGO
ONE MILE FROM HEAVEN
PASSION
PEARL OF THE SOUTH PACIFIC

Eason, B. Reeves
RIMFIRE

Eastwood, Clint
THE EIGER SANCTION
THE OUTLAW JOSEY WALES

Edwards, Blake
A SHOT IN THE DARK

Eichberg, Richard
THE FLAME OF LOVE

Elliott, Clyde E.
BOOLOO

English, John
HILLS OF UTAH

Enright, Ray
CHINA SKY
FLAMING FEATHER
RIVERS END

Eriksen, Dan
SLAVES

Farrow, John
CHINA
TWO YEARS BEFORE THE MAST

Feist, Felix
PIRATES OF TRIPOLI

Fernandez, Emilio
THE PEARL
THE TORCH

Ferrer, Mel
GREEN MANSIONS

Firstenberg, Sam
REVENGE OF THE NINJA

Fleischer, Richard
ASHANTI
CHE
MANDINGO
THE NEW CENTURIONS

Fleming, Victor
GONE WITH THE WIND

Flemyng, Gordon
THE SPLIT

Flicker, Theodore
UP IN THE CELLAR

Florey, Robert
DANGEROUS TO KNOW
DAUGHTER OF SHANGHAI
OUTPOST IN MOROCCO
TARZAN AND THE MERMAIDS

Ford, John
CHEYENNE AUTUMN
THE FUGITIVE
THE HORSE SOLDIERS
THE HURRICANE
MY DARLING CLEMENTINE
THE SEARCHERS

Forde, Walter
CHU CHIN CHOW

Forman, Milos
RAGTIME

Foster, Lewis R.
TROPIC ZONE

Foster, Norman
INDIAN PAINT
THE MYSTERIOUS MR. MOTO
NAVAJO
NINE LIVES OF ELFEGO BACA
SOMBRERO
THANK YOU, MR. MOTO
THINK FAST, MR. MOTO

Fowler, Gene Jr.
THE OREGON TRAIL

Fowley, Douglas
MACUMBA LOVE

Fox, Wallace
THE DARING CABALLERO
THE GAY AMIGO

Frank, Melvin
THAT CERTAIN FEELING

Frankenheimer, John
BLACK SUNDAY
THE HORSEMEN

Franklin, Sidney
THE GOOD EARTH

Freedman, Jerrold
BORDERLINE

Freeland, Thornton
DARK SANDS
FLYING DOWN TO RIO

Fregonese, Hugo
MARK OF THE RENEGADE

Freund, Karl
THE MUMMY

Friend, Robert L.
TARZAN'S DEADLY SILENCE

Fuller, Samuel
CHINA GATE
HOUSE OF BAMBOO
RUN OF THE ARROW

Furie, Sidney J.
THE APPALOOSA
LADY SINGS THE BLUES

Garen, Leo
HEX

Gering, Marion
MADAME BUTTERFLY
ROSE OF THE RANCHO
RUMBA
SARUMBA

Gilbert, Lewis
THE ADVENTURERS
7TH DAWN
YOU ONLY LIVE TWICE

Gilbert, Stuart
THE HALF-BREED

Girard, Bernard
RIDE OUT FOR REVENGE

Girdier, William
ABBY
SHEBA BABY

Glendon, J. Frank
CIRCLE OF DEATH

Goldbeck, Willis
TEN TALL MEN

Goldman, Martin
THE LEGEND OF NIGGER CHARLEY

Goldstone, James
BROTHER JOHN

Goodwins, Leslie
THE GIRL FROM MEXICO

HI, BEAUTIFUL
LADIES DAY
MEXICAN SPITFIRE
MEXICAN SPITFIRE AT SEA
MEXICAN SPITFIRE OUT WEST
MEXICAN SPITFIRE SEES A GHOST
MEXICAN SPITFIRE'S BABY
MEXICAN SPITFIRE'S BLESSED
  EVENT
MEXICAN SPITFIRE'S ELEPHANT

Gordon, Michael
TEXAS ACROSS THE RIVER

Gordon, Robert
THE GATLING GUN
THE JOE LOUIS STORY

Gordy, Berry
MAHOGANY

Goulding, Edmund
DOWN AMONG THE SHELTERING PALMS
THE GREAT LIE

Graham, William
CHANGE OF HABIT
CHOICE OF BULLETS
HONKY

Green, Alfred E.
COPACABANA
THE JACKIE ROBINSON STORY
SOUTH OF PAGO-PAGO
A THOUSAND AND ONE NIGHTS

Green, Guy
DIAMOND HEAD
A PATCH OF BLUE

Greville, Arthur
PARADISE ISLE

Gries, Tom
THE HAWAIIANS
JOURNEY THROUGH ROSEBUD
100 RIFLES

Griffith, Edward H.
BAHAMA PASSAGE

Grinde, Nick
KING OF CHINATOWN

Gillermin, John
EL CONDOR
SHAFT IN AFRICA
SKYJACKED
TARZAN GOES TO INDIA

Gunn, Bill
GANJA AND HESS

Haas, Hugo
NIGHT OF THE QUARTER MOON

Haig, Roul
OKEFENOKEE

Haley, Earl
THE KING OF THE WILD HORSES

Hall, Alexander
LIMEHOUSE BLUES

Hamilton, Guy
THE MAN IN THE MIDDLE

Hartford-Davis, Robert
BLACK GUNN

Haskin, Byron
CAPTAIN SINBAD
HIS MAJESTY O'KEEFE
MAN-EATER OF KUMAON
TARZAN'S PERIL

Hathaway, Henry
CHINA GIRL
LEGEND OF THE LOST
NEVADA SMITH

Hawks, Howard
THE BIG SKY
THE OUTLAW
TIGER SHARK

Heard, Paul F.
HONG KONG AFFAIR

Heisler, Stuart
TULSA

Henreid, Paul
A WOMAN'S DEVOTION

Hessler, Gordon
THE GOLDEN VOYAGE OF SINBAD

Hibbs, Jesse
MAD ABOUT LOVE
RIDE A CROOKED TRAIL
WALK THE PROUD LAND

Hill, Bob
CYCLONE RANGER

Hill, Jack
COFFY
FOXY BROWN

Hillyer, Lambert
THE CALIFORNIA TRAIL
THE GIRL FROM RIO
SOUTH OF THE RIO GRANDE

Hitchcock, Alfred
TOPAZ

Hittleman, Carl
GUN BATTLE AT MONTEREY

Hogan, James
ELLERY QUEEN'S PENTHOUSE MYSTERY

Hopper, Dennis
THE LAST MOVIE

Hopper, Jerry
HURICANE SMITH

Horner, Harry
A LIFE IN THE BALANCE
MAN FROM DEL RIO

Hough, John
TRIUMPHS OF A MAN CALLED HORSE

Howard, David
THE FIGHTING GRINGO
THE MARINES ARE COMING
THE RENEGADE RANGER

Hughes, Howard
THE OUTLAW

Hughes, Ken
DROP DEAD, DARLING

Humberstone, Bruce
TEN WANTED MEN

Huston, John
THE BARBARIAN AND THE GEISHA
THE LIFE AND TIMES OF JUDGE ROY
BEAN
THE MAN WHO WOULD BE KING
THE UNFORGIVEN
WE WERE STRANGERS

Hyams, Peter
CAPRICORN ONE

Ivory, James
THE GURU

Jackson, Pat
THE VIRGIN ISLAND

Jason, Will
TAHITI NIGHTS
THIEF OF DAMASCUS

Johnson, Robert
LIVINC BETWEEN TWO WORLDS

Jones, Harmon
BULLWHIP
PRINCESS OF THE NILE

Jorkman, Stig B.
GEORGIA, GEORGIA

Juran, Nathan
THE GOLDEN BLADE
LAND RAIDERS
THE 7TH VOYAGE OF SINBAD

Kane, Joseph
CALIFORNIA PASSAGE
DUEL AT APACHE WELLS
FAIR WIND TO JAVA
OLD LOS ANGELES
ROCK ISLAND TRAIL
SAN ANTONE

Kaplan, Jonathan
THE SLAMS

Karlson, Phil
BLACK GOLD

GUNMAN'S WALK
THE WRECKING CREW

Katzin, Lee H.
HEAVEN WITH A GUN

Kazan, Elia
PINKY
VIVA ZAPATA

Keighley, William
GEORGE WASHINGTON SLEPT HERE
HONEYMOON

Keljan, Bob
SCREAM BLACULA SCREAM

Keller, Harry
ROSE OF CIMARRON

Kemp, Jack
MIRACLE IN HARLEM

Kennedy, Burt
DIRTY DINGUS MAGEE

Kenton, Erle C.
DEVIL'S PLAYGROUND
ISLAND OF LOST SOULS
PARDON MY SARONG

Kershner, Irvin
THE RETURN OF A MAN CALLED HORSE

King, Henry
THE BRAVADOS
CAPTAIN FROM CASTILE
LOVE IS A MANY SPLENDORED THING
MARGIE
RAMONA

King, Louis
CHARLIE CHAN IN EGYPT
DANGEROUS MISSION
TYPHOON

Kjellin, Alf
THE McMASTERS

Klane, Robert
THANK GOD IT'S FRIDAY

Kline, Herbert
THE FIGHTER

Knight, John
THE MAIN CHANCE

Knowles, Bernard
JASSY

Koch, Howard W.
FORT BOWIE

Korda, Zoltan
JUNGLE BOOK
SANDERS OF THE RIVER

Korty, John
ALEX AND THE GYPSY

Koster, Henry
FLOWER DRUM SONG
MY BLUE HEAVEN

Kotcheff, William T.
TIARA TAHITI
TWO GENTLEMEN SHARING

Kowalski, Bernard L.
STILETTO

Krish, John
THE WILD AFFAIR

Kulik, Buzz
VILLA RIDES

La Cava, Gregory
THE HALF-NAKED TRUTH

Lamont, Charles
BAGDAD
FLAME OF ARABY
MOONLIGHT IN HAWAII
SLAVE GIRL

Landers, Lew
ALADDIN AND HIS LAMP
BORDER CAFE
CAPTAIN JOHN SMITH AND POCAHONTAS
THE GIRL AND THE GAMBLER
THE GIRL FROM HAVANA
HURRICANE ISLAND
LA CONGA NIGHTS
THE MAGIC CARPET
REDHEAD FROM MANHATTAN
TOKYO ROSE

UNDER THE TONTO RIM

Landres, Paul
OREGON PASSAGE
SON OF A GUNFIGHTER

Lang, Richard
THE MOUNTAIN MEN

Lang, Walter
GREENWICH VILLAGE
THE KING AND I
SONG OF THE ISLANDS
WEEK-END IN HAVANA

Lathan, Stan
AMAZING GRACE

Laughlin, Frank
THE MASTER GUNFIGHTER

Laven, Arnold
ANNA LUCASTA
GERONIMO

Leacock, Philip
TAKE A GIANT STEP
TAMAHINE

Le Borg, Reginald
JUNGLE WOMAN
WAR DRUMS
WEIRD WOMAN
THE WHITE ORCHID

Lee, Rowland V.
THE BRIDGE OF SAN LUIS REY

Leeds, Herbert I.
RIDE ON, VAQUERO
ROMANCE OF THE RIO GRANDE

Leewood, Jack
THUNDER ISLAND

Leisen, Mitchell
BEHOLD MY WIFE
GOLDEN EARRINGS
SWING HIGH, SWING LOW

Leonard Robert Z.
NANCY GOES TO RIO

Lerner, Irving
CRY OF BATTLE

Lester, Richard
CUBA
HELP!

Lewin, Albert
THE MOON AND SIXPENCE
SAADIA

Lewis, Joseph H.
BOMBS OVER BURMA
THE MAD DOCTOR OF MARKET STREET

Lloyd, Frank
BLOOD ON THE SUN
THE LASH
THE LAST COMMAND
MUTINY ON THE BOUNTY (1935)

Logan, Joshua
ENSIGN PULVER
SAYONARA
SOUTH PACIFIC

Locoy, Joseph
THE GYPSY AND THE GENTLEMAN
THE LAWLESS

Lubin, Arthur
ALI BABA AND THE FORTY THIEVES
IMPACT
A NIGHT IN PARADISE
RIDE 'EM COWBOY
WHITE SAVAGE

Ludwig, Edward
THE BLACK SCORPION

Lumet, Sidney
THE WIZ

Lyon, Francis D.
CULT OF THE COBRA
THE GIRL WHO KNEW TOO MUCH
THE OKLAHOMAN

MacDonald, David
ALONG THE NAVAJO TRAIL

APACHE CHIEF

MacDonald, Wallace
GUNMEN FROM LAREDO

MacKenna, Kenneth
WALLS OF GOLD

MacKenzie, John
BEYOND THE LIMIT

Maddow, Ben
AN AFFAIR OF THE SKIN

Malmuth, Bruce
NIGHTHAWKS

Mamoulian, Rouben
THE MARK OF ZORRO

Mander, Miles
MORALS OF MARCUS

Manduke, Joe
CORNBREAD, EARL AND ME

Mankiewicz, Joseph L.
NO WAY OUT
THE QUIET AMERICAN

Mann, Anthony
BORDER INCIDENT
SERENADE

Mann, Daniel
FOR LOVE OF IVY
LOST IN THE STARS
THE MOUNTAIN ROAD
OUR MAN FLINT
THE TEAHOUSE OF THE AUGUST MOON
WHO'S BEEN SLEEPING IN MY BED

Marin, Edwin L.
STUDY IN SCARLET

Marks, Arthur
FRIDAY FOSTER

Marshall, George
CRY FOR HAPPY
A MESSAGE TO GARCIA
THE SAVAGE
SCARED STIFF

Martin, Charles
IF HE HOLLERS, LET HIM GO!

Marton, Andrew
THE WILD NORTH

Mason, Noel
YANKEE DON

Mate, Rudolph
FAR HORIZONS
FORBIDDEN

Mayer, Gerald
BRIGHT ROAD

Mayo, Archie
ADVENTURES OF MARCO POLO

McCarey, Leo
SATAN NEVER SLEEPS

McCarthy, John P.
THE CISCO KID RETURNS

McCowan, George
SHADOW OF THE HAWK

McDonald, Frank
THE BIG SOMBRERO
SNOW DOG
SON OF BELLE STARR
TWILIGHT ON THE RIO GRANDE

McGann, William
ON THE BORDER
WHEN WERE YOU BORN?

McLaglen, Andrew V.
ONE MORE TRAIN TO ROB

McLeod, Norman Z.
ROAD TO RIO

Medak, Peter
ZORRO THE GAY BLADE

Medford, Don
THE ORGANIZATION

Meins, Gus
THE CALIFORNIAN

Melford, George
EAST OF BORNEO

Menzies, William C.
CHANDU, THE MAGICIAN

Merrill, Kieth
THREE WARRIORS
WINDWALKER

Meyer, Russ
BEYOND THE VALLEY OF THE DOLLS

Milestone, Lewis
MUTINY ON THE BOUNTY (1962)

Miller, Robert Ellis
THE HEART IS A LONELY HUNTER

Miner, Allen
GHOST TOWN
THE RIDE BACK

Minnelli, Vincente
CABIN IN THE SKY
KISMET
THE PIRATE
YOLANDA AND THE THIEF

Moguy, Leonide
ACTION IN ARABIA

Montgomery, Robert
RIDE THE PINK HORSE

Moody, Don
POPI

Moore, Michael
KILL A DRAGON

Morse, Terry
BELLS OF SAN FERNANDO

Moxey, John
FOXHOLE IN CAIRO

Murphy, Dudley
EMPEROR JONES

Murphy, Ralph
RAINBOW ISLAND

Nassour, Edward
THE BEAST OF HOLLOW MOUNTAIN

Nazarro, Ray
CHINA CORSAIR
DOMINO KID
EL DORADO PASS
THE PALOMINO
ROSE OF SANTA ROSA
THE WHITE SQUAW

Neame, Ronald
ESCAPE FROM ZAHRAIN

Neill, Roy William
BLACK MOON
FURY OF THE JUNGLE
GYPSY WILDCAT
RHYTHM OF THE ISLANDS

Nelson, Gene
HARUM SCARUM

Nelson, Ralph
FATE IS THE HUNTER
A HERO AIN'T NOTHING BUT A SANDWICH
...tick...tick...tick...
THE WILBY CONSPIRACY
THE WRATH OF GOD

Neumann, Kurt
THE DEERSLAYER
HIAWATHA
ISLAND OF LOST MEN
MOHAWK
RAINBOW ON THE RIVER
TARZAN AND THE LEOPARD WOMAN

Newfield, Sam
JUNGLE SIREN

Newman, Joseph M.
FLIGHT TO HONG KONG
FORT MASSACRE

Nigh, William
BEAUTY AND THE BANDIT
THE MYSTERIOUS MR. WONG
ROSE OF THE RIO GRANDE
ROGUE OF THE RIO GRANDE
SOUTH OF MONTEREY

Nosseck, Max
KOREA PATROL

Nugent, Elliott
MY FAVORITE BRUNETTE
MY OUTLAW BROTHER

STRICTLY DYNAMITE

O'Hara, Gerry
MAROC 7

O'Neal, Ron
SUPER FLY, TNT

Orlebeck, Les
GAUCHOS OF EL DORADO

O'Steen, Sam
SPARKLE

Panama, Norman
THAT CERTAIN FEELING

Parker, Alan
FAME

Parks, Gordon Jr.
AARON LOVES ANGELA
THE LEARNING TREE
SHAFT
SUPER FLY
THOMASINE AND BUSHROD
THREE THE HARD WAY

Parrish, Robert
THE PURPLE PLAIN

Paul, Byron
LT. ROBIN CRUSOE, U.S.N.

Peckinpah, Sam
BRING ME THE HEAD OF ALFREDO
  GARCIA

Peerce, Larry
THE INCIDENT
ONE POTATO, TWO POTATO

Penn, Arthur
ALICE'S RESTAURANT
LITTLE BIG MAN
THE MIRACLE WORKER

Penn, Leo
A MAN CALLED ADAM

Petrie, Daniel
THE MAIN ATTRACTION

Peverall, John
TERROR OF THE TONGS

Pevney, Joseph
DESERT LEGION
FOXFIRE
TAMMY AND THE BACHELOR

Pichel, Irving
A MEDAL FOR BENNY

Pierce, Charles B.
WINTERHAWK

Pierson, Frank
KING OF THEY GYPSIES

Pine, William
SWAMP FIRE

Poitier, Sidney
BUCK AND THE PREACHER
LET'S DO IT AGAIN
A PIECE OF THE ACTION
UPTOWN SATURDAY NIGHT
A WARM DECEMBER

Pollack, Barry
COOL BREEZE

Pollack, Sydney
JEREMIAH JOHNSON
THE YAKUZA

Polonsky, Abraham
TELL THEM WILLIE BOY IS HERE

Popkin, Leo C.
THE WELL

Potter, H.C.
MR. BLANDINGS BUILDS HIS DREAM
  HOUSE
THE SHOPWORN ANGEL

Powell, Michael
BLACK NARCISSUS
GONE TO EARTH

Preminger, Otto
CARMEN JONES
HURRY SUNDOWN
PORGY AND BESS

Pressburger, Emeric
BLACK NARCISSUS
GONE TO EARTH

Pressman, Michael
BOULEVARD NIGHTS

Quine, Richard
SIREN OF BAGDAD
SYNANON
THE WORLD OF SUZIE WONG

Rafkin, Alan
NOBODY'S PERFECT

Rapper, Irving
THE BRAVE ONE

Rash, Steve
THE BUDDY HOLLY STORY

Ratoff, Gregory
CARNIVAL IN COSTA RICA

Rawlins, John
ARABIAN NIGHTS
RAIDERS OF THE DESERT
SIX LESSONS FROM MADAME LA ZONGA
SUDAN

Ray, Nicholas
55 DAYS AT PEKING
HOT BLOOD

Reed, Carol
FLAP
OUTCAST OF THE ISLANDS

Reed, Theodore
TROPIC HOLIDAY

Reisch, Walter
SONG OF SCHEHERAZADE

Richardson, Tony
THE BORDER

SANCTUARY

Rilla, Wolf
CAIRO

Ritt, Martin
EDGE OF THE CITY
THE GREAT WHITE HOPE
PARIS BLUES
SOUNDER

Roach, Hal
MEN OF THE NORTH

Robbins, Jerome
WEST SIDE STORY

Roberts, Stephen
TRUMPET BLOWS

Robertson, Hugh A.
MELINDA

Robson, Mark
LOST COMMAND
NINE HOURS TO RAMA
RETURN TO PARADISE

Roemer, Michael
NOTHING BUT A MAN

Rogell, Albert
HAWAIIAN NIGHTS
SONG OF INDIA

Romero, Eddie
BLACK MAMA, WHITE MAMA
SAVAGE SISTERS

Rosen, Phil
PHANTOM OF CHINATOWN
WEST OF THE PECOS

Rossen, Robert
THE BRAVE BULLS
ISLAND IN THE SUN

Rothman, Stephanie
TERMINAL ISLAND

Rouse, Russell
THE WELL

Rowland, William
WOMEN IN THE NIGHT

Ruben, J. Walter
JAVA HEAD

Sagal, Boris
THE OMEGA MAN

St. Clair, Mal
THE BULLFIGHTERS

St. Jacques, Raymond
BOOK OF NUMBERS

Sale, Richard
SPOILERS OF THE NORTH

Salkow, Sidney
GUN BROTHERS
SWORD OF THE AVENGER
TOUGHEST MAN ALIVE

Sandrich, Mark
HOLIDAY INN

Santell, Alfred
ALOMA OF THE SOUTH SEAS
THE ARIZONA KID
BEYOND THE BLUE HORIZON
MEXICANA

Schaefer, George
DOCTORS' WIVES

Schertzinger, Victor
ROAD TO SINGAPORE

Schlatter, George
NORMAN...IS THAT YOU?

Schultz, Michael
COOLEY HIGH
GREASED LIGHTNING
WHICH WAY IS UP

Schrader, Paul
CAT PEOPLE

Schuster, Harold
WINGS OF THE MORNING

Scoppa, Pete
POPI

Scorsese, Martin
THE KING OF COMEDY

Scott, Ewing
ARCTIC MANHUNT

Scott, Oz
BUSTIN' LOOSE

Sears, Fred F.
AMBUSH AT TOMAHAWK GAP
APACHE AMBUSH
EL ALAMEIN
MASSACRE CANYON

Seiler, Lewis
SOMETHING FOR THE BOYS

Seiter, William A.
YOU WERE NEVER LOVELIER

Seitz, George B.
THE FIGHTING RANGER

Sekely, Steve
KENNER

Selander, Leslie
THE BARRIER
THE BROKEN STAR
DESERT SANDS
FORT VENGEANCE
FORT YUMA
INDIAN AGENT
THE MYSTERIOUS DESPERADO
THE RAIDERS
SADDLE LEGION
TOMAHAWK
WAR PAINT
THE YELLOW TOMAHAWK

Shah, Krishna
THE RIVER NIGER

Sharp, Don
THE BRIDES OF FU MANCHU
THE FACE OF FU MANCHU

Sheldon, Sidney
DREAM WIFE

Shenson, Walter
WELCOME TO THE CLUB

Sherman, George
BATTLE AT APACHE PASS
BLACK BART
BORDER RIVER
CHIEF CRAZY HORSE
COMANCHE
THE GOLDEN HORDE
THE LAST OF THE FAST GUNS
MEXICALI ROSE
SOUTH OF THE BORDER
TEN DAYS TO TULARA
TOMAHAWK
THE TREASURE OF PANCHO VILLA
THE VEILS OF BAGDAD
WAR ARROW
THE WIZARD OF BAGDAD

Sherwood, John
RAW EDGE

Sholem, Lee
CANNIBAL ATTACK
MA AND PA KETTLE AT WAIKIKI
PHARAOH'S CURSE
TARZAN AND THE SLAVE GIRL

Shores, Lynn
REBELLION
UNDER STRANGE FLAGS

Sidney, Geroge
SHOW BOAT (1951)

Siegel, Don
FLAMING STAR

Silverstein, Elliot
A MAN CALLED HORSE

Sirk, Douglas
IMITATION OF LIFE (1959)
TAZA, SON OF COCHISE

Smith, Noel
CATTLE TOWN

Smithee, Allen
DEATH OF A GUNFIGHTER

Spangler, Larry G.
THE SOUL OF NIGGER CHARLEY

Springsteen, R.G.
BELLE OF OLD MEXICO
FABULOUS SENORITA

TROPICAL HEAT WAVE

Spottiswoode, Roger
UNDER FIRE

Stafford, John
THE REVENGE OF GENERAL LING

Stahl, John M.
IMITATION OF LIFE (1934)

Stanley, Paul
CRY TOUGH

Starrett, Jack
CLEOPATRA JONES
CRY BLOOD APACHE
THE LOSERS
THE STRANGE VENGEANCE OF ROSALIE

Stein, Paul L.
RED WAGON

Stevens, George
GUN FEVER

Stevens, Robert
CHANGE OF MIND

Stevenson, Robert
TO THE ENDS OF THE EARTH

Stone, Andrew
THE DECKS RAN RED
STORMY WEATHER

Strick, Joseph
THE BALCONY

Sturges, John
A GIRL NAMED TAMIKO
JOE KIDD
THE MAGNIFICENT SEVEN

Summers, Jerry
THE VENGEANCE OF FU MANCHU

Sunasky, Irving
THE YEAR OF THE HORSE

Sutherland, Edward
MR. ROBINSON CRUSOE

Swackhamer, E.W.
MAN AND BOY

Swanson, Donald
THE MAGIC GARDEN

Taurog, Norman
BLUE HAWAII

Taylor, Don
THE ISLAND OF DR. MOREAU
RIDE THE WILD SURF

Taylor, Ray
RETURN OF CHANDU
WEST TO GLORY

Tetzlaff, Ted
SON OF SINBAD

Tewksbury, Peter
STAY AWAY, JOE

Thiele, William
THE JUNGLE PRINCESS
TARZAN TRIUMPHS

Thomas, Ralph
THE WIND CANNOT READ

Thompson, J. Lee
BATTLE FOR THE PLANET OF THE
  APES
KINGS OF THE SUN
MACKENNA'S GOLD

Thorpe, Richard
ALL THE BROTHERS WERE VALIANT
BORDER ROMANCE
A DATE WITH JUDY
FIESTA
FUN IN ACAPULCO
LAST OF THE PAGANS
MALAYA
WHITE CARGO

Tinling, James
PASSPORT HUSBAND

Tourneur, Jacques
THE LEOPARD MAN
PHANTOM RAIDERS
STRANGER ON HORSEBACK
WAY OF A GAUCHO

Towne, Robert
PERSONAL BEST

Twist, Derek
THE END OF THE RIVER

Ulmer, Edgar G.
BABES IN BAGDAD
CLUB HAVANA
THE NAKED DAWN

Vajda, Ladislaus
THE REVENGE OF GENERAL LING

Valdez, Luis
ZOOT SUIT

Van Dyke, W.S.
THE CUBAN LOVE SONG
LAUGHING BOY
NEVER THE TWAIN SHALL MEET

Vernevil, Henri
GUNS FOR SAN SEBASTIAN

Vidor, Charles
THE LOVES OF CARMEN
THE TUTTLES OF TAHITI

Vidor, King
BIRD OF PARADISE
DUEL IN THE SUN
JAPANESE WAR BRIDE

Vogel, Virgil
SWORD OF ALI BABA

von Sternberg, Josef
SHANGHAI EXPRESS
THE SHANGHAI GESTURE

Waggner, George
OUTLAW EXPRESS
PAWNEE
SOUTH OF TAHITI
WOLF CALL
THE WOLF MAN

Wagner, Fernando
VIRGIN SACRIFICE

Walker, Hal
ROAD TO BALI

Wallace, Richard
THE LITTLE MINISTER
SINBAD THE SAILOR

Walsh, Raoul
BAND OF ANGELS
COLORADO TERRITORY

Wanamaker, Sam
CATLOW
SINBAD AND THE EYE OF THE TIGER

Warren, Charles Marquis
ARROWHEAD

Warren, Mark
COME BACK CHARLESTON BLUE

Watt, Nate
LAW OF THE PAMPAS

Webb, Jack
THE LAST TIME I SAW ARCHIE

Webb, Robert D.
SEVEN CITIES OF GOLD
WHITE FEATHER

Weber, Lois
WHITE HEAT

Webster, Nicholas
GONE ARE THE DAYS

Weis, Don
THE ADVENTURES OF HAJJI BABA

Wellman, William a.
ACROSS THE WIDE MISSOURI
BUFFALO BILL
THE HATCHET MAN
THE ROBIN HOOD OF EL DORADO

Wendkos, Paul
GUNS OF THE MAGNIFICENT SEVEN
TEMPLE OF THE SWINGING DOLL

Wecker, Alfred
THE GAY CABALLERO
LOST BOUNDARIES
PIRATES OF MONTEREY

Whale, James
SHOW BOAT (1936)

Wilcox, Fred M.
I PASSED FOR WHITE

Willat, I.V.
UNDER STRANGE FLAGS

Williams, Elmo
APACHE WARRIOR

Williams, Oscar
FIVE ON THE BLACK HAND SIDE

Williamson, Fred
THE LEGEND OF NIGGER CHARLEY

Wilson, Richard
THREE IN THE ATTIC

Winner, Michael
CHATO'S LAND

Wise, Robert
ODDS AGAINST TOMORROW
THE SAND PEBBLES
WEST SIDE STORY

Witney, William H.
APACHE RIFLES
ARIZONA RAIDERS
DARKTOWN STRUTTERS
DOWN·LAREDO WAY
THE GAY RANCHERO
THE GOLDEN STALLION
IN OLD AMARILLO
THE LONG ROPE
ON THE OLD SPANISH TRAIL
PALS OF THE GOLDEN WEST
SANTA FE PASSAGE
SOUTH PACIFIC TRAIL
SUNSET IN THE WEST
SUSANNA PASS
TWILIGHT IN THE SIERRAS

Wood, Sam
THE BARBARIAN
SARATOGA TRUNK

Wright, Mark V.
ROOTIN' TOOTIN' RHYTHM

Wyler, William
THE LIBERATION OF L.B. JONES

Yarbrough, Jean
HOLIDAY IN HAVANA

Young, Harold
JUNGLE CAPTIVE

Young, Terence
THE KLANSMAN

Yust, Larry
TRICK BABY

Zinnemann, Fred
HIGH NOON
MEMBER OF THE WEDDING

Zugsmith, Albert
CONFESSIONS OF AN OPIUM EATER

MINORITY/THIRD WORLD CLASSIFICATION INDEX

ARABIAN NIGHTS

THE ADVENTURES OF HAJJI BABA
ALADDIN AND HIS LAMP
ALI BABA AND THE FORTY THIEVES
ALI BABA GOES TO TOWN
ARABIAN ADVENTURE
ARABIAN NIGHTS
BABES IN BAGDAD
CAPTAIN SINBAD
CHU CHIN CHOW
THE GOLDEN BLADE
THE GOLDEN HORDE
THE GOLDEN VOYAGE OF SINBAD
KISMET (1930, 1944, 1955)
THE MAGIC CARPET
PRINCESS OF THE NILE
PRISONERS OF THE CASBAH
THE 7TH VOYAGE OF SINBAD
SINBAD AND THE EYE OF THE TIGER
SINBAD THE SAILOR
SIREN OF BAGDAD
SON OF SINBAD
SWORD OF ALI BABA
THIEF OF BAGDAD
THIEF OF DAMASCUS
A THOUSAND AND ONE NIGHTS
THE VEILS OF BAGDAD
THE WIZARD OF BAGDAD

ALICE'S RESTAURANT
ANNA AND THE KING OF SIAM
BATTLE FOR THE PLANET OF THE
    APES
CULT OF THE COBRA
DIMENSION 5
DROP DEAD, DARLING
HELP!
IMPACT
THE KING AND I
LADY OF THE TROPICS
THE LAST TIME I SAW ARCHIE
LORD JIM
THE LOSERS

THE MAIN ATTRACTION
THE MAN IN THE MIDDLE
OUR MAN FLINT
SAVAGE SISTERS
THE STORY OF DR. WASSELL
TO THE ENDS OF THE EARTH
THE WRECKING CREW

Balinese
ROAD TO BALI

Burmese
THE PURPLE PLAIN

Chinese
ADVENTURES OF MARCO POLO
THE BITTER TEA OF GENERAL YEN
BLOOD ON THE SUN
BOMBS OVER BURMA
THE BRIDES OF FU MANCHU
CHINA
CHINA DOLL
CHINA GIRL
CHINA SKY
CLEOPATRA JONES AND THE CASINO OF
    GOLD
CONFESSIONS OF AN OPIUM EATER
DANGEROUS TO KNOW
DAUGHTER OF SHANGHAI
DAUGHTER OF THE DRAGON
DRAGON SEED
EAST IS WEST
ELLERY QUEEN'S PENTHOUSE MYSTERY
ENTER THE DRAGON
THE FACE OF FU MANCHU
FATE IS THE HUNTER
55 DAYS AT PEKING
FIVE GATES TO HELL
THE FLAME OF LOVE
FLIGHT TO HONG KONG
FLOWER DRUM SONG
THE GIRL WHO KNEW TOO MUCH
THE GOOD EARTH
THE HATCHET MAN
HELL'S HALF ACRE
HONG KONG AFFAIR
HUSBANDS

ISLAND OF LOST MEN
JAVA HEAD
KILL A DRAGON
KING OF CHINATOWN
LIMEHOUSE BLUES
THE MASK OF FU MANCHU
THE MOUTAIN ROAD
THE MYSTERIOUS MR. WONG
ONE MORE TRAIN TO ROB
PHANTOM OF CHINATOWN
THE REVENGE OF GENERA LING
THE SAND PEBBLES
SATAN NEVER SLEEPS
SHANGHAI EXPRESS
THE SHANGHAI GESTURE
THE SON-DAUGHTER
STUDY IN SCARLET
TERROR OF THE TONGS
THANK YOU, MR. MOTO
THINK FAST, MR. MOTO
13 FRIGHTENED GIRLS
THE VENGEANCE OF FU MANCHU
WALK LIKE A DRAGON
WHEN WERE YOU BORN?
THE WILD AFFAIR
WOMEN IN THE NIGHT
THE WORLD OF SUZIE WONG
THE YEAR OF THE HORSE

Eurasian
CHINA CORSAIR
CHINA GATE
IN LOVE AND WAR
LOVE IS A MANY SPLENDORED THING
7TH DAWN

Filipino
CRY OF BATTLE
SURRENDER-HELL
SWORD OF THE AVENGER

Japanese
THE BARBARIAN AND THE GEISHA
BEHIND THE RISING SUN
CRY FOR HAPPY
DREAMS OF GLASS
A GIRL NAMED TAMIKO
HOUSE OF BAMBOO
JAPANESE WAR BRIDE
LITTLE TOKYO, U.S.A.
MADAME BUTTERFLY
MY GEISHA
THE MYSTERIOUS MR. MOTO
NAVY WIFE
NOBODY'S PERFECT

REVENGE OF THE NINJA
SAYONARA
THE TEAHOUSE OF THE AUGUST MOON
TOKYO ROSE
WELCOME TO THE CLUB
WHO'S BEEN SLEEPING IN MY BED
THE WIND CANNOT READ
THE YAKUZA

Javanese
FAIR WIND TO JAVA

Korean
KOREA PATROL

Macaoan
FORBIDDEN

Malayan
BOOLOO
THE VIRGIN SOLDIERS

Malaysian
MALAYA

Mandalayan
GIRL FROM MANDALAY

Thai
TARZAN'S THREE CHALLENGES

Vietnamese
THE QUIET AMERICAN

African
ASHANTI
CRY THE BELOVED COUNTRY
DARK SANDS
DRUMS OF THE CONGO
MARK OF THE HAWK
SHAFT IN AFRICA
TARZAN'S PERIL
A WARM DECEMBER

American
ABBY
ALL THE FINE YOUNG CANNIBALS
AN AFFAIR OF THE SKIN
AMAZING GRACE
ANNA LUCASTA
THE BALCONY

BAND OF ANGELS
BEYOND THE VALLEY OF THE DOLLS
BLACK BELT JONES
BLACK CAESAR
BLACK GIRL
BLACK GUNN
BLACK MAMA, WHITE MAMA
BLACULA
BOOK OF NUMBERS
BRIGHT ROAD
BROTHER JOHN
BROTHERS
BUCK AND THE PREACHER
BUSTIN' LOOSE
CABIN IN THE SKY
CAPRICORN ONE
CARMEN JONES
CAT PEOPLE
CHANGE OF HABIT
CHANGE OF MIND
CLAUDINE
CLEOPATRA JONES
CLEOPATRA JONES AND THE CASINO
   OF GOLD
COFFY
COME BACK CHARLESTON BLUE
COOL BREEZE
THE COOL WORLD
COOLEY HIGH
CORNBREAD, EARL AND ME
COTTON COMES TO HARLEM
COUNTDOWN AT KUSINI
DARKER THAN AMBER
DARKTOWN STRUTTERS
DEATH OF A GUNFIGHTER
DEVILS OF DARKNESS
DOCTOR'S WIVES
EDGE OF THE CITY
EDUCATION OF SONNY CARSON
THE EIGER SANCTION
EMPEROR JONES
FAME
FAMILY HONEYMOON
FIVE ON THE BLACK HAND SIDE
FOR LOVE OF IVY
FOXY BROWN
FRIDAY FOSTER
GANJA AND HESS
GEORGE WASHINGTON SLEPT HERE
GEORGIA, GEORGIA
GONE ARE THE DAYS
GONE WITH THE WIND
GREASED LIGHTNING
THE GREAT LIE
THE GREAT WHITE HOPE

HALLS OF ANGER
HAMMER
THE HEART IS A LONELY HUNTER
A HERO AIN'T NOTHING BUT A SANDWICH
HI, BEAUTIFUL
HICKEY & BOGGS
HIT MAN
HOLIDAY INN
HONEYMOON
HONKY
THE HORSE SOLDIERS
HURRY SUNDOWN
I PASSED FOR WHITE
IF HE HOLLERS, LET HIM GO!
IMITATION OF LIFE (1934, 1959)
THE INCIDENT
THE JACKIE ROBINSON STORY
THE JOE LOUIS STORY
THE KING OF COMEDY
KINGS GO FORTH
THE KLANSMAN
LADY SINGS THE BLUES
THE LANDLORD
THE LEARNING TREE
THE LEGEND OF NIGGER CHARLEY
LEO THE LAST
LET'S DO IT AGAIN
THE LIBERATION OF L.B. JONES
LIVING BETWEEN TWO WORLDS
LOST BOUNDARIES
LOST IN THE STARS
THE LOST MAN
THE MACK
THE MAGIC GARDEN
MAHOGANY
THE MAIN CHANCE
MAN AND BOY
A MAN CALLED ADAM
MANDINGO
MAROC 7
MELINDA
MEMBER OF THE WEDDING
MILDRED PIERCE
MIRACLE IN HARLEM
MR. BLANDINGS BUILDS HIS DREAM HOUSE
MY BLUE HEAVEN
THE NEW CENTURIONS
NIGHT OF THE QUARTER MOON
NO WAY OUT
NORMAN...IS THAT YOU?
OLD DRACULA
THE OMEGA MAN
ONE MILE FROM HEAVEN
ONE POTATO, TWO POTATO
PARIS BLUES

A PATCH OF BLUE
A PIECE OF THE ACTION
PINKY
PORGY AND BESS
PUTNEY SWOPE
RAGTIME
RAINBOW ON THE RIVER
THE RIVER NIGER
SANCTUARY
SANDERS OF THE RIVER
SAVAGE SISTERS
SCREAM BLACULA SCREAM
SHADOWS
SHAFT
SHEBA BABY
THE SHOPWORN ANGEL
SHOW BOAT (1936, 1951)
SINCE YOU WENT AWAY
SKIN GAME
SLAVES
SMOOTH AS SILK
THE SOUL OF NIGGER CHARLEY
SOUL SOLDIER
SOUNDER
SPARKLE
THE SPLIT
STILETTO
STORMY WEATHER
SUPER FLY
SUPER FLY, TNT
SYNANON
TAKE A GIANT STEP
TAMMY AND THE BACHELOR
TARZAN'S DEADLY SILENCE
TERMINAL ISLAND
TERROR IN THE CITY
THANK GOD IT'S FRIDAY
THAT CERTAIN FEELING
THEY CALL ME MISTER TIBBS
THOMASINE AND BUSHROD
THREE IN THE ATTIC
...tick...tick...tick...
TRICK BABY
UP IN THE CELLAR
UPTIGHT
WALK ON THE WILD SIDE
WELCOME TO THE CLUB
THE WELL
WEST OF THE PECOS
WHAT EVER HAPPENED TO BABY JANE
WIZ
YOUNGBLOOD

Jamaican
TWO GENTLEMEN SHARING

West Indian
BAHAMA PASSAGE
BLACK MOON
ISLAND IN THE SUN
THE VIRGIN ISLAND

CAJUN
BAYOU
NEVADA SMITH
SWAMP FIRE

CREOLE
DUEL ON THE MISSISSIPPI
THE IRON MISTRESS
RIDE A CROOKED TRAIL
SARATOGA TRUNK

GYPSY
ALEX AND THE GYPSY
ALONG THE NAVAJO TRAIL
CARAVAN (1934, 1946)
DEVILS OF DARKNESS
DOWN LAREDO WAY
GOLDEN EARRINGS
GONE TO EARTH
GUERILLA GIRL
THE GYPSY AND THE GENTLEMAN
GYPSY WILDCAT
HOT BLOOD
THE HUNCHBACK OF NOTRE DAME
JASSY
KING OF THE GYPSIES
THE LITTLE MINISTER
THE LOVES OF CARMEN
MADONNA OF THE SEVEN MOONS
RED WAGON
SOMBRERO
WINGS OF THE MORNING
THE WOLF MAN

INDIAN
BENGAL BRIGADE
BHOWANI JUNCTION
BLACK NARCISSUS
THE DIAMOND QUEEN
THE GURU
JAGUAR
THE JUNGLE
JUNGLE BOOK
KENNER
THE LONG DUEL

MAN-EATER OF KUMAON
THE MAN WHO WOULD BE KING
NINE HOURS TO RAMA
THE RAINS CAME
RETURN OF CHANDU
SONG OF INDIA
TARZAN GOES TO INDIA
THIRTEEN WOMEN
THE WILBY CONSPIRACY

JUNGLE EXOTIC

BELA LUGOSI MEETS A BROOKLYN
   GORILLA
BOMBA AND THE HIDDEN CITY
CANNIBAL ATTACK
CAPTIVE WILD WOMAN
EAST OF BORNEO
ELEPHANT STAMPEDE
FURY OF THE CONGO
FURY OF THE JUNGLE
GREEN MANSIONS
HER JUNGLE LOVE
ISLAND OF LOST SOULS
JUNGLE CAPTIVE
JUNGLE JIM
THE JUNGLE PRINCESS
JUNGLE SIREN
JUNGLE WOMAN
THE LOST VOLCANO
MARK OF THE GORILLA
TARZAN AND THE LEOPARD WOMAN
TARZAN AND THE MERMAIDS
TARZAN AND THE SLAVE GIRL
TARZAN TRIUMPHS
VOODOO TIGER
VOODOO WOMAN
WHITE CARGO

LATIN AMERICAN

THE ADVENTURERS
BANDIT QUEEN
CARNIVAL IN COSTA RICA
CLUB HAVANA
COPACABANA
CRISIS
A DATE WITH JUDY
DEVILS OF DARKNESS
THE GANG'S ALL HERE
THE GIRL FROM RIO
GREENWICH VILLAGE
THE HALF-NAKED TRUTH

HAVANA ROSE
HOT PEPPER
I LIVE FOR LOVE
JACK AHOY
KILLER SHARK
LA CONGA KNIGHTS
LADIES DAY
LAUGHING AT LIFE
LAW OF THE PAMPAS
THE LEOPARD MAN
MARLOWE
A MEDAL FOR BENNY
MY FAVORITE BRUNETTE
NANCY GOES TO RIO
PAN AMERICANA
PASSPORT HUSBAND
THE PIRATE
RIDE ON, VAQUERO
ROAD TO RIO
SIX LESSONS FROM MADAME LA ZONGA
SOMETHING FOR THE BOYS
STORM OVER THE ANDES
STRICTLY DYNAMITE
TEMPLE OF THE SWINGING DOLL
TEN DAYS TO TULARA
TEN WANTED MEN
THAT NIGHT IN RIO
THUNDER ISLAND
TOUGHEST MAN ALIVE
TROPIC FURY
TROPIC ZONE
WALLS OF GOLD
WONDER BAR
YOLANDA AND THE THIEF
YOU WERE NEVER LOVELIER

Argentine
HI GAUCHO
WAY OF A GAUCHO

Brazilian
THE AMERICANO
THE END OF THE RIVER
THE FALCON'S ADVENTURE
FLYING DOWN TO RIO
MACUMBA LOVE

Cuban
AFFAIR IN HAVANA
CHE
CUBA
CUBAN FIREBALL
FABULOUS SENORITA
THE GIRL FROM HAVANA
HOLIDAY IN HAVANA

A MESSAGE TO GARCIA
RUMBA
SANTIAGO
SARUMBA
SCARED STIFF
TOPAZ
TROPICAL HEAT WAVE
TWILIGHT IN THE SIERRAS
WE WERE STRANGERS
WEEK-END IN HAVANA

Guatamalan
VIRGIN SACRIFICE

Mexican
AMBUSH AT CIMARRON PASS
APACHE AMBUSH
THE APPALOOSA
THE ARIZONA KID
BACKTRACK
THE BADLANDERS
BANDOLERO!
THE BEAST OF HOLLOW MOUNTAIN
BEAUTY AND THE BANDIT
BELLE OF OLD MEXICO
BELLS OF SAN FERNANDO
THE BIG SOMBRERO
BLACK BART
THE BLACK SCORPION
THE BORDER
BORDER CAFE
BORDER INCIDENT
BORDER RIVER
BORDER ROMANCE
BORDERLINE
THE BRAVADOS
THE BRAVE BULLS
BRING ME THE HEAD OF ALFREDO
  GARCIA
THE BROKEN STAR
THE BROKEN WING
THE BULLFIGHTER AND THE LADY
THE BULLFIGHTERS
CALIFORNIA PASSAGE
THE CALIFORNIA TRAIL
THE CALIFORNIAN
CAPTAIN THUNDER
CATLOW
CATTLE TOWN
CHILDREN OF SANCHEZ
THE CISCO KID
THE CISO KID RETURNS
COMANCHE
CONQUEST OF COCHISE
CRIMINALS OF THE AIR

CYCLONE RANGER
THE DANCING PIRATE
THE DARING CABALLERO
DOMINO KID
DUEL AT APACHE WELLS
EL CONDOR
EL DORADO PASS
THE FALCON IN MEXICO
FIESTA
THE FIGHTER
THE FIGHTING RANGER
THE FIREBRAND
FUN IN ACAPULCO
GAUCHOS OF EL DORADO
THE GAY AMIGO
THE GAY CABALLERO
THE GAY RANCHERO
GIANT
THE GIRL AND THE GAMBLER
THE GIRL FROM MEXICO
GIRL OF THE RIO
THE GOLDEN STALLION
GUN BATTLE AT MONTEREY
HIGH NOON
HUMAN CARGO
IN CALIENTE
IN OLD AMARILLO
IT HAPPENED OUT WEST
JOE KIDD
THE KISSING BANDIT
THE LAND RAIDERS
THE LASH
THE LAST COMMAND
THE LAST OF THE FAST GUNS
THE LAWLESS
THE LIFE AND TIMES OF JUDGE ROY
  BEAN
A LIFE IN THE BALANCE
LONE WOLF McQUADE
THE LONG ROPE
MAD ABOUT LOVE
THE MAGNIFICENT SEVEN
MAN AND BOY
MAN FROM DEL RIO
THE MARINES ARE COMING
MARK OF THE RENEGADE
THE MARK OF ZORRO
THE MASKED RIDER
THE MASTER GUNFIGHTER
MEXICALI ROSE
MEXICAN HAYRIDE
MEXICAN SPITFIRE
MEXICAN SPITFIRE AT SEA
MEXICAN SPITFIRE OUT WEST
MEXICAN SPITFIRE SEES A GHOST

MEXICAN SPITFIRE'S BABY
MEXICAN SPITFIRE'S BLESSED
   EVENT
MEXICAN SPITFIRE'S ELEPHANT
MEXICANA
MY OUTLAW BROTHER
THE MYSTERIOUS DESPERADO
THE NAKED DAWN
NINE LIVES OF ELFEGO BACA
OLD LOS ANGELES
ON THE BORDER
ON THE OLD SPANISH TRAIL
ONE-EYED JACKS
THE OUTLAW
OUTLAW EXPRESS
THE PALOMINO
PALS OF THE GOLDEN WEST
PASSION
THE PEARL
PIRATES OF MONTEREY
PLAYMATES
THE PROFESSIONALS
THE RAIDERS
REBELLION
THE RENEGADE RANGER
THE RIDE BACK
RIMFIRE
THE ROBIN HOOD OF EL DORADO
ROMANCE OF THE RIO GRANDE
ROOTIN' TOOTIN' RHYTHM
ROSE OF THE RANCHO
ROSE OF THE RIO GRANDE
ROGUE OF THE RIO GRANDE
SADDLE LEGION
SALT OF THE EARTH
SAN ANTONE
THE SANTA FE TRAIL
THE SAVAGE GUNS
SENOR AMERICANO
SERENADE
SINGER NOT THE SONG
SON OF A GUNFIGHTER
SON OF BELLE STARR
SOUTH OF MONTEREY
SOUTH OF THE BORDER
SOUTH OF THE RIO GRANDE
SOUTH PACIFIC TRAIL
STRANGE VOYAGE
SUNSET IN THE WEST
SUSANNA PASS
THE TEXAN
THIS REBEL BREED
TIGER SHARK
THE TORCH
TRAIL TO MEXICO

THE TREASURE OF PANCHO VILLA
TROPIC HOLIDAY
TROUBLE IN TEXAS
TRUMPET BLOWS
TWILIGHT ON THE RIO GRANDE
UNDER A TEXAS MOON
UNDER STRANGE FLAGS
UNDER THE TONTO RIM
VERA CRUZ
VILLA RIDES
VIVA VILLA
VIVA ZAPATA
WALK ON THE WILD SIDE
WEST TO GLORY
THE WHITE ORCHID
WINGS OF THE HAWK
A WOMAN'S DEVOTION
YANKEE DON
ZOOT SUIT
ZORRO THE GAY BLADE

Nicaraguan
UNDER FIRE

Panamanian
THE ISLAND OF DR. MOREAU
PHANTOM RAIDERS
SWING HIGH, SWING LOW

Peruvian
THE BRIDGE OF SAN LUIS REY
THE LAST MOVIE

Puerto Rican
AARON LOVES ANGELA
THE BUDDY HOLLY STORY
CRY TOUGH
FAME
HARBOR LIGHTS
POPI
WEST SIDE STORY

MIDDLE EASTERN

Afghan
THE HORSEMEN

Algerian
CASBAH
FLIGHT FROM ASHIYA

Arab
ARABESQUE
BAGDAD

DESERT LEGION
DESERT SANDS
DREAM WIFE
EL ALAMEIN
ESCAPE FROM ZAHRAIN
HAREM GIRL
HARUM SCARUM
LEGEND OF THE LOST
LOST COMMAND
NIGHTHAWKS
OMAR KHAYYAM
RAIDERS OF THE DESERT
SHE
SLAVE GIRL
TEN TALL MEN

Egyptian
THE BARBARIAN
CAIRO
CAIRO ROAD
CHANDU, THE MAGICIAN
CHARLIE CHAN IN EGYPT
FOXHOLE IN CAIRO
JUNGLE MOON MEN
LITTLE EGYPT
THE MUMMY
PHARAOH'S CURSE
SUDAN

Libyan
PIRATES OF TRIPOLI

Moroccan
THE LONG SHIPS
OUTPOST IN MOROCCO
ROAD TO MOROCCO
SAADIA
SONG OF SCHEHERAZADE

Palestinian
BLACK SUNDAY

Persian
THE DESERT HAWK
A NIGHT IN PARADISE

Syrian
ACTION IN ARABIA
MORALS OF MARCUS

Tunisian
FLAME OF ARABY

Turkish
YOU CAN'T WIN THEM ALL

NATIVE AMERICAN

ACROSS THE WIDE MISSOURI
THE ADVENTURES OF FRONTIER FREMONT
AGAINST A CROOKED SKY
BEHOLD MY WIFE
BELLS OF SAN FERNANDO
BLACK GOLD
BROKEN LANCE
BUFFALO BILL
CALL HER SAVAGE
CANCEL MY RESERVATION
CAPTAIN JOHN SMITH AND POCAHONTAS
CATTLE QUEEN OF MONTANA
THE CHARGE AT FEATHER RIVER
CHOICE OF BULLETS
DANGEROUS MISSION
DAUGHTER OF THE WEST
THE DEERSLAYER
DIRTY DINGUS MAGEE
DUEL IN THE SUN
FLAMING FEATHER
FLAP
FORT TI
GHOST TOWN
GOLD OF THE SEVEN SAINTS
GUN BROTHERS
GUN FEVER
GUNMAN'S WALK
GUNMEN FROM LAREDO
THE HALF-BREED
HIAWATHA
HILLS OF UTAH
HURRICANE ISLAND
INDIAN AGENT
THE INDIAN FIGHTER
INDIAN PAINT
THE LAST HUNT
LAUGHING BOY
THE LEGEND OF NIGGER CHARLEY
MASSACRE
THE McMASTERS
THE MOUNTAIN MEN
OREGON PASSAGE
THE OREGON TRAIL
PERSONAL BEST
THE QUIET GUN
RAMONA
RAW EDGE
THE RETURN OF A MAN CALLED HORSE
RIDE 'EM COWBOY
RIDE OUT FOR REVENGE
ROCK ISLAND TRAIL
SANTA FE PASSAGE
SHADOW OF THE HAWK

SPOILERS OF THE NORTH
THE SQUAW MAN
STAY AWAY, JOE
THE STRANGE VENGEANCE OF ROSALIE
TEXAS ACROSS THE RIVER
TOMAHAWK
WAR PAINT
WOLF CALL
THE YELLOW TOMAHAWK

Apache
AMBUSH AT TOMAHAWK GAP
APACHE
APACHE CHIEF
APACHE WARRIOR
APACHE WOMAN
ARROWHEAD
BATTLE AT APACHE PASS
BROKEN ARROW
CHATO'S LAND
CRY BLOOD APACHE
FORT BOWIE
FORT YUMA
FOXFIRE
THE GATLING GUN
GERONIMO
MACKENNA'S GOLD
MY DARLING CLEMENTINE
RIO CONCHOS
TAZA, SON OF COCHISE
TOMAHAWK TRAIL
WALK THE PROUD LAND
WAR DRUMS

Arapaho
YELLOWSTONE KELLY

Blackfoot
THE BIG SKY
WINTERHAWK

Californian
ISLAND OF BLUE DOLPHINS
SEVEN CITIES OF GOLD

Cherokee
OKLAHOMA TERRITORY
THE OKLAHOMAN
ROSE OF CIMARRON
TULSA

Cheyenne
BULLWHIP
CHEYENNE AUTUMN
LITTLE BIG MAN

WHITE MAN
WINDWALKER

Chippewa
THE WILD NORTH

Comanche
APACHE RIFLES
THE SEARCHERS

Crow
TRIUMPHS OF A MAN CALLED HORSE

Eskimo
ARCTIC MANHUNT

Flathead
JEREMIAH JOHNSON

Hopi
HEAVEN WITH A GUN

Kiowa
FLAMING STAR
NEVADA SMITH
THE UNFORGIVEN

Modoc
DRUM BEAT

Mohawk   ·
MOHAWK

Navajo
KING OF THE WILD HORSES
NAVAJO
THE OUTLAW JOSEY WALES

Paiute
FORT MASSACRE
TELL THEM WILLIE BOY IS HERE

Pawnee
PAWNEE

Pueblo
COLORADO TERRITORY

Seminole
JOE PANTHER
OKEFENOKEE
WAR ARROW

Seneca
UNCONQUERED

Shoshoni
FAR HORIZONS

Sioux
CHIEF CRAZY HORSE
HEX
JOURNEY THROUGH ROSEBUD
A MAN CALLED HORSE
RUN OF THE ARROW
THE SAVAGE
TRIUMPHS OF A MAN CALLED HORSE
THE WHITE SQUAW

Canadian Indian
THE BARRIER
MEN OF THE NORTH
NORTHERN PATROL
NORTHWEST MOUNTED POLICE
RIVER'S END
SNOW DOG

Central American Indian
THE WRATH OF GOD

      MEXICAN INDIAN
THE FUGITIVE
RIDE THE PINK HORSE

Aztec
CAPTAIN FROM CASTILE

Mayan
KINGS OF THE SUN

Yaqui
ARIZONA RIFLES
100 RIFLES

South American Indian
BEYOND THE LIMIT

      SOUTH SEA ISLAND

ALL THE BROTHERS WERE VALIANT
ALOMA OF THE SOUTH SEAS
BEYOND THE BLUE HORIZON
BOMBA ON PANTHER ISLAND
COBRA WOMAN
DOWN AMONG THE SHELTERING PALMS
DRUMS OF TAHITI
EAST OF SUMATRA
ENCHANTED ISLAND
ENSIGN PULVER
ISLE OF ESCAPE

LAST OF THE PAGANS
LT. ROBIN CRUSOE, U.S.N.
THE MAD DOCTOR OF MARKET STREET
MR. ROBINSON CRUSOE
OUTCAST OF THE ISLANDS
PARADISE ISLE
PARDON MY SARONG
PEARL OF THE SOUTH PACIFIC
RAINBOW ISLAND
RETURN TO PARADISE
RHYTHM OF THE ISLANDS
ROAD TO SINGAPORE
SAVAGE DRUMS
SONG OF THE ISLANDS
SOUTH OF PAGO-PAGO
SOUTH PACIFIC
TYPHOON
WEIRD WOMAN
WHITE HEAT
WHITE SAVAGE

Hawaiian
BLUE HAWAII
DIAMOND HEAD
HAWAII CALLS
HAWAIIAN NIGHTS
THE HAWAIIANS
MA AND PA KETTLE AT WAIKIKI
MOONLIGHT IN HAWAII
NAKED PARADISE
RIDE THE WILD SURF

Maori
THE DECKS RAN RED

Polynesian
BIRD OF PARADISE (1932, 1951)
HIS MAJESTY O'KEEFE
THE HURRICANE
HURRICANE SMITH
NEVER THE TWAIN SHALL MEET
SOUTH OF TAHITI
TAMAHINE

Samoan
ON THE ISLE OF SAMOA

Tahitian
MAROC 7
THE MOON AND SIXPENCE
MUTINY ON THE BOUNTY (1935, 1962)
PAGAN LOVE SONG

TAHITI NIGHTS
TIARA TAHITI
THE TUTTLES OF TAHITI